ALL·IN·ONE

CompTIA
Security+®

EXAM GUIDE

Fifth Edition (Exam SY0-501)

Dr. Wm. Arthur Conklin
Dr. Gregory White
Chuck Cothren
Roger L. Davis
Dwayne Williams

New York   Chicago   San Francisco
Athens   London   Madrid   Mexico City
Milan   New Delhi   Singapore   Sydney   Toronto

Cataloging-in-Publication Data is on file with the Library of Congress

Names: Conklin, Wm. Arthur (William Arthur), author.
Title: CompTIA security+ all-in-one exam guide, (Exam SY0-501) / Dr. Wm. Arthur Conklin, Dr. Gregory White, Chuck Cothren, Roger L. Davis, Dwayne Williams.
Description: Fifth edition. | New York : McGraw-Hill Education, [2018]
Identifiers: LCCN 2017052997| ISBN 9781260019322 (set : alk. paper) | ISBN 9781260019315 (book : alk. paper) | ISBN 9781260019308 (CD) | ISBN 1260019322 (set : alk. paper) | ISBN 1260019314 (book : alk. paper) | ISBN 1260019306 (CD)
Subjects: LCSH: Computer security—Examinations—Study guides. | Computer networks—Security measures—Examinations—Study guides. | Computer technicians—Certification—Study guides. | Electronic data processing personnel—Certification—Study guides.
Classification: LCC QA76.9.A25 .C667565 2018 | DDC 005.8—dc23 LC record available at https://lccn.loc.gov/2017052997

McGraw-Hill Education books are available at special quantity discounts to use as premiums and sales promotions, or for use in corporate training programs. To contact a representative, please visit the Contact Us pages at www.mhprofessional.com.

CompTIA Security+® All-in-One Exam Guide, Fifth Edition (Exam SY0-501)

56789 LCR 212019

ISBN: Book p/n 978-1-260-01931-5 and CD p/n 978-1-260-01930-8
of set 978-1-260-01932-2

MHID: Book p/n 1-260-01931-4 and CD p/n 1-260-01930-6
of set 1-260-01932-2

Sponsoring Editor Amy Stonebraker	**Technical Editor** Chris Crayton	**Production Supervisor** James Kussow
Editorial Supervisor Janet Walden	**Copy Editor** William McManus	**Composition** Cenveo® Publisher Services
Project Editor Patty Mon	**Proofreader** Claire Splan	**Illustration** Cenveo Publisher Services
Acquisitions Coordinator Claire Yee	**Indexer** Ted Laux	**Art Director, Cover** Jeff Weeks

This book is dedicated to the many information security professionals who quietly work to ensure the safety of our nation's critical infrastructures. We want to recognize the thousands of dedicated individuals who strive to protect our national assets but who seldom receive praise and often are only noticed when an incident occurs. To you, we say thank you for a job well done!

ABOUT THE AUTHORS

Dr. Wm. Arthur Conklin, CompTIA Security+, CISSP, CSSLP, GISCP, GCFA, GRID, CRISC, CASP, is an Associate Professor and Director of the Center for Information Security Research and Education in the College of Technology at the University of Houston. He holds two terminal degrees, a Ph.D. in business administration (specializing in information security), from The University of Texas at San Antonio (UTSA), and the degree Electrical Engineer (specializing in space systems engineering) from the Naval Postgraduate School in Monterey, CA. He is a fellow of ISSA and a senior member of ASQ, IEEE, and ACM. His research interests include the use of systems theory to explore information security, specifically in cyber-physical systems. He has a strong interest in cybersecurity education, and is involved with the NSA/DHS Centers of Academic Excellence in Cyber Defense (CAE CD) and the NIST National Initiative for Cybersecurity Education (NICE) Cybersecurity Workforce Framework (NICE Framework). He has coauthored six security books and numerous academic articles associated with information security. He is active in the DHS-sponsored Industrial Control Systems Joint Working Group (ICSJWG) efforts associated with workforce development and cybersecurity aspects of industrial control systems. He has an extensive background in secure coding and has been co-chair of the DHS/DoD Software Assurance Forum Working Group for workforce education, training, and development.

Dr. Gregory White has been involved in computer and network security since 1986. He spent 19 years on active duty with the United States Air Force and 11 years in the Air Force Reserves in a variety of computer and security positions. He obtained his Ph.D. in computer science from Texas A&M University in 1995. His dissertation topic was in the area of computer network intrusion detection, and he continues to conduct research in this area today. He is currently the Director for the Center for Infrastructure Assurance and Security (CIAS) and is a professor of computer science at the University of Texas at San Antonio (UTSA). Dr. White has written and presented numerous articles and conference papers on security. He is also the coauthor of five textbooks on computer and network security and has written chapters for two other security books. Dr. White continues to be active in security research. His current research initiatives include efforts in community incident response, intrusion detection, and secure information sharing.

Chuck Cothren, CISSP, Security+, is a Field Engineer at Ionic Security applying over 20 years of information security experience in consulting, research, and enterprise environments. He has assisted clients in a variety of industries including healthcare, banking, information technology, retail, and manufacturing. He advises clients on topics such as security architecture, penetration testing, training, consultant management, data loss prevention, and encryption. He is coauthor of the books *Voice and Data Security* and *Principles of Computer Security*.

Roger L. Davis, CISSP, CISM, CISA, is a Technical Account Manager for Microsoft supporting enterprise-level companies. He has served as president of the Utah chapter of the Information Systems Security Association (ISSA) and various board positions for the Utah chapter of the Information Systems Audit and Control Association (ISACA). He is a retired Air Force lieutenant colonel with 30 years of military and information systems/security experience. Mr. Davis served on the faculty of Brigham Young University and the Air Force Institute of Technology. He coauthored McGraw-Hill Education's *Principles of Computer Security* and *Voice and Data Security*. He holds a master's degree in computer science from George Washington University, a bachelor's degree in computer science from Brigham Young University, and performed post-graduate studies in electrical engineering and computer science at the University of Colorado.

Dwayne Williams, CISSP, CASP, is Associate Director, Technology and Research, for the Center for Infrastructure Assurance and Security at the University of Texas at San Antonio and is the Director of the National Collegiate Cyber Defense Competition. Mr. Williams has over 24 years of experience in information systems and network security. Mr. Williams's experience includes six years of commissioned military service as a Communications-Computer Information Systems Officer in the United States Air Force, specializing in network security, corporate information protection, intrusion detection systems, incident response, and VPN technology. Prior to joining the CIAS, he served as Director of Consulting for SecureLogix Corporation, where he directed and provided security assessment and integration services to Fortune 100, government, public utility, oil and gas, financial, and technology clients. Mr. Williams graduated in 1993 from Baylor University with a bachelor of arts in computer science. Mr. Williams is a coauthor of *Voice and Data Security*, *Principles of Computer Security*, and *CompTIA Security + All-in-One Exam Guide*.

About the Technical Editor

Chris Crayton (MCSE) is an author, technical consultant, and trainer. He has worked as a computer technology and networking instructor, information security director, network administrator, network engineer, and PC specialist. Chris has authored several print and online books on PC repair, CompTIA A+, CompTIA Security+, and Microsoft Windows. He has also served as technical editor and content contributor on numerous technical titles for several leading publishing companies. He holds numerous industry certifications, has been recognized with many professional teaching awards, and has served as a state-level SkillsUSA competition judge.

Becoming a CompTIA Certified IT Professional Is Easy

It's also the best way to reach greater professional opportunities and rewards.

Why Get CompTIA Certified?

Growing Demand

Labor estimates predict some technology fields will experience growth of more than 20% by the year 2020. (Source: CompTIA 9th Annual Information Security Trends study: 500 U.S. IT and Business Executives Responsible for Security.) CompTIA certification qualifies the skills required to join this workforce.

Higher Salaries

IT professionals with certifications on their resume command better jobs, earn higher salaries, and have more doors open to new multi-industry opportunities.

Verified Strengths

91% of hiring managers indicate CompTIA certifications are valuable in validating IT expertise, making certification the best way to demonstrate your competency and knowledge to employers. (Source: CompTIA Employer Perceptions of IT Training and Certification.)

Universal Skills

CompTIA certifications are vendor neutral—which means that certified professionals can proficiently work with an extensive variety of hardware and software found in most organizations.

 **Learn** 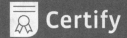 **Certify**  **Work**

Learn more about what the exam covers by reviewing the following:

- Exam objectives for key study points.

- Sample questions for a general overview of what to expect on the exam and examples of question format.

- Visit online forums, like LinkedIn, to see what other IT professionals say about CompTIA exams.

Purchase a voucher at a Pearson VUE testing center or at CompTIAstore.com.

- Register for your exam at a Pearson VUE testing center.

- Visit pearsonvue.com/CompTIA to find the closest testing center to you.

- Schedule the exam online. You will be required to enter your voucher number or provide payment information at registration.

- Take your certification exam.

Congratulations on your CompTIA certification!

- Make sure to add your certification to your resume.

- Check out the CompTIA Certification Roadmap to plan your next career move.

Learn More: Certification.CompTIA.org/securityplus

CompTIA Disclaimer

CONTENTS AT A GLANCE

CONTENTS

PREFACE

Information and computer security has moved from the confines of academia to mainstream America in the last decade. From the ransomware attacks to data disclosures such as Equifax and U.S. Office of Personnel Management that were heavily covered in the media and broadcast into the average American's home, information security has become a common topic. In boardrooms, the topic has arrived with the technical attacks against intellectual property and the risk exposure from cybersecurity incidents. It has become increasingly obvious to everybody that something needs to be done in order to secure not only our nation's critical infrastructure, but also the businesses we deal with on a daily basis. The question is, "Where do we begin?" What can the average information technology professional do to secure the systems that he or she is hired to maintain?

The answer to these questions is complex, but certain aspects can guide our actions. First, no one knows what the next big threat will be. The APT, ransomware, data disclosures … these were all known threats long before they became the major threat *du jour*. What is next? No one knows, so we can't buy a magic box to fix it. Yet. But we do know that we will do it with the people we have, at their current level of training, when it arrives. The one investment that we know will be good is in our people, through education and training. For that will be what we bring to the next incident, problem, challenge, or, collectively, our national defense in the realm of cybersecurity. One could say security today begins and ends with our people. And trained people will result in better outcomes.

So, where do you, the IT professional seeking more knowledge on security, start your studies? The IT world is overflowing with certifications that can be obtained by those attempting to learn more about their chosen profession. The security sector is no different, and the CompTIA Security+ exam offers a basic level of certification for security. CompTIA Security+ is an ideal starting point for one interested in a career in security. In the pages of this exam guide, you will find not only material that can help you prepare for taking the CompTIA Security+ examination, but also the basic information that you will need in order to understand the issues involved in securing your computer systems and networks today. In no way is this exam guide the final source for learning all about protecting your organization's systems, but it serves as a point from which to launch your security studies and career.

One thing is certainly true about this field of study—it never gets boring. It constantly changes as technology itself advances. Something else you will find as you progress in your security studies is that no matter how much technology advances and no matter how many new security devices are developed, at its most basic level, the human is still the weak link in the security chain. If you are looking for an exciting area to delve into, then you have certainly chosen wisely. Security offers a challenging blend of technology and people issues. We, the authors of this exam guide, wish you luck as you embark on an exciting and challenging career path.

—*Wm. Arthur Conklin, Ph.D.*
—*Gregory B. White, Ph.D.*

ACKNOWLEDGMENTS

We, the authors of *CompTIA Security+ All-in-One Exam Guide, Fifth Edition*, have many individuals who we need to acknowledge—individuals without whom this effort would not have been successful.

The list needs to start with those folks at McGraw-Hill Education who worked tirelessly with the project's multiple authors and led us successfully through the minefield that is a book schedule and who took our rough chapters and drawings and turned them into a final, professional product we can be proud of. We thank the good people from the Acquisitions team, Amy Stonebraker and Claire Yee; from the Editorial Services team, Janet Walden; and from the Production team, James Kussow. We also thank the technical editor, Chris Crayton; the project editor, Patty Mon; the copyeditor, William McManus; the proofreader, Claire Splan; and the indexer, Jack Lewis, for all their attention to detail that made this a finer work after they finished with it. And to Tim Green, who made these journeys possible.

We also need to acknowledge our current employers who, to our great delight, have seen fit to pay us to work in a career field that we all find exciting and rewarding. There is never a dull moment in security because it is constantly changing.

We would like to thank Art Conklin for again herding the cats on this one.

Finally, we would each like to individually thank those people who—on a personal basis—have provided the core support for us individually. Without these special people in our lives, none of us could have put this work together.

—The Author Team

To Bill McManus, we have worked on several books together and your skill never ceases to amaze me—may I someday learn to express complex ideas with the grace and simplicity you deliver. Thank you again for making this a better book.

—Art Conklin

I would like to thank my wife, Charlan, for the tremendous support she has always given me.

—Gregory B. White

Josie, Macon, and Jet, thank you for the love, support, and laughs.

—Chuck Cothren

Geena, all I am is because of you. Thanks for being my greatest support. As always, love to my powerful children and wonderful grandkids!

—Roger L. Davis

To my wife and best friend Leah for your love, energy, and support—thank you for always being there. To my kids—this is what Daddy was typing on the computer!

—Dwayne Williams

INTRODUCTION

Computer security has become paramount as the number of security incidents steadily climbs. Many corporations now spend significant portions of their budget on security hardware, software, services, and personnel. They are spending this money not because it increases sales or enhances the product they provide, but because of the possible consequences should they not take protective actions.

Why Focus on Security?

Security is not something that we want to have to pay for; it would be nice if we didn't have to worry about protecting our data from disclosure, modification, or destruction from unauthorized individuals, but that is not the environment we find ourselves in today. Instead, we have seen the cost of recovering from security incidents steadily rise along with the number of incidents themselves. Cyber-attacks and information disclosures are occurring so often that one almost ignores them on the news. But with the theft of over 145 million consumers' credit data from Equifax, with the subsequent resignation of the CSO and CEO, and hearings in Congress over the role of legislative oversight with respect to critical records, a new sense of purpose with regard to securing data may be at hand. The days of paper reports and corporate "lip-service" may be waning, and the time to meet the new challenges of even more sophisticated attackers has arrived. This will not be the last data breach, nor will attackers stop attacking our systems, so our only path forward is to have qualified professionals defending our systems.

A Growing Need for Security Specialists

In order to protect our computer systems and networks, we need a significant number of new security professionals trained in the many aspects of computer and network security. This is not an easy task as the systems connected to the Internet become increasingly complex with software whose lines of code number in the millions. Understanding why this is such a difficult problem to solve is not hard if you consider just how many errors might be present in a piece of software that is several million lines long. When you add the factor of how fast software is being developed—from necessity as the market is constantly changing—understanding how errors occur is easy.

Not every "bug" in the software will result in a security hole, but it doesn't take many to have a drastic effect on the Internet community. We can't just blame the vendors for this situation, because they are reacting to the demands of government and industry. Many vendors are fairly adept at developing patches for flaws found in their software, and patches are constantly being issued to protect systems from bugs that may introduce security problems. This introduces a whole new problem for managers and administrators—patch management. How important this has become is easily illustrated by how many of the most recent security events have occurred as a result of a security bug that was discovered months prior to the security incident, and for which a patch has been available, but for which the community has not correctly installed the patch, thus making the incident possible. The reasons for these failures are many, but in the end the solution is a matter of trained professionals at multiple levels in an organization working together to resolve these problems.

But the issue of trained people does not stop with security professionals. Every user, from the board room to the mail room, plays a role in the cybersecurity posture of a firm. Training the non-security professional in the enterprise to use the proper level of care when interacting with systems will not make the problem go away either, but it will substantially strengthen the posture of the enterprise. Understanding the needed training and making it a reality is another task on the security professional's to-do list.

Because of the need for an increasing number of security professionals who are trained to some minimum level of understanding, certifications such as the CompTIA Security+ have been developed. Prospective employers want to know that the individual they are considering hiring knows what to do in terms of security. The prospective employee, in turn, wants to have a way to demonstrate his or her level of understanding, which can enhance the candidate's chances of being hired. The community as a whole simply wants more trained security professionals.

The goal of taking the CompTIA Security+ exam is to prove that you've mastered the worldwide standards for foundation-level security practitioners. The exam gives you a perfect opportunity to validate your knowledge and understanding of the computer security field, and it is an appropriate mechanism for many different individuals, including network and system administrators, analysts, programmers, web designers, application developers, and database specialists, to show proof of professional achievement in security. According to CompTIA, the exam is aimed at individuals who have

- A minimum of two years of experience in IT administration with a focus on security

- Day-to-day technical information security experience

- Broad knowledge of security concerns and implementation, including the topics that are found in the specific CompTIA Security+ domains

The exam objectives were developed with input and assistance from industry and government agencies. The CompTIA Security+ exam is designed to cover a wide range of security topics—subjects about which a security practitioner would be expected to know. The test includes information from six knowledge domains:

Domain	Percent of Exam
1.0 Threats, Attacks and Vulnerabilities	21%
2.0 Technologies and Tools	22%
3.0 Architecture and Design	15%
4.0 Identity and Access Management	16%
5.0 Risk Management	14%
6.0 Cryptography and PKI	12%

The *Threats, Attacks and Vulnerabilities* domain covers indicators of compromise and types of malware; types of attacks; threat actor types and attributes; penetration testing concepts; vulnerability scanning concepts; and the impact of types of vulnerabilities. The *Technologies and Tools* domain examines installing and configuring network components, both hardware and software-based, to support organizational security; using the appropriate software tools to assess the security posture of an organization; troubleshooting common security issues; analyzing and interpreting output from security technologies; deploying mobile devices securely; and implementing secure protocols.

The *Architecture and Design* domain examines the use cases and purposes for frameworks, best practices, and secure configuration guides; secure network architecture concepts; secure systems design; secure staging deployment concepts; the security implications of embedded systems; secure application development and deployment concepts; cloud and virtualization concepts; resiliency and automation strategies to reduce risk; and the importance of physical security controls. The fourth domain, *Identity and Access Management*, covers identity and access management concepts; identity and access services; identity and access management controls; and common account management practices.

The *Risk Management* domain covers the importance of policies, plans, and procedures related to organizational security; concepts of business impact analysis; concepts of risk management processes; incident response procedures; basic concepts of forensics; concepts of disaster recovery and continuity of operations; types of security controls; and data security and privacy practices. The last domain, *Cryptography and PKI*, covers the basic concepts of cryptography; cryptography algorithms and their basic characteristics; how to install and configure wireless security settings, and how to implement public key infrastructure.

The exam consists of a series of questions, each designed to have a single best answer or response. The other available choices are designed to provide options that an individual might choose if he or she had an incomplete knowledge or understanding of the security topic represented by the question. The exam will have both multiple-choice and performance-based questions. Performance-based questions present the candidate with a task or a problem in a simulated IT environment. The candidate is given an opportunity to demonstrate his or her ability in performing skills. The exam questions are based on the CompTIA Security+ Certification Exam Objectives: SY0-501 document obtainable from the CompTIA website at https://certification.comptia.org/certifications/security.

CompTIA recommends that individuals who want to take the CompTIA Security+ exam have the CompTIA Network+ certification and two years of IT administration experience with an emphasis on security. Originally administered only in English, the exam is now offered in testing centers around the world in the English, Japanese, Portuguese, and Simplified Chinese. Consult the CompTIA website at www.comptia.org to determine a test center location near you.

The exam consists of a maximum of 90 questions to be completed in 90 minutes. A minimum passing score is considered 750 out of a possible 900 points. Results are available immediately after you complete the exam. An individual who fails to pass the exam the first time will be required to pay the exam fee again to retake the exam, but no mandatory waiting period is required before retaking it the second time. If the individual again fails the exam, a minimum waiting period of 30 days is required for each subsequent retake. For more information on retaking exams, consult CompTIA's retake policy, which can be found on its website.

Preparing Yourself for the CompTIA Security+ Exam

CompTIA Security+ All-in-One Exam Guide, Fifth Edition, is designed to help prepare you to take the CompTIA Security+ certification exam SY0-501.

How This Book Is Organized

The book is divided into sections and chapters to correspond with the objectives of the exam itself. Some of the chapters are more technical than others—reflecting the nature of the security environment, where you will be forced to deal with not only technical details, but also other issues such as security policies and procedures as well as training and education. Although many individuals involved in computer and network security have advanced degrees in math, computer science, information systems, or computer or electrical engineering, you do not need this technical background to address security effectively in your organization. You do not need to develop your own cryptographic algorithm, for example; you simply need to be able to understand how cryptography is used, along with its strengths and weaknesses. As you progress in your studies, you will learn that many security problems are caused by the human element. The best technology in the world still ends up being placed in an environment where humans have the opportunity to foul things up—and all too often do.

As you can see from the table of contents, the overall structure of the book is designed to mirror the objectives of the CompTIA Security+ exam. The majority of the chapters are designed to match the objectives order as posted by CompTIA. There are occasions where the order differs slightly, mainly to group terms by contextual use.

In addition, there are two appendixes in this book. Appendix A provides an additional in-depth explanation of the OSI Model and Internet protocols, should this information be new to you, and Appendix B explains how best to use the CD-ROM included with the book.

Located just before the Index, you will find a useful Glossary of security terminology, including many related acronyms and their meaning. We hope that you use the Glossary frequently and find it to be a useful study aid as you work your way through the various topics in this exam guide.

Special Features of the All-in-One Series

To make these exam guides more useful and a pleasure to read, the All-in-One series has been designed to include several features.

Objective Map

The objective map that follows this introduction has been constructed to allow you to cross-reference the official exam objectives with the objectives as they are presented and covered in this book. References have been provided for the objective exactly as CompTIA presents it, the section of the exam guide that covers that objective and a chapter reference.

Icons

To alert you to an important bit of advice, a shortcut, or a pitfall, you'll occasionally see Notes, Tips, Cautions, and Exam Tips peppered throughout the text.

 NOTE Notes offer nuggets of especially helpful stuff, background explanations, and information, and terms are defined occasionally.

 TIP Tips provide suggestions and nuances to help you learn to finesse your job. Take a tip from us and read the Tips carefully.

 CAUTION When you see a Caution, pay special attention. Cautions appear when you have to make a crucial choice or when you are about to undertake something that may have ramifications you might not immediately anticipate. Read them now so you don't have regrets later.

 EXAM TIP Exam Tips give you special advice or may provide information specifically related to preparing for the exam itself.

End-of-Chapter Reviews and Questions

An important part of this book comes at the end of each chapter, where you will find a brief review of the high points along with a series of questions followed by the answers to those questions. Each question is in multiple-choice format. The answers provided also include a small discussion explaining why the correct answer actually is the correct answer.

The questions are provided as a study aid to you, the reader and prospective CompTIA Security+ exam taker. We obviously can't guarantee that if you answer all of our questions correctly you will absolutely pass the certification exam. Instead, what we can guarantee is that the questions will provide you with an idea about how ready you are for the exam.

The Total Tester

CompTIA Security+ All-in-One Exam Guide, Fifth Edition, also provides you with a test engine containing even more practice exam questions and their answers to help you prepare for the certification exam. Read more about the companion Total Tester practice exam software in Appendix B.

Onward and Upward

At this point, we hope that you are now excited about the topic of security, even if you weren't in the first place. We wish you luck in your endeavors and welcome you to the exciting field of computer and network security.

Objective Map: Exam SY0-501

Official Exam Objective	All-in-One Coverage	Chapter No.
1.0 Threats, Attacks, and Vulnerabilities		
1.1 Given a scenario, analyze indicators of compromise and determine the type of malware.	Malware and Indicators of Compromise	1
1.2 Compare and contrast types of attacks.	Attacks	2
1.3 Explain threat actor types and attributes.	Threat Actors	3
1.4 Explain penetration testing concepts.	Vulnerability Scanning and Penetration Testing	4
1.5 Explain vulnerability scanning concepts.	Vulnerability Scanning and Penetration Testing	4
1.6 Explain the impact associated with types of vulnerabilities.	Vulnerabilities and Impacts	5
2.0 Technologies and Tools		
2.1 Install and configure network components, both hardware- and software-based, to support organizational security.	Network Components	6
2.2 Given a scenario, use appropriate software tools to assess the security posture of an organization.	Security Tools and Technologies	7
2.3 Given a scenario, troubleshoot common security issues.	Troubleshoot Common Security Issues	8
2.4 Given a scenario, analyze and interpret output from security technologies.	Security Tools and Technologies	7
2.5 Given a scenario, deploy mobile devices securely.	Mobile Devices	9
2.6 Given a scenario, implement secure protocols.	Implementing Secure Protocols	10
3.0 Architecture and Design		
3.1 Explain use cases and purpose for frameworks, best practices and secure configuration guides.	Architecture Frameworks and Secure Network Architectures	11
3.2 Given a scenario, implement secure network architecture concepts.	Architecture Frameworks and Secure Network Architectures	11
3.3 Given a scenario, implement secure systems design.	Secure Systems Design and Deployment	12
3.4 Explain the importance of secure staging deployment concepts.	Secure Systems Design and Deployment	12
3.5 Explain the security implications of embedded systems.	Embedded Systems	13
3.6 Summarize secure application development and deployment concepts.	Application Development and Deployment	14
3.7 Summarize cloud and virtualization concepts.	Cloud and Virtualization	15

PART I

Threats, Attacks, and Vulnerabilities

Malware and Indicators of Compromise

In this chapter, you will

- Examine the types of malware
- Understand the different types of malicious software that exist, including viruses, worms, Trojan horses, logic bombs, and rootkits
- Learn how artifacts called indicators of compromise can tell you if a system has been attacked

There are various forms of malicious software, software that is designed to compromise an end system, leaving it vulnerable to attack. In this chapter we examine the various types of malware (malicious software) and indicators of compromise that demonstrate a system has been attacked.

Certification Objective   This chapter covers CompTIA Security+ exam objective 1.1, Given a scenario, analyze indicators of compromise and determine the type of malware. This is a performance-based question testable objective, which means expect a question in which one must employ the knowledge based on a scenario. The best answer to a question will depend upon details in the scenario, not just the question. The question may also involve tasks other than just picking the best answer from a list. Instead, choices, such as order things on a diagram, rank order answers, match two columns of items, may be found.

Malware

Malware refers to software that has been designed for some nefarious purpose. Such software can be designed to cause damage to a system, such as by deleting all files, or it can be designed to create a backdoor in the system to grant access to unauthorized individuals. Generally the installation of malware is done so that it is not obvious to the authorized users. Several different types of malicious software can be used, such as viruses, Trojan horses, logic bombs, spyware, and worms, and they differ in the ways they are installed and their purposes.

Polymorphic Malware

The detection of malware by anti-malware programs is primarily done through the use of a signature. Files are scanned for sections of code in the executable that act as markers, unique patterns of code that enable detection. Just as the human body creates antigens that match marker proteins, anti-malware programs detect malware through unique markers present in the code of the malware.

Malware writers are aware of this functionality and have adapted methods to defeat it. One of the primary means of avoiding detection by sensors is the use of polymorphic code, which is code that changes on a regular basis. These changes or mutations are designed not to affect the functionality of the code, but rather to mask any signature from detection. *Polymorphic malware* is malware that can change its code after each use, making each replicant different from a detection point of view.

Viruses

The best-known type of malicious code is the virus. Much has been written about viruses because several high-profile security events have involved them. A *virus* is a piece of malicious code that replicates by attaching itself to another piece of executable code. When the other executable code is run, the virus also executes and has the opportunity to infect other files and perform any other nefarious actions it was designed to do. The specific way that a virus infects other files, and the type of files it infects, depends on the type of virus. The first viruses created were of two types—boot sector viruses and program viruses.

Armored Virus

When a new form of malware/virus is discovered, antivirus companies and security researchers will decompile the program in an attempt to reverse engineer its functionality. Much can be determined from reverse engineering, such as where the malware came from, how it works, how it communicates, how it spreads, and so forth. Armoring malware can make the process of determining this information much more difficult, if not impossible. Some malware, such as the Zeus Trojan, employs encryption in ways to prevent criminals from stealing the intellectual property of the very malware that they use.

Crypto-malware

Crypto-malware is an early name given to malware that encrypts files on a system and then leaves them unusable either permanently, acting as a denial of service, or temporarily until a ransom is paid, making it ransomware, which is discussed in the next section. Crypto-malware is typically completely automated, and when targeted as a means of denial of service, the only repair mechanism is to rebuild the system. This can be time consuming and/or impractical in some cases, making this attack mechanism equivalent to physical destruction of assets.

In May of 2017, a crypto-worm form of malware, WannaCry, was released, resulting in a ransomware attack that swept across many government computers in Europe, including medical devices in England's National Health Service (NHS). This ransomware created havoc by exploiting a vulnerability in Microsoft Windows systems that was exposed by the group known as Shadow Brokers.

Ransomware

Ransomware is a form of malware that performs some action and extracts ransom from a user. A current ransomware threat, first appearing in 2013, is CryptoLocker. CryptoLocker is a Trojan horse that will encrypt certain files using RSA public key encryption. When the user attempts to get the files, they are provided with a message instructing them how to purchase the decryption key. Because the system is using 2048-bit RSA encryption, brute force decryption is out of the realm of recovery options. RSA encryption is covered in more detail in Chapter 27. The system is highly automated and users have a short time window to get the private key. Failure to get the key will result in the loss of the data.

EXAM TIP Cryto-malware and ransomware are both new to the Security+ objectives. Adding these attack vectors and how to differentiate them from other attacks to your knowledgebase will be useful for the exam.

Worm

It was once easy to distinguish between a worm and a virus. Recently, with the introduction of new breeds of sophisticated malicious code, the distinction has blurred. *Worms* are pieces of code that attempt to penetrate networks and computer systems. Once a penetration occurs, the worm will create a new copy of itself on the penetrated system. Reproduction of a worm thus does not rely on the attachment of the virus to another piece of code or to a file, which is the definition of a virus.

Viruses were generally thought of as a system-based problem, and worms were network-based. If the malicious code is sent throughout a network, it may subsequently be called a worm. The important distinction, however, is whether the code has to attach itself to something else (a virus) or if it can "survive" on its own (a worm).

Some examples of worms that have had high profiles include the Sobig worm of 2003, the SQL Slammer worm of 2003, the 2001 attacks of Code Red and Nimba, and the 2005 Zotob worm that took down CNN Live. Nimba was particularly impressive in that it used five different methods to spread: via e-mail, via open network shares, from browsing infected websites, using the directory traversal vulnerability of Microsoft IIS 4.0/5.0, and most impressively through the use of backdoors left by Code Red II and sadmind worms.

EXAM TIP Worms act like a virus but also have the ability to travel without human action.

Trojan

A Trojan horse, or simply *Trojan*, is a piece of software that appears to do one thing (and may, in fact, actually do that thing) but hides some other functionality. The analogy to the famous story of antiquity is very accurate. In the original case, the object appeared to be a large wooden horse, and in fact it was. At the same time, it hid something much more sinister and dangerous to the occupants of the city of Troy. As long as the horse was left outside the city walls, it could cause no damage to the inhabitants. It had to be taken in by the inhabitants, and it was inside that the hidden purpose was activated. A computer Trojan works in much the same way. Unlike a virus, which reproduces by attaching itself to other files or programs, a Trojan is a stand-alone program that must be copied and installed by the user—it must be "brought inside" the system by an authorized user. The challenge for the attacker is enticing the user to copy and run the program. This generally means that the program must be disguised as something that the user would want to run—a special utility or game, for example. Once it has been copied and is inside the system, the Trojan will perform its hidden purpose with the user often still unaware of its true nature.

A good example of a Trojan is Back Orifice (BO), originally created in 1999 and now offered in several versions. BO can be attached to a number of types of programs. Once it is attached, and once an infected file is run, BO will create a way for unauthorized individuals to take over the system remotely, as if they were sitting at the console. BO is designed to work with Windows-based systems. Many Trojans communicate to the outside through a port that the Trojan opens, and this is one of the ways Trojans can be detected.

 EXAM TIP Ensure you understand the differences between viruses, worms, Trojans, and various other types of threats for the exam.

Rootkit

Rootkits are a form of malware that is specifically designed to modify the operation of the operating system in some fashion to facilitate nonstandard functionality. The history of rootkits goes back to the beginning of the UNIX operating system, where rootkits were sets of modified administrative tools. Originally designed to allow a program to take greater control over operating system function when it fails or becomes unresponsive, the technique has evolved and is used in a variety of ways. One high-profile case occurred at Sony BMG Corporation, when rootkit technology was used to provide copy protection technology on some of the company's CDs. Two major issues led to this being a complete debacle for Sony: first, the software modified systems without the users' approval; and second, the software opened a security hole on Windows-based systems, creating an exploitable vulnerability at the rootkit level. This led the Sony case to be labeled as *malware*, which is the most common use of rootkits.

A rootkit can do many things—in fact, it can do virtually anything that the operating system does. Rootkits modify the operating system kernel and supporting functions, changing the nature of the system's operation. Rootkits are designed to avoid, either by subversion or evasion, the security functions of the operating system to avoid detection. Rootkits act as a form of malware that can change thread priorities to boost an application's performance, perform keylogging, act as a sniffer, hide other files from other applications, or create backdoors in the authentication system. The use of rootkit functionality to hide other processes and files enables an attacker to use a portion of a computer without the user or other applications knowing what is happening. This hides exploit code from antivirus and anti-spyware programs, acting as a cloak of invisibility.

Rootkits can load before the operating system loads, acting as a virtualization layer, as in SubVirt and Blue Pill. Rootkits can exist in firmware, and these have been demonstrated in both video cards and expansion cards. Rootkits can exist as loadable library modules, effectively changing portions of the operating system outside the kernel. Further information on specific rootkits in the wild can be found at www.antirootkit.com.

 EXAM TIP Five types of rootkits exist: firmware, virtual, kernel, library, and application level.

Once a rootkit is detected, it needs to be removed and cleaned up. Because of rootkits' invasive nature, and the fact that many aspects of rootkits are not easily detectable, most system administrators don't even attempt to clean up or remove a rootkit. It is far easier to use a previously captured clean system image and reimage the machine than to attempt to determine the depth and breadth of the damage and attempt to fix individual files.

Keylogger

As the name suggests, a *keylogger* is a piece of software that logs all of the keystrokes that a user enters. Keyloggers in their own respect are not necessarily evil, for you could consider Microsoft Word to be a keylogger. What makes a keylogger a malicious piece of software is when its operation is 1) unknown to the user, and 2) not under the user's control. Keyloggers have been marketed for a variety of uses, from surveillance over your children's activity, to that of a spouse, to maintaining records of what has been done on a machine. Malicious keyloggers have several specific characteristics; they are frequently hidden from the user's view, even when you look at task manager; and they are used against the end-user's interests. Hackers use keyloggers to obtain passwords and other sensitive pieces of information, enabling them to use these secrets to act as the user without the user's consent. Keylogger functionality has even been found in legitimate programs, where keystrokes are recorded for "legitimate" purposes and then are stored in a fashion that enables unauthorized users to steal the data.

Adware

The business of software distribution requires a form of revenue stream to support the cost of development and distribution. One form of revenue stream is advertising. Software that is supported by advertising is called *adware*. Adware comes in many different forms. With legitimate adware, the user is aware of the advertising and agrees to the arrangement in return for free use of the software. This type of adware often offers an alternative, ad-free version for a fee. Adware can also refer to a form of malware, which is characterized by software that presents unwanted ads. These ads are sometimes an irritant, and at other times represent an actual security threat. Frequently, these ads are in the form of pop-up browser windows, and in some cases they cascade upon any user action.

Spyware

Spyware is software that "spies" on users, recording and reporting on their activities. Typically installed without user knowledge, spyware can perform a wide range of activities. It can record keystrokes (commonly called *keylogging*) when the user logs onto specific websites. It can monitor how a user applies a specific piece of software, such as to monitor attempts to cheat at games. Many uses of spyware seem innocuous at first, but the unauthorized monitoring of a system can be abused very easily. In other cases, the spyware is specifically designed to steal information. Many states have passed legislation banning the unapproved installation of software, but spyware can circumvent this issue through complex and confusing end-user license agreements.

Bots

A *bot* is a functioning piece of software that performs some task, under the control of another program. A series of bots is controlled across the network in a group, and the entire assembly is called a botnet (combining the terms bot and network). Some botnets are legal and perform desired actions in a distributed fashion. Illegal botnets work in the same fashion, with bots distributed and controlled from a central set of servers. Bots can do a wide array of things, from spam to fraud to spyware and more.

Botnets continue to advance malware threats. Some of the latest botnets are designed to mine bitcoins, using distributed processing power for gain. Some of the more famous botnets include Zeus, a botnet that performs keystroke logging and is used primarily for the purpose of stealing banking information. Zeus has been linked to the delivery of cryptolocker ransomware. Another famous botnet is conficker, which has infected millions of machines worldwide. The conficker botnet is one of the most studied pieces of malware, with a joint industry–government working group convened to battle it.

RAT

A *remote-access Trojan (RAT)* is a toolkit designed to provide the capability of covert surveillance and/or the capability to gain unauthorized access to a target system. RATs often mimic similar behaviors of keylogger or packet sniffer applications using the automated collection of keystrokes, usernames, passwords, screenshots, browser history, e-mails, chat logs, and more, but they also do so with a design of intelligence. RATs can also employ malware to infect a system with code that can be used to facilitate the exploitation of a target. Rather than just collect the information, RATs present it to an attacker in a form to facilitate the capability to gain unauthorized access to the target machine.

This frequently involves the use of specially configured communication protocols that are set up upon initial infection of the target computer. This backdoor into the target machine can allow an attacker unfettered access, including the ability to monitor user behavior, change computer settings, browse and copy files, access connected systems, and more. RATs are commonly employed by the more skilled threat actors, although there are RATs that are easy enough for even beginners to employ.

A RAT should be considered as another form of malware, but rather than just being a program, it has an operator behind it, guiding it to do even more persistent damage. RATs can be delivered via phishing e-mails, watering holes, or any of a myriad of other malware infection vectors. RATs typically involve the creation of hidden file structures on a system and are vulnerable to detection by modern anti-malware programs. There are several major families of RATs, but an exhaustive list would be long and ever increasing. When facing a more skilled adversary, it is not uncommon to find RAT packages that have been modified for specific use, such as the program used in the Ukraine electric grid attack in 2015.

Logic Bomb

Logic bombs, unlike viruses and Trojans, are a type of malicious software that is deliberately installed, generally by an authorized user. A *logic bomb* is a piece of code that sits dormant for a period of time until some event or date invokes its malicious payload. An example of a logic bomb might be a program that is set to load and run automatically, and that periodically checks an organization's payroll or personnel database for a specific employee. If the employee is not found, the malicious payload executes, deleting vital corporate files.

If the event is a specific date or time, the program will often be referred to as a *time bomb*. In one famous example of a time bomb, a disgruntled employee left a time bomb in place just prior to being fired from his job. Two weeks later, thousands of client records were deleted. Police were eventually able to track the malicious code to the disgruntled ex-employee, who was prosecuted for his actions. He had hoped that the two weeks that had passed since his dismissal would have caused investigators to assume he could not have been the individual who had caused the deletion of the records.

Logic bombs are difficult to detect because they are often installed by authorized users and, in particular, have been installed by administrators who are also often responsible for security. This demonstrates the need for a separation of duties and a periodic review of all programs and services that are running on a system. It also illustrates the need to maintain an active backup program so that if your organization loses critical files to this sort of malicious code, it loses only transactions that occurred since the most recent backup, resulting in no permanent loss of data.

Backdoor

Backdoors were originally (and sometimes still are) nothing more than methods used by software developers to ensure that they could gain access to an application even if something were to happen in the future to prevent normal access methods. An example would be a hard-coded password that could be used to gain access to the program in the event that administrators forgot their own system password. The obvious problem with this sort of backdoor (also sometimes referred to as a *trapdoor*) is that, since it is hard-coded, it cannot be removed. Should an attacker learn of the backdoor, all systems running that software would be vulnerable to attack.

The term *backdoor* is also, and more commonly, used to refer to programs that attackers install after gaining unauthorized access to a system to ensure that they can continue to have unrestricted access to the system, even if their initial access method is discovered and blocked. Backdoors can also be installed by authorized individuals inadvertently, should they run software that contains a Trojan horse (introduced earlier). Common backdoors include NetBus and Back Orifice. Both of these, if running on your system, can allow an attacker remote access to your system—access that allows them to perform any function on your system. A variation on the backdoor is the rootkit, discussed in a previous section, which is established not to gain root access but rather to ensure continued root access.

 EXAM TIP The Security+ exam objectives include the ability to compare and contrast different forms of attacks, including keyloggers, adware, spyware, bots, RATs, logic bombs, and backdoors. To prepare for the exam, you should understand the differences between these attacks.

Indicators of Compromise

Indicators of compromise (IOCs) are just as the name suggests: indications that a system has been compromised by unauthorized activity. When a threat actor makes changes to a system, either by direct action, malware, or other exploit, forensic artifacts are left behind in the system. IOCs act as bread crumbs for investigators, providing little clues that can help identify the presence of an attack on a system. The challenge is in looking for, collecting, and analyzing these bits of information and then determining what they mean for a given system. This is one of the primary tasks for an incident responder, gathering and processing these disparate pieces of data and creating a meaningful picture of the current state of a system.

Fortunately, there are toolsets to aid the investigator in this task. Tools such as YARA can take a set of signatures (also called IOCs) and then scan a system for them, determining whether or not a specific threshold is met indicating a particular infection. Although the specific list will vary based on the system and the specific threat that one is looking for, a common set of IOCs that firms should monitor include

- Unusual outbound network traffic
- Anomalies in privileged user account activity
- Geographical irregularities in network traffic

- Account login red flags
- Increases in database read volumes
- HTML response sizes
- Large numbers of requests for the same file
- Mismatched port-application traffic, including encrypted traffic on plain ports
- Suspicious registry or system file changes
- Unusual DNS requests
- Unexpected patching of systems
- Mobile device profile changes
- Bundles of data in the wrong place
- Web traffic with nonhuman behavior
- Signs of DDoS activity, even if temporary

No single compromise will exhibit everything on this list, but monitoring these items will tend to catch most compromises, because at some point in the compromise life-cycle, every compromise will exhibit one or more of the preceding behaviors. Then, once detected, a responder can zero in on the information and fully document the nature and scope of the problem.

As with many other sophisticated systems, IOCs have developed their own internal languages, protocols, and tools. Two major, independent systems for communicating IOC information exist:

- **OpenIOC**   Originally developed by Mandiant (acquired by FireEye) to facilitate information of IOC data. Mandiant subsequently made OpenIOC open source.
- **STIX/TAXII/CybOx**   MITRE designed Structured Threat Information Expression (STIX), Trusted Automated Exchange of Indicator Information (TAXII), and Cyber Observable Expression (CybOX) to specifically facilitate automated information sharing between organizations.

Chapter Review

This chapter examined the types of malware commonly found in today's environment, including viruses, polymorphic malware, ransomware, worms, Trojans, keyloggers, root-kits, and more. The chapter then looked at systems including RATs, logic bombs, and backdoors. The chapter concluded with an examination of the topic of indicators of compromise, examining this as a means of determining a past or active infection.

Questions

To help you prepare further for the CompTIA Security+ exam, and to test your level of preparedness, answer the following questions and then check your answers against the correct answers at the end of the chapter.

1. A disgruntled administrator is fired for negligence at your organization. Thirty days later, your organization's internal file server and backup server crash at exactly the same time. Examining the servers, it appears that critical operating system files were deleted from both systems. If the disgruntled administrator was responsible for administering those servers during her employment, this is most likely an example of what kind of malware?

   A. Crypto-malware

   B. Trojan

   C. Worm

   D. Logic bomb

2. A desktop system on your network has been compromised. Despite loading different operating systems using different media on the same desktop, attackers appear to have access to that system every time it is powered up and placed on the network. This could be an example of what type of rootkit?

   A. Application

   B. Kernel

   C. Firmware

   D. Virtual

3. A colleague has been urging you to download a new animated screensaver he has been using for several weeks. While he is showing you the program, the cursor on his screen moves on its own and a command prompt window opens and quickly closes. You can't tell what if anything was displayed in that command prompt window. Your colleague says "It's been doing that for a while, but it's no big deal." Based on what you've seen, you suspect the animated screensaver is really what type of malware?

   A. A worm

   B. A Trojan

   C. Ransomware

   D. Adware

4. Several desktops in your organization are displaying a red screen with the message "Your files have been encrypted. Pay 1 bitcoin to recover them." These desktops have most likely been affected by what type of malware?

   A. Zotob worm

   B. Adware

C. Ransomware

D. Rootkit

5. While port scanning your network for unauthorized systems, you notice one of your file servers has TCP port 31337 open. When you connect to the port with netcat, you see a prompt that reads "Enter password for access:". Your server may be infected with what type of malware?

   A. Virus

   B. Cryptolocker

   C. Backdoor

   D. Spyware

6. A user in your organization is having issues with her laptop. Every time she opens a web browser, she sees different pop-ups every few minutes. It doesn't seem to matter which websites are being visited—the pop-ups still appear. What type of malware does this sound like?

   A. Adware

   B. Virus

   C. Ransomware

   D. BitLocker

7. Your organization is struggling to contain a recent outbreak of malware. On some of the PCs, your antivirus solution is able to detect and clean the malware. On other PCs exhibiting the exact same symptoms, your antivirus solution reports the system is "clean." These PCs are all running the same operating system and same antivirus software. What might be happening?

   A. Your firewall rules are allowing attackers to backdoor those PCs.

   B. The antivirus solution is reporting false negatives on some of the PCs.

   C. The antivirus solution isn't properly licensed on all systems.

   D. Your systems are infected with polymorphic malware.

8. Malware engineers sometimes take steps to prevent reverse engineering of their code. A virus, such as Zeus, that uses encryption to resist reverse engineering attempts is what type of malware?

   A. Armored virus

   B. Rootkit

   C. RAT

   D. Cryptolocker

9. A colleague can't open any Word document he has stored on his local system. When you force open one of the documents to analyze it, you see nothing but seemingly random characters. There's no visible sign the file is still a Word document. Regardless of what you use to view or open the Word documents, you don't see anything but random characters. Your colleague was most likely a victim of what type of malware?

   A. Virus

   B. Crypto-malware

   C. RAT

   D. Backdoor

10. An employee at your organization is concerned because her ex-spouse "seems to know everything she does." She tells you her ex keeps accessing her e-mail and social media accounts even after she has changed her passwords multiple times. She is using a laptop at home that was a gift from her ex. Based on what you've been told, you suspect the laptop has what type of malware loaded on it?

   A. Adware

   B. Keylogger

   C. Logic bomb

   D. Ransomware

11. Users at your organization are complaining about slow systems. Examining several of them, you see that CPU utilization is extremely high and a process called "btmine" is running on each of the affected systems. You also notice each of the affected systems is communicating with an IP address outside your country on UDP port 43232. If you disconnect the network connections on the affected systems, the CPU utilization drops significantly. Based on what you've observed, you suspect these systems are infected with what type of malware?

   A. Adware

   B. Bot

   C. Cryptolocker

   D. Armored Virus

12. A piece of malware is infecting the desktops in your organization. Every hour more systems are infected. The infections are happening in different departments and in cases where the users don't share any files, programs, or even e-mails. What type of malware can cause this type of infection?

   A. Virus

   B. RAT

   C. BitLocker

   D. Worm

13. Which of the following could be an indicator of compromise?

    A. Unusual outbound network traffic

    B. Increased number of logins

    C. Large numbers of requests for the same file

    D. All of the above

14. You notice some unusual network traffic and discover several systems in your organization are communicating with a rather dubious "market research" company on a regular basis. When you investigate further you discover that users of the affected systems all installed the same piece of freeware. What might be happening on your network?

    A. These users unwittingly installed spyware.

    B. These systems are all infected with ransomware.

    C. This could be normal behavior and nothing to worry about.

    D. These systems are infected with logic bombs.

15. Which of the following are characteristics of remote-access Trojans?

    A. They can be deployed through malware such as worms.

    B. They allow attacks to connect to the system remotely.

    C. They give attackers the ability to modify files and change settings.

    D. All of the above.

Answers

    1. D. As both servers crashed at exactly the same time, this is most likely a logic bomb. A *logic bomb* is a piece of code that sits dormant for a period of time until some event or date invokes its malicious payload—in this case, 30 days after the disgruntled employee was fired.

    2. C. This is most likely a firmware rootkit, possibly in the video card or expansion card. In the given scenario, the rootkit has to reside outside of the operating system and applications loaded on that system.

    3. B. The animated screensaver is most likely a Trojan. The software appears to do one thing, but contains hidden, additional functionality. Your colleague brought the Trojan "inside the walls" when he downloaded and installed the software on his desktop.

    4. C. This is quite clearly ransomware. The malware has encrypted files on the affected systems and is demanding payment for recovery of the files.

    5. C. This prompt most likely belongs to a backdoor—an alternate way of accessing the system. The TCP service is listening for incoming connections and prompts for a password when connections are established. Providing the correct password would grant command-line access to the system.

6. **A.** This is classic adware behavior. Unwanted pop-ups that appear during browsing sessions regardless of the website being viewed are very typical of adware.

7. **D.** This is most likely an infection with polymorphic malware. Polymorphic malware is designed to change its own code on a regular basis, but retain the same functionality. The changes in code are designed to mask the malware from signature-based detection. The "clean" PCs in this example are still infected, but with a variant of the malware that no longer matches any signature in the antivirus solution.

8. **A.** An armored virus is a piece of malware specifically designed to resist reverse engineering attempts. Zeus uses encryption in its attempts to prevent security researchers from learning how it works, how it communicates, and so on.

9. **B.** If specific file types are no longer usable and seem to be nothing but strings of random characters, it's likely your colleague was a victim of crypto-malware. Crypto-malware encrypts files on a system to make them unusable to anyone without the decryption key.

10. **B.** This is most likely a keylogger, a piece of software that records all keystrokes entered by the user. If the ex was able to access the logs generated by the keylogger, he would be able to see the new passwords for e-mail and social media accounts as they were being changed.

11. **B.** These systems are most likely infected with a bot and are now part of a botnet. The systems are running an unknown/unauthorized process and communicating with an external IP address on UDP port 43232. These are all classic signs of bots and botnet activity.

12. **D.** This infection pattern is typical of a worm. Worms are self-propagating and don't require any human interaction to spread to additional systems.

13. **D.** Unusual network traffic, additional logins, and large numbers of requests for the same file are all potential indicators of compromise. Individually, they could be considered suspicious, but seen together and affecting the same system would definitely warrant a deeper inspection of that system.

14. **A.** If all the users installed the same piece of freeware, it is likely they are all infected with spyware. Spyware records and reports user behavior and can do everything from recording keystrokes to monitoring web usage. Spyware is often bundled with freeware.

15. **D.** All of these are characteristics of remote-access Trojans (RATs). RATs are often deployed through other malware, allow remote access to the affected system, and give the attacker the ability to manipulate and modify the affected system.

2

Attacks

In this chapter, you will

- Learn how to compare and contrast different types of attacks
- Learn about the different types of attacks, including social engineering, application/service attacks, wireless attacks, and cryptographic attacks

Attacks can be made against virtually any layer or level of software, from network protocols to applications. When an attacker finds a vulnerability in a system, he exploits the weakness to attack the system. The effect of an attack depends on the attacker's intent and can result in a wide range of effects, from minor to severe. An attack on a system might not be visible on that system because the attack is actually occurring on a different system, and the data the attacker will manipulate on the second system is obtained by attacking the first system. Attacks can be against the user, as in social engineering, or against the application, the network, or the cryptographic elements being employed in a system. This chapter compares and contrasts these types of attacks.

Although hackers and viruses receive the most attention in the news, they are not the only methods used to attack computer systems and networks. This chapter addresses many different ways computers and networks are attacked on a daily basis. Each type of attack threatens at least one of the three security requirements: confidentiality, integrity, and availability (the CIA of security).

From a high-level standpoint, attacks on computer systems and networks can be grouped into two broad categories: attacks on specific software (such as an application or the operating system) and attacks on a specific protocol or service. Attacks on a specific application or operating system are generally possible because of an oversight in the code (and possibly in the testing of that code) or because of a flaw, or bug, in the code (again indicating a lack of thorough testing). Attacks on specific protocols or services are attempts either to take advantage of a specific feature of the protocol or service or to use the protocol or service in a manner for which it was not intended. This chapter discusses various forms of attacks of which security professionals need to be aware.

Certification Objective   This chapter covers CompTIA Security+ exam objective 1.2, Compare and contrast types of attacks.

Social Engineering Methods

Social engineering is an attack against a user, and typically involves some form of social interaction. The weakness that is being exploited in the attack is not necessarily one of technical knowledge, or even security awareness. Social engineering at its heart involves manipulating the very social nature of interpersonal relationships. It in essence preys on several characteristics that we tend to desire. The willingness to help, for instance, is a characteristic one would like to see in a team environment. We want employees who help each other, and we tend to reward those who are helpful and punish those who are not.

If our work culture is built around collaboration and teamwork, then how can this be exploited? It is not simple, but it can be accomplished through a series of subtle ruses. One is built around the concept of developing a sense of familiarity—making it seem as if you belong to the group. For example, by injecting yourself into a conversation or encounter, armed with the right words and the correct information, you can make it seem as if you belong. Through careful name dropping and aligning your story with current events and expectations, you can just slip in unnoticed. Another example is by arriving at a door at the same time as a person with an ID card, carrying something in both your hands, you probably can get them to open and hold the door for you. An even more successful technique is to have a conversation on the way to the door over something that makes you fit in. People want to help, and this tactic empowers the person to help you.

A second method involves creating a hostile situation. People tend to want to avoid hostility, so if you are engaged in a heated argument with someone as you enter the group you wish to join—making sure not only that you are losing the argument, but that it also seems totally unfair—you instantly can build a connection to anyone who has been similarly mistreated. Play on sympathy, their desire for compassion, and use that moment to bypass the connection moment.

A good social engineer understands how to use body language to influence others—how to smile at the right time, how to mirror movements, how to influence others not through words but through body language cues. Any woman who has used body language to get a man to do something without directly asking him to do it understands this game. Men understand as well, and they play because they are attempting to get something as well. When someone has the key information you need for a project, a proposal, or any other important thing, trading a quid quo pro is an unspoken ritual. And if you do this with someone who has malicious intent, then remember the saying, "Beware of Greeks bearing gifts."

NOTE Much of social engineering will play to known stereotypical behavior. Detailing this material is not meant to justify the behaviors, for they are in fact wrong. But it is important to watch for them, for these are the tools used by social engineers—crying babies, flirting, hiding in plain sight (the janitor, plant waterer, pizza delivery person)—we are all blinded by biases and conditioning, and social engineers know and exploit these weaknesses. And if called out on the behavior, they will even go with that and protest too much, agree too much, whatever it takes to win a person over. Don't be that person—in either case, using stereotypes or falling prey to them.

PART I

The best defense against social engineering attacks is a comprehensive training and awareness program that includes social engineering, but this does not mean that employees should be trained to be stubborn and unhelpful. Rather, training should emphasize the value of being helpful and working as a team, but doing so in an environment where trust is verified and is a ritual without social stigma. No one will get past TSA employees with social engineering techniques when checking in at an airport, because they dispassionately enforce and follow set procedures, but they frequently do so with kindness, politeness, and helpfulness while also ensuring that the screening procedures are always completed.

 EXAM TIP For the exam, be familiar with all of the various social engineering attacks and the associated effectiveness of each attack.

Phishing

Phishing (pronounced "fishing") is a type of social engineering in which an attacker attempts to obtain sensitive information from users by masquerading as a trusted entity in an e-mail or instant message sent to a large group of often random users. The attacker attempts to obtain information such as usernames, passwords, credit card numbers, and details about the users' bank accounts. The message that is sent often encourages the user to go to a website that appears to be for a reputable entity such as PayPal or eBay, both of which have frequently been used in phishing attempts. The website the user actually visits is not owned by the reputable organization, however, and asks the user to supply information that can be used in a later attack. Often the message sent to the user states that the user's account has been compromised and requests, for security purposes, the user to enter their account information to verify the details.

In another very common example of phishing, the attacker sends a bulk e-mail, supposedly from a bank, telling the recipients that a security breach has occurred and instructing them to click a link to verify that their account has not been tampered with. If the individual actually clicks the link, they are taken to a site that appears to be owned by the bank but is actually controlled by the attacker. When they supply their account and password for "verification" purposes, they are actually giving it to the attacker.

Spear Phishing

Spear phishing is the term that has been created to refer to a phishing attack that targets a specific group with something in common. By targeting a specific group, the ratio of successful attacks (that is, the number of responses received) to the total number of e-mails or messages sent usually increases because a targeted attack will seem more plausible than a message sent to users randomly.

Whaling

High-value targets are referred to as whales. A *whaling* attack is thus one where the target is a high-value person, such as a CEO or CFO. Whaling attacks are not performed by attacking multiple targets and hoping for a reply, but rather are custom-built to increase the odds of success. Spear phishing is a common method used against whales, as it is designed to appear to be ordinary business for the target, being crafted to imitate a non-suspicious communication. Whales can be deceived in the same manner as any other person; the difference is that the target group is limited, hence an attacker cannot rely upon random returns from a wide population of targets.

Vishing

Vishing is a variation of phishing that uses voice communication technology to obtain the information the attacker is seeking. Vishing takes advantage of the trust that some people place in the telephone network. Users are unaware that attackers can spoof (simulate) calls from legitimate entities using Voice over IP (VoIP) technology. Voice messaging can also be compromised and used in these attempts. This is used to establish a form of trust that is then exploited by the attacker over the phone. Generally, the attackers are hoping to obtain credit card numbers or other information that can be used in identity theft. The user may receive an e-mail asking him or her to call a number that is answered by a potentially compromised voice message system. Users may also receive a recorded message that appears to come from a legitimate entity. In both cases, the user will be encouraged to respond quickly and provide the sensitive information so that access to their account is not blocked. If a user ever receives a message that claims to be from a reputable entity and asks for sensitive information, the user should not provide it but instead should use the Internet or examine a legitimate account statement to find a phone number that can be used to contact the entity. The user can then verify that the message received was legitimate or report the vishing attempt.

Tailgating

Tailgating (or piggybacking) is the simple tactic of following closely behind a person who has just used their own access card or personal identification number (PIN) to gain physical access to a room or building. People are often in a hurry and will frequently not follow good physical security practices and procedures. Attackers know this and may attempt to exploit this characteristic in human behavior. An attacker can thus gain access to the facility without having to know the access code or having to acquire an access card. It is similar to shoulder surfing in that it relies on the attacker taking advantage of an authorized user who is not following security procedures. Frequently the attacker may even start a conversation with the target before reaching the door so that the user may be more comfortable with allowing the individual in without challenging them. In this sense piggybacking is related to social engineering attacks.

Both the piggybacking and shoulder surfing attack techniques rely on the poor security practices of an authorized user in order to be successful. Thus, both techniques can be easily countered by training employees to use simple procedures to ensure nobody follows them too closely or is in a position to observe their actions. A more sophisticated counter-measure to piggybacking is a *mantrap*, which utilizes two doors to gain access to the facility. The second door does not open until the first one is closed, and the doors are closely spaced so that an enclosure is formed that only allows one individual through at a time.

Impersonation

Impersonation is a common social engineering technique and can be employed in many ways. It can occur in person, over a phone, or online. In the case of an impersonation attack, the attacker assumes a role that is recognized by the person being attacked, and in assuming that role, the attacker uses the potential victim's biases against their better judgment to follow procedures. Impersonations can occur in a variety of manners, from third parties, to help desk operators, to vendors, or even online sources.

Third-Party Authorization

Using previously obtained information about a project, deadlines, bosses, and so on, the attacker arrives with 1) something the victim is quasi-expecting or would see as normal, 2) uses the guise of a project in trouble or some other situation where the attacker will be viewed as helpful or as someone not to upset, and 3) they name-drop "Mr. Big," who happens to be out of the office and unreachable at the moment, avoiding the reference check. And the attacker seldom asks for anything that on the face of it seems unreasonable, or is unlikely to be shared based on the circumstances. These actions can create the appearance of a third-party authorization, when in fact there is none.

Help Desk/Tech Support

Calls to or from help desk and tech support units can be used to elicit information. Posing as an employee, an attacker can get a password reset, information about some system, or other useful information. The call can go the other direction as well, where the social engineer is posing as the help desk or tech support. Then, by calling employees, the attacker can get information on system status and other interesting elements that they can use later.

Contractors/Outside Parties

It is common in many organizations to have outside contractors clean the building, water the plants, and do other routine chores. In many of these situations, without proper safeguards, an attacker can simply put on clothing that matches a contractor's uniform, show up to do the job at a slightly different time than it's usually done, and, if challenged, play on the sympathy of the workers by saying they are filling in for X or covering for Y. The attacker then roams the halls unnoticed because they blend in, all the while photographing desks and papers and looking for information.

Online Attacks

Impersonation can be employed in online attacks as well. In these cases, technology plays an intermediary role in the communication chain. Some older forms, such as pop-up windows, tend to be less effective today, because users are wary of them. Yet phishing attempts via e-mail and social media scams abound.

Defenses

In all of the cases of impersonation, the best defense is simple—have processes in place that require employees to ask to see a person's ID before engaging with them if the employees do not personally known them. That includes challenging people such as delivery drivers and contract workers. Don't let people in through the door, piggyback-ing, without checking their ID. If this is standard process, then no one becomes offended, and if someone fakes offense, it becomes even more suspicious. Training and awareness do work, as proven by trends such as the diminished effectiveness of pop-up windows. But the key to this defense is to make the training periodic and to tailor it to what is cur-rently being experienced, rather than a generic recitation of best practices.

 EXAM TIP A training and awareness program is still the best defense against social engineering attacks.

Dumpster Diving

The process of going through a target's trash in hopes of finding valuable information that might be used in a penetration attempt is known in the security community as *dumpster diving*. One common place to find information, if the attacker is in the vicin-ity of the target, is in the target's trash. The attacker might find little bits of information that could be useful for an attack. The tactic is not, however, unique to the computer community; it has been used for many years by others, such as identity thieves, private investigators, and law enforcement personnel, to obtain information about an individual or organization. If the attackers are very lucky, and the target's security procedures are very poor, they may actually find user IDs and passwords.

An attacker may gather a variety of information that can be useful in a social engineer-ing attack. In most locations, trash is no longer considered private property after it has been discarded (and even where dumpster diving is illegal, little enforcement occurs). An organization should have policies about discarding materials. Sensitive information should be shredded and the organization should consider securing the trash receptacle so that individuals can't forage through it. People should also consider shredding personal or sensitive information that they wish to discard in their own trash. A reasonable quality shredder is inexpensive and well worth the price when compared with the potential loss that could occur as a result of identity theft.

Shoulder Surfing

Shoulder surfing does not necessarily involve direct contact with the target, but instead involves the attacker directly observing the individual entering sensitive information on a form, keypad, or keyboard. The attacker may simply look over the shoulder of the user at work, for example, or may set up a camera or use binoculars to view the user enter-ing sensitive data. The attacker can attempt to obtain information such as a PIN at an automated teller machine (ATM), an access control entry code at a secure gate or door, or a calling card or credit card number. Many locations now use a small shield to surround a keypad so that it is difficult to observe somebody as they enter information. More sophisticated systems can actually scramble the location of the numbers so that the top row at one time includes the numbers 1, 2, and 3 and the next time includes 4, 8, and 0.

While this makes it a bit slower for the user to enter information, it thwarts an attacker's attempt to observe what numbers are pressed and then enter the same buttons/pattern, since the location of the numbers constantly changes.

Hoax

At first glance, it might seem that a hoax related to security would be considered a nuisance and not a real security issue. This might be the case for some hoaxes, especially those of the urban legend type, but the reality of the situation is that a *hoax* can be very damaging if it causes users to take some sort of action that weakens security. One real hoax, for example, described a new, highly destructive piece of malicious software. It instructed users to check for the existence of a certain file and to delete it if the file was found. In reality, the file mentioned was an important file used by the operating system, and deleting it caused problems the next time the system was booted. The damage caused by users modifying security settings can be serious. As with other forms of social engineering, training and awareness are the best and first line of defense for both users and administrators. Users should be trained to be suspicious of unusual e-mails and stories and should know who to contact in the organization to verify their validity if they are received. A hoax often also advises the user to send it to their friends so that they know about the issue as well—and by doing so, they help spread the hoax. Users need to be suspicious of any e-mail telling them to "spread the word."

Watering Hole Attack

The most commonly recognized attack vectors are those that are direct to a target. Because of their incoming and direct nature, defenses are crafted to detect and defend against them. But what if the user "asked" for the attack by visiting a website? Just as a hunter waits near a watering hole for animals to come drink, attackers can plant malware at sites where users are likely to frequent. First identified by RSA, a *watering hole attack* involves the infecting of a target website with malware. In some of the cases detected, the infection was constrained to a specific geographical area. These are not simple attacks, yet they can be very effective at delivering malware to specific groups of end users. Watering hole attacks are complex to achieve and appear to be backed by nation states and other high-resource attackers. In light of the stakes, the typical attack vector will be a zero day attack to further avoid detection.

Social Engineering Principles

Social engineering is very successful for two general reasons. The first is the basic desire of most people to be helpful. When somebody asks a question for which we know the answer, our normal response is not to be suspicious but rather to answer the question. The problem with this is that seemingly innocuous information can be used either directly in an attack or indirectly to build a bigger picture that an attacker can use to create an aura of authenticity during an attack—the more information an individual has about an organization, the easier it will be to convince others that he is part of the organization and has a right to even sensitive information.

The second reason that social engineering is successful is that individuals normally seek to avoid confrontation and trouble. If the attacker attempts to intimidate the target, threatening to call the target's supervisor because of a lack of help, the target may give in and provide the information to avoid confrontation.

Tools

The tools in a social engineer's toolbox are based on a knowledge of psychology and don't necessarily require a sophisticated knowledge of software or hardware. The social engineer will employ strategies aimed to exploit people's own biases and beliefs in a manner to momentarily deny them the service of good judgment and the use of standard procedures. Employing social engineering tools is second nature to a social engineer, and with skill they can switch these tools in and out in any particular circumstance, just as a plumber uses various hand tools and a system administrator uses OS commands to achieve complex tasks. When watching any of these professionals work, we may marvel at how they wield their tools, and the same is true for social engineers—except their tools are more subtle, and the target is people and trust. The "techniques" that are commonly employed in many social engineering attacks are described next.

NOTE A great video showing the use of several social engineering tools can be found at https://www.youtube.com/watch?v=lc7scxvKQOo ("This is how hackers hack you using simple social engineering"). This video demonstrates the use of vishing to steal someone's cell phone credentials.

Authority

The use of *authority* in social situations can lead to an environment where one party feels at risk in challenging another over an issue. If an attacker can convince a target that he has *authority* in a particular situation, he can entice the target to act in a particular manner or risk adverse consequences. In short, if you act like a boss when requesting something, people are less likely to withhold it.

The best defense against this and many social engineering attacks is a strong set of policies that has no exceptions. Much like security lines in the airport, when it comes to the point of screening, everyone gets screened, even flight crews, so there is no method of bypassing the critical step.

Intimidation

Intimidation can be either subtle, through perceived power, or more direct, through the use of communications that build an expectation of superiority.

Consensus

Consensus is a group-wide decision. It frequently comes not from a champion, but rather through rounds of group negotiation. These rounds can be manipulated to achieve desired outcomes. The social engineer simply motivates others to achieve her desired outcome.

Scarcity

If something is in short supply and is valued, then arriving with what is needed can bring rewards—and acceptance. "Only *X* widgets left at this price" is an example of this technique. Even if something is not scarce, implied scarcity, or implied future change in availability, can create a perception of scarcity. By giving the impression of *scarcity*, or short supply, of a desirable product, an attacker can motivate a target to make a decision quickly without deliberation.

Familiarity

People do things for people they like or feel connected to. Building this sense of *familiarity* and appeal can lead to misplaced trust. The social engineer can focus the conversation on familiar items, not the differences. Again, leading with persuasion that one has been there before and done something, even if they haven't, for perception will lead to the desired familiar feeling.

Trust

Trust is defined as having an understanding of how something will act under specific conditions. Social engineers can shape the perceptions of a target to where they will apply judgments to the trust equation and come to false conclusions. The whole objective of social engineering is not to force people to do things they would not do, but rather to give them a pathway that leads them to feel they are doing the correct thing in the moment.

Urgency

Time can be manipulated to drive a sense of *urgency* and prompt shortcuts that can lead to opportunities for interjection into processes. Limited-time offers should always be viewed as suspect. Perception is the key. Giving the target a reason to believe that they can take advantage of a time situation, whether it really is present or not, achieves the outcome of them acting in a desired manner.

 EXAM TIP The key in all social engineering attacks is that you are manipulating a person and their actions by manipulating their perception of a situation. A social engineer preys on people's beliefs, biases, and stereotypes—to the victim's detriment. This is hacking the human side of a system.

Application/Service Attacks

In the beginning of the computer security era, most attacks were against the network and operating system layers because both had easily exploitable vulnerabilities and were relatively ubiquitous. As the networking companies and OS vendors cleaned up their code bases, exploiting these layers became much more difficult. Attackers shifted their focus to applications. The application layer was a much less homogenous target because there were many different applications, but the ubiquity of vulnerabilities made up for the lower level of homogeneity. Certain desktop applications, like Adobe Flash and Acrobat, became frequent targets.

Application security controls and techniques are important in ensuring that the applications deployed are as secure as possible. Establishing the security of an application begins with secure coding techniques and then adding security controls to provide defense in depth. Using application hardening techniques and proper configuration and change controls provides a process-driven method to ensure continued security per a defined risk profile.

DoS

Denial-of-service (DoS) attacks can exploit a known vulnerability in a specific application or operating system, or they can attack features (or weaknesses) in specific protocols or services. In a DoS attack, the attacker attempts to deny authorized users access either to specific information or to the computer system or network itself. This can be accomplished by crashing the system—taking it offline—or by sending so many requests that the machine is overwhelmed.

The purpose of a DoS attack can be simply to prevent access to the target system, or the attack can be used in conjunction with other actions to gain unauthorized access to a computer or network. For example, a SYN flooding attack can be used to prevent service to a system temporarily in order to take advantage of a trusted relationship that exists between that system and another.

SYN flooding is an example of a DoS attack that takes advantage of the way TCP/IP networks were designed to function, and it can be used to illustrate the basic principles of any DoS attack. SYN flooding uses the TCP three-way handshake that establishes a connection between two systems. Under normal circumstances, the first system sends a SYN packet to the system with which it wants to communicate. The second system responds with a SYN/ACK if it is able to accept the request. When the initial system receives the SYN/ACK from the second system, it responds with an ACK packet, and communication can then proceed. This process is shown in Figure 2-1.

In a SYN flooding attack, the attacker sends fake communication requests to the targeted system. Each of these requests will be answered by the target system, which then waits for the third part of the handshake. Since the requests are fake (a nonexistent IP address is used in the requests, so the target system is responding to a system that doesn't exist), the target will wait for responses that never come, as shown in Figure 2-2. The target system will drop these connections after a specific time-out period, but if the attacker

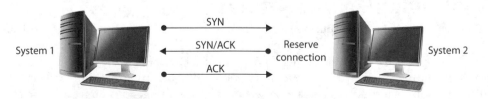

Figure 2-1   The TCP three-way handshake

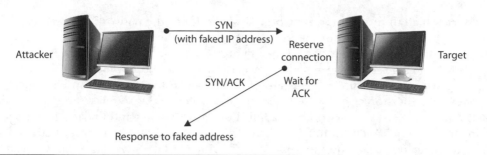

Figure 2-2 A SYN flooding DoS attack

sends requests faster than the time-out period eliminates them, the system will quickly be filled with requests. The number of connections a system can support is finite, so when more requests come in than can be processed, the system will soon be reserving all its connections for fake requests. At this point, any further requests are simply dropped (ignored), and legitimate users who want to connect to the target system will not be able to do so, because use of the system has been denied to them.

Another simple DoS attack is the infamous ping of death (POD), and it illustrates the other type of attack—one targeted at a specific application or operating system, as opposed to SYN flooding, which targets a protocol. In the POD attack, the attacker sends an Internet Control Message Protocol (ICMP) ping packet equal to, or exceeding, 64KB (which is to say, greater than $64 \times 1024 = 65,536$ bytes). This type of packet should not occur naturally (there is no reason for a ping packet to be larger than 64KB). Certain systems are not able to handle this size of packet, and the system will hang or crash.

DDoS

DoS attacks are conducted using a single attacking system. A DoS attack employing multiple attacking systems is known as a *distributed denial-of-service (DDoS)* attack. The goal of a DDoS attack is also to deny the use of or access to a specific service or system. DDoS attacks were made famous in 2000 with the highly publicized attacks on eBay, CNN, Amazon, and Yahoo!.

In a DDoS attack, service is denied by overwhelming the target with traffic from many different systems. A network of attack agents (sometimes called zombies) is created by the attacker, and upon receiving the attack command from the attacker, the attack agents commence sending a specific type of traffic against the target. If the attack network is large enough, even ordinary web traffic can quickly overwhelm the largest of sites, such as the 400-Gbps CloudFlare attack in early 2014.

Creating a DDoS network is no simple task. The attack agents are not willing agents—they are systems that have been compromised and on which the DDoS attack software has been installed. To compromise these agents, the attacker has to have gained unauthorized access to the system or tricked authorized users to run a program that installed the attack software. The creation of the attack network may in fact be a multistep process in which the attacker first compromises a few systems that are then used as handlers or masters, which in turn compromise other systems. Once the network has been created, the agents (zombies) wait for an attack message that will include data on the specific target before launching the attack. One important aspect of a DDoS attack is that with just a few messages to the agents, the attacker can have a flood of messages sent against the targeted system. Figure 2-3 illustrates a DDoS network with agents and handlers.

How can you stop or mitigate the effects of a DoS or DDoS attack? One important precaution is to ensure that you have applied the latest patches and updates to your systems and the applications running on them. Once a specific vulnerability is discovered, it does not take long before multiple exploits are written to take advantage of it. Generally, you will have a small window of opportunity in which to patch your system between the time the vulnerability is discovered and the time exploits become widely available. A vulnerability can also be discovered by hackers, and exploits provide the first clues that a system has been compromised. Attackers can also reverse-engineer patches to learn what vulnerabilities have been patched, allowing them to attack unpatched systems.

Another approach involves changing the time-out option for TCP connections so that attacks such as the SYN flooding attack are more difficult to perform, because unused connections are dropped more quickly.

For DDoS attacks, much has been written about distributing your own workload across several systems so that any attack against your system would have to target several hosts to be completely successful. While this is true, if large enough DDoS networks are created (with tens of thousands of zombies, for example), any network, no matter how much the load is distributed, can be successfully attacked. Such an approach also involves additional costs to your organization to establish this distributed environment. Addressing the problem in this manner is actually an attempt to mitigate the effect of the attack, rather than preventing or stopping an attack.

To prevent a DDoS attack, you must either be able to intercept or block the attack messages or keep the DDoS network from being established in the first place. Tools have been developed that will scan your systems, searching for sleeping zombies waiting for an attack signal. Many of the current antivirus/spyware security suite tools will detect known

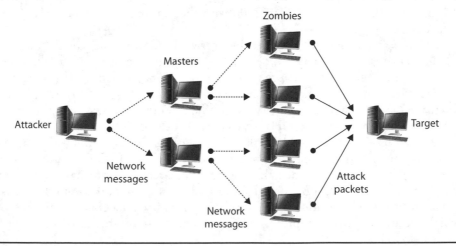

Figure 2-3   DDoS attacks

zombie-type infections. The problem with this type of prevention approach, however, is that it is not something you can do to prevent an attack on your network—it is something you can do to keep your network from being used to attack other networks or systems. You have to rely on the community of network administrators to test their own systems to prevent attacks on yours.

A final option you should consider that will address several forms of DoS and DDoS attacks is to block ICMP packets at your border, since many attacks rely on ICMP. Carefully consider this approach before implementing it, however, because it will also prevent the use of some possibly useful troubleshooting tools.

Man-in-the-Middle

A *man-in-the-middle* attack, as the name implies, generally occurs when an attacker is able to place himself in the middle of two other hosts that are communicating. Ideally (from the attacker's perspective), this is done by ensuring that all communication going to or from the target host is routed through the attacker's host (which can be accomplished if the attacker can compromise the router for the target host). The attacker can then observe all traffic before relaying it, and can actually modify or block traffic. To the target host, it appears that communication is occurring normally, since all expected replies are received. Figure 2-4 illustrates this type of attack.

There are numerous methods of instantiating a man-in-the-middle attack. One of the common methods is via *session hijacking*, which can occur when information such as a cookie is stolen, allowing the attacker to impersonate the legitimate session. This attack can be a result of a cross-site scripting attack, which tricks a user into executing code resulting in cookie theft. The amount of information that can be obtained in a man-in-the-middle attack will be limited if the communication is encrypted. Even in this case, however, sensitive information can still be obtained, since knowing what communication is being conducted, and between which individuals, may in fact provide information that is valuable in certain circumstances.

Buffer Overflow

If there's one item that could be labeled as the "Most Wanted" in coding security, it would be the buffer overflow. The CERT Coordination Center (CERT/CC) at Carnegie Mellon University estimates that nearly half of all exploits of computer programs stem historically from some form of buffer overflow. Finding a vaccine to buffer overflows would stamp

Figure 2-4
A man-in-the-middle attack

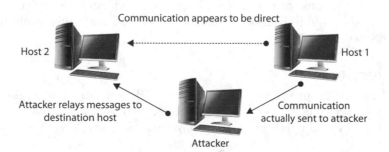

Communication appears to be direct

Host 2

Host 1

Attacker relays messages to destination host

Communication actually sent to attacker

Attacker

out half of these security-related incidents, by type, and probably 90 percent by volume. The Morris finger worm in 1988 was an exploit of an overflow, as were more recent big-name events such as Code Red and Slammer. The generic classification of buffer overflows includes many variants, such as static buffer overruns, indexing errors, format string bugs, Unicode and ANSI buffer size mismatches, and heap overruns.

The concept behind these vulnerabilities is relatively simple. In a *buffer overflow*, the input buffer that is used to hold program input is overwritten with data that is larger than the buffer can hold. The root cause of this vulnerability is a mixture of two things: poor programming practice and programming language weaknesses. For example, what would happen if a program that asks for a 7- to 10-character phone number instead receives a string of 150 characters? Many programs will provide some error checking to ensure that this will not cause a problem. Some programs, however, cannot handle this error, and the extra characters continue to fill memory, overwriting other portions of the program. This can result in a number of problems, including causing the program to abort or the system to crash. Under certain circumstances, the program can execute a command supplied by the attacker. Buffer overflows typically inherit the level of privilege enjoyed by the program being exploited. This is why programs that use root-level access are so dangerous when exploited with a buffer overflow, as the code that will execute does so at root-level access.

Programming languages such as C were designed for space and performance constraints. Many functions in C, like **gets()**, are unsafe in that they will permit unsafe operations, such as unbounded string manipulation into fixed buffer locations. The C language also permits direct memory access via pointers, a functionality that provides a lot of programming power, but carries with it the burden of proper safeguards being provided by the programmer.

 EXAM TIP Buffer overflows can occur in any code, and code that runs with privilege has an even greater risk profile. In 2014, a buffer overflow in the OpenSSL library, called Heartbleed, left hundreds of thousands of systems vulnerable and exposed critical data for tens to hundreds of million users worldwide.

Buffer overflows are input validation attacks, designed to take advantage of input routines that do not validate the length of inputs. Surprisingly simple to resolve, all that is required is the validation of all input lengths (input validation) prior to writing to memory. This can be done in a variety of manners, including the use of safe library functions for inputs. This is one of the vulnerabilities that has been shown to be solvable, and in fact the prevalence is declining substantially among major security-conscious software firms.

Injection

When user input is used without input validation, this results in an opportunity for an attacker to craft input to create specific events to occur when the input is parsed and used by an application. SQL *injection* attacks involve the manipulation of input, resulting in a SQL statement that is different than intended by the designer. XML and LDAP injections are done in the same fashion. As SQL, XML, and LDAP are used to store data, this can give an attacker access to data against business rules. Command injection attacks can occur when input is used in a fashion that allows command-line manipulation. This can give an attacker command-line access at the privilege level of the application.

Cross-Site Scripting

Cross-site scripting (XSS) is one of the most common web attack methodologies. The cause of the vulnerability is weak user input validation. If input is not validated properly, an attacker can include a script in their input and have it rendered as part of the web process. There are several different types of XSS attacks, which are distinguished by the effect of the script:

- **Non-persistent XSS attack**   The injected script is not persisted or stored, but rather is immediately executed and passed back via the web server.
- **Persistent XSS attack**   The script is permanently stored on the web server or some back-end storage. This allows the script to be used against others who log in to the system.
- **DOM-based XSS attack**   The script is executed in the browser via the Document Object Model (DOM) process as opposed to the web server.

Cross-site scripting attacks can result in a wide range of consequences, and in some cases, the list can be anything that a clever scripter can devise. Common uses that have been seen in the wild include

- Theft of authentication information from a web application
- Session hijacking
- Deploying hostile content
- Changing user settings, including future users
- Impersonating a user
- Phishing or stealing sensitive information

Controls to defend against XSS attacks include the use of anti-XSS libraries to strip scripts from the input sequences. Various other ways to mitigate XSS attacks include limiting types of uploads and screening the size of uploads, whitelisting inputs, and so on, but attempting to remove scripts from inputs can be a tricky task. Well-designed anti-XSS input library functions have proven to be the best defense. Cross-site scripting vulnerabilities are easily tested for and should be a part of the test plan for every application. Testing a variety of encoded and unencoded inputs for scripting vulnerability is an essential test element.

Cross-Site Request Forgery

Cross-site request forgery (XSRF) attacks utilize unintended behaviors that are proper in defined use but are performed under circumstances outside the authorized use. This is an example of a "confused deputy" problem, a class of problems where one entity mistakenly performs an action on behalf of another. An XSRF attack relies upon several conditions to be effective. It is performed against sites that have an authenticated user and exploits the site's trust in a previous authentication event. Then, by tricking a user's browser to send an HTTP request to the target site, the trust is exploited. Assume your bank allows you to log in and perform financial transactions, but does not validate the authentication for each subsequent transaction. If a user is logged in and has not closed their browser, then an action in another browser tab could send a hidden request to the bank, resulting in a transaction that appears to be authorized but in fact was not done by the user.

There are many different mitigation techniques that can be employed, from limiting authentication times, to cookie expiration, to managing some specific elements of a web page like header checking. The strongest method is the use of random XSRF tokens in form submissions. Subsequent requests cannot work, as the token was not set in advance. Testing for XSRF takes a bit more planning than for other injection-type attacks, but this, too, can be accomplished as part of the design process.

Privilege Escalation

Cyberattacks are multistep processes. Most attacks begin at a privilege level associated with an ordinary user. From this level, the attacker exploits vulnerabilities that enable them to achieve root- or admin-level access. This step in the attack chain is called *privilege escalation* and is essential for many attack efforts.

There are a couple of ways to achieve privilege escalation. On pathway is to use existing privilege and do an act that allows you to steal a better set of credentials. The use of sniffers to grab credentials, getting the SAM or etc/passwd file, is one method of obtaining "better" credentials. Another method is through vulnerabilities or weaknesses in processes that are running with escalated privilege. Injecting malicious code into these processes can also achieve escalated privilege.

 EXAM TIP Blocking privilege escalation is an important defensive step in a system. This is the rationale behind Microsoft's recent reduction in processes and services that run in elevated mode. This greatly reduces the attack surface available for an attacker to perform this essential task.

ARP Poisoning

In moving packets between machines, a device sometimes needs to know where to send a packet using the MAC or layer 2 address. Address Resolution Protocol (ARP) handles this problem through four basic message types:

- **ARP request** "Who has this IP address?"
- **ARP reply** "I have that IP address; my MAC address is…"

- **Reverse ARP request (RARP)**   "Who has this MAC address?"
- **RARP reply**   "I have that MAC address; my IP address is…"

These messages are used in conjunction with a device's ARP table, where a form of short-term memory associated with these data elements resides. The commands are used as a simple form of lookup. When a machine sends an ARP request to the network, the reply is received and entered into all devices that hear the reply. This facilitates efficient address lookups, but also makes the system subject to attack.

When the ARP table gets a reply, it automatically trusts the reply and updates the table. Some operating systems will even accept ARP reply data if they never heard the original request. There is no mechanism to verify the veracity of the data received. An attacker can send messages, corrupt the ARP table, and cause packets to be misrouted. This form of attack is called *ARP poisoning* and results in malicious address redirection. This can allow a mechanism whereby an attacker can inject themselves into the middle of a conversation between two machines, a man-in-the-middle attack.

Amplification

Certain types of attacks could be considered to be dependent upon volume, such as DoS and DDoS attacks. For these attacks to generate a sufficient volume of packets to overwhelm a host, typically a large server, they require more than a single home PC. *Amplification* is a trick where an attacker uses a specific protocol aspect to achieve what a single machine cannot by itself. As an example, consider the ICMP command **ping**. If you issue an ICMP **ping** command, the machine receiving it provides a ping reply packet. What if you were to send the ICMP request to a network address, in essence all active hosts within that network? They would all reply with a packet. Now, suppose that an attacker forges the requesting packet so that the reply address is a specific machine. The net effect is all of those machines will reply to the forged address—one machine, with an amplified response.

DNS Poisoning

The DNS system is used to convert a name into an IP address. There is not a single DNS system, but rather a hierarchy of DNS servers, from root servers on the backbone of the Internet, to copies at your ISP, your home router, and your local machine, each in the form of a DNS cache. To examine a DNS query for a specific address, you can use the **nslookup** command. Figure 2-5 shows a series of DNS queries executed on a Windows machine. In the first request, the DNS server was from an ISP, while on the second request, the DNS server was from a VPN connection. Between the two requests, the network connections were changed, resulting in different DNS lookups. The changing of where DNS is resolved can be a *DNS poisoning* attack. The challenge in detecting these attacks is knowing what the authoritative DNS entry should be, and detecting when it changes in an unauthorized fashion. Using a VPN can change a DNS source, and this may be desired, but unauthorized changes can be attacks.

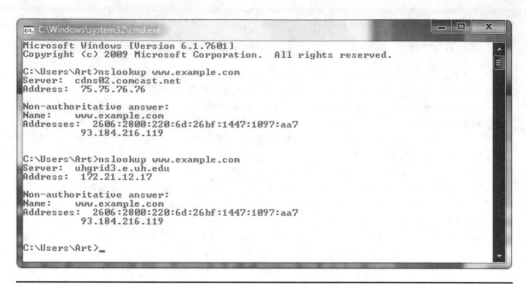

Figure 2-5   nslookup of a DNS query

At times, **nslookup** will return a nonauthoritative answer, as shown in Figure 2-6. This typically means the result is from a cache as opposed to a server that has an authoritative (that is, known to be current) answer.

There are other commands you can use to examine and manipulate the DNS cache on a system. In Windows, the **ipconfig /displaydns** command will show the current DNS cache on a machine. Figure 2-7 shows a small DNS cache. This cache was recently emptied using the **ipconfig /flushdns** command to make it fit on the screen.

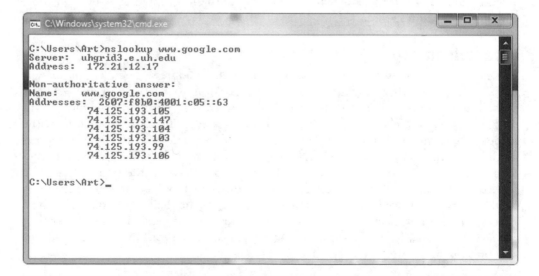

Figure 2-6   Cache response to a DNS query

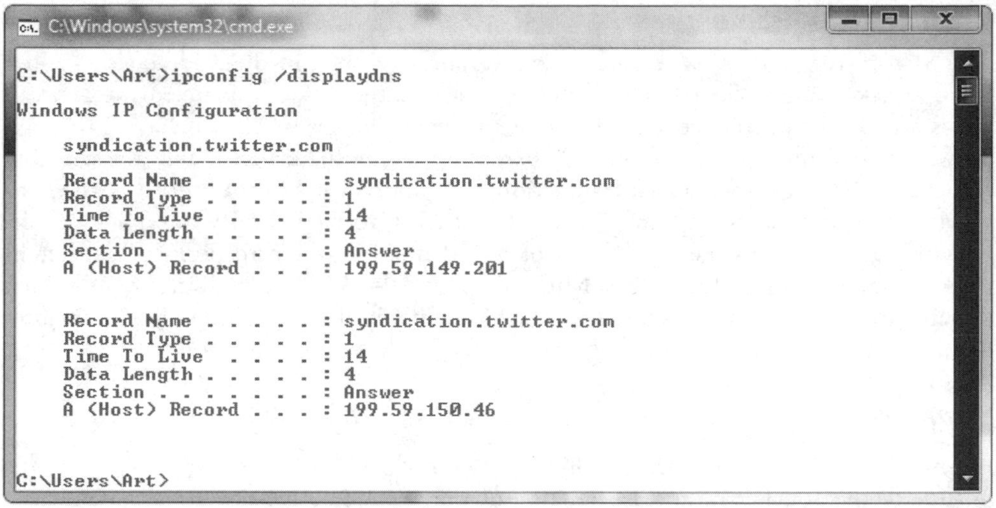

```
C:\Windows\system32\cmd.exe                                    _  □  X

C:\Users\Art>ipconfig /displaydns

Windows IP Configuration

   syndication.twitter.com
   ----------------------------------------------------------
   Record Name . . . . . : syndication.twitter.com
   Record Type . . . . . : 1
   Time To Live  . . . . : 14
   Data Length . . . . . : 4
   Section . . . . . . . : Answer
   A (Host) Record . . . : 199.59.149.201


   Record Name . . . . . : syndication.twitter.com
   Record Type . . . . . : 1
   Time To Live  . . . . : 14
   Data Length . . . . . : 4
   Section . . . . . . . : Answer
   A (Host) Record . . . : 199.59.150.46


C:\Users\Art>
```

Figure 2-7 Cache response to a DNS table query

Looking at DNS as a complete system shows that there are hierarchical levels from the top (root server) down to the cache in an individual machine. DNS poisoning can occur at any of these levels, with the effect of the poisoning growing wider the higher up it occurs. In 2010, a DNS poisoning event resulted in the "Great Firewall of China" censoring Internet traffic in the United States until caches were resolved.

DNS poisoning is a variant of a larger attack class referred to as DNS spoofing. In DNS spoofing, an attacker changes a DNS record through any of a multitude of means. There are many ways to perform DNS spoofing, a few of which include compromising a DNS server, the use of the Kaminsky attack, and the use of a false network node advertising a false DNS address. An attacker can even use DNS cache poisoning to result in DNS spoofing. By poisoning an upstream DNS cache, all of the downstream users will get spoofed DNS records.

Because of the importance of integrity on DNS requests and responses, a project has begun to secure the DNS infrastructure using digital signing of DNS records. This project, initiated by the U.S. government and called Domain Name System Security Extensions (DNSSEC), works by digitally signing records. This is done by adding records to the DNS system, a key and a signature attesting to the validity of the key. With this information, requestors can be assured that the information they receive is correct. It will take a substantial amount of time (years) for this new system to propagate through the entire DNS infrastructure, but in the end, the system will have much greater assurance.

Domain Hijacking

Domain hijacking is the act of changing the registration of a domain name without the permission of its original registrant. Technically a crime, this act can have devastating consequences because the DNS system will spread the false domain location far and wide automatically. The original owner can request it to be corrected, but this can take time.

Man-in-the-Browser

The *man-in-the-browser (MitB)* attack is a variant of a man-in-the-middle attack. In a MitB attack, the first element is a malware attack that places a Trojan element that can act as a proxy on the target machine. This malware changes browser behavior through browser helper objects or extensions. When a user connects to their bank, the malware recognizes the target (a financial transaction) and injects itself in the stream of the conversation. When the user approves a transfer of $150 to pay a utility bill, for example, the malware intercepts the user's keystrokes and modifies them to perform a different transaction. A famous example of a MitB attack was the financial malware, Zeus, which targeted financial transactions on users' machines, manipulating and changing them after the users had entered password credentials.

Zero Day

A *zero day* attack is one that uses a vulnerability for which there is no previous knowledge outside of the attacker, or at least not the software vendor. Zero day attacks are critical as there is no known defense to the vulnerability itself, leaving the only security solution to be secondary solutions, such as catching subsequent hacker activity. Zero day vulnerabilities are highly valued by attackers because they are almost sure bets when attacking a system. There is a market in zero day vulnerabilities, where hackers trade them. There is also an interesting question with respect to government collection of zero days, which they use for intelligence operations. Should governments keep secret libraries of zero days, or should they alert the software vendors, allowing patching and protection across the broader environment of systems?

 EXAM TIP Zero day attacks are becoming more common as collections of zero day vulnerabilities are being released by hackers outing government collections of zero day methods. Understanding this term and how it relates to risk in a system is important to differentiate this attack pattern, which is part of the "compare and contrast" aspect of the Security+ objective associated with understanding attacks.

Replay

A *replay* attack occurs when the attacker captures a portion of a communication between two parties and retransmits it at a later time. For example, an attacker might replay a series of commands and codes used in a financial transaction to cause the transaction to be conducted multiple times. Generally, replay attacks are associated with attempts to circumvent authentication mechanisms, such as the capturing and reuse of a certificate or ticket.

The best way to prevent replay attacks is with encryption, cryptographic authentication, and time stamps. If a portion of the certificate or ticket includes a date/time stamp or an expiration date/time, and this portion is also encrypted as part of the ticket or certificate, replaying it at a later time will prove useless, since it will be rejected as having expired.

EXAM TIP The best method for defending against replay attacks is through the use of encryption and short time frames for legal transactions. Encryption can protect the contents from being understood, and a short time frame for a transaction prevents subsequent use.

Pass the Hash

Pass the hash is a hacking technique where the attacker captures the hash used to authenticate a process. They can then use this hash by injecting it into a process in place of the password. This is a highly technical attack, targeting the Windows authentication process, injecting a copy of the password hash directly into the system. The attacker does not need to know the password, but instead can use a captured hash and inject it directly, which will verify correctly, granting access. As this is a very technically specific hack, tools have been developed to facilitate its operation.

Hijacking and Related Attacks

Hijacking is a form of attack where the attacker hijacks a user's experience, typically after the exchange of credentials, or in the background in a manner where the user is not even aware of the attack process.

Clickjacking

Clickjacking is an attack against the design element of a user interface. Clickjacking tricks a web browser user into clicking something different from what the user perceives, by means of malicious code in the web page. This malicious code may be a transparent overlay or other means of disguising rouge elements, but the net result is the user thinks they are clicking one thing but in reality are clicking the attacker's hidden control, causing the browser to execute the attacker's code. If the attacker modifies a page so that a transparent overlay with invisible clickable elements aligns with actual elements, then the code that runs when a click occurs can be the attacker's code.

Session Hijacking

TCP/IP hijacking and *session hijacking* are terms used to refer to the process of taking control of an already existing session between a client and a server. The advantage to an attacker of hijacking over attempting to penetrate a computer system or network is that the attacker doesn't have to circumvent any authentication mechanisms, since the user has already authenticated and established the session. Once the user has completed the authentication sequence, the attacker can then usurp the session and carry on as if the attacker, and not the user, had authenticated with the system. To prevent the user from noticing anything unusual, the attacker can decide to attack the user's system and perform a DoS attack on it, taking it down so that the user, and the system, will not notice the extra traffic that is taking place.

Hijack attacks generally are used against web and Telnet sessions. Sequence numbers as they apply to spoofing also apply to session hijacking, since the hijacker will need to provide the correct sequence numbers to continue the appropriate sessions.

URL Hijacking

URL hijacking is a generic name for a wide range of attacks that target the URL. The URL is the primary means by which a user receives web content. If the correct URL is used, you get the desired content. If the URL is tampered with or altered, you can get different content. There are a wide range of URL-based attacks, from malware manipulations, to typo squatting, to ad-based attacks that make the user think they are clicking the correct link. The net result is the same: the user thinks they are asking for content A, and they get B instead.

Typo Squatting

Typo squatting is an attack form that involves capitalizing upon common typo errors. If a user mistypes a URL, then the result should be a 404 error, or "resource not found." But if an attacker has registered the mistyped URL, then you would land on the attacker's page. This attack pattern is also referred to as *URL hijacking*, *fake URL*, or *brandjacking* if the objective is to deceive based on branding.

There are several reasons that an attacker will pursue this avenue of attack. The most obvious is one of a phishing attack. The fake site collects credentials, passing them on to the real site, and then steps out of the conversation to avoid detection once the credentials are obtained. It can also be used to plant drive-by malware on the victim machine. It can move the packets through an affiliate network, earning click-through revenue based on the typos. There are numerous other forms of attacks that can be perpetrated using a fake URL as a starting point.

Driver Manipulation

Drivers are pieces of software that sit between the operating system and a peripheral device. In one respect, drivers are a part of the OS, an extension. In another respect, drivers are code that is not part of the OS and is developed by firms other than the OS developer. *Driver manipulation* is the attack on a system by changing drivers, thus changing the behavior of the system. Drivers may not be as protected as other parts of the core system, yet they join it when invoked. This has led to drivers being signed and significantly tightening up the environment of drivers and ancillary programs.

Shimming

Shimming is a process of putting a layer of code between the driver and the OS. Shimming allows flexibility and portability, for it enables changes between different versions of an OS without modifying the original driver code. Shimming also represents a means by which malicious code can change a driver's behavior without changing the driver itself.

Refactoring

Refactoring is the process of restructuring existing computer code without changing its external behavior. Refactoring is done to improve nonfunctional attributes of the software, such as improving code readability and/or reducing complexity. Refactoring can uncover design flaws that lead to exploitable vulnerabilities, allowing these to be closed without changing the external behavior of the code. Refactoring is a means by which an attacker can add functionality to a drive, yet maintain its desired functionality. Although this goes against the original principle of refactoring, improving code efficiency, it speaks to the ingenuity of attackers.

Spoofing

Spoofing is nothing more than making data look like it has come from a different source. This is possible in TCP/IP because of the friendly assumptions behind the protocols. When the protocols were developed, it was assumed that individuals who had access to the network layer would be privileged users who could be trusted.

When a packet is sent from one system to another, it includes not only the destination IP address and port but the source IP address as well. You are supposed to fill in the source with your own address, but nothing stops you from filling in another system's address. This is one of the several forms of spoofing.

MAC Spoofing

MAC spoofing is the act of changing a MAC address to bypass security checks based on the MAC address. This can work when the return packets are being routed by IP address and can be correctly linked to the correct MAC address. Not all MAC spoofing is an attack; small firewall routers commonly have a MAC clone function by which the device can clone a MAC address to make it seem transparent to other devices such as the cable modem connection.

IP Address Spoofing

IP is designed to work so that the originators of any IP packet include their own IP address in the From portion of the packet. While this is the intent, nothing prevents a system from inserting a different address in the From portion of the packet. This is known as *IP address spoofing*. An IP address can be spoofed for several reasons.

Smurf Attack

In a specific DoS attack known as a Smurf attack, the attacker sends a spoofed packet to the broadcast address for a network, which distributes the packet to all systems on that network. In the Smurf attack, the packet sent by the attacker to the broadcast address is an echo request with the From address forged so that it appears that another system (the target system) has made the echo request. The normal response of a system to an echo request is an echo reply, and it is used in the ping utility to let a user know whether a remote system is reachable and is responding. In the Smurf attack, the request is sent to all systems on the network, so all will respond with an echo reply to the target system, as shown in Figure 2-8. The attacker has sent one packet and has been able to generate as many as 254 responses aimed at the target. Should the attacker send several of these spoofed requests, or send them to several different networks, the target can quickly become overwhelmed with the volume of echo replies it receives.

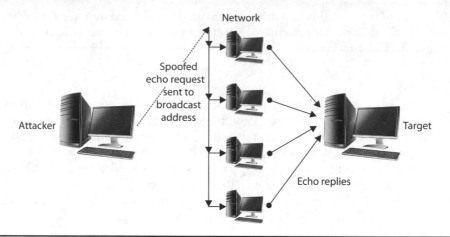

Figure 2-8 Spoofing used in a Smurf DoS attack

EXAM TIP A Smurf attack allows an attacker to use a network structure to send large volumes of packets to a victim. By sending ICMP requests to a broadcast IP address, with the victim as the source address, the multitudes of replies will flood the victim system.

Spoofing and Trusted Relationships

Spoofing can also take advantage of a trusted relationship between two systems. If two systems are configured to accept the authentication accomplished by each other, an individual logged on to one system might not be forced to go through an authentication process again to access the other system. An attacker can take advantage of this arrangement by sending a packet to one system that appears to have come from a trusted system. Since the trusted relationship is in place, the targeted system may perform the requested task without authentication.

Since a reply will often be sent once a packet is received, the system that is being impersonated could interfere with the attack, since it would receive an acknowledgment for a request it never made. The attacker will often initially launch a DoS attack (such as a SYN flooding attack) to temporarily take out the spoofed system for the period of time that the attacker is exploiting the trusted relationship. Once the attack is completed, the DoS attack on the spoofed system would be terminated and the administrators, apart from having a temporarily nonresponsive system, possibly may never notice that the attack occurred. Figure 2-9 illustrates a spoofing attack that includes a SYN flooding attack.

Because of this type of attack, administrators are encouraged to strictly limit any trusted relationships between hosts. Firewalls should also be configured to discard any packets from outside of the firewall that have From addresses indicating they originated from inside the network (a situation that should not occur normally and that indicates spoofing is being attempted).

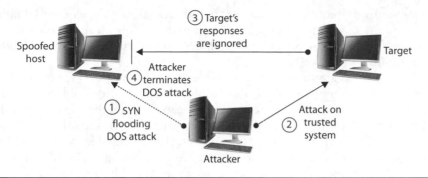

Figure 2-9   Spoofing to take advantage of a trusted relationship

Spoofing and Sequence Numbers

How complicated the spoofing is depends heavily on several factors, including whether the traffic is encrypted and where the attacker is located relative to the target. Spoofing attacks from inside a network, for example, are much easier to perform than attacks from outside of the network, because the inside attacker can observe the traffic to and from the target and can do a better job of formulating the necessary packets.

Formulating the packets is more complicated for external attackers because a sequence number is associated with TCP packets. A sequence number is a 32-bit number established by the host that is incremented for each packet sent. Packets are not guaranteed to be received in order, and the sequence number can be used to help reorder packets as they are received and to refer to packets that may have been lost in transmission.

In the TCP three-way handshake, two sets of sequence numbers are created, as shown in Figure 2-10. The first system chooses a sequence number to send with the original SYN packet. The system receiving this SYN packet acknowledges with a SYN/ACK. It sends an acknowledgment number back, which is based on the first sequence number plus one (that is, it increments the sequence number sent to it by one). It then also creates its own sequence number and sends that along with it. The original system receives the SYN/ACK with the new sequence number. It increments the sequence number by one and uses it as the acknowledgment number in the ACK packet with which it responds.

The difference in the difficulty of attempting a spoofing attack from inside a network and from outside involves determining the sequence number. If the attacker is inside of the network and can observe the traffic with which the target host responds, the attacker can easily see the sequence number the system creates and can respond with the correct

Figure 2-10
Three-way
handshake
with sequence
numbers

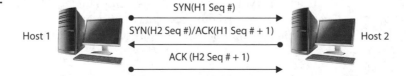

sequence number. If the attacker is external to the network and the sequence number the target system generates is not observed, it is next to impossible for the attacker to provide the final ACK with the correct sequence number. So the attacker has to guess what the sequence number might be.

Sequence numbers are somewhat predictable. Sequence numbers for each session are not started from the same number, so that different packets from different concurrent connections will not have the same sequence numbers. Instead, the sequence number for each new connection is incremented by some large number to keep the numbers from being the same. The sequence number may also be incremented by some large number every second (or some other time period). An external attacker has to determine what values are used for these increments. The attacker can do this by attempting connections at various time intervals to observe how the sequence numbers are incremented. Once the pattern is determined, the attacker can attempt a legitimate connection to determine the current value, and then immediately attempt the spoofed connection. The spoofed connection sequence number should be the legitimate connection incremented by the determined value or values.

EXAM TIP The Security+ exam objective for attacks (1.2) is to compare and contrast different attack types. This means that you need to be able to differentiate attacks based on a set of given symptoms and indications. Learning how these attacks are performed, what they look like, and how to recognize specific attacks is essential for the exam.

Wireless Attacks

Wireless is a common networking technology that has a substantial number of standards and processes to connect users to networks via a radio signal, freeing machines from wires. As in all software systems, wireless networking is a target for hackers. This is partly because of the simple fact that wireless removes the physical barrier.

Replay

A *replay* attack in wireless uses the same principle as replay attacks presented earlier in the "Application/Service Attacks" section. By repeating information, one can try to get repeated behavior from a system. Because wireless systems are not constrained by wires, attackers can copy traffic rather easily between endpoints and the wireless access point. Replay protections are essential in wireless systems to prevent exploitation of the open signal.

EXAM TIP The best method for defending against replay attacks is through the use of encryption and short time frames for legal transactions. Encryption can protect the contents from being understood, and a short time frame for a transaction prevents subsequent use.

IV

The *initialization vector (IV)* is used in wireless systems as the randomization element at the beginning of a connection. Attacks against the IV aim to determine it, thus finding the repeating key sequence.

The IV is the primary reason for the weaknesses in WEP. The IV is sent in the plaintext part of the message, and because the total keyspace is approximately 16 million keys, the same key will be reused. Once the key has been repeated, an attacker has two ciphertexts encrypted with the same key stream. This allows the attacker to examine the ciphertext and retrieve the key. This attack can be improved by examining only packets that have weak IVs, reducing the number of packets needed to crack the key. Using only weak IV packets, the number of required captured packets is reduced to around four or five million, which can take only a few hours to capture on a fairly busy access point (AP). For a point of reference, this means that equipment with an advertised WEP key of 128 bits can be cracked in less than a day, whereas to crack a normal 128-bit key would take roughly 2,000,000,000,000,000,000 years on a computer able to attempt one trillion keys a second. AirSnort is a modified sniffing program that takes advantage of this weakness to retrieve the WEP keys. The biggest weakness of WEP is that the IV problem exists regardless of key length, because the IV always remains at 24 bits.

Evil Twin

The *evil twin* attack is in essence an attack against the wireless protocol via substitute hardware. This attack uses an access point owned by an attacker that usually has been enhanced with higher-power and higher-gain antennas to look like a better connection to the users and computers attaching to it. By getting users to connect through the evil access point, attackers can more easily analyze traffic and perform man-in-the-middle–type attacks. For simple denial of service, an attacker could use interference to jam the wireless signal, not allowing any computer to connect to the access point successfully.

Rogue AP

By setting up a rogue access point, or *rogue AP*, an attacker can attempt to get clients to connect to it as if it were authorized and then simply authenticate to the real AP, a simple way to have access to the network and the client's credentials. Rogue APs can act as a man in the middle and easily steal users' credentials. Enterprises with wireless APs should routinely scan for and remove rogue APs, as users have difficulty avoiding them.

Jamming

Jamming is a form of denial of service that specifically targets the radio spectrum aspect of wireless. Just as other DoS attacks can manipulate things behind the scenes, so can jamming on a wireless AP, enabling things such as attachment to a rogue AP.

WPS

Wi-Fi Protected Setup (WPS) is a network security standard that was created to provide users with an easy method of configuring wireless networks. Designed for home networks and small business networks, this standard involves the use of an eight-digit PIN to configure wireless devices. WPS consists of a series of Extensible Authentication Protocol (EAP) messages and has been shown to be susceptible to a brute force attack. A successful attack can reveal the PIN and subsequently the WPA/WPA2 passphrase and allow unauthorized parties to gain access to the network. Currently, the only effective mitigation is to disable WPS.

Bluejacking

Bluejacking is a term used for the sending of unauthorized messages to another Bluetooth device. This involves sending a message as a phonebook contact:

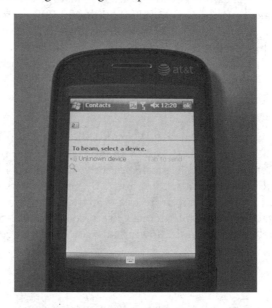

Then the attacker sends the message to the possible recipient via Bluetooth. Originally, this involved sending text messages, but more recent phones can send images or audio as well. A popular variant of this is the transmission of "shock" images, featuring disturbing or crude photos. As Bluetooth is a short-range protocol, the attack and victim must be within roughly 10 yards of each other. The victim's phone must also have Bluetooth enabled and must be in discoverable mode. On some early phones, this was the default configuration, and while it makes connecting external devices easier, it also allows attacks against the phone. If Bluetooth is turned off, or if the device is set to nondiscoverable, bluejacking can be avoided.

Bluesnarfing

Bluesnarfing is similar to bluejacking in that it uses the same contact transmission protocol. The difference is that instead of sending an unsolicited message to the victim's phone, the attacker copies off the victim's information, which can include e-mails, contact lists, calendar, and anything else that exists on that device. More recent phones with media capabilities can be snarfed for private photos and videos. Bluesnarfing used to require a laptop with a Bluetooth adapter, making it relatively easy to identify a possible attacker, but bluesnarfing applications are now available for mobile devices. Bloover, a combination of Bluetooth and Hoover, is one such application that runs as a Java applet. The majority of Bluetooth phones need to be discoverable for the bluesnarf attack to work, but it does not necessarily need to be paired. In theory, an attacker can also brute force the device's unique 48-bit name. A program called RedFang attempts to perform this brute force attack by sending all possible names and seeing what gets a response. This approach was addressed in Bluetooth 1.2 with an anonymity mode.

 EXAM TIP The Security+ exam objective is to compare and contrast attacks, and in the case of bluejacking and bluesnarfing, these are both attacks against Bluetooth. They differ in that bluejacking is the sending of unauthorized data via Bluetooth, whereas bluesnarfing is the unauthorized taking of data over a Bluetooth channel. Understanding this difference is important.

RFID

Radio frequency identification (RFID) tags are used in a wide range of use cases. From tracking devices to keys, the unique serialization of these remotely sensible devices has made them useful in a wide range of applications. RFID tags come in several different forms and can be classified as either active or passive. Active tags have a power source, while passive tags utilize the RF energy transmitted to them for power. RFID tags are used as a means of identification, and have the advantage over bar codes that they do not have to be visible, just within radio wave range, typically centimeters to 200 meters depending upon tag type. RFID tags are used in a range of security situations including contactless identification systems such as smart cards.

RFID tags have multiple security concerns. First and foremost, because they are connected via RF energy, physical security is a challenge. Security is an important issue for RFID tag systems because they form a means of identification and there is a need for authentication and confidentiality of the data transfers. There are several standards associated with securing the RFID data flow, including ISO/IEC 18000 and ISO/IEC 29167 for cryptography methods to support confidentiality, untraceability, tag and reader authentication, and over-the-air privacy, while ISO/IEC 20248 specifies a digital signature data structure for use in RFID systems.

There are several different attack types that can be performed against RFID systems:

- Against the RFID devices themselves, the chips and readers
- Against the communication channel between the device and the reader
- Against the reader and back-end system

The last type is more of a standard IT/IS attack depending upon the interfaces used (web, database, etc.) and is not covered any further. Attacks against the communication channel are relatively easy because the radio frequencies are known and devices exist to interface with tags. Two main attacks are replay and eavesdropping. In a replay attack, the RFID information is recorded and then replayed later. In the case of an RFID-based access badge, it could be read in a restaurant from a distance and then replayed at the appropriate entry point to gain entry. In the case of eavesdropping, the data can be collected, monitoring the movement of tags for whatever purpose needed by an unauthorized party. Both of these attacks are easily defeated using the ISO/IEC security standards previously listed.

If eavesdropping is possible, then what about man-in-the-middle attacks? These are certainly possible, as they would be a combination of a sniffing (eavesdropping) action, followed by a replay (spoofing) attack. This leads to the question as to whether an RFID can be cloned. And again, the answer is yes, if the RFID information is not protected via a cryptographic component.

NFC

Near field communication (NFC) is a set of wireless technologies that enables smartphones and other devices to establish radio communication over a short proximity, typically a distance of 10 cm (3.9 in) or less. This technology did not see much use until recently when it started being employed to move data between cell phones and in mobile payment systems. Now that NFC has become the mainstream method of payments via mobile phones, it is becoming ubiquitous, and in many cases connected directly to financial information, the importance of understanding and protecting this communication channel is paramount.

Disassociation

Disassociation attacks against a wireless system are attacks designed to disassociate a host from the wireless access point, and from the wireless network. Disassociation attacks stem from the deauthentication frame that is in the IEEE 802.11 (Wi-Fi) standard. The deauthentication frame is designed as a tool to remove unauthorized stations from a Wi-Fi access point, but because of the design of the protocol, they can be implemented by virtually anyone. An attacker only needs to have the MAC address of the intended victim, which enables them to send a spoofed message to the access point, specifically spoofing the MAC address of the victim machine. This results in the disconnection of the victim machine, making this attack a form of denial of service.

Disassociation attacks are not typically used alone, but rather in concert with another attack objective. For instance, if you disassociate a connection and then sniff the reconnect, you can steal passwords. After disassociating a machine, the user attempting to reestablish a WPA or WPA2 session will need to repeat the WPA four-way handshake. This gives the hacker a chance to sniff this event, the first step in gathering needed information for a brute force or dictionary-based WPA password-cracking attack. Forcing users to reconnect creates a chance to mount a man-in-the-middle attack against content provided during a connection. This has been used by the Wifiphisher tool to collect passwords.

Cryptographic Attacks

Attacks against the cryptographic system are referred to as *cryptographic attacks*. These attacks are designed to take advantage of two specific weaknesses. First, users widely view cryptography as magic, or otherwise incomprehensible "stuff," leading them to trust the results without valid reasons. Second, although understood by computer scientists, algorithmic weaknesses that can be exploited are frequently overlooked by developers.

Birthday

The *birthday* attack is a special type of brute force attack that gets its name from something known as the birthday paradox, which states that in a group of at least 23 people, the chance that two individuals will have the same birthday is greater than 50 percent. Mathematically, we can use the equation $1.25k^{1/2}$ (with k equaling the size of the set of possible values), and in the birthday paradox, k would be equal to 365 (the number of possible birthdays). This same phenomenon applies to passwords, with k (number of passwords) being quite a bit larger.

Known Plaintext/Ciphertext

If an attacker has the original plaintext and ciphertext for a message, then they can determine the key used through brute force attempts targeting the keyspace. These *known plaintext/ciphertext* attacks can be difficult to mitigate, as some messages are particularly prone to this problem. For example, by having known messages, such as the German weather reports, during WWII, the Allies were able to use cryptanalysis techniques to eventually determine the Enigma machine rotor combinations, leading to the breakdown of that system. Modern cryptographic algorithms have protections included in the implementations to guard against this form of attack. One is the use of large keyspaces, making the brute force spanning of the keyspace, or even a significant portion of it, no longer possible.

Password Attacks

The most common form of authentication is the user ID and password combination. While it is not inherently a poor mechanism for authentication, the combination can be attacked in several ways. All too often, these attacks yield favorable results for the attacker, not as a result of a weakness in the scheme but usually due to the user not following good password procedures.

Poor Password Choices

The least technical of the various password-attack techniques consists of the attacker simply attempting to guess the password of an authorized user of the system or network. It is surprising how often this simple method works, and the reason it does is because people are notorious for picking poor passwords. Users need to select a password that they can remember, so they create simple passwords, such as their birthday, their mother's maiden name, the name of their spouse or one of their children, or even simply their user ID itself. All it takes is for the attacker to obtain a valid user ID (often a simple matter, because organizations tend to use an individual's names in some combination—first letter of their first name combined with their last name, for example) and a little bit of information about the user before guessing can begin. Organizations sometimes make it even easier for attackers to obtain this sort of information by posting the names of their "management team" and other individuals, sometimes with short biographies, on their websites.

Even if a person doesn't use some personal detail as their password, the attacker may still get lucky, since many people use a common word for their password. Attackers can obtain lists of common passwords—a number of such lists exist on the Internet. Words such as "password" and "secret" have often been used as passwords. Names of favorite sports teams also often find their way onto lists of commonly used passwords.

Rainbow Tables

Rainbow tables are precomputed tables or hash values associated with passwords. Using rainbow tables can change the search for a password from a computational problem to a lookup problem. This can tremendously reduce the level of work needed to crack a given password. The best defense against rainbow tables is *salted hashes*, as the addition of a salt value increases the complexity of the problem by making the precomputing process not replicable between systems. A *salt* is merely a random set of characters designed to increase the length of the item being hashed, effectively making rainbow tables too big to compute.

Dictionary

Another method of determining passwords is to use a password-cracking program that uses a list of dictionary words to try to guess the password, hence the name *dictionary* attack. The words can be used by themselves, or two or more smaller words can be combined to form a single possible password. A number of commercial and public-domain password-cracking programs employ a variety of methods to crack passwords, including using variations on the user ID.

These programs often permit the attacker to create various rules that tell the program how to combine words to form new possible passwords. Users commonly substitute certain numbers for specific letters. If the user wanted to use the word *secret* for a password, for example, the letter *e* could be replaced with the number *3*, yielding *s3cr3t*. This password will not be found in the dictionary, so a pure dictionary attack would not crack it, but the password is still easy for the user to remember. If a rule were created that tried all words in the dictionary and then tried the same words substituting the number *3* for the letter *e*, however, the password would be cracked.

Rules can also be defined so that the password-cracking program will substitute special characters for other characters or combine words. The ability of the attacker to crack passwords is directly related to the method the user employs to create the password in the first place, as well as the dictionary and rules used.

Brute Force

If the user has selected a password that is not found in a dictionary, even if various numbers or special characters are substituted for letters, the only way the password can be cracked is for an attacker to attempt a *brute force* attack, in which the password-cracking program attempts all possible password combinations.

The length of the password and the size of the set of possible characters in the password will greatly affect the time a brute force attack will take. A few years ago, this method of attack was very time consuming, since it took considerable time to generate all possible combinations. With the increase in computer speed, however, generating password combinations is much faster, making it more feasible to launch brute force attacks against certain computer systems and networks.

A brute force attack on a password can take place at two levels: It can attack a system, where the attacker is attempting to guess the password at a login prompt, or it can attack the list of password hashes contained in a password file. The first attack can be made more difficult if the account locks after a few failed login attempts. The second attack can be thwarted if the password file is securely maintained so that others cannot obtain a copy of it.

Online vs. Offline

When the brute force attack occurs in real time against a system, it is frequently being done to attack a single account with multiple examples of passwords. Success or failure is determined by the system under attack, and the attacker either gets in or doesn't. *Online* brute force attacks tend to be very noisy and easy to see by network security monitoring, and are also limited by system response time and bandwidth.

Offline, brute force can be employed to perform hash comparisons against a stolen password file. This has the challenge of stealing the password file, but if accomplished, it is possible to use high-performance GPU-based parallel machines to try passwords at very high rates and against multiple accounts at the same time.

Hybrid Attack

A hybrid password attack is an attack that combines the preceding methods. Most cracking tools have this option built in, first attempting a dictionary attack, and then moving to brute force methods.

Collision

A *collision* attack is where two different inputs yield the same output of a hash function. Through the manipulation of data, creating subtle changes that are not visible to the user yet create different versions of a digital file and the creation of many different versions, then using the birthday attack to find a collision between any two of the many versions, an attacker has a chance to create a file with changed visible content but identical hashes.

Downgrade

As part of a Transport Layer Security/Secure Sockets Layer (TLS/SSL) setup, there is a specification of the cipher suite to be employed. This is done to enable the highest form of encryption that both server and browser can support. In a *downgrade* attack, the attacker takes advantage of a commonly employed principle to support backward compatibility, to downgrade the security to a lower or nonexistent state.

Replay

Replay attacks work against cryptographic systems like they do against other systems. If an attacker can record a series of packets and then replay them, what was valid before may well be valid again. There is a wide range of defenses against replay attacks, and as such this should not be an issue. But developers that do not follow best practices can create implementations that lack replay protections, enabling this attack path to persist.

Weak Implementations

Weak implementations are another problem associated with backward compatibility. The best example of this is SSL. SSL, in all of its versions, has now fallen to attackers. TLS, an equivalent methodology that does not suffer these weaknesses, is the obvious solution, yet many websites still employ SSL. Cryptography has long been described as an arms race between attackers and defenders, with multiple versions and improvements over the years. Whenever an older version is allowed to continue operation, there is a risk associated with weaker implementations.

Chapter Review

This chapter examined the attack methods used by hackers. Four major categories of attack were covered: social engineering attacks against the people/user component, application/service attacks against specific types of components, wireless attacks against the network connection, and cryptographic attacks.

The social engineering section examined phishing/spear phishing, whaling, vishing, tailgating, impersonation, dumpster diving, shoulder surfing, hoaxes, and watering hole attacks and then described the tools and principles that make these attacks so successful.

The section on application/service attacks first examined DoS, DDoS, man-in-the-middle, buffer overflows, injections, cross-site scripting, cross-site request forgery, privilege escalation, and ARP poisoning. The section continued with amplification attacks, DNS poisoning, domain hijacking, man-in-the-browser attacks, zero days, replays, and pass the hash methods. The section concluded with hijacking methods, driver manipulation, and a wide array of spoofing techniques.

The wireless section covered replay, IV, evil twin, and rogue IP attacks. It also covered jamming, attacking WPS, bluejacking, bluesnarfing, attacks on RFID and NFC, and disassociation attacks.

The chapter concluded with a section on cryptographic attacks, including birthday attacks, known plaintext/ciphertext attacks, password attacks, dictionary attacks, brute force, and hybrid methods. Collision, downgrade, replay, and weak implementations were also covered.

What is important to remember is that this material is designed to assist you in understanding CompTIA exam objective 1.2: Compare and contrast types of attacks. Be prepared to differentiate between the types of attacks.

Questions

To help you prepare further for the CompTIA Security+ exam, and to test your level of preparedness, answer the following questions and then check your answers against the correct answers at the end of the chapter.

1. While waiting in the lobby of your building for a guest, you notice a man in a red shirt standing close to a locked door with a large box in his hands. He waits for someone else to come along and open the locked door, then proceeds to follow her inside. What type of social engineering attack have you just witnessed?

   A. Impersonation

   B. Phishing

   C. Boxing

   D. Tailgating

2. A user reports seeing "odd certificate warnings" on her web browser this morning whenever she visits Google. Looking at her browser, you see certificate warnings. Looking at the network traffic, you see all HTTP and HTTPS requests from that system are being routed to the same IP regardless of destination. Which of the following attack types are you seeing in this case?

   A. Phishing

   B. Man-in-the-middle

   C. Cryptolocker

   D. DDoS

3. Users are reporting the wireless network on one side of the building is broken. They can connect, but can't seem to get to the Internet. While investigating, you notice all of the affected users are connecting to an access point you don't recognize. These users have fallen victim to what type of attack?

   A. Rogue AP

   B. WPS

   C. Bluejacking

   D. Disassociation

4. When an attacker captures network traffic and retransmits it at a later time, what type of attack are they attempting?

   A. Denial of service attack

   B. Replay attack

   C. Bluejacking attack

   D. Man-in-the-middle attack

5. What type of attack involves an attacker putting a layer of code between an original device driver and the operating system?

   A. Refactoring

   B. Trojan horse

   C. Shimming

   D. Pass the hash

6. A colleague asks you for advice on why he can't log in to his Gmail account. Looking at his browser, you see he has typed www.gmal.com in the address bar. The screen looks very similar to the Gmail login screen. Your colleague has just fallen victim to what type of attack?

   A. Jamming

   B. Rainbow table

   C. Whale phishing

   D. Typo squatting

7. You've been asked to try and crack the password of a disgruntled user who was recently fired. Which of the following could help you crack that password in the least amount of time?

   A. Rainbow tables

   B. Brute force

   C. Dictionary

   D. Hybrid attack

8. You're sitting at the airport when your friend gets a message on her phone. In the text is a picture of a duck with the word "Pwnd" as the caption. Your friend doesn't know who sent the message. Your friend is a victim of what type of attack?

   A. Snarfing

   B. Bluejacking

   C. Quacking

   D. Collision

9. All of the wireless users on the third floor of your building are reporting issues with the network. Every 15 minutes, their devices disconnect from the network. Within a minute or so they are able to reconnect. What type of attack is most likely underway in this situation?

    A. WPS attack

    B. Downgrade attack

    C. Brute force attack

    D. Disassociation attack

10. Your organization's web server was just compromised despite being protected by a firewall and IPS. The web server is fully patched and properly configured according to industry best practices. The IPS logs show no unusual activity, but your network traffic logs show an unusual connection from an IP address belonging to a university. What type of attack is most likely occurring?

    A. Cross-site scripting attack

    B. Authority attack

    C. Zero day attack

    D. URL hijacking attack

11. Your e-commerce site is crashing under an extremely high traffic volume. Looking at the traffic logs, you see tens of thousands of requests for the same URL coming from hundreds of different IP addresses around the world. What type of attack are you facing?

    A. DoS

    B. DDoS

    C. DNS poisoning

    D. Snarfing

12. A user wants to know if the network is down, because she is unable to connect to anything. While troubleshooting, you notice the MAC address for her default gateway doesn't match the MAC address of your organization's router. What type of attack has been used against this user?

    A. Consensus attack

    B. ARP poisoning

    C. Refactoring

    D. Smurf attack

13. A user in your organization contacts you to see if there's any update to the "account compromise" that happened last week. When you ask him to explain what he means, the user tells you he received a phone call earlier in the week from your department and was asked to verify his userid and password. The user says he gave the caller his userid and password. This user has fallen victim to what specific type of attack?

    A. Spear phishing

    B. Vishing

    C. Phishing

    D. Replication

14. Coming into your office, you overhear a conversation between two security guards. One guard is telling the other she caught several people digging through the trash behind the building early this morning. The security guard says the people claimed to be looking for aluminum cans, but only had a bag of papers—no cans. What type of attack has this security guard witnessed?

    A. Spear phishing

    B. Pharming

    C. Dumpster diving

    D. Combing

15. A user calls to report a problem with an application you support. The user says when she accidentally pasted an entire paragraph into an input field, the application crashed. You are able to consistently reproduce the results using the same method. What vulnerability might that user have accidentally discovered in that application?

    A. Poison apple

    B. Shoulder surfing

    C. Smurfing

    D. Buffer overflow

Answers

1. **D.** Tailgating (or piggybacking) is the simple tactic of following closely behind a person who has just used their own access card, key, or PIN to gain physical access to a room or building. The large box clearly impedes the person in the red shirt's ability to open the door, so they let someone else do it for them and follow them in.

2. **B.** This is most likely some type of man-in-the-middle attack. This attack method is usually done by routing all of the victim's traffic to the attacker's host, where the attacker can view it, modify it, or block it. The attacker inserts himself into the middle of his victim's network communications.

3. A. This is a rogue AP attack. Attackers set up their own access points in an attempt to get wireless devices to connect to the rogue AP instead of the authorized access points.

4. B. A replay attack occurs when the attacker captures a portion of the communication between two parties and retransmits it at a later time. For example, an attacker might replay a series of commands and codes used in a financial transaction to cause the transaction to be conducted multiple times. Generally, replay attacks are associated with attempts to circumvent authentication mechanisms, such as the capturing and reuse of a certificate or ticket.

5. C. *Shimming* is the process of putting a layer of code between the device driver and the operating system.

6. D. Typo squatting capitalizes on common typing errors, such as gmal instead of gmail. The attacker registers a domain very similar to the real domain and attempts to collect credentials or other sensitive information from unsuspecting users.

7. A. Rainbow tables are precomputed tables or hash values associated with passwords. When used correctly in the right circumstances, they can dramatically reduce the amount of work needed to crack a given password.

8. B. This is most likely a bluejacking attack. If a victim's phone has Bluetooth enabled and is in discoverable mode, it may be possible for an attacker to send unwanted texts, images, or audio to the victim's phone.

9. D. Disassociation attacks against a wireless system are attacks designed to disassociate a host from the wireless access point and from the wireless network. If the attacker has a list of MAC addresses for the wireless devices, they can spoof deauthentication frames, causing the wireless devices to disconnect from the network.

10. C. If a "properly secured" and patched system is suddenly compromised, it is most likely the result of a zero day attack. A zero day attack is one that uses a vulnerability for which there is no previous knowledge outside of the attacker.

11. B. This is a DDoS attack. DDoS (or distributed denial of service) attacks attempt to overwhelm their targets with traffic from many different sources. Botnets are quite commonly used to launch DDoS attacks.

12. B. ARP poisoning is an attack that involves sending spoofed ARP or RARP replies to a victim in an attempt to alter the ARP table on the victim's system. If successful, an ARP poisoning attack will replace one of more MAC addresses in victim's ARP table with the MAC address the attacker supplies in their spoofed responses.

13. B. Vishing is a social engineering attack that uses voice communication technology to obtain the information the attacker is seeking. Most often the attacker will call a victim and pretend to be someone else in an attempt to extract information from the victim.

14. **C.** Dumpster diving is the process of going through a target's trash in the hopes of finding valuable information such as user lists, directories, organization charts, network maps, passwords, and so on.

15. **D.** This user may have discovered a buffer overflow vulnerability in the application. A buffer overflow can occur when more input is supplied than the program is designed to process (for example, 150 characters supplied to a 10-character input field). If the application doesn't reject the additional input, the extra characters can continue to fill up memory and overwrite other portions of the program, causing instability or undesirable results.

Threat Actors

In this chapter, you will
- Explain threat actor types
- Explain threat actor attributes
- Explore open source threat intelligence

This chapter examines the types and attributes of threat actors. Threat actors can take many forms and represent different levels of threats, so understanding the type and motivation of an actor can be critical for proper defensive measures. The chapter also explores open source intelligence as used to understand the current threat environment, and to lead the proper resource deployment of cyber defenses.

Certification Objective   This chapter covers CompTIA Security+ exam objective 1.3, Explain threat actor types and attributes.

Types of Actors

The act of deliberately accessing computer systems and networks without authorization is generally referred to as *hacking*, with individuals who conduct this activity being referred to as hackers. The term "hacking" also applies to the act of exceeding one's authority in a system. This would include authorized users who attempt to gain access to files they aren't permitted to access or who attempt to obtain permissions that they have not been granted. While the act of breaking into computer systems and networks has been glorified in the media and movies, the physical act does not live up to the Hollywood hype. Intruders are, if nothing else, extremely patient, since the process to gain access to a system takes persistence and dogged determination. The attacker will conduct many pre-attack activities in order to obtain the information needed to determine which attack will most likely be successful. Typically, by the time an attack is launched, the attacker will have gathered enough information to be very confident that the attack will succeed.

Generally, attacks by an individual or even a small group of attackers fall into the *unstructured threat* category. Attacks at this level generally are conducted over short periods of time (lasting at most a few months), do not involve a large number of individuals, have little financial backing, and are accomplished by insiders or outsiders who do not seek collusion with insiders. Intruders, or those who are attempting to conduct an intrusion, definitely come in many different varieties and have varying degrees of sophistication (see Figure 3-1).

Script Kiddies

At the low end of the spectrum technically are what are generally referred to as *script kiddies*, individuals who do not have the technical expertise to develop scripts or discover new vulnerabilities in software but who have just enough understanding of computer systems to be able to download and run scripts that others have developed. These individuals generally are not interested in attacking specific targets, but instead simply want to find any organization that may not have patched a newly discovered vulnerability for which the script kiddie has located a script to exploit the vulnerability. It is hard to estimate how many of the individuals performing activities such as probing networks or scanning individual systems are part of this group, but it is undoubtedly the fastest growing group and the vast majority of the "unfriendly" activity occurring on the Internet is probably carried out by these individuals.

Hacktivists

As shown in Figure 3-1, at the next level above script kiddies are those people who are capable of writing scripts to exploit known vulnerabilities. These individuals are much more technically competent than script kiddies and account for an estimated 8 to 12 percent of malicious Internet activity. When hackers work together for a collectivist effort, typically on behalf of some cause, they are referred to as *hacktivists*. Hacktivist groups may include script kiddies, but in general script kiddies do not have the skills to participate in a meaningful manner in advancing a hacktivist cause, although they may be enlisted as ground troops to add volume to an attack.

Figure 3-1
Distribution of attacker skill levels

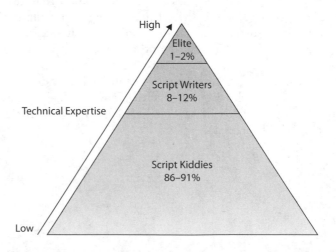

Organized Crime

As businesses became increasingly reliant upon computer systems and networks, and as the amount of financial transactions conducted via the Internet increased, it was inevitable that *organized crime* would eventually turn to the electronic world as a new target to exploit. One of the major changes over the past decade in cybersecurity has been the ability for hackers to monetize their efforts. Part of this is due to the rise in cryptocurrency, such as bitcoin, but an entire marketplace on the dark web for stolen identities, financial data, and intellectual property has created a criminal cybersecurity marketplace that, in terms of dollars, is larger than the international drug trade. This has led to a whole new class of organized crime figure, cybersecurity criminals, who can lurk in the shadows of anonymity and create malware and other attacks, as well as perform attacks, all with an eye on making money.

Criminal activity on the Internet at its most basic is no different from criminal activity in the physical world. Fraud, extortion, theft, embezzlement, and forgery all take place in the electronic environment.

One difference between criminal groups and the "average" hacker is the level of organization that criminal elements employ in their attack. Criminal groups typically have more money to spend on accomplishing the criminal activity and are willing to spend extra time accomplishing the task, provided the level of reward at the conclusion is great enough. With the tremendous amount of money that is exchanged via the Internet on a daily basis, the level of reward for a successful attack is high enough to interest criminal elements. Attacks by criminal organizations usually fall into the *structured threat* category, which is characterized by a greater amount of planning, a longer period of time to conduct the activity, more financial backing to accomplish it, and possibly corruption of, or collusion with, insiders.

Nation States/APT

At the top end of this spectrum shown in Figure 3-1 are those highly technical individuals, often referred to as *elite hackers*, who not only have the ability to write scripts that exploit vulnerabilities but also are capable of discovering new vulnerabilities. This group is the smallest of the lot, however, and is responsible for, at most, only 1 to 2 percent of intrusive activity. Many of these elite hackers are employed by major cybersecurity firms in an effort to combat criminal activity. Others are employed by *nation states* and other international organizations, to train and run large groups of skilled hackers to conduct nation-state attacks against a wide range of adversaries. In the United States, government rules and regulations prevent government workers from attacking companies for reasons of economic warfare. Not all countries live by this principle, and many have organized hacking efforts designed to gather information from international companies, stealing intellectual property for the express purpose of advancing their own country's national companies.

As nations have increasingly become dependent on computer systems and networks, the possibility that these essential elements of society might be targeted by organizations or nations determined to adversely affect another nation has become a reality. Many nations today have developed to some extent the capability to conduct *information warfare*. There are several definitions for information warfare, but a simple one is that it is warfare conducted against the information and information processing equipment used by an adversary. In practice, this is a much more complicated subject, because information not only may be the target of an adversary, but also may be used as a weapon. Whatever definition you use, information warfare falls into the *highly structured threat* category. This type of threat is characterized by a much longer period of preparation (years is not uncommon), tremendous financial backing, and a large and organized group of attackers. The threat may include attempts not only to subvert insiders but also to plant individuals inside of a potential target in advance of a planned attack.

An interesting aspect of information warfare is the list of possible targets available. We have grown accustomed to the idea that, during war, military forces will target opposing military forces but will generally attempt to destroy as little civilian infrastructure as possible. In information warfare, military forces are certainly still a key target, but much has been written about other targets, such as the various infrastructures that a nation relies on for its daily existence. Water, electricity, oil and gas refineries and distribution, banking and finance, telecommunications—all fall into the category of critical infrastructures for a nation. Critical infrastructures are those whose loss would have severe repercussions on the nation. With countries relying so heavily on these infrastructures, it is inevitable that they will be viewed as valid targets during conflict. Given how dependent these infrastructures are on computer systems and networks, it is also inevitable that these same computer systems and networks will be targeted for a cyberattack in an information war.

Another major advance in cyberattacks is the development of the *advanced persistent threat (APT)*. APT attacks are characterized by using toolkits to achieve a presence on a target network and then, instead of just moving to steal information, focusing on the long game, maintaining a persistence on the target network. The tactics, tools, and procedures of APTs are focused on maintaining administrative access to the target network and avoiding detection. Then, over the long haul, the attacker can remove intellectual property and more from the organization, typically undetected.

Operation Night Dragon is the name given to an intellectual property attack executed against oil, gas, and petrochemical companies in the United States in 2006. Using a set of global servers, attackers from China raided global energy companies for proprietary and highly confidential information such as bidding data for leases. The attack shed new light on what constitute critical data and associated risks. Further, as demonstrated by the Stuxnet attacks against Iranian uranium plants, the cyberattacks in Estonia, and the attacks on electricity distribution in the Ukraine, the risk of nation-state attacks is real. There have been numerous accusations of intellectual property theft being sponsored by, and in some cases even performed by, nation-state actors. In a world where information dominates government, business, and economies, the collection of information is the key to success, and with large rewards, the list of characters willing to spend significant resources is high.

Insiders

It is generally acknowledged by security professionals that *insiders* are more dangerous in many respects than outside intruders. The reason for this is simple—insiders have the access and knowledge necessary to cause immediate damage to an organization.

Most security is designed to protect against outside intruders and thus lies at the boundary between the organization and the rest of the world. Insiders may actually already have all the access they need to perpetrate criminal activity such as fraud. In addition to unprecedented access, insiders also frequently have knowledge of the security systems in place and are better able to avoid detection. Attacks by insiders are often the result of employees who have become disgruntled with their organization and are looking for ways to disrupt operations. It is also possible that an "attack" by an insider may be an accident and not intended as an attack at all. An example of this might be an employee who deletes a critical file without understanding its critical nature.

 EXAM TIP One of the hardest threats that security professionals will have to address is that of the insider. Since employees already have access to the organization and its assets, additional mechanisms need to be in place to detect attacks by insiders and to lessen the ability of these attacks to succeed.

Employees are not the only insiders that organizations need to be concerned about. Often, numerous other individuals have physical access to company facilities. Custodial crews frequently have unescorted access throughout the facility, often when nobody else is around. Other individuals, such as contractors or partners, may have not only physical access to the organization's facilities but also access to computer systems and networks. A contractor involved in U.S. intelligence computing, Edward Snowden, was charged with espionage in 2013 after he released a wide range of data illustrating the technical capabilities of U.S. intelligence surveillance systems. He is the ultimate insider, with his name becoming synonymous with the insider threat issue.

Competitors

In today's world of global economic activity, much of it enabled by the interconnected nature of businesses, many businesses have an information component. And this information component is easier to copy, steal, or disrupt than older, more physical assets, making it an alluring target for *competitors*. There have been cases of people moving from competitor to competitor, taking insider information with them for years, even decades, before the Internet was developed. The interconnectedness and digital nature of modern business has enabled this sort of corporate crime to be committed to an even greater degree. Where, in decades past, it would take significant risk to copy the detailed engineering specifications of a major process for a firm, today the same might be accomplished with a few clicks and a USB drive.

 EXAM TIP Being able to differentiate the different types of threat actors based on their characteristics is important for the exam. What differentiates an insider from a nation state from a competitor when examining a potential attack?

Attributes of Actors

Threat actors can be divided into groups based on abilities, as shown previously in the chapter. There are other ways to differentiate the threat actors, by location, internal or external, by level of sophistication, level of resources, and intent. These attributes are described below.

Internal/External

Internal threat actors have one significant advantage over external actors. Internal actors have access to the system, and although it may be limited to user access, access provides the threat actor the ability to pursue their attack. External actors have an additional step, the establishment of access to the system under attack.

Level of Sophistication

As shown earlier in Figure 3-1, attacker skill or sophistication can be divided into several categories. When examining a group of threat actors and considering the individual skills of members of the group, there may well be a mix, with a few highly skilled individuals acting to move larger numbers of less skilled participants. The greater the skill level the more an individual will be expected to lead and design the attacks. When it comes to the sophistication level of the attack itself, one notable trend is that as the skill level goes up, so too does the use of minimal methods. Although zero day attacks are widely covered in the news, true zero day vulnerabilities are rarely used; they are reserved for the few cases where there are no other options, because once used they will be patched. Even with highly sophisticated and resourced nation-state teams employing APT methods, a surprising number of attacks are being performed using old attacks, old vulnerabilities, and simple methods that take advantage of "low-hanging fruit." This is not to say that newer, more advanced methods are not used, but rather there is an economy of mechanism in the attacks themselves, using just what is needed at each step. There is also a lot of missing data to this picture, as we do not know of the methods that have been used successfully if the threat actor remains undetected.

Resources/Funding

As mentioned earlier, criminal organizations and nation states have larger budgets, bigger teams, and the ability to pursue campaigns for longer periods of time. Cybersecurity is challenging for attackers as well as defenders, and there are expenses associated with maintaining teams and tools used as threat actors against a system. APTs, with their penchant for long-term attacks, some lasting for years, require significant resources to engage in this type of activity, so there is a need for long-term resources that only major organizations or governments can manage over time.

Intent/Motivation

The intent or motivation behind an attack can be simple or multifold in nature. A script kiddie is just trying to make a technique work. A more skilled threat actor is usually pursuing a specific objective, such as trying to make a point as a hacktivist. At the top of the intent pyramid is the APT threat actor, whose intent or motivation is at least three-fold. First is the drive to persist access mechanisms so that the threat actor has continued access. Second is the drive to remain undetected. In most APTs that are discovered, the length of intrusion is greater than a year and in many cases determining the original date of infection is not possible, as it is limited by length of logs. Third is the goal of stealing something of value on the network. APTs do not go to all the trouble of maintaining access and remaining invisible just to crash a system or force a rebuild.

 EXAM TIP When taking the Security+ exam, threat actors will be described in terms of attributes: resources, level of sophistication, location, and motivation. Be sure to understand how these differences matter with respect to types of attacks.

Use of Open Source Intelligence

Open source intelligence, sometimes called *open source threat intelligence*, refers to intelligence data collected from public sources. There is a wide range of public sources of information concerning current cybersecurity activity. From news articles, to blogs, to government reports, there seems to be a never-ending stream of news concerning what is happening, to whom, and how. This leads to the overall topic of information sharing and the greater topic of threat intelligence (not just open source).

Cybersecurity is a game of resource management. No firm has the resources to protect everything against all threats, and even attempting to do so would add complexity that would open up other threat avenues. One of the important decisions is where to apply one's resources in the complex landscape of cybersecurity defense. Threat intelligence is the gathering of information from a variety of sources, including non-public sources, to allow an entity to properly focus their defenses against the most likely threat actors.

There are several major sources besides the wide range of open source feeds. Examples include Information Sharing and Analysis Organizations (ISAOs) and Information Sharing Analysis Centers (ISACs). ISAOs vary greatly in capability but essentially include any organization, whether an industry sector or geographic region, that is sharing cyber-related information for the purpose of enhancing their members' cybersecurity posture. ISACs are a special category of ISAO consisting of privately run, but government approved, industry-based cybersecurity. ISACs may be considered fusion centers where real-time information can be shared between members. ISAOs and ISACs work on a very simple premise: share what is happening to you, and together learn what is happening in your industry. The sharing is anonymized, the analysis is performed by highly skilled workers in a security operations center, and the resulting information is fed back to members as close to real time as possible. Highly skilled analysts are expensive, and this mechanism shares the costs across all of the member institutions. A U.S. government program, InfraGard, is run by the FBI and also acts as a means of sharing, although timeliness and level of analysis are nowhere near that of an ISAC, but the price is right (free).

At the end of the day, a combination of open source information, ISAC information (if available—not everyone can join), and InfraGard information provides a picture of what the current threat landscape looks like and what the most effective options for defense are against each threat. Using this information is critical in the deployment of proper cybersecurity defenses.

Chapter Review

The chapter opened with an examination of the types of threat actors. From script kiddies, to hacktivists, to organized crime and nation states, the primary differentiation is level of resources. The threat actors of insiders and competitors were also covered. Switching to the attributes of threat actors, they can be internal or external, and possess varying levels of skill, resources, and motivation. The chapter closed with an examination of open source intelligence.

Questions

To help you prepare further for the CompTIA Security+ exam, and to test your level of preparedness, answer the following questions and then check your answers against the correct answers at the end of the chapter.

1. Which of the following is the term generally used to refer to the act of deliberately accessing computer systems and networks without authorization?

    A. Phishing

    B. Threat

    C. Vulnerability

    D. Attack

2. Attacks by an individual or even a small group of attackers fall into which threat category?

    A. Unorganized threat

    B. APT

    C. Singular threat

    D. Hactivist

3. Which of the following is the term used to refer to individuals who do not have the technical expertise to develop scripts or discover new vulnerabilities in software but who have just enough understanding of computer systems to be able to download and run scripts that others have developed?

    A. Script kiddies

    B. Hackers

    C. Simple intruders

    D. Intermittent attackers

4. What is the name given to a group of hackers who work together for a collectivist effort, typically on behalf of some cause?

   A. Script kiddies

   B. Hacktivists

   C. Motivated hackers

   D. Organized intruders

5. Attacks by individuals from organized crime are generally considered to fall into which threat category?

   A. Highly structure threats

   B. Unstructured threat

   C. Structured threat

   D. Advanced persistent threat

6. What is the name given to the group of individuals who not only have the ability to write scripts that exploit vulnerabilities but also are capable of discovering new vulnerabilities?

   A. Elite hackers

   B. Hacktivists

   C. Uber hackers

   D. Advanced persistent threat actors

7. Criminal activity on the Internet can include which of the following? (Choose all that apply.)

   A. Fraud

   B. Extortion

   C. Theft

   D. Embezzlement

   E. Forgery

8. Warfare conducted against the information and information processing equipment used by an adversary is known as which of the following?

   A. Information warfare

   B. Cyber warfare

   C. Offensive cyber operations

   D. Computer espionage

9. What term is used to describe the type of threat that is characterized by a much longer period of preparation (years is not uncommon), tremendous financial backing, and a large and organized group of attackers?

   A. Advanced capability threat

   B. Structured threat

   C. Nation-state threat

   D. Highly structured threat

10. What is the term used to define attacks that are characterized by using toolkits to achieve a presence on a target network, with a focus on the long game—maintaining a persistence on the target network?

    A. Covert network threat

    B. Advanced persistent threat

    C. Covert channel attack

    D. Concealed network presence

11. Which of the following are reasons that the insider threat is considered so dangerous? (Choose all that apply.)

    A. Insiders have the access and knowledge necessary to cause immediate damage to an organization.

    B. Insiders may actually already have all the access they need to perpetrate criminal activity such as fraud.

    C. Insiders generally do not have knowledge of the security systems in place, so system monitoring will allow for any inappropriate activity to be detected.

    D. Attacks by insiders are often the result of employees who have become disgruntled with their organization and are looking for ways to disrupt operations.

12. When discussing threat concerns regarding competitors, which of the following is true?

    A. There are no known cases of criminal activity involving people moving from competitor to competitor, taking insider information with them for years.

    B. Where in the past it would take significant risk to copy the detailed engineering specifications of a major process for a firm, today it can be accomplished with a few clicks and a USB drive.

    C. Modern search engines make it less likely that a competitor could steal intellectual property without being detected.

    D. With increases in digital forensics, it is now more difficult to copy and steal proprietary digital information or disrupt operations.

13. Which of the following are true concerning attacker skill and sophistication? (Choose all that apply.)

   A. The level of complexity for modern networks and operating systems has grown so that it is nearly impossible for anyone but the most skilled of hackers to gain unauthorized access to computer systems and networks.

   B. Attackers do not have magic skills, but rather the persistence and skill to keep attacking weaknesses.

   C. With the introduction of cloud computing during the last decade, attackers now primarily focus on the cloud, thus reducing the level of sophistication required to conduct attacks since they can focus on a more limited environment.

   D. There is a surprising number of attacks being performed using old attacks, old vulnerabilities, and simple methods that take advantage of "low-hanging fruit."

14. Which of the following is the term used to describe the processes used in the collection of information from public sources?

   A. Media exploitation

   B. Open source intelligence

   C. Social media intelligence

   D. Social engineering

15. What term is used to describe the gathering of information from a variety of sources, including non-public sources, to allow an entity to properly focus their defenses against the most likely threat actors?

   A. Infosec analysis

   B. Data intelligence

   C. Threat intelligence

   D. Information warfare

Answers

   1. **D.** Attack is the term that is now generally accepted when referring to the act of gaining unauthorized access to computer systems and networks. The terms phishing, threat, vulnerability all relate to attacks, but are not the act of attacking.

   2. **D.** Attacks by an individual or even a small group of attackers fall into the hactivist threat category. Attacks by criminal organizations usually fall into the structured threat category. The other two answers are not categories of threats used by the security community.

3. A. Script kiddies is the label used to refer to individuals who do not have the technical expertise to develop scripts or discover new vulnerabilities in software but who have just enough understanding of computer systems to be able to download and run scripts that others have developed. Hackers is the more general term used to refer to individuals at all levels who attempt to gain unauthorized access to computer systems and networks. The other two answers are not terms used in the security community.

4. B. When hackers work together for a collectivist effort, typically on behalf of some cause, they are referred to as hacktivists. Hacktivist groups may include script kiddies, but in general script kiddies do not have the skills to participate in a meaningful manner in advancing a hacktivist cause, although they may be enlisted as ground troops to add volume to an attack. The other two terms are not generally used in the security community.

5. C. Attacks by criminal organizations usually fall into the structured threat category characterized by a greater amount of planning, a longer period of time to conduct the activity, more financial backing to accomplish it, and possibly corruption of, or collusion with, insiders. Highly structured threats require greater planning, while unstructured threats require less, and APT attacks are typically nation state in origin, not organized criminals.

6. A. Elite hackers is the name given to those who not only have the ability to write scripts that exploit vulnerabilities but also are capable of discovering new vulnerabilities.

7. A, B, C, D, and **E.** Criminal activity on the Internet at its most basic is no different from criminal activity in the physical world. Fraud, extortion, theft, embezzlement, and forgery all take place in the electronic environment.

8. A. Information warfare is warfare conducted against the information and information processing equipment used by an adversary. Cyber warfare and offensive cyber operations are terms that you may encounter, but the more generally accepted term for this type of activity is information warfare. Computer espionage is generally associated with intelligence gathering and not general computer warfare.

9. D. A highly structured threat is characterized by a much longer period of preparation (years is not uncommon), tremendous financial backing, and a large and organized group of attackers. The threat may include attempts not only to subvert insiders but also to plant individuals inside of a potential target in advance of a planned attack. This type of threat generally is much more involved and extensive than a structured threat. The other terms are not commonly used in the security industry.

10. **B.** Advanced persistent threats (APTs) are attacks characterized by using toolkits to achieve a presence on a target network and then, instead of just moving to steal information, focusing on the long game, maintaining a persistence on the target network. Their tactics, tools, and procedures are focused on maintaining administrative access to the target network and avoiding detection. Covert channels are indeed a concern in security but are a special category of attack. The other terms are not generally used in the security community.

11. **A, B,** and **D.** Insiders frequently *do* have knowledge of the security systems in place and are thus better able to avoid detection.

12. **B.** In today's world of global economic activity, much of it is enabled by the interconnected nature of businesses. Many businesses have an information component that is easier to copy, steal, or disrupt than older, more physical assets. Additionally, there have been cases of people moving from competitor to competitor, taking insider information with them for years, even decades, before the Internet was developed.

13. **B** and **D.** While the complexity of systems is indeed increasing, there still exists a large number of computers and networks that have not been adequately protected, making it possible for less sophisticated attackers to gain unauthorized access. Additionally, while cloud computing has added another focus for attackers, it has not eliminated computer systems and networks in general as potential targets.

14. **B.** Open source intelligence is the term used to describe the processes used in the collection of intelligence from public sources. Human intelligence (HUMINT) is a specific category of intelligence gathering focused on obtaining information directly from individuals. The other terms are not generally used by security professionals.

15. **C.** Threat intelligence is the gathering of information from a variety of sources, including non-public sources, to allow an entity to properly focus their defenses against the most likely threat actors. Information warfare is conducted against the information and information processing equipment used by an adversary and consists of a larger range of activities. The other two terms are not generally used by security professionals.

Vulnerability Scanning and Penetration Testing

In this chapter, you will
- Explain penetration testing concepts
- Explain vulnerability scanning concepts

This chapter explores the employment of vulnerability scanning and penetration testing to determine security control effectiveness. These techniques can provide significant insight into the actual effectiveness of a system security solution against actual threats.

Certification Objectives   This chapter covers CompTIA Security+ exam objective 1.4, Explain penetration testing concepts, and exam objective 1.5, Explain vulnerability scanning concepts.

Penetration Testing Concepts

A *penetration test* (or *pen test*) simulates an attack from a malicious outsider probing your network and systems for a way in (often any way in). Pen tests are often the most aggressive form of security testing and can take on many forms, depending on what is considered "in" or "out" of scope. For example, some pen tests simply seek to find a way into the network—any way in. This can range from an attack across network links, to social engineering, to having a tester physically break into the building. Other pen tests are limited—only attacks across network links are allowed, with no physical attacks.

Regardless of the scope and allowed methods, the goal of a pen test is the same: to determine if an attacker can bypass your security and access your systems. Unlike a vulnerability assessment, which typically just catalogs vulnerabilities, a pen test attempts to exploit vulnerabilities to see how much access that vulnerability allows. Pen tests are very useful in that they

- Can show relationships between a series of "low-risk" items that can be sequentially exploited to gain access (making them a "high-risk" item in the aggregate).

- Can be used to test the training of employees, the effectiveness of your security measures, and the ability of your staff to detect and respond to potential attackers.
- Can often identify and test vulnerabilities that are difficult or even impossible to detect with traditional scanning tools.

 EXAM TIP Penetration tests are focused efforts to determine the effectiveness of the security controls used to protect a system.

An effective pen test offers several critical elements. First, it focuses on the most commonly employed threat vectors seen in the current threat environment. Using zero days that no one else has discovered does not help an organization understand its security defenses against the existing threat environment. It is important to mimic real-world attackers if that is what the organization wants to test its defenses against. The second critical element is to focus on the objectives of real-world attackers, such as getting to and stealing intellectual property. Bypassing defenses but not obtaining the attacker's objectives, again, does not provide a full exercise of security capabilities.

Active Reconnaissance

Reconnaissance is the first step of performing a pen test. The objective of reconnaissance is to obtain an understanding of the system and its components that attackers may want to attack. Pen testers can employ multiple methods to achieve this objective, and in most cases, multiple methods will be employed to ensure good coverage of the systems and the potential vulnerabilities that may be present. There are two classifications for reconnaissance activities, active and passive. *Active reconnaissance* testing involves tools that actually interact with the network and systems in a manner that their use can be observed. Active reconnaissance can provide a lot of useful information, but you should be aware as a pen tester that its use may alert defenders to the impending attack.

Passive Reconnaissance

Passive reconnaissance is the use of tools that do not provide information to the network or systems under investigation. Using information obtained via Google or other third-party search engines such as Shodan is a prime example. This allows the gathering of information without the actual sending of packets to a system where they could be observed. If a company announces the upgrade or adoption of a particular software package via a PR release, for example, this information can be used to determine potential threat measures to employ.

Passive vs. Active Tools

Tools can be classified as active or passive. *Active tools* interact with a target system in a fashion where their use can be detected. Scanning a network with Nmap (Network Mapper) is an active act that can be detected. In the case of Nmap, the tool may not be specifically detectable, but its use, the sending of packets, can be detected. When you need to map out your network or look for open services on one or more hosts, a port scanner is probably the most efficient tool for the job. Figure 4-1 shows a screenshot of Zenmap, a cross-platform version of the very popular Nmap port scanner available from Insecure.org.

Passive tools are those that do not interact with the system in a manner that would permit detection, as in sending packets or altering traffic. An example of a passive tool is Tripwire, which can detect changes to a file based on hash values. Another passive example is the OS mapping by analyzing TCP/IP traces with a tool such as Wireshark. Passive sensors can use existing traffic to provide data for analysis.

EXAM TIP Passive tools receive traffic only and do nothing to the traffic flow that would permit others to know they are interacting with the network. Active tools modify or send traffic and are thus discoverable by their traffic patterns.

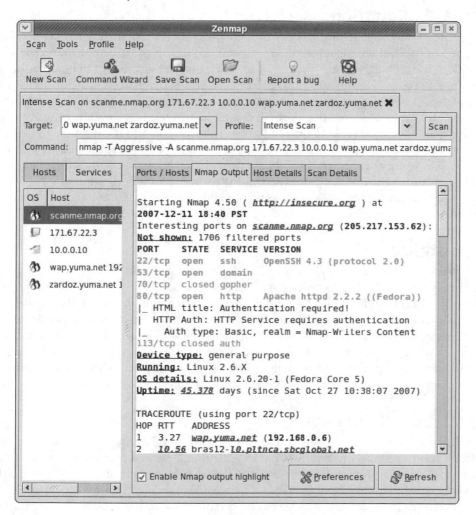

Figure 4-1   Zenmap—a port scanner based on Nmap

Pivot

Pivoting is a key method used by a pen tester or attacker to move across a network. The first step is the attacker obtaining a presence on a machine, call it Machine A. The attacker then remotely through this machine examines the network again, using Machine A's IP address. This enables an attacker to see sections of networks that were not observable from their previous position. Performing a *pivot* is not easy, as the attacker not only must establish access to Machine A, but also must move their tools to Machine A, and control those tools remotely from another machine, all while not being detected. This activity, also referred to as traversing a network, is one place where defenders can observe the attacker's activity. When an attacker traverses the network, network security monitoring tools will detect the activity as unusual with respect to both the account being utilized and the actual traversing activity.

Initial Exploitation

A key element of a penetration test is the actual exploitation of a vulnerability. Exploiting the vulnerabilities encountered serves two purposes. First, it demonstrates the level of risk that is actually present. Second, it demonstrates the viability of the mechanism of the attack vector. During a pen test, the exploitation activity stops short of destructive activity. The *initial exploitation* is intended to demonstrate only that a vulnerability is present and exploitable, not that the objective of the pen test is achievable. In many cases, multiple methods, including pivoting (network traversal) and escalation of privilege to perform activities at administrator privilege, are used to achieve the final desired effect.

One key element to remember is that all activities on a system occur using an account, and pen testing is no different. Attackers will attempt to compromise an ordinary or standard user account in their initial exploitation, and then use that account and their tools to perform more attacks to gain access to other systems and accounts.

Persistence

Persistence is one of the key elements of a whole class of attacks referred to as advanced persistent threats (APTs). As covered in Chapter 3, APTs place two elements at the forefront of all activity: invisibility from defenders and persistence. APT actors tend to be very patient and use techniques that make it very difficult to remove them once they have gained a foothold. Persistence can be achieved via a wide range of mechanisms, from agents that beacon back out, to malicious accounts, to vulnerabilities introduced to enable reinfection. Each of these has advantages and disadvantages, but when used together in multiple places, closing all the doors opened by an attacker becomes very difficult.

Escalation of Privilege

Escalation of privilege is the movement from a lower-level account to an account that enables root-level activity. Typically, the attacker uses a normal user account to exploit a vulnerability on a process that is operating at root, enabling the attacker to assume the privileges of the exploited process—at root level. Once this level of privilege is achieved, the attacker takes additional steps to ensure persistent access back to the privileged level.

With root access, things like log changes and other changes are possible, expanding the ability of the attacker to achieve their objective and to remove information, particularly logs that could lead to detection of the attack.

Black Box

Black box testing is a software-testing technique that consists of finding implementation bugs using malformed/semi-malformed data injection in an automated fashion. Black box techniques test the functionality of the software, usually from an external or user perspective. Testers using black box techniques typically have no knowledge of the internal workings of the software they are testing. They treat the entire software package as a "black box"—they put input in and look at the output. They have no visibility into how the data is processed inside the application, only the output that comes back to them. Test cases for black box testing are typically constructed around intended functionality (what the software is supposed to do) and focus on providing both valid and invalid inputs.

Black box software testing techniques are very useful for examining any web-based application. Web-based applications are typically subjected to a barrage of valid, invalid, malformed, and malicious input from the moment they are exposed to public traffic. By performing black box testing before an application is released, developers can potentially find and correct errors in the development or testing stages.

Black box testing can also be applied to networks or systems. Pen tests and vulnerability assessments are often performed from a purely external perspective, where the testers have no inside knowledge of the network or systems they are examining.

White Box

White box testing is almost the polar opposite of black box testing. Sometimes called clear box testing, white box techniques test the internal structures and processing within an application for bugs, vulnerabilities, and so on. A white box tester will have detailed knowledge of the application they are examining—they'll develop test cases designed to exercise each path, decision tree, input field, and processing routine of the application.

White box testing is often used to test paths within an application (if X, then go do this; if Y, then go do that), data flows, decision trees, and so on. Sometimes the term "white box testing" is applied to network assessments where the tester will have detailed knowledge of the network, including but not limited to IP addresses, network routes, valid user credentials, and so on. In those cases, the tester is typically referred to as a "white hat."

Gray Box

So what happens when you mix a bit of black box testing and a bit of white box testing? You get *gray box* testing. In a gray box test, the testers typically have some knowledge of the software, network, or systems they are testing. For this reason, gray box testing can be very efficient and effective because testers can often quickly eliminate entire testing paths, test cases, and toolsets and can rule out things that simply won't work and are not worth trying.

EXAM TIP The key difference between black box, gray box, and white box testing is the perspective and knowledge of the tester. Black box testers have no knowledge of the inner workings and perform their tests from an external perspective. White box testers have detailed knowledge of the inner workings and perform their tests from an internal perspective. Gray box testers have partial knowledge.

Pen Testing vs. Vulnerability Scanning

Vulnerability scanning is the scanning of a system for vulnerabilities, whether they are exploitable or not. Penetration testing is the examination of a system for vulnerabilities that can be exploited. The key is exploitation. There may be vulnerabilities in a system, in fact, one of the early steps in penetration testing is the examination for vulnerabilities, but the differentiation comes in the follow-on steps—the examination of the system in terms of exploitability.

Vulnerability Scanning Concepts

One very valuable method that can help administrators secure their systems is vulnerability scanning. *Vulnerability scanning* is the process of examining your systems and network devices for holes, weaknesses, and issues and finding them before a potential attacker does. Specialized tools called *vulnerability scanners* are designed to help administrators discover and address vulnerabilities. But there is much more to vulnerability scanning than simply running tools and examining the results—administrators must be able to analyze any discovered vulnerabilities and determine their severity, how to address them if needed, and whether any business processes will be affected by potential fixes. Vulnerability scanning can also help administrators identify common misconfigurations in account setup, patch level, applications, and operating systems. Most organizations look at vulnerability scanning as an ongoing process, as it is not enough to scan systems once and assume they will be secure from that point on.

Passively Test Security Controls

When an automated vulnerability scanner is used to examine a system for vulnerabilities, one of the side effects is the passive testing of the security controls. This is referred to as *passive testing* because the target of the vulnerability scanner is the system, not the controls. If the security controls are effective, then the vulnerability scan may not properly identify the vulnerability. If the security control prevents a vulnerability from being attacked, then it may not be exploitable.

Identify Vulnerability

Vulnerabilities are known entities; otherwise, the scanners would not have the ability to scan for them. When a scanner finds a vulnerability present in a system, it makes a log of the fact. In the end, an enumeration of the vulnerabilities that were discovered is part of the vulnerability analysis report.

Identify Lack of Security Controls

If a vulnerability is exposed to the vulnerability scanner, then a security control is needed to prevent the vulnerability from being exploited. As vulnerabilities are discovered, the specific environment of each vulnerability is documented. As the security vulnerabilities are all known in advance, the system should have controls in place to protect against exploitation. Part of the function of the vulnerability scan is to learn where controls are missing or are ineffective.

Identify Common Misconfigurations

One source of failure with respect to vulnerabilities is in the misconfiguration of a system. Common misconfigurations include access control failures and failure to protect configuration parameters. Vulnerability scanners can be programmed to test for these specific conditions and report on them.

Intrusive vs. Non-intrusive

Vulnerability scanners need a method of detecting whether or not a vulnerability is present and exploitable. One method is to perform a test that changes the system state, an *intrusive* test. The other method is to perform a test in a manner that does not directly interact with the specific vulnerability. This *non-intrusive* method can be significantly less accurate in the actual determination of a vulnerability. If a vulnerability scan is going to involve a lot of checks, the non-intrusive method can be advantageous, as the servers may not have to be rebooted all the time.

Credentialed vs. Non-credentialed

A vulnerability scanner can be programmed with the credentials of a system, giving it the same access as an authorized user. This is assumed to be easier than running the same tests without credentials, widely considered to be a more real-world attempt. It is important to run both, for if an attacker is able to compromise an account, they may well have insider credentials. *Credentialed* scans will be more accurate in determining whether the vulnerabilities exist, as they are not encumbered by access controls. *Non-credentialed* scans demonstrate what the system may be vulnerable to against an outside attacker without access to a user account.

 EXAM TIP Understanding how to recognize credentialed vs. non-credentialed scans is testable on the exam. Little scenario details can make the difference between correct and incorrect—watch for the details.

False Positive

Tools are not perfect. Sometimes they will erroneously report things as an issue when they really are not a problem—and other times they won't report an issue at all. A *false positive* is an incorrect finding—something that is incorrectly reported as a vulnerability.

The scanner tells you there is a problem when in reality nothing is wrong. A *false negative* is when the scanner fails to report a vulnerability that actually does exist—the scanner simply missed the problem or didn't report it as a problem.

 EXAM TIP False positive and false negative are terms used in several contexts. Understanding the difference is important to get exam questions correct. For a given question, one needs to have an understanding of the expected answer for a test. If they get a positive result as an answer, but if in reality this result is wrong, that is a false positive. If a woman takes a pregnancy test and it returns a positive result, but the woman in fact is not pregnant, that is a false positive.

Chapter Review

In this chapter, you learned about penetration testing and vulnerability scanning. Under the topic of penetration testing, you explored the concepts of active and passive reconnaissance, the pivot operation, and the initial exploitation, followed by escalation of privilege and persistence. Black box, white box, and gray box testing were also covered. The vulnerability scanning coverage introduced you to passive scanning, followed by the identification of vulnerabilities, lack of security controls, and common misconfigurations. It examined intrusive versus non-intrusive scans, credentialed versus non-credentialed scans, and finished with false positives.

Questions

To help you prepare further for the CompTIA Security+ exam, and to test your level of preparedness, answer the following questions and then check your answers against the correct answers at the end of the chapter.

1. You've been asked to perform an assessment of a new software application. Your client wants you to perform the assessment without providing you any information about how the software was developed or how data is processed by the application. This is an example of what type of testing?

   A. White box testing

   B. Passive testing

   C. Black box testing

   D. Active testing

2. While examining log files on a compromised Linux system, you notice an unprivileged user account was compromised, followed by several processes crashing and restarting, and finally the shadow file was accessed and modified. Which of the following techniques might the attacker have used?

   A. Active scanning

   B. Escalation of privilege

    C. Passive scanning

    D. Credentialed attack

3. While running a vulnerability scanner against a Windows 2016 server, the tool reports the server may be affected by an offset2lib patch vulnerability. You find this odd because the offset2lib patch vulnerability only applies to Linux-based systems. Your vulnerability scanner has most likely reported which of the following?

    A. System misconfiguration

    B. Overflow finding

    C. Actual negative

    D. False positive

4. While responding to a security incident, your team examines network traffic logs. You see incoming connections to a web server in the DMZ. Several hours later in the same traffic logs you see connections from the web server to other systems in the DMZ as well as internal systems. This is an example of what type of technique?

    A. Buffer overflow

    B. SQL injection

    C. Passive injection

    D. Pivoting

5. You've been asked to examine network traffic for evidence of compromise. You have 1TB of tcpdump logs to review. Which of the following tools would you use to examine these logs?

    A. Nmap

    B. Zenmap

    C. Wireshark

    D. Nessus

6. A colleague calls you to ask for assistance. He is having trouble keeping an attacker out of his network. He tells you no matter what he tries, he can't seem to keep the attacker out of his network and he has no idea how the attacker keeps getting in. This is an example of what kind of attack?

    A. Gray box attack

    B. Whack-a-mole attack

    C. Advanced persistent threat

    D. Privilege escalation

7. Your network traffic logs show a large spike in traffic to your DNS server. Looking at the logs, you see a large number of TCP connection attempts from a single IP address. The destination port of the TCP connections seems to increment by one with each new connection attempt. This is most likely an example of what activity?

   A. Active reconnaissance

   B. Passive reconnaissance

   C. Buffer overflow

   D. Initial exploitation

8. You've been asked to examine a custom web application your company is developing. You will have access to design documents, data structure descriptions, data flow diagrams, and any other details about the application you think would be useful. This is an example of what type of testing?

   A. Active testing

   B. White box testing

   C. Gray box testing

   D. Active testing

9. You are attempting to perform an external vulnerability assessment for a client, but your source IP addresses keep getting blocked every time you attempt to run a vulnerability scan. The client confirms this is "as expected" behavior. You aren't able to scan for vulnerabilities, but you have been able to do which of the following?

   A. Identify vulnerability controls

   B. Identify common misconfigurations

   C. Passively test security controls

   D. All of the above

10. What is the main difference between a credentialed and non-credentialed vulnerability scan?

    A. A credentialed scan is performed by a certified professional.

    B. A credentialed scan is performed with a valid userid/password.

    C. A non-credentialed scan uses passive techniques.

    D. A non-credentialed scan will identify more vulnerabilities.

11. While validating a vulnerability, your colleague changes the password of the administrator account on the Windows Server she is examining (as proof of success). This is an example of what type of testing?

    A. Intrusive testing

    B. Credentialed testing

    C. Passive testing

    D. Security control testing

12. A colleague shows you a scanning report indicating your web server is not vulnerable to the Heartbleed bug. You know this isn't true as you've personally verified that web server is vulnerable. You believe the scanner used to examine your web server is reporting which of the following?

   A. Common misconfiguration

   B. False positive

   C. False negative

   D. SSL mismatch

13. Which of the following would be an example of initial exploitation?

   A. Scanning a network using Nmap

   B. Using a SQL injection attack to successfully bypass a login prompt

   C. Using cracked credentials to delete customer data

   D. Installing a backdoor to provide future access if needed

14. Which of the following is a passive tool?

   A. Tripwire

   B. Nmap

   C. Zenmap

   D. Nessus

15. What is the primary difference between penetration tests and vulnerability scans?

   A. Penetration tests use active tools.

   B. Vulnerability scans are performed from internal and external perspectives.

   C. Penetration tests exploit discovered vulnerabilities.

   D. Vulnerability scans never use credentials.

Answers

1. **C.** Black box testing is performed with no knowledge of the internal workings of the software being tested. The application is treated as a "black box"—the tester cannot see what's inside the box.

2. **B.** Escalation of privilege is the movement to an account that enables root-level activity. Typically, the attacker uses a normal user account to exploit a vulnerability on a process that is operating at root, enabling the attacker to assume the privileges of the exploited process—at root level. With root-level access, the attacker was able to access and modify the shadow file.

3. **D.** A false positive is the erroneous reporting of an issue when none really exists. In this case the scanner incorrectly identified the presence of a Linux-specific vulnerability on a Windows system.

4. **D.** This is an example of pivoting. Pivoting occurs when an attacker gains access to a system and then uses that system to scan/attack other systems on the same network.

5. **C.** Wireshark is a network protocol analyzer used for capturing and examining network traffic. Nmap and Zenmap are port scanners. Nessus is a vulnerability scanner.

6. **C.** This is most likely persistence efforts from an advanced persistent threat (APT). APTs typically try to avoid detection and employ methods that provide them with continued access to compromised systems.

7. **A.** This is most likely an example of active reconnaissance. This particular traffic would be indicative of a TCP port scanning attempt where the attacker is probing the system for any open TCP ports.

8. **B.** This is an example of white box testing. In white box testing, the tester has access to detailed knowledge of the things they are examining, whether it's an application, host, or network.

9. **C.** If your source IP addresses are blocked every time you attempt a vulnerability scan, you've successfully done a passive test of the client's security controls. Your goal was to test for vulnerabilities, but the side effect of your testing validated the client's security controls were working as intended.

10. **B.** A credentialed scan is performed with a valid set of user credentials. Credentialed scans are performed with "valid user" access and have the potential to identify vulnerabilities inside an application or environment.

11. **A.** This is an example of intrusive testing. Intrusive testing to validate a vulnerability involves exploiting the vulnerability and then making changes to the tested item to prove the vulnerability is present and exploitable. In this case, changing the administrator password proves your colleague could exploit the vulnerability she found.

12. **C.** A false negative is when the scanner fails to report a vulnerability that actually does exist—the scanner simply missed the problem or didn't report it as a problem.

13. **B.** Using a SQL injection attack to successfully bypass a login prompt is an example of initial exploitation. The vulnerability was identified and exploited, but no further action was taken. This proves the existence of the vulnerability and demonstrates the risk associated with the vulnerability.

14. **A.** Tripwire is the only passive tool listed. Tripwire detects changes to files based on hash values. Nmap and Zenmap are active tools that generate and send packets to systems being examined. Nessus is a vulnerability scanning tool.

15. **C.** Penetration testing is the examination of a system for vulnerabilities that can be exploited. The key is exploitation. There may be vulnerabilities in a system, in fact, one of the early steps in penetration testing is the examination for vulnerabilities, but the differentiation comes in the follow-on steps—the examination of the system in terms of exploitability. Discovered vulnerabilities are exploited during penetration testing.

Vulnerabilities and Impacts

In this chapter, you will

- Explore the sources and types of vulnerabilities
- Explain the impact associated with types of vulnerabilities

Vulnerabilities are the source of virtually all security concerns. Vulnerabilities are specific characteristics of a system that an attacker exploits to violate the security posture of the system. When an attacker exploits a vulnerability, the impact can vary from minimal to disastrous. This chapter examines the technical source and business impact of the types of vulnerabilities commonly found in systems.

Certification Objective   This chapter covers CompTIA Security+ exam objective 1.6, Explain the impact associated with types of vulnerabilities.

    EXAM TIP   Per exam objective 1.6, be prepared for questions that require you to identify the impact associated with a specific vulnerability. Vulnerabilities open or expand risk, which can result in impact to an organization. The key is in tracing the problem to how it affects the enterprise in terms of impact or cost.

Race Conditions

A *race condition* is an error condition that occurs when the output of a function is dependent on the sequence or timing of the inputs. It becomes a bug when the inputs do not happen in the order the programmer intended. The term race condition relates to the idea of multiple inputs racing each other to influence the output first. Race conditions can occur in multithreaded or distributed programs when the sequence or timing of processes or threads is important for the program to operate properly. Race conditions are very difficult to detect, for they are typically transient or nondeterministic and may depend upon other processes running on a system, even if not connected programmatically. The impact of a race condition is usually the failure of a system in the form of a crash. Race conditions can be combated with reference counters, kernel locks, and thread synchronization. Reference counters are structures in the kernel that detail whether a resource is actively being used or not at the current moment. Locking the kernel was an early method, but it causes performance issues. Thread synchronization prevents threads from accessing the shared data at the same time.

 EXAM TIP Race conditions can be used for privilege elevation and denial-of-service attacks. Programmers can use reference counters, kernel locks, and thread synchronization to prevent race conditions.

System Vulnerabilities

Systems can have a wide range of vulnerabilities, many of which are related to specific components. But other vulnerabilities are associated with the whole system, including end-of-life issues, embedded system issues, and issues caused by lack of vendor support. It is important to understand these major vulnerabilities and have mitigation plans to protect the system from risk due to these conditions.

End-of-Life Systems

All systems eventually reach an end-of-life stage. *End-of-life* is defined as when the system has reached a point where it can no longer function as intended. End-of-life status can be reached for many reasons, such as lack of vendor support, a failure to instantiate on newer hardware, or incompatibility with other aspects of a system. Old software systems are frequently referred to as legacy systems, especially when they are still in use post end-of-life.

After software has reached end-of-life and the original vendor no longer supports it with updates and patches, security becomes an issue because the vendor will no longer fix newly discovered vulnerabilities. If an organization decides to continue to use end-of-life software, it must implement external controls to prevent access to the vulnerability. When the hardware is also end-of-life, the organization must have a substantial investment in spare hardware/parts, and in many cases newer hardware systems will not run old software. Incompatibilities between newer, current systems and old systems require intermediate patch layers to be built to allow communications to and from the old systems. All of these efforts increase costs and risk associated with end-of-life software and systems. In most cases in which an organization continues to use end-of-life software, the organization has determined that the software is critical to its operations and that replacing it is too expensive in terms of the capital costs, time, and resources.

The decision to continue using Windows XP represents a common example of end-of-life problems. Microsoft has discontinued Windows XP and has stopped its vendor support, such as updates, patches, and drivers. The effect is that Windows XP machines are vulnerable to new forms of attack. Many institutions, from manufacturing plants to hospitals, and a whole host between, find themselves trapped with the legacy Windows XP OS because of cost, compatibility, and/or legacy issues associated with moving to a newer OS. Recent ransomware attacks have plagued older OS's that are no longer being patched, making them easy targets.

Embedded Systems

Embedded systems are systems that are included within other systems. This term can apply to a stand-alone, single-purpose system designed to provide specific functionality to an overall system. It can also be used to refer to some module or component of a larger system that comes from another source. One of the risks of embedded systems comes from the software that is in the system yet separate from any update/patch methodology. The software includes any inherent vulnerabilities that exist as a part of its build but are separate from the overall system build. Old versions of Linux and software libraries have known vulnerabilities. When these programs are part of an embedded system, if they are not updated/patched, they can bring hidden vulnerabilities into the overall system.

Lack of Vendor Support

Lack of vendor support can become an issue at several different levels of vendor. The most obvious scenario is when the original manufacturer of the item, be it hardware or software, no longer offers support. When an item reaches end-of-life from the original manufacturer's standpoint, this signifies the finality of its life under almost all circumstances. After the manufacturer stops supporting an item, options to keep it up to date with patches and fixes seldom exist. At this point, an organization that continues to use the product assumes all of the risk associated with issues uncovered after the product has entered end-of-life status, and the options to address these risks are limited to compensating controls.

Another scenario in which lack of vendor support arises is when the system under question was implemented by a third-party vendor and that vendor either no longer supports the configuration or, in some cases, is no longer in business. The underlying technology may still be supported by the original manufacturers, but the lack of support for the middleware provided by the third-party implementer raises questions as to whether the underlying products can be updated or patched. This places the testing burden on the end user, and in many cases the end user does not have the knowledge or skills necessary to conduct thorough regression testing.

 EXAM TIP A system can have vulnerabilities related to the age of the system. Whether the system is composed of old parts, as in an embedded system, or has become an end-of-life legacy system, the lack of vendor support can result in the owner's inability to address many newly discovered issues.

Improper Input Handling

Improper input handling is the true number one cause of software vulnerabilities. Improper input handling or input validation is the root cause behind most overflows, injection attacks, and canonical structure errors. Users have the ability to manipulate input, so it is up to the developer to handle the input appropriately to prevent malicious entries from having an effect. Buffer overflows (discussed later in the chapter) have long been recognized as a class of improper input handling. Newer input handling attacks include canonicalization attacks and arithmetic attacks. Probably the most effective defensive mechanism that you can employ is input validation. Considering all inputs to be hostile until properly validated can mitigate many attacks based on common vulnerabilities. This is a challenge, as the validation efforts need to occur after all parsers have completed manipulating input streams, a common function in web-based applications using Unicode and other international character sets.

Input validation is especially well suited for the following vulnerabilities: buffer overflow, reliance on untrusted inputs in a security decision, cross-site scripting (XSS), cross-site request forgery (XSRF), path traversal, and incorrect calculation of buffer size. Input validation may seem suitable for various injection attacks, but given the complexity of the input and the ramifications from legal but improper input streams, this method falls short for most injection attacks. What can work is a form of recognition and whitelisting approach, where the input is validated and then parsed into a standard structure that is then executed. This restricts the attack surface to not only legal inputs but also expected inputs.

The impact of improper input handling can be catastrophic, allowing an attacker to either gain a foothold on a system or increase his level of privilege. Because this type of error is dependent upon the process being attacked, the results can vary, but they almost always result in attackers advancing their kill chain.

 EXAM TIP Input validation is especially well suited for the following vulnerabilities: buffer overflow, reliance on untrusted inputs in a security decision, cross-site scripting (XSS), cross-site request forgery (XSRF), path traversal, and incorrect calculation of buffer size. When taking the Security+ exam, look for questions that address a large number of related problems with a common potential cause.

Improper Error Handling

Every application will encounter errors and exceptions, and these need to be handled in a secure manner. One attack methodology includes forcing errors to move an application from normal operation to exception handling. During an exception, it is common practice to record/report the condition, typically in a log file, including supporting information such as the data that resulted in the error. This information can be invaluable in diagnosing the cause of the error condition. The challenge is in where this information is captured. The best method is to capture it in a log file, where it can be secured by an access control list (ACL). The worst method is to echo the information to the user. Echoing error condition details to users can provide valuable information to attackers when they cause errors on purpose.

Improper error handling can lead to a wide range of disclosures. Errors associated with SQL statements can disclose data structures and data elements. Remote procedure call (RPC) errors can give up sensitive information such as filenames, paths, and server names. Programmatic errors can disclose line numbers that an exception occurred on, the method that was invoked, and information such as stack elements. Attackers can use the information they gather from errors to further their attack on a system, as the information typically gives them details about the composition and inner workings of the system that they can exploit.

Misconfiguration/Weak Configuration

Most systems have significant configuration options that administrators can adjust to enable or disable functionality based on usage. When a system suffers from *misconfiguration* or *weak configuration*, it may not achieve all of the desired performance or security objectives. Configuring a database server to build a complete replica of all actions as a backup system can result in a system that is bogged down and not capable of proper responses when usage is high. Similarly, old options, such as support for legacy protocols, can lead to vulnerabilities. Misconfiguration can result from omissions as well, such as when the administrator does not change default credentials, which is equivalent to having no credentials at all, leaving the system vulnerable. This form of vulnerability provides a means for an attacker to gain entry or advance their level of privilege, and because this can happen on components with a wide span of control, such as a router or a switch, in some cases an attacker can effectively gain total ownership of an enterprise.

Default Configuration

Default configuration is the configuration that a system enters upon start, upon recovering from an error, and at times when operating. This configuration acts as a system baseline, a position from which all other states can be measured. It is very important for the default configuration to be secure from the beginning, for if not, then a system will be vulnerable whenever entering this configuration, which in many conditions is common.

"Secure by Default" is an initiative by Microsoft to ensure that all of its systems are designed to be secure by default when installed and operated. One of the key elements of this initiative is to force the system installer to provide unique and secure credentials upon installation. This prevents the misconfiguration by omission issue (discussed in the previous section) that enables attackers to reuse default admin credentials to gain admin- or root-level control over a system. As with misconfigurations, this form of vulnerability provides a means for an attacker to gain entry or advance their level of privilege, and because this can happen on components with a wide span of control, such as a router or a switch, in some cases an attacker can effectively gain total ownership of an enterprise.

 EXAM TIP Configuration issues are common causes of problems and are easy targets for questions on the Security+ exam. Pay attention to the details of the question to determine what the specific issue is, be it default configuration, misconfiguration, or weak configuration, as you will likely see all of these as choices.

Resource Exhaustion

All systems are defined as a process that creates specific outputs as a result of a defined set of inputs. The internals of the system use a variety of resources to achieve the transition of input states to output states. *Resource exhaustion* is the state where a system does not have all of the resources it needs to continue to function. Two common resources are capacity and memory, which are interdependent in some scenarios but completely separate in others. Capacity is defined by a system having the necessary amount of communication bandwidth, processing bandwidth, and memory to manage intermediate states. When one of these resources becomes exhausted, failure can ensue. For instance, if a system has more TCP SYN requests than it can handle, it fails to complete handshakes and enable additional connections. If a program runs out of memory, it will fail to operate correctly. This is an example of a resource exhaustion attack, where the attack's aim is to deplete resources.

 EXAM TIP Like race conditions, resource exhaustion vulnerabilities tend to result in a system crash. These attacks can result in less damage, but from the aspect of an attacker advancing a persistence, it's necessary to change system functions as part of an overall attack strategy. However, in some cases, the outages can stop essential services, including customer-facing systems.

Untrained Users

Untrained users are users who do not know how to operate a system properly because they haven't received training associated with the system's capabilities. Unfortunately, untrained users are fairly common in most modern organizations. Whether they are end users who don't know how to navigate standard GUIs or highly technical people like software developers who don't understand how to properly use the interface of their IDE, the end result is the same: the system of protections and efficiencies built into a program goes unused. Untrained users typically are less efficient because they do not use the system to its designed performance level. Untrained users can also add risk to a system by not using designed-in mitigations, in essence bypassing controls designed to reduce risk.

Training of users begins with policies and procedures. These elements explain the what and how of workers daily tasks. The procedures should also hand exceptions and abnormal conditions, for they occur and should be handled according to procedure. Training also needs to include general user security training including things like password policies and defending against social engineering attacks.

 EXAM TIP Users are part of the overall system, and users have the ability to be configured during training. Training users how to properly use their tools, including general security items such as security policies and how to defend against social engineering is essential. Untrained users are easier targets for an attacker to compromise.

Improperly Configured Accounts

Accounts form the basis for access control, for they define the user, and this leads to the list of allowed actions via an access control list (ACL). Improperly configured accounts can lead to improper allowances via ACLs. Individual accounts quickly become too numerous to efficiently manage on an individual basis, and as a response to this problem, administrators create group accounts to reduce the number of controlling entries to a manageable number. But when a user account ends up in the wrong group, the user may receive permissions that are inappropriate for that user, and even worse, there is no distinct warning flag that this has occurred. This is one of the reasons that Linux system administrators do not log in as root even when they need to perform root actions. If they were logged in as root, then an inadvertent typo or a command in the wrong directory could result in catastrophic failure. Forcing them to use the **su** command to take a root action reminds them of the gravity of the action and to proceed cautiously.

A common misconfiguration suites on Windows computers is the use of a local administrator account. This may seem harmless as it is only a local account, but if an attacker is able to access a local administrator account, he then has numerous potential paths leading to domain administrator access; thus, organizations need to limit the use of local admin accounts, or take specific mitigating actions to ensure they can't be used to gain domain admin access.

Vulnerable Business Processes

Virtually all work is a combination of technology, people, and processes. Just as technology and users often have vulnerabilities that can be comprised, as previously discussed, *vulnerable business processes* are subject to compromise. When a business process that contains an inherent vulnerability is automated, then all that automation can do is increase the speed of the failure. A simple example would be paying an invoice without matching it to an approved purchase order. A common form of fraud is to send an invoice to an organization for goods or services that were not provided, typically for something common like office supplies. If someone in the organization processes the invoice for payment without verifying that the organization ordered and received the supplies, then this is clearly a business process failure. If the payment process is automated and works similarly, the vulnerability is even greater.

Weak Cipher Suites and Implementations

Cryptographic errors come from several common causes. One typical mistake is choosing to develop your own cryptographic algorithm. Development of a secure cryptographic algorithm is far from an easy task, and even when attempted by experts, weaknesses can be discovered that make the algorithm unusable. Cryptographic algorithms become trusted only after years of scrutiny and repelling attacks, so any new algorithms would take years to join the trusted set. If you instead decide to rely on secret algorithms, be warned that secret or proprietary algorithms have never provided the desired level of protection. A similar mistake to attempting to develop your own cryptographic algorithm is to attempt to write your own implementation of a known cryptographic algorithm. Errors in coding implementations are common and lead to *weak implementations* of secure algorithms that are vulnerable to bypass. Do not fall prey to creating a weak implementation; instead, use a proven, vetted cryptographic library.

The second major cause of cryptographic weakness is the employment of deprecated or weak cryptographic algorithms. *Weak cipher suites* are those that at one time were considered secure but are no longer considered secure. As the ability to use ever faster hardware has enabled attackers to defeat some cryptographic methods, the older, weaker methods have been replaced by newer, stronger ones. Failure to use the newer, stronger methods can result in weakness. A common example of this is SSL; all versions of SSL are now considered deprecated, and should not be used. Everyone should switch their systems to TLS-based solutions.

The impact of cryptographic failures is fairly easy to understand: whatever protection that was provided is no longer there, even if it is essential for the security of the system.

Memory/Buffer Vulnerability

When computer programs take inputs for a variable, they are put into buffers in memory. These buffers are located where the variable is stored in memory, so when the program needs to reference the value of a variable, it uses the memory location to obtain the value. Some languages, referred to as type safe, verify the length of an input before assigning it to the memory location. Other languages, such as C/C++, rely upon the programmer to handle this verification task. When this task is not properly performed, there exists a chance to overwrite the allocated area in memory, potentially corrupting other values of other variables, and certainly not storing what was requested in the variable in question. This is a *memory/buffer vulnerability* and it can exist in software without issue until input that exceeds the allocated space is received. Then the memory/buffer vulnerability becomes an input overflow or buffer overflow error.

Other forms of memory vulnerabilities include DLL injections, where additional code can be put into a program's memory space and used, and issues associated with pointers, including pointer errors, commonly associated with dereference errors.

The impact of memory and buffer vulnerabilities is the same as for input-handling issues. An attacker can use the access to program flow to either obtain access or advance privilege level.

Memory Leak

Memory leaks are programming errors caused when a computer program does not properly handle memory resources. Over time, while a program runs, if it does not clean memory resources as they are no longer needed, it can grow in size, with chunks of dead memory being scattered across the program's footprint in memory. If a program executes for a long time, these chunks can grow and consume resources, causing a system to crash. Even if the program only runs for a short time, in some cases, leaks can cause issues when referencing values later in a run, returning improper values.

The impact of memory leaks is similar to that of race conditions and resource exhaustion: the system can crash. Thus, based on what function the affected system performs, the loss of that function or capacity is the result.

Integer Overflow

An *integer overflow* is a programming error condition that occurs when a program attempts to store a numeric value, an integer, in a variable that is too small to hold it. The results vary by language and numeric type. In some cases, the value saturates the variable, assuming the maximum value for the defined type and no more. In other cases, especially with signed integers, it can roll over into a negative value, as the most significant bit is usually reserved for the sign of the number. This can create significant logic errors in a program. As with most errors, integer overflow errors are targets for attackers to exploit, as they can be manipulated to create incorrect results in a system.

Integer overflows are easily tested for, and static code analyzers can point out where they are likely to occur. Given this, there are not any good excuses for having these errors end up in production code.

Buffer Overflow

Buffer overflow attacks are input validation attacks, designed to take advantage of input routines that do not validate the length of inputs. Surprisingly simple to resolve, all that is required is the validation of all input lengths prior to writing to memory. This can be done in a variety of manners, including the use of safe library functions for inputs. This is one of the vulnerabilities that has been shown to be solvable, and in fact the prevalence is declining substantially among major security-conscious software firms.

The concept behind the buffer overflow vulnerability is relatively simple. The input buffer that is used to hold program input is overwritten with data that is larger than the buffer can hold. The root cause of this vulnerability is a mixture of two things: poor programming practice and programming language weaknesses. For example, what would happen if a program that asks for a 7- to 10-character phone number instead receives a string of 150 characters? Many programs will provide some error checking to ensure that this will not cause a problem. Some programs, however, cannot handle this error, and the extra characters continue to fill memory, overwriting other portions of the program. This can result in a number of problems, including causing the program to abort or the system to crash. Under certain circumstances, the program can execute a command supplied by the attacker. Buffer overflows typically inherit the level of privilege enjoyed by the program being exploited. This is why programs that use root-level access are so dangerous when exploited with a buffer overflow, as the code that will execute does so at root-level access.

Pointer Dereference

Some computer languages use a construct referred to as a pointer, a variable that refers to the memory location that holds a variable as opposed to the value in the memory location. To get the value at the memory location denoted by a pointer variable, one must dereference the pointer. The act of *pointer dereference* now changes the meaning of the object to the contents of the memory location, not the memory location as identified by the pointer. Pointers can be very powerful and allow fast operations across a wide range of structures. But they can also be dangerous, as mistakes in their use can lead to unexpected consequences. When a programmer uses user inputs in concert with pointers, for example, lets the user pick a place in an array, and uses a pointer to reference the value, mistakes in the input validation can lead to errors in pointer dereference, which may or may not trigger an error, as the location will contain data and it will be returned.

DLL Injection

Dynamic link libraries (DLLs) are pieces of code that can add functionality to a program through the inclusion of library routines linked at run time. *DLL injection* is the process of adding to a program at run time a DLL that has a specific vulnerability of function that can be capitalized upon by an attacker. A good example of this is Microsoft Office, a suite of programs that use DLLs loaded at run time. Adding an "evil" DLL in the correct directory, or via a registry key, can result in "additional functionality" being incurred.

 EXAM TIP There are several different vulnerabilities with similar causes. Memory leaks and buffer overflows can be caused by a variety of input-related vulnerabilities. What distinguishes many of these causes is the actual target of the vulnerability. Integer overflows target math operations, SQL injection targets SQL engine operations, and so forth. The key to the correct answer lies in the details of the quest.

System Sprawl/Undocumented Assets

The foundation of a comprehensive security program is understanding all of your assets and how they are connected. This applies to hardware, software, and data. Understanding your network diagram, including all the systems and how they are connected, is essential to managing the flow of traffic. Understanding what software you have, where it is installed, and how it is configured is essential when updates and patches become necessary. These elements are all important, not to mention correct access control lists for the above. Data is its own asset category because it moves around and can't be diagrammed. Data can be in transit, at rest, or in use, and typically it is the most important asset to protect. All of these topics are covered throughout this book and listed in the Security+ exam objectives.

System sprawl is when the systems expand over time, adding elements and functionality, and over time the growth and change exceeds the documentation. This addition of *undocumented assets* means that these specific assets are not necessarily included in plans for upgrades, security, etc. Enterprises inevitably end up with system sprawl and undocumented assets. What begins as correct, over time moves to complete failure to understand because we seldom manage the documentation of the architecture as built and deployed.

As changes occur, we always seem to miss updating the diagrams, architectures, and rules associated with security. System sprawl occurs because we continually "improve" systems by adding functionality and frequently fail to update the architecture plans. The new elements that are not documented become undocumented assets and contribute to misunderstandings and issues when they are not considered for future changes. Undocumented assets also have a higher chance of becoming an unknown vulnerability primarily because of their undocumented status that precludes their inclusion in routine security checks.

EXAM TIP As time passes, an enterprise may lose the ability to properly manage all of the systems, devices, software, and data assets that have accumulated. This results in overprovisioning provisioned resources and is commonly known as system sprawl. Don't confuse the Security+ exam objective terms system sprawl and VM sprawl. Although they are similar in concept, VM sprawl applies to virtual machines and is covered in Chapter 15.

Architecture/Design Weaknesses

System architectures can have strengths and weaknesses. Most of these are the result of design. *Architecture/design weaknesses* are issues that result in vulnerabilities and increased risk in a systematic manner. These flaws are not easily corrected without addressing the specific architecture or design vulnerability that created them in the first place. An example of this is a flat network design without any segmentation. This increases the likelihood that an attacker can traverse the network and get access to sensitive data from an entry point that is significantly less trusted.

New Threats/Zero Day

Zero day is a term used to define vulnerabilities that are newly discovered and not yet addressed by a patch. Most vulnerabilities exist in an unknown state until discovered by a researcher or developer. If a researcher or developer discovers a vulnerability but does not share the information, then this vulnerability can be exploited without a vendor's ability to fix it, because for all practical knowledge the issue is unknown, except to the person who found it. From the time of discovery until a fix or patch is made available, the vulnerability goes by the name zero day, indicating that it has not been addressed yet. The most frightening thing about a zero day threat is the unknown factor—their capability and effect on risk are unknown because they are unknown. Although there are no patches for zero day vulnerabilities, you can use compensating controls to mitigate the risk.

EXAM TIP Zero day threats have become a common topic in the news and are a likely target for exam questions. Keep in mind that defenses exist, such as compensating controls, which are controls that mitigate the risk indirectly; for example, a mitigating control may block the path to the vulnerability rather than directly address the vulnerability.

Improper Certificate and Key Management

Certificates are the most common method of transferring and managing cryptographic keys between parties. *Improper certificate management* can lead to key problems and cryptographic failures. Failure to properly validate a key before use can result in an expired or compromised key being used. *Improper key management* can result in failure to secure data if, for example, a compromised key continues to be used. The PKI system has established processes and procedures to ensure proper key hygiene and limit the potential issues associated with public key cryptography. To receive these benefits from a PKI system, it is important to follow the established procedures and methods for both certificate usage and subsequent key usage.

Chapter Review

In this chapter, you became acquainted with the impact associated with various types of vulnerabilities. The chapter began with a discussion of the impacts associated with a series of specific types of vulnerabilities, including race conditions, system vulnerabilities, improper input handling, and improper error handling. The chapter continued with coverage of impacts associated with misconfiguration/weak configurations, default configurations, resource exhaustion, untrained users, improperly configured accounts, and vulnerable business practices. The next set of impacts examined included those associated weak cipher suites and implementations and memory/buffer vulnerabilities. The chapter concluded with an examination of the impacts of system sprawl/undocumented assets, architecture/design weaknesses, new threats/zero days, and improper certificate and key management.

Questions

To help you prepare further for the CompTIA Security+ exam, and to test your level of preparedness, answer the following questions and then check your answers against the correct answers at the end of the chapter.

1. You're reviewing a custom web application and accidentally type a number in a text field. The application returns an error message containing variable names, filenames, and the full path of the application. This is an example of which of the following?

   A. Resource exhaustion

   B. Improper error handling

   C. Generic error message

   D. Common misconfiguration

2. A web server in your organization has been defaced. The server is patched and properly configured as far as anyone can tell. Your logs show unusual traffic from external IP addresses just before the defacement occurred. It's possible your server was attacked by which of the following?

   A. Misconfiguration attack

   B. Insider threat

    C. Zero day exploit

    D. Design weakness attack

3. You're working with a group testing a new application. You've noticed that when three or more of you click Submit on a specific form at the same time, the application crashes every time. This is most likely an example of which of the following?

    A. A race condition

    B. A nondeterministic error

    C. Undocumented feature

    D. DLL injection

4. Which of the following is a vulnerability related to a lack of vendor support?

    A. The product has been declared "end-of-life" by the vendor.

    B. The vendor is no longer in business.

    C. The vendor does not support nonstandard configurations for its products.

    D. All of the above.

5. An externally facing web server in your organization keeps crashing. Looking at the server after a reboot, you notice CPU usage is pegged and memory usage is rapidly climbing. The traffic logs show a massive amount of incoming HTTP and HTTPS requests to the server. Which type of attack is this web server experiencing?

    A. Input validation

    B. Distributed error handling

    C. Resource exhaustion

    D. Race condition

6. A colleague on your team takes three times longer than you do to complete common tasks in a particular application. When you go to help him, you notice immediately that he doesn't use any of the shortcuts designed into the application. When you ask him why he is not using shortcuts, he tells you he didn't know the shortcuts exist. This is an example of which of the following?

    A. An untrained user

    B. Improper application configuration

    C. Memory leak

    D. Lack of vendor support

7. Your organization is considering using a new ticket identifier with your current help desk system. The new identifier would be a 16-digit integer created by combining the date, time, and operator ID. Unfortunately, when you've tried using the new identifier in the "ticket number" field on your current system, the application crashes every time. The old method of using a 5-digit integer works just fine. This is most likely an example of which of the following?

A. Common misconfiguration

B. Zero day vulnerability

C. Memory leak

D. Integer overflow

8. While examining a laptop infected with malware, you notice the malware loads on startup and also loads a file called netutilities.dll each time Microsoft Word is opened. This is an example of which of the following?

A. Zero day exploit

B. DLL injection

C. System infection

D. Memory overflow

9. You're providing incident response services for a small company after a breach. The first thing you notice is the entire network is completely flat once you get behind the firewall. Services, user workstations, and printers are all on the same subnet with no VLANs or network segmentation. This is an example of what type of weakness?

A. Architecture/design weakness

B. Network traversal weakness

C. TCP overflow weakness

D. Memory leak weakness

10. A web application you are reviewing has an input field for username and indicates the username should be between 6 and 12 characters. You've discovered that if you input a username 150 characters or more in length, the application crashes. What is this is an example of?

A. Memory leak

B. Buffer overflow

C. Directory traversal

D. Integer overflow

11. You've been asked to help address some findings from a recent PCI (Payment Card Industry) audit, one of which is support for SSL 2.0 on a web server. Your CFO wants to know why SSL 2.0 support is a problem. You tell her SSL 2.0 support is an example of which of the following vulnerabilities?

    A. Separation of duties

    B. Default configuration

    C. Resource exhaustion

    D. Weak cipher suites

12. Your organization is having issues with a custom web application. The application seems to run fine for a while but starts to lock up or crash after 7 to 10 days of continuous use. Examining the server, you notice that memory usage seems to climb every day until the server runs out of memory. The application is most likely suffering from which of the following?

    A. Memory leak

    B. Overflow leak

    C. Zero day exploit

    D. Pointer dereference

13. While examining internal network traffic, you notice a large amount of suspicious traffic coming from an IP address in the development environment. The IP address isn't listed on any network diagram and shouldn't be active on your network as far as you can tell. When you ask the developers about it, one of them tells you he set up that server over 12 months ago for a temporary project and forgot all about it. This is an example of which of the following?

    A. Single server contingency

    B. DLL injection

    C. Undocumented asset

    D. Insider threat

14. While auditing an organization, you discover that new users are added to the domain by sending an e-mail request to the IT department, but the e-mails don't always come from Human Resources, and IT doesn't always check with HR to ensure the new user request corresponds to an authorized user. This is an example of which of the following?

    A. Process overflow

    B. Vulnerable business process

    C. Insider threat

    D. Trojan e-mail attack

15. Which of the following is an example of an embedded system?

   A. A user workstation

   B. A web server

   C. A network-enabled thermostat

   D. A database server

Answers

1. **B.** When an application fails to properly trap an error and generates error messages containing potentially sensitive information, this is known as *improper error handling*.

2. **C.** If a completely patched, properly configured server is successfully attacked, the most likely culprit is a zero day exploit. With zero day exploits, the vulnerability being exploited is unknown to the general public or the developer, so even a "fully patched" system is potentially vulnerable to zero day exploits.

3. **A.** This is most likely an example of a race condition. A race condition is an error condition that occurs when the output of a function is dependent on the sequence or timing of the inputs. In this case, the application crashes when multiple inputs are submitted at the same time because the application is not receiving the inputs or handling the inputs in the expected order.

4. **D.** All of these are potential vulnerabilities associated with a lack of vendor support. When a vendor declares a product to be end-of-life, the vendor typically ends support for that product, which typically means it will provide no updates, patches, or maintenance even if critical vulnerabilities are later discovered. A vendor that no longer exists clearly can't provide support or patches. Vendors that support only specific configurations may not provide maintenance, features, or patches that allow their product to work securely in your specific environment.

5. **C.** *Resource exhaustion* is the state where a system does not have all of the resources it needs to continue to function. In this case the server does not have the memory or CPU capacity to handle the massive volume of HTTP/HTTPS requests that are coming into the server.

6. **A.** Your colleague is an untrained user. *Untrained users* are users who do not know how to operate a system efficiently or securely because they haven't received training associated with the system's capabilities.

7. **D.** An *integer overflow* is a programming error condition that occurs when a program attempts to store a numeric value, an integer, in a variable that is too small to hold it. In this case the 16-digit integer is too large for the field that's working just fine with the 5-digit integer.

8. **B.** This is an example of DLL injection. *DLL injection* is the process of adding to a program at run time a DLL that has a specific vulnerability of function that can be capitalized upon by an attacker.

9. **A.** A flat network designed with no network segmentation increases the likelihood an attacker can easily traverse the network and gain access to sensitive information. The problem lies with the how the network was designed/built. This is known as an *architecture/design weakness*.

10. **B.** This is a fairly classic example of a *buffer overflow*. The input routine does not validate the provided input to ensure a maximum of 12 characters are received and processed. In this case, the application tries to store all 150 or more characters of the username, resulting in areas of memory being overwritten and causing the application to crash.

11. **D.** SSL 2.0 is an example of a *weak cipher suite*. While technically the protocol used for SSL 2.0 is not a "vulnerability," the cipher suites used in SSL 2.0 are cryptographically insecure—meaning an attacker can "break them" and access the content you are trying to protect.

12. **A.** *Memory leaks* are programming errors caused when a computer program does not properly handle memory resources. Over time, while a program runs, if it does not clean memory resources as they are no longer needed, it can grow in size, with chunks of dead memory being scattered across the program's footprint in memory. If a program executes for a long time, these can grow and consume resources, causing a system to crash.

13. **C.** This is a good example of an *undocumented asset*. The server was added to the environment, but the appropriate network documentation was never updated.

14. **B.** This is an example of a *vulnerable business process*. If IT is creating new user accounts based on e-mails it receives without validating that the requests are valid, then an attacker could take advantage of this process.

15. **C.** The network-enabled thermostat is an example of an *embedded system*. This device is a stand-alone, single-purpose system that is a component of a larger system (the HVAC system in this case).

PART II

Technologies and Tools

Network Components

In this chapter, you will

- Install and configure network components, both hardware- and software-based, to support organizational security

Large systems are composed of a highly complex set of integrated components. These components can be integrated into a system designed to perform complex operations. System integration is the set of processes designed to produce synergy from the linkage of all of the components. In most business cases, third parties will be part of the value chain, necessitating the sharing of business information, processes, and data with them. This has security and risk implications that need to be understood before these relationships are established.

Certification Objective   This chapter covers CompTIA Security+ exam objective 2.1, Install and configure network components, both hardware- and software-based, to support organizational security.

 EXAM TIP   This chapter contains topics under exam objective 2.1 that can be tested with performance-based questions. It is not enough to simply learn the terms associated with the material. You should be familiar with installing and configuring the components to support organizational security.

Firewall

A *firewall* can be hardware, software, or a combination of both whose purpose is to enforce a set of network security policies across network connections. It is much like a wall with a window: the wall serves to keep things out, except those permitted through the window (see Figure 6-1). Network security policies act like the glass in the window; they permit some things to pass, such as light, while blocking others, such as air. The heart of a firewall is the set of security policies that it enforces. Management determines what is allowed in the form of network traffic between devices, and these policies are used to build rulesets for the firewall devices used to filter network traffic across the network.

Security policies are rules that define what traffic is permissible and what traffic is to be blocked or denied. These are not universal rules, and many different sets of rules are

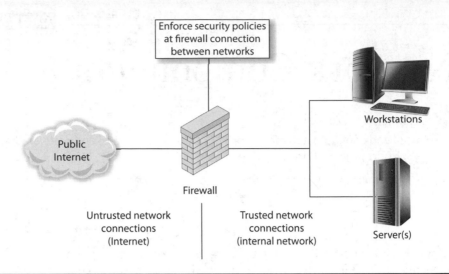

Figure 6-1 How a firewall works

created for a single organization with multiple connections. A web server connected to the Internet may be configured to allow traffic only on port 80 for HTTP and have all other ports blocked, for example. An e-mail server may have only necessary ports for e-mail open, with others blocked. The network firewall can be programmed to block all traffic to the web server except for port 80 traffic, and to block all traffic bound to the mail server except for port 25. In this fashion, the firewall acts as a security filter, enabling control over network traffic, by machine, by port, and in some cases based on application-level detail. A key to setting security policies for firewalls is the same as for other security policies—the principle of least access: allow only the necessary access for a function; block or deny all unneeded functionality. How an organization deploys its firewalls determines what is needed for security policies for each firewall.

As will be discussed later, the security topology will determine what network devices are employed at what points in a network. At a minimum, your organization's connection to the Internet should pass through a firewall. This firewall should block all network traffic except that specifically authorized by the organization. Blocking communications on a port is simple—just tell the firewall to close the port. The issue comes in deciding what services are needed and by whom, and thus which ports should be open and which should be closed. This is what makes a security policy useful. The perfect set of network security policies, for a firewall, is one that the end user never sees and that never allows even a single unauthorized packet to enter the network. As with any other perfect item, it will be rare to find the perfect set of security policies for firewalls in an enterprise. When developing rules for a firewall, the principle of least access is best to use; you want the firewall to block as much traffic as possible, while allowing the authorized traffic through.

To develop a complete and comprehensive security policy, you first need to have a complete and comprehensive understanding of your network resources and their uses. Once you know how the network will be used, you will have an idea of what to permit.

In addition, once you understand what you need to protect, you will have an idea of what to block. Firewalls are designed to block attacks before they reach a target machine. Common targets are web servers, e-mail servers, DNS servers, FTP services, and databases. Each of these has separate functionality, and each has unique vulnerabilities. Once you have decided who should receive what type of traffic and what types should be blocked, you can administer this through the firewall.

How Do Firewalls Work?

Firewalls enforce the established security policies through a variety of mechanisms, including the following:

- Network Address Translation (NAT)
- Basic packet filtering
- Stateful packet filtering
- Access control lists (ACLs)
- Application layer proxies

One of the most basic security functions provided by a firewall is NAT, which allows you to mask significant amounts of information from outside of the network. This allows an outside entity to communicate with an entity inside the firewall without truly knowing its address. NAT is a technique used in IPv4 to link private IP addresses to public ones. Private IP addresses are sets of IP addresses that can be used by anyone and, by definition, are not routable across the Internet. NAT can assist in security by preventing direct access to devices from outside the firm, without first having the address changed at a NAT device. The benefit is that fewer public IP addresses are needed, and from a security point of view the internal address structure is not known to the outside world. If a hacker attacks the source address, he is simply attacking the NAT device, not the actual sender of the packet.

NAT was conceived to resolve an address shortage associated with IPv4 and is considered by many to be unnecessary for IPv6. However, the added security features of enforcing traffic translation and hiding internal network details from direct outside connections will give NAT life well into the IPv6 timeframe.

Basic packet filtering, the next most common firewall technique, involves looking at packets, their ports, protocols, and source and destination addresses, and checking that information against the rules configured on the firewall. Telnet and FTP connections may be prohibited from being established to a mail or database server, but they may be allowed for the respective service servers. This is a fairly simple method of filtering based on information in each packet header, such as IP addresses and TCP/UDP ports. Packet filtering will not detect and catch all undesired packets, but it is fast and efficient.

 EXAM TIP Firewalls operate by examining packets and selectively denying some based on a set of rules. Firewalls act as gatekeepers or sentries at select network points, segregating traffic and allowing some to pass and blocking others.

Firewalls can also act as network traffic regulators in that they can be configured to mitigate specific types of network-based attacks. In denial-of-service and distributed denial-of-service (DoS/DDoS) attacks, an attacker can attempt to flood a network with traffic. Firewalls can be tuned to detect these types of attacks and act as a flood guard, mitigating the effect on the network. Firewalls can be very effective in blocking a variety of flooding attacks, including port floods, SYN floods, and ping floods.

Firewall Rules

Firewalls operate by enforcing a set of rules on the traffic attempting to pass. This set of *firewall rules*, also called the firewall ruleset, is a mirror of the policy constraints at a particular point in the network. Thus, the ruleset will vary from firewall to firewall, as it is the operational implementation of the desired traffic constraints at each point. Firewall rules state whether the firewall should allow particular traffic to pass through or block it. The structure of a firewall rule can range from simple to very complex, depending upon the type of firewall and the type of traffic. A packet filtering firewall can act on IP addresses and ports, either allowing or blocking based on this information.

 EXAM TIP Firewall rules make great performance-based questions—what rules belong on which firewall. Understanding how a rule blocks or permits traffic is essential, but so is seeing the overall network flow picture regulated by the rules. Be able to place rules to a network diagram to meet objectives.

ACL

Access control lists (ACLs) are lists of users and their permitted actions. Users can be identified in a variety of ways, including by a user ID, a network address, or a token. The simple objective is to create a lookup system that allows a device to determine which actions are permitted and which are denied. A router can contain an ACL that lists permitted addresses or blocked addresses, or a combination of both. The most common implementation is for file systems, where named user IDs are used to determine which file system attributes are permitted to the user. This same general concept is reused across all types of devices and situations in networking.

Just as the implicit deny rule applies to firewall rulesets (covered later in the chapter), the explicit deny principle can be applied to ACLs. When using this approach to ACL building, allowed traffic must be explicitly allowed by a **permit** statement. All of the specific **permit** commands are followed by a **deny all** in the ruleset. ACL entries are typically evaluated in a top-to-bottom fashion, so any traffic that does not match a **permit** entry will be dropped by a **deny all** statement placed as the last line in the ACL.

Application-Based vs. Network-Based

Application-based firewalls (aka application-layer firewalls) can analyze traffic at an even deeper level, examining the application characteristics of traffic and blocking specific actions while allowing others, even inside web-connected applications. This gives application-based firewalls much greater specificity than *network-based firewalls* that only look at IP addresses and ports.

Some high-security firewalls also employ application layer proxies. Packets are not allowed to traverse the firewall, but data instead flows up to an application that in turn decides what to do with it. For example, a Simple Mail Transfer Protocol (SMTP) proxy may accept inbound mail from the Internet and forward it to the internal corporate mail server. While proxies provide a high level of security by making it very difficult for an attacker to manipulate the actual packets arriving at the destination, and while they provide the opportunity for an application to interpret the data prior to forwarding it to the destination, they generally are not capable of the same throughput as stateful packet inspection firewalls. The trade-off between performance and speed is a common one and must be evaluated with respect to security needs and performance requirements.

Stateful vs. Stateless

The typical network firewall operates on IP addresses and ports, in essence a *stateless* interaction with the traffic. A *stateful* packet inspection firewall can act upon the state condition of a conversation—is this a new conversation or a continuation of a conversation, and did it originate inside or outside the firewall? This provides greater capability, but at a processing cost that has scalability implications.

To look at all packets and determine the need for each and its data requires stateful packet filtering. Stateful means that the firewall maintains, or knows, the context of a conversation. In many cases, rules depend on the context of a specific communication connection. For instance, traffic from an outside server to an inside server may be allowed if it is requested but blocked if it is not. A common example is a request for a web page. This request is actually a series of requests to multiple servers, each of which requests can be allowed or blocked. Advanced firewalls employ stateful packet filtering to prevent several types of undesired communications. Should a packet come from outside the network, in an attempt to pretend that it is a response to a message from inside the network, the firewall will have no record of it being requested and can discard it, blocking the undesired external access attempt. As many communications will be transferred to high ports (above 1023), stateful monitoring will enable the system to determine which sets of high port communications are permissible and which should be blocked. A disadvantage of stateful monitoring is that it takes significant resources and processing to perform this type of monitoring, and this reduces efficiency and requires more robust and expensive hardware.

Implicit Deny

All firewall rulesets should include an *implicit deny* rule that is in place to prevent any traffic from passing that is not specifically recognized as allowed. Firewalls execute their rules upon traffic in a top-down manner, with any allow or block rule whose conditions are met ending the processing. This means the order of rules is important. It also means that the last rule should be a deny all rule, for any traffic that gets to the last rule and has not met a rule allowing it to pass should be blocked.

 EXAM TIP To invoke implicit deny, the last rule should be a deny all rule, because any traffic that gets to the last rule and has not met a rule allowing it to pass should be blocked.

Secure Network Administration Principles

Secure network administration principles are the principles used to ensure network security and include properly configuring hardware and software and properly performing operations and maintenance. Networks are composed of a combination of hardware and software, operated under policies and procedures that define desired operating conditions. All of these elements need to be done with security in mind, from planning, to design, to operation.

Rule-Based Management

Rule-based management is a common methodology for configuring systems. Desired operational states are defined in such manner that they can be represented as rules, and a control enforces the rules in operation. This methodology is used for firewalls, proxies, switches, routers, anti-malware, IDS/IPS, and more. As each packet is presented to the control device, the set of rules is applied and interpreted. This is an efficient manner of translating policy objectives into operational use.

 EXAM TIP   To be prepared for performance-based questions, you should be familiar with installing and configuring the firewall components, including rules, types of firewalls, and administration of firewalls to support organizational security.

VPN Concentrator

A *VPN concentrator* acts as a VPN endpoint, providing a method of managing multiple separate VPN conversations, each isolated from the others and converting each encrypted stream to its unencrypted, plaintext form, on the network. VPN concentrators can provide a number of services, including but not limited to securing remote access and site-to-site communications. A VPN offers a means of cryptographically securing a communication channel, and the concentrator is the endpoint for this activity. It is referred to as a concentrator because it typically converts many different, independent conversations into one channel. Concentrators are designed to allow multiple, independent encrypted communications across a single device, simplifying network architectures and security.

Remote Access vs. Site-to-Site

VPNs can connect machines from different networks over a private channel. When the VPN is set up to connect specific machines between two networks on an ongoing basis, with no setup per communication required, it is referred to as a *site-to-site* VPN configuration. If the VPN connection is designed to allow remote hosts to connect to a network, they are called *remote access* VPNs. Both of these VPNs offer the same protection from outside eavesdropping on the communication channel they protect, the difference is in why they are set up.

IPSec

IPSec is a set of protocols developed by the IETF to securely exchange packets at the network layer (layer 3) of the OSI model (RFCs 2401–2412). Although these protocols work only in conjunction with IP networks, once an IPSec connection is established, it is possible to tunnel across other networks at lower levels of the OSI model. The set of security services provided by IPSec occurs at the network layer of the OSI model, so higher-layer protocols, such as TCP, UDP, Internet Control Message Protocol (ICMP), Border Gateway Protocol (BGP), and the like, are not functionally altered by the implementation of IPSec services.

The IPSec protocol series has a sweeping array of services it is designed to provide, including but not limited to access control, connectionless integrity, traffic-flow confidentiality, rejection of replayed packets, data security (encryption), and data-origin authentication. IPSec has two defined modes—transport and tunnel—that provide different levels of security. IPSec also has three modes of connection: host-to-server, server-to-server, and host-to-host.

The transport mode encrypts only the data portion of a packet, thus enabling an outsider to see source and destination IP addresses. The transport mode protects the higher-level protocols associated with a packet and protects the data being transmitted but allows knowledge of the transmission itself. Protection of the data portion of a packet is referred to as content protection.

Tunnel mode provides encryption of source and destination IP addresses, as well as of the data itself. This provides the greatest security, but it can be done only between IPSec servers (or routers) because the final destination needs to be known for delivery. Protection of the header information is known as context protection.

 EXAM TIP In *transport mode* (end-to-end), security of packet traffic is provided by the endpoint computers. In *tunnel mode* (portal-to-portal), security of packet traffic is provided between endpoint node machines in each network and not at the terminal host machines.

It is possible to use both methods at the same time, such as using transport within one's own network to reach an IPSec server, which then tunnels to the target server's network, connecting to an IPSec server there, and then using the transport method from the target network's IPSec server to the target host. IPSec uses the term security association (SA) to describe a unidirectional combination of specific algorithm and key selection to provide a protected channel. If the traffic is bidirectional, two SAs are needed and can in fact be different.

Basic Configurations

Four basic configurations can be applied to machine-to-machine connections using IPSec. The simplest is a host-to-host connection between two machines, as shown in Figure 6-2. In this case, the Internet is not a part of the SA between the machines. If bidirectional security is desired, two SAs are used. The SAs are effective from host to host.

Case I:
Two SAs from host to host for bidirectional secure communications

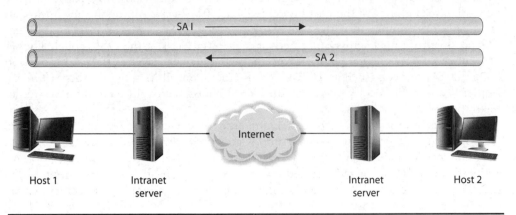

Figure 6-2   A host-to-host connection between two machines

The second case places two security devices in the stream, relieving the hosts of the calculation and encapsulation duties. These two gateways have an SA between them. The network is assumed to be secure from each machine to its gateway, and no IPSec is performed across these hops. Figure 6-3 shows the two security gateways with a tunnel across the Internet, although either tunnel mode or transport mode could be used.

The third case combines the first two. A separate SA exists between the gateway devices, but an SA also exists between hosts. This could be considered a tunnel inside a tunnel, as shown in Figure 6-4.

Remote users commonly connect through the Internet to an organization's network. The network has a security gateway through which it secures traffic to and from its servers and authorized users. In the last case, illustrated in Figure 6-5, the user establishes an

Case 2:
IPSec between machines using gateway security devices

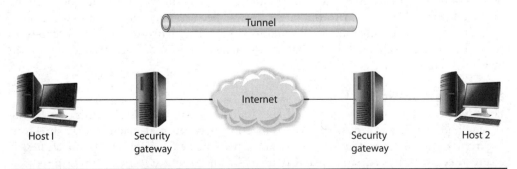

Figure 6-3   Two security gateways with a tunnel across the Internet

Case 3:
Separate IPSec tunnels, host to host and gateway to gateway

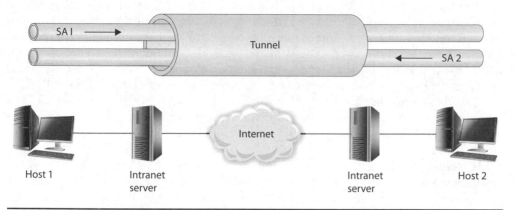

Figure 6-4   A tunnel inside a tunnel

SA with the security gateway and then a separate SA with the desired server, if required. This can be done using software on a remote laptop and hardware at the organization's network.

Windows can act as an IPSec server, as can routers and other servers. The primary issue is CPU usage and where the computing power should be implanted. This consideration has led to the rise of IPSec appliances, which are hardware devices that perform the IPSec function specifically for a series of communications. Depending on the number of connections, network bandwidth, and so on, these devices can be inexpensive for small office or home office use or quite expensive for large, enterprise-level implementations.

Figure 6-5
Tunnel from host to gateway

Case 4:
Tunnel from host to gateway
Optional: Two SAs for bidirectional secure communications

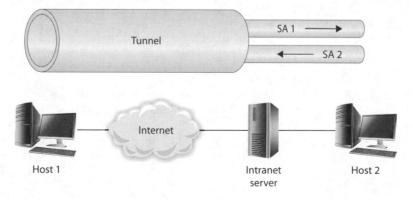

Tunnel Mode

Tunnel mode for IPSec is a means of encapsulating packets inside a protocol that is understood only at the entry and exit points of the tunnel. This provides security during transport in the tunnel, because outside observers cannot decipher packet contents or even the identities of the communicating parties. IPSec has a tunnel mode that can be used from server to server across a public network. Although the tunnel endpoints are referred to as servers, these devices can be routers, appliances, or servers. In tunnel mode, the tunnel endpoints merely encapsulate the entire packet with new IP headers to indicate the endpoints, and they encrypt the contents of this new packet. The true source and destination information is contained in the inner IP header, which is encrypted in the tunnel. The outer IP header contains the addresses of the endpoints of the tunnel.

As mentioned, AH and ESP can be employed in tunnel mode. When AH is employed in tunnel mode, portions of the outer IP header are given the same header protection that occurs in transport mode, with the entire inner packet receiving protection. This is illustrated in Figure 6-6. ESP affords the same encryption protection to the contents of the tunneled packet, which is the entire packet from the initial sender, as illustrated in Figure 6-7. Together, in tunnel mode, AH and ESP can provide complete protection across the packet, as shown in Figure 6-8. The specific combination of AH and ESP is referred to as a security association in IPSec.

In IPv4, IPSec is an add-on, and its acceptance is vendor driven. It is not a part of the original IP—one of the short-sighted design flaws of the original IP. In IPv6, IPSec is integrated into IP and is native on all packets. Its use is still optional, but its inclusion in the protocol suite will guarantee interoperability across vendor solutions when they are compliant with IPv6 standards.

Transport Mode

In *transport mode*, the two communication endpoints are providing security primarily for the upper-layer protocols. The cryptographic endpoints, where encryption and decryption occur, are located at the source and destination of the communication channel. For AH

Figure 6-6

IPSec use of AH in tunnel mode

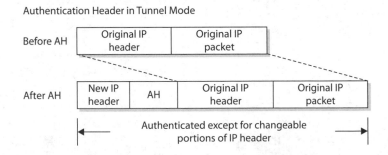

Authentication Header in Tunnel Mode

Figure 6-7

IPSec use of ESP in tunnel mode

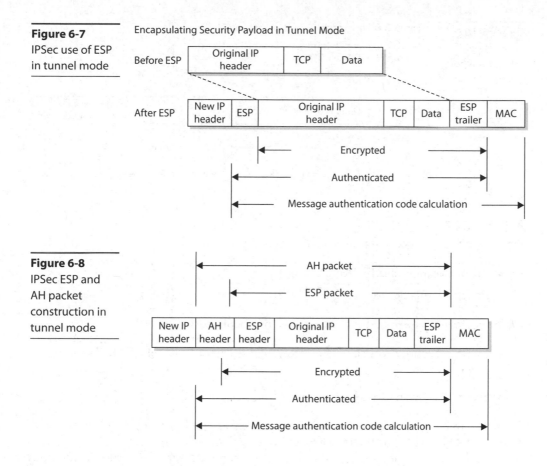

Encapsulating Security Payload in Tunnel Mode

Figure 6-8

IPSec ESP and AH packet construction in tunnel mode

in transport mode, the original IP header is exposed, but its contents are protected via the AH block in the packet, as illustrated in Figure 6-9. For ESP in transport mode, the data contents are protected by encryption, as illustrated in Figure 6-10.

Figure 6-9

IPSec use of AH in transport mode

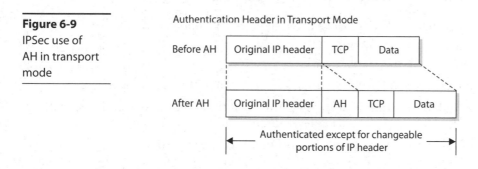

Authentication Header in Transport Mode

Figure 6-10
IPSec use of
ESP in transport
mode

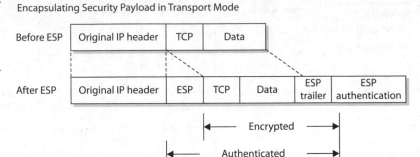

AH and ESP

IPSec uses two protocols to provide traffic security:

- Authentication Header (AH)
- Encapsulating Security Payload (ESP)

For key management and exchange, three protocols exist:

- Internet Security Association and Key Management Protocol (ISAKMP)
- Oakley
- Secure Key Exchange Mechanism for Internet (SKEMI)

These key management protocols can be collectively referred to as Internet Key Management Protocol (IKMP) or Internet Key Exchange (IKE).

IPSec does not define specific security algorithms, nor does it require specific methods of implementation. IPSec is an open framework that allows vendors to implement existing industry-standard algorithms suited for specific tasks. This flexibility is key in IPSec's ability to offer a wide range of security functions. IPSec allows several security technologies to be combined into a comprehensive solution for network-based confidentiality, integrity, and authentication. IPSec uses the following:

- Diffie-Hellman key exchange between peers on a public network
- Public key signing of Diffie-Hellman key exchanges to guarantee identity and avoid man-in-the-middle attacks
- Bulk encryption algorithms, such as IDEA and 3DES, for encrypting data
- Keyed hash algorithms, such as HMAC, and traditional hash algorithms, such as MD5 and SHA-1, for packet-level authentication
- Digital certificates to act as digital ID cards between parties

To provide traffic security, two header extensions have been defined for IP datagrams. The *AH*, when added to an IP datagram, ensures the integrity of the data and also the authenticity of the data's origin. By protecting the nonchanging elements in the IP header, the AH protects the IP address, which enables data-origin authentication. The *ESP* provides security services for the higher-level protocol portion of the packet only, not the IP header.

EXAM TIP   IPSec *AH* protects integrity, but it does not provide privacy. IPSec *ESP* provides confidentiality, but it does not protect integrity of the packet. To cover both privacy and integrity, both headers can be used at the same time.

AH and ESP can be used separately or in combination, depending on the level and types of security desired. Both also work with the transport and tunnel modes of IPSec protocols.

IPSec uses cryptographic keys in its security process and has both manual and automatic distribution of keys as part of the protocol series. Manual key distribution is included, but it is practical only in small, static environments and does not scale to enterprise-level implementations. The default method of key management, IKE, is automated. IKE authenticates each peer involved in IPSec and negotiates the security policy, including the exchange of session keys. IKE creates a secure tunnel between peers and then negotiates the SA for IPSec across this channel. This is done in two phases: the first develops the channel, and the second the SA.

Split Tunnel vs. Full Tunnel

Split tunnel is a form of VPN where not all traffic is routed via the VPN. Split tunneling allows multiple connection paths, some via the protected route such as the VPN, whereas other traffic from, say, public Internet sources is routed via non-VPN paths. The advantage of split tunneling is the ability to avoid bottlenecks from all traffic having to be encrypted across the VPN. A split tunnel would allow a user private access to information from locations over the VPN and less secure access to information from other sites. The disadvantage is that attacks from the non-VPN side of the communication channel can affect the traffic requests from the VPN side. A *full tunnel* solution routes all traffic over the VPN, providing protection to all networking traffic.

EXAM TIP   For performance-based questions, simply learning the terms associated with VPNs and IPSec in particular is insufficient. You should be familiar with the configuration and use of IPSec components, including types of configurations, and their use to support organizational security.

TLS

Transport Layer Security (TLS), the successor to Secure Sockets Layer (SSL), can be used to exchange keys and create a secure tunnel that enables a secure communications across a public network. TLS-based VPNs have some advantages over IPSec-based VPNs when networks are heavily NAT encoded, because IPSec-based VPNs can have issues crossing multiple NAT domains.

Always-on VPN

One of the challenges associated with VPNs is the establishment of the secure connection. In many cases, this requires additional end-user involvement, either in the form of launching a program, entering credentials, or both. This acts as an impediment to use, as users avoid the extra steps. *Always-on VPNs* are a means to avoid this issue, through the use of pre-established connection parameters and automation. Always-on VPNs can self-configure and connect once an Internet connection is sensed and provide VPN functionality without user intervention.

NIPS/NIDS

Network-based intrusion detection systems (NIDSs) are designed to detect, log, and respond to unauthorized network or host use, both in real time and after the fact. NIDSs are available from a wide selection of vendors and are an essential part of network security. These systems are implemented in software, but in large systems, dedicated hardware is required as well.

A *network-based intrusion prevention system (NIPS)* has as its core an intrusion detection system. However, whereas a NIDS can only alert when network traffic matches a defined set of rules, a NIPS can take further actions. A NIPS can take direct action to block an attack, its actions governed by rules. By automating the response, a NIPS significantly shortens the response time between detection and action.

 EXAM TIP Recognize that a NIPS has all the same characteristics of a NIDS but, unlike a NIDS, can automatically respond to certain events, such as by resetting a TCP connection, without operator intervention.

Whether network-based or host-based, an IDS will typically consist of several specialized components working together, as illustrated in Figure 6-11. These components are often logical and software-based rather than physical and will vary slightly from

Figure 6-11
Logical
depiction of IDS
components

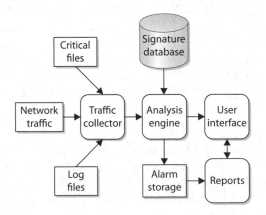

vendor to vendor and product to product. Typically, an IDS will have the following logical components:

- **Traffic collector (or sensor)** This component collects activity/events for the IDS to examine. On a host-based IDS, this could be log files, audit logs, or traffic coming to or leaving a specific system. On a network-based IDS, this is typically a mechanism for copying traffic off the network link—basically functioning as a sniffer. This component is often referred to as a sensor.

- **Analysis engine** This component examines the collected network traffic and compares it to known patterns of suspicious or malicious activity stored in the signature database. The analysis engine is the "brains" of the IDS.

- **Signature database** The signature database is a collection of patterns and definitions of known suspicious or malicious activity.

- **User interface and reporting** This component interfaces with the human element, providing alerts when appropriate and giving the user a means to interact with and operate the IDS.

Most IDSs can be tuned to fit a particular environment. Certain signatures can be turned off, telling the IDS not to look for certain types of traffic. For example, if you are operating in a pure Linux environment, you may not wish to see Windows-based alarms, as they will not affect your systems. Additionally, the severity of the alarm levels can be adjusted depending on how concerned you are over certain types of traffic. Some IDSs will also allow the user to exclude certain patterns of activity from specific hosts. In other words, you can tell the IDS to ignore the fact that some systems generate traffic that looks like malicious activity, because it really isn't.

NIDSs/NIPSs can be divided into three categories based on primary methods of detection used: signature-based, heuristic/behavioral-based, and anomaly-based. These are described in the following sections.

Signature-Based

This model relies on a predefined set of patterns (called *signatures*). The IDS has to know what behavior is considered "bad" ahead of time before it can identify and act upon suspicious or malicious traffic. *Signature-based* systems work by matching signatures in the network traffic stream to defined patterns stored in the system. Signature-based systems can be very fast and precise, with low false-positive rates. The weakness of signature-based systems is that they rely on having accurate signature definitions beforehand, and as the number of signatures expand, this creates an issue in scalability.

Heuristic/Behavioral

The *behavioral* model relies on a collected set of "normal behavior"—what should happen on the network and is considered "normal" or "acceptable" traffic. Behavior that does not fit into the "normal" activity categories or patterns is considered suspicious or malicious. This model can potentially detect zero day or unpublished attacks but carries a high false-positive rate because any new traffic pattern can be labeled as "suspect."

The *heuristic* model uses artificial intelligence (AI) to detect intrusions and malicious traffic. This is typically implemented through algorithms that help an IDS decide if a traffic pattern is malicious or not. For example, a URL containing a character repeated 10 times may be considered "bad" traffic as a single signature. With a heuristic model, the IDS will understand that if 10 repeating characters is bad, 11 is still bad, and 20 is even worse. This implementation of fuzzy logic allows this model to fall somewhere between signature-based and behavior-based models.

Anomaly

This detection model is similar to behavior-based methods. The IDS is first taught what "normal" traffic looks like and then looks for deviations from those "normal" patterns. An *anomaly* is a deviation from an expected pattern or behavior. Specific anomalies can also be defined, such as Linux commands sent to Windows-based systems, and implemented via an artificial intelligence–based engine to expand the utility of specific definitions.

Inline vs. Passive

For an NIDS/NIPS to function, it must have a means of examining the network data stream. There are two methods that can be employed, an *inline* sensor or a *passive* sensor. An inline sensor monitors the data packets as they actually pass through the device. A failure of an inline sensor would block traffic flow. A passive sensor monitors the traffic via a copying process, so the actual traffic does not flow through or depend upon the sensor for connectivity. Most sensors are passive sensors, but in the case of NIPSs, an inline sensor coupled directly to the NIPS logic allows for the sensor to act as a gate and enable the system to block selected traffic based on rules in the IPS, without additional hardware.

In-Band vs. Out-of-Band

The distinction between in-band and out-of-band NIDS/NIPS is similar to the distinction between inline and passive sensors. An *in-band* NIDS/NIPS is an inline sensor coupled to a NIDS/NIPS that makes its decisions in-band and enacts changes via the sensor. This has the advantage of high security, but it also has implications related to traffic levels and traffic complexity. In-band solutions work great for protecting network segments that have high-value systems and a limited number of traffic types, such as in front of a set of database servers with serious corporate data, where the only types of access would be via database connections.

An *out-of-band* system relies on a passive sensor, or set of passive sensors, and has the advantage of greater flexibility in detection across a wider range of traffic types. The disadvantage is the delay in reacting to the positive findings, as the traffic has already passed to the end host.

Rules

NIDS/NIPS solutions make use of an analytics engine that uses *rules* to determine whether an event of interest has occurred or not. These rules may be simple signature-based rules, such as Snort rules, or they may be more complex Bayesian rules associated with heuristic/behavioral systems or anomaly-based systems. Rules are the important part of the NIDS/NIPS capability equation—without an appropriate rule, the system will not detect the desired condition. One of the things that has to be updated when new threats are discovered is a rule to enable their detection.

EXAM TIP To be prepared for performance-based questions, you should be familiar with the types of NIDS and NIPS configurations and their use to support organizational security.

Analytics

Big data *analytics* is currently all the rage in the IT industry, with varying claims of how much value can be derived from large datasets. A NIDS/NIPS can certainly create large data sets, especially when connected to other data sources such as log files in a SIEM solution (covered later in this chapter). Using analytics to increase accurate detection of desired events and decrease false positives and false negatives requires planning, testing, and NIDS/NIPS/SIEM solutions that support this level of functionality. In the past, being able to write Snort rules was all that was needed to have a serious NIDS/NIPS solution. Today, it is essential to integrate the data from a NIDS/NIPS with other security data to detect advanced persistent threats (APTs). Analytics is essential today, and tomorrow it will be AI determining how to examine packets.

False Positive

As with all data-driven systems that use a "rule" to determine the presence or absence of an event, there exists a chance of errors in a NIDS/NIPS. If you are testing for the presence of an unauthorized user, and the system says the user is not the authorized person, yet in reality the user is who they say they are, then this is a *false positive*. The positive result is not really true.

False Negative

False negatives are in essence the opposite of a false positive. If you are looking for a forensic artifact that shows deletion of a file by a user, and the test result is negative, there is no artifact, telling you the user did not delete the file, but in reality they did, then this result is a *false negative*.

Whenever you get a test result, you should understand the rate of false positives and the rate of false negatives (these rates can be different) and incorporate that information into your decision making based on the test result.

EXAM TIP Understand the specific difference between false-positive and false-negative results with respect to IDS solutions. It is easy to ask this type of question, and depending on the way the question is asked determines the correct solution. Perform the logic on the test presented: What was the expected result? What result was achieved? And compare to reality and see if it was a false positive or false negative.

Router

Routers are network traffic management devices used to connect different network segments together. Routers operate at the network layer of the OSI reference model, routing traffic using the network address and utilizing routing protocols to determine optimal paths across a network. Routers form the backbone of the Internet, moving traffic from network to network, inspecting packets from every communication as they move traffic in optimal paths.

Routers operate by examining each packet, looking at the destination address, and using algorithms and tables to determine where to send the packet next. This process of examining the header to determine the next hop can be done in quick fashion.

One serious operational security issue with routers concerns the access to a router and control of its internal functions. Routers can be accessed using the Simple Network Management Protocol (SNMP) and Telnet/SSH and can be programmed remotely. Because of the geographic separation of routers, this can become a necessity, for many routers in the world of the Internet can be hundreds of miles apart, in separate locked structures. Physical control over a router is absolutely necessary, for if any device, be it server, switch, or router, is physically accessed by a hacker, it should be considered compromised; thus, such access must be prevented. It is important to ensure that the administrative password is never passed in the clear, that only secure mechanisms are used to access the router, and that all of the default passwords are reset to strong passwords. This eliminates methods such as Telnet in managing routers securely; SSH should be used instead.

Just like switches, the most assured point of access for router management control is via the serial control interface port or specific router management Ethernet interface. This allows access to the control aspects of the router without having to deal with traffic-related issues. For internal company networks, where the geographic dispersion of routers may be limited, third-party solutions to allow out-of-band remote management exist. This allows complete control over the router in a secure fashion, even from a remote location, although additional hardware is required.

Routers are available from numerous vendors and come in sizes big and small. A typical small home office router for use with cable modem/DSL service is shown in Figure 6-12. Larger routers can handle traffic of up to tens of gigabytes per second per channel, using fiber-optic inputs and moving tens of thousands of concurrent Internet connections across the network. These routers, which can cost hundreds of thousands of dollars, form an essential part of e-commerce infrastructure, enabling large enterprises such as Amazon and eBay to serve many customers concurrently.

Figure 6-12
A small home office router for cable modem/DSL use

ACLs

Routers use *ACLs* (access control lists) as a method of deciding whether a packet is allowed to enter the network. With ACLs, it is also possible to examine the source address and determine whether or not to allow a packet to pass. This allows routers equipped with ACLs to drop packets according to rules built in the ACLs. This can be a cumbersome process to set up and maintain, and as the ACL grows in size, routing efficiency can be decreased. It is also possible to configure some routers to act as quasi–application gateways, performing stateful packet inspection and using contents as well as IP addresses to determine whether or not to permit a packet to pass. This can tremendously increase the time for a router to pass traffic and can significantly decrease router throughput. Configuring ACLs and other aspects of setting up routers for this type of use are beyond the scope of this book.

 EXAM TIP Establishing and maintaining ACLs can require significant effort. Creating them is a straightforward task, but their judicious use will yield security benefits with a limited amount of maintenance. This can be very important in security zones such as a DMZ and at edge devices, blocking undesired outside contact while allowing known inside traffic.

Antispoofing

One of the persistent problems at edge devices is verifying that the source IP address on a packet matches the expected source IP address at the interface. Many DDoS attacks rely upon bots sending packets with spoofed IP addresses. *Antispoofing* measures are performed to prevent this type of attack from happening. When a machine in your network begins sending packets with incorrect source IP addresses, one of the primary actions that the gateway router should perform is to recognize that the source IP address on a packet does not match the assigned IP address space for the interface, and not send the packet. In this case, the router should drop the packet. Enabling source IP checking on routers at the edge of networks is done using networking commands associated with your router's OS, and these commands will vary between vendors, but all vendors support this functionality. It is important to enable source IP checking to prevent spoofing from propagating across a network.

Switch

A *switch* forms the basis for connections in most Ethernet-based local area networks (LANs). Although hubs and bridges still exist, in today's high-performance network environment, switches have replaced both. A switch has separate collision domains for each port. This means that for each port, two collision domains exist: one from the port to the client on the downstream side and one from the switch to the network upstream. When full duplex is employed, collisions are virtually eliminated from the two nodes, host and client. This also acts as a security factor in that a sniffer can see only limited traffic, as opposed to a hub-based system, where a single sniffer can see all of the traffic to and from connected devices.

PART II

One of the security concerns with switches is that, like routers, they are intelligent network devices and are therefore subject to hijacking by hackers. Should a hacker break into a switch and change its parameters, he might be able to eavesdrop on specific or all communications, virtually undetected. Switches are commonly administered using the SNMP and Telnet protocols, both of which have a serious weakness in that they send passwords across the network in clear text. Just as in the case with routers, secure administrative connections should be by SSH rather than Telnet to prevent clear text transmission of critical data such as passwords.

EXAM TIP   Simple Network Management Protocol (SNMP) provides management functions to many network devices. SNMPv1 and SNMPv2 authenticate using a cleartext password, allowing anyone monitoring packets to capture the password and have access to the network equipment. SNMPv3 adds cryptographic protections, making it a preferred solution.

A hacker armed with a sniffer that observes maintenance on a switch can capture the administrative password. This allows the hacker to come back to the switch later and configure it as an administrator. An additional problem is that switches are shipped with default passwords, and if these are not changed when the switch is set up, they offer an unlocked door to a hacker. Commercial-quality switches have a local serial console port or a management Ethernet interface for guaranteed access to the switch for purposes of control. Some products in the marketplace enable an out-of-band network, using these dedicated channels to enable remote, secure access to programmable network devices.

CAUTION   To secure a switch, you should disable all access protocols other than a secure serial line or a secure protocol such as Secure Shell (SSH). Using only secure methods to access a switch will limit the exposure to hackers and malicious users. Maintaining secure network switches is even more important than securing individual boxes, for the span of control to intercept data is much wider on a switch, especially if it's reprogrammed by a hacker.

Port Security

Switches can also perform a variety of security functions. Switches work by moving packets from inbound connections to outbound connections. While moving the packets, it is possible for switches to inspect the packet headers and enforce security policies. *Port security* is a capability provided by switches that enables you to control which devices and how many of them are allowed to connect via each port on a switch. Port security operates through the use of MAC addresses. Although not perfect—MAC addresses can be spoofed—port security can provide useful network security functionality.

Port address security based on Media Access Control (MAC) addresses can determine whether a packet is allowed or blocked from a connection. This is the very function that a firewall uses for its determination, and this same functionality is what allows an 802.1X device to act as an "edge device."

Port security has three variants:

- **Static learning** A specific MAC address is assigned to a port. This is useful for fixed, dedicated hardware connections. The disadvantage is that the MAC addresses need to be known and programmed in advance, making this good for defined connections but not good for visiting connections.

- **Dynamic learning** Allows the switch to learn MAC addresses when they connect. Dynamic learning is useful when you expect a small, limited number of machines to connect to a port.

- **Sticky learning** Also allows multiple devices to a port, but also stores the information in memory that persists through reboots. This prevents the attacker from changing settings through power cycling the switch.

Layer 2 vs. Layer 3

Switches operate at the data link layer of the OSI model, while routers act at the network layer. For intranets, switches have become what routers are on the Internet—the device of choice for connecting machines. As switches have become the primary network connectivity device, additional functionality has been added to them. A switch is usually a *layer 2* device, operating at the data link layer, but *layer 3* switches that operate at the network layer can incorporate routing functionality.

Loop Prevention

Switches operate at layer 2 of the OSI model, and at this level there is no countdown mechanism to kill packets that get caught in loops or on paths that will never resolve. This means that another mechanism is needed for *loop prevention*. The layer 2 space acts as a mesh, where potentially the addition of a new device can create loops in the existing device interconnections. Open Shortest Path First (OSPF) is a link-state routing protocol that is commonly used between gateways in a single autonomous system. To prevent loops, a technology called spanning trees is employed by virtually all switches. The Spanning Tree Protocol (STP) allows for multiple, redundant paths, while breaking loops to ensure a proper broadcast pattern. STP is a data link layer protocol, and is approved in IEEE standards 802.1D, 802.1w, 802.1s, and 802.1Q. It acts by trimming connections that are not part of the spanning tree connecting all of the nodes.

Flood Guard

One form of attack is a flood. There are numerous types of flooding attacks: ping floods, SYN floods, ICMP floods (Smurf attacks), and traffic flooding. Flooding attacks are used as a form of denial of service to a network or system. Detecting flooding attacks is relatively easy, but there is a difference between detecting the attack and mitigating the attack. Flooding can be actively managed through dropping connections or managing traffic. *Flood guards* act by managing traffic flows. By monitoring the traffic rate and percentage of bandwidth occupied by broadcast, multicast, and unicast traffic, a flood guard can detect when to block traffic to manage flooding.

EXAM TIP Flood guards are commonly implemented in firewalls and IDS/IPS solutions to prevent DoS and DDoS attacks.

Proxy

Though not strictly a security tool, a *proxy* server can be used to filter out undesirable traffic and prevent employees from accessing potentially hostile websites. A proxy server takes requests from a client system and forwards them to the destination server on behalf of the client. Several major categories of proxy servers are described in the following sections.

Deploying a proxy solution within a network environment is usually done either by setting up the proxy and requiring all client systems to configure their browsers to use the proxy or by deploying an intercepting proxy that actively intercepts all requests without requiring client-side configuration.

From a security perspective, proxies are most useful in their ability to control and filter outbound requests. By limiting the types of content and websites employees can access from corporate systems, many administrators hope to avoid loss of corporate data, hijacked systems, and infections from malicious websites. Administrators also use proxies to enforce corporate acceptable use policies and track use of corporate resources.

Forward and Reverse Proxy

Proxies can operate in two directions. A *forward proxy* operates to forward requests to servers based on a variety of parameters, as described in the other portions of this section. A *reverse proxy* is typically installed on the server side of a network connection, often in front of a group of web servers, and intercepts all incoming web requests. It can perform a number of functions, including traffic filtering, Secure Sockets Layer (SSL)/Transport Layer Security (TLS) decryption, serving of common static content such as graphics, and performing load balancing.

Transparent

Proxy servers can be completely *transparent* (these are usually called *gateways* or *tunneling proxies*), or they can modify the client request before sending it on or even serve the client's request without needing to contact the destination server.

Application/Multipurpose

Proxies can come in many forms, two of which are *application* proxies and *multipurpose* proxies. Application proxies act as proxies for a specific application only, while multipurpose proxies act as a proxy for multiple systems or purposes. Proxy servers can provide a wide range of services in a system including:

- **Anonymizing proxy** An anonymizing proxy is designed to hide information about the requesting system and make a user's web browsing experience "anonymous." This type of proxy service is often used by individuals concerned with the amount of personal information being transferred across the Internet and the use of tracking cookies and other mechanisms to track browsing activity.

- **Caching proxy** This type of proxy keeps local copies of popular client requests and is often used in large organizations to reduce bandwidth usage and increase performance. When a request is made, the proxy server first checks to see whether it has a current copy of the requested content in the cache; if it does, it services the client request immediately without having to contact the destination server. If the content is old or the caching proxy does not have a copy of the requested content, the request is forwarded to the destination server.

- **Content-filtering proxy** Content-filtering proxies examine each client request and compare it to an established acceptable use policy (AUP). Requests can usually be filtered in a variety of ways, including by the requested URL, the destination system, or the domain name or by keywords in the content itself. Content-filtering proxies typically support user-level authentication so access can be controlled and monitored and activity through the proxy can be logged and analyzed. This type of proxy is very popular in schools, corporate environments, and government networks.

- **Open proxy** An open proxy is essentially a proxy that is available to any Internet user and often has some anonymizing capabilities as well. This type of proxy has been the subject of some controversy, with advocates for Internet privacy and freedom on one side of the argument, and law enforcement, corporations, and government entities on the other side. As open proxies are often used to circumvent corporate proxies, many corporations attempt to block the use of open proxies by their employees.

- **Web proxy** A web proxy is solely designed to handle web traffic and is sometimes called a web cache. Most web proxies are essentially specialized caching proxies.

Load Balancer

Certain systems, such as servers, are more critical to business operations and should therefore be the object of fault-tolerance measures. A common technique that is used in fault tolerance is load balancing through the use of a *load balancer*, which move loads across a set of resources in an effort not to overload individual servers. This technique is designed to distribute the processing load over two or more systems. It is used to help improve resource utilization and throughput but also has the added advantage of increasing the fault tolerance of the overall system since a critical process may be split across several systems. Should any one system fail, the others can pick up the processing it was handling. While there may be an impact to overall throughput, the operation does not go down entirely. Load balancing is often utilized for systems handling websites, high-bandwidth file transfers, and large Internet Relay Chat (IRC) networks. Load balancing works by a series of health checks that tell the load balancer which machines are operating, and by a scheduling mechanism to spread the work evenly. Load balancing is best for stateless systems, as subsequent requests can be handled by any server, not just the one that processed the previous request.

Scheduling

When a load balancer move loads across a set of resources, it decides which machine gets a request via a *scheduling* algorithm. There are a couple of commonly used scheduling algorithms: affinity-based scheduling and round-robin scheduling.

Affinity

Affinity-based scheduling is designed to keep a host connected to the same server across a session. Some applications, such as web applications, can benefit from affinity-based scheduling. The method used by affinity-based scheduling is to have the load balancer keep track of where it last balanced a particular session and direct all continuing session traffic to the same server. If it is a new connection, the load balancer establishes a new affinity entry and assigns the session to the next server in the available rotation.

Round-Robin

Round-robin scheduling involves sending each new request to the next server in rotation. All requests are sent to servers in equal amounts, regardless of the server load. Round-robin schemes are frequently modified with a weighting factor to take server load or other criteria into account when assigning the next server.

Active-Passive

For high-availability solutions, having a single load balancer creates a single point of failure. It is common to have multiple load balancers involved in the balancing work. In an *active-passive* scheme, the primary load balancer is actively doing the balancing while the secondary load balancer passively observes and is ready to step in at any time the primary system fails.

Active-Active

In an *active-active* scheme, all the load balancers are active, sharing the load balancing duties. Active-active load balancing can have performance efficiencies, but it is important to watch the overall load. If the overall load cannot be covered by $N-1$ load balancers (i.e., one fails), then failure of a load balancer will lead to session interruption and traffic loss. Without a standby passive system to recover the lost load, the system will trim load based on capacity, dropping requests that the system lacks capacity to service.

Virtual IPs

In a load balanced environment, the IP addresses for the target servers of a load balancer will not necessarily match the address associated with the router sending the traffic. Load balancers handle this through the concept of virtual IP addresses, *virtual IPs*, that allow for multiple systems to be reflected back as a single IP address.

EXAM TIP Preparing for performance-based questions requires more than simply learning the terms associated with network-based security solutions such as routers, switches, proxies, and load balancers. You should be familiar with the configuration and use of these components against specific threats such as spoofing, loops, floods, and traffic issues. Understanding how and when to configure each device based on a scenario is important and testable.

Access Point

Wireless *access points* are the point of entry and exit for radio-based network signals into and out of a network. As wireless has become more capable in all aspects of networking, wireless-based networks are replacing cabled, or wired, solutions. In this scenario, one could consider the access point to be one half of a network interface card (NIC), with the other half being the wireless card in a host.

SSID

The 802.11 protocol designers expected some security concerns and attempted to build provisions into the 802.11 protocol that would ensure adequate security. The 802.11 standard includes attempts at rudimentary authentication and confidentiality controls. Authentication is handled in its most basic form by the 802.11 access point (AP), forcing the clients to perform a handshake when attempting to "associate" to the AP. Association is the process required before the AP will allow the client to talk across the AP to the network.

The authentication function is known as the *service set identifier (SSID)*. This unique 32-character identifier is attached to the header of the packet. Association occurs only if the client has all the correct parameters needed in the handshake, among them the SSID. This SSID setting should limit access to only authorized users of the wireless network. The SSID is broadcast by default as a network name, but broadcasting this beacon frame can be disabled. Many APs also use a default SSID; for example, for many versions of Cisco APs, this default is *tsunami*, which can indicate an AP that has not been configured for any security. Renaming the SSID and disabling SSID broadcast are both good ideas; however, because the SSID is part of every frame, these measures should not be considered securing the network. As the SSID is, hopefully, a unique identifier, only people who know the identifier will be able to complete association to the AP.

While the SSID is a good idea in theory, it is sent in plaintext in the packets, so in practice the SSID offers little security significance—any sniffer can determine the SSID, and many operating systems—Windows XP and later, for instance—will display a list of SSIDs active in the area and prompt the user to choose which one to connect to. This weakness is magnified by most APs' default settings to transmit beacon frames. The beacon frame's purpose is to announce the wireless network's presence and capabilities so that WLAN cards can attempt to associate to it. This can be disabled in software for many APs, especially the more sophisticated ones. From a security perspective, the beacon frame is damaging because it contains the SSID, and this beacon frame is transmitted at a set interval (ten times per second by default). Since a default AP without any other traffic is sending out its SSID in plaintext ten times a second, you can see why the SSID does not provide true authentication. Scanning programs such as NetStumbler work by capturing the beacon frames, and thereby the SSIDs, of all APs.

EXAM TIP   Although not considered the strongest security measures, renaming the SSID and disabling SSID broadcast are important concepts to know for the exam.

MAC Filtering

MAC filtering is the selective admission of packets based on a list of approved Media Access Control (MAC) addresses. Employed on switches, this method is used to provide a means of machine authentication. In wired networks, this enjoys the protection afforded by the wires, making interception of signals to determine their MAC addresses difficult. In wireless networks, this same mechanism suffers from the fact that an attacker can see the MAC addresses of all traffic to and from the access point, and then can spoof the MAC addresses that are permitted to communicate via the access point.

EXAM TIP   MAC filtering can be employed on wireless access points, but can be bypassed by attackers observing allowed MAC addresses and spoofing the allowed MAC address for the wireless card.

Signal Strength

The usability of a wireless signal is directly related to its *signal strength*. Too weak of a signal and the connection can drop out or lose data. Signal strength can be influenced by a couple of factors: the transmitting power level and the environment across which the signal is transmitted. In buildings with significant metal in the walls and roofs, additional power may be needed to have sufficient signal strength at the receivers. Wi-Fi power levels can be controlled by the hardware for a variety of reasons. The lower the power used, the less the opportunity for interference. But if the power levels are too low, then signal strength limits range. Access points can have the power level set either manually or via programmatic control. For most users, power level controls are not very useful, and leaving the unit in default mode is the best option. In complex enterprise setups, with site surveys and planned overlapping zones, this aspect of signal control can be used to increase capacity and control on the network.

Band Selection/Width

In today's wireless environments, there are multiple different bands employed, each with different bandwidths. *Band selection* may seem trivial, but with 802.11a, b/g, n, and ac radios, the deployment of access points should support the desired bands based on client needs. Multiband radio access points exist and are commonly employed to resolve these issues. Wi-Fi operates over two different frequencies, 2.4 GHz for b/g and n, and 5 GHz for a, n, and ac.

Antenna Types and Placement

Wi-Fi is by nature a radio-based method of communication, and as such uses antennas to transmit and receive the signals. The actual design and placement of the antennas can have a significant effect on the usability of the radio frequency (RF) medium for carrying the traffic.

Antennas come in a variety of *types*, each with its own transmission pattern and gain factor. Gain is a measurement of antenna efficiency. High-gain antennas can deal with weaker signals, but also have more-limited coverage. Wide-coverage, omnidirectional antennas can cover wider areas, but at lower levels of gain. The objective of antenna *placement* is to maximize the coverage over a physical area and reduce low-gain areas. This can be very complex in buildings with walls, electrical interference, and other sources of interference and frequently requires a site survey to determine proper placement.

EXAM TIP Because wireless antennas can transmit outside a facility, tuning and placement of antennas can be crucial for security. Adjusting radiated power through the power level controls will assist in keeping wireless signals from being broadcast outside areas under physical access control.

The standard access point is equipped with an omnidirectional antenna. Omnidirectional antennas operate in all directions, making the relative orientation between devices less important. Omnidirectional antennas cover the greatest area per antenna. The weakness occurs in corners and hard-to-reach areas, as well as boundaries of a facility where directional antennas are needed to complete coverage. Figure 6-13 shows a sampling of common Wi-Fi antennas: 6-13(a) is a common home wireless router, (b) is a commercial indoor wireless access point (WAP), and (c) is an outdoor directional antenna. Indoor WAPs can be visible as shown, or hidden above ceiling tiles.

Wireless networking problems caused by weak signal strength can sometimes be solved by installing upgraded Wi-Fi radio antennas on the access points. On business networks, the complexity of multiple access points typically requires a comprehensive site survey to map the Wi-Fi signal strength in and around office buildings. Additional wireless access points can then be strategically placed where needed to resolve dead spots in coverage. For small businesses and homes, where a single access point may be all that is needed, an antenna upgrade may be a simpler and more cost-effective option to fix Wi-Fi signal problems.

Figure 6-13
Wireless access
point antennas

a   b   c

Two common forms of upgraded antennas are the Yagi antenna and the panel antenna. An example of a Yagi antenna is shown in Figure 6-13(c). Both Yagi and panel antennas are directional in nature, spreading the RF energy in a more limited field, increasing effective range in one direction while limiting it in others. Panel antennas can provide solid room performance while preventing signal bleed behind the antennas. This works well on the edge of a site, limiting the stray emissions that could be captured offsite. Yagi antennas act more like a rifle, funneling the energy along a beam. This allows much longer communication distances using standard power. This also enables eavesdroppers to capture signals from much greater distances because of the gain provided by the antenna itself.

Fat vs. Thin

Fat (or thick) *access points* are standalone access points, while *thin access* points are controller-based access points. These solutions differ in their handling of common functions such as configuration, encryption, updates, and policy settings. Determining which is more effective requires a closer examination of the difference, presented in the next section, and a particular site's needs and budget.

Controller-Based vs. Standalone

Small *standalone* Wi-Fi access points can have substantial capabilities with respect to authentication, encryption, and even, to a degree, channel management. These are also called fat or thick controllers, referring to the level of work the AP performs. As the wireless deployment grows in size and complexity, there are some advantages to a *controller-based* access point solution. Controller-based, or thin AP, solutions allow for centralized management and control, which can facilitate better channel management for adjacent access points, better load balancing, and easier deployment of patches and firmware updates. From a security standpoint, controller-based solutions offer large advantages in overall network monitoring and security controls. In large-scale environments, controller-based access points can enable network access control (NAC, discussed later in the chapter) based on user identity, managing large sets of users in subgroups. Internet access can be blocked for some users (e.g., clerks), while internal access can be blocked for others (e.g., guests).

SIEM

Security Information and Event Management (SIEM) systems are a combination of hardware and software designed to classify and analyze security data from numerous sources. SIEMs were once considered to be appropriate only for the largest of enterprises, but nowadays the large number of data sources associated with security have made SIEMs essential in almost all security organizations. There is a wide range of vendor offerings in this space, from virtually free to systems large enough to handle any enterprise, with a budget to match.

Aggregation

One of the key functions of a SIEM solution is the *aggregation* of security information sources. In this instance, aggregation refers to the collecting of information in a central place, in a common format, to facilitate analysis and decision making. The sources that can feed a SIEM are many, including system event logs, firewall logs, security application logs, and specific program feeds from security appliances. Having this material in a central location that facilitates easy exploration by a security analyst is very useful during incident response events.

Correlation

Correlation is the connection of events based on some common basis. Events can correlate based on time, based on common events, based on behaviors, and so on. Although correlation is not necessarily causation, it is still useful to look for patterns, and then use these patterns to find future issues. Many activities are multistep events and determining their presence before they get to the end of their cycle and commit the final act, or early detection, is one of the values of correlation. Correlation can identify things like suspicious IP addresses based on recent behavior. For instance, a correlation rule can identify port scanning, a behavior that in and of itself is not hostile but also is not normal, hence future activity from that IP address would be considered suspect. SIEMs can use multiple rules and patterns with correlation to provide earlier warning of hostile activity.

Automated Alerting and Triggers

SIEMs have the ability through a set of rules and the use of analytical engines to identify specific predetermined patterns and either issue an alert or react to them. *Automated alerting* can remove much of the time delay between specific activity and security operations reaction. Consider a SIEM like an IDS on steroids, for it can use external information in addition to current traffic information to provide a much richer pattern-matching environment. A *trigger* event, such as the previously mentioned scanning activity, or the generation of ACL failures in log events, can result in the SIEM highlighting a connection on an analyst's workstation or, in some cases, responding automatically.

Time Synchronization

Time synchronization is a common problem for computer systems. When multiple systems handle aspects of a particular transaction, having a common time standard for all the systems is essential if you want to be able to compare their logs. This problem becomes even more pronounced when an enterprise has geographically dispersed operations across multiple time zones. Most systems record things in local time, and when multiple time zones are involved, analysts need to be able to work with two time readings synchronously: local time and UTC time. UTC (Coordinated Universal Time) is a global time standard and does not have the issues of daylight saving settings, or even different time zones. UTC is in essence a global time zone. Local time is still important to compare events to local activities. SIEMs can handle both time readings simultaneously, using UTC for correlation across the entire enterprise, and local time for local process meaning.

Event Deduplication

In many cases, multiple records related to the same event can be generated. For example, an event may be noted in both the firewall log and the system log file. As another example, NetFlow data, because of how and where it is generated, is full of duplicate records for the same packet. Having multiple records in a database representing the same event wastes space and processing and can skew analytics. To avoid these issues, SIEMs use a special form of correlation to determine which records are duplicates of a specific event, and then delete all but a single record. This *event deduplication* assists security analysts by reducing clutter in a dataset that can obscure real events that have meaning. For this to happen, the events records require a central store, something a SIEM solution provides.

 EXAM TIP To answer questions regarding how and why an organization would use a SIEM system, keep in mind that SIEMS are designed to aggregate information, correlate events, synchronize times, and deduplicate records/events from numerous systems for the purpose of expediting automated detection, alerting, and triggers.

Logs/WORM

Log files, or *logs*, exist across a wide array of sources, and have a wide range of locations and details recorded. One of the valuable features of a SIEM solution is the capability to collect these disparate data sources into a standardized data structure that security administrators can then exploit using database tools to create informative reports. Logs are written once into this SIEM datastore, and then can be read many times by different rules and analytical engines for different decision-support processes. This *write once read many (WORM)* concept is commonly employed to achieve operational efficiencies, especially when working with large data sets, such as log files on large systems.

DLP

Data loss prevention (DLP) refers to technology employed to detect and prevent transfers of data across an enterprise. Employed at key locations, DLP technology can scan packets for specific data patterns. This technology can be tuned to detect account numbers, secrets, specific markers, or files. When specific data elements are detected, the system can block the transfer. The primary challenge in employing DLP technologies is the placement of the sensor. The DLP sensor needs to be able observe the data, so if the channel is encrypted, DLP technology can be thwarted.

USB Blocking

USB devices offer a convenient method of connecting external storage to a system and an easy means of moving data between machines. They also provide a means by which data can be infiltrated from a network by an unauthorized party. There are numerous methods of performing *USB blocking*, from the extreme of physically disabling the ports, to software solutions that enable a wide range of controls. Most enterprise-level DLP solutions include a means of blocking or limiting USB devices. Typically, this involves preventing the use of USB devices for transferring data to the device without specific authorization codes. This acts as a barrier, allowing USBs to import data but not export data.

Cloud-Based

As data moves to the cloud, so does the need for data loss prevention. But performing *cloud-based DLP* is not a simple matter of moving the enterprise edge methodology to the cloud. There are several attributes of cloud systems that can result in issues for DLP deployments. Enterprises move data to the cloud for many reasons, but two primary ones are size (cloud data sets can be very large) and availability (cloud-based data can be highly available across the entire globe to multiple parties), and both of these are challenges for DLP solutions. The DLP industry has responded with cloud-based DLP solutions designed to manage these and other cloud-related issues while still affording the enterprise visibility and control over data transfers.

E-mail

E-mail is a common means of communication in the enterprise, and files are commonly attached to e-mail messages to provide additional information. Transferring information out of the enterprise via e-mail attachments is a concern for many organizations. Blocking e-mail attachments is not practical given their ubiquity in normal business, so a solution is needed to scan e-mails for unauthorized data transfers. This is a common chore for enterprise-class DLP solutions, which can connect to the mail server and use the same scanning technology used for other network connections.

 EXAM TIP DLP has become integral in enterprises, is widespread, and has several aspects that can be tested on the exam. DLP solutions can include e-mail solutions, USB solutions, and cloud solutions. DLPs detect the data is moving somewhere using different hooks to block the different paths (file transfers, to and from cloud, e-mail). Read the question carefully to determine what is specifically being asked.

NAC

Networks comprise connected workstations and servers. Managing security on a network involves managing a wide range of issues related not only to the various connected hardware but also to the software operating those devices. Assuming that the network is secure, each additional connection involves risk. Managing the endpoints on a case-by-case basis as they connect is a security methodology known as *network access control (NAC)*. Two main competing methodologies exist: Network Access Protection (NAP) is a Microsoft technology for controlling network access to a computer host, and Network Admission Control (NAC) is Cisco's technology for controlling network admission.

Microsoft's NAP system is based on measuring the system health of the connecting machine, including patch levels of the OS, antivirus protection, and system policies.

NAP was first utilized in Windows XP Service Pack 3, Windows Vista, and Windows Server 2008, and it requires additional infrastructure servers to implement the health checks. The system includes enforcement agents that interrogate clients and verify admission criteria. The client side is initiated whenever network connections are made. Response options include rejection of the connection request or restriction of admission to a subnet.

Cisco's NAC system is built around an appliance that enforces policies chosen by the network administrator. A series of third-party solutions can interface with the appliance, allowing the verification of a whole host of options, including client policy settings, software updates, and client security posture. The use of third-party devices and software makes this an extensible system across a wide range of equipment.

Neither Cisco NAC nor Microsoft NAP is widely adopted across enterprises. The client pieces are all in place, but enterprises have been slow to fully deploy the server side of this technology. The concept of automated admission checking based on client device characteristics is here to stay, as it provides timely control in the ever-changing network world of today's enterprises. With the rise of bring your own device (BYOD) policies in organizations, there is renewed interest in using NAC to assist in protecting the network from unsafe devices.

 EXAM TIP For the Security+ exam, the term NAC refers to network access control. The Microsoft and Cisco solutions referenced in this section are examples of this type of control—their names and acronyms are not relevant to the exam. The concept of NAC and what it accomplishes is relevant and testable.

Dissolvable vs. Permanent

The use of NAC technologies requires an examination of a host before allowing it to connect to the network. This examination is performed by a piece of software, frequently referred to as an agent. Agents can be permanently deployed to hosts, so that the functionality is already in place, or provided on an as-needed basis by the endpoint at time of use. When agents are predeployed to endpoints, these *permanent agents* act as the gateway to NAC functionality. One of the first checks is agent integrity, then machine integrity. In cases where deployment on an as-needed basis is chosen, an agent can be deployed upon request and later discarded after use. These agents are frequently referred to as *dissolvable agents*, for they in essence disappear after use.

Host Health Checks

One of the key benefits of a NAC solution is the ability to enforce a specific level of *host health checks* on clients before they are admitted to the network. Some common host health checks include verifying an antivirus solution is present, has the latest patches, and has been run recently, and verifying that the OS and applications are patched. The policy options vary based on implementation, but a client that does not pass the health checks can be denied connection to the network, forced to have its health fixed before connection, or placed on a separate isolated network segment.

Agent vs. Agentless

In recognition that deploying agents to machines can be problematic in some instances, vendors have also developed agentless solutions for NAC. Rather than have the agent wait on the host for activation and use, the agent can operate from within the network itself, rendering the host in effect agentless. In *agent*-based solutions, code is stored on the host machine for activation and use at time of connection. In *agentless* solutions, the code resides on the network and is deployed to memory for use in a machine requesting connections, but since it never persists on the host machine, it is referred to as agentless. In most instances, there is no real difference in the performance of agent versus agentless solutions when properly deployed. The real difference comes in the issues of having agents on boxes versus persistent network connections for agentless.

Mail Gateway

E-mail is one of the reasons for connecting networks together, and *mail gateways* can act as solutions to handle mail-specific traffic issues. Mail gateways are used to process e-mail packets on a network, providing a wide range of e-mail-related services. From filtering spam, to managing data loss, to handling the encryption needs, mail gateways are combinations of hardware and software optimized to perform these tasks in the enterprise.

Spam Filter

The bane of users and system administrators everywhere, *spam* is essentially unsolicited and undesired bulk electronic messages. While typically conveyed via e-mail, spam can be transmitted via text message to phones and mobile devices, as postings to Internet forums, and by other means. If you've ever used an e-mail account, chances are you've received spam. Enter the concept of the *spam filterg*, software that is designed to identify and remove spam traffic from an e-mail stream as it passes through the mail gateway.

From a productivity and security standpoint, spam costs businesses and users billions of dollars each year, and it is such a widespread problem that the U.S. Congress passed the CAN-SPAM Act of 2003 to empower the Federal Trade Commission to enforce the act and the Department of Justice to enforce criminal sanctions against spammers. The act establishes requirements for those who send commercial e-mail, spells out penalties for spammers and companies whose products are advertised in spam if they violate the law, and gives consumers the right to ask spammers to stop spamming them. Despite all our best efforts, however, spam just keeps coming; as the technologies and techniques developed to stop the spam get more advanced and complex, so do the tools and techniques used to send out the unsolicited messages.

Here are a few of the more popular methods used to fight the spam epidemic; most of these techniques are used to filter e-mail but could be applied to other mediums as well:

- **Blacklisting**   Blacklisting is essentially noting which domains and source addresses have a reputation for sending spam, and rejecting messages coming from those domains and source addresses. This is basically a permanent "ignore" or "call block" type capability. Several organizations and a few commercial companies provide lists of known spammers.

- **Content or keyword filtering** Similar to Internet content filtering, this method filters e-mail messages for undesirable content or indications of spam. Much like content filtering of web content, filtering e-mail based on something like keywords can cause unexpected results, as certain terms can be used in both legitimate and spam e-mail. Most content-filtering techniques use regular expression matching for keyword filtering.

- **Trusted servers** The opposite of blacklisting, a trusted server list includes SMTP servers that are being "trusted" not to forward spam.

- **Delay-based filtering** Some SMTP servers are configured to insert a deliberate pause between the opening of a connection and the sending of the SMTP server's welcome banner. Some spam-generating programs do not wait for that greeting banner, and any system that immediately starts sending data as soon as the connection is opened is treated as a spam generator and dropped by the SMTP server.

- **PTR and reverse DNS checks** Some e-mail filters check the origin domain of an e-mail sender. If the reverse checks show the mail is coming from a dial-up user, home-based broadband, or a dynamically assigned address, or has a generic or missing domain, then the filter rejects it, as these are common sources of spam messages.

- **Callback verification** Because many spam messages use forged "from" addresses, some filters attempt to validate the "from" address of incoming e-mail. The receiving server can contact the sending server in an attempt to validate the sending address, but this is not always effective, as spoofed addresses are sometimes valid e-mail addresses that can be verified.

- **Statistical content filtering** Statistical filtering is much like a document classification system. Users mark received messages as either spam or legitimate mail and the filtering system learns from the users' input. The more messages that are seen and classified as spam, the better the filtering software should get at intercepting incoming spam. Spammers counteract many filtering technologies by inserting random words and characters into the messages, making it difficult for content filters to identify patterns common to spam.

- **Rule-based filtering** Rule-based filtering is a simple technique that merely looks for matches in certain fields or keywords. For example, a rule-based filtering system may look for any message with the words "get rich" in the subject line of the incoming message. Many popular e-mail clients have the ability to implement rule-based filtering.

- **Egress filtering** Some organizations perform spam filtering on e-mail leaving their organization as well, and this is called egress filtering. The same types of anti-spam techniques can be used to validate and filter outgoing e-mail in an effort to combat spam.

- **Hybrid filtering** Most commercial anti-spam methods use hybrid filtering, a combination of several different techniques, to fight spam. For example, a filtering solution may take each incoming message and match it against known spammers, then against a rule-based filter, then a content filter, and finally against a statistical-based filter. If the message passes all filtering stages, it will be treated as a legitimate message; otherwise, it is rejected as spam.

Much spam filtering is done at the network or SMTP server level. It's more efficient to scan all incoming and outgoing messages with a centralized solution than it is to deploy individual solutions on user desktops throughout the organization. E-mail is essentially a proxied service by default: messages generally come into and go out of an organization's mail server. (Users don't typically connect to remote SMTP servers to send and receive messages, but they can.) Anti-spam solutions are available in the form of software that is loaded on the SMTP server itself or on a secondary server that processes messages either before they reach the SMTP server or after the messages are processed by the SMTP server. Anti-spam solutions are also available in appliance form, where the software and hardware are a single integrated solution. Many centralized anti-spam methods allow individual users to customize spam filtering for their specific inbox, specifying their own filter rules and criteria for evaluating inbound e-mail.

The central issue with spam is that, despite all the effort placed into building effective spam filtering programs, spammers continue to create new methods for flooding inboxes. Spam filtering solutions are good, but are far from perfect, and continue to fight the constant challenge of allowing in legitimate messages while keeping the spam out. The lack of central control over Internet traffic also makes anti-spam efforts more difficult. Different countries have different laws and regulations governing e-mail, which range from draconian to nonexistent. For the foreseeable future, spam will continue to be a burden to administrators and users alike.

DLP

As mentioned previously, *data loss prevention (DLP)* is also an issue for outgoing mail, particularly e-mail attachments. There are two options for preventing the loss of data via e-mail: use an integrated DLP solution that scans both outgoing traffic and mail, or use a separate standalone system that scans only e-mail. The disadvantage of using a separate standalone system is that it requires maintaining two separate DLP keyword lists. Most enterprise-level DLP solutions have built-in gateway methods for integration with mail servers to facilitate outgoing mail scanning. This allows outgoing mail traffic to be checked against the same list of keywords that other outgoing traffic is scanned against.

Encryption

E-mail is by default a plaintext protocol, making e-mail and e-mail attachments subject to eavesdropping anywhere between sender and receiver. E-mail *encryption* can protect e-mail from eavesdropping as well as add authentication services. Encrypting e-mail has been a challenge for enterprises, not because the process of encryption is difficult, but due to the lack of a uniform standardized protocol that would allow complete automation of the process, making it transparent to users.

Many e-mail encryption solutions exist, from add-in programs, such as Pretty Good Privacy (PGP) and others, to encryption gateways that handle the process post-mail server, or after the e-mail has passed through the mail server. Each solution has its challenges and limitations, including compatibility across other systems (both sender and receiver have to have the same support). Using the built-in S/MIME (Secure/Multipurpose Internet Mail Extensions) standard provides a means for public key infrastructure (PKI) use across e-mail channels, but challenges still remain. Specifically, to use PKI, one relies upon certificates on both sides, and the passing of certificates, and the maintenance of certificate stores across an enterprise can lead to challenges. This is alleviated within an organization, as the enterprise can handle the certificates. In enterprise situations, there are PKI handlers to handle the certificates, but to standalone external users, the handling of certificates is a challenge that continues to exist.

 EXAM TIP E-mail is ubiquitous and has its own set of security issues. Mail gateways can act as a focal point for security concerns, so whether it is spam filtering, DLP functionality, or encryption and signing, it can be accomplished at a mail gateway.

Bridge

A *bridge* is a network segregation device that operates at layer 2 of the OSI model. It operates by connecting two separate network segments and allows communication between the two segments based on the layer 2 address on a packet. Separating network traffic into separate communication zones can enhance security. Traffic can be separated using bridges, switches, and VLANs. Traffic separation prevents sensitive traffic from being sniffed by limiting the range over which the traffic travels. Keeping highly sensitive traffic separated from areas of the network where less trusted traffic and access may occur prevents the inadvertent disclosure by traffic interception. Network separation can be used to keep development, testing, and production networks separated, preventing accidental cross-pollination of changes.

SSL/TLS Accelerators

The process of encrypting traffic per SSL/TLS protocols can be a computer-intensive effort. For large-scale web servers, this becomes a bottleneck in the throughput of the web server. Rather than continue to use larger and larger servers for web pages, organization with significant SSL/TLS needs use a specialized device that is specifically designed to handle the computations. This device, called an *SSL/TLS accelerator*, includes hardware-based SSL/TLS operations to handle the throughput, and it acts as a transparent device between the web server and the Internet. When an enterprise experiences web server bottlenecks due to SSL/TLS demands, an accelerator can be an economical solution.

SSL Decryptors

Networks with encrypted traffic entering and leaving pose an interesting dilemma for network security monitoring: how can the traffic be examined if it can't be seen? *SSL decryptors* are a solution to this problem. They can be implemented in hardware or software, or in a combination of both, and they act as a means of opening the SSL/TLS traffic using the equivalent of a man-in-the-middle method to allow for the screening of the traffic. Then, the traffic can be re-encrypted and sent on its way. This functionality is included in many high-end next-generation firewall (NGFW) systems and provides the additional ability to selectively determine what traffic is decrypted and screened. Configuration of these channels can be tedious, as most of these devices are limited in their computational power, making complete network-wide decrypting not feasible. Most of these systems use a certificate-copying mechanism to obtain the necessary credentials. If the credentials are not available, the traffic can be flagged for further investigation, such as outbound traffic to unknown destinations—as in an encrypted command and control (C&C) botnet connection.

Media Gateway

One of the elements that the Internet has brought to enterprise networks is digital media channels. A wide range of media protocols exist and have found use in the communication of voice and video signals. *Media gateways* have been built to handle all of these different protocols, including translating them to other common protocols used in a network. Depending upon desired complexity and throughput needs, these devices can exist as a standalone device or as part of a switch/firewall.

Hardware Security Module

A *hardware security module (HSM)* is a device used to manage or store encryption keys. It can also assist in cryptographic operations such as encryption, hashing, or the application of digital signatures. HSMs are typically peripheral devices, connected via USB or a network connection. HSMs have tamper protection mechanisms to prevent physical access to the secrets they protect. Because of their dedicated design, they can offer significant performance advantages over general-purpose computers when it comes to cryptographic operations. When an enterprise has significant levels of cryptographic operations, HSMs can provide throughput efficiencies.

 EXAM TIP Storing private keys anywhere on a networked system is a recipe for loss. HSMs are designed to allow the use of the key without exposing it to the wide range of host-based threats.

Chapter Review

In this chapter, you became acquainted with the network components used in an enterprise network. This has been a long chapter, with 17 different major topics and numerous subtopics. What is important to focus on when you review this chapter is the objective: Install and configure network components, both hardware- and software-based, to support organizational security. For each of the components covered in the major topic areas, you should understand when and how you would employ the component in response to a scenario that lists some security objective. This is how installation and configuration can be tested. Understanding the similarities and difference between the various components with respect to security objectives is the key to questions for this exam objective.

Questions

To help you prepare further for the CompTIA Security+ exam, and to test your level of preparedness, answer the following questions and then check your answers against the correct answers at the end of the chapter.

1. After you implement a new firewall on your corporate network, a coworker comes to you and asks why he can no longer connect to a Telnet server he has installed on his home DSL line. This failure to connect is likely due to:

   A. Network Address Translation (NAT)

   B. Basic packet filtering

   C. Blocked by policy, Telnet not considered secure

   D. A denial-of-service attack against Telnet

2. Why will NAT likely continue to be used even in IPv6 networks?

   A. Even IPv6 does not have enough IP addresses.

   B. It is integral to how access control lists work.

   C. It allows faster internal routing of traffic.

   D. It can hide the internal addressing structure from direct outside connections.

3. You are asked to present to senior management virtual private network methodologies in advance of your company's purchase of new VPN concentrators. Why would you strongly recommend IPSec VPNs?

   A. Connectionless integrity

   B. Data-origin authentication

   C. Traffic-flow confidentiality

   D. All of the above

4. Why is Internet Key Exchange preferred in enterprise VPN deployments?

   A. IKE automates key management by authenticating each peer to exchange session keys.

   B. IKE forces the use of Diffie-Hellman, ensuring higher security than consumer VPNs.

   C. IKE prevents the use of flawed hash algorithms such as MD5.

   D. IKE mandates the use of the IPSec ESP header.

5. After an upgrade to your VPN concentrator hardware, your manager comes to you with a traffic graph showing a 50 percent increase in VPN traffic since the new hardware was installed. What is a possible cause of this increase?

   A. Mandatory traffic shaping.

   B. VPN jitter causing multiple IKE exchanges per second.

   C. The new VPN defaults to full tunneling.

   D. The new VPN uses transport mode instead of tunneling mode.

6. A network-based intrusion prevention system (NIPS) relies on what other technology at its core?

   A. VPN

   B. IDS

   C. NAT

   D. ACL

7. You have been asked to prepare a report on network-based intrusion detection systems that compares the NIDS solutions from two potential vendors your company is considering. One solution is signature based and one is behavioral based. Which of the following lists what your report will identify as the key advantage of each?

   A. Behavioral: low false-negative rate; Signature: ability to detect zero day attacks

   B. Behavioral: ability to detect zero day attacks; Signature: low false-positive rates

   C. Behavioral: high false-positive rate; Signature: high speed of detection

   D. Behavioral: low false-positive rate; Signature: high false-positive rate

8. Why are false negatives more critical than false positives in NIDS/NIPS solutions?

   A. A false negative is a missed attack, whereas a false positive is just extra noise.

   B. False positives are indications of strange behavior, whereas false negatives are missed normal behavior.

   C. False negatives show what didn't happen, whereas false positives show what did happen.

   D. False negatives are not more critical than false positives.

9. You are managing a large network with several dozen switches when your monitoring system loses control over half of them. This monitoring system uses SNMPv2 to read traffic statistics and to make configuration changes to the switches. What has most likely happened to cause the loss of control?

    A. A zero day Cisco bug is being used against you.

    B. One of the network administrators may be a malicious insider.

    C. An attacker has sniffed the SNMP password and made unauthorized configuration changes.

    D. Nothing, just reboot the machine, the switches are likely to reconnect to the monitoring server.

10. How can proxy servers improve security?

    A. They use TLS-based encryption to access all sites.

    B. They can control which sites and content employees access, lessening the chance of malware exposure.

    C. They enforce appropriate use of company resources.

    D. They prevent access to phishing sites.

11. List three key functions of a Security Information and Event Management system:

    _____, _____, _____

12. What technology can check the client's health before allowing access to the network?

    A. DLP

    B. Reverse proxy

    C. NIDS/NIPS

    D. NAC

13. How does a mail gateway's control of spam improve security?

    A. It prevents users from being distracted by spam messages.

    B. It can defeat many phishing attempts.

    C. It can encrypt messages.

    D. It prevents data leakage.

14. Why is e-mail encryption difficult?

    A. E-mail encryption prevents DLP scanning of the message.

    B. E-mail encryption ensures messages are caught in spam filters.

    C. Because of a lack of a uniform standardized protocol and method for encryption.

    D. Because of technical key exchange issues.

15. What kind of device provides tamper protection for encryption keys?

    A. HSM

    B. DLP

    C. NIDS/NIPS

    D. NAC

Answers

1. **C.** Because Telnet is considered unsecure, default firewall policies will more than likely block it.

2. **D.** NAT's capability to hide internal addressing schemes and prevent direct connections from outside nodes will likely keep NAT technology relevant even with broader adoption of IPv6.

3. **D.** The IPSec protocol supports a wide variety of services to provide security. These include access control, connectionless integrity, traffic-flow confidentiality, rejection of replayed packets, data security, and data-origin authentication.

4. **A.** IKE automates the key exchange process in a two-phase process to exchange session keys.

5. **C.** If a VPN defaults to full tunneling, all traffic is routed through the VPN tunnel, versus split tunneling, which allows multiple connection paths.

6. **B.** A NIPS relies on the technology of an intrusion detection system at its core to detect potential attacks.

7. **B.** The key advantage of a behavioral-based NIDS is its ability to detect zero day attacks, whereas the key advantage of a signature-based NIDS is low false-positive rates.

8. **A.** A false negative is more critical as it is a potential attack that has been completely missed by the detection system; a false positive consumes unnecessary resources to be analyzed but is not an actual attack.

9. **C.** An attacker has likely sniffed the cleartext SNMP password and used it to access and make changes to the switching infrastructure.

10. **B.** Proxy servers can improve security by limiting the sites and content accessed by employees, limiting the potential access to malware.

11. SIEM should have these key functions: aggregation, correlation, alerting, time synchronization, event deduplication, and log collection.

12. **D.** NAC, or network access control, is a technology that can enforce the security health of a client machine before allowing it access to the network.

13. **B.** A mail gateway that blocks spam can prevent many phishing attempts from reaching your users.

14. **C.** A lack of a uniform standardized protocol for encryption makes encrypting e-mail end to end difficult.

15. **A.** A hardware security module (HSM) has tamper protections to prevent the encryption keys they manage from being altered.

Security Tools and Technologies

In this chapter, you will be able to
- Understand how to use appropriate software tools to assess the security posture of an organization
- Given a scenario, analyze and interpret output from security technologies

Software tools and security technologies are the methods by which professionals can address vulnerabilities and risk in the enterprise. Tools enable a security analyst to assess the current security posture of a system. Various security technologies provide information that can be analyzed and interpreted by security analysts to determine risk profiles.

Certification Objective   This chapter covers CompTIA Security+ exam objectives 2.2, Given a scenario, use appropriate software tools to assess the security posture of an organization, and 2.4, Given a scenario, analyze and interpret output from security technologies. These exam objectives are good candidates for performance-based questions, which means you should expect questions in which you must apply your knowledge of the topic to a scenario. The best answer to a question will depend upon specific details in the scenario preceding the question, not just the question. The questions may also involve tasks other than just picking the best answer from a list. Instead, they may involve actual simulations of steps to take to solve a problem.

Protocol Analyzer

A *protocol analyzer* is simply a tool (either hardware or software) that can be used to capture and analyze traffic passing over a communications channel, such as a network. Although protocol analyzers exist for many types of communication channels, such as telecommunications traffic and system buses, the most common use of a protocol analyzer is for the capture and examination of network traffic. In the networking world, this tool is commonly referred to by a variety of names such as packet sniffer, network analyzer, network sniffer, packet analyzer, or simply sniffer. Packet analyzers can be used to capture and analyze wired or wireless traffic and can be software based (most common) or a dedicated hardware/software platform. An effective packet analyzer must have the capability to place a network interface in promiscuous mode, which tells the interface to accept and process every packet it sees—not just packets destined for this specific system or sent to a broadcast, multicast, or unicast address. On a switched network, packet analyzers are typically plugged into a SPAN (discussed in the next section) or monitor ports that are configured to receive copies of packets passing through one or more interfaces on the same switch. Capabilities of packet analyzers vary greatly—some do nothing more than simple packet capture, whereas others attempt to reconstruct entire TCP/IP sessions with decoded packets and color-coded traffic streams.

From a security perspective, protocol analyzers are very useful and effective tools. Want to see if any system on your network is transmitting traffic on a specific port? Want to see if any packets are being sent to an address at a rival company? Want to see which employees spend all day surfing eBay? Want to find the system that's flooding the local network with broadcast traffic? A protocol analyzer can help you address all these issues and more—if you have the analyzer plugged into the right location of your network and can "see" the traffic you are concerned about. Most organizations have multiple points in the network where traffic can be sniffed—in the core switch, between the user base and the server farm, between remote users and the core network, between the organization and any link to the Internet, and so on. Knowing how to ensure the packet analyzer can "see" the traffic you want to analyze, knowing where to place the analyzer, and knowing how to use the analyzer are all keys to getting the best results from a protocol analyzer. An example of a free and widely used protocol analyzer is Wireshark.

Switched Port Analyzer

The term *Switched Port Analyzer (SPAN)* is usually associated with Cisco switches—other vendors refer to the same capability as *port mirroring* or *port monitoring*. A SPAN has the ability to copy network traffic passing through one or more ports on a switch or one or more VLANs on a switch and forward that copied traffic to a port designated for traffic capture and analysis (as shown in Figure 7-1). A SPAN port or mirror port creates the collection point for traffic that will be fed into a protocol analyzer or IDS/IPS. SPAN or mirror ports can usually be configured to monitor traffic passing into interfaces, passing

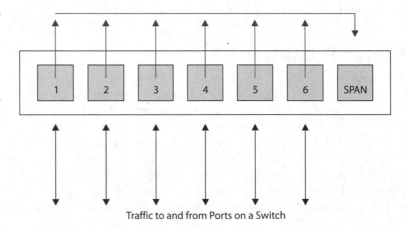

Figure 7-1
A SPAN port collects traffic from other ports on a switch.

Traffic to and from Ports on a Switch

out of interfaces, or passing in both directions. When configuring port mirroring, you need to be aware of the capabilities of the switch you are working with. Can it handle the volume of traffic? Can it successfully mirror all the traffic, or will it end up dropping packets to the SPAN if traffic volume gets too high?

Network Scanners

A *network scanner* is a tool designed to probe a network or systems for open ports, and hence machines that are on the network. Its job is to probe for open (or listening) ports and report back to the user which ports are closed, which are filtered, and which are open. Network scanners are capable of working on any IP network—including virtually every operating system and every popular mobile computing platform, from tablets to smartphones—because they operate by examining network connections. Having a good network scanning tool in your toolset and knowing how to use it properly can be very beneficial. The most commonly used scanner is the freeware tool Nmap (Network Mapper). Network scanners are also called port scanners and can be used to do the following:

- *Search for "live" hosts on a network.* Most network scanners enable you to perform a quick scan using ICMP, TCP, or UDP packets to search for active hosts on a given network or network segment. ICMP is still very popular for this task, but with the default blocking of ICMPv4 in many modern operating systems, such as Windows 7 and beyond, users are increasingly turning to TCP or UDP scans for these tasks.

- *Search for any open ports on the network.* Network scanners are most often used to identify any open ports on a host, group of hosts, or network. By scanning a large number of ports over a large number of hosts, a network scanner can provide you (or an attacker) with a very good picture of what services are running on which hosts on your network. Scans can be done for the "default" set of popular ports, a large range of ports, or every possible port (from 1 to 65535).

- *Search for specific ports.* Only looking for web servers? Mail servers? Network scanners can also be configured to just look for specific services.

- *Identify services on ports.* Some network scanners can help identify the services running on open ports based on information returned by the service or the port/service assigned (if standards have been followed). For example, a service running on port 80 is likely to be a web server.

- *Look for TCP/UDP services.* Most network scanners can perform scans for both TCP and UDP services, although some tools do not allow you to scan for both protocols at the same time.

As a security professional, you'll use network scanners in much the same way an attacker would: to probe the systems in your network for open services. When you find open services, you'll need to determine if those services should be running at all, if they should be running on the system(s) you found them on, and if you can do anything to limit what connections are allowed to those services. For example, you may want to scan your network for any system accepting connections on TCP port 1433 (Microsoft SQL Server). If you find a system accepting connections on TCP port 1433 in your Sales group, chances are someone has installed something they shouldn't have (or someone installed something for them). It is important to note that network scanning activity can trigger an incident response activity when detected. Because of this, it is important that when using these types of tools inside a network that the security team is aware of the scope and timing of use to prevent unnecessary IR activity.

So how does a network scanner actually work? Much will depend on the options you select when configuring your scan, but for the sake of this example, assume you're running a standard TCP connect scan against 192.168.1.20 for ports 1–1000. The scanner will attempt to create a TCP connection to each port in the range 1–1000 on 192.168.1.20. When the scanner sends out that SYN packet, it waits for the responding SYN/ACK. If a SYN/ACK is received, the scanner will attempt to complete the three-way handshake and mark the port as "open." If the sent packet times out or an RST packet is received, the scanner will likely mark that port as "closed." If an "administratively prohibited" message or something similar comes back, the scanner may mark that port as "filtered." When the scan is complete, the scanner will present the results in a summary format— listing the ports that are open, closed, filtered, and so on. By examining the responses from each port, you can typically deduce a bit more information about the system(s) you are scanning, as detailed here:

- **Open** Open ports accept connections. If you can connect to these with a network scanner, the ports are not being filtered at the network level. However, there are instances where you may find a port that is marked as "open" by a network scanner that will immediately drop your connections if you attempt to connect to it in some other manner. For example, port 22 for SSH may appear "open" to a network scanner but will immediately drop your SSH connections. In such a case, the service is likely being filtered by a host-based firewall or a firewall capability within the service itself.

- **Closed** You will typically see this response when the scanned target returns an RST packet.

- **Filtered** You will typically see this response when an ICMP unreachable error is returned. This usually indicates that port is being filtered by a firewall or other device.

- **Additional types** Some network scanners will attempt to further classify responses, such as dropped, blocked, denied, timeout, and so on. These are fairly tool specific, and you should refer to any documentation or help file that accompanies that network scanner for additional information.

In general, you will want to run your scanning efforts multiple times using different options to ensure you get a better picture. A SYN scan may return different results than a NULL scan or FIN scan. You'll want to run both TCP and UDP scans as well. You may need to alter your scanning approach to use multiple techniques at different times of the day/night to ensure complete coverage. The bad guys are doing this against your network right now, so you might as well use the same tools they do to see what they see. Network scanners can also be very useful for testing firewall configurations because the results of the port scans can show you exactly which ports are open, which ones you allow through, which ports are carrying services, and so on.

So how do you defend against port scans? Well, it's tough. Port scans are pretty much a part of the Internet traffic landscape now. Although you can block IP addresses that scan you, most organizations don't because you run the risk of an attacker spoofing source addresses as decoys for other scanning activity. The best defense is to carefully control what traffic you let in and out of your network, using firewalls, network filters, and host filters. Then carefully monitor any traffic that you do allow in.

 EXAM TIP The previous two sections have described two of the most widely used and versatile tools, Wireshark and Nmap. Understanding what these tools can do and when and how they can be employed on your network covers a lot of testable areas of this objective.

Rogue System Detection

One of the challenges of network engineers is to determine if unauthorized equipment is attached to a network. Rogue systems are unauthorized systems and fall outside of the enterprise operations umbrella, adding risk to a system. This is why the first elements of the top 20 security controls consist of knowing the authorized software and hardware in your environment. You should do *rogue system detection* on a regular basis, which you can do in two ways with a network scanner. First, you can do active scans of the network to detect any devices not authorized. Second, you can do a passive scan via an examination of packets to see if anyone is communicating who is not authorized.

Network Mapping

Network mapping tools are another name for network scanners. Network mappers are designed to create network diagrams of how machines are connected. And then they stop there, while network scanners can do additional tasks, such as identify systems, services, and open ports. By definition, this makes network analyzers also mappers, albeit with more capabilities. The process of network mapping is the use of network mapping tools to identify the nodes of a network and characterize them as to OS, purpose, systems, etc.

Wireless Scanners/Cracker

You can use *wireless scanners/crackers* to perform network analysis of the wireless side of your networks. Who is connecting to them? What are they accessing? Is everything in conformance with your security plan? You need to actively pursue and answer these questions on a regular basis. There are a wide variety of wireless scanners that can assist in developing this form of monitoring.

Some common examples of wireless scanners are Kismet, NetStumbler, and Mini-Stumbler. If you wish to add cracking ability, then AirSnort, AirCrack and CoWPAtty are common solutions.

Password Cracker

Password crackers are used by hackers to find weak passwords. Why would a system administrator use one? Same reason. Running your system's password lists through a password cracker provides two things: an early warning of a crackable password, and peace of mind that your passwords are safe when you can't crack any in a reasonable period of time.

Password crackers work using dictionary lists and brute force. On the dictionary lists, they make passwords by combining words with each other, with numbers, special symbols and test those against the system. They also can do brute force attacks. Password crackers can work on-line against a live system, but then they can be subject to timeouts after a limited number of false entries. But if they can steal the password file, they can operate a maximum speed until a match is found. On a modern Core I-7 machine, ten character passwords will fall in roughly a month of work.

Vulnerability Scanner

A *vulnerability scanner* is a program designed to probe a system for weaknesses, misconfigurations, old versions of software, and so on. There are essentially three main categories of vulnerability scanners: network, host, and application. A network vulnerability scanner probes a host or hosts for issues across their network connections. Typically, a network scanner will either contain or use a port scanner to perform an initial assessment of the network to determine which hosts are alive and which services are open on those hosts. It then probes each system and service. Network scanners are very broad tools that can run potentially thousands of checks, depending on the OS and services being examined. This makes them a very good "broad sweep" for network-visible vulnerabilities. Due to the number of checks they can perform, network scanners can generate a great deal of traffic and a large number of connections to the systems being examined, so you should take care to minimize the impact on production systems and production networks. Network scanners are essentially the equivalent of a Swiss army knife for assessments. They do lots of tasks and are extremely useful to have around—they may not be as good as a tool dedicated to examining one specific type of service, but if you can only run a single tool to examine your network for vulnerabilities, you'll want that tool to be a network vulnerability scanner. Figure 7-2 shows a screenshot of Nessus from Tenable Network Security, a very popular network vulnerability scanner.

Bottom line: If you need to perform a broad sweep for vulnerabilities on one or more hosts across the network, a network vulnerability scanner is the right tool for the job.

Host vulnerability scanners are designed to run on a specific host and look for vulnerabilities and misconfigurations on that host. Host vulnerability scanners tend to be more specialized than network vulnerability scanners because they're looking for issues

Figure 7-2 Nessus—a network vulnerability scanner

associated with a specific operating system or set of operating systems. A good example of a host vulnerability scanner is the Microsoft Baseline Security Analyzer (MBSA), shown in Figure 7-3. MBSA is designed to examine the security state of a Windows host and offer guidance to address any vulnerabilities, misconfigurations, or missing patches. Although MBSA can be run against remote systems across the network, it is typically run on the host being examined and requires you to have access to that local host (at the Administrator level). The primary thing to remember about host vulnerability scanners is that they are typically looking for vulnerabilities on the system they are running on.

EXAM TIP   If you want to scan a specific host for vulnerabilities, weak password policies, or unchanged passwords, and you have direct access to the host, a host vulnerability scanner might be just the tool to use.

It's worth nothing that some tools (such as Nessus) really cross the line between network-based and host-based vulnerability scanners. If you supply Nessus with host, login, and domain credentials, it can perform many checks that would be considered "host based."

Selecting the right type of vulnerability scanner isn't that difficult. Just focus on what types of vulnerabilities you need to scan for and how you will be accessing the host, services, or applications being scanned. It's also worth noting that to do a thorough job, you will likely need both network-based and host-based scanners—particularly for

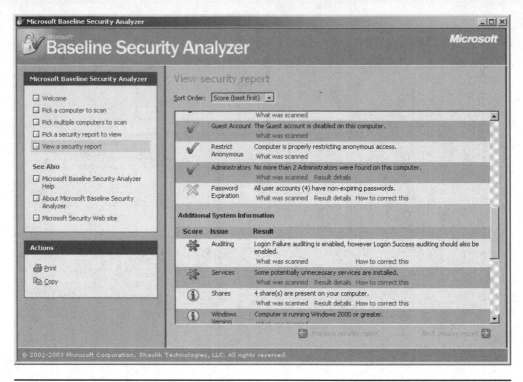

Figure 7-3 Microsoft Baseline Security Analyzer

critical assets. Host- and network-based scanners perform different tests and provide visibility into different types of vulnerabilities. If you want to ensure the best coverage, you'll need to run both.

Application vulnerability scanners are designed to look for vulnerabilities in applications or certain types of applications. Application vulnerability scanners are some of the most specialized scanners—even though they contain hundreds or even thousands of checks, they only look for misconfigurations or vulnerabilities in a specific type of application. Different types of application vulnerability scanners operate against different types of applications. Some scanners are specific to an application, while others are specific to a type of application, as in web-based applications.

Arguably the most popular type of application vulnerability scanners are designed to test for weaknesses and vulnerabilities in web-based applications. Web applications are designed to be visible, interact with users, and accept and process user input—all things that make them attractive targets for attackers. As such, a relatively large number of web application scanners are available, ranging from open source to subscription fee basis. To be an effective web application scanner, the tool must be able to perform thousands of checks for vulnerabilities, misconfigurations, default content, settings,

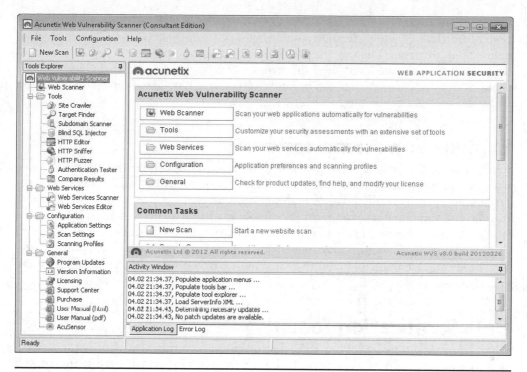

Figure 7-4   Acunetix WVS

issues, and so on, with a variety of web technologies from IIS to Apache to PHP to ASP and everything else in between. Application vulnerability scanners are usually capable of performing advanced checks, such as SQL injection or JavaScript injection, that require interacting with the web application being examined and modifying requests and responses based on feedback from the application. Figure 7-4 shows a screenshot of Acunetix WVS (Web Vulnerability Scanner), an application vulnerability scanner specifically for web technologies.

EXAM TIP   If you want to examine a specific application or multiple instances of the same type of application (such as a website), an application vulnerability scanner is the tool of choice.

Configuration Compliance Scanner

The need to automate configuration checks has existed for years, and became important enough that a standard format was developed. SCAP, Security Content Automation Protocol, is a protocol to manage information related to security configurations and the automated validation of them. There is a wide variety of *configuration compliance scanners* that can perform this task, some SCAP compliant, some not, all with the intended purpose of informing system administrators whether or not their systems align with their defined requirements. The use of these tools requires that a baseline set of defined configurations is established and then the tools can track changes as the defined baseline changes. In most cases, the tool can be used to establish a baseline upon its first operation and set to measure deviations in future cycles.

Exploitation Frameworks

Exploitation frameworks are tool sets designed to assist hackers in the tasks associated with exploiting vulnerabilities in a system. These frameworks are important because the exploitation path typically involves multiple steps, all done in precise order on a system to gain meaningful effect. The most commonly used framework is Metasploit, a set of "tools" designed to assist a penetration tester in carrying out the steps needed to exploit a vulnerability on a system. These frameworks can be used by security personnel as well, specifically to test the exploitability of a system based on existing vulnerabilities and employed security controls.

Data Sanitization Tools

Data sanitization tools are tools used to destroy, purge, or otherwise identify for destruction specific types of data on systems. Before a system can be retired and disposed of, you need to sanitize the data needs. There are several approaches, the first being the whole disk approach. You can use a data sanitization tool to erase or wipe the entire storage of the system, making the data no longer recoverable. One method of doing this is to use self-encrypting disks, and the destruction of the key leaves the disk unrecoverable. A second, more targeted approach is to identify the sensitive data and deal with it specifically. Tools such as Identity Finder excel at this aspect of data sanitization. As with all tools, it is not the tool that provides the true value, but rather the processes and procedures that ensure the work is done and done correctly when required.

Steganography Tools

Steganography tools are designed to perform the act of steganography. Steganography is the science of hidden writing, or more specifically the hiding of messages in other content. Historically, this has been done by painting over messages, and later removing the cover paint, as well as other methods. Today, this is done within digital data streams. Because of the nature of digital images, videos, and audio files and the excess coding capacity in the stream, it is possible to embed additional content in the file. If this content is invisible to the typical user, then it is considered to be steganography. The same techniques are used to add visible (or invisible) watermarks to files so that their lineage can be traced. These watermarks can be used to trace documents, even serialize copies, so a firm can tell who leaks critical information, as each copy of a document is unique and traceable to a specific authorized user.

Honeypot

A *honeypot* is a server that is designed to act like the real server on a corporate network, but rather than having the real data, the data it possesses is fake. Honeypots serve as attractive targets to attackers. A honeypot acts as a trap for attackers, as traffic in the honeypot can be assumed to be malicious.

A *honeynet* is a network designed to look like a corporate network, but is made attractive to attackers. A honeynet is a collection of honeypots. It looks like the corporate network, but because it is known to be a false copy, all of the traffic is assumed to be illegitimate. This makes it easy to characterize the attacker's traffic and also to understand where attacks are coming from.

Backup Utilities

Backup utilities are tools designed to perform one of the most important tasks in computer security, the backing up of data in case of loss. Backing up a single system isn't that hard; a simple utility can manage it. Backing up an enterprise full of servers and workstations is a completely different problem with issues of segregating data, scale, and management of the actual backup files. This requires real tools to manage the process and scale it to enterprise class. Managing backups is a critical security task, for only by understanding the current backup posture does the security team know the status of this critical security function.

Banner Grabbing

Banner grabbing is a technique used to gather information from a service that publicizes information via a banner. Banners can be used for many things; for example, they can be used to identify services by type, version, and so forth, and they enable administrators to post information, including warnings, to users when they log in. Attackers can use banners to determine what services are running, and typically do for common banner-issuing services such as HTTP, FTP, SMTP, and Telnet. Figure 7-5 shows a couple of banner grabs being performed from a Telnet client against a web server. In this example, Telnet sends information to two different web servers and displays the responses (the banners). The top response is from an Apache instance (Apache/2.0.65) and the bottom is from Microsoft IIS (Microsoft-HTTPAPI/2.0).

If an organization wishes to raise the bar for attackers, they can change the banners to be less specific, masking the true revision and, in some cases, the actual type of service provider. This will only serve to slow down an adversary, but each element that forces more attempts, more time acts in the defenders interests, it provides time to catch an attacker.

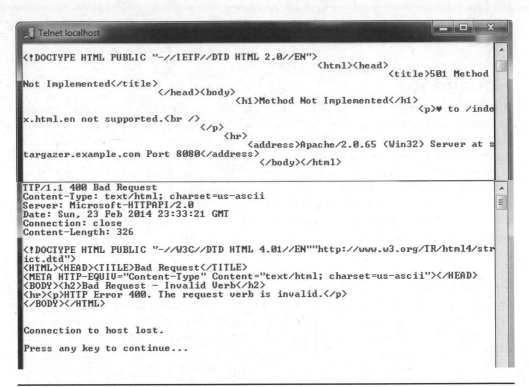

Figure 7-5 Banner grabbing using Telnet

Passive vs. Active

Tools can be classified as passive or active. *Passive tools* are those that do not interact with the system in a manner that would permit detection, as in sending packets or altering traffic. An example of a passive tool is Tripwire, which can detect changes to a file based on hash values. Another example of a passive tool is Wireshark, which, among other passive activities, performs OS mapping by analyzing TCP/IP traces. Passive sensors can use existing traffic to provide data for analysis.

Active tools interact with a target system in a fashion where their use can be detected. Scanning a network with Nmap is an active interaction that can be detected. In the case of Nmap, the tool itself may not be specifically detectable, but its use, the sending of packets, can be detected. When you need to map out your network or look for open services on one or more hosts, a network scanner is probably the most efficient tool for the job.

When determining whether to use a passive tool or an active tool, attackers may consider how much time they have available to carry out the attack. If an attacker has plenty of time, he likely will choose a passive scanner rather than a more invasive tool, such as Nmap, because he can collect the same information with less risk of detection.

But the passive tool is subject to a couple of limitations; it can only detect systems based on their behavior on a network, and its collection point must be on the path between source and destination of conversations associated with the system being examined. An active tool can use the network to carry its interrogatory packets to a host and back, eliminating the location issue (to a degree), but also at the cost of alerting the system that it is being interrogated.

EXAM TIP   Passive tools receive traffic only and do nothing to the traffic flow that would permit detection that they are interacting with the network. Active tools modify or send traffic and thus are discoverable by their traffic patterns.

Command-Line Tools

There are many command-line tools that provide a user direct information concerning a system. These are built into the operating system itself, or are common programs that are used by system administrators and security professionals on a regular basis.

EXAM TIP   The fact that exam objective 2.2 enumerates a specific set of command-line tools means you should be prepared for performance-based questions targeting specific tools. You should know how and when to use each of these tools.

ping

The *ping* command sends echo requests to a designated machine to determine if communication is possible. The syntax is **ping [*options*] *targetname/address***. The options include items such as name resolution, how many pings, data size, TTL counts, and more. Figure 7-6 shows a **ping** command on a Windows machine.

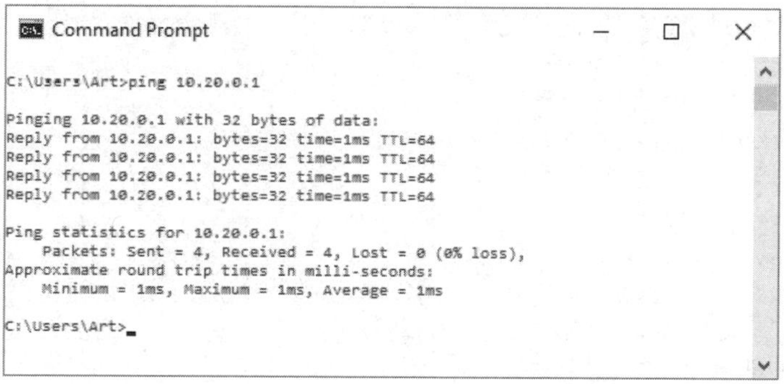

Figure 7-6
Ping command

```
C:\Users\Art>ping 10.20.0.1

Pinging 10.20.0.1 with 32 bytes of data:
Reply from 10.20.0.1: bytes=32 time=1ms TTL=64
Reply from 10.20.0.1: bytes=32 time=1ms TTL=64
Reply from 10.20.0.1: bytes=32 time=1ms TTL=64
Reply from 10.20.0.1: bytes=32 time=1ms TTL=64

Ping statistics for 10.20.0.1:
    Packets: Sent = 4, Received = 4, Lost = 0 (0% loss),
Approximate round trip times in milli-seconds:
    Minimum = 1ms, Maximum = 1ms, Average = 1ms

C:\Users\Art>
```

PART II

netstat

The *netstat* command is used to monitor network connections to and from a system. The following are some examples of how you can use **netstat**:

- **netstat –a**   Lists all active connections and listening ports
- **netstat –at**   Lists all active TCP connections
- **netstat –an**   Lists all active UDP connections

Many more options are available and useful. The **netstat** command is available on Windows and Linux, but availability of certain **netstat** command switches and other **netstat** command syntax may differ from operating system to operating system.

tracert

The *tracert* command is a Windows command for tracing the route that packets take over the network. The **tracert** command provides a list of the hosts, switches, and routers in the order that a packet passes by them, providing a trace of the network route from source to target. As **tracert** uses ICMP, if ICMP is blocked, **tracert** will fail to provide information. On Linux and macOS systems, the command with similar functionality is **traceroute**.

nslookup/dig

The DNS system is used to convert a name into an IP address. There is not a single DNS system, but rather a hierarchy of DNS servers, from root servers on the backbone of the Internet, to copies at your ISP, your home router, and your local machine, each in the form of a DNS cache. To examine a DNS query for a specific address, you can use the *nslookup* command. Figure 7-7 shows a series of DNS queries executed on a Windows machine. In the first request, the DNS server was with an ISP, while on the

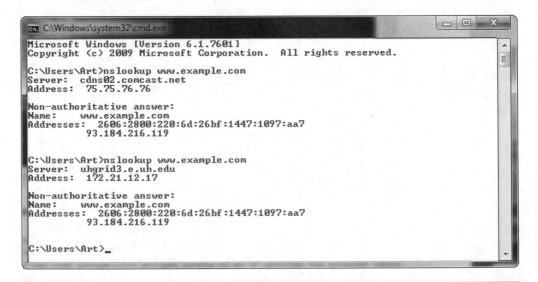

Figure 7-7   nslookup of a DNS query

second request, the DNS server was from a VPN connection. Between the two requests, the network connections were changed, resulting in different DNS lookups.

At times, **nslookup** will return a nonauthoritative answer, as shown in Figure 7-8. This typically means the result is from a cache as opposed to a server that has an authoritative (that is, known to be current) answer, such as from a DNS server.

While **nslookup** works on Windows systems, the command *dig* works on Linux systems. One difference is that **dig** is designed to return answers in a format that is easy to parse and include in scripts, a common trait of Linux command-line utilities.

arp

The *arp* command is designed to interface with the operating system's Address Resolution Protocol (ARP) caches on a system. In moving packets between machines, a device sometimes needs to know where to send a packet using the MAC or layer 2 address. ARP handles this problem through four basic message types:

- **ARP request**   "Who has this IP address?"
- **ARP reply**   "I have that IP address; my MAC address is…"
- **Reverse ARP (RARP) request**   "Who has this MAC address?"
- **RARP reply**   "I have that MAC address; my IP address is…"

These messages are used in conjunction with a device's ARP table, where a form of short-term memory associated with these data elements resides. The commands are used as a simple form of lookup. When a machine sends an ARP request to the network, the reply is received and entered into all devices that hear the reply. This facilitates efficient address lookups, but also makes the system subject to attack.

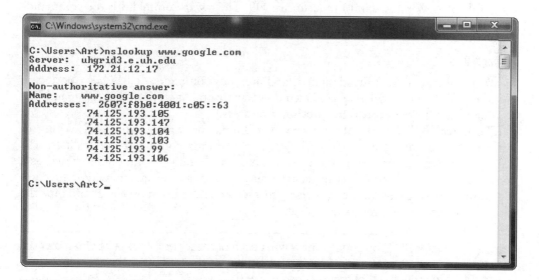

```
C:\Windows\system32\cmd.exe

C:\Users\Art>nslookup www.google.com
Server:  uhgrid3.e.uh.edu
Address:  172.21.12.17

Non-authoritative answer:
Name:    www.google.com
Addresses:  2607:f8b0:4001:c05::63
          74.125.193.105
          74.125.193.147
          74.125.193.104
          74.125.193.103
          74.125.193.99
          74.125.193.106


C:\Users\Art>_
```

Figure 7-8   Cache response to a DNS query

The arp command allows a system administrator the ability to see and manipulate the ARP cache on a system. This way they can see if entries have been spoofed or if other problems, such as errors, occur.

ipconfig/ip/ifconfig

Both *ipconfig* (for Windows) and *ifconfig* (for Linux) are command-line tools to manipulate the network interfaces on a system. They have the ability to list the interfaces and connection parameters, alter parameters, and refresh/renew connections. If you are having network connection issues, this is one of the first tools you should use, to verify the network setup of the operating system and its interfaces.

The *ip* command in Linux is used to show and manipulate routing, devices, policy routing, and tunnels.

tcpdump

The *tcpdump* utility is designed to analyze network packets either from a network connection or a recorded file. You also can use **tcpdump** to create files of packet captures, called pcap files, and perform filtering between input and output, making it a valuable tool to lessen data loads on other tools. For example, if you have a complete packet capture file that has hundreds of millions of records, but you are only interested in one server's connections, you can make a copy of the pcap file containing only the packets associated with the server of interest. This file will be smaller and easier to analyze with other tools.

nmap

Nmap is a program developed by Gordon Lyon and has been the standard network mapping utility for Windows and Linux since 1999. The *nmap* command is the command-line command to launch and run the nmap utility.

netcat

Netcat is the network utility designed for Linux environments. It has been ported to Windows, but is not regularly used in windows environments. The actual command-line command to invoke **netcat** is **nc –options –address**.

The **netcat** utility is the tool of choice in Linux for reading from and writing to network connections using TCP or UDP. Like all Linux command-line utilities, it is designed for scripts and automation. **Netcat** has a wide range of functions. It acts as a connection to the network and can act as a transmitter, or a receiver, and with redirection it can turn virtually any running process into a server. It can listen on a port and pipe the input it receives to the process identified.

 EXAM TIP   You should know what each of these tools looks like when being used. If presented with output from one of the tools, you should be able to identify the tool that was used.

Security Technologies

There are several security technologies that you can employ to analyze security situations. The following technologies are presented to prepare you to answer performance-based exam questions related to CompTIA Security+ objective 2.4, Given a scenario, analyze and interpret output from security technologies. You should focus on understanding what information each of these technologies can provide and how to analyze and interpret that output to address a security problem.

HIDS/HIPS

Both a *host-based intrusion detection system (HIDS)* and a *host-based intrusion prevention system (HIPS)* alert on behaviors that match specified behavioral patterns. Unlike antivirus detection, where the likelihood of a false negative is low, a HIDS/HIPS can have significant false positive rates depending upon the specificity of the ruleset. For this reason, coupled with the basic purpose of these systems, they serve to act as an alerting mechanism to provide a signal to start incident response activities. The primary difference between a HIDS and a HIPS is that a HIPS is designed to provide automated responses to conditions to prevent intrusions. Rather than just alerting an operator, a HIPS can send a TCP reset signal to a device, breaking the communication path.

Antivirus

Antivirus (AV) applications check files for matches to known viruses and other forms of malware. Should your AV solution alert you, the only wise course of action is to either quarantine the file or erase it using the AV utility.

File Integrity Check

Whenever you download a file from an online source, even if from the vendor of the file, you should perform a *file integrity check* to ensure that the file has not been tampered with in any fashion. This will alert you to a changed binary, even if the hosting agent of the file doesn't know about the specific issue. File integrity checks operate by taking a hash of the file and comparing this value to an offline store of correct values. If the hashes match, then the file is unaltered. On Microsoft Windows machines, a system file integrity check can be performed using the command line command **sfc /scannow**.

Host-Based Firewall

A *host-based firewall* is a firewall located on a host system. Because of the firewall's proximity to a single system, you can tune it to the exact specifications of that machine, making it highly specific in its granularity of function. When you have high-value servers, a host-based firewall can provide specific connection specificity, allowing only permitted addresses and ports to access the machine. If properly tuned, a host-based firewall will have a very low false positive rate, and when it blocks connections, if there are repeated attempts, this is a sign of an active attack against the server.

Application Whitelisting

Application whitelisting is a technology that marks files as safe to run on a system based upon their hash values. This allows only specified binaries to be run on a system. For machines with a limited number of applications, this can be a powerful tool to combat many forms of malware. On Microsoft Windows machines using the Enterprise version of the OS, whitelisting can be done natively in the OS via a tool called applocker.

Removable Media Control

Removable media represents a potential data exfiltration pathway, as well as a pathway for malware into a system. *Removable media controls* are designed to prevent the transfer of data from a system to a removable media location, such as a flash drive or an external hard drive. There are multiple ways of doing this, but one of the most common is an encryption-based method, by which the files being transferred are encrypted to a key kept on the original system. This allows external media to be used to back up files, but they cannot be used to transfer data, as the key is on the original system and not accessible outside that machine.

Advanced Malware Tools

Advanced malware tools include tools such as Yara, a command-line pattern matcher that looks for indicators of compromise in a system. Yara assists security engineers in hunting down malware infections based on artifacts that the malware leaves behind in memory. Another type of advanced malware tool is a threat prevention platform that analyzes a system and its traffic in real time and alerts engineers to common malware artifacts such as callbacks to external devices.

Patch Management Tools

Patch management can be a daunting task. Administrators have to consider patches not only for the operating systems, but also for applications. In an enterprise with multiple machines that have different configurations, the task of maintaining software in a patched state is a significant chore. *Patch management tools* assist administrators by keeping lists of the software on a system and alerting users when patches become available. Some of these tools can even assist in the application of the patches. Having the tool alert users when patches are available is only part of the necessary solution; it is also necessary to ensure that the patches are installed, and there are tools to alert administrators when patches have not been updated in a timely fashion.

UTM

Unified threat management (UTM) is a marketing term used to describe all-in-one devices employed in network security. UTM devices typically provide a wide range of services, including switching, firewall, IDS/IPS, anti-malware, anti-spam, content filtering, and traffic shaping. These devices are designed to simplify security administration and are targeted for small and midsized networks. Because of the wide range of services UTMs provide, they are typically located at the edge of the network, managing traffic in and out of the network. When a UTM alerts, it is best to treat the alert like any other action that triggers an incident response and investigate the cause.

DLP

Data loss prevention (DLP) refers to technology employed to detect and prevent transfers of data across an enterprise. Employed at key locations, DLP technology can scan packets for specific data patterns. You can tune this technology to detect account numbers, secrets, specific markers, or files. When specific data elements are detected, the system can block the transfer. The primary challenge in employing DLP technologies is the placement of the sensor. The DLP sensor needs to be able to observe the data, so if the channel is encrypted, DLP technology can be thwarted. When a DLP system alerts that an issue has arisen with respect to blocking the potential exfiltration of protected information, this alarm should result in an investigation by an incident response team.

Data Execution Prevention

Data execution protection (DEP) is the protection of specific memory areas as nonexecutable in a Windows system. Implemented post Windows XP DEP combines with other technologies to prevent attackers from changing the operation of a program through code injection into a data storage location and then subsequently executing the code. Should a system detect a DEP violation, the OS will kill the program. Should this issue repeat, it is highly suspect that the program has been tampered with and needs to be reloaded.

Web Application Firewall

A *web application firewall (WAF)* is a device that performs restrictions based on rules associated with HTTP/HTTPS traffic. By definition, web application firewalls are a form of content filter, and their configuration capabilities allow them to provide significant capability and protections. The level of specificity in what can be allowed or blocked can be as precise as "allow Facebook but block Facebook games." WAFs can detect and block disclosure of critical data, such as account numbers, credit card numbers, and so on. WAFs can also be used to protect websites from common attack vectors such as cross-site scripting, fuzzing, and buffer overflow attacks.

PART II

You can configure a web application firewall to examine inside an SSL session. This is important if an attacker is attempting to use an encrypted channel such as SSL to mask her activity. Because legitimate SSL channels are instantiated by the system, you can pass the appropriate credentials internally to the WAF to enable SSL inspection.

 EXAM TIP This last section of the chapter has covered a bunch of different tools, each designed for a different purpose. Do not lose sight of the objective: Given a scenario, analyze and interpret output from security technologies. What can you do or not do with each of these technologies?

Chapter Review

In this chapter, you became acquainted with the appropriate software tools to assess the security posture of an organization. These tools include protocol analyzers, network scanners, rogue system detectors, network mapping tools, wireless scanners/crackers, password crackers, vulnerability scanners, configuration compliance scanners, exploitation frameworks, data sanitization tools, steganography tools, honeypots, backup utilities, and banner grabbing tools. You also learned the difference between passive and active tools. The chapter then explored a series of command-line tools and their application in security. The tools covered include ping, netstat, tracert, nslookup/dig, arp, ipconfig/ifconfig, tcpdump, nmap, and netcat.

The chapter closed with an overview of analyzing and interpreting the output from security technologies, including HIDS/HIPS, antivirus, file integrity checkers, host-based firewalls, application whitelisting, removable media controls, advanced malware tools, patch management tools, UTM, DLP, DEP, and web application firewalls. It is important to note that this chapter covers scenario-based performance objectives, and as such, you should be ready to demonstrate how you would employ the utilities described in the chapter.

Questions

To help you prepare further for the CompTIA Security+ exam, and to test your level of preparedness, answer the following questions and then check your answers against the correct answers at the end of the chapter.

 1. What kind of tool is Wireshark?

    A. Scanner

    B. Steganography

    C. Malware

    D. Protocol analyzer

2. There are reports of a worm going through your company that communicates to other nodes on port TCP/1337. What tool would you use to find infected nodes on your network?

    A. Protocol analyzer

    B. Advanced malware tool

    C. Network scanner

    D. Password cracker

3. Why should you never use a network scanner on a network you are not authorized to scan?

    A. A network scanner or port scanner is the same tool that an attacker would use.

    B. It might crash the network switch.

    C. Being too efficient at finding network information will cause you to get more work.

    D. It will slow down your work machine with ancillary traffic.

4. Your manager comes to you with an audit finding that 85 percent of the machines on your network are vulnerable to a variety of different exploits. He wants you to verify the findings of the report. What would be the best tool for this?

    A. Protocol analyzer

    B. Network scanner

    C. Vulnerability scanner

    D. All of the above

5. What is the most common use of data sanitization tools?

    A. Clearing web-form fields between user sessions

    B. Erasing hard drives before computers are recycled

    C. Removing PII from a database

    D. Integrating with a data loss prevention system

6. Your organization has been hit with multiple targeted network attacks over the last few months resulting in two data breaches. To attempt to discover how the attackers are getting into your systems, you set up a few vulnerable virtual machines with fake data on them that look like the organization's real machines. What defense mechanism have you built?

    A. Passive sensors

    B. Network-based intrusion detection system (NIDS)

    C. DMZ

    D. A honeynet

7. The **tcpdump** command-line tool is classified as which of the following?

   A. Network scanner

   B. Password cracker

   C. Protocol analyzer

   D. Data sanitization tool

8. Why should you compare hashes of the files you download from the Internet to a library of known hash values?

   A. It prevents the spread of malware by checking a file's integrity.

   B. It prevents you from running the incorrect application.

   C. It protects the data stored in the file.

   D. The hash is needed to decrypt the file.

9. What two things can removable media control do to improve security?

   A. Prevent data sharing and prevent executables from running

   B. Prevent infiltration of malware and prevent exfiltration of data

   C. Provide secure log storage and provide portable encryption

   D. Provide a sandbox location for malware and provide network access control

10. Which of the following describes most network tools that are designed to detect an attack?

    A. Active

    B. Passive

    C. Linux based

    D. Windows based

11. List at least three ways host vulnerability scanners are different from network vulnerability scanners: _____ _____ _____.

12. A network scanner will usually list a port on a remote machine as one of which three classifications? _____ _____ _____

Answers

1. **D.** Wireshark is a protocol analyzer that can make visual displays of IP traffic.

2. **C.** A network scanner that searches for particular ports can help detect infected machines.

3. **A.** Because a network scanner operates the same way that an attacker would operate a port scanner against your network to search for vulnerable machines, many companies prohibit the use of a network scanner on any corporate machines.

PART II

4. **C.** A vulnerability scanner is the best tool for the task. A protocol analyzer allows you to examine packets, not systems for vulnerabilities. A network scanner maps systems, but has limited vulnerability scanning capability.

5. **B.** The most common use of a data sanitization tool is to erase hard drives of any potential sensitive data before they are recycled.

6. **D.** A honeynet is composed of several vulnerable machines deployed to purposely be attacked.

7. **C.** The **tcpdump** command-line tool is a protocol analyzer that allows you to filter and display all the network traffic going to a machine, or save it in files for later viewing.

8. **A.** Comparing the file's hash ensures that the file has not been altered from the known good file, which prevents the spread of malware because most changes are due to a virus being implanted in the file.

9. **B.** Removable media control can prevent a path for malware to enter the organization, and can prevent the exfiltration of sensitive data from the organization.

10. **B.** The majority of detection tools are passive, in that they wait for something in the environment to change as an indicator of an attack. Most tools have equivalents for both Windows and Linux, since the detection is not dependent upon the host system being attacked.

11. Host vulnerability scanners are different from network vulnerability scanners by:
    - Being more specialized
    - Requiring high-level access to the local host, typically Administrative access
    - Scanning for vulnerabilities on a specific operating system
    - Generally only running against a single host
    - Being able to find more in-depth issues such as missing patches and unchanged passwords

12. Network scanners will typically return a port's status as either open, closed, or filtered.

Troubleshooting Common Security Issues

In this chapter, you will

- Identify common security issues
- Given a scenario, troubleshoot common security issues

Troubleshooting common security issues is a common aspect of a security professional's daily job. Learning to recognize common security issues and the solutions to fixing them is an important skill to master.

Certification Objective   This chapter covers CompTIA Security+ exam objective 2.3, Given a scenario, troubleshoot common security issues. This exam objective is a good candidate for performance-based questions, which means you should expect questions in which you must apply your knowledge of the topic to a scenario. The best answer to a question will depend upon specific details in the scenario preceding the question, not just the question. The question may also involve tasks other than just picking the best answer from a list. Instead, it may involve actual simulation of steps to take to solve a problem.

Unencrypted Credentials/Clear Text

Unencrypted credentials or *cleartext credentials* are unfortunately still a common security issue. When credentials are transferred from one machine to another, it is important to protect the transfer of this information from unauthorized observation. When information is sent between machines in cleartext or unencrypted form, the information being transmitted is subject to eavesdropping by any machine in the communication pathway. The information is also subject to release in the event of an error that results in the credential information being persisted in a log or displayed on someone's screen. Maintaining security over credentials is essential to prevent their disclosure to unauthorized parties, and as such they should never be transmitted across cleartext forms of communication in unencrypted form.

Logs and Events Anomalies

Logs, or log files, are an everyday part of computing. What makes log files useful is the exercise of careful discrimination when choosing what is logged. The objective of logging is to record *event anomalies.* Event anomalies are conditions that differ from expected outcomes. One of the challenges is in determining what to log and what not to log. When logging something, it is important to determine whether that information has a potential security implication, or will be used in some form at a later time. Take the example of successful logins. This can be an important element to log on some resources. And if the successful login data is missing from a log when you expect it to be there because of other factors, this is an anomalous event. Was the log erased? Was there an error in the machine setup?

On a workstation, successful logins can be used to establish the beginning of a session. On some high-value assets, this information is important because the set of users accessing the information is most likely limited, and because of the value of the information, this information can be useful. If you notice, for example, that a particular user, who only accesses the system monthly to audit the machine, has started logging in every day, and late at night, this is clearly an anomalous event.

Permission Issues

Permission issues are problems associated with user permissions involving access and using resources. Verifying user rights and permission issues is a practice that should occur at a reasonable interval and be based on the level of user. Periodic review of rights and permissions is one of the more powerful security controls. But the strength of this control depends upon rights and permissions kept up to date and properly maintained. Ensuring that the list of users and associated rights is complete and up to date is a challenging task in anything bigger than the smallest enterprises. A compensating control that can assist in keeping user rights lists current is a set of periodic audits of the user base and associated permissions.

Access Violations

Access violations occur when someone attempts to access a resource that they do not have permission to access. There are two reasons for this error. First, the user is unauthorized and is either making a mistake or attempting to get past security. The other option is that permissions are set inappropriately. This second option is not as rare as one would think, but it also tends to be self-correcting, for if the user should have permission, they typically request the issue be fixed.

As attackers probe a network, looking for information to steal, they can frequently trigger access violations. Tracking and investigating unusual access violations can be an important tool to find intruders, especially intruders of the advanced persistent threat (APT) type. Finding the "unusual access violations" typically requires a security information and event management (SIEM) system to sort through and group violations and other indicators to highlight the data points of interest.

Certificate Issues

Certificates are means for carrying public keys and vouching for their authenticity. A common *certificate issue* is when a user attempts to use a certificate that lacks a complete chain of trust back to a trusted root, leaving the certificate hanging without any means of validation. These chain of trust violations can sometimes be "fixed" when the end user installs the certificate into the trust repository. But this then begs the question, should that certificate be trusted? Maintaining the repository of trusted certificates across an enterprise is another exercise in distributed configuration maintenance, a challenge to keep up to date. Failure to install a needed trust chain makes a key that should be trusted, untrusted. Failure by accepting a trust chain that should not be trusted means accepting certificates in the future that should not be trusted.

Data Exfiltration

Data is the primary target of most attackers. The value of the data can vary, making some data more valuable and, hence, more at risk of theft. *Data exfiltration* is where an attacker attempts to steal a copy of your data and export it from your system.

To prevent theft, a variety of controls can be employed. Some are risk mitigation steps, such as data minimization, which is the act of not storing data that isn't needed by the enterprise for a specific business purpose in the future. If it must be stored and has value, then use technologies such as data loss prevention (DLP) to provide a means of protection. Simple security controls such as firewalls and network segmentation can also act to make data theft more difficult.

Another preventative measure for data exfiltration is the DLP (data loss prevention) technology. DLP is discussed in detail in Chapter 6. With respect to this section, DLP technology offers a way to observe in real time if there is an attempt to exfiltrate data that has been labeled as sensitive, and to some degrees offer ways to stop the transfer. USB devices can be of particular concern and one option available to Windows users is the extension of Bitlocker technology to USB drives, forcing encryption onto the drive and encrypting all data that moves to the drive, with a key that remains in the enterprise. This makes the data unreadable outside the enterprise.

 EXAM TIP We have covered six different common security issues—can you troubleshoot them? What are the symptoms of each, and how would you identify and differentiate each?

Misconfigured Devices

Misconfigured devices represent one of the more common security issues and can go completely unnoticed. Many security controls depend upon a properly configured device to function properly. Consider access control lists, for example; suppose you carefully select the users from the list to grant access to a system, limiting who can open a file, but you fail to notice that the top entry in the list, "everyone," is checked. The result is that this one check box overrides all of your selections and nonselections, automatically granting everyone access by default. Without any warnings, this oversight just destroyed your attempt at access control.

Firewalls, content filters, and access points are all common systems with configurations that are critical for proper operation. This misconfiguration issue is common enough that the NIST Risk Management Framework (https://csrc.nist.gov/projects/risk-management/risk-management-framework-(RMF)-Overview) states specifically that controls must be tested once they are put in place to ensure they actually work as desired.

Firewall

Firewalls essentially are devices to enforce network access policy. Using a set of rules, a firewall either allows or blocks passage of packets. The key is the ruleset. A solid ruleset enables solid controls, whereas a sloppy ruleset enables sloppy controls. Over time, rulesets become less orderly and have issues due to exceptions. For example, while troubleshooting a connection issue, a network tech may request that a particular port be opened on a firewall, in response to which a "temporary" rule is created. After the testing is complete, another pressing issue might lead to the "temporary" rule being forgotten about and never removed. Consequently, an attacker could target the open port for exploitation. Auditing firewall rulesets against the business policy requirements will find these issues, but audits are time consuming and tedious. And when an auditor finds a rule that is clearly for testing, it must be determined if the test or exception that the rule is in place for is still ongoing, or is it over and the rule should be removed.

Content Filter

Content filters are used to limit specific types of content across the Web to users. A common use is to block sites that are not work related, and to limit items such as Google searches and other methods of accessing content determined to be inappropriate. Like all other policy enforcement devices, content filters rely upon a set of rules, and rule maintenance is an issue. One of the most common issues with content filters is too broad of a blocking. In a medical environment, blocking the word "breast" will not work, nor in a chicken plant. There needs to be a mechanism in place to lift blocks easily and quickly if a user objects and it is easy to determine they should have access.

Access Points

Access points are the first line of defense, where access to a network is either granted or denied. Access points, whether RJ-45 physical jacks or wireless, need a method of determining entry criteria, before allowing access to network resources. Whether by local ACL, advanced systems such as RADIUS, or network access control (NAC), access points are only as good as the rules behind them. They must be configured with appropriate criteria for determining which traffic to grant or deny access to the network. Maintaining the proper entry criteria across the backend systems that the access point depends upon to enforce these rules can be a challenge. This challenge grows in scale when hardware checks are incorporated and there is a lot of changing hardware, or personnel changes.

EXAM TIP In this section, we looked at common issues with misconfigured devices, specifically firewalls, content filters, and access points. Consider how these would be described in terms of a scenario for exam questions.

Weak Security Configurations

Weak security configurations refer to the choice of a set of configuration parameters associated with a software application or operating system that results in greater than necessary security risk. One of the advantages of software is its ability to be configured to fit different situations, and some of these configurations are inherently more secure.

An example is in choosing cipher suites (algorithms) when setting up HTTPS. The most common example of a weak security configuration in this context is the choice of SHA-1 signature-based certificates. Although technically still usable, SHA-1 has been replaced by SHA-2, and many security professionals consider SHA-1 to be weak. Other examples would be to pick a configuration of SSLv2, or an RSA key length of 1024 bits. Using outdated or weak cipher suites is hard to justify when picking stronger options is merely a configuration setting away.

Another example is in establishing password policies with respect to an operating system or domain. Allowing users to choose weak passwords and allowing users unlimited password tries without locking the account are legitimate options, although ill-advised choices. Either of these choices would result in a weak security configuration of the OS.

Personnel Issues

Personnel issues in the context of security are the problems caused by users, through their actions and errors. People form an important part of the security environment in an organization. Poorly trained users can weaken even well-thought-out security plans by clicking e-mail links and the like. In many cases, the final line of defense is not the security team, but regular users, as they are the ones who are likely to be phished. People are easily attacked via social engineering, allowing an attacker to get the initial foothold on a system from which they can advance an attack.

Policy Violation

Policy violations occur when personnel do not adhere to written polices established by the organization. Enterprises set up a wall of policies to cover a wide range of security behaviors, from acceptable use policies, to password policies, to clean desk and vacation policies, and more. The purpose behind these policies is to provide guidance to the personnel in the organization regarding what is proper and acceptable behavior and what behaviors should be avoided. Personnel violate these policies for multiple reasons, including lack of knowledge, lack of situational awareness, and failure to follow directions (willful disobedience).

For personnel who lack knowledge of the policy, policy-specific training is the answer. For those who have problems with situational awareness, they may understand the policy but not recognize when it is applied, in which case the best answer is training with respect to awareness of the problem. Whereas both of these reasons for policy violations can be addressed and resolved through training, the third category, willful disobedience, requires a different approach. Every organization typically has a small percentage of employees who don't care and will routinely violate policy. These personnel need to be identified and isolated in such a manner that they do not jeopardize the security for the entire organization. For punishments, it is important to integrate with HR and to use terms like "up to and including termination," but not to specify punishments, as circumstances may preclude predetermining punishments in some cases.

Insider Threat

All activity on a system takes place under an account. An account defines a user, to which items such as the levels of privilege to objects can be assigned. Users have access granted to their account because trust is required for them to perform their duties, and this trust is reflected in the permissions given to their account. An insider who acts maliciously abuses this trust, and is considered an *insider threat*. An insider threat is a more significant challenge to the organization than an outside attacker because the insider already has at least basic privileges on the system. In the attack chain, one of the early steps, and sometimes a difficult step for outside attackers, is establishing basic user access on a system. The insider threat, in essence, begins with this step already completed.

If the malicious insider is someone with elevated privileges, such as a system administrator, then this form of attack can be especially harmful. A malicious insider with root-level access and skills can bypass many security measures and perform many damaging tasks while avoiding detection. The recent case of the NSA insider Edward Snowden shows how devastating this form of attack vector can be to an organization.

The best defense against insiders lies in a layered defense consisting of two parts. The first is through HR screening of new hires and monitoring of employee activity and morale. The other tool is separation of duties, which ensures that no single individual has the ability to conduct transactions alone (covered in more detail in Chapter 21). Ensuring that system admins do not have the ability to manipulate the logs on the systems they administer can be managed with multiple log servers and multiple sets of administrative controls.

 EXAM TIP Managing the malicious insider problem is a combination of people management through HR and separation of duties on the technical side.

Social Engineering

Social engineering is a form of hacking a user (see Chapter 2 for in-depth coverage). Training users to have an awareness of social engineering, enabling them to recognize social engineering is the best defense. If users are falling victim to social engineering, the best troubleshooting strategy is to provide them with comprehensive awareness training of social engineering techniques, enabling them to recognize and report social engineering attacks without falling victim. Social engineering is not just an isolated attack, but can act together with a phishing campaign to increase the odds that a user will click the item and become a victim. Social engineering is a pernicious problem that will continue to evolve, so users should receive awareness training on a regular basis.

Social Media

Social media is a popular method of communicating with friends, family, associates, and others across the Web. Sharing can be a valuable character quality in a person, but over-sharing on social media can lead to risk. If employees are sharing company information via social media, that can result in a lot of security issues such as an employee inadvertently sharing confidential company information. Social engineers have been known to use social media postings to gain information that is used to socially engineer personnel, using their own information to allow a stranger to create a false sense of trust.

Most organizations have some form of social media policy that, in broad terms, prohibits sharing of work-related details via social media. But even posting non-work-related issues on social media can lead to work-related issues. For example, if an organization discovers that an employee is expressing extremist views on social media that coworkers are aware of and feel threatened by, the organization could face claims of a "hostile" work environment, a serious work issue. Social media has become one of the newest HR issues, and conducting awareness campaigns helping employees steer clear of the mines in this minefield is about the best defense.

Personal E-mail

The use of *personal e-mail* at work can cause a variety of issues. Personal e-mail can offer a data exfiltration pathway that is outside of corporate control. Personal e-mail can also act as a path for malware to enter the network, and the user's machine specifically. For these and other reasons, many companies have a policy prohibiting personal e-mail in the workplace.

 EXAM TIP   People are an integral part of a security system, whether normal users or security personnel. Having security-based HR policies associated with user behaviors, such as personal e-mail, content filters (web browsing behavior), acceptable use agreements, and more, is an important element in system security. Be prepared to recognize the types of issues associated with personnel and how they are resolved.

Unauthorized Software

One of the security challenges in an enterprise is the addition of *unauthorized software* to a system, which poses additional risks to the enterprise. This is why the first elements of the top 20 security controls (covered in Chapter 11) consist of knowing the authorized software and hardware in your environment. Unauthorized software can be either the use of an unapproved program or the use of an approved program with improper licensing (covered a bit later in the chapter).

There are several methods of controlling unauthorized software, including removing users' ability to add software, and the use of whitelisting or deep-freeze technologies that restrict what can run on a machine. Deep-freeze software prohibits any lasting changes to a machine by reverting the disk drives back to the state they were in when the user logged in, preventing a whole host of issues from occurring. Regular audits of installed software can also identify systems with unauthorized software.

 EXAM TIP Unauthorized software can lead to baseline deviations or license compliance violations, and can be uncovered via asset management, so these topics are related. But if given a scenario, can you separate the issues and pick the one that best fits the details? Focusing on the scenario can help you identify the best answer.

Baseline Deviation

Baselining is the measuring of a system's current state of security readiness. Various tools are available that you can use to examine a system to see if it has specific weaknesses that make it vulnerable to attack—weaknesses like default passwords, issues with permissions, and so forth. The way baselining is supposed to work is simple: you set up a system, measure the baseline, fix the issues, and declare the resulting system configuration as your baseline. Then, in the future, after changing applications, etc., you can measure the baseline again and look for any deviations. Whenever you update, patch, add a new application, it is possible to measure the security risk gap based on before and after baseline measurements.

A *baseline deviation* is a change from the original baseline value. This change can be positive, lowering risk, or negative, increasing risk. If the change increases risk, then you need to evaluate this new risk level for possible remediation. The biggest challenge is in running the baseline scans, or automating them, to determine when deviations occur.

License Compliance Violation (Availability/Integrity)

Software license violations can result in software disabling key functions. In many corporate environments, software licenses are administered via key servers and other mechanisms. When a user gets a message that the software license is not valid, or expired, that may be an error, but it might still affect the functioning of the software. Software that is in an improper license state may not receive proper updates. *License compliance violations* need to be resolved in a timely manner to prevent inadvertent availability issues. Even if the violation is in error, resolving the error is an important task to take care of in a timely fashion.

Asset Management

Asset management is an important fundamental security task, so much so that it is at the top of the top 20 common security controls. Understanding what hardware and software you have in the enterprise, where it is specifically located, and how it is configured is the foundation for many security elements. Poor asset management adds to system and application sprawl in the enterprise. Maintaining accurate asset records can be a challenge in an ever-changing IT environment, yet it remains an important task. There are many automated solutions to assist in this effort, and if your organization is large, you should take advantage of these tools. It is also important to understand the patch state of all the assets, and keep this up to date as well.

Authentication Issues

Authentication is a key process in maintaining security. When there are *authentication issues*, such as default passwords, the end result can be a vulnerability. When users log into a system, the system can create log entries. For high-value assets, your organization likely wants the system to log both the entry and exit of the user. For the vast majority of systems, it is more important to just look at authentication failures. Authentication failures occur when the system fails to present proper user identification to the access control system. An authentication failure may occur because a user just changed her password or mistyped the password. These errors are typically resolved after a couple of tries.

More concerning is a wave of hundreds or thousands of failed logins to a specific account, as this is a sign of brute-force hacking. Another concern is a distributed method of brute forcing, where a password is tried against multiple users in rapid fashion. Compared to a common brute-force attack, this method will show up in the logs as lower numbers of failed authentication across the accounts, but all of them will have the same IP address from where the attack was launched. This attack is hard to see in the logs, as it is scattered across numerous data points over time, but can be detected by many SIEM devices. Finding and blocking these types of authentication hacks is useful when the numbers of failed logins indicate attempts at breaking into the system, either via a single account or multiple accounts.

Chapter Review

In this chapter, you became acquainted with troubleshooting common security problems. Following the presentation of topics listed in exam objective 2.3, the chapter began with coverage of unencrypted credentials/clear text issues, logs and events anomalies, permission issues, access violations, and certificate issues. The chapter continued with data exfiltration issues and misconfigured devices, including firewalls, content filters, access points, and weak security configurations. The topic of personnel issues, including policy violations, insider threat, social engineering, social media, and personal e-mail, were presented. The chapter closed with the topics of unauthorized software, baseline deviations, license compliance violations (availability/integrity), asset management issues, and authentication issues.

PART II

Questions

To help you prepare further for the CompTIA Security+ exam, and to test your level of preparedness, answer the following questions and then check your answers against the correct answers at the end of the chapter.

1. Your friend in another department asks you to help him understand some fundamental principles about encryption and clear text. Identify three important principles about the risk incurred by unencrypted credentials and clear text.

2. Which of the following is a valid principle relevant to logs and event anomalies?

   A. It's important to determine what to log and what not to log.

   B. You should gather and log as much information as you can.

   C. Context doesn't matter much when logging information.

   D. Logs should be actively maintained and never be destroyed or overwritten.

3. Which of the following is true about managing user permission issues?

   A. User rights and permissions reviews are not powerful security controls.

   B. Ensuring that user lists and associated rights are complete and current is a straightforward task with today's tools.

   C. Compensating controls are unnecessary.

   D. The strength of this control is highly dependent on it being kept current and properly maintained.

4. What is the most likely reason for access violation errors?

   A. Intruders are trying to hide their footprints.

   B. The user is unauthorized and is either making a mistake or is attempting to get past security.

   C. A SIEM system will not identify access violations.

   D. An APT intrusion won't usually trigger access violations.

5. Which of the following is a risk typically related to certificates?

   A. Failure to install a needed trust chain makes a key that should be trusted, untrusted.

   B. A chain of trust violation can always be "fixed" when the end user installs a certificate into the trust repository.

   C. Maintaining the repository of trusted certificates across an enterprise is a simple task.

   D. Accepting a trust chain that should not be trusted means accepting certificates in the past that should be trusted.

6. Which of the following properly defines data exfiltration?

   A. A means for carrying public keys and vouching for their authenticity.

   B. Someone attempts to access a resource that they do not have permission to access.

   C. An attacker attempts to steal a copy of your data and export it from your system.

   D. Ensuring that the list of users and associated rights is complete and up to date.

7. Which of the following is true about firewalls?

   A. Firewalls are encrypted remote terminal connections.

   B. Over time, rulesets stabilize and become easier to maintain.

   C. Firewalls are network access policy enforcement devices that allow or block passage of packets based on a ruleset.

   D. Auditing firewall rules is a straightforward process.

8. Your manager asks you to help her understand some fundamental principles about device configuration. Identify three important principles about device configuration.

9. A friend approaches you at a personal social event and says he was unable to access a popular website at work, but other sites such as new sites seemed to work. Identify the most likely culprit.

10. Identify three reasons why poorly trained users present a significant security challenge.

11. Which of the following is not true about insider threats?

   A. Segregation of duties can help manage insider threats.

   B. Ensuring that system admins do not have the ability to manipulate the logs on the systems they administer can mitigate the insider threat.

   C. The best defense against insider threats is a single strong layer of defense.

   D. Managing the malicious insider problem is a combination of people management through HR and separation of duties.

12. Which of the following is not a risk related to social media?

   A. An employee can inadvertently share confidential company information.

   B. Extreme viewpoints can present a legal liability to the company.

   C. Viable training programs can help mitigate social media risks.

   D. The use of social media can facilitate social engineering.

13. Identify three essential policies an enterprise should have to properly manage the human aspects of network security.

14. Identify the primary reason why personal e-mail presents risks to the corporation.

15. List three methods of controlling unauthorized software.

Answers

1. Important principles about the risk incurred by unencrypted credentials and clear text include

   - It is important to protect the transfer of authorizing credentials between computer systems from unauthorized observation.

   - When information is sent between machines in cleartext or unencrypted form, the information being transmitted is subject to eavesdropping by any machine in the communication pathway.

   - The information is also subject to release in the event of an error that results in the credential information being persisted in a log or displayed on someone's screen.

   - To prevent credential disclosure to unauthorized parties, they should never be transmitted across cleartext forms of communication in unencrypted form.

2. **A.** A valid principle relevant to logs and event anomalies is that you should determine what to log and what not to log.

3. **D.** When managing user permissions, it is important to recall that the strength of this control is highly dependent on being kept current and properly maintained.

4. **B.** The most likely reason for access violation errors is that the user is unauthorized and is either making a mistake or is attempting to get past security.

5. **A.** A risk typically related to certificates is the failure to install a needed trust chain, which makes a key that should be trusted, untrusted.

6. **C.** Data exfiltration is when an attacker attempts to steal a copy of your data and export it from your system.

7. **C.** Firewalls are network access policy enforcement devices that allow or block passage of packets based on a ruleset.

8. Important principles about device configuration are

   - Misconfigured devices are one of the more common security issues and can go completely unnoticed.

   - Many security controls depend upon a properly configured device to function properly.

   - Firewalls, content filters, and access points are all common systems with configurations that are critical for proper operation.

   - The misconfiguration issue is common enough that the NIST Risk Management Framework specifies that one must test controls once in place to ensure they actually do work as desired.

9. Content filters are used to limit specific types of content across the Web to users. A common use is to block sites that are not work related. They are used to limit items such as Google searches and other methods of accessing content determined to be inappropriate. Content filters typically rely upon a set of rules.

10. Poorly trained users present a significant security challenge because personnel can violate policies because they don't understand why a policy exists or they lack situational awareness of how a policy is applied. It can also be the result of willful disobedience. Each of these can result in increased risk to the enterprise.

11. **C.** The best defense against insider threats is to have multiple strong layers of defense.

12. **C.** While social media significantly facilitates collaboration, it does introduce risks such as an employee inadvertently sharing confidential company information. An employee expressing extreme viewpoints can present a legal liability to the company. Viable training programs can help mitigate social media risks.

13. Essential policies an enterprise should have to properly manage the human aspects of network security include policies on personal e-mail, content filtering (web browsing behavior), and acceptable use.

14. Personal e-mail presents at least three risks to a corporation in that it offers a data exfiltration pathway that is outside of corporate control, it can act as a path for malware to enter the network, and it can act as a path for malware to enter user machines.

15. Three methods of controlling unauthorized software are

- Removing the user's ability to add software
- Using whitelisting or freeze technologies to restrict what can run on a machine
- Conducting regular audits to identify unauthorized software

Mobile Devices

In this chapter, you will

- Examine the connection methods used by mobile devices
- Study mobile device management concepts
- Understand mobile device policy and enforcement
- Identify deployment models based on a given scenario

There has been an amazing convergence of business and individual usage of mobile devices. The convergence of cloud storage capabilities and Software as a Service (SaaS) is dramatically changing the landscape of mobile device usage. The ubiquitous presence of mobile devices and the need for continuous data access across multiple platforms have led to significant changes in the way mobile devices are being used for personal and business purposes. In the past, companies provided mobile devices to their employees for primarily business usage but they were available for personal usage. With continuously emerging devices and constantly changing technologies, many companies are allowing employees to bring their own devices (BYOD: bring your own device) for both personal and business usage.

Certification Objective   This chapter covers CompTIA Security+ exam objective 2.5, Given a scenario, deploy mobile devices securely. This chapter contains topics under exam objective 2.5 that can be tested with performance-based questions. It is not enough to simply learn the terms associated with the material. You should be familiar with how to deploy mobile devices securely based on a given scenario. The scenario will provide the necessary information to determine the best answer to the question.

Connection Methods

Mobile devices, by their mobile nature, require a non-wired means of connection to a network. Typically, this connection on the enterprise side is via the Internet, but on the mobile device side a wide range of options exist for connectivity. Where and how mobile devices connect to a network is manageable by the enterprise in architecting the mobile connection aspect of their wireless network.

Cellular

Cellular connections use mobile telephony circuits, today typically fourth-generation (4G) or LTE in nature, although some 3G services still exist. One of the strengths of cellular is that robust nationwide networks have been deployed, making strong signals available virtually anywhere with reasonable population density. The corresponding weakness is that gaps in cellular service still exist is remote areas.

Wi-Fi

Wi-Fi (listed as WiFi under exam objective 2.5) refers to the radio communication methods developed under the Wi-Fi Alliance. These systems exist on 2.4- and 5-GHz frequency spectrums and networks are constructed by both the enterprise you are associated with and third parties. This communication methodology is ubiquitous with computing platforms and is relatively easy to implement and secure. Securing Wi-Fi networks is covered extensively in this and other chapters, as it is a mainstream method of constructing networks today.

SATCOM

SATCOM (satellite communications) is the use of terrestrial transmitters and receivers and satellites in orbit to transfer the signals. SATCOM can be one way, as in satellite radio, but for most communications two-way signals are needed. Satellites are expensive, and for high-density urban areas, both cost and line-of-sight issues make SATCOM a more expensive option. But in rural areas or remote areas, such as in the wilderness or at sea, SATCOM is one of the only options for communications.

Bluetooth

Bluetooth was originally developed by Ericsson and known as multi-communicator link; in 1998, Nokia, IBM, Intel, and Toshiba joined Ericsson and adopted the Bluetooth name. This consortium became known as the Bluetooth Special Interest Group (SIG), which now has more than 24,000 members and drives the development of the technology and controls the specification to ensure interoperability. Bluetooth is a short-range, low-power wireless protocol that transmits in the 2.4-GHz band, the same band used for 802.11. The concept for this short-range (approx. 32 feet) wireless protocol is to transmit data in personal area networks (PANs).

Bluetooth transmits and receives data from a variety of devices, the most common being mobile phones, laptops, printers, and audio devices. The mobile phone has driven a lot of Bluetooth growth and has even spread Bluetooth into new cars as a mobile phone hands-free kit.

Bluetooth has gone through a few releases. Version 1.1 was the first commercially successful version, with version 1.2 released in 2007 and correcting some of the problems found in 1.1. Version 1.2 allows speeds up to 721 Kbps and improves resistance to interference. Version 1.2 is backward-compatible with version 1.1. With the rate of advancement and the life of most tech items, Bluetooth 1 series is basically extinct. Bluetooth 2.0 introduced enhanced data rate (EDR), which allows the transmission of up to 3.0 Mbps. Bluetooth 3.0 has the capability to use an 802.11 channel to achieve speeds up to 24 Mbps.

The current version is the Bluetooth 4.0 standard with support for three modes: classic, high speed, and Low Energy.

Bluetooth 4 introduces a new method to support collecting data from devices that generate data at a very low rate. Some devices, such as medical devices, may only collect and transmit data at low rates. This feature, called Low Energy (LE), was designed to aggregate data from various sensors, like heart rate monitors, thermometers, and so forth, and carries the commercial name Bluetooth Smart.

As Bluetooth became popular, people started trying to find holes in it. Bluetooth features easy configuration of devices to allow communication, with no need for network addresses or ports. Bluetooth uses pairing to establish a trust relationship between devices. To establish that trust, the devices advertise capabilities and require a passkey. To help maintain security, most devices require the passkey to be entered into both devices; this prevents a default passkey–type attack. The Bluetooth's protocol advertisement of services and pairing properties is where some of the security issues start. Bluetooth should always have discoverable mode turned off unless you're deliberately pairing a device. The following table displays Bluetooth versions and speeds.

Bluetooth Data Rates

Different versions of Bluetooth have differing maximum data transfer rates.

Bluetooth Version	Speed
Bluetooth v1.0 and v1.0B	768 Kbps
Bluetooth v1.1	768 Kbps
Bluetooth v1.2	1 Mbps
Bluetooth v2.0 and v2.1 + EDR (Enhanced Data Rate)	3 Mbps
Bluetooth v3.0 + HS (High Speed)	24 Mbps
Bluetooth Smart (v4.0, 4.1, and 4.2)	24 Mbps

NFC

Near Field Communication (NFC) is a set of wireless technologies that enables smartphones and other devices to establish radio communication when they are within close proximity to each other, typically a distance of 10 cm (3.9 in) or less. This technology did not see much use until recently when it started being employed to move data between cell phones and in mobile payment systems. NFC is likely to become a high-use technology in the years to come as multiple uses exist for the technology, and the next generation of smartphones is sure to include this as a standard function. Currently, NFC relies to a great degree on its very short range for security, although apps that use it have their own security mechanisms as well.

ANT

ANT is a multicast wireless sensor network technology that operates in the 2.4-GHz ISM band. ANT is a proprietary method, but has open access and a protocol stack to facilitate communication by establishing standard rules for co-existence, data representation, signaling, authentication, and error detection within a PAN. ANT is conceptually similar to Bluetooth Low Energy, but is oriented toward usage with sensors, such as heart rate monitors, fitness devices, and personal devices. ANT uses a unique isosynchronous network technology that allows it to manage communications in a crowded 2.4-GHz spectrum, and to work well with multiple devices without interference.

Infrared

Infrared (IR) is a band of electromagnetic energy just beyond the red end of the visible color spectrum. IR has been used in remote-control devices for years. IR made its debut in computer networking as a wireless method to connect to printers. Now that wireless keyboards, wireless mice, and mobile devices exchange data via IR, it seems to be everywhere. IR can also be used to connect devices in a network configuration, but it is slow compared to other wireless technologies. IR cannot penetrate walls but instead bounces off them. Nor can it penetrate other solid objects, so if you stack a few items in front of the transceiver, the signal is lost. Because IR can be seen by all in range, any desired security must be on top of the base transmission mechanism.

USB

Universal Serial Bus (USB) has become the ubiquitous standard for connecting devices with cables. Mobile phones can transfer data and charge their battery via USB. Laptops, desktops, even servers have USB ports for a variety of data connection needs. USB ports have greatly expanded users' ability to connect devices to their computers. USB ports automatically recognize a device being plugged into the system and usually work without the user needing to add drivers or configure software. This has spawned a legion of USB devices, from music players to peripherals to storage devices—virtually anything that can consume or deliver data connects via USB.

The most interesting of these devices, for security purposes, are the USB flash memory–based storage devices. USB drive keys, which are basically flash memory with a USB interface in a device typically about the size of your thumb, provide a way to move files easily from computer to computer. When plugged into a USB port, these devices automount and behave like any other drive attached to the computer. Their small size and relatively large capacity, coupled with instant read-write ability, present security problems. They can easily be used by an individual with malicious intent to conceal the removal of files or data from the building or to bring malicious files into the building and onto the company network.

USB connectors come in a wide range of sizes and shapes. For mobile use there is USB mini, USB micro, and now USB Type-C, which is faster and reversible (does not care which side is up).

 EXAM TIP The various mobile device connection methods are conducive to performance-based questions, which means you need to pay attention to the scenario presented and choose the best connection methodology. Consider data rate, purpose, distances, and so forth in picking the best choice.

Mobile Device Management Concepts

Knowledge of *mobile device management (MDM)* concepts is essential in today's environment of connected devices. MDM began as a marketing term for a collective set of commonly employed protection elements associated with mobile devices. When viewed as a comprehensive set of security options for mobile devices, every corporation should have and enforce an MDM policy. The policy should require

- Device locking with a strong password
- Encryption of data on the device
- Device locking automatically after a certain period of inactivity
- The capability to remotely lock the device if it is lost or stolen
- The capability to wipe the device automatically after a certain number of failed login attempts
- The capability to remotely wipe the device if it is lost or stolen

Password policies should extend to mobile devices, including lockout and, if possible, the automatic wiping of data. Corporate policy for data encryption on mobile devices should be consistent with the policy for data encryption on laptop computers. In other words, if you don't require encryption of portable computers, then should you require it for mobile devices? There is not a uniform answer to this question because mobile devices are much more mobile in practice than laptops, and more prone to loss. This is ultimately a risk question that management must address: What is the risk and what are the costs of the options employed? This also raises a bigger question: Which devices should have encryption as a basic security protection mechanism? Is it by device type, or by user based on what data would be exposed to risk? Fortunately, MDM solutions exist, making the choices manageable.

 EXAM TIP   Mobile device management (MDM) is a marketing term for a collective set of commonly employed protection elements associated with mobile devices.

Application Management

Most mobile device vendors provide some kind of application store for finding and purchasing apps for their mobile devices. The vendors do a reasonable job of making sure that offered apps are approved and don't create an overt security risk. Yet many apps request access to various information stores on the mobile device as part of their business model. Understanding what access is requested and approved upon installation of apps is an important security precaution. These are all potential problems for mobile users concerned over data security and drive the need for a mobile *application management* solution. Your company may have to restrict the types of applications that can be downloaded and used on mobile devices. If you need very strong protection, your company can be very proactive and provide an enterprise application store where only company-approved applications are available, with a corresponding policy that apps cannot be obtained from any other source. Another method is to restrict apps through the use of an MDM solution, discussed in the previous section.

Content Management

Applications are not the only information moving to mobile devices. Content is moving as well, and organizations need a means of content management for mobile devices. For instance, it might be fine to have, and edit, some types of information on mobile devices, whereas other, more sensitive information should be blocked from mobile device access. *Content management* is the set of actions used to control content issues, including what content is available and to what apps, on mobile devices. Most organizations have a data ownership policy that clearly establishes their ownership rights over data, regardless of whether the data is stored on a device owned by the organization or a device owned by the employee. But enterprise content management goes a step further, examining what content belongs on specific devices and then using mechanisms to enforce these rules. Again, MDM solutions exist to assist in this security issue with respect to mobile devices.

Remote Wipe

Today's mobile devices are ubiquitous and are very susceptible to loss and theft. When enterprise data exists on these devices, management of the data, even if the device is lost is a concern. Further, it is unlikely that a lost or stolen device will be recovered by the owner, thus making even encrypted data stored on a device more vulnerable to decryption. If the thief can have your device for a long time, he can take all the time he wants to try to decrypt your data. Therefore, many companies prefer to just remotely wipe a lost or stolen device. *Remote wiping* a mobile device typically removes data stored on the device and resets the device to factory settings. There is a dilemma in the use of BYOD devices that store both personal and enterprise data. Wiping the device usually removes all data, both personal and enterprise. Therefore, a corporate policy that requires wiping a lost device may mean the device's user loses personal photos and data. The software controls for separate data containers, one for business and one for personal, have been proposed but are not a mainstream option yet.

For most devices, remote wipe can only be managed via apps on the device, such as Outlook for e-mail, calendar and contacts, and MDM solutions for all data. For Apple and Android devices, the OS also has the ability to set the device up for remote locking and factory reset, which effectively wipes the device.

Geofencing

Geofencing is the use of the Global Positioning System (GPS) and/or radio frequency identification (RFID) technology to create a virtual fence around a particular location and detect when mobile devices cross the fence. This enables devices to be recognized by others, based on location and have actions taken. Geofencing is used in marketing to send messages to devices that are in a specific area such as near a point of sale, or just to count potential customers. Geofencing has been used for remote workers, notifying management when they have arrived at remote work sites, allowing things like network connections to be enabled for them. The uses of geofencing are truly only limited by one's imagination.

Turning off geofencing is possible via the device. On Apple devices, just turn off location services. Although to completely prevent tracking of the device, you must turn off the radio using airplane mode.

Geolocation

Most mobile devices are now capable of using GPS for tracking device location. Many apps rely heavily on GPS location, such as device-locating services, mapping applications, traffic monitoring apps, and apps that locate nearby businesses such as gas stations and restaurants. Such technology can be exploited to track movement and location of the mobile device, which is referred to as *geolocation*. This tracking can be used to assist in the recovery of lost devices.

EXAM TIP Know the difference between geofencing and geolocation. These make great distractors.

Screen Locks

Most corporate policies regarding mobile devices require the use of the mobile device's *screen-locking* capability. This usually consists of entering a passcode or PIN to unlock the device. It is highly recommended that screen locks be enforced for all mobile devices. Your policy regarding the quality of the passcode should be consistent with your corporate password policy. However, many companies merely enforce the use of screen-locking. Thus, users tend to use convenient or easy-to-remember passcodes. Some devices allow complex passcodes. As shown in Figure 9-1, the device screen on the left supports only a simple iOS passcode, limited to four numbers, while the device screen on the right supports a passcode of indeterminate length and can contain alphanumeric characters.

Some more advanced forms of screen locks work in conjunction with device wiping. If the passcode is entered incorrectly a specified number of times, the device is automatically wiped. Apple has made this an option on iOS devices. Apple also allows remote locking of a device from the user's iCloud account. Android devices have a wide range of options including the use of apps as screen locks.

EXAM TIP Mobile devices require basic security mechanisms of screen locks, lockouts, device wiping, and encryption to protect sensitive information contained on them.

Push Notification Services

Push notification services are services that deliver information to mobile devices without a specific request from the device. Push notifications are used by a lot of apps in mobile devices to indicate that content has been updated. Push notification methods

Figure 9-1
iOS lock screens

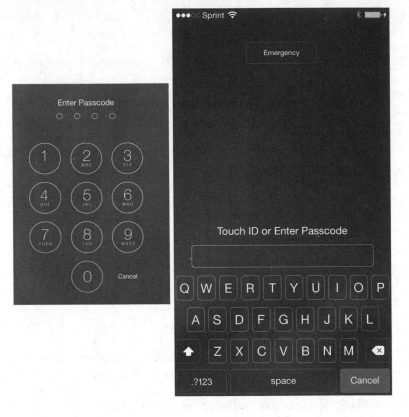

are typically unique to the platform, with Apple Push Notification service for Apple devices and Android Cloud to Device Messaging as examples. Many other back-end server services have similar server services for updating their content. As push notifications enable the movement of information from external sources to the device, this has some security implications, such as device location, and potential interaction with the device. For instance, it is possible to push the device to emit a sound, even if the sound is muted on the device.

Passwords and Pins

Passwords and *pins* are common security measures used to protect mobile devices from unauthorized use. These are essential tools and should be used in all cases, and mandated by company policy. The rules for passwords covered throughout this book apply to mobile devices as well, in fact maybe even more so. Having a simple gesture-based wipe on the screen as a pin can at times be discovered by looking at the oil pattern on the screen. If the only swipes are for unlocking the phone, then you will see the pattern and security is lost via this method. Either cleaning or dirtying the whole screen is the obvious solution.

Biometrics

Biometrics are used across a wide range of mobile devices as a means of access control. Many of these devices have less than perfect recognition, and various biometric sensors have proven to be hackable, as demonstrated in many security presentations at conferences. The newest biometric method, facial recognition, based on a camera image of the user's face while they are holding the phone, offers some promise, but similar concerns. Because these biometric sensors have been shown to be bypassable, they should be considered convenience features, not security features. Management policies should reflect this fact and should dictate that these methods not be relied upon for securing important data.

Context-Aware Authentication

Context-aware authentication is the use of contextual information such as who the user is, what resource they are requesting, what machine they are using, how they are connected, and so on, to make the authentication decision as to whether to permit the user access to the requested resource. The goal is to prevent unauthorized end users, devices, or network connections from being able to access corporate data. This approach can be used, for example, to allow an authorized user to access network-based resources from inside the office but deny the same user access if they are connecting via a public Wi-Fi network.

Containerization

Containerization on mobile devices refers to dividing the device into a series of containers, one container holding work-related materials, the other personal. The containers can separate apps, data … virtually everything on the device. Some mobile device management solutions support remote control over the work container. This enables a much stronger use case for mixing business and personal matters on a single device. Most MDM solutions offer the ability to encrypt the containers, especially the work-related container, providing another layer of protection for the data.

Storage Segmentation

On mobile devices, it can be very difficult to keep personal data separate from corporate data. *Storage segmentation* is similar to containerization in that it represents a logical separation of the storage in the unit. Some companies have developed capabilities to create separate virtual containers to keep personal data separate from corporate data and applications. For devices that are used to handle highly sensitive corporate data, this form of protection is highly recommended.

Full Device Encryption

Just as laptop computers should be protected with whole disk encryption to protect the data in case of loss or theft, you may need to consider *full device encryption* for mobile devices used by your organization's employees. Mobile devices are much more likely to be lost or stolen, so you should consider encrypting data on your organization's mobile devices. More and more, mobile devices are used when accessing and storing business-critical data or other sensitive information. Protecting the information on mobile devices is becoming a business imperative. This is an emerging technology, so you'll need to complete some rigorous market analysis to determine what commercial product meets your needs.

 EXAM TIP Protection of data on a mobile device is accomplished via multiple tools and methods. For the exam, pay careful attention to the details of the question to determine which protection method is applicable, as each defends against a different issue. Full device encryption offers completely different protection from screen locks, and the details of the question will steer you to the correct answer. Don't jump on the choice that appears to be obvious; take a moment to understand the details.

Enforcement and Monitoring

Your organization's policies regarding mobile devices should be consistent with your existing computer security policies. Your training programs should include instruction on mobile device security. Disciplinary actions should be consistent. Your monitoring programs should be enhanced to include monitoring and control of mobile devices.

Third-Party App Stores

Many mobile devices have manufacturer-associated app stores from which apps can be downloaded to their respective devices. These app stores are considered by an enterprise to be *third-party app stores*, as the contents they offer come from neither the user nor the enterprise in nature. Currently there are two main app stores, the Apple App Store for iOS devices and Google Play for Android devices. The Apple App Store is built on a principle of exclusivity, and stringent security requirements are highly enforced for the apps that are offered. Google Play has fewer restrictions, which has translated into some security issues stemming from apps. Managing what apps a user can add to the device is essential because many of these apps can create security risks for an organization. This issue becomes significantly more complex with employee-owned devices and access to corporate data stores. The segmentation options discussed earlier to separate work and personal spaces are offered on a limited number of mobile devices, so the ability to control this access becomes problematic. Virtually all segmentation is done via an additional app, the MDM solution. Devices permitted access to sensitive corporate information should be limited to company-owned devices, allowing more stringent control.

Rooting/Jailbreaking

A common hack associated with mobile devices is the jailbreak. *Jailbreaking* is a process by which the user escalates their privilege level, bypassing the operating system's controls and limitations. The user still has the complete functionality of the device, but also has additional capabilities, bypassing the OS-imposed user restrictions. There are several schools of thought concerning the utility of jailbreaking, but the important issue from a security point of view is that running any device with enhanced privileges can result in errors that cause more damage, because normal security controls are typically bypassed.

Rooting a device is a process by which OS controls are bypassed, and this is the term frequently used for Android devices. Whether the device is rooted or jailbroken, the effect is the same: the OS controls designed to constrain operations are no longer in play and the device can do things it was never intended to do, good or bad.

 EXAM TIP   Rooting is used to bypass OS controls on Android and jailbreaking is used to escalate privileges and do the same on iOS devices. Both processes stop OS controls from inhibiting user behaviors.

Sideloading

Sideloading is the process of adding apps to a mobile device without using the authorized store associated with the device. Currently, sideloading only works on Android devices, as Apple has not enabled execution of any apps except those coming through the App Store. Sideloading is an alternative means of instantiating an app on the device without having to have it hosted on the requisite app store. The downside, simply put, is that without the vendor app store screening, one is at greater risk of installing malicious software in the guise of a desired app.

Custom Firmware

Custom firmware is firmware for a device that has been altered from the original factory settings. This firmware can bring added functionality, but it can also result in security holes. Custom firmware should be used only on devices that do not have access to critical information.

Carrier Unlocking

Most mobile devices in the United States come locked to a carrier, while in other parts of the world they are unlocked, relying upon a subscriber identity module (SIM) for connection and billing information. This is a byproduct of the business market decisions made early in the mobile phone market lifecycle and has remained fairly true to date. If you have a carrier-locked device and you attempt to use a SIM from another carrier, the device will not accept it unless you unlock the device. *Carrier unlocking* is the process of programming the device to sever itself from the carrier. This is usually done through the inputting of a special key sequence that unlocks the device.

Firmware OTA Updates

Firmware essentially is software. It may be stored in a chip, but like all software, it sometimes requires updating. With mobile devices being literally everywhere, the scale does not support bringing the devices to a central location or connection for updating. *Firmware OTA (over the air) updates* are a solution to this problem. Similar to adding or updating an app from an app store, you can tap a menu option on a mobile device to connect to an app store and update the device firmware. All major device manufacturers support this model, for it is the only real workable solution.

Camera Use

Many mobile devices include on-board cameras, and the photos/videos they take can divulge information. This information can be associated with anything the camera can image—whiteboards, documents, even the location of the device when the photo/video was taken via geo-tagging (discussed in the upcoming "GPS Tagging" section). Another challenge presented by mobile devices is the possibility that they will be used for illegal purposes. This can create liability for the company if it is a company-owned device. Despite all the potential legal concerns, possibly the greatest concern of mobile device users is that their personal photos will be lost during a device wipe originated by the company.

SMS/MMS

Short Message Service (SMS) and *Multimedia Messaging Service (MMS)* are standard protocols used to send messages, including multimedia content in the case of MMS, to and from mobile devices over a cellular network. SMS is limited to short, text-only messages of fewer than 160 characters and is carried over the signaling path of the cellular network when signaling data is not being sent. SMS dates back to the early days of mobile telephony in the 1980s, while MMS is a more recent development designed to support sending multimedia content to and from mobile devices. Because of the content connections that can be sent via MMS in particular, and SMS in certain cases, it is important to at least address these communication channels in relevant policies.

External Media

External media refers to any item or device that can store data. From flash drives to hard drives, music players, smartphones, even smart watches, if it can store data, it is a pathway for data exfiltration. External media can also deliver malware into the enterprise. The risk is evident: these devices can carry data into and out of the enterprise, yet they have become synonymous with today's tech worker. The key is to develop a policy that determines where these devices can exist and where they should be banned. And then follow the plan with monitoring and enforcement.

USB OTG

Universal Serial Bus is a common method of connecting mobile devices to computers and other host-based platforms. Connecting mobile devices directly to each other required changes to USB connections. Enter *USB OTG (USB On-The-Go)*, an extension of USB technology that facilitates direct connection between USB OTG–enabled mobile devices. USB OTG allows those devices to switch back and forth between the roles of host and device, including deciding which provides power (host) and which consumes power across the interface. USB OTG also allows the connection of USB-based peripherals, such as keyboards, mice, and external storage, to mobile devices. Although USB OTG is relatively new, most mobile devices made since 2015 are USB OTG compatible.

Recording Microphone

Many of today's electronic devices, from smartphones and smartwatches to devices such as the online assistants from Amazon and Google, even toys, have the ability to record audio information. *Recording microphones* can be used to record conversations, collecting sensitive data without the parties under observation even being aware of the activity. As with other high-tech gadgets, the key is to determine the policy of where recording microphones can be used and the rules for their use.

GPS Tagging

Photos taken on mobile devices or with cameras that have GPS capabilities can have location information embedded in the digital photo. This is called GPS tagging by CompTIA, and *geo-tagging* by others. Posting photos with geo-tags embedded in them has its use, but it can also unexpectedly publish information that users may not want to share. For example, if you use your smartphone to take a photo of your car in the driveway and then post the photo on the Internet in an attempt to sell your car, if geo-tagging was enabled on the smartphone, the location of where the photo was taken is embedded as metadata in the digital photo. Such a posting could inadvertently expose where your home is located. There has been much public discussion on this topic, and geo-tagging can be disabled on most mobile devices. It is recommended that it be disabled unless you have a specific reason for having the location information embedded in the photo.

Wi-Fi Direct/Ad Hoc

Wi-Fi typically connects a Wi-Fi device to a network via a wireless access point. Other methods exist, namely Wi-Fi direct and Wi-Fi ad hoc. In *Wi-Fi direct*, two Wi-Fi devices connect to each other via a single-hop connection. In essence, one of the two devices acts as an access point for the other device. The key element is the single-hop nature of a Wi-Fi direct connection. Wi-Fi direct connects only two devices, but these two devices can be connected with all of the bells and whistles of modern wireless networking, including WPA2.

Wi-Fi direct uses a couple of services to establish secure connections between two devices. The first is Wi-Fi Direct Device and Service Discovery. This protocol provides a way for devices to discover each other based on the services they support before connecting. A device can see all compatible devices in the area and then narrow down the list to only devices that allow a specific service, say printing, before displaying to the user a list of available printers for pairing. The second protocol used is WPA2. This protocol is used to protect the connections and prevent unauthorized parties from pairing to Wi-Fi Direct devices, or intercepting communications from paired devices.

The primary difference with *Wi-Fi ad hoc* is that in the ad hoc network, multiple devices can communicate with each other, with each device capable of communicating with all other devices.

Tethering

Tethering is the connection of a device to a mobile device that has a means of accessing a network for the purpose of sharing the network access. Connecting a mobile phone to a laptop to charge the phone's battery is not tethering. Connecting a mobile phone to a laptop so that the laptop can use the phone to connect to the Internet is tethering. When you tether a device, you create additional external network connections.

Payment Methods

Twenty years ago, *payment methods* were cash, check, or charge. Today we have new intermediaries; smart devices with Near Field Communication (NFC) linked to credit cards offer a convenient alternative form of payment. While the actual payment is still a credit/debit card charge, the payment pathway is through the digital device. Utilizing the security features of the device, NFC, biometrics/pin, this form of payment has some advantages over the other methods as it allows additional specific security measures, such as biometric-based approval for the transaction, before accessing the payment method.

EXAM TIP This section contains topics that can be tested with performance-based questions. It is not enough to simply learn the terms associated with the material. You should be familiar with how to determine the correct enforcement and monitoring solution based on a given scenario. The scenario will provide the necessary information to determine the best answer to the question. You should understand the differences between the items—from app stores, to OS protections, to connectivity options—sufficiently to be able to select the correct item based on the stated scenario.

Deployment Models

When determining how to incorporate mobile devices securely in your organization, you need to consider a wide range of issues, including how security will be enforced, how all the policies will be enforced, and ultimately, what devices will be supported. You can choose from a variety of device deployment models to support your security strategy, ranging from a pure employee-owned model (BYOD) to a strict corporate-owned model, with several hybrid models in between. Each of these models has advantages and disadvantages.

EXAM TIP Be prepared for performance-based questions that ask you to determine the correct mobile deployment model based on a given scenario.

BYOD

The *bring your own device (BYOD)* deployment model has many advantages in business, and not just from the perspective of minimizing device cost for the organization. Users tend to prefer to have a single device rather than carry multiple devices. Users have less of a learning curve on devices they already know how to use or have an interest in learning. This model is popular in small firms and in organizations that employ a lot of temporary workers. The big disadvantage is that employees will not be eager to limit their use of their personal device based on corporate policies, so corporate control will be limited.

CYOD

The *choose your own device (CYOD)* deployment model is similar to BYOD in concept in that it gives users a choice in the type of device. In most cases, the organization constrains this choice to a list of acceptable devices that can be supported in the organization. Because the device is owned by the organization, it has greater flexibility in imposing restrictions on device use in terms of apps, data, updates, and so forth.

COPE

In the *corporate owned, personally enabled (COPE)* deployment model, employees are supplied a mobile device that is chosen and paid for by the organization, but they are given permission to use it for personal activities. The organization can decide how much choice and freedom employees get with regard to personal use of the device. This allows the organization to control security functionality while dealing with the employee dissatisfaction associated with the traditional method of device supply, corporate-owned business only (COBO).

Corporate-Owned

In the *corporate-owned* deployment model, also known as corporate-owned, business only (COBO), the company supplies employees with a mobile device that is restricted to company-only use. The disadvantage of this model is that employees have to carry two devices, one personal and one for work, and then separate functions between the devices based on purpose of use in each instance. The advantage is that the corporation has complete control over its devices and can apply any security controls desired without interference from other device functionality.

 EXAM TIP Expect performance-based questions for the different deployment models: BYOD, CYOD, COPE, and corporate-owned. The correct answer to the question will lie in the details of the scenario, so look carefully at the details to determine the best answer.

VDI

While it seems the deployment models are only associated with phones, this is really not the case, for personal computers can also be external mobile devices requiring connections at times. In the case of laptops, a *virtual desktop infrastructure (VDI)* solution can bring control to the mobile environment associated with non-corporate-owned equipment. The enterprise can set up virtual desktop machines that are fully security compliant and contain all the necessary applications needed by the employee, and then let the employee access the virtual machine via either a virtual connection or a remote desktop connection. This can solve most if not all of the security and application functionality issues associated with mobile devices. It does require an IT staff that is capable of setting up, maintaining, and managing the VDI in the organization, which is not necessarily a small task depending on the number of instances needed. Interaction with these VDI's can be accomplished easily on many of today's mobile devices because of their advanced screens and compute power.

Chapter Review

In this chapter, you became acquainted with the elements required to deploy mobile devices securely. The chapter opened with a description of the various communication connection methods. Specifically, the chapter covered cellular, Wi-Fi, SATCOM, Bluetooth, NFC, ANT, infrared, and USB connection methods. From there, the chapter explored the concepts of mobile device management. In this section the topics included application and content management, remote wiping, geofencing and geolocation, screen locks, push notification services, passwords and pins, biometrics, context-aware authentication, containerization, storage segmentation, and full device encryption. The chapter next examined the enforcement and monitoring requirements for third-party app stores, rooting/jailbreaking, sideloading, custom firmware, carrier unlocking, firmware OTA updates, camera use, SMS/MMS, external media, USB OTG, recording microphones, GPS tagging, Wi-Fi direct/ad hoc, tethering, and payment methods. The chapter closed with a discussion of the deployment models, including BYOD, CYOD, COPE, corporate-owned, and VDI.

Questions

To help you prepare further for the CompTIA Security+ exam, and to test your level of preparedness, answer the following questions and then check your answers against the correct answers at the end of the chapter.

1. Which of the following is a weakness of cellular technology?
    A. Multiple vendors in a nationwide network
    B. Less availability in rural areas
    C. Multiple cell towers in close proximity in urban areas
    D. Strong signals in areas of reasonable population
2. What frequency spectrum does Wi-Fi use?
    A. 1.9 Hz
    B. 2.7 GHz

    C. 5 GHz

    D. 5.4 GHz

3. What is the most common scenario for the use of satellite communications (SATCOM)?

    A. In densely populated areas

    B. Rural and remote areas or at sea

    C. As a backup for cell phone coverage

    D. Where line-of-sight issues exist

4. What frequency spectrum does Bluetooth use?

    A. 1.7 GHz

    B. 2.4 GHz

    C. 5 GHz

    D. 6.4 GHz

5. Which of the following is the data rate for Bluetooth 4.0?

    A. 768 Kbps

    B. 1 Mbps

    C. 3 Mbps

    D. 24 Mbps

6. Which of the following are the three modes supported by Bluetooth 4.0?

    A. Classic, low speed, high energy

    B. Enhanced data rate, backward compatible, high energy

    C. Classic, high speed, Low Energy

    D. Synchronous, high speed, Low Energy

7. What mechanism does Bluetooth use to establish a trust relationship?

    A. Pairing

    B. Kerberos

    C. PKI

    D. Public key

8. What is the primary use of Near Field Communication (NFC)?

    A. Establish radio communications over a short proximity

    B. Communication in sparsely populated areas

    C. Long-distance connectivity

    D. Communication in noisy industrial environments

9. Which of the following correctly describes ANT?

   A. It is similar to Bluetooth enhanced mode.

   B. It operates in the 5-GHz spectrum.

   C. It encrypts HTTP traffic.

   D. It functions well in the crowded 2.4-GHz spectrum.

10. What is a disadvantage of infrared (IR) technology?

    A. It has a high data rate.

    B. It cannot penetrate solid objects.

    C. It can penetrate walls.

    D. It uses a slow encryption technology.

11. What is the main security concern with Universal Serial Bus (USB) technology?

    A. It connects to cell phones for easy charging.

    B. It uses proprietary encryption.

    C. It automounts and acts like a hard drive attached to the computer.

    D. It uses older encryption technology.

12. Which of the following is not an element of a good Mobile Device Management (MDM) policy?

    A. The ability to decrypt data on the device

    B. The ability to lock the device if it is lost or stolen

    C. The ability to remotely wipe the device if it is lost or stolen

    D. The ability to wipe the device automatically after several failed login attempts

13. Which of the following correctly defines Mobile Device Management (MDM)?

    A. A marketing term for commonly employed protections for mobile devices

    B. The ability to lock mobile devices after a period of inactivity

    C. A method of locking devices with a strong password

    D. The set of standard protocols for communicating with mobile devices

14. Why is it important to establish policies governing remote wiping of mobile devices?

    A. Mobile devices typically do not mix personal and business data.

    B. Mobile devices are more easily secured.

    C. Thieves cannot decrypt mobile devices.

    D. They are more susceptible to loss than other devices.

15. What is the purpose of geofencing?

   A. It can be used to remotely wipe a lost device.

   B. It makes securing the mobile device simpler.

   C. It enables devices to be recognized by location and have actions taken.

   D. It can enforce device locking with a strong password.

Answers

1. **B.** A weakness of cellular technology is that it is less available in rural areas.

2. **C.** Wi-Fi uses both 2.4-GHz and 5-GHz frequency spectrums.

3. **B.** SATCOM usage is most common in rural and remote areas or at sea, where other technologies are not available.

4. **B.** Bluetooth uses the 2.4-GHz frequency spectrum.

5. **D.** 24 Mbps is the data rate for Bluetooth 4.0.

6. **C.** The three modes supported by Bluetooth 4.0 are classic, high speed, and Low Energy.

7. **A.** Bluetooth uses pairing to establish a trust relationship.

8. **A.** The primary use of NFC is to establish radio communications over a short proximity.

9. **D.** ANT functions well in the crowded 2.4-GHz spectrum.

10. **B.** A disadvantage of IR technology is that it cannot penetrate solid objects.

11. **C.** The main security concern with USB technology is that it automounts and acts like a hard drive attached to the computer.

12. **A.** Decryption of data on the device is not an element of a good MDM policy.

13. **A.** MDM is a marketing term for commonly employed protections for mobile devices.

14. **D.** It is important to establish policies governing remote wiping of mobile devices because they are more susceptible to loss than other devices.

15. **C.** The purpose of geofencing is to enable devices to be recognized by location and have actions taken.

CHAPTER 10

Implementing Secure Protocols

In this chapter, you will

- Learn to implement secure protocols for given scenarios
- Explore use cases for secure protocols

Protocols enable communication between components, independent of vendor, and act as a language that specifies how communications are to be conducted, and what can be communicated. As is true of many communications technologies, protocols have both secure and nonsecure versions. This chapter examines common protocols that can be secured and their use cases.

Certification Objective   This chapter covers CompTIA Security+ exam objective 2.6, Given a scenario, implement secure protocols. This exam objective is a good candidate for performance-based questions, which means you should expect questions in which you must apply your knowledge of the topic to a scenario. The best answer to a question will depend upon specific details in the scenario preceding the question, not just the question. The question may also involve tasks other than just picking the best answer from a list. Instead, it may involve actual simulation of steps to take to solve a problem.

Secure Protocols

Protocols act as common language allowing different components to talk using a common, known set of commands. *Secure protocols* are those that have built-in security mechanisms, so that by default security can be enforced via the protocol. Many different protocols exist, all of which are used to achieve specific communication goals.

EXAM TIP   During the exam, you should expect to be asked to implement common protocols and services when given a basic scenario. Pay very close attention to the protocol details and port numbers covered throughout this chapter!

DNSSEC

The *Domain Name Service (DNS)* is a protocol for the translation of names into IP addresses. When users enter a name such as www.example.com, the DNS system converts this name into the actual numerical IP address. DNS records are also used for e-mail delivery. The DNS protocol uses UDP over port 53 for standard queries, although TCP can be used for large transfers such as zone transfers. DNS is a hierarchical system of servers, from local copies of records, up through Internet providers to root-level servers. DNS is one of the primary underlying protocols used on the Internet and is involved in almost all addressing lookups. The problem with DNS is that requests and replies are sent in plaintext and are subject to spoofing.

DNSSEC (Domain Name System Security Extensions) is a set of extensions to the DNS protocol that, through the use of cryptography, enables origin authentication of DNS data, authenticated denial of existence, and data integrity, but does not extend to availability or confidentiality. DNSSEC records are signed so that all DNSSEC responses are authenticated but not encrypted. This prevents unauthorized DNS responses from being interpreted as correct. Authenticated denial of existence also allows a resolver to validate that a certain domain name does not exist.

Data transfers over UDP 53 are size limited to 512 bytes, and DNSSEC packets can be larger. For this reason, DNSSEC typically uses TCP port 53 for its work. It is possible to extend UDP packet size to 4096 to cope with DNSSEC, and this is covered in RFC 2671.

SSH

The *Secure Shell (SSH)* protocol is an encrypted remote terminal connection program used for remote connections to a server. SSH uses asymmetric encryption but generally requires an independent source of trust with a server, such as manually receiving a server key, to operate. SSH uses TCP port 22 as its default port.

 EXAM TIP SSH uses public-key cryptography for secure remote terminal access and was designed as a secure replacement for Telnet.

S/MIME

MIME (Multipurpose Internet Mail Extensions) is a standard for transmitting binary data via an e-mail. E-mails are sent as plaintext files, and any attachments need to be encoded so as to fit the plaintext format, and MIME specifies how this is done with base64 encoding. Because it is plaintext, there is no security associated with the attachments; they can be seen by any machine between sender and receiver. *S/MIME (Secure/Multipurpose Internet Mail Extensions)* is a standard for public key encryption and signing of MIME data in e-mails. S/MIME is designed to provide cryptographic protections to e-mails and is built into the majority of modern e-mail software to facilitate interoperability.

SRTP

The *Secure Real-time Transport Protocol (SRTP)* is a network protocol for securely delivering audio and video over IP networks. SRTP uses cryptography to provide encryption, message authentication and integrity, and replay protection to the RTP data.

LDAPS

LDAP is the primary protocol for transmitting directory information. Directory services may provide any organized set of records, often with a hierarchical structure, and are used in a wide variety of situations including Active Directory datasets. By default, Lightweight Directory Access Protocol (LDAP) traffic is transmitted insecurely. You can make LDAP traffic secure by using it with SSL/TLS, known as *LDAP Secure (LDAPS)*. Commonly, LDAP is enabled over SSL/TLS by using a certificate from a trusted certificate authority (CA).

LDAPS uses a TLS/SSL tunnel to connect LDAP services. Technically, this method was retired with LDAPv2, and replaced with Simple Authentication and Security Layer (SASL) in LDAPv3. SASL (which is not listed in the exam objectives) is a standard method of using TLS to secure services across the Internet.

 EXAM TIP LDAPS communication occurs over port TCP 636. LDAPS communication to a global catalog server occurs over TCP 3269. When connecting to ports 636 or 3269, SSL/TLS is negotiated before any LDAP traffic is exchanged.

FTPS

FTPS is the implementation of FTP over an SSL/TLS secured channel. This supports complete FTP compatibility, yet provides the encryption protections enabled by SSL/TLS. FTPS uses TCP ports 989 and 990.

SFTP

SFTP is the use of FTP over an SSH channel. This leverages the encryption protections of SSH to secure FTP transfers. Because of its reliance on SSH, it uses TCP port 22.

SNMPv3

The *Simple Network Management Protocol version 3 (SNMPv3)* is a standard for managing devices on IP-based networks. SNMPv3 was developed specifically to address the security concerns and vulnerabilities of SNMPv1 and SNMPv2. SNMP is an application layer protocol, part of the IP suite of protocols, and can be used to manage and monitor devices, including network devices, computers, and other devices connected to the IP network. All versions of SNMP require ports 161 and 162 to be open on a firewall.

SSL/TLS

Secure Sockets Layer (SSL) is an application of encryption technology developed for transport-layer protocols across the Web. This protocol uses public key encryption methods to exchange a symmetric key for use in confidentiality and integrity protection as well as authentication. The current version, V3, is outdated, having been replaced by the IETF standard *TLS*. All versions of SSL have been deprecated due to security issues, and in the vast majority of commercial servers employing SSL/TLS, SSL has been retired. Because of the ubiquity of the usage of the term, the term SSL will last for quite a while, but in function, it is now done via TLS.

Transport Layer Security (TLS) is an IETF standard for the employment of encryption technology and replaces SSL. Using the same basic principles, TLS updates the mechanisms employed by SSL. Although sometimes referred to as SSL, it is a separate standard. The standard port for SSL and TLS is undefined, for it depends upon what the protocol that is being protected uses; for example, port 80 for HTTP becomes port 443 when it is for HTTPS.

HTTPS

Hypertext Transfer Protocol Secure (HTTPS) is the use of SSL or TLS to encrypt a channel over which HTTP traffic is transmitted. Because of issues with all versions of SSL, only TLS is recommended for use. This uses TCP port 443. HTTPS is the most widely used method to secure HTTP traffic.

Secure POP/IMAP

Secure POP/IMAP listed under exam objective 2.6 basically refers to POP3 and IMAP (respectively) over an SSL/TLS session. Secure POP3 utilizes TCP port 995 and Secure IMAP uses TCP port 993. Encrypted data from the e-mail client is sent to the e-mail server over a SSL/TLS session. With the deprecation of SSL, TLS is the preferred protocol today. If e-mail connections are started in nonsecure mode, the STARTTLS directive tells the clients to change to the secure ports. The other mail protocol, SMTP uses port 25, and SSL/TLS encrypted SMTP uses port 465.

EXAM TIP IMAP uses port 143, but secure IMAP uses port 993. POP uses port 110, but secure POP uses port 995.

Use Cases

Protocols enable parties to have a common understanding of how communications will be handled and they define the expectations for each party. Since different use cases have different communication needs, different protocols are used in different use cases. Various IETF working groups have been working to standardize some general-purpose security protocols, ones that can be reused over and over instead of inventing new ones for each use case. SASL, introduced earlier in the chapter, is an example of such an effort;

SASL is a standardized method of invoking a TLS tunnel to secure a communication channel. This method is shown to work with a wide range of services, currently more than 15 and increasing.

This section examines some common use cases and the associated secure protocols used in them.

 EXAM TIP This section covers how the various protocols are used in different use cases. Given a use case on the exam, you need to be able to identify the correct protocol(s), as well as be able to do the same in reverse, identify use cases for a given protocol.

Voice and Video

Voice and *video* are frequently streaming media and, as such, have their own protocols for the encoding of the data streams. To securely transfer this material, you can use the *Secure Real-time Transport Protocol (SRTP)*, which securely delivers audio and video over IP networks. SRTP is covered in RFC 3711 (https://tools.ietf.org/html/rfc3711).

Time Synchronization

Network Time Protocol (NTP) is the standard for *time synchronization* across servers and clients. NTP is transmitted over UDP port 123. NTP has no assurance against a man-in-the-middle attack, and although this has raised concerns over the implications, to date, nothing has been done to secure NTP directly, or to engineer an out-of-band security check. If you are hypersensitive to this risk, you could enclose all time communications using a TLS tunnel, although this is not an industry practice.

E-mail and Web

E-mail and the *Web* are both native plaintext-based systems. As discussed previously in this chapter, HTTPS, which relies on SSL/TLS, is used to secure web connections. Use of HTTPS is widespread and common. Keep in mind that SSL is no longer considered secure. E-mail is a bit more complicated to secure, and the best option is via S/MIME, also discussed previously in this chapter.

File Transfer

Secure *file transfer* can be accomplished via a wide range of methods, ensuring the confidentiality and integrity of file transfers across networks. FTP is not secure, but as previously discussed, SFTP and FTPS are secure alternatives that can be used.

Directory Services

Directory services use LDAP as the primary protocol. When security is required, LDAPS is a common option, as described previously. Directory services are frequently found behind the scenes with respect to logon information.

Remote Access

Remote access is the means by which users can access computer resources across a network. Securing remote access can be done via many means, some for securing the authentication process and others for the actual data access itself. As with many situations that require securing communication channels or data in transit, organizations commonly use SSL/TLS to secure remote access. Depending upon the device being accessed, a variety of secure protocols exist. For networking equipment, such as routers and switches, SSH is the secure alternative to Telnet. For servers and other computer connections, access via VPN, or use of IPSec, is common.

Domain Name Resolution

Domain name resolution is performed primarily by the DNS protocol. DNS is a plaintext protocol and the secure version, DNSSEC, is not widely deployed as yet. For local deployments, DNSSEC has been available in Windows Active Directory domains since 2012. From an operational perspective, both TCP and UDP port 53 can be used for DNS, with the need of firewall protection between the Internet and TCP port 53 to prevent attackers from accessing zone transfers.

Routing and Switching

Routing and *switching* are the backbone functions of networking in a system. Managing the data associated with networking is the province of SNMPv3. SNMPv3 enables applications to manage data associated with networking and devices. Local access to the boxes may be accomplished by Telnet, although for security reasons SSH should be used instead.

Network Address Allocation

Managing *network address allocation* functions in a network requires multiple decision criteria, including the reduction of complexity and the management of device names and locations. SNMPv3 has many functions that can be employed to manage the data flows of this information to management applications that can assist administrators in network assignments.

IP addresses can be allocated either statically, which means manually configuring a fixed IP address for each device, or via DHCP, which allows the automation of assigning IP addresses. In some cases, a mix of static and DHCP is used. IP address allocation is part of proper network design, which is crucial to the performance and expandability of a network. Learn how to properly allocate IP addresses for a new network—and know your options if you run out of IP addresses.

 EXAM TIP The past several use cases are related but different. Pay careful attention to the exact wording of the question being asked when you have to choose among options such as domain name resolution, routing, and address allocation. These are all associated with IP networking, but they perform separate functions.

Subscription Services

Subscription services is the management of data flows to and from a system based on either a push (publish) or pull (subscribe) model. Managing what data elements are needed by which nodes is a problem that you can tackle by using directory services, such as LDAP.

Another use of subscription services is the Software as a Service (SaaS) model, where software is licensed on a subscription basis. The actual software is hosted centrally, commonly in the cloud, and user access is based on subscriptions. This is becoming a common software business model.

Chapter Review

In this chapter, you became acquainted with secure protocols used in an enterprise and the use cases to which they apply. Specifically, you examined DNSSEC, SSH, S/MIME, SRTP, LDAPS, FTPS, SFTP, SNMPv3, SSL/TLS, HTTPS, and Secure POP3/IMAP and then learned which protocols apply in use cases involving voice and video, time synchronization, e-mail, the Web, file transfer, directory services, remote access, domain name resolution, routing and switching, network address allocation, and subscription services. The key element of this chapter is that it prepared you to choose the correct secure protocols for use cases when given a scenario on the CompTIA Security+ exam.

Questions

To help you prepare further for the CompTIA Security+ exam, and to test your level of preparedness, answer the following questions and then check your answers against the correct answers at the end of the chapter.

1. Which of the following accurately describes the purpose of computer protocols?

    A. They provide security and scalability.

    B. They allow developers to use any programming language on any platform.

    C. They define the state of a virtual machine at a point in time.

    D. They act as a common language to allow different components to communicate.

2. What is the purpose of the DNS protocol?

    A. It provides a function for charging SaaS on a per-use basis.

    B. It translates names into IP addresses.

    C. It supports the networking infrastructure.

    D. It defines tenants in a public cloud.

3. A user reports to the help desk that he is getting "cannot resolve address" error messages from his browser. Which port is likely a problem on his firewall?

    A. 22

    B. 53

    C. 440

    D. 553

4. What is a weakness of the DNS protocol?

   A. Requests and replies are sent in plaintext.

   B. It doesn't provide billing standardization in cloud infrastructures.

   C. TCP can be used for large transfers such as zone transfers.

   D. Its encryption capabilities are slow.

5. Which of the following is a benefit of DNSSEC?

   A. Scalability

   B. Lower expenditures from operations capital (OpsCap) expenditures

   C. Enables origin authentication, authenticated denial of existence, and data integrity

   D. Availability and confidentiality

6. What is the Secure Shell (SSH) protocol?

   A. It is an encrypted remote terminal connection program used for remote connections to a server.

   B. It provides dynamic network address translation.

   C. It provides Software as a Service (SaaS).

   D. It provides snapshots of physical machines at a point in time.

7. What is the purpose of the Secure/Multipurpose Internet Mail Extensions (S/MIME) protocol?

   A. It is used in audio encryption.

   B. It optimizes the use of ports 80 and 443.

   C. It encrypts HTTP traffic.

   D. It provides cryptographic protections to e-mails.

8. What is the purpose of Secure Real-time Transport Protocol (SRTP)?

   A. It encrypts SMTP traffic.

   B. It encrypts port 22.

   C. It securely delivers audio and video over IP networks.

   D. It encrypts e-mails with a public key.

9. What is the purpose of Lightweight Directory Access Protocol Secure (LDAPS)?

   A. It leverages encryption protections of SSH to secure FTP transfers.

   B. It uses an SSL/TLS tunnel to connect LDAP services.

   C. It digitally signs DNS records.

   D. It provides both symmetric and asymmetric encryption.

10. Which port does FTPS use?

    A. 53

    B. 83

    C. 990

    D. 991

11. You are a security admin for XYZ company. You suspect that company e-mails using default POP and IMAP e-mail protocols and ports are getting intercepted while in transit. Which of the following ports should you consider using?

    A. Port 995 and 993

    B. Port 53 and 22

    C. Port 110 and 143

    D. Port 161 and 16240

12. What is the purpose of the Simple Network Management Protocol (SNMP)?

    A. It provides asymmetric encryption values.

    B. It achieves specific communication goals.

    C. It provides a common language for developers.

    D. It is used to manage devices on IP-based networks.

13. What is the purpose of the Secure Sockets Layer (SSL) protocol?

    A. It provides monitoring capabilities on IP networks.

    B. It provides static network address translation.

    C. It supports the implementation of a private cloud.

    D. It provides encryption for transport-layer protocols across the Web.

14. Which of the following correctly describes Transport Layer Security (TLS)?

    A. It replaces SSL.

    B. It extends SNMP.

    C. It provides Port Address Translation.

    D. It uses port 22 for encryption.

15. What is the purpose of HTTPS?

    A. To allow enumeration and monitoring of network resources

    B. To use SSL or TLS to encrypt a channel over which HTTP traffic is transmitted

    C. To implement single sign-on

    D. To enhance communication protocols

Answers

1. **D.** Computer protocols act as a common language to allow different components to communicate.

2. **B.** Domain Name Service (DNS) translates names into IP addresses.

3. **B.** Domain Name Service (DNS) uses TCP and UDP port 53 for standard queries and responses.

4. **A.** A major weakness of the DNS protocol is that requests and replies are sent in plaintext.

5. **C.** A major benefit of DNSSEC is that it enables origin authentication, authenticated denial of existence, and data integrity.

6. **A.** The SSH protocol is an encrypted remote terminal connection program used for remote connections to a server.

7. **D.** The purpose of the S/MIME protocol is to provide cryptographic protections to e-mail attachments

8. **C.** The purpose of SRTP is to deliver audio and video securely over IP networks.

9. **B.** LDAPS uses an SSL/TLS tunnel to connect LDAP services.

10. **C.** FTPS uses port 990.

11. **A.** The default POP3 and IMAP ports are 110 and 143 respectively. These are not secure. As a security admin, you should consider using secure POP using port 995 and secure IMAP using port 993.

12. **D.** The purpose of SNMP is to manage devices on IP-based networks.

13. **D.** The purpose of SSL is to provide encryption for transport-layer protocols across the Web.

14. **A.** TLS replaces SSL.

15. **B.** HTTPS uses SSL or TLS to encrypt a channel over which HTTP traffic is transmitted.

PART III

Architecture and Design

CHAPTER 11

Architecture Frameworks and Secure Network Architectures

In this chapter, you will

- Explore use cases and purpose for frameworks
- Examine the best practices for system architectures
- Explain the use of secure configuration guides
- Given a scenario, implement secure network architecture concepts

Architectures play an important role in the establishment of a secure enterprise. Implementing security controls on computer systems may seem to be independent of architecture, but it is the architecture that determines *which* security controls are implemented and how they are configured. Architectures are intended to be in place for a fairly long term and are difficult to change, so carefully choosing and implementing the correct architecture for an organization's computer systems up front makes them easier to maintain and more effective over time.

Certification Objective   This chapter covers CompTIA Security+ exam objectives 3.1, Explain use cases and purpose for frameworks, best practices and secure configuration guides, and 3.2, Given a scenario, implement secure network architecture concepts.

Objective 3.2 is a good candidate for performance-based questions, which means you should expect questions in which you must apply your knowledge of the topic to a scenario. The best answer to a question will depend upon specific details in the scenario preceding the question, not just the question. The questions may also involve tasks other than just picking the best answer from a list. Instead, you may be instructed to order things on a diagram, put options in rank order, match two columns of items, or perform a similar task.

Industry-Standard Frameworks and Reference Architectures

Industry-standard frameworks and *reference architectures* are conceptual blueprints that define the structure and operation of the IT systems in the enterprise. Just as in an architecture diagram that provides a blueprint for constructing a building, the enterprise architecture provides the blueprint and roadmap for aligning IT and security with the enterprise's business strategy. A framework is more generic than the specifics that are specified by an architecture. An enterprise can use both a framework describing the objectives and methodology desired, while an architecture will specify specific components, technologies, and protocols to achieve those design objectives.

There are numerous sources of frameworks and reference architectures, and they can be grouped in a variety of ways. The Security+ exam groups them in the following groups: regulatory, non-regulatory, national vs. international, and industry-specific frameworks.

Regulatory

Industries under governmental regulation frequently have an approved set of architectures defined by *regulatory* bodies. For example, the electric industry has the NERC (North American Electric Reliability Corporation) Critical Infrastructure Protection (CIP) standards. This is a set of 14 individual standards that, when taken together, drives a reference framework/architecture for this bulk electric system in North America. Most industries in the United States are regulated in one manner or another. When it comes to cybersecurity, more and more regulations are beginning to apply, from privacy, to breach notification, to due diligence and due care provisions.

Non-regulatory

Some reference architectures are neither industry specific nor regulatory, but rather are technology focused and considered *non-regulatory*, such as the National Institute of Standards and Technology (NIST) Cloud Computing Security Reference Architecture (Special Publication 500-299) and the NIST Framework for Improving Critical Infrastructure Cybersecurity (commonly known as the Cybersecurity Framework, or CSF). The latter being a consensus-created overarching framework to assist enterprises in their cybersecurity programs.

To give you a sense of how a non-regulatory framework is structured, consider the structure of the CSF. The CSF has three main elements: the Framework Core, the Framework Implementation Tiers, and the Framework Profiles. The Framework Core is built around five Functions: Identify, Protect, Detect, Respond, and Recover. The Framework Core then has Categories and Subcategories for each of these Functions, with Informative References to standards, guidelines, and practices matching the Subcategories. The Framework Implementation Tiers are a way of representing an organization's level of achievement, from Partial (Tier 1), to Risk Informed (Tier 2), to Repeatable (Tier 3), to Adaptive (Tier 4). These Tiers are similar to maturity model levels. The Framework

Profiles section describes current state of alignment for the elements and the desired state of alignment, a form of gap analysis. The NIST CSF is being mandated for government agencies, but is completely voluntary in the private sector. This framework has been well received, partly because of its comprehensive nature and partly because of its consensus approach, which created a usable document. NIST has been careful to promote its Cybersecurity Framework (CSF), not as a government-driven requirement but as an optional, non-regulatory based framework.

National vs. International

The U.S. federal government has its own cloud-based reference architecture for systems that use the cloud. Called the Federal Risk and Authorization Management Program (FedRAMP), this process is a government-wide program that provides a standardized approach to security assessment, authorization, and continuous monitoring for systems using cloud products and services.

One of the more interesting international frameworks has been the harmonization between the United States and European Union with respect to data privacy (U.S.) or data protection (EU) issues. The EU rules and regulations covering privacy issues and data protection were so radically different from those in the U.S. that they had to forge a special framework, originally called the U.S.-EU Safe Harbor Framework, to harmonize the concepts and enable U.S. and EU corporations to effectively do business with each other. Changes in EU law, coupled with EU court determinations that the U.S.-EU Safe Harbor Framework is not a valid mechanism to comply with EU data protection requirements when transferring personal data from the European Union to the United States, forced a complete refreshing of the methodology. The new privacy-sharing methodology is called the EU-U.S. Privacy Shield Framework and became effective in the summer of 2016.

Industry-Specific Frameworks

There are several examples of *industry-specific frameworks*. Industry-specific frameworks have been developed by entities within a particular industry—sometimes to address regulatory needs, other times because of industry-specific concerns or risks. Although some of these may not seem to be complete frameworks, they provide instructive guidance on how systems should be architected. Some of these frameworks are regulatory based, like the NERC CIP standards previously referenced. Another industry-specific framework is the HITRUST Common Security Framework (CSF) for use in the medical industry and enterprises that must address HIPAA/HITECH rules and regulations.

Benchmarks/Secure Configuration Guides

Benchmarks and *secure configuration guides* offer guidance for setting up and operating computer systems to a secure level that is understood and documented. As each organization may differ, the standard for a benchmark is a consensus-based set of knowledge designed to deliver a reasonable set of security across as wide a base as possible.

There are numerous sources for these guides, but three main sources exist for a large number of these systems. You can get benchmark guides from manufacturers of the software, from the government, and from an independent organization called Center for Internet Security (CIS). Not all systems have benchmarks, nor do all sources cover all systems, but searching for and following the correct configuration and setup directives can go a long way in establishing security.

The vendor/manufacturer guidance source is easy—go to the website of the vendor of your product. The government sources are a bit more scattered, but two solid sources are the NIST Computer Security Resource Center's National Vulnerability Database (NVD) National Checklist Program (NCP) Repository, https://nvd.nist.gov/ncp/repository. A different source is the U.S. Department of Defense's Defense Information Security Agency (DISA) Security Technical Implementation Guides (STIGs). These are detailed step-by-step implementation guides, a list of which is available at https://iase.disa.mil/stigs/Pages/index.aspx.

Platform/Vendor-Specific Guides

Setting up secure services is important to enterprises, and some of the best guidance comes from the manufacturer in the form of *platform/vendor-specific guides*. These guides include installation and configuration guidance, and in some cases operational guidance as well.

Web Server

Many different web servers are used in enterprises, but the market leaders are Microsoft, Apache, and nginx. By definition, *web servers* offer a connection between users (clients) and web pages (data being provided), and as such they are prone to attacks. Setting up any external-facing application properly is key to prevent unnecessary risk. Fortunately, for web servers, several authoritative and proscriptive sources of information are available to help administrators properly secure the application. In the case of Microsoft's IIS and SharePoint Server, the company provides solid guidance on the proper configuration of the servers. The Apache Software Foundation provides some information for its web server products as well.

Another good source of information is from the Center for Internet Security, as part of its benchmarking guides. The CIS guides provide authoritative, proscriptive guidance developed as part of a consensus effort between consultants, professionals, and others. This guidance has been subject to significant peer review and has withstood the test of time. CIS guides are available for multiple versions of Apache, Microsoft, and other vendors' products.

Operating System

The *operating system (OS)* is the interface for the applications that we use to perform tasks and the actual physical computer hardware. As such, the OS is a key component for the secure operation of a system. Comprehensive, proscriptive configuration guides for all major operating systems are available from their respective manufacturers, from the Center for Internet Security, and from the DoD DISA STIGs program.

Application Server

Application servers are the part of the enterprise that handle specific tasks we associate with IT systems. Whether it is an e-mail server, a database server, a messaging platform, or any other server, application servers are where the work happens. Proper configuration of an application server depends to a great degree on the server specifics. Standard application servers, such as e-mail and database servers, have guidance from the manufacturer, CIS, and STIGs. The less standard servers—ones with significant customizations, such as a custom set of applications written in-house for your inventory control operations, or order processing, or any other custom middleware—also require proper configuration, but the true vendor in these cases is the in-house builders of the software. Ensuring proper security settings and testing of these servers should be part of the build program so that they can be integrated into the normal security audit process to ensure continued proper configuration.

Network Infrastructure Devices

Network infrastructure devices are the switches, routers, concentrators, firewalls, and other specialty devices that make the network function smoothly. Properly configuring these devices can be challenging but is very important because failures at this level can adversely affect the security of traffic being processed by them. The criticality of these devices makes them targets, for if a firewall fails, in many cases there are no indications until an investigation finds that it failed to do its job. Ensuring these devices are properly configured and maintained is not a job to gloss over, but one that requires professional attention by properly trained personnel, and backed by routine configuration audits to ensure they stay properly configured. With respect to most of these devices, the greatest risk lies in the user configuration of the device via rulesets, and these are specific to each user and cannot be mandated by a manufacturer's installation guide. Proper configuration and verification is site specific and, many times, individual device specific. Without a solid set of policies and procedures to ensure this work is properly performed, these devices, while they may work, will not perform in a secure manner.

General Purpose Guides

The best general purpose guide is the CIS Controls, a common set of 20 security controls. This project began as a consensus project out of the U.S. Department of Defense and has over nearly 20 years morphed into the de facto standard for selecting an effective set of security controls. The framework is now maintained by the Center for Internet Security and can be found at https://www.cisecurity.org/controls/.

 EXAM TIP Determining the correct configuration information is done by the careful parsing of the scenario in the question. It is common for IT systems to be composed of multiple major components, web server, database server, and application server, so read the question carefully to see what is being requested. The scenario specifics matter as they will point to the best answer.

Defense-in-Depth/Layered Security

Secure system design relies upon many elements, a key one being *defense-in-depth*, or *layered security*. Defense-in-depth is a security principle by which multiple, differing security elements are employed to increase the level of security. Should an attacker be able to bypass one security measure, one of the overlapping controls can still catch and block the intrusion. For instance, in networking, a series of defenses, including access control lists, firewalls, intrusion detection systems, and network segregation, can be employed in an overlapping fashion to achieve protection.

Vendor Diversity

Having multiple suppliers creates *vendor diversity*, which reduces the risk from any single supplier. Having multiple operating systems, such as both Linux and Windows, reduces the total risk should something happen to one of them. Having only a monoculture raises risks when something specific to that environment fails. Having two vendors supply parts means that should one vendor run into any problem, you have a second vendor to turn to. Having two connections to the Internet provides redundancy, and having them operated by separate vendors adds diversity and lowers the risks even more.

Having multiple vendors in a layered defense also adds security through the removal of a single failure mode scenario. Two firewalls, from different vendors, will be more robust should one firewall have a flaw. The odds of the other vendor having the same exploitable flaw is relatively low, making your overall security higher, even during a vendor failure.

Control Diversity

Security controls are the mechanisms by which security functions are achieved. It is important to have *control diversity*, both administrative and technical, providing layered security to ensure the controls are effective in producing the desired results. One area frequently overlooked is the value of policies and procedures to guide workers' actions. If these policies and procedures are aligned with reducing risk, they act as controls. If there are technical controls backing up those policies, then policy violations may still not create a complete vulnerability, as the technical control can stop a problem from occurring. Total reliance on technical controls without policy provides insufficient security because users who lack policy guidance may utilize a system in ways not foreseen by the implementers of the technical controls, resulting in another risk.

Administrative

Administrative controls are those that operate on the management aspects of an organization. They include controls such as policies, regulations, and laws. Management activities such as planning and risk assessment are common examples of administrative controls. Having multiple independent, overlapping administrative controls can act as a form of layered security.

Technical

Technical controls are those that operate through a technological intervention in the system. Examples include elements such as user authentication (passwords), logical access controls, antivirus/anti-malware software, firewalls, intrusion detection and prevention systems, and so forth. Having multiple independent, overlapping technical controls, such as firewalls and access control lists to limit entry, is an example of layered security through technical controls.

 EXAM TIP Know the difference between administrative and technical controls. You may be given a list of controls and asked to choose which is an administrative control (or a technical control).

User Training

Users represent an essential link in the security defenses of an enterprise. Users also represent a major point of vulnerability, as most significant attacks have a user component. Whether it is phishing, spear phishing, clickbaiting, or some other form of manipulating a user, history has shown it will succeed a portion of the time, and the attacker only needs one person to let them in. The best defense is to implement a strong *user training* program that instructs users to recognize safe and unsafe computing behaviors. The best form of user training has proven to be user-specific training, training that is related to the tasks that individuals use computers to accomplish. That means you need separate training for executives and management.

Another line of defense is to monitor users and mandate retraining when you notice that their training is no longer effective (for example, they begin clicking unverified links in e-mails). And for users who continually have problems following training/retraining instructions, you need to add additional layers of protection to their machines so that if they are compromised, the damage is limited.

 EXAM TIP Users require security training that is specific to how they utilize computers in the enterprise, and they require periodic retraining.

Zones/Topologies

The first aspect of security is a layered defense. Just as a castle has a moat, an outside wall, an inside wall, and even a keep, so, too, does a modern secure network have different layers of protection. Different *zones/topologies* are designed to provide layers of defense, with the outermost layers providing basic protection and the innermost layers providing the highest level of protection. The outermost zone is the Internet, a free area, beyond any specific controls. Between the inner, secure corporate network and the Internet is an area where machines are considered at risk. A constant issue is that accessibility tends to be inversely related to level of protection, so it is more difficult to provide complete protection and unfettered access at the same time. Trade-offs between access and security are handled through zones, with successive zones guarded by firewalls enforcing ever-increasingly strict security policies.

DMZ

The zone that is between the untrusted Internet and the trusted internal network is called the *DMZ*, after its military counterpart, the demilitarized zone, where neither side has any specific controls. Within the inner, secure network, separate branches are frequently carved out to provide specific functional areas.

A DMZ in a computer network is used in the same way; it acts as a buffer zone between the Internet, where no controls exist, and the inner, secure network, where an organization has security policies in place. To demarcate the zones and enforce separation, a firewall is used on each side of the DMZ. The area between these firewalls is accessible from either the inner, secure network or the Internet. Figure 11-1 illustrates these zones as caused by firewall placement. The firewalls are specifically designed to prevent access across the DMZ directly, from the Internet to the inner, secure network.

Pay special attention to the security settings of network devices placed in the DMZ, and consider them to be compromised by unauthorized use at all times. Machines whose functionality is locked down to preserve security are commonly called hardened operating systems in the industry. This lock-down approach needs to be applied to the machines in the DMZ, and although it means that their functionality is limited, such precautions ensure that the machines will work properly in a less-secure environment.

Many types of servers belong in the DMZ, including web servers that are serving content to Internet users, as well as remote-access servers and external e-mail servers. In general, any server directly accessed from the outside, untrusted Internet zone needs to be in the DMZ. Other servers should not be placed in the DMZ. Domain name servers for your inner, trusted network and database servers that house corporate databases should not be accessible from the outside. Application servers, file servers, print servers—all of the standard servers used in the trusted network—should be behind both firewalls, along with the routers and switches used to connect these machines.

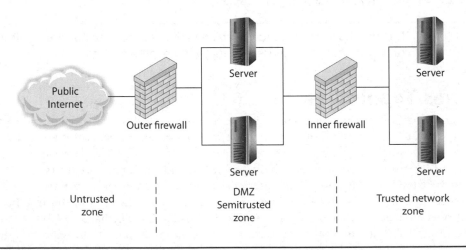

Figure 11-1 The DMZ and zones of trust

The idea behind the use of the DMZ topology is to force an outside user to make at least one hop in the DMZ before he can access information inside the trusted network. If the outside user makes a request for a resource from the trusted network, such as a data element from a database via a web page, then this request needs to follow this scenario:

1. A user from the untrusted network (the Internet) requests data via a web page from a web server in the DMZ.

2. The web server in the DMZ requests the data from the application server, which can be in the DMZ or in the inner, trusted network.

3. The application server requests the data from the database server in the trusted network.

4. The database server returns the data to the requesting application server.

5. The application server returns the data to the requesting web server.

6. The web server returns the data to the requesting user from the untrusted network.

This separation accomplishes two specific, independent tasks. First, the user is separated from the request for data on a secure network. By having intermediaries do the requesting, this layered approach allows significant security levels to be enforced. Users do not have direct access or control over their requests, and this filtering process can put controls in place. Second, scalability is more easily realized. The multiple-server solution can be made to be very scalable, literally to millions of users, without slowing down any particular layer.

 EXAM TIP DMZs act as a buffer zone between unprotected areas of a network (the Internet) and protected areas (sensitive company data stores), allowing for the monitoring and regulation of traffic between these two zones.

Extranet

An *extranet* is an extension of a selected portion of a company's intranet to external partners. This allows a business to share information with customers, suppliers, partners, and other trusted groups while using a common set of Internet protocols to facilitate operations. Extranets can use public networks to extend their reach beyond a company's own internal network, and some form of security, typically VPN, is used to secure this channel. The use of the term *extranet* implies both privacy and security. Privacy is required for many communications, and security is needed to prevent unauthorized use and events from occurring. Both of these functions can be achieved through the use of technologies described in this chapter and other chapters in this book. Proper firewall management, remote access, encryption, authentication, and secure tunnels across public networks are all methods used to ensure privacy and security for extranets.

 EXAM TIP An extranet is a semiprivate network that uses common network technologies (such as HTTP, FTP, and so on) to share information and provide resources to business partners. Extranets can be accessed by more than one company, because they share information between organizations.

Intranet

An *intranet* describes a network that has the same functionality as the Internet for users but lies completely inside the trusted area of a network and is under the security control of the system and network administrators. Typically referred to as campus or corporate networks, intranets are used every day in companies around the world. An intranet allows a developer and a user the full set of protocols—HTTP, FTP, instant messaging, and so on—that is offered on the Internet, but with the added advantage of trust from the network security. Content on intranet web servers is not available over the Internet to untrusted users. This layer of security offers a significant amount of control and regulation, allowing users to fulfill business functionality while ensuring security.

Two methods can be used to make information available to outside users: Duplication of information onto machines in the DMZ can make it available to other users. Proper security checks and controls should be made prior to duplicating the material to ensure security policies concerning specific data availability are being followed. Alternatively, *extranets* (discussed in the previous section) can be used to publish material to trusted partners.

 EXAM TIP An intranet is a private, internal network that uses common network technologies (such as HTTP, FTP, and so on) to share information and provide resources to organizational users.

Should users inside the intranet require access to information from the Internet, a proxy server can be used to mask the requestor's location. This helps secure the intranet from outside mapping of its actual topology. All Internet requests go to the proxy server. If a request passes filtering requirements, the proxy server, assuming it is also a cache server, looks in its local cache of previously downloaded web pages. If it finds the page in its cache, it returns the page to the requestor without needing to send the request to the Internet. If the page is not in the cache, the proxy server, acting as a client on behalf of the user, uses one of its own IP addresses to request the page from the Internet. When the page is returned, the proxy server relates it to the original request and forwards it on to the user. This masks the user's IP address from the Internet. Proxy servers can perform several functions for a firm; for example, they can monitor traffic requests, eliminating improper requests such as inappropriate content for work. They can also act as a cache server, cutting down on outside network requests for the same object. Finally, proxy servers protect the identity of internal IP addresses using NAT, although this function can also be accomplished through a router or firewall using NAT as well.

Wireless

Wireless networking is the transmission of packetized data by means of a physical topology that does not use direct physical links. This definition can be narrowed to apply to networks that use radio waves to carry the signals over either public or private bands, instead of using standard network cabling.

The topology of a wireless network is either hub and spoke or mesh. In the hub and spoke model, the wireless access point is the hub and is connected to the wired network. Wireless clients then connect to this access point via wireless, forming the spokes. In most enterprises, multiple wireless access points are deployed, forming an overlapping set of radio signals allowing clients to connect to the stronger signals. With tuning and proper antenna alignment and placement of the access points, administrators can achieve the desired areas of coverage and minimize interference.

The other topology supported by wireless is a mesh topology. In a mesh topology, the wireless units talk directly to each other, without a central access point. This is a form of ad hoc networking (discussed in more detail later in the chapter). A new breed of wireless access points have emerged on the market that combine both of these characteristics. These wireless access points talk to each other in a mesh network method, and once they have established a background network where at least one station is connected to the wired network, then wireless clients can connect to any of the access points as if the access points were normal access points. But instead of the signal going from wireless client to access point to wired network, the signal is carried across the wireless network from access point to access point until it reaches the master device that is wired to the outside network.

Guest

A *guest* zone is a network segment that is isolated from systems that guests should never have access to. Administrators commonly configure on the same hardware multiple logical wireless networks, including a guest network, providing separate access to separate resources based on login credentials.

Honeynets

As introduced in Chapter 7, a *honeynet* is a network designed to look like a corporate network, but is made attractive to attackers. A honeynet is a collection of honeypots, servers that are designed to act like real network servers but possess only fake data. A honeynet looks like the corporate network, but because it is known to be a false copy, all of the traffic is assumed to be illegitimate. This makes it easy to characterize the attacker's traffic and also to understand where attacks are coming from.

NAT

If you're thinking that a 32-bit address space that's chopped up and subnetted isn't enough to handle all the systems in the world, you're right. While IPv4 address blocks are assigned to organizations such as companies and universities, there usually aren't enough Internet-visible IP addresses to assign to every system on the planet a unique, Internet-routable IP address. To compensate for this lack of available IP address space, organizations use *Network Address Translation (NAT)*, which translates private (nonroutable) IP addresses into public (routable) IP addresses.

Certain IP address blocks are reserved for "private use," and not every system in an organization needs a direct, Internet-routable IP address. Actually, for security reasons, it's much better if most of an organization's systems are hidden from direct Internet access. Most organizations build their internal networks using the private IP address ranges (such as 10.1.1.X) to prevent outsiders from directly accessing those internal networks. However, in many cases those systems still need to be able to reach the Internet. This is accomplished by using a NAT device (typically a firewall or router) that translates the many internal IP addresses into one of a small number of public IP addresses.

For example, consider a fictitious company, ACME.com. ACME has several thousand internal systems using private IP addresses in the 10.X.X.X range. To allow those IP addresses to communicate with the outside world, ACME leases an Internet connection and a few public IP addresses, and deploys a NAT-capable device. ACME administrators configure all their internal hosts to use the NAT device as their default gateway. When internal hosts need to send packets outside the company, they send them to the NAT device. The NAT device removes the internal source IP address out of the outbound packets and replaces it with the NAT device's public, routable address and sends the packets on their way. When response packets are received from outside sources, the device performs NAT in reverse, stripping off the external, public IP address from the destination address field and replacing it with the correct internal, private IP address before sending the packets into the private ACME.com network. Figure 11-2 illustrates this NAT process.

In Figure 11-2, we see an example of NAT being performed. An internal workstation (10.10.10.12) wants to visit a website at 199.181.132.250. When the packet reaches the NAT device, the device translates the 10.10.10.12 source address to the globally routable 63.69.110.110 address, the IP address of the device's externally visible interface. When the website responds, it responds to the device's address just as if the NAT device had originally requested the information. The NAT device must then remember which internal workstation requested the information and route the packet to the appropriate destination.

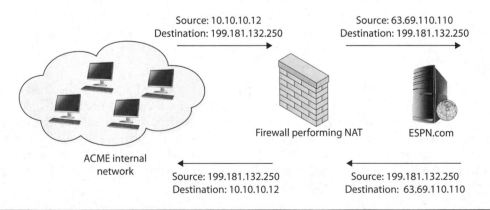

Source: 10.10.10.12
Destination: 199.181.132.250

Source: 63.69.110.110
Destination: 199.181.132.250

Firewall performing NAT

ESPN.com

ACME internal
network

Source: 199.181.132.250
Destination: 10.10.10.12

Source: 199.181.132.250
Destination: 63.69.110.110

Figure 11-2 Logical depiction of NAT

While the underlying concept of NAT remains the same, there are actually several different approaches to implementing NAT. For example:

- **Static NAT**   Maps an internal, private address to an external, public address. The same public address is always used for that private address. This technique is often used when hosting something you wish the public to be able to get to, such as a web server, behind a firewall.

- **Dynamic NAT**   Maps an internal, private IP address to a public IP address selected from a pool of registered (public) IP addresses. This technique is often used when translating addresses for end-user workstations and the NAT device must keep track of internal/external address mappings.

- **Port Address Translation (PAT)**   Allows many different internal, private addresses to share a single external IP address. Devices performing PAT replace the source IP address with the NAT IP address and replace the source port field with a port from an available connection pool. PAT devices keep a translation table to track which internal hosts are using which ports so that subsequent packets can be stamped with the same port number. When response packets are received, the PAT device reverses the process and forwards the packet to the correct internal host. PAT is a very popular NAT technique and in use at many organizations.

Ad Hoc

An *ad hoc* network is one where the systems on the network direct packets to and from their source and target locations without using a central router or switch. Windows supports ad hoc networking, although it is best to keep the number of systems relatively small. A common source of ad hoc networks is in the wireless space. From Zigbee devices that form ad hoc networks to Wi-Fi Direct, a wireless ad hoc network is one where the devices talk to each other without an access point or a central switch to manage traffic.

Ad hoc networks have several advantages. Without the need for access points, ad hoc networks provide an easy and cheap means of direct client-to-client communication. Ad hoc wireless networks can be easy to configure and provide a simple way to communicate with nearby devices when running cable is not an option.

Ad hoc networks have disadvantages as well. In enterprise environments, managing an ad hoc network is difficult because there isn't a central device through which all traffic flows. This means there isn't a single place to visit for traffic stats, security implementations, and so forth. This also makes monitoring ad hoc networks more difficult.

 EXAM TIP   This section has introduced a lot of zones and topologies, all of which are testable. You need to understand how to construct a network with each type because the exam may provide block diagrams and ask you to fill in the blanks. Know the differences among the zones/topologies and how each is configured.

Segregation/Segmentation/Isolation

As networks have become more complex, with multiple layers of tiers and interconnections, a problem can arise in connectivity. One of the limitations of the Spanning Tree Protocol (STP) is its inability to manage Layer 2 traffic efficiently across highly complex networks. STP was created to prevent loops in Layer 2 networks and has been improved to the current version of Rapid Spanning Tree Protocol (RSTP). RSTP creates a spanning tree within the network of Layer 2 switches, disabling links that are not part of the spanning tree. RSTP, IEEE 802.1w, provides a more rapid convergence to a new spanning tree solution after topology changes are detected. The problem with the spanning tree algorithms is that the network traffic is interrupted while the system recalculates and reconfigures. These disruptions can cause problems in network efficiencies and have led to a push for flat network designs, which avoid packet-looping issues through an architecture that does not have tiers.

One name associated with flat network topologies is network fabric, a term meant to describe a flat, depthless network. Network fabrics are becoming increasingly popular in data centers, and other areas of high traffic density, as they can offer increased throughput and lower levels of network jitter and other disruptions. While this is good for efficiency of network operations, this "everyone can talk to everyone" idea is problematic with respect to security.

Modern networks, with their increasingly complex connections, result in systems where navigation can become complex between nodes. Just as a DMZ-based architecture allows for differing levels of trust, the isolation of specific pieces of the network using security rules can provide differing trust environments. There are several terms used to describe the resulting architecture, including network *segmentation*, *segregation*, *isolation*, and *enclaves*. "Enclaves" is the most commonly used term to describe sections of a network that are logically isolated by segmentation at the networking protocol. The concept of segregating a network into enclaves can create areas of trust where special protections can be employed and traffic from outside the enclave is limited or properly screened before admission.

Enclaves are not diametrically opposed to the concept of a flat network structure; they are just carved-out areas, like gated neighborhoods, where one needs special credentials to enter. A variety of security mechanisms can be employed to create a secure enclave. Layer 2 addressing (subnetting) can be employed, making direct addressability an issue. Firewalls, routers, and application-level proxies can be employed to screen packets before entry or exit from the enclave. Even the people side of the system can be restricted by dedicating one or more systems administrators to manage the systems.

Enclaves are an important tool in modern secure network design. Figure 11-3 shows a network design with a standard two-firewall implementation of a DMZ. On the internal side of the network, multiple firewalls can be seen, carving off individual security enclaves, zones where the same security rules apply. Common enclaves include those for high-security databases, low-security users (call centers), public-facing kiosks, and the management interfaces to servers and network devices. Having each of these in its own zone provides for more security control. On the management layer, using a nonroutable IP address scheme for all of the interfaces prevents them from being directly accessed from the Internet.

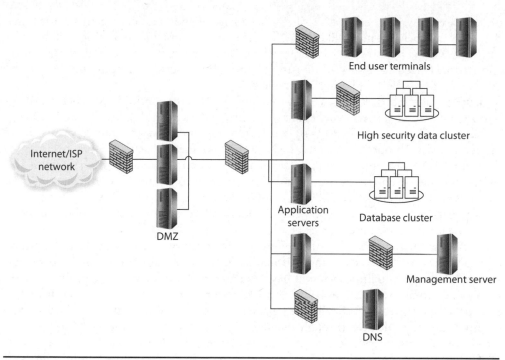

End user terminals

High security data cluster

Application servers

Database cluster

Management server

DMZ

Internet/ISP network

DNS

Figure 11-3   Secure enclaves

Physical

Physical segregation is where you have separate physical equipment to handle different classes of traffic, including separate switches, separate routers, separate cables. This is the most secure method of separating traffic, but also the most expensive. Organizations commonly have separate physical paths in the outermost sections of the network where connections to the Internet are made. This is mostly for redundancy, but it also acts to separate the traffic.

Contractual obligations sometimes require physical segregation of equipment, such as in the Payment Card Industry Data Security Standards (PCI DSS). Under PCI DSS, if an organization wishes to have a set of assets be considered out of scope with respect to the security audit for card number processing systems, then that set of assets must be physically segregated from the processing systems. Enclaves are an example of physical separation.

Logical (VLAN)

A LAN is a set of devices with similar functionality and similar communication needs, typically co-located and operated off a single switch. This is the lowest level of a network hierarchy and defines the domain for certain protocols at the data link layer for communication. A virtual LAN (VLAN) is a logical implementation of a LAN and allows computers connected to different physical networks to act and communicate as if they were on the same physical network. A VLAN has many of the same characteristic attributes of a LAN and behaves much like a physical LAN but is implemented using switches and software. This very powerful technique allows significant network flexibility, scalability, and performance and allows administrators to perform network reconfigurations without having to physically relocate or recable systems.

Trunking is the process of spanning a single VLAN across multiple switches. A trunk-based connection between switches allows packets from a single VLAN to travel between switches, as shown in Figure 11-4. Two trunks are shown in the figure: VLAN 10 is implemented with one trunk and VLAN 20 is implemented with the other. Hosts on different VLANs cannot communicate using trunks and thus are switched across the switch network. Trunks enable network administrators to set up VLANs across multiple switches with minimal effort. With a combination of trunks and VLANs, network administrators can subnet a network by user functionality without regard to host location on the network or the need to recable machines.

VLANs are used to divide a single network into multiple subnets based on functionality. This permits the accounting and marketing departments, for example, to share a switch because of proximity yet still have separate traffic domains. The physical placement of equipment and cables is logically and programmatically separated so that adjacent ports on a switch can reference separate subnets. This prevents unauthorized use of physically close devices through separate subnets that are on the same equipment. VLANs also allow a network administrator to define a VLAN that has no users and map all of the unused ports to this VLAN (some managed switches allow administrators to simply disable unused ports as well). Then, if an unauthorized user should gain access

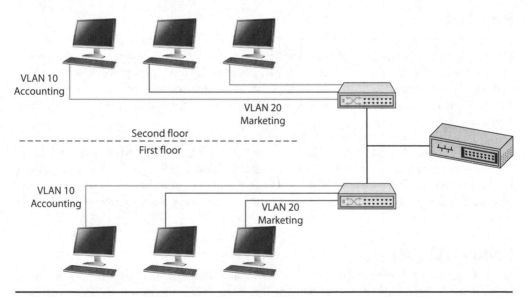

Figure 11-4 VLANs and trunks

to the equipment, that user will be unable to use unused ports, as those ports will be securely defined to nothing. Both a purpose and a security strength of VLANs is that systems on separate VLANs cannot directly communicate with each other.

EXAM TIP   Physical vs. logical segregation: Physical segregation requires creating two or more physical networks, each with its own servers, switches, and routers. Logical segregation uses one physical network with firewalls and/or routers separating and facilitating communication between the logical networks.

Virtualization

Virtualization offers server isolation logically while still enabling physical hosting. Virtual machines allow you to run multiple servers on a single piece of hardware, enabling the use of more powerful machines in the enterprise at higher rates of utilization. By definition, a virtual machine provides a certain level of isolation from the underlying hardware, operating through a hypervisor layer. If a single piece of hardware has multiple virtual machines running, they are isolated from each other by the hypervisor layer as well. Virtualization is covered in depth in Chapter 15.

Air Gaps

Air gaps is the term used to describe when no data path exists between two networks that are not connected in any way except via a physical air gap between them. Physically or logically there is no direct path between them. It is a conceptual term that refers to isolating a secure network or computer from all other networks (particularly the Internet) and computers by ensuring that it can't establish external communication, the goal of which is to prevent any possibility of unauthorized access. Air gaps are considered by some to be a security measure, but this topology has several weaknesses. First, sooner or later, some form of data transfer is needed between air-gapped systems. When this happens, administrators transfer files via USB-connected external media, which effectively breaches the air gap.

Air gaps as a security measure fail because people can move files and information between the systems with external devices. Second, and because of the false sense of security imparted by the air gap, these transfers are not subject to serious security checks. About the only thing that air gaps can prevent are automated connections such as reverse shells and other connections used to contact servers outside the network from within.

EXAM TIP   Air gaps have to be architected into a system to exist in reality, and then strictly enforced with near-draconian policies. The bottom line is that they are hard to control, and when they break down, the failures can be significant.

Tunneling/VPN

Tunneling/virtual private networking (VPN) technologies allow two networks to connect surely across an unsecure stretch of network. These technologies are achieved with protocols discussed in multiple chapters throughout this book, such as IPsec, L2TP, SSL/TLS, and SSH. At this level, understand that these technologies enable two sites, such as a remote worker's home network and the corporate network, to communicate across unsecure networks, including the Internet, at a much lower risk profile. The two main uses for tunneling/VPN technologies are site-to-site communications and remote access to a network.

Site-to-Site

Site-to-site communication links are network connections that connect two or more networks across an intermediary network layer. In almost all cases, this intermediary network is the Internet or some other public network. To secure the traffic that is going from site to site, encryption in the form of either a VPN or a tunnel can be employed. In essence, this makes all of the packets between the endpoints in the two networks unreadable to nodes between the two sites.

Remote Access

Remote access is when a user requires access to a network and its resources, but is not able to make a physical connection. Remote access via a tunnel or VPN has the same effect as directly connecting the remote system to the network—it's as if the remote user just plugged a network cable directly into her machine. So, if you do not trust a machine to be directly connected to your network, you should not use a VPN or tunnel, for if you do, that is what you are logically doing.

 EXAM TIP   Tunneling/VPN technology is a means of extending a network either to include remote users or to connect two sites. Once the connection is made, it is like the connected machines are locally on the network.

Security Device/Technology Placement

The placement of each security device is related to the purpose of the device and the environment that it requires. (See Chapter 1 for deeper coverage of many of the security devices discussed in this section.) Technology placement has similar restrictions; these devices must be in the flow of the network traffic that they use to function. If an enterprise has two Internet connections, with half of the servers going through one connection and the other half going through the other connection, then at least two of each technology that is to be deployed between the Internet and the enterprise is needed, with one each for placement between the connection and the Internet. As we will see with different devices, the placement needs are fairly specific and essential for the devices to function properly.

Sensors

Sensors are devices that capture data and act upon it. There are multiple kinds of sensors and various placement scenarios. Each type of sensor is different, and no single type of sensor can sense everything. Sensors can be divided into two types based on where they are placed: network or host. Network-based sensors can provide coverage across multiple machines, but are limited by traffic engineering to systems that packets pass the sensor. They may have issues with encrypted traffic, for if the packet is encrypted and they cannot read it, they are unable to act upon it. Lastly, network-based sensors have limited knowledge of what hosts they see are doing, so the sensor analysis is limited in its ability to make precise decisions on the content. Host-based sensors provide more specific and accurate information in relation to what the host machine is seeing and doing, but are limited to just that host. A good example of the differences in sensor placement and capabilities is seen in the host-based intrusion detection and network-based intrusion detection systems.

Sensors have several different actions they can take: they can report on what they observe, they can use multiple readings to match a pattern and create an event, and they can act based on proscribed rules. Not all sensors can take all actions, and the application of specific sensors is part of a monitoring and control deployment strategy. This deployment strategy must consider network traffic engineering, the scope of action, and other limitations.

Collectors

Collectors are sensors, or concentrators that combine multiple sensors that collect data for processing by other systems. Collectors are subject to the same placement rules and limitations as sensors.

Correlation Engines

Correlation engines take sets of data and match the patterns against known patterns. They are a crucial part of a wide range of tools, such as antivirus or intrusion detection devices, to provide a means of matching a collected pattern of data against a set of patterns associated with known issues. Should incoming data match one of the stored profiles, the engine can alert or take other actions. Correlation engines are limited by the strength of the match when you factor in time and other variants that create challenges in a busy traffic environment. The placement of correlation engines is subject to the same issues as all other network placements; the traffic you desire to study must pass the sensor feeding the engine. If the traffic is routed around the sensor, the engine will fail.

Filters

Packet *filters* process packets at a network interface based on source and destination addresses, ports, or protocols, and either allow passage or block them based on a set of rules. Packet filtering is often part of a firewall program for protecting a local network from unwanted traffic. The filters are local to the traffic being passed, so they must be placed inline with a system's connection to the network and Internet, or else they will not be able to see traffic to act upon it.

Another example of a filter is a spam filter. Spam filters work like all other filters; they act as a sorter—good e-mail to your inbox, spam to the trash. There are many cases where you wish to divide a sample into conforming, which are permitted, and non-conforming, which are blocked.

Proxies

Proxies are servers that act as a go-between between clients and other systems; in essence, they are designed to act on the clients' behalf. See Chapter 6 for in-depth coverage of proxies. This means that the proxies must be in the normal path of network traffic for the system being proxied. As networks become segregated, the proxy placement must be such that it is in the natural flow of the routed traffic for it to intervene on the clients' behalf.

Firewalls

Firewalls at their base level are policy enforcement engines that determine whether traffic can pass or not based on a set of rules. Regardless of the type of firewall, the placement is easy: firewalls must be inline with the traffic they are regulating. If there are two paths for data to get to a server farm, then either one firewall must have both paths go through it or two firewalls are necessary. Firewalls are commonly placed between network segments, enabling them to examine traffic that enters or leaves a segment. This gives them the ability to isolate a segment while avoiding the cost or overhead of doing this segregation on each and every system. Chapter 6 covers firewalls in detail.

VPN Concentrators

A *VPN concentrator* takes multiple individual VPN connections and terminates them into a single network point. This single endpoint is what should define where the VPN concentrator is located in the network. The VPN side of the concentrator is typically outward facing, exposed to the Internet. The internal side of the device should terminate in a network segment where you would allow all of the VPN users to connect their machines directly. If you have multiple different types of VPN users with different security profiles and different connection needs, then you might have multiple concentrators with different endpoints that correspond to appropriate locations inside the network.

SSL Accelerators

An *SSL accelerator* is used to provide SSL/TLS encryption/decryption at scale, removing the load from web servers. Because of this, it needs to be placed between the appropriate web servers and the clients they serve, typically Internet facing.

Load Balancers

Load balancers take incoming traffic from one network location and distribute it across multiple network operations. A load balancer must reside in the traffic path between the requestors of a service and the servers that are providing the service. The role of the load balancer is to manage the workloads on multiple systems by distributing the traffic to and from them. To do this, it must be located within the traffic pathway. For reasons of efficiency, load balancers are typically located close to the systems that they are managing the traffic for.

DDoS Mitigator

DDoS mitigators by nature must exist outside the area that they are protecting. They act as an umbrella, shielding away the unwanted DDoS packets. As with all of the devices in this section, the DDoS mitigator must reside in the network path of the traffic it is shielding the inner part of the networks from. Because the purpose of the DDoS mitigator is to stop unwanted DDoS traffic, it should be positioned at the very edge of the network, before other devices.

Aggregation Switches

An *aggregation switch* is a switch that provides connectivity for several other switches. Think of it as a one-to-many type of device. It's the one switch that many other switches connect to. It is placed upstream from the multitude of devices and takes the place of a router or a much larger switch. Assume you have ten users on each of three floors. You can place a 16-port switch on each floor, and then consume three router ports. Now make that ten floors of ten users, and you are consuming ten ports on your router for the ten floors. An aggregate switch will reduce this to one connection, while providing faster switching between users than the router would. These traffic management devices are located based on network layout topologies to limit unnecessary router usage.

Taps and Port Mirror

Most enterprise switches have the ability to copy the activity of one or more ports through a Switch Port Analyzer (SPAN) port, also known as a *port mirror*. This traffic can then be sent to a device for analysis. Port mirrors can have issues when traffic levels get heavy as the aggregate SPAN traffic can exceed the throughput of the device. For example, a 16-port switch, with each port running at 100 Mbps, can have traffic levels of 1.6 GB if all circuits are maxed, which gives you a good idea of why this technology can have issues in high-traffic environments.

A *Test Access Point (TAP)* is a passive signal-copying mechanism installed between two points on the network. The TAP can copy all packets it receives, rebuilding a copy of all messages. TAPs provide the one distinct advantage of not being overwhelmed by traffic levels, at least not in the process of data collection. The primary disadvantage is that a TAP is a separate piece of hardware and adds to network costs.

 EXAM TIP To work properly, every security device covered in this section must be placed inline with the traffic flow that it is intended to interact with. If there are network paths around the device, it will not perform as designed. Understanding the network architecture is important when placing devices.

PART III

SDN

Software-defined networking (SDN) is a relatively new method of managing the network control layer separate from the data layer, and under the control of computer software. This enables network engineers to reconfigure the network by making changes via a software program, without the need for re-cabling. SDN allows for network function deployment via software, so you could program a firewall between two segments by telling the SDN controllers to make the change. They then feed the appropriate information into switches and routers to have the traffic pattern switch, adding the firewall into the system. SDN is relatively new and just beginning to make inroads into local networks, but the power it presents to network engineers is compelling, enabling them to reconfigure networks at the speed of a program executing change files.

Chapter Review

This first half of this chapter presented use cases and purpose for frameworks, best practices, and secure configuration guides. You first became acquainted with industry-standard frameworks and reference architectures, including regulatory, non-regulatory, national, international, and industry-specific frameworks. You then learned about benchmarks and secure configuration guides, starting with platform/vendor-specific guides for web servers, operating systems, application servers, and network infrastructure devices, and then general purpose guides. Next, the chapter presented defense-in-depth/layered security, describing the roles of vendor diversity, control diversity (both technical and administrative), and user training in support of adding depth to your security posture.

The latter half of the chapter presented secure network architecture concepts, beginning with zones and topologies. The topics in this section included examination of the zones/topologies of the following architectural elements; DMZ, extranet, intranet, wireless, guest, honeynets, NAT, and ad hoc network designs. The concepts of segregation/segmentation/isolation, both physical and logical, were covered. Also covered were virtualization and air gaps. The use of tunneling or VPN to create site-to-site connections, or remote access was presented. You also learned about security device and technology placement, including the placement of sensors, collectors, correlation engines, filters, proxies, firewalls, VPN concentrators, SSL accelerators, load balancers, DDoS mitigators, aggregation switches, TAPs, and port mirrors. The chapter wrapped up with a look at software-defined networking, a relatively new network architecture concept.

Questions

To help you prepare further for the CompTIA Security+ exam, and to test your level of preparedness, answer the following questions and then check your answers against the correct answers at the end of the chapter.

1. From the Internet going into the network, which of the following is the first device a packet would encounter (assuming all devices are present)?

   A. Firewall

   B. Load balancer

    C. DMZ

    D. DDoS mitigator

2. Tunneling is used to achieve which of the following?

    A. Eliminate an air gap

    B. Connect users to a honeynet

    C. Remote access from users outside the building

    D. Intranet connections to the DMZ

3. Connections to third-party content associated with your business, such as a travel agency website for corporate travel, is an example of which of the following?

    A. Intranet

    B. Extranet

    C. Guest network

    D. Proxy service

4. Which of the following is not a standard practice to support defense-in-depth?

    A. Vendor diversity

    B. User diversity

    C. Control diversity

    D. Redundancy

5. Industry-standard frameworks are useful for which of the following purposes?

    A. Aligning with an audit-based standard

    B. Aligning IT and security with the enterprise's business strategy

    C. Providing high-level organization over processes

    D. Creating diagrams to document system architectures

6. Which of the following represents the greatest risk if improperly configured?

    A. Operating system on a server

    B. Web server

    C. Application server

    D. Network infrastructure device

7. What is the primary purpose of a DMZ?

    A. Prevent direct access to secure servers from the Internet

    B. Provide a place for corporate servers to reside so they can access the Internet

    C. Create a safe computing environment next to the Internet

    D. Slow down traffic coming and going to the network

8. If you wish to monitor 100 percent of the transmissions from your customer service representatives to the Internet and other internal services, which is the best tool?

   A. SPAN port

   B. TAP

   C. Mirror port

   D. Aggregator switches

9. For traffic coming from the Internet into the network, which of the following is the correct order in which devices should receive the traffic?

   A. – Firewall – DMZ – SSL accelerator – load balancer – web server

   B. – Firewall – DMZ – firewall – load balancer – SSL accelerator – web server

   C. – DMZ – firewall – SSL accelerator – load balancer – web server

   D. – Firewall – DMZ – firewall – SSL accelerator – load balancer – web server

10. Which type of network enables networking without intervening network devices?

    A. Ad hoc

    B. Honeynet

    C. NAT

    D. Intranet

11. Air gaps offer protection from which of the following?

    A. Malware

    B. Ransomware

    C. Reverse shells

    D. Pornography or other not safe for work (NSFW) materials

12. For traffic coming from the Internet into the network, which of the following is the correct order in which devices should receive the traffic?

    A. – Firewall – DMZ – proxy server – client

    B. – Firewall – DMZ – firewall – DDoS mitigator – web server

    C. – DMZ – Firewall – load balancer – web server

    D. – Firewall – DMZ – firewall – load balancer – database server

13. Your boss asks you to set up a new server. Where can you get the best source of information on configuration for secure operations?

    A. User group website for the server

    B. Secure configuration guide from the Center for Internet Security

    C. Ask the senior admin for his notes from the last install

    D. A copy of the configuration files of another server in your enterprise

14. To have the widest effect on security, which of the following controls should be addressed and maintained on a regular basis?

    A. User training

    B. Vendor diversity

    C. Administrative controls

    D. Technical controls

15. VLANs provide which of the following?

    A. Physical segregation

    B. Physical isolation

    C. Logical segmentation

    D. All of the above

Answers

1. **D.** When present, the DDoS mitigator is first in the chain of devices to screen incoming traffic. It blocks the DDoS traffic that would otherwise strain the rest of the network.

2. **C.** Remote access is one of the primary uses of tunneling and VPNs.

3. **B.** External network connections to sections of a third-party network as a part of your business's network is an extranet.

4. **B.** Although diversity among users can have many benefits, defense-in-depth isn't one of them. All of the other choices are valid components of a defense-in-depth program.

5. **B.** Industry frameworks provide a method to align IT and security with the enterprise's business strategy.

6. **D.** When improperly configured, network infrastructure devices can allow unauthorized access to traffic traversing all devices they carry traffic to and from.

7. **A.** The primary purpose of a DMZ is to provide separation between the untrusted zone of the Internet and the trusted zone of enterprise systems. It does so by preventing direct access to secure servers from the Internet.

8. **B.** A Test Access Point (TAP) is required to monitor 100 percent of the transmissions from your customer service representatives to the Internet and other internal services.

9. **D.** Firewall – DMZ – Firewall – SSL accelerator – load balancer – web server. A is missing the second firewall, B has the load balancer and SSL accelerator in the wrong order, and C is missing the first firewall.

10. **A.** An ad hoc network is constructed without central networking equipment and supports direct machine-to-machine communications.

PART III

11. **C.** Reverse shells or other items that call out of a network are stopped by the air gap. All of the other problems can occur by connection such as a USB.

12. **D.** Firewall – DMZ – firewall – load balancer – database server. A has a missing second firewall, B has the DDoS mitigator in the wrong position, and C is missing the first firewall.

13. **B.** The Center for Internet Security (CIS) maintains a collection of peer-reviewed, consensus-driven guidance for secure system configuration. All of the other options represent choices with potential errors from unvetted or previous bad choices.

14. **A.** User training has the widest applicability, because users touch all systems, while the other controls only touch some of them. Users also require maintenance in the form of retraining as they lose their focus on security over time.

15. **C.** VLANs are logical segmentation devices. They have no effect on the physical separation of traffic.

Secure Systems Design and Deployment

In this chapter, you will

- Learn to implement secure systems design for a given scenario
- Understand the importance of secure staging development concepts

System design has a great effect on the security of a system once it is in operation. Errors in system design are very difficult to correct later, and almost impossible once a system is in production. Ensuring that security concerns are considered and addressed during the design phase of a project will go a long way in establishing a system that can be secured using security controls.

Certification Objective   This chapter covers CompTIA Security+ exam objectives 3.3, Given a scenario, implement secure systems design, and 3.4, Explain the importance of secure staging deployment concepts.

These exam objectives are good candidates for performance-based questions, which means you should expect questions in which you must apply your knowledge of the topic to a scenario. The best answer to a question will depend upon specific details in the scenario preceding the question, not just the question. The question may also involve tasks other than just picking the best answer from a list. Instead, you may be instructed to order things on a diagram, put options in rank order, match two columns of items, or perform a similar task.

Hardware/Firmware Security

Hardware, in the form of servers, workstations, and even mobile devices, can represent a weakness or vulnerability in the security system associated with an enterprise. While you can easily replace hardware if it is lost or stolen, you can't retrieve the information the lost or stolen hardware contains. You can safeguard against complete loss of data through backups, but this does little in the way of protecting it from disclosure to an unauthorized party who comes into possession of your lost or stolen hardware. You can implement software measures such as encryption to hinder the unauthorized party's access to the data, but these measures also have drawbacks in the form of scalability and key distribution.

There are some hardware protection mechanisms that your organization should consider employing to safeguard servers, workstations, and mobile devices from theft, such as placing cable locks on mobile devices and using locking cabinets and safes to secure portable media, USB drives, and CDs/DVDs.

A lot of hardware has firmware that provides the necessary software instructions to facilitate the hardware functionality. *Firmware* is a source of program code for the system, and if an adversary changes the firmware, this can result in an open attack vector into the trusted core of the enterprise. This is because most systems will trust the firmware of a trusted system. Monitoring and managing firmware security is a time-intensive task because few tools exist for that purpose, and even fewer for automation of the task. This makes physical security of the system and its peripheral hardware important.

 EXAM TIP Physical security is an essential element of a security plan. Unauthorized access to hardware and networking components can make many security controls ineffective.

FDE/SED

Full disk encryption (FDE) and *self-encrypting disks (SEDs)* are methods of implementing cryptographic protection on hard disk drives and other similar storage media with the express purpose of protecting the data even if the disk drive is removed from the machine. Portable machines, such as laptops, have a physical security weakness in that they are relatively easy to steal, after which they can be attacked offline at an attacker's leisure. The use of modern cryptography, coupled with hardware protection to the keys, makes this vector of attack much more difficult. In essence, both of these methods offer a transparent, seamless manner of encrypting the entire hard disk drive using keys that are only available to someone who can properly log into the machine.

TPM

The *Trusted Platform Module (TPM)* is a hardware solution on the motherboard, one that assists with key generation and storage as well as random number generation. When the encryption keys are stored in the TPM, they are not accessible via normal software channels and are physically separated from the hard drive or other encrypted data locations. This makes the TPM a more secure solution than storing the keys on the machine's normal storage.

HSM

A *hardware security module (HSM)* is a device used to manage or store encryption keys. It can also assist in cryptographic operations such as encryption, hashing, or the application of digital signatures. HSMs typically are peripheral devices, connected via USB or a network connection. HSMs have tamper protection mechanisms to prevent physical access to the secrets they protect. Because of their dedicated design, they can offer significant performance advantages over general-purpose computers when it comes to cryptographic operations. When an enterprise has significant levels of cryptographic operations, HSMs can provide throughput efficiencies.

EXAM TIP Storing private keys anywhere on a networked system is a recipe for loss. HSMs are designed to allow the use of the key without exposing it to the wide range of host-based threats.

UEFI/BIOS

Basic Input/Output System (BIOS) is the firmware that a computer system uses as a connection between the actual hardware and the operating system. BIOS is typically stored on nonvolatile flash memory, which allows for updates yet persists when the machine is powered off. The purpose behind BIOS is to initialize and test the interfaces to any actual hardware in a system. Once the system is running, the BIOS functions to translate low-level access to the CPU, memory, and hardware devices, making a common interface for the OS to connect to. This facilitates multiple hardware manufacturers and differing configurations against a single OS install.

Unified Extensible Firmware Interface (UEFI) is the current replacement for BIOS. UEFI offers significant modernization over the decades-old BIOS, including the capability to deal with modern peripherals such as high-capacity storage and high-bandwidth communications. UEFI also has more security designed into it, including provisions for secure booting. From a system design aspect, UEFI offers advantages in newer hardware support, and from a security point of view, secure boot has some specific advantages. For these reasons, all new systems are UEFI based.

Secure Boot and Attestation

One of the challenges in securing an OS is that it has myriad drivers and other add-ons that hook into it and provide specific added functionality. If you do not properly vet these additional programs before installation, this pathway can provide a means by which malicious software can attack a machine. And since these attacks can occur at boot time, at a level below security applications such as antivirus software, they can be very difficult to detect and defeat. UEFI offers a solution to this problem, called Secure Boot. *Secure Boot* is a mode that, when enabled, only allows signed drivers and OS loaders to be invoked. Secure Boot requires specific setup steps, but once enabled, it blocks malware that attempts to alter the boot process. Secure Boot enables the *attestation* that the drivers and OS loaders being used have not changed since they were approved for use. Secure Boot is supported by Microsoft Windows and all major versions of Linux.

 EXAM TIP Understand how TPM, UEFI, Secure Boot, hardware root of trust (covered shortly), and integrity measurement (covered near the end of the chapter) work together to solve a specific security issue.

Supply Chain

Hardware and firmware security is ultimately dependent upon the manufacturer for the root of trust (discussed in the next section). In today's world of global manufacturing with global outsourcing, attempting to identify all the suppliers in a hardware manufacturer's *supply chain*, which commonly changes from device to device, and even between lots, is practically futile in most cases. Who manufactured all the components of the device you are ordering? If you're buying a new PC, where did the hard drive come from? Is it possible the new PC comes preloaded with malware? (Yes, it has happened.)

Unraveling the supply chain for assembled equipment can be very tricky, because even when purchasing equipment from a highly trusted vendor, you don't know where they got the components, the software, the libraries, and so forth, and even if you could figure that out, you can't be sure the suppliers don't have their own supply chains. As major equipment manufacturers have become global in nature, and use parts from all over the world, specifying national content is both difficult and expensive. Global supply chains can be very difficult to negotiate if you have very strict rules concerning country of origin.

Hardware Root of Trust

A *hardware root of trust* is a concept that if one has a trusted source of specific security functions, this layer can be used to promote security to higher layers of a system. Because roots of trust are inherently trusted, they must be secure by design. This is usually accomplished by keeping them small and limiting their functionality to a few specific tasks. Many roots of trust are implemented in hardware that is isolated from the OS and the rest of the system so that malware cannot tamper with the functions they provide. Examples of roots of trust include TPM chips in computers and Apple's Secure Enclave coprocessor in its iPhones and iPads. Apple also uses a signed Boot ROM mechanism for all software loading.

EMI/EMP

Electromagnetic interference (EMI) is an electrical disturbance that affects an electrical circuit. EMI is due to either electromagnetic induction or radiation emitted from an external source, either of which can induce currents into the small circuits that make up computer systems and cause logic upsets. An *electromagnetic pulse (EMP)* is a burst of current in an electronic device as a result of a current pulse from electromagnetic radiation. EMP can produce damaging current and voltage surges in today's sensitive electronics. The main sources of EMPs would be industrial equipment on the same circuit, solar flares, and nuclear bursts high in the atmosphere.

It is important to shield computer systems from circuits with large industrial loads, such as motors. These power sources can produce significant noise, including EMI and EMPs, that will potentially damage computer equipment. Another source of EMI is fluorescent lights. Be sure any cabling that goes near fluorescent light fixtures is well shielded and grounded. Shielding and grounding are the tools used to protect from stray electric fields, although the challenge is that the effort needs to be exacting, for even little gaps can be catastrophic.

Operating Systems

Operating systems are complex programs designed to provide a platform for a wide variety of services to run. Some of these services are extensions of the OS itself, while others are stand-alone applications that use the OS as a mechanism to connect to other programs and hardware resources. It is up to the OS to manage the security aspects of the hardware being utilized. Things such as access control mechanisms are great in theory, but it is the practical implementation of these security elements in the OS that provides the actual security profile of a machine.

Early versions of home operating systems did not have separate named accounts for separate users. This was seen as a convenience mechanism; after all, who wants the hassle of signing into the machine? This led to the simple problem that all users could then see and modify and delete everyone else's content. Content could be separated by using access control mechanisms, but that required configuration of the OS to manage every user's identity. Early versions of many OSs came with literally every option turned on. Again, this was a convenience factor, but it led to systems running processes and services that they never used, and increasing the attack surface of the host unnecessarily.

Determining the correct settings and implementing them correctly is an important step in securing a host system. This section explores the multitude of controls and options that need to be employed properly to achieve a reasonable level of security on a host system.

Types

Many different systems have the need for an operating system. Hardware in networks requires an operating system to perform the networking function. Servers and workstations require an OS to act as the interface between applications and the hardware. Specialized systems such as kiosks and appliances, both of which are forms of automated single-purpose systems, require an OS between the application software and hardware.

Network

Network components use a *network operating system* to provide the actual configuration and computation portion of networking. There are many vendors of networking equipment, and each has its own proprietary operating system. Cisco has the largest footprint with its IOS, internetworking operating system, the operating system that runs on all Cisco routers and switches. Other vendors such as Juniper have Junos, which is built off of a stripped Linux core. As networking moves to software-defined networking (SDN), introduced in Chapter 11, the concept of the network operating system will become more important and mainstream because it will become a major part of day-to-day operations in the IT enterprise.

Server

Server operating systems bridge the gap between the server hardware and the applications that are being run on the server. Currently, server OSs include Microsoft Windows Server, many flavors of Linux, and an ever-increasing number of virtual machine/hypervisor environments. For performance reasons, Linux had a significant market share in the realm of server OSs, although Windows Server with its Active Directory technology and built-in Hyper-V capability has assumed a commanding lead in market share.

PART III

Workstation

The *workstation OS* exists to provide a functional working space, typically a graphical interface, for a user to interact with the system and its various applications. Because of the high level of user interaction on workstations, it is very common to see Windows in the role of workstation OS. In large enterprises, administrators tend to favor Windows client workstations because Active Directory enables them to manage users, configurations, and settings easily across the entire enterprise.

Appliance

Appliances are stand-alone devices, wired into the network and designed to run an application to perform a specific function on traffic. These systems operate as headless servers, preconfigured with applications that run and perform a wide range of security services on the network traffic that they see. For reasons of economics, portability, and functionality, the vast majority of *appliances OS*s are built using a Linux-based OS. As these are often customized distributions, keeping them patched becomes a vendor problem because most IT people aren't properly trained to manage that task. Enterprise class intrusion detection appliances, loss prevention appliances, backup appliances, and more, are all examples of systems that bring Linux OSs into the enterprise, but not under the enterprise patch process, for the maintenance is a vendor issue.

Kiosk

Kiosks are stand-alone machines, typically operating a browser instance on top of a Windows OS. These machines are usually set up to autologin to a browser instance that is locked to a website that allows all of the functionality desired. These are commonly used for interactive customer service applications, such as interactive information sites, menus, and so on. The OS on a kiosk needs to be able to be locked down to minimal functionality so that users can't make any configuration changes. It also should have elements such as autologin and an easy way to construct the applications.

Mobile OS

Mobile devices began as a phone, with limited other abilities. *Mobile OS*s come in two main types: Apple's iOS and Google's Android OS. These OSs are optimized to both device capability and desired set of functionality. These systems are not readily expandable at the OS level, but serve as stable platforms from which users can run apps to do tasks. As the Internet and functionality spread to mobile devices, the capability of these devices has expanded as well. From smartphones to tablets, today's mobile system is a computer, with virtually all compute capability one could ask for, with a phone attached. Chapter 9 covers how to manage mobile device security in depth.

 EXAM TIP   Pay attention to the nuances in a scenario-based question that asks you to identify the correct type of operating system types, for the details in the scenario will dictate the correct or best response.

Patch Management

Every OS, from Linux to Windows, requires software updates, and each OS has different methods of assisting users in keeping their systems up to date. Microsoft, for example, typically makes updates available for download from its website. While most administrators or technically proficient users may prefer to identify and download updates individually, Microsoft recognizes that nontechnical users prefer a simpler approach, which Microsoft has built into its operating systems. In Windows 7 forward, Microsoft provides an automated update functionality that will, once configured, locate any required updates, download them to your system, and even install the updates if that is your preference.

How you patch a Linux system depends a great deal on the specific version in use and the patch being applied. In some cases, a patch will consist of a series of manual steps requiring the administrator to replace files, change permissions, and alter directories. In other cases, the patches are executable scripts or utilities that perform the patch actions automatically. Some Linux versions, such as Red Hat, have built-in utilities that handle the patching process. In those cases, the administrator downloads a specifically formatted file that the patching utility then processes to perform any modifications or updates that need to be made.

Regardless of the method you use to update the OS, it is critically important to keep systems up to date. New security advisories come out every day, and while a buffer overflow may be a "potential" problem today, it will almost certainly become a "definite" problem in the near future. Much like the steps taken to baseline and initially secure an OS, keeping every system patched and up to date is critical to protecting the system and the information it contains.

Vendors typically follow a hierarchy for software updates:

- **Hotfix** This term refers to a (usually) small software update designed to address a specific problem, such as a buffer overflow in an application that exposes the system to attacks. Hotfixes are typically developed in reaction to a discovered problem and are produced and released rather quickly.

- **Patch** This term refers to a more formal, larger software update that can address several or many software problems. Patches often contain enhancements or additional capabilities as well as fixes for known bugs. Patches are usually developed over a longer period of time.

- **Service pack** This refers to a large collection of patches and hotfixes rolled into a single, rather large package. Service packs are designed to bring a system up to the latest known good level all at once, rather than requiring the user or system administrator to download dozens or hundreds of updates separately.

Disabling Unnecessary Ports and Services

An important management issue for running a secure system is to identify the specific needs of a system for its proper operation and to enable only items necessary for those functions. *Disabling unnecessary ports and services* prevents their use by unauthorized users and improves system throughput and increases security. Systems have ports and connections that need to be disabled if not in use.

EXAM TIP Disabling unnecessary ports and services is a simple way to improve system security. This minimalist setup is similar to the implicit deny philosophy and can significantly reduce an attack surface.

Least Functionality

Just as we have a principle of least privilege, we should follow a similar track with *least functionality* on systems. A system should do what it is supposed to do, and only what it is supposed to do. Any additional functionality is an added attack surface for an adversary and offers no additional benefit to the enterprise.

Secure Configurations

Operating systems can be configured in a variety of manners, from completely open with lots of functionality, whether it is needed or not, to relatively closed and stripped down to only the services needed to perform its intended function. Operating system developers and manufacturers all share a common problem: they cannot possibly anticipate the many different configurations and variations that the user community will require from their products. So, rather than spending countless hours and funds attempting to meet every need, manufacturers provide a "default" installation for their products that usually contains the base OS and some more commonly desirable options, such as drivers, utilities, and enhancements. Because the OS could be used for any of a variety of purposes, and could be placed in any number of logical locations (LAN, DMZ, WAN, and so on), the manufacturer typically does little to nothing with regard to security. The manufacturer may provide some recommendations or simplified tools and settings to facilitate securing the system, but in general, end users are responsible for securing their own systems. Generally, this involves removing unnecessary applications and utilities, disabling unneeded services, setting appropriate permissions on files, and updating the OS and application code to the latest version.

This process of securing an OS is called *hardening*, and it is intended to make the system more resistant to attack, much like armor or steel is hardened to make it less susceptible to breakage or damage. Each OS has its own approach to security, and while the process of hardening is generally the same, different steps must be taken to secure each OS. The process of securing and preparing an OS for the production environment is not trivial; it requires preparation and planning. Unfortunately, many users don't understand the steps necessary to secure their systems effectively, resulting in hundreds of compromised systems every day. Having systems properly configured prior to use can limit the number of user caused incidents.

EXAM TIP System hardening is the process of preparing and securing a system and involves the removal of all unnecessary software and services.

You must meet several key requirements to ensure that the system hardening processes described in this section achieve their security goals. These are OS independent and should be a normal part of all system maintenance operations:

- The base installation of all OS and application software comes from a trusted source, and is verified as correct by using hash values.

- Machines are connected only to a completely trusted network during the installation, hardening, and update processes.

- The base installation includes all current patches and updates for both the OS and applications.

- Current backup images are taken after hardening and updates to facilitate system restoration to a known state.

These steps ensure that you know what is on the machine, can verify its authenticity, and have an established backup version.

Trusted Operating System

A *trusted operating system* is one that is designed to allow multilevel security in its operation. This is further defined by its ability to meet a series of criteria required by the U.S. government. Trusted OSs are expensive to create and maintain because any change must typically undergo a recertification process. The most common criteria used to define a trusted OS is the Common Criteria for Information Technology Security Evaluation (abbreviated as Common Criteria, or CC), a harmonized security criteria recognized by many nations, including the United States, Canada, Great Britain, and most of the EU countries, as well as others. Versions of Windows, Linux, mainframe OSs, and specialty OSs have been qualified to various Common Criteria levels. Trusted OSs are most commonly used by government agencies and contractors for sensitive systems that require this level of protection.

Application Whitelisting/Blacklisting

Applications can be controlled at the OS at the time of start via blacklisting or whitelisting. *Application blacklisting* is essentially noting which applications should not be allowed to run on the machine. This is basically a permanent "ignore" or "call block" type capability. *Application whitelisting* is the exact opposite: it consists of a list of allowed applications. Each of these approaches has advantages and disadvantages. Blacklisting is difficult to use against dynamic threats, as the identification of a specific application can easily be avoided through minor changes. Whitelisting is easier to employ from the aspect of the identification of applications that are allowed to run—hash values can be used to ensure the executables are not corrupted. The challenge in whitelisting is the number of potential applications that are run on a typical machine. For a single-purpose machine, such as a database server, whitelisting can be relatively easy to employ. For multipurpose machines, it can be more complicated.

Microsoft has two mechanisms that are part of the OS to control which users can use which applications:

- **Software restrictive policies** Employed via group policies and allow significant control over applications, scripts, and executable files. The primary mode is by machine and not by user account.

- **User account level control** Enforced via AppLocker, a service that allows granular control over which users can execute which programs. Through the use of rules, an enterprise can exert significant control over who can access and use installed software.

On a Linux platform, similar capabilities are offered from third-party vendor applications.

Disable Default Accounts/Passwords

Because accounts are necessary for many systems to be established, default accounts with default passwords are a way of life in computing. Whether the OS or an application, these defaults represent a significant security vulnerability if not immediately addressed as part of setting up the system or installing of the application. *Disable default accounts/passwords* should be such a common mantra for people that no systems exist with this vulnerability. This is a simple task, and one that you must do for any new system. If you cannot disable the default account—and there will be times when this is not a viable option—the other alternative is to change the password to a very long password that offers strong resistance to brute force attacks.

Peripherals

Peripherals used to be basically dumb devices with low to no interaction, but with the low cost of compute power and the vendors' desire to offer greater functionality, many of these devices have embedded computers in them. This has led to hacking of peripherals and the need for security pros to understand the security aspects of peripherals. From wireless keyboards and mice, to printers, to displays and storage devices, these items have all become sources of risk.

Wireless Keyboards

Wireless keyboards operate via a short-range wireless signal between the keyboard and the computer. The main method of connection is via either a USB Bluetooth connector, in essence creating a small personal area network (PAN), or a 2.4-GHz dongle. Wireless keyboards are frequently paired with wireless mice, removing troublesome and annoying cables off the desktop. Because of the wireless connection, the signals to and from the peripherals are subject to interception, and attacks have been made on these devices. Having the keystrokes recorded between the keyboard and the computer is equivalent to keylogging, and since it is external to the system it can be very difficult to detect.

Because of the usefulness of wireless keyboards, banning them because of the risk of signal interception is not a solid security case, but ensuring that you get them from reputable firms that patch their products is important.

Wireless Mice

Wireless mice are similar in nature to wireless keyboards. They tend to connect as a human interface device (HID) class of USB. This is part of the USB specification and is used for mice and keyboards, simplifying connections, drivers, and interfaces through a common specification.

One of the interesting security problems with wireless mice and keyboards has been the development of the mousejacking attack. This is when an attacker performs a man-in-the-middle attack on the wireless interface and can control the mouse and or intercept the traffic. When this attack first hit the environment, manufacturers had to provide updates to their software interfaces to block this form of attack. Some of the major manufacturers, like Logitech, took this effort for their mainstream product line, but a lot of mice that are older were never patched. And smaller vendors have never addressed the vulnerability, so it still exists.

Displays

Computer *displays* are primarily connected to machines via a cable to one of several types of display connectors on a machine. But for conferences and other group settings, there are a wide array of devices today that can enable a machine to connect to a display via a wireless network. These devices are available from Apple, Google, and a wide range of AV companies. The risk of using these is simple: who else within range of the wireless signal can watch what you are beaming to the display in the conference room? And if the signal was intercepted, would you even know? In a word, you wouldn't. This doesn't mean these devices should not be used in the enterprise, just that they should not be used when transmitting sensitive data to the screen.

Wi-Fi-Enabled MicroSD Cards

A class of *Wi-Fi-enabled MicroSD cards* was developed to eliminate the need to move the card from device to device to move the data. Primarily designed for digital cameras, these cards are very useful for creating Wi-Fi devices out of devices that had an SD slot. These devices work by having a tiny computer embedded in the card running a stripped-down version of Linux. One of the major vendors in this space uses a stripped-down version of BusyBox and has no security invoked at all, making the device completely open to hackers. Putting devices such as these into an enterprise network can introduce a wide variety of unpatched vulnerabilities.

Printers/MFDs

Printers have CPUs and a lot of memory. The primary purpose for this is to offload the printing from the device sending the print job to the print queue. Modern printers now come standard with a bidirectional channel, so that you can send a print job to the printer and it can send back information as to job status, printer status, and other items. *Multifunction devices (MFDs)* are like printers on steroids. They typically combine printing, scanning, and faxing all into a single device. This has become a popular market segment as it reduces costs and device proliferation in the office.

Connecting printers to the network allows multiple people to connect and independently print jobs, sharing a fairly expensive high-speed duplexing printer. But with the CPU, firmware, and memory comes the risk of an attack vector, and hackers have demonstrated malware passed by a printer to another computer that shares the printer. This is not a mainstream issue yet, but it has passed the proof-of-concept phase and in the future we will need to have software protect us from our printers.

External Storage Devices

The rise of network-attached storage (NAS) devices moved quickly from the enterprise into form factors that are found in homes. As users have developed large collections of digital videos and music, these *external storage devices*, running on the home network, solve the storage problem. These devices are typically fairly simple Linux-based appliances, with multiple hard drives in a RAID arrangement. With the rise of ransomware, these devices can spread infections to any and all devices that connect to the network. For this reason, precautions should be taken with respect to always-on connections to storage arrays. If not necessary, always-on should be avoided.

Digital Cameras

Digital cameras are sophisticated computing platforms that can capture images, perform image analysis, connect over networks, and even send files across the globe directly from a camera into a production system in a newsroom, for instance. The capabilities are vast, and the ability to move significant data quantities is built in for up to live 4K video streaming. Most cameras that have all of this capability are designed for high-end professional use, and the data streams are encrypted, as the typical use would require an encrypted channel.

 EXAM TIP All sorts of peripherals are used in today's systems, and each of them needs to be properly configured to reduce the threat environment. When given a scenario-based question, the key is to use the context of the question to determine which peripheral is the correct answer. The necessary details will be in the context, not the answer choices.

Sandboxing

Sandboxing refers to the quarantine or isolation of a system from its surroundings. It has become standard practice for some programs with an increased risk surface to operate within a sandbox, limiting the interaction with the CPU and other processes, such as memory. This works as a means of quarantine, preventing problems from getting out of the sandbox and onto the OS and other applications on a system.

Virtualization can be used as a form of sandboxing with respect to an entire system. You can build a VM, test something inside the VM, and, based on the results, make a decision with regard to stability or whatever concern was present.

Environment

Most organizations have multiple, separate computing *environments* designed to provide isolation between the functions of development, test, staging, and production. The primary purpose of having these separate environments is to prevent security incidents arising from untested code ending up in the production environment. The hardware of these environments is segregated and access control lists are used to prevent users from accessing more than one environment at a time. Moving code between environments requires a special account that can access both, minimizing issues of cross-contamination.

Development

The *development environment* is sized, configured, and set up for developers to develop applications and systems. Unlike production hardware, the development hardware does not have to be scalable, and it probably does not need to be as responsive for given transactions. The development platform does need to use the same OS type and version as used in the production environment, for developing on Windows and deploying to Linux is fraught with difficulties that can be avoided by matching the environments in terms of OS type and version. After code is successfully developed, it is moved to a test system.

Test

The *test environment* fairly closely mimics the production environment—same versions of software, down to patch levels, same sets of permissions, same file structures, and so forth. The purpose of the test environment is to test a system fully prior to deploying it into production to ensure that it is bug-free and will not disrupt the production environment. The test environment may not scale like production, but from a software/hardware footprint, it will look exactly like production. This is important to ensure that system-specific settings are tested in an environment identical to that in which they will be run.

Staging

The staging environment is an optional environment, but it is commonly used when an organization has multiple production environments. After passing testing, the system moves into staging, from where it can be deployed to the different production systems. The primary purpose of staging is to serve as a sandbox after testing, so the test system can test the next set, while the current set is deployed across the enterprise. One method of deployment is a staged deployment, where software is deployed to part of the enterprise and then a pause occurs to watch for unseen problems. If none occur, the deployment continues, stage by stage, until all of the production systems are changed.

PART III

By moving software in this manner, you never lose the old production system until the end of the move, giving you time to monitor and catch any unforeseen problems. This also prevents the total loss of production to a failed update.

Production

The *production environment* is where the systems work with real data, doing the business that the system is intended to perform. This is an environment where, by design, very few changes occur, and those that do must first be approved and tested via the system's change management process.

 EXAM TIP Understand the structure and purpose of the different environments so that when given a scenario and asked to identify which environment is appropriate, you can pick the best answer: development, test, staging, or production.

Secure Baseline

To secure the software on a system effectively and consistently, you must take a structured and logical approach. Start by examining the system's intended functions and capabilities to determine what processes and applications will be housed on the system. As a best practice, you should remove or disable anything that is not required for operations; then, apply all the appropriate patches, hotfixes, and settings to protect and secure the system.

This process of establishing software's base security state is called *baselining*, and the resulting product is a *secure baseline* that allows the software to run safely and securely. Software and hardware can be tied intimately when it comes to security, so you must consider them together. Once you have completed the baselining process for a particular hardware and software combination, you can configure any similar systems with the same baseline to achieve the same level and depth of security and protection. Uniform software baselines are critical in large-scale operations, because maintaining separate configurations and security levels for hundreds or thousands of systems is far too costly.

After administrators have finished patching, securing, and preparing a system, they often create an initial baseline configuration. This represents a secure state for the system or network device and a reference point of the software and its configuration. This information establishes a reference that can be used to help keep the system secure by establishing a known safe configuration. If this initial baseline can be replicated, it can also be used as a template when deploying similar systems and network devices.

Integrity Measurement

Integrity measurement is the measuring and identification of changes to a specific system away from an expected value. From the simple changing of data as measured by a hash value to the TPM-based integrity measurement of the system boot process and attestation of trust, the concept is the same. Take a known value, perform a storage of a hash or other keyed value, and then, at time of concern, recalculate and compare.

In the case of a TPM-mediated system, where the TPM chip provides a hardware-based root of trust anchor, the TPM system is specifically designed to calculate hashes of a system and store them in a Platform Configurations Register (PRC). This register can be read later and compared to a known, or expected, value, and if they differ, there is a trust violation. Certain BIOSs, UEFIs, and boot loaders can work with the TPM chip in this manner, providing a means of establishing a trust chain during system boot.

Chapter Review

In this chapter, you became acquainted with the elements of secure system design and deployment. The chapter opened with hardware/firmware security, exploring FDE/SED, TPM, and HSM devices, UEFI/BIOS, Secure Boot and attestation, supply chain, hardware root of trust, and EMI/EMP issues. Next, we surveyed the various types of operating systems, including network, server, workstation, appliance, kiosk, and mobile OSs, and then looked at hardening those systems via patch management, disabling unnecessary functions, ports, and services, and adhering to the concept of least functionality. We continued with the secure OS design concepts of secure configurations, trusted operating systems, application whitelisting/blacklisting, and disabling default accounts and passwords.

The chapter then explored security aspects of peripheral devices, including wireless keyboards and mice, displays, Wi-Fi-enabled MicroSD cards, printers and MFDs, external storage devices, and digital cameras.

The chapter closed with an examination of secure staging deployment concepts, including sandboxing, maintaining independent environments of development, test, staging, and production, creating a secure baseline, and monitoring change through integrity measurement.

Questions

To help you prepare further for the exam, and to test your level of preparedness, answer the following questions and then check your answers against the correct answers at the end of the chapter.

1. Why is physical security an essential element of a security plan?
    A. Because employees telecommute, physical security is of lesser concern.
    B. Physical security is not necessary with capabilities like encrypted hard drives and UEFI.
    C. Unauthorized access to hardware and networking components can make many security controls ineffective.
    D. Physical security has no impact to software security.

2. Which of the following is true concerning the purpose of full disk encryption and self-encrypting drives?

   A. They significantly affect user response times during the encryption process.

   B. They make offline attacks easier.

   C. They eliminate the need for physical security measures.

   D. They protect the data even if the disk is removed from the machine.

3. What is the primary purpose of the TPM?

   A. To store encryption keys and make them inaccessible via normal software channels

   B. To ensure platforms can run in a trusted environment

   C. To facilitate storage of keys in the machine's normal storage

   D. To safely use system-provided key generation and storage and random number generation capabilities

4. Which of the following is not true about HSMs?

   A. They are devices used to manage or store encryption keys.

   B. Their limiting factor is performance.

   C. They allow the use of keys without exposing them to host-based threats.

   D. They typically have tamper-protection mechanisms to prevent physical access.

5. Why is UEFI preferable to BIOS?

   A. UEFI resides on the hardware, making it faster than BIOS.

   B. UEFI is stored in volatile hardware storage.

   C. UEFI has limited ability to deal with high-capacity storage and high-bandwidth communications and thus is more optimized.

   D. UEFI has more security designed into it, including provisions for secure booting.

6. Secure Boot performs all of the following except:

   A. It provides all approved drivers needed.

   B. It enables attestation that drivers haven't changed since they were approved.

   C. It only allows signed drivers and OS loaders to be invoked.

   D. It blocks malware that attempts to alter the boot process.

7. When researching the security of a device manufacturer's supply chain, which of the following is most difficult to determine?

   A. Once a device is ordered, the purchaser can be sure its source won't change.

   B. Specifications are consistent between lots.

   C. Country of origin.

   D. The purchaser can rely on the root of trust to be consistent.

8. Which of the following is not true regarding hardware roots of trust?

   A. They are secure by design.

   B. They have very specific functionality.

   C. They are typically implemented in hardware that is isolated from the operating system.

   D. They provide security only at their level, not to higher layers of a system.

9. Which of the following is true about electromagnetic interference (EMI)?

   A. It is a well-known issue and computer systems are protected from it.

   B. Fluorescent lights can produce EMI that can affect computer systems.

   C. Industrial equipment doesn't produce EMI.

   D. Shielding protects most devices from EMI.

10. What is an important step in securing a host system?

    A. Determining the correct settings and implementing them correctly

    B. Using the operating system's embedded options for ease of configuration

    C. Increasing the attack surface by enabling all available settings

    D. Use manufacturer settings to provide a secure baseline to work from

11. Which of the following is a stand-alone machine, typically operating a browser on top of a Windows OS and set up to autologin to a browser instance locked to a specific website?

    A. Workstation

    B. Kiosk

    C. Appliance

    D. Server

12. Which of the following is a more formal, larger software update that addresses many software problems, often containing enhancements or additional capabilities as well as fixes for known bugs?

    A. Hotfix

    B. Service pack

    C. Patch

    D. Rollup

13. What is a simple way to improve system security?

    A. Enabling all ports and services

    B. Maintaining comprehensive access control rules

    C. Disabling unnecessary ports and services

    D. Optimizing system throughput

14. Why is the principle of least functionality important?

    A. A system needs to be flexible in the functions it performs.

    B. Manufacturer settings control known vulnerabilities.

    C. Dynamically assigning functions reduces the attack surface.

    D. Unnecessary functionality adds to the attack surface.

15. All of the following are steps in the OS hardening process except for:

    A. Removing unnecessary applications and utilities

    B. Disabling unneeded services

    C. Updating the OS and application code to the latest version

    D. Accepting default permissions

Answers

1. **C.** Physical security is an essential element of a security plan because unauthorized access to hardware and networking components can make many security controls ineffective.

2. **D.** The purpose of full disk encryption (FDE) and self-encrypting drives (SEDs) is to protect the data even if the disk is removed from the machine.

3. **A.** The primary purpose of Trusted Platform Module (TPM) is to store encryption keys and make them inaccessible via normal software channels.

4. **B.** Performance is not a limiting factor for HSMs.

5. **D.** UEFI is preferable to BIOS because it has more security designed into it, including provisions for secure booting.

6. **A.** Secure Boot does not provide all drivers; rather, it ensures they are signed and unchanged.

7. **C.** The country of origin of all the device's components.

8. **D.** Hardware roots of trust are built on the principle that if one "trusts" one layer, that layer can be used to promote security to higher layers of a system.

9. **B.** Fluorescent lights can produce EMI that can affect computer systems.

10. **A.** An important step in securing a host system is determining the correct settings and implementing them correctly.

11. **B.** A kiosk is a stand-alone machine, typically operating a browser on top of a Windows OS and set up to autologin to a browser instance locked to a specific website.

12. **C.** A patch is a more formal, larger software update that addresses many software problems, often containing enhancements or additional capabilities as well as fixes for known bugs.

13. C. Disabling unnecessary ports and services is a simple way to improve system security.

14. D. The principle of least functionality is important because unnecessary or unused functions add to the attack surface.

15. D. Accepting default permissions is not part of the OS hardening process.

CHAPTER 13

Embedded Systems

In this chapter, you will

- Explain the security implications of embedded systems
- Explain the security implications of smart devices/IoT
- Explain the security implications of SCADA systems

Embedded systems is the name given to computers that are included as an integral part of a larger system, typically hardwired in. From computer peripherals like printers, to household devices like smart TVs and thermostats, to the car you drive, embedded systems are everywhere. Embedded systems can be as simple as a microcontroller with fully integrated interfaces (a system on a chip) or as complex as the tens of interconnected embedded systems in a modern automobile. Embedded systems are designed with a single control purpose in mind and have virtually no additional functionality, but this does not mean that they are free of risk or security concerns. The vast majority of security exploits involve getting a device or system to do something it is capable of doing, and technically designed to do, even if the resulting functionality was never an intended use of the device or system.

The designers of embedded systems typically are focused on minimizing costs, with security seldom seriously considered as part of either the design or the implementation. Because most embedded systems operate as isolated systems, the risks have not been significant. However, as capabilities have increased, and these devices have become networked together, the risks have increased significantly. For example, smart printers have been hacked as a way into enterprises, and as a way to hide from defenders. And when next-generation automobiles begin to talk to each other, passing traffic and other information between them, and begin to have navigation and other inputs being beamed into systems, the risks will increase and security will become an issue. This has already been seen in the airline industry, where the separation of in-flight Wi-Fi, in-flight entertainment, and cockpit digital flight control networks has become a security issue.

EXAM TIP   Understand static environments, systems in which the hardware, OS, applications, and networks are configured for a specific function or purpose. These systems are designed to remain unaltered through their lifecycle, rarely requiring updates.

Certification Objective   This chapter covers CompTIA Security+ exam objective 3.5, Explain the security implications of embedded systems.

SCADA/ICS

SCADA is an acronym for *supervisory control and data acquisition*, a system designed to control automated systems in cyber-physical environments. SCADA systems have their own smart components, each of which is an example of an embedded system. Together they form a SCADA system, which can control manufacturing plants, traffic lights, refineries, energy networks, water plants, building automation and environmental controls, and a host of other systems. A SCADA system is also known by names such as distributed control system (DCS) and *industrial control system (ICS)*, the variations depending on the industry and the configuration. Where computers control a physical process directly, a SCADA system likely is involved.

Most SCADA systems involve multiple components networked together to achieve a set of functional objectives. These systems frequently include a human–machine interface (HMI), where an operator can exert a form of directive control over the operation of the system under control. SCADA systems historically have been isolated from other systems, but the isolation is decreasing as these systems are being connected across traditional networks to improve business functionality. Many older SCADA systems were air gapped from the corporate network; that is, they shared no direct network connections. This meant that data flows in and out were handled manually and took time to accomplish. Modern systems wished to remove this constraint and added direct network connections between the SCADA networks and the enterprise IT network. These connections increase the attack surface and the risk to the system, and the more they resemble an IT networked system, the greater the need for security functions.

SCADA systems have been drawn into the security spotlight with the Stuxnet attack on Iranian nuclear facilities, initially reported in 2010. Stuxnet is malware designed to attack a specific SCADA system and cause failures resulting in plant equipment damage. This attack was complex and well designed, crippling nuclear fuel processing in Iran for a significant period of time. This attack raised awareness of the risks associated with SCADA systems, whether connected to the Internet or not (Stuxnet crossed an air gap to hit its target).

Smart Devices/IoT

Smart devices and devices that comprise the *Internet of Things (IoT)* have taken the world's markets by storm. From key fobs that can track the location of things via GPS, to cameras that can provide surveillance, to connected household appliances, TVs, dishwashers, refrigerators, crock pots, washers, and dryers—anything with a microcontroller now seems to be connected to the Web so that it can be controlled remotely. Artificial intelligence (AI) has also entered into the mix, enabling even greater functionality, embodied in products such as Amazon Echo, Google Home, Microsoft Cortana, and Apple Siri.

Computer-controlled light switches, LED light bulbs, thermostats, and baby monitors—the smart home is also becoming a reality, connecting everything to the Internet. You can carry a key fob that your front door recognizes, unlocking before you get to it. Of course, the security camera sees you first and alerts the system that someone is coming up the driveway. The only thing that can be said with confidence about this revolution is someone will figure out a how and a why to connect virtually anything to the network.

All of these devices have a couple similarities. They all have a network interface, for their connectivity is their purpose as a smart device or a member of the Internet of Things club. On that network interface is some form of compute platform. With complete computer functionality now included on a system on a chip platform (covered in a later section), these tiny devices can have a complete working computer for a few dollars in cost. The use of a Linux-type kernel as the core engine makes programming easier, as the base of programmers is very large. These devices also can be mass produced and at relatively low cost. The scaling of the software development over literally millions of units makes costs scalable. Functionality is king, meaning that security or anything that might impact new expanded functionality has taken a back seat.

Wearable Technology

Wearable technologies include everything from biometric sensors measuring heart rate, to step counters measuring how far one walks, to smart watches that combine all these functions and more. By measuring biometric signals, such as pulse rate, and body movements, it is possible to measure fitness and even sleep. These wearable devices are built using very small computers that run a real-time operating system, usually built from a stripped-down Linux kernel. As with all information containing devices, how does one protect the data? As wearables learn more and more of your personal data, they become a source of interest for hackers. Protecting the data is the security objective for these devices.

Home Automation

Home automation is one of the driving factors behind the IoT movement. From programmable smart thermostats to electrical control devices that replace wall switches to enable voice-operated lights, the home environment is awash with tech. Other home automation technologies include locks that are operated electronically, allowing you to lock or unlock them remotely from your smartphone; surveillance cameras connected to your smartphone that tell you when someone is at your door and allow you to talk to them without even being home; appliances that can be set up to run when energy costs are lower, or to automatically order more food when you take the last of an item from the pantry or refrigerator. No longer the props of a futuristic TV show, these technologies are available today and at fairly reasonable costs.

The tech behind the home automation technologies is the same tech behind a lot of recent advances: a small system on a chip, a complete computer system, with a real-time operating system designed to accomplish a limited set of functions; a network connection, usually wireless; some sensors to measure light, heat, or sound; and an application to integrate the functionality. The security challenge is that most of these devices literally have no security. Poor networking software led to a legion of baby monitors and other home devices being exploited to become a large botnet called Mirai, which attacked Krebs on Security (among others) with a DDoS rate that exceeded 600 Gbps in the fall of 2016.

HVAC

Building-automation systems, climate control systems, *HVAC* (heating, ventilation, and air conditioning) systems, are examples of systems that are managed by embedded systems. Although these systems used to be independent and stand-alone systems, the rise of hyperconnectivity has shown value in integrating them. Having a "smart building" that reduces building resources in accordance with the number and distribution of people inside increases efficiency and reduces costs. Interconnecting these systems and adding in Internet-based central control mechanisms does increase the risk profile from outside attacks. These outside attacks could result in HVAC malfunction or failure, rendering a major office building uninhabitable due to heat and safety.

SoC

System on a chip (SoC) refers to a complete computer system miniaturized on a single integrated circuit, designed to provide the full functionality of a computing platform on a single chip. This includes networking and graphics display. Some SoC solutions come with memory, while others have the memory separate. SoCs are very common in the mobile computing market (both phones and tablets) because of their low power consumption and efficient design. Some SoC brands have become household names because mobile phone companies have advertised their inclusion in a system, such as the Snapdragon processor in Android devices. Quad-core and eight-core SoC systems are already in place, and they even have advanced designs such as quad plus one, where the fifth processor is slower and designed for simple processes and uses extremely small amounts of power. So when the quad cores are not needed, there is not significant energy usage.

The programming of SoC systems can occur at several different levels. Dedicated OSs and applications can be written for them, such as the Android fork of Linux, which is specific to the mobile device marketplace. Because these devices represent computing platforms with billions of devices worldwide, they have become a significant force in the marketplace. The security implications of SoC-based systems is associated not with the specifics of SoC, but in the fact that they are ubiquitous in our technology-driven lives. Security issues are handled by the device, not the specific SoC aspect itself.

RTOS

Real-time operating systems (RTOSs) are designed for systems where the processing must occur in real time and data cannot be queued or buffered for any significant length of time. RTOSs are not general-purpose machines, but are programmed for a specific purpose.

They still have to deal with contention, and they have scheduling algorithms to deal with timing collisions, but in general an RTOS processes each input as it is received, or within a specific time slice defined as the response time. Examples of RTOS are from something as common as an anti-lock braking computer in a car, to as complex as a robotic system used on an assembly line.

Most general-purpose computer operating systems are capable of multitasking by design. This includes Windows and Linux. Multitasking systems make poor real-time processors, primarily because of the overhead associated with separating tasks and processes. Windows and Linux may have interrupts, but these are the exception, not the rule, for the processor. RTOS-based software is written in a completely different fashion, designed to emphasize the thread in processing rather than handling multiple threads.

The security implications surrounding RTOS systems lie in their timing. Should an event do something that interferes with the system's ability to respond within its time allotment, then the system itself can fail in its task. RTOS systems also tend to be specific to the degree that updates and patches tend not to be common as the manufacturer of the system does not provide that level of support. As items such as cars become more networked, these weaknesses are becoming apparent and one can expect this situation to change over time.

Printers/MFDs

Printers and *multifunction devices (MFDs)*, which combine a printer, scanner, and fax, have embedded compute power to act as a print server, manage the actual printing or scanning process, and allow complete network connectivity. These devices communicate in a bidirectional fashion, accepting print jobs and sending back job status, printer status, and other information to the computer. This has decoupled printing from the computer, making it a stand-alone entity. The system that runs all these functions was designed to provide maximum functionality for the device, and security is more of an afterthought than a design element. As such, these devices have been shown to be hackable and capable of passing malware from the printer to the computer. These attacks still exist primarily as a proof of concept as opposed to a real-world threat, which is fortunate, because the current generation of security software does not monitor printer activity to and from the computer very well.

Camera Systems

Digital *camera systems* have entered the computing world through a couple of different portals. First, there is the world of high-end digital cameras that have networking stacks, image processors, and even 4K video feeds. These are used in enterprises such as news organizations, which rely on getting the data live without extra processing delays. What is important to note is that most of these devices, although they are networked into other networks, have built-in VPNs that are always on, because the content is considered valuable enough to protect as a feature.

The next set of cameras reverses the quantity and quality characteristics. Where the high-end devices are fairly small in number, there is a growing segment of video surveillance cameras, including cameras for household surveillance, baby monitoring, and the like. Hundreds of millions of these devices are sold and they all have a sensor, a processor, a network stack, and so forth. These are part of the Internet of Things revolution, where millions of devices connect together either on purpose or by happenstance. It was a network of these devices, along with a default username and password, that led to the Mirai botnet that actually broke the Internet for a while in the fall of 2016. The true root cause was a failure to follow a networking RFC concerning source addressing, coupled with the default username and password and remote configuration that enabled the devices to be taken over. Two sets of fails, working together, created weeks' worth of problems.

Special Purpose

As the name indicates, *special-purpose systems* are systems designed for special purposes. Three primary types of special-purpose systems targeted by CompTIA are the systems in medical devices, vehicles, and aircraft/UAV. Each of these categories has significant computer systems providing much of the functionality control for the device, and each of these systems has its own security issues.

Medical Devices

Medical devices are a very diverse group, from small implantable devices, such as pacemakers, to multi-ton MRI machines. In between is a wide range of devices, from those that measure vital signs to those that actually control vital functions. Each of these has several interesting characteristics, and they all have an interesting caveat—they can have a direct effect on a human's life. This makes security of these devices also a safety function.

Medical devices, such as lab equipment and infusion pumps and other computer-controlled equipment, have been running on computer controls for years. The standard of choice has been an embedded Linux kernel that has been stripped of excess functionality and pressed into service in the embedded device. One of the problems with this approach is how to patch this kernel when vulnerabilities are found. Another, related problem is that as the base system gets updated to a newer version, the embedded system stays trapped on the old version. This requires regression testing for problems, and most manufacturers will not undertake such labor-intensive chores.

Medical devices are manufactured under strict regulatory guidelines that are designed for static systems that do not need patching, updating, or changes. Any change would force a requalification, a lengthy, time-consuming, and expensive process. As such, these devices tend to never be patched. With the advent of several high-profile vulnerabilities, including Heartbleed and Bash shell attacks, most manufacturers simply recommended that the devices be isolated and never connected to an outside network. In concept, this is fine, but in reality this can never happen, as all the networks in a hospital or medical center are connected.

A recent recall of nearly a half million pacemakers in 2017 for a software vulnerability that would allow a hacker to access and change the performance characteristics of the device is proof of the problem. The good news is that the devices can be updated without removing them, but it will take a doctor's visit to have the new firmware installed.

Vehicles

A modern *vehicle* has not a single computer in it, but actually hundreds of them, all interconnected on a bus. The controller area network (CAN) bus is designed to allow multiple microcontrollers to communicate with each other without a central host computer. Before the CAN bus was invented, individual microcontrollers were used to control the engine, emissions, transmission, braking, heating, electrical, and other systems, and the wiring harnesses used to interconnect everything became unwieldy. Robert Bosch developed the CAN bus for cars, specifically to address the wiring harness issue, and when first deployed in 1986 at BMW, the weight reduction was over 100 pounds.

As of 2008, all new U.S. and European cars must use a CAN bus, per SAE regulations, a mandate engineers have willingly embraced as they continue to add more and more subsystems. The CAN bus has a reference protocol specification, but recent auto hacking discoveries have shown several interesting things. First, in defending allegations that some of its vehicles could suddenly accelerate without driver action, Toyota's claim that the only way to make a vehicle accelerate quickly is to step on the gas pedal, that software alone won't do it, was proven to be false. Hackers have demonstrated almost complete control over all functions of their Prius using computers and CAN bus commands. Second, every automobile manufacturer has interpreted/ignored the reference protocol specification to varying degrees. Finally, as demonstrated by hackers at DEF CON, it is possible to disable cars in motion, over the Internet, as well as fool around with the entertainment console settings and other systems.

The bottom line is that, to function properly, newer vehicles rely on multiple computer systems, all operating semi-autonomously and with very little security. The U.S. Department of Transportation is pushing for vehicle-to-vehicle communication technology, so that vehicles can tell each other when traffic is changing ahead of them. Couple that with the advances in self-driving technology, and the importance of stronger security in the industry is clear. There is evidence that this is beginning, that security is improving, but the pace of improvement is slow when compared to typical computer innovation speeds.

Aircraft/UAV

Aircraft also have significant computer footprints inside, as most modern jets have what is called an "all-glass cockpit," meaning the old individual gauges and switches have been replaced with a computer display that includes a touch screen. This enables greater functionality and is more reliable than the older systems. But as with vehicles, the connecting of all of this equipment onto busses that are then eventually connected to outside networks has led to a lot of security questions for the aviation industry. And, as is true of medical devices, patching the OS for aircraft systems is a difficult process because the industry is heavily regulated, with strict testing requirements. This makes for systems that, over time, will become vulnerable as the base OS has been thoroughly explored and every vulnerability mapped and exploited in non-aviation systems, and these use cases can port easily to aircraft.

Recent revelations have shown that the in-flight entertainment systems, on standard Linux distros, are separated from flight controls not by separate networks, but by a firewall. This has led hackers to sound the alarm over aviation computing safety.

Unmanned aerial vehicles (UAVs) represent the next frontier of flight. These machines range from the small drones that hobbyists can play with for under $300 to full-size aircraft that can fly across oceans. What makes these systems different from regular aircraft is that the pilot is on the ground, flying the device via remote control. UAVs have cameras, sensors, and processors to manage the information, and even the simple hobbyist versions have sophisticated autopilot functions. Because of the remote connection, UAVs are networked and operated either under direct radio control (rare) or via a networked system (much more common).

 EXAM TIP This chapter presented a cornucopia of different embedded systems. For the exam, remember three main elements: the technology components, SoC and RTOS; the connectivity component—Internet of Things; and the different marketplaces, home automation, wearables, medical devices, vehicles, and aviation. Read the question for clues as to what the specific question is being asked.

Chapter Review

In this chapter, you became acquainted with the security implications of embedded systems, which have become ubiquitous in our everyday lives. The chapter opened with a discussion of the SCADA/ICS space and how operational technology is its own world and one of significant size. The chapter then moved to the world of smart devices and the Internet of Things, including wearable technology and home automation. It then discussed HVAC systems. Examples of security implications are provided in each of these topics.

The chapter moved into system on a chip (SoC) solutions and real-time operating systems (RTOSs). It briefly examined printers and MFDs, as well as camera systems. The chapter closed with an examination of some special-purpose ecosystems, including medical devices, vehicles, and aircraft/UAVs. As these systems are in our lives almost every day, understanding them and the security implications associated with the nature of their system's operation is important.

Questions

To help you prepare further for the exam, and to test your level of preparedness, answer the following questions and then check your answers against the correct answers at the end of the chapter.

1. Which of the following statements is not true?

   A. Embedded systems are designed with a single control purpose in mind and typically have no additional functionality.

   B. Embedded systems are free of risk or security concerns.

   C. *Embedded* is the name given to a computer that is included as an integral part of a larger system.

   D. Embedded systems can be as complex as the tens of interconnected embedded systems in a modern automobile.

2. Which of the following is true regarding risk of next-generation vehicles?

   A. There are minimal risks when next-generation automobiles share information.

   B. Passing traffic and other information between vehicles does not increase security risks.

   C. The sharing of navigation and other inputs between vehicles presents a potential security issue.

   D. Time-to-market and cost minimization have minimal impact on potential risks being exploited.

3. Which of the following is true about in-flight networks?

   A. Wi-Fi, in-flight entertainment, and cockpit digital flight control networks are segregated.

   B. The integration of Wi-Fi, in-flight entertainment, and cockpit digital flight control networks does not introduce potential security risks.

   C. Wi-Fi and cockpit digital flight control networks can be integrated without increasing potential security risks.

   D. Wi-Fi, in-flight entertainment, and cockpit digital flight control networks can present potential security risks.

4. Which of the following is true about static environments?

   A. They are often designed to be fully integrated into a company's network security strategy.

   B. They are designed to remain unaltered through their lifecycle.

   C. Because they perform a very specific function, they have no need for security updates.

   D. They cannot be exploited because hackers can't find them on a network.

5. Which of the following is true about building-automation systems, climate control systems, HVAC systems, elevator control systems, and alarm systems?

   A. They are independent and stand-alone systems that offer little integration value.

   B. Interconnecting these systems and adding Internet-based central control mechanisms doesn't increase the risk profile from outside attacks.

   C. These systems are being integrated to increase efficiency and reduce costs.

   D. Integrating these systems into building management systems introduces minimal risk.

6. Which of the following properly defines supervisory control and data acquisition (SCADA)?

   A. A scaled-down version of Linux designed for use in an embedded system

   B. The standard used for communicating between intelligent car systems

   C. The risk created by connecting control systems in buildings

   D. A system designed to control automated systems in cyber-physical environments

7. Which of the following is true about SCADA systems?

   A. SCADA systems continue to be air-gapped from other systems.

   B. The ongoing integration of SCADA environments has reduced potential risks.

   C. The introduction of human machine interfaces to manage SCADA systems has eliminated potential risks.

   D. The historical isolation of SCADA systems from other systems is decreasing as SCADA systems are being connected across traditional networks to improve business functionality.

8. Which of the following is true about smart devices and the Internet of Things (IoT)?

   A. The use of a Linux-type kernel as the core engine makes programming more complex.

   B. Mass production introduces significant security risks.

   C. The scaling of the software development over large numbers of units makes costs scalable, and functionality is paramount.

   D. Security or anything that might impact new expanded functionality is considered early and gets the focus and resources necessary.

9. Which of the following is true about home automation devices?

   A. They have been used in botnet exploitations with significant impacts.

   B. They don't impose significant potential risks as they are isolated on the home network.

   C. Because home automation systems are exploding in use, they have been designed with security in mind from the very beginning.

   D. Their network connection is usually wireless, which is not easily exploited.

10. Which of the following is true about HVAC and building automation systems?

    A. They have not been exploited to any significant degree yet.

    B. Interconnecting these systems and using Internet-based central control mechanisms increases the risk profile from outside attacks.

    C. Having a "smart building" that reduces building resources in accordance with the number and distribution of people inside has not increased efficiency or reduced costs.

    D. The rise of hyperconnectivity has introduced no additional security concerns.

11. Which of the following is not true about systems on a chip?

    A. They provide the full functionality of a computing platform on a single chip.

    B. They typically have low power consumption and efficient design.

    C. Programming of SoC systems can occur at several different levels and thus potential risks are easily mitigated.

    D. Because these devices represent computing platforms with billions of devices worldwide, they have become a significant force in the marketplace.

12. What distinguishes real-time operating systems (RTOSs) from general-purpose operating systems?

    A. Unlike RTOSs, most general-purpose operating systems handle interrupts within defined time constraints.

    B. Unlike general-purpose OSs, most RTOSs are capable of multitasking by design.

    C. Unlike RTOSs, most general-purpose operating systems are multitasking by design.

    D. Unlike general-purpose OSs, RTOSs are designed to handle multiple threads.

13. Which of the following is true about printers and multifunction devices?

    A. They rely on the computer to manage the printing and scanning processes.

    B. Because of their long history and widespread use, security is designed into these products.

    C. These devices communicate in a bidirectional fashion, accepting print jobs and sending back job status, printer status, and so forth.

    D. So far, they have not been shown to be hackable or capable of passing malware from the printer to the computer.

14. Which of the following is a very important aspect to always remember when dealing with security of medical devices?

    A. They are still relatively new in their usage.

    B. They can directly affect human life.

    C. Security is not related to safety.

    D. They are almost exclusively stand-alone devices, without Internet connectivity.

15. Which of the following poses a significant potential risk of unmanned aerial vehicles?

   A. They have sophisticated autopilot functions.

   B. They have cameras, sensors, and payloads.

   C. Low prices for some models.

   D. Because they are pilotless, their remote-control systems may be networked and vulnerable to potential risks.

Answers

1. **B.** Embedded systems are not free of risk or security concerns, as hackers have demonstrated.

2. **C.** The sharing of navigation and other inputs presents a potential security issue for next-generation vehicles. False information when shared can cause problems.

3. **D.** Wi-Fi, in-flight entertainment, and cockpit digital flight control networks can present potential security risks.

4. **B.** Static environments are designed to remain unaltered through their lifecycle.

5. **C.** Building-automation systems, climate control systems, HVAC systems, elevator control systems, and alarm systems are being integrated to increase efficiency and reduce costs.

6. **D.** SCADA is a system designed to control automated systems in cyber-physical environments.

7. **D.** Historical isolation of SCADA systems is decreasing as these systems are being connected across traditional networks to improve business functionality.

8. **C.** The scaling of the software development over large numbers of units makes costs scalable, and functionality is paramount in smart devices and IoT.

9. **A.** Home automation devices have been used in botnet exploitations with significant impacts.

10. **B.** Interconnecting HVAC and building automation systems and using Internet-based central control mechanisms to manage them increases the risk profile from outside attacks.

11. **C.** Programming of SoC systems can occur at several different levels and thus potential risks are difficult to mitigate.

12. **C.** One thing that distinguishes real-time operating systems (RTOSs) from general-purpose operating systems is that most general-purpose operating systems are designed for multitasking.

13. C. Printers and multifunction devices communicate in a bidirectional fashion, accepting print jobs and sending back job status, printer status, and so forth.

14. B. A very important aspect to always remember when dealing with security of medical devices is that they can directly affect human life.

15. D. A significant potential risk of unmanned aerial vehicles is that, because they are pilotless, their remote-control systems may be networked and thus vulnerable to potential risks.

CHAPTER 14

Application Development and Deployment

In this chapter, you will

- Examine secure development lifecycle models
- Explore secure coding concepts
- Learn to summarize secure application development and deployment concepts

Secure application development and deployment are foundational elements of cybersecurity. Poor application development practices lead to a greater number and severity of vulnerabilities, increasing the security problems for implementers.

Certification Objective   This chapter covers CompTIA Security+ exam objective 3.6, Summarize secure application development and deployment concepts.

Development Lifecycle Models

The production of software is the result of a process. There are a multitude of tasks, from gathering requirements, planning, design, coding, testing and support. These tasks are performed by a team of people according to a process model. There are several different process models that can be employed to facilitate the proper development steps in the proper order. Two of these, the waterfall model and the agile model, are examples of models and are discussed in the following section.

Waterfall vs. Agile

The *waterfall* model is a development model based on simple manufacturing design. The work process begins with the requirements analysis phase and progresses through a series of four more phases, with each phase being completed before progressing to the next phase—without overlap. This is a linear, sequential process, and the model discourages backing up and repeating earlier stages (after all, you can't reverse the flow of a waterfall). Depicted in Figure 14-1, this is a simple model where the requirements phase precedes the design phase, which precedes the implementation phase, and so on through verification and maintenance. Should a new requirement "be discovered" after the requirements

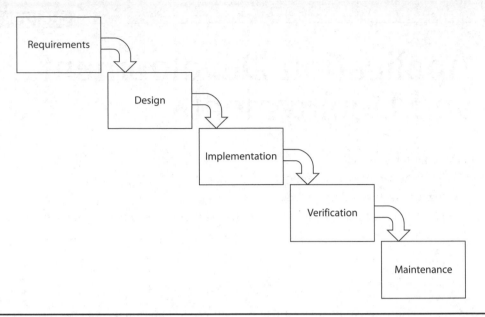

Figure 14-1 Waterfall development model

phase has ended, for example, it can be added, but the work does not go back to that phase. This makes the model very nonadaptive and difficult to use unless the developers implement a rigid method to ensure that each phase is truly completed before advancing to the next phase of the work. This can add to development time and cost. For these and other reasons, the waterfall model, although conceptually simple, is considered by most experts as nonworkable in practice.

The waterfall methodology is particularly poorly suited for complex processes and systems where many of the requirements and design elements will be unclear until later stages of development. It is useful for small, bite-sized pieces, and in this manner is incorporated within other models such as the spiral, incremental, and Agile methods. One of the major weaknesses of the waterfall model is that it is difficult to incorporate late in the cycle changes from a customer, making the development process inflexible.

The *agile* model is not a single development methodology, but a whole group of related methods. Designed to increase innovation and efficiency of small programming teams, Agile methods rely on quick turns involving small increases in functionality. The use of repetitive, small development cycles can enable different developer behaviors, which in turn can result in more efficient development. There are many different methods and variations, but some of the major forms of Agile development are Scrum and Extreme Programming (XP). XP is built around the people side of the process, while Scrum is centered on the process perspective. More information on the foundations of the agile method, see the Agile Manifesto (http://agilemanifesto.org/).

Scrum

The Scrum programming methodology is built around a 30-day release cycle. It is highly dependent upon a prioritized list of high-level requirements, and program changes are managed on a 24-hour and 30-day basis. The concept is to keep the software virtually always ready for release. The master list of all tasks is called the product backlog. The 30-day work list is referred to as a sprint, and the chart that tracks what is accomplished daily is called the burn-down chart.

From a security perspective, nothing in the Scrum model prevents the application of secure programming practices. To include security requirements into the development process, they must appear on the product and sprint backlogs. This can be accomplished during the design phase of the project. As additions to the backlogs can occur at any time, the security team can make a set of commonly used user stories that support required security elements. The second method of incorporating security functionality is through developer training. Developers should be trained on security-related elements of programming, such as validating user input, using only approved libraries, and so forth.

The advantage of Scrum is that it enables quick turns of incremental changes to a software base. This makes change management easier. There are limitations in the amount of planning, but in a mature Agile environment, the security user stories can be already built and understood. The only challenge is ensuring that the security elements on the product and sprint backlogs get processed in a timely manner, but this is a simple management task. Security tasks tend to be less exciting than features, so keeping them in the process stack takes management effort.

XP

Extreme Programming is a structured process that is built around user stories. These stories are used to architect requirements in an iterative process that uses acceptance testing to create incremental advances. The XP model is built around the people side of the software development process and works best in smaller development efforts. Like other Agile methods, the idea is to have many small, incremental changes on a regular time schedule. XP stresses team-level communication, and as such, is highly amenable to the inclusion of security methods, if the development team includes one or more security-conscious developers.

 EXAM TIP   Understanding the differences between Agile and waterfall development, including when each is advantageous, is testable.

Secure DevOps

DevOps is a combination of development and operations, and a blending of tasks performed by a company's application development and systems operations teams. DevOps emphasizes communication and collaboration between product management, software development, and operations professionals in order to facilitate continuous development, continuous integration, continuous delivery, and continuous monitoring processes. DevOps can be considered the anti-waterfall model, for rather than going from phase to phase, in DevOps, as small changes are ready to advance, they advance. This leads to many small, incremental changes, but also equates to less time between updates and less time to fix or change things. *Secure DevOps* is the addition of security steps to the DevOps process. Just as you can add security steps to the waterfall model, or any other software development model, you can add them to DevOps as well, promoting a secure DevOps outcome.

Security Automation

One of the key elements of DevOps is automation. DevOps relies upon automation for much of its efficiencies. *Security automation* can do the same for security with respect to improving efficiencies that automation has in DevOps. Automating routine and extensive security processes allows fewer resources to cover more environment in a more effective and efficient manner. Automation removes the manual labor that costs money to employ, especially skilled cybersecurity personnel. And rather than replacing the personnel with scripts, the use of automation allows the personnel to spend their time doing value-added work such as analysis. Take the issues associated with patching systems. One has to identify which patches belong on which systems, apply the patches and then verify periodically that the system is working and systems are patched. All of these steps can be highly automated, making a small group capable of patching and monitoring patch levels on a large base of systems.

Continuous Integration

Continuous integration is the DevOps manner of continually updating and improving the production code base. By using high levels of automation, and safety nets of automated backout routines, continuous integration allows the DevOps team to test and update even very minor changes without a lot of overhead. Instead of running a few large updates, with many integrated and potentially cross-purpose update elements, all squeezed into a single big package, the DevOps team runs a series of smaller, single-purpose integrations throughout the process. This means that when testing, the team can isolate the changes to a small, manageable number, without the significance of multiple potential interactions. This can make DevOps more secure by reducing interaction errors and other errors that are difficult to detect and time consuming to track down.

Baselining

Baselining is the process of determining a standard set of functionality and performance. This is a metrics-driven process, where later changes can be compared to the baseline to gauge their impact on performance and other variables. If a change improves the baseline elements in a positive fashion, a new baseline can be established. If the new values are of lesser quality, then a decision can be made as to accept the changes or change the baseline. It is through baselining that performance and feature creep are countered by the management team. If a new feature negatively impacts performance, then the new feature might be withheld. Baselining is important to DevOps and security in general as it provides a reference point when making changes. Without the reference point, it is hard to show changes are improvements. Development teams should baseline systems at time of development, and at periods of major changes.

Immutable Systems

An *immutable system* is a system that, once deployed, is never modified, patched, or upgraded. If a patch or update is required, the system is merely replaced with a new system that is patched and updated. In a typical system, one that is mutable or changeable, that is patched and updated before deployment, it is extremely difficult to know conclusively if future changes to the system are authorized or not, and if they are correctly applied or not. Linux makes this determination especially difficult. On a Linux system, the binaries and libraries are scattered over many directories: /boot, /bin, /usr/bin, /lib, /usr/lib, /opt/bin, /usr/local/bin, and many more. Configuration files are similarly scattered over /etc, /opt/etc, /usr/local/etc, /usr/lib, and so on. These directories have some files that should never be modified and others that are regularly updated. When the system update services run, they often create temporary files in these directories as well. Consequently, it is very difficult to lock down all these directories and perform authorized system and software updates at the same time. Immutable systems resolve these issues.

Infrastructure as Code

Infrastructure as code is the use of code to build systems, rather than manually configuring them via normal configuration mechanisms. It is a way of using automation to build out systems, reproducible, efficient and is a key attribute of enabling best practices in DevOps. Developers become more involved in defining system configuration, and the Ops team gets more involved in the actual development process. The objective is to avoid having developers write applications and toss them over a wall to the implementers, the Ops team, and expect them to make the applications work in the environment. As systems have become larger, more complex, and interrelated, interconnecting developer input and production input has created an environment of infrastructure as code, a version of Infrastructure as a Service.

 EXAM TIP Understand how DevOps interacts with and can be supported by a secure development lifecycle. Also understand the major methods, such as immutable systems and continuous integration, and where they can be employed effectively to secure DevOps.

Version Control and Change Management

Programs are developed, released, used and then changes are desired, either to change functionality, fix errors, or improve performance. This leads to multiple versions of programs. *Version control* is as simple as tracking which version of a program is being worked on, whether in development, testing, or production. Version control systems tend to use primary numbers to indicate major releases, and numbers after a decimal point to indicate minor changes.

Having the availability of multiple versions brings into focus the issue of *change management*, which addresses how an organization manages which versions are currently being used, and how it coordinates changes as they are released by a manufacturer.

Tracking version numbers, and bug fixes, including what is being fixed, with the why and how behind the changes is important documentation for the internal development team. Advanced teams keep track not only of what went wrong, but the root cause analysis—how did it get past testing. This documentation is important to ensure that later code changes do not reintroduce old vulnerabilities into the code base.

In traditional software publishing, a new version required a new install and fairly significant testing, as the level of change in a new version could be drastic and introduce issues of compatibility, functionality, and even correctness. DevOps turned the tables on this equation by introducing the idea that developers and production work together to create, in essence, a series of micro releases, so that any real problems are associated with single changes and not bogged down by interactions between multiple module changes.

Whether you are operating in the traditional world or in the DevOps world, you need a change management process that ensures that all changes in production are authorized, properly tested, and, in case of failure, rolled back. It should also ensure that accurate documentation is produced and kept up to date.

Provisioning and Deprovisioning

Provisioning is the process of assigning to users permissions or authorities to access objects. Users can be provisioned into groups, enabling them to be managed as a group rather than individually. Computer processes or threads can be provisioned to operate at higher levels of authority when executing, and best practice includes removing higher levels of permission when not needed, to reduce the number of threads at elevated privilege. *Deprovisioning* is the removal of permissions or authorities. In secure coding, the practice is to provision a thread to an elevated execution permission level (e.g., root) only during the time that the administrative permissions are needed. After those steps have passed, the thread can be deprovisioned to a lower access level. This combination shortens the period of time an application is at an increased level of authority, reducing the risk exposure should the program get hijacked or hacked.

Secure Coding Techniques

Application security begins with code that is secure and free of vulnerabilities. Unfortunately, all code has weaknesses and vulnerabilities, so instantiating the code in a manner that has effective defenses preventing the exploitation of vulnerabilities can maintain a desired level of security. Proper handling of configurations, errors and exceptions, and inputs can assist in the creation of a secure application. Testing of the application throughout the software development lifecycle (SDLC) can be used to determine the actual security risk profile of a system.

There are numerous individual elements in a *Software Development Life Cycle Methodology (SDLM)* that can assist a team in developing secure code. Correct SDLM processes, such as input validation, proper error and exception handling, and cross-site scripting and cross-site request forgery mitigations, can improve the security of code. Process elements such as security testing, fuzzing, and patch management also help to ensure applications meet a desired risk profile.

There are two main enumerations of common software errors: the Top 25 list maintained by MITRE, and the OWASP Top Ten list for web applications. Depending on the type of application being evaluated, these lists provide a solid starting point for security analysis of known error types. MITRE is the repository of the industry-standard list for standard programs, and OWASP for web applications. As the causes of common errors do not change quickly, these lists are not updated every year.

Proper Error Handling

Every application will encounter errors and exceptions, and these need to be handled in a secure manner. One attack methodology includes forcing errors to move an application from normal operation to exception handling. During an exception, it is common practice to record/report the condition, including supporting information such as the data that resulted in the error. This information can be invaluable in diagnosing the cause of the error condition. The challenge is in where this information is captured. The best method is to capture it in a log file, where it can be secured by an ACL. The worst case is when it is echoed to the user. Echoing error condition details to users can provide valuable information to attackers when they cause errors on purpose.

 EXAM TIP All errors/exceptions should be trapped and handled in the generating routine.

Improper exception handling can lead to a wide range of disclosures. Errors associated with SQL statements can disclose data structures and data elements. Remote procedure call (RPC) errors can give up sensitive information such as filenames, paths, and server names. Programmatic errors can give up line numbers that an exception occurred on, the method that was invoked, and information such as stack elements.

Proper Input Validation

With the move to web-based applications, the errors have shifted from buffer overflows to input-handling issues. Users have the ability to manipulate input, so it is up to the developer to handle the input appropriately to prevent malicious entries from having an effect. Buffer overflows could be considered a class of improper input, but newer attacks include canonicalization attacks and arithmetic attacks. Probably the most important defensive mechanism that can be employed is input validation. Considering all inputs to be hostile until properly validated can mitigate many attacks based on common vulnerabilities. This is a challenge, as the validation efforts need to occur after all parsers have completed manipulating input streams, a common function in web-based applications using Unicode and other international character sets.

Proper input validation is especially well suited for the following vulnerabilities: buffer overflow, reliance on untrusted inputs in a security decision, cross-site scripting (XSS), cross-site request forgery (XSRF), path traversal, and incorrect calculation of buffer size. Input validation may seem suitable for various injection attacks, but given the complexity of the input and the ramifications from legal but improper input streams, this method falls short for most injection attacks. What can work is a form of recognition and whitelisting approach, where the input is validated and then parsed into a standard structure that is then executed. This restricts the attack surface to not only legal inputs, but also expected inputs.

EXAM TIP Consider all input to be hostile. Input validation is one of the most important secure coding techniques employed, mitigating a wide array of potential vulnerabilities.

Output validation is just as important in many cases as input validation. If querying a database for a username and password match, the expected forms of the output of the match function should be either one match or none. If using record count to indicate the level of match, which is a common practice, then a value other than 0 or 1 would be an error. Defensive coding using output validation would not act on values >1, as these are clearly an error and should be treated as a failure.

Normalization

Normalization is an initial step in the input validation process. Specifically, it is the step of creating the canonical form, or simplest form, of a string before processing. Strings can be encoded using Unicode and other encoding methods. This makes byte-by-byte comparisons meaningless when trying to screen user input of strings. Checking to see if the string is "rose" can be difficult when: A Rose, is a rose, is a r%6fse (all of these represent the same string, just different forms). The process of normalization converts all of these to rose, where it can then be screened as valid input.

Different libraries exist to assist developers in performing this part of input validation. Developers should always normalize their inputs prior to validation steps to remove Unicode and other encoding issues. Per the Unicode standard, "when implementations keep strings in a normalized form, they can be assured that equivalent strings have a unique binary representation."

Stored Procedures

Stored procedures are precompiled methods implemented within a database engine. Stored procedures act as a secure coding mechanism because they offer an isolation of user input from the actual SQL statements being executed. This is the primary defense mechanism against SQL injection attacks, separation of user input from the SQL statements. User-supplied input data is common in interactive applications that use databases. This input can allow the user to define the specificity of search, match, and so forth. But what cannot happen is to allow a user to write the actual SQL code that is executed. There are too many things that could go wrong, too much power to allow a user to directly wield it, and eliminating SQL injection attacks by "fixing" input has never worked.

All major database engines support stored procedures. Stored procedures have a performance advantage over other forms of data access. The downside is that stored procedures are written in another language, SQL, and a database programmer typically is needed to implement the more complex ones.

Code Signing

An important factor in ensuring that software is genuine and has not been altered is a method of testing the software integrity. With software being updated across the Web, how can you be sure that the code received is genuine and has not been tampered with? The answer is a process known as *code signing*, which involves applying a digital signature to code, providing a mechanism where the end user can verify the code integrity. In addition to verifying the integrity of the code, digital signatures provide evidence as to the source of the software. Code signing rests upon the established public key infrastructure (PKI). To use code signing, a developer needs a key pair. For this key, the public key, to be recognized by the end user, it needs to be signed by a recognized certificate authority.

Encryption

Encryption is one of the elements where secure coding techniques have some unique guidance: "never roll your own crypto." This not only means you should not write your own cryptographic algorithms, but also means you should not attempt to implement standard algorithms by yourself. Vetted, proven cryptographic libraries exist for all major languages, and the use of these libraries is considered best practice. The guidance has a variety of interrelated rationales, but the simple explanation is that crypto is almost impossible to invent, and very hard to implement correctly. Thus, to have usable, secure encryption in your application, you need to adopt proven algorithms and utilize proven code bases.

Obfuscation/Camouflage

Obfuscation or *camouflage* is the hiding of obvious meaning from observation. While obscurity is not considered adequate security under most circumstances, adding obfuscation or camouflage to a system to make it harder for an attacker to understand and exploit is a good thing. Numbering your e-mail servers email1, email2, email3, . . . tells an attacker what namespace to explore. Removing or hiding these hints makes the work harder and offers another layer of protection.

This works well for data names and other exposed elements that have to be exposed to the outside. Where this does not work well is in the construction of code. Obfuscated code, or code that is hard or even nearly impossible to read, is a ticking time bomb. The day will come that someone will need to read the code to figure out how it works, either to modify it or to fix it if it is not working. If programmers have issues reading and understanding the code, how it functions, and what it is supposed to do, how can they contribute to its maintenance?

Code Reuse/Dead Code

Modern software development includes extensive reuse of components. From component libraries to common functions across multiple components, there is significant opportunity to reduce development time and costs through *code reuse*. This can also simplify a system through the reuse of known elements. The downside of massive code reuse is that failure of a widely reused code component has a ripple effect across many applications.

During the design phase, the development team should make decisions as to the appropriate level of reuse. For some complex functions, such as cryptography, reuse is the preferred path. In other cases, where the lineage of a component cannot be established, then the risk of use may outweigh the benefit. Additionally, the inclusion of previously used code, sometimes referred to as legacy code, can reduce development efforts and risk.

EXAM TIP The use of legacy code in current projects does not exempt that code from security reviews. All code should receive the same scrutiny, especially legacy code that may have been developed prior to the adoption of SDLC processes.

Dead code is code that while it may be executed, the results that it produces are never used elsewhere in the program. There are compiler options that can remove dead code, called dead code elimination, but you must use these options with care. Assume you have a section of code that you put in specifically to set a secret value to all zeros. The logic is as follows: generate secret key, use secret key, set secret key to zero. You do this last step to remove the key from memory and keep it from being stolen. But along comes the dead code removal routine. It sees that you set the value of secretkey == 0, but then you never use it again. So the compiler, in optimizing your code, removes your protection step.

Server-Side vs. Client-Side Execution and Validation

Input validation can be performed either on the server side of a client-server architecture or on the client side. In all client-server and peer-to-peer operations, one universal truth applies: never trust input without validation. Systems that are designed and configured without regard to this truth are subject to client-side attacks. Systems can be designed where the client has the functionality needed to assure input veracity, but there is always the risk that the client can become corrupted, whether by malware, a disgruntled user, or simple misconfiguration. The veracity of client-side execution actions cannot be guaranteed. Server-side execution of code can be secured making it the preferred location for sensitive operations such as input validation.

The lure of doing validation on the client side is to save the round-trip communication time, especially for input errors such as missing values. Applications commonly have client-side code to validate the input as correct in terms of it being complete and approximately correct. This validation on the client side does not mean that the data is safe to use, only that it appears that the data has been completely filled in. All input validation with respect to completeness, correctness, and security checks must be done on the server side, and must be done before the user input is used in any way.

EXAM TIP Attackers have significant advantages on clients because of access issues. Because one cannot guarantee the security of the environment of client machines and code, all sensitive operations should be performed on server-side environments.

Memory Management

Memory management comprises the actions used to control and coordinate computer memory, assigning memory to variables and reclaiming it when it is no longer being used. Errors in memory management can result in a program that has a memory leak, and the leak can grow over time, consuming more and more resources. The routine to clean up memory that has been allocated in a program but is no longer needed is called garbage collection. In the C programming language, where there is no automatic garbage collector, the programmer must allocate and free memory explicitly. One of the advantages of newer programming languages such as Java, C#, Python, and Ruby is that they provide automatic memory management with garbage collection. This may not be as efficient as when specifically coded in C, but it is significantly less error prone.

Use of Third-Party Libraries and SDKs

Programming today is, to a great extent, an exercise in using *third-party libraries* and *software development kits (SDKs)*. This is because once code has been debugged and proven to work, rewriting it is generally not a valuable use of time. Also, some fairly complex routines, such as encryption, have vetted, proven library sets that remove a lot of risk from programming these functions. Using these proven resources can reduce errors and vulnerabilities in code, making this a positive move for secure development. Using third-party elements brings baggage in that is code you have not developed and don't necessarily have all the dependency details. If the development team manages dependencies correctly, the benefits greatly outweigh the risks.

Data Exposure

Data exposure is the loss of control over data from a system during operations. Data must be protected during storage (data at rest), during communication (data in transit), and at times during use. It is up to the programming team to chart the flow of data through a system and ensure that it is protected from exposure throughout the process. Exposed data can be lost to unauthorized parties (a failure of confidentiality) or, equally dangerous, can be changed by an unauthorized party (a failure of integrity). Protection of the data will typically be done using various forms of cryptography, which is covered in Chapter 26.

 EXAM TIP The list of elements under secure coding techniques is long and specific. It is important to understand the differences among the techniques so that you can recognize which one best fits the context of the question.

Code Quality and Testing

When coding operations commence, application developers can use tools and techniques to assist them in the assessment of the security level of the code under development. They can analyze code either statically or dynamically to find weaknesses and vulnerabilities. Manual code reviews by the development team can provide benefits both to the code and the team. *Code quality* does not end with development, as the code needs to be delivered and installed both intact and correctly on the target system.

Code analysis encompasses the processes used to inspect code for weaknesses and vulnerabilities. Code analysis can be divided into two forms: static and dynamic. Static analysis involves examination of the code without execution. Dynamic analysis involves the execution of the code as part of the testing. Both static and dynamic analyses are typically performed with tools, which are much better at the detailed analysis steps needed for any but the smallest code samples.

Code testing is the verification that the code meets to functional requirements as laid out in the requirements process. While code analysis makes certain the code works properly doing what it is supposed to do and only what it is supposed to do, code testing makes certain it meets the business requirements.

Code analysis can be performed at virtually any level of development, from unit level to subsystem to system to complete application. The higher the level, the greater the test space and more complex the analysis. When the analysis is done by teams of humans reading the code, typically at the smaller unit level, it is referred to as a code review. Code analysis should be done at every level of development, because the sooner that weaknesses and vulnerabilities are discovered, the easier they are to fix. Issues found in design are cheaper to fix than those found in coding, which are cheaper to fix than those found in final testing, and all of these are cheaper to fix than errors discovered after the software has been deployed.

Static Code Analyzers

Static code analysis is when the code is examined without being executed. This analysis can be performed on both source code and object code bases. The term "source code" is typically used to designate the high-level language code, although technically, source code is the original code base in any form, from high-level language to machine code. Static analysis can be performed by humans or tools, although humans are limited to the high-level language, while tools can be used against virtually any form of code base.

Static code analysis is frequently performed using automated tools. These tools are given a variety of names, but are commonly called *static code analyzers* or source code analyzers. Sometimes, extra phrases, such as "binary scanners" or "byte code scanners," are used to differentiate the tools. Static tools use a variety of mechanisms to search for weaknesses and vulnerabilities. Automated tools can provide advantages when checking syntax, approved function/library calls, and examining rules and semantics associated with logic and calls. They can catch elements a human could overlook.

Dynamic Analysis (e.g., Fuzzing)

Dynamic analysis is performed while the software is executed, either on a target system or an emulated system. The system is fed specific test inputs designed to produce specific forms of behaviors. Dynamic analysis can be particularly important on systems such as embedded systems, where a high degree of operational autonomy is expected. As a case in point, the failure to perform adequate testing of software on the Ariane rocket program led to the loss of an Ariane V booster during takeoff. Subsequent analysis showed that if proper software testing had been performed, the error conditions could have been detected and corrected without the loss of the flight vehicle. Many times you can test software in use without the rest of the system, and for some use cases, where failure costs are high, extensive testing before actual use is standard practice.

Dynamic analysis requires specialized automation to perform specific testing. Among the tools available are dynamic test suites designed to monitor operations for programs that have high degrees of parallel functions, thread-checking routines to ensure multicore processors and software are managing threads correctly, and programs designed to detect race conditions and memory addressing errors.

Fuzzing (or *fuzz testing*) is a brute force method of addressing input validation issues and vulnerabilities. The basis for fuzzing a program is the application of large numbers of inputs to determine which ones cause faults and which ones might be vulnerable to exploitation. Fuzz testing can be applied to anywhere data is exchanged to verify that input validation is being performed properly. Network protocols can be fuzzed, file protocols can be fuzzed, and web protocols can be fuzzed. The vast majority of browser errors are found via fuzzing.

Fuzz testing works well in white, black, or gray box testing, as it can be performed without knowledge of the specifics of the application under test. Fuzz testing works by sending a multitude of input signals and seeing how the program handles them. Specifically, malformed inputs can be used to vary parser operation and to check for memory leaks, buffer overflows, and a wide range of input validation issues. Since input validation errors are one of the top issues in software vulnerabilities, fuzzing is the best method of testing against these issues, such as cross-site scripting and injection vulnerabilities.

There are several ways to classify fuzz testing. It can be classified as smart testing or dumb testing, indicating the type of logic used in creating the input values. Smart testing uses knowledge of what could go wrong, and malforms the inputs using this knowledge. Dumb testing just uses random inputs.

 EXAM TIP   Fuzz testing is a staple of SDLC-based testing, finding a wide range of errors with a single test method.

Fuzz testing also can be classified as generation-based or mutation-based. Generation-based fuzz testing uses the specifications of input streams to determine the data streams that are to be used in testing. Mutation-based fuzz testing takes known good traffic and mutates it in specific ways to create new input streams for testing. Each of these has its advantages, and the typical fuzzing environment involves both used together.

Stress Testing

The typical objective in performance testing is not to find specific bugs, but rather to determine bottlenecks and performance factors for the systems under test. These tests are frequently referred to as load testing and stress testing. Load testing involves running the system under a controlled speed environment. *Stress testing* takes the system past this operating point to see how it responds to overload conditions. One of the reasons stress testing is performed on software under development is to determine the service levels that can be expected from the software in a production environment. Typically, these are expressed in the terms of a service level agreement (SLA).

Sandboxing

Sandboxing refers to the execution of computer code in an environment designed to isolate the code from direct contact with the target system. Sandboxes are used to execute untrusted code, code from guests, and unverified programs. Sandboxes work like a virtual machine (VM) and can mediate a wide range of system interactions, from memory access to network access, and access to other programs, the file system, and devices. The level of protection offered by a sandbox depends upon the level of isolation and mediation offered.

Model Verification

Ensuring the code does what the code is supposed to do, verification, is more complex than just running the program and looking for runtime errors. The program results for a given set of inputs need to match the expected results per the system model. For instance, if applying a simple mathematical operation, is the calculation correct? This is simple to verify on a case-by-case basis, but when a program has many interdependent calculations, verifying that the result matches the desired design model can be a fairly complex task.

Validation and verification are the terms used to describe this testing. Validation is the process of checking whether the program specification captures the requirements from the customer. Verification is the process of checking that the software developed meets the model specification. Performing *model verification* testing is important, as this is the assurance that the code as developed meets the design requirements.

 EXAM TIP   Understand the different quality and testing elements so that you can apply the correct one to the context of a question.

Compiled vs. Runtime Code

Compiled code is code that is written in one language, then run through a compiler and transformed into executable code that can be run on a system. Compilers can do many things to optimize code and create smaller, faster-running programs on the actual hardware. But compilers have problems with dynamic code capable of changing at runtime. Interpreters create *runtime code* that can be executed via an interpreter engine, like a Java virtual machine (JVM), on a computer system. Although slower than compilers in execution, there are times that interpreters excel. To run a program with a compiler, the compiler first has to compile the source program into the target program and then load and execute the target program. These steps must all occur, and can take time. With an interpreter, the interpreter manages the conversion of the high-level code into the machine code on the fly, removing the compile steps. So, while an interpreter may be slow at running the code, if a lot of changes are happening that force recompiles, it can be faster.

In today's world, we have both compilers and interpreters for most languages, so that the correct tool can be used for the correct situation. We also have systems such as just-in-time compilers and bytecode interpreters that blur the traditional categorizations of compilers and interpreters.

Chapter Review

In this chapter, you became acquainted with secure application development and deployment concepts. The chapter opened with the waterfall and Agile development models. From there it moved into a discussion of secure DevOps. The topics under secure DevOps included security automation, continuous integration, baselining, immutable systems, and infrastructure as code. The chapter finished this segment with version control, change management, provisioning, and deprovisioning.

The chapter then looked at secure coding techniques, beginning with proper error handling and proper input validation, followed by a discussion of normalization and stored procedures. Code signing, encryption, and obfuscation/camouflage were covered next. The secure coding section wrapped up with a look at code reuse/dead code, server-side versus client-side execution, memory management, use of third-party libraries, and data exposure.

The chapter then explored code quality and testing, including the topics of static code analyzers, dynamic analysis (fuzzing), stress testing, sandboxing, and model verification. The chapter concluded with an examination of compiled code versus runtime code.

Questions

To help you prepare further for the CompTIA Security+ exam, and to test your level of preparedness, answer the following questions and then check your answers against the list of correct answers at the end of the chapter.

1. Which of the following methodologies progresses through a series of phases, with each phase being completed before progressing to the next phase?

   A. Scrum

   B. Waterfall

   C. Agile

   D. Extreme Programming (XP)

2. Which of the following methodologies is a structured process that is built around user stories that are used to architect requirements in an iterative process that uses acceptance testing to create incremental advances?

   A. Agile

   B. Scrum

   C. Extreme Programming (XP)

   D. Waterfall

3. Which of the following are elements of software development that will help to improve the security of code? (Choose all that apply.)

   A. Input validation

   B. Proper error and exception handling

   C. Cross-site scripting mitigations

   D. Patch management

4. Where should all errors/exceptions be trapped and handled?

   A. In the main program or routing that called the routine that generated the error/exception

   B. In the generating routine itself

   C. In a special routine designed to handle all errors/exceptions

   D. In a separate routine designed to handle each specific error/exception

5. Which of the following is a system that, once deployed, is never modified, patched, or upgraded?

   A. Baseline

   B. Immutable system

   C. Frozen system

   D. Fixed configuration

6. What is the term used to describe removing users' permissions or authorities to objects?

   A. Provisioning

   B. Version control

   C. Change management

   D. Deprovisioning

7. The process describing how an organization manages which versions are currently being used, and how it coordinates updates or new versions as they are released by a manufacturer, is known as which of the following?

   A. Version control

   B. Provisioning

   C. Change management

   D. Deprovisioning

8. Which of the following is an initial step in the input validation process that creates the canonical form, or simplest form, of a string before processing?

   A. Implementing stored procedures

   B. Code signing

   C. Code reuse

   D. Normalization

9. Which of the following is true about what is known as *dead code*?

    A. Dead code is code that is never executed and thus can be removed from the program without a negative impact.

    B. Dead code is code that is never executed but should remain in the program because removing it may have unintended consequences.

    C. Dead code is code that while it may be executed, the results that it produces are never used elsewhere in the program. There are compiler options that can remove dead code, which is called dead code elimination, but these must be used with care because dead code elimination may have unintended consequences.

    D. Dead code is code that while it may be executed, the results that it produces are never used elsewhere in the program. It should be removed through automated or manual means to improve the program.

10. What is the term used to describe the loss of control over data from a system during operations?

    A. Sandboxing

    B. Data exposure

    C. Data breach

    D. Runtime release

11. What term is used to refer to testing a system under a controlled speed environment?

    A. Load testing

    B. Stress testing

    C. Sandboxing

    D. Static code analysis

12. Fuzz testing works best in which of the following testing environments?

    A. White box testing

    B. Gray box testing

    C. Black box testing

    D. Fuzz testing works equally well in all of the above.

13. Code analysis can be performed at which of the following levels of development? (Choose all that apply.)

    A. Unit level

    B. Subsystem level

    C. System level

    D. Complete application

PART III

14. Which code analysis method is performed while the software is executed, either on a target system or an emulated system?

   A. Static analysis

   B. Runtime analysis

   C. Sandbox analysis

   D. Dynamic analysis

15. Which of the following is true concerning *verification*? (Choose all that apply.)

   A. Ensuring the code does what the code is supposed to do, verification, is more complex than just running the program and looking for runtime errors.

   B. Verification also checks whether the program specification captures the requirements from the customer.

   C. Verification is simple on a case-by-case basis, but when a program has many interdependent calculations, verifying that the results match the desired design model can be a fairly complex task.

   D. Verification is the process of checking that the software developed meets the model specification.

Answers

1. **B.** The *waterfall* model is a development model based on simple manufacturing design. The work process begins with the requirements analysis phase and progresses through a series of four more phases, with each phase being completed before progressing to the next phase. The *Scrum* programming methodology is built around a 30-day release cycle. The *Agile* model is not a single development methodology, but a whole group of related methods. Designed to increase innovation and efficiency of small programming teams, Agile methods rely on quick turns involving small increases in functionality. *Extreme Programming* is a structured process that is built around user stories. These stories are used to architect requirements in an iterative process that uses acceptance testing to create incremental advances.

2. **C.** *Extreme programming (XP)* is a structured process that is built around user stories. These stories are used to architect requirements in an iterative process that uses acceptance testing to create incremental advances. *Agile* methods are not a single development methodology, but a whole group of related methods. Designed to increase innovation and efficiency of small programming teams, Agile methods rely on quick turns involving small increases in functionality. The *waterfall* model is a development model based on simple manufacturing design. The work process begins with the requirements analysis phase and progresses through a series of four more phases, with each phase being completed before progressing to the next phase. The *Scrum* programming methodology is built around a 30-day release cycle.

3. **A, B,** and **C.** All are elements of software development that will help to improve the security of code. While *patch management* is an important aspect of security, it occurs after code development and delivery and is considered a process element and not a part of the software development lifecycle.

4. **B.** All errors/exceptions should be trapped and handled in the generating routine.

5. **B.** An *immutable system* is a system that, once deployed, is never modified, patched, or upgraded. If a patch or update is required, the system is merely replaced with a new system that is patched and updated. *Baselining* is the process of determining a standard set of functionality and performance. This is a metrics-driven process, where later changes can be compared to the baseline to gauge their impact on performance and other variables. If a change improves the baseline elements in a positive fashion, a new baseline can be established. The other terms are not commonly used in industry.

6. **D.** *Deprovisioning* is the removal of users' permissions or authorities to access objects. *Provisioning* is the process of assigning to users permissions or authorities to access objects. *Version control* is as simple as tracking which version of a program is being worked on, whether in development, testing, or production. *Change management* addresses how an organization manages which versions are currently being used, and how it coordinates changes as they are released by a manufacturer.

7. **C.** *Change management* addresses how an organization manages which versions are currently being used, and how it coordinates changes as they are released by a manufacturer. *Version control* is as simple as tracking which version of a program is being worked on, whether in development, testing, or production. *Provisioning* is the process of assigning permissions or authorities to objects for users. *Deprovisioning* is the removal of permissions or authorities to objects for users.

8. **D.** *Normalization* is an initial step in the input validation process. Specifically, it is the step of creating the canonical form, or simplest form, of a string before processing. *Stored procedures* are precompiled methods implemented within a database engine. Stored procedures act as a secure coding mechanism because they offer an isolation of user input from the actual SQL statements being executed. *Code signing* involves applying a digital signature to code, providing a mechanism where the end user can verify the code integrity. *Code reuse* is reusing code from one application to another.

9. **C.** *Dead code* is code that while it may be executed, the results that it obtains are never used elsewhere in the program. There are compiler options that can remove dead code, called dead code elimination, but these options must be used with care because dead code elimination may have unintended consequences.

10. **B.** *Data exposure* is the loss of control over data from a system during operations. *Sandboxing* refers to the execution of computer code in an environment designed to isolate the code from direct contact with the target system. A data breach occurs when an unauthorized user gains access to your system and its data. Runtime release is not a term used in the industry.

PART III

11. **A.** *Load testing* involves running the system under a controlled speed environment. *Stress testing* takes the system past this operating point to see how it responds to overload conditions. *Sandboxing* refers to the execution of computer code in an environment designed to isolate the code from direct contact with the target system. *Static code analysis* is when the code is examined without being executed.

12. **D.** *Fuzz testing* works well in white, black, or gray box testing, as it can be performed without knowledge of the specifics of the application under test.

13. **A, B, C,** and **D.** Code analysis can be performed at virtually any level of development, from unit level to subsystem to system to complete application.

14. **D.** *Dynamic analysis* is performed while the software is executed, either on a target system or an emulated system. *Static code analysis* is when the code is examined without being executed. *Sandboxing* refers to the execution of computer code in an environment designed to isolate the code from direct contact with the target system. Runtime analysis is descriptive of the type of analysis but is not the term used in industry.

15. **A, C,** and **D.** Ensuring the code does what the code is supposed to do, *verification*, is more complex than just running the program and looking for runtime errors. The program results for a given set of inputs need to match the expected results per the system model. For instance, if applying a simple mathematical operation, is the calculation correct? This is simple to verify on a case-by-case basis, but when a program has many interdependent calculations, verifying that the result matches the desired design model can be a fairly complex task. *Verification* is the process of checking that the software developed meets the model specification. *Validation* is the process of checking whether the program specification captures the requirements from the customer.

CHAPTER 15

Cloud and Virtualization

In this chapter, you will
- Explore virtualization concepts
- Become familiar with cloud concepts

Virtualization and cloud services are becoming common enterprise tools to manage cost, capacity, complexity, and risk. You need to understand how these services contribute to a security solution in today's enterprise, as described in this chapter.

Certification Objective This chapter covers CompTIA Security+ exam objective 3.7, Summarize cloud and virtualization concepts.

Hypervisor

Virtualization technology is used to enable a computer to have more than one OS present and, in many cases, operating at the same time. Virtualization is an abstraction of the OS layer, creating the ability to host multiple OSs on a single piece of hardware. To enable virtualization, a hypervisor is employed. A *hypervisor* is a low-level program that allows multiple operating systems to run concurrently on a single host computer. Hypervisors use a thin layer of code to allocate resources in real time. The hypervisor acts as the traffic cop that controls I/O and memory management. One of the major advantages of virtualization is the separation of the software and the hardware, creating a barrier that can improve many system functions, including security. The underlying hardware is referred to as the host machine, and on it is a host OS. Either the host OS has built-in hypervisor capability or an application is needed to provide the hypervisor function to manage the virtual machines (VMs). The virtual machines are typically referred to as guest OSs. Two types of hypervisors exist, Type I and Type II.

EXAM TIP A hypervisor is the interface between a virtual machine and the host machine hardware. Hypervisors are the layer that enables virtualization.

Type I

Type I hypervisors run directly on the system hardware. They are referred to as a native, bare-metal, or embedded hypervisors in typical vendor literature. Type I hypervisors are designed for speed and efficiency, as they do not have to operate through another OS layer. Examples of Type I hypervisors include KVM (Kernel-based Virtual Machine, a Linux implementation), Xen (Citrix Linux implementation), Microsoft Windows Server Hyper-V (a headless version of the Windows OS core), and VMware's vSphere/ESXi platforms. All of these Type I hypervisors are designed for the high-end server market in enterprises, and are designed to allow multiple VMs on a single set of server hardware. These platforms come with management tool sets to facilitate VM management in the enterprise.

Type II

Type II hypervisors run on top of a host operating system. In the beginning of the virtualization movement, Type II hypervisors were most popular. Administrators could buy the VM software and install it on a server they already had running. Typical Type II hypervisors include Oracle's VirtualBox and VMware's VMware Player. These are designed for limited numbers of VMs, typically running in a desktop or small server environment.

Application Cells/Containers

A hypervisor-based virtualization system enables multiple OS instances to coexist on a single hardware platform. The concept of *application cells/containers* is similar, but rather than having multiple independent OSs, a container holds the portions of an OS that it needs separate from the kernel. So, in essence, multiple containers can share an OS, yet have separate memory, CPU, and storage threads, guaranteeing that they will not interact with other containers. This allows multiple instances of an application or different applications to share a host OS with virtually no overhead. This also allows portability of the application to a degree separate from the OS stack. Multiple major container platforms exist, but the industry has coalesced around a standard form called the Open Container Initiative (OCI), designed to enable standardization and the market stability of the environment. Different vendors in the container space have slightly different terminologies, so you need to check with your specific implementation by vendor to understand the exact definition of container and cell in their environment.

You can think of containers as the evolution of the VM concept to the application space. A container consists of an entire runtime environment bundled into one package: an application, including all its dependencies, libraries, and other binaries, and the configuration files needed to run it. This eliminates the differences between a development, test, or production environment, as the differences are in the container as a standard solution. By containerizing the application platform, including its dependencies, any differences in OS distributions, libraries, and underlying infrastructure are abstracted away and rendered moot.

VM Sprawl Avoidance

Sprawl is the uncontrolled spreading and disorganization caused by lack of an organizational structure when many similar elements require management. Just as you can lose track of a file in a large file directory and have to hunt for it, you can lose track of a VM among many others that have been created. VMs basically are files that contain a copy of a working machine's disk and memory structures. Creating a new VM is a simple process. If an organization has only a couple of VMs, keeping track of them is relatively easy. But as the number of VMs grows rapidly over time, sprawl can set in. VM sprawl is a symptom of a disorganized structure. An organization needs to implement *VM sprawl avoidance* through policy. It can avoid VM sprawl through naming conventions and proper storage architectures, so that the files are in the correct directory, making finding the correct VM easy and efficient. But as in any filing system, it works only if everyone routinely follows the established policies and procedures to ensure that proper VM naming and filing are performed.

One of the strongest business cases for integrated VM management tools, such as ESX sever from VMware, is its ability to enable administrators to manage VMs and avoid sprawl. Being able to locate and use resources when required is an element of security, specifically availability, and sprawl causes availability issues.

VM Escape Protection

When multiple VMs are operating on a single hardware platform, one concern is *VM escape*, where software, either malware or an attacker, escapes from one VM to the underlying OS. Once the VM escape occurs, the attacker can attack the underlying OS, or resurface in a different VM. When you examine the problem from a logical point of view, both VMs use the same RAM, the same processors, and so forth; the difference is one of timing and specific combinations. While the VM system is designed to provide protection, as with all things of larger scale, the devil is in the details. Large-scale VM environments have specific modules designed to detect escape and provide *VM escape protection* to other modules.

 EXAM TIP   Virtual environments have several specific concepts that the exam may address. Understand the difference between Type I and Type II hypervisors, and where you would use each. Understand the differences between VM sprawl and VM escape and the issues each poses. Expect questions for which you are given several of these terms as options and have to choose the correct one.

Cloud Storage

Cloud storage is a common term used to describe computer storage provided over a network. One of the characteristics of cloud storage is transparency to the end user. This improves usability of this form of service provisioning. Cloud storage offers much to the user: improvements in performance, scalability, flexibility, security, and reliability, among other items. These improvements are a direct result of the specific attributes associated with how cloud services are implemented.

Security is a particular challenge when data and computation are handled by a remote party, as in cloud computing. The specific challenge is how to allow data to be stored outside your enterprise and yet remain in control over the use of the data. The common answer is encryption. By properly encrypting its data before transferring it to cloud storage, an organization can ensure that the data is stored securely with the cloud service provider.

Use of cloud storage services is already becoming mainstream with ordinary users through such services as Apple iCloud, Microsoft OneDrive (formerly SkyDrive), and Dropbox. These are easy to use, easy to configure, and provide the basic services desired with minimal user difficulty.

Cloud Deployment Models

There are many different *cloud deployment models*. Clouds can be created by many entities, internal and external to an organization. Many commercial cloud services are available, and are offered from a variety of firms as large as Google and Amazon, to smaller, local providers. Internally, an organization's own services can replicate the advantages of cloud computing while improving the utility of limited resources. The promise of cloud computing is improved utility and is marketed under the concepts of Platform as a Service, Software as a Service, and Infrastructure as a Service.

SaaS

Software as a Service (SaaS) is the offering of software to end users from within the cloud. Rather than installing software on client machines, SaaS acts as software on demand, where the software runs from the cloud. This has several advantages: updates can be seamless to end users, and integration between components can be enhanced. Common examples of SaaS are products that are offered via the Web by subscription services, such as Microsoft Office 365 and Adobe Creative Suite.

PaaS

Platform as a Service (PaaS) is a marketing term used to describe the offering of a computing platform in the cloud. Multiple sets of software working together to provide services, such as database services, can be delivered via the cloud as a platform. PaaS offerings generally focus on security and scalability, both of which are characteristics that fit with cloud and platform needs.

IaaS

Infrastructure as a Service (IaaS) is a term used to describe cloud-based systems that are delivered as a virtual solution for computing. Rather than building data centers, IaaS allows firms to contract for utility computing as needed. IaaS is specifically marketed on a pay-per-use basis, scalable directly with need.

EXAM TIP Be sure you understand the differences between cloud computing service models Platform as a Service, Software as a Service, and Infrastructure as a Service.

Private

If your organization is highly sensitive to sharing resources, you may wish to consider the use of a *private cloud*. Private clouds are essentially reserved resources used only for your organization—your own little cloud within the cloud. This service will be considerably more expensive, but it should also carry less exposure and should enable your organization to better define the security, processing, handling of data, and so on that occurs within your cloud.

Public

The term *public cloud* refers to when the cloud service is rendered over a system that is open for public use. In most cases, there is little operational difference between public and private cloud architectures, but the security ramifications can be substantial. Although public cloud services will separate users with security restrictions, the depth and level of these restrictions, by definition, will be significantly less in a public cloud.

Hybrid

A *hybrid cloud* structure is one where elements are combined from private, public, and community cloud structures. When examining a hybrid structure, you need to remain cognizant that, operationally, these differing environments may not actually be joined, but rather used together. Sensitive information can be stored in the private cloud and issue-related information can be stored in the community cloud, all of which information is accessed by an application. This makes the overall system a hybrid cloud system.

Community

A *community cloud* system is one where several organizations with a common interest share a cloud environment for the specific purposes of the shared endeavor. For example, local public entities and key local firms may share a community cloud dedicated to serving the interests of community initiatives. This can be an attractive cost-sharing mechanism for specific data-sharing initiatives.

EXAM TIP Be sure to understand and recognize the different cloud systems, private, public, hybrid, and community, because you may see all four as answer choices for a cloud question. The best answer will typically depend upon a single factor in the question.

On-Premise vs. Hosted vs. Cloud

Systems can exist in a wide array of places, from on-premises, to hosted, to in the cloud. *On-premises* (or *on-premise* according to CompTIA) means the system resides locally in the building of the organization. Whether a VM, storage, or even services, if the solution is locally hosted and maintained, it is referred to as on-premises. The advantage is that the organization has total control and generally high connectivity. The disadvantage is that it requires local resources and is not as easy to scale. *Hosted* services refers to having the services hosted somewhere else, commonly in a shared environment. Using third-party services for hosted services provides you a set cost based on the amount you use. This has cost advantages, especially when scale is included—does it make sense to have all the local infrastructure, including personnel, for a small, informational-only website? Of course not; you would have that website hosted. Storage works the opposite with scale. Small-scale storage needs are easily met in-house, whereas large-scale storage needs are typically either hosted or in the cloud.

 EXAM TIP On-premise means it is on your site. Hosted means it is somewhere else, a specific location. In the cloud refers to having it distributed across a remotely accessible infrastructure via a network, with specific cloud characteristics—scalability, etc.

VDI/VDE

Virtual desktop infrastructure (VDI) and *virtual desktop environment (VDE)* are terms used to describe the hosting of a desktop environment on a central server. VDI refers to all the components needed to set up the environment. VDE is what the user sees, the actual user environment. There are several advantages to this type of desktop environment. From a user's perspective, her "machine" and all of its data are persisted in the server environment. This means that a user can move from machine to machine and have a singular environment following her around. And since the end-user devices are just simple doors back to the server instance of the user's desktop, the computing requirements at the edge point are considerably lower and can be provided on older machines. Users can use a wide range of machines, even mobile phones, to access their desktop and perform their work. VDI/VDE can provide tremendous security advantages because all data, even when being processed, resides on servers inside the enterprise, so if a user's device or laptop is lost or stolen, it holds nothing from the desktop environment to compromise.

Cloud Access Security Broker

Cloud access security brokers (CASBs) act as security policy enforcement points between cloud service providers and their customers to ensure that enterprise security policies are maintained as the cloud-based resources are utilized. CASBs belong to the broader category of managed security service providers (MSSPs), which offer Security as a

Service to organizations. CASB vendors provide a range of security services designed to protect cloud infrastructure and data. CASBs act as security policy enforcement points between cloud service providers and their customers to enact enterprise security policies as the cloud-based resources are utilized.

Security as a Service

Just as you can get Software as a Service and Infrastructure as a Service, you can contract with an MSSP for Security as a Service. *Security as a Service* is the outsourcing of security functions to a vendor that can offer advantages in scale, costs, and speed. Security is a complex, wide-ranging cornucopia of technical specialties, all working together to provide appropriate risk reductions in today's enterprise. This means effective security requires technically savvy security pros, experienced management, specialized hardware and software, and fairly complex operations, both routine and in response to incidents. Any or all of this can be outsourced to a security vendor, and firms routinely examine vendors for solutions where the business economics makes outsourcing attractive.

Different security vendors offer different specializations, from network security, web application security, or e-mail security, to incident response services and even infrastructure updates. Depending upon architecture, needs, and scale, these third-party vendors often can offer an organization a compelling economic advantage in provisioning all or part of its security solution.

 EXAM TIP Be sure to understand the differences among the several types of services that can be delivered via the cloud, including storage, software, infrastructure, platform, and security, each with a specific deliverable and value proposition. Read cloud service–related questions carefully to determine which is the best solution, for at times the differentiating factor may be a single word in the question.

Chapter Review

In this chapter, you became acquainted with virtualization and cloud services. The chapter opened with a description of hypervisors, both Type I and II, and then covered application cells and containers. The problems with VM sprawl and VM escape were covered next. The chapter then moved to cloud-based storage and cloud deployment models, including SaaS, PaaS, and IaaS. The models of private, public, hybrid, and community clouds were explored. The issues associated with on-premises, hosted, and cloud-based provisioning were covered. The chapter concluded with an examination of VDI/VDE, cloud access security brokers, and Security as a Service in more general terms.

Questions

To help you prepare further for the CompTIA Security+ exam, and to test your level of preparedness, answer the following questions and then check your answers against the list of correct answers at the end of the chapter.

1. How does a hypervisor enable multiple guest operating systems to run concurrently on a host computer?

   A. Via a specialized driver package

   B. By abstracting the hardware from the guest operating systems

   C. By providing specific virtual hardware to each guest OS

   D. By hiding the underlying Linux operating system

2. Your supervisor asks you to analyze virtualization options for an upcoming project to move several critical servers onto virtual machines. He asks you to find a solution that maximizes the number of guest OSs per server and optimizes speed and efficiency. What solution should you recommend?

   A. A Type I hypervisor, such as VMware Sphere/ESXi or Hyper-V

   B. A Type II hypervisor, such as VirtualBox or VMware Player

   C. Both A and B

   D. Neither A nor B

3. Your new application has multiple small processes that provide services to the network. You want to make this application run more efficiently by virtualizing it. What is the best approach for virtualization of this application?

   A. Type II hypervisor

   B. Linux KVM

   C. Containerization

   D. Type I hypervisor

4. Why is VM sprawl an issue?

   A. VM sprawl uses too many resources on parallel functions.

   B. The more virtual machines in use, the harder it is to migrate a VM to a live server.

   C. Virtual machines are so easy to create, you end up with hundreds of small servers only performing a single function.

   D. When servers are no longer physical, it can be difficult to locate a specific machine.

5. When doing incident response for your company, you are reviewing the forensics of several virtual servers and you see the attacker on the web server injecting code into uninitialized memory blocks. What attack is the attacker likely attempting?

   A. Denial-of-service attack on the hypervisor

   B. VM escape

   C. Containerization attack

   D. Crashing the CASB

6. Your manager was just in a meeting about the security risks of storing data in the cloud and now is frantically requesting that you immediately shut off all access to cloud storage providers such as Dropbox, Box, OneDrive, and others, services that your company relies on for daily operations. What solution should you recommend to allow these services to be continued while protecting the corporate data in the cloud?

   A. VM escape

   B. Type II hypervisor

   C. Containerization

   D. Encryption

7. You are planning to move some applications to the cloud, including your organization's accounting application, which is highly customized and does not scale well. Which cloud deployment model is best for this application?

   A. SaaS

   B. PaaS

   C. IaaS

   D. None of the above

8. You need to move to the cloud a specific customer service module that has a web front end. This application is highly scalable and can be provided on demand. Which cloud deployment model is best for this application?

   A. SaaS

   B. PaaS

   C. IaaS

   D. None of the above

9. One of the primary resources in use at your organization is a standard database that many applications tie into. Which cloud deployment model is best for this kind of application?

   A. SaaS

   B. PaaS

   C. IaaS

   D. None of the above

10. Which cloud deployment model has the fewest security controls?

    A. Private

    B. Public

    C. Hybrid

    D. Community

11. Which cloud deployment model is shared by several organizations with a specific purpose?

    A. Private

    B. Public

    C. Hybrid

    D. Community

12. What is the primary downside of a private cloud model?

    A. Restrictive access rules

    B. Cost

    C. Scalability

    D. Lack of vendor support

13. The desktop support team wants to virtualize the desktop environment on a central server. What is the advantage for adopting VDI?

    A. Users can move to different machines and their applications will follow them.

    B. A wide array of devices, even low-powered ones, can be used to access a user's desktop.

    C. No data would be compromised if the hardware was lost.

    D. All of the above.

    E. None of the above.

14. The CIO asks you to provide guidance on implementing security now that many of the corporate applications are moving to the cloud. Which of the following should you recommend implementing?

    A. Encryption

    B. CASBs

    C. SaaS

    D. Containerization

15. What is the greatest advantage of outsourcing an organization's IT security to a Security as a Service provider?

   A. A lost or damaged encryption key can be recovered by the provider.

   B. Security can be provided seamlessly in all geographic locations.

   C. The provider can offer scale, cost, and speed efficiencies.

   D. Regulatory compliance is easier to achieve.

Answers

1. **B.** The hypervisor abstracts the hardware from the guest operating system to enable multiple guest operating systems to run concurrently on a host computer.

2. **A.** Speed and efficiency are maximized by a Type I hypervisor.

3. **C.** Containerization runs small applications on a host OS with virtually no overhead.

4. **D.** VM sprawl is an issue because when virtual machines proliferate, they can be easily moved and potentially easily copied to random locations. This can make finding a specific machine difficult without a specific organizational structure.

5. **B.** Although all hypervisors actively try to prevent it, any flaw in memory handling could allow code that is maliciously placed in a block to be read by the hypervisor or another machine. This is known as VM escape. The scenario states virtual server, eliminating C and D, and operational code blocks in uninitialized memory would not cause DOS.

6. **D.** Data encryption can protect corporate data that is stored in cloud storage provider locations.

7. **C.** Infrastructure as a Service is appropriate for highly customized, poorly scaling solutions that require specific resources to run.

8. **A.** Software as a Service is suitable for delivering highly scalable, on-demand applications without installing endpoint software.

9. **B.** Platform as a Service is suitable for standard resources in use by many other applications.

10. **B.** The shared environment of a public cloud has the least amount of security controls.

11. **D.** Community clouds are shared resources for a specific purpose.

12. **B.** A private cloud model is considerably more expensive as it is a dedicated resource, negating some of the advantages of outsourcing the infrastructure in the first place.

13. **D.** All of the above. Adopting VDI can provide multiple advantages, including: the session can follow the user, the desktop can be accessed from a variety of devices, and if a device is lost, it contains no corporate data.

14. **B.** Cloud access security brokers (CASBs) are specialized tools or services used to protect cloud infrastructure and data.

15. **C.** The greatest advantage to outsourcing cloud security to a Security as a Service provider is that the provider can offer scale, cost, and speed efficiencies.

CHAPTER 16

Resiliency and Automation Strategies

In this chapter, you will
- Learn how resiliency strategies reduce risk
- Discover automation strategies to reduce risk

Resilient systems are those that can return to normal operating conditions after a disruption. You can improve the resiliency of your systems, and thereby reduce risk associated with their failure, through the proper use of various configuration and setup strategies, such as snapshots and the capability to revert to known states, and by implementing redundant and fault-tolerant systems. Automation is used to improve efficiency and accuracy when administering machines using commands.

Certification Objective   This chapter covers CompTIA Security+ exam objective 3.8, Explain how resiliency and automation strategies reduce risk.

Automation/Scripting

Automation and *scripting* are valuable tools for system administrators and others to safely and efficiently execute tasks. Automation in the context of systems administration is the use of tools and methods to perform tasks otherwise performed manually by humans, thereby improving efficiency and accuracy and reducing risk. While many tasks can be performed by simple command-line execution or through the use of GUI menu operations, the use of scripts has three advantages. First, prewritten and tested scripts remove the chance of user error, either typos at the command line or clicking the wrong GUI option. Keyboard errors are common and can take significant time to undo or fix. For instance, you can erase an entire directory very quickly, while the recovery can take significant time to locate and restore the lost directory from a backup. The second advantage is that scripts can be chained together to provide a means of automating complex actions that require multiple commands in a structured sequence. Lastly, automation via scripts can save significant time, allowing complex operations to run at machine speed versus human input speed. When invoking an operation across multiple systems, a script that has a loop for all the machines can make some impossible tasks possible because of the reduction in human input time.

Automation is a major element of an enterprise security program. Many protocols, standards, methods, and architectures have been developed to support automation. The security community has developed automation methods associated with vulnerability management, including the Security Content Automation Protocol (SCAP), Common Vulnerabilities and Exposures (CVE), and more. You can find details about these protocols and others at http://measurablesecurity.mitre.org/, SCAP is at https://scap.nist.gov/ and CVE is at https://cve.mitre.org/.

Automated Courses of Action

Scripts are the best friend of administrators, analysts, investigators, and any other professional who values efficient and accurate technical work. Scripts are small computer programs that allow *automated courses of action.* As with all programs, the subsequent steps can be tested and, when necessary, approved before use in the production environment. Scripts and automation are important enough that they are specified in National Institute of Standards and Technology Special Publication 800-53 series, which specifies security and privacy controls for the U.S. government. For instance, under patching, SP 800-53 not only specifies using an automated method of determining which systems need patches, but also specifies that the patching mechanism be automated (see SI-2 flaw remediation in 800-53). Automated courses of action reduce errors.

Automated courses of action can save time as well. If, during an investigation, you need to take an image of a hard drive on a system, calculate hash values, and record all of the details in a file for chain of custody, you can do so manually by entering a series of commands at the command line, or you can run a single script that has been tested and approved for use.

Continuous Monitoring

Continuous monitoring is the term used to describe a system that has monitoring built into it, so rather than monitoring being an external event that may or may not happen, monitoring is an intrinsic aspect of the action. From a big picture point of view, continuous monitoring is the name used to describe a formal risk assessment process that follows the NIST Risk Management Framework (RMF) methodology. Part of that methodology is the use of security controls. Continuous monitoring is the operational process by which you can monitor controls and determine if they are functioning in an effective manner.

As most enterprises have a large number of systems and an even larger number of security controls, part of an effective continuous monitoring plan is the automated handling of the continuous monitoring status data, to facilitate consumption in a meaningful manner. Automated dashboards and alerts that show out-of-standard conditions allow operators to focus on the parts of the system that need attention rather than sifting through terabytes of data.

Configuration Validation

Configuration validation is a challenge as systems age and change over time. When you place a system into service, you should validate its configuration against security standards, ensuring that the system will do what it is supposed to do, and only what it is supposed to do, with no added functionality. You should ensure that all extra ports, services, accounts, and so forth are disabled, removed, or turned off, and that the configuration files, including ACLs for the system, are correct and working as designed.

Over time, as things change, software is patched, and other things are added to or taken away from the system. Updates to the application, the OS, and even other applications on the system change the configuration. Is the configuration still valid? How does an organization monitor all of its machines to ensure valid configurations? It is common for large enterprises to group systems by functions—standard workstations, manager workstations, etc.—to facilitate management of software and hardware configurations at sacle.

Automated testing is a method that can scale and resolve issues revolving around managing multiple configurations, making it just another part of the continuous monitoring system. Any other manual method eventually fails because of fluctuating priorities that will result in routine maintenance being deferred.

 EXAM TIP Automation/scripting plays a key role in automated courses of action, continuous monitoring, and configuration validation. These elements work together. On the exam, read the context of the question carefully and determine what specific question you are being asked, as this will identify the best answer from the related options.

Templates

Templates are master recipes for the building of objects, be they servers, programs, or even entire systems. Templates are what make Infrastructure as a Service possible. To establish a business relationship with an IaaS firm, they need to collect billing information, and there are a lot of terms and conditions that you should review with your legal team. But, then, the part you want, is the standing up of some piece of infrastructure. Templates enable the setting up of standard business arrangements, as well as the technology stacks used by customers.

As an example of how templates fit into an automation strategy, consider a scenario in which you want to contract with an IaaS vendor to implement a LAMP stack, a popular open source web platform that is ideal for running dynamic sites. It is composed of Linux, Apache, MySQL, and PHP/Python/Perl, hence the term LAMP. Naturally, you want your LAMP stack to be secure, patched, and have specific accounts for access. You fill out a web form for the IaaS vendor, which uses your information to match to an appropriate template. You specify all the conditions and click the Create button. If you were going to stand up this LAMP stack on your own, it might take days to configure all of these elements, from scratch, on hardware in-house. After you click the Create button, the IaaS firm uses templates and master images to provide your solution online in a matter of minutes. If you have very special needs, it might take a bit longer, but you get the idea: templates allow rapid, error-free creation of configurations, connection of services, testing, deployment, and more.

Master Image

A *master image* is a premade, fully patched image of your organization's systems. A master image in the form of a virtual machine can be configured and deployed in seconds to replace a system that has become tainted or is untrustworthy because of an incident. Master images provide the true clean backup of the operating systems, applications, everything but the data. When you architect your enterprise to take advantage of master images, you make many administrative tasks easier to automate, easier to do, and substantially freer of errors. Should an error be found, you have one image to fix and then deploy. Master images work very well for enterprises with multiple desktops, for you can create a master image that can be quickly deployed on new or repaired machines, bringing the systems to an identical and fully patched condition.

 EXAM TIP Master images are key elements of template-based systems and, together with automation and scripting, make many previously laborious and error-prone tasks fast, efficient, and error free. Understanding the role each of these technologies plays is important when examining the context of the question on the exam. Be sure to answer what the question asks for, because all of these technologies may play a role in a scenario.

Non-persistence

Non-persistence is when a change to a system is not permanent. Making a system non-persistent can be a useful tool when you wish to prevent certain types of malware attacks. A system that cannot preserve changes cannot have persistent files added into their operations. A simple reboot wipes out the new files, malware, etc. A system that has been made non-persistent is not able to save changes to its configuration, its applications, or anything else. There are utility programs that can freeze a machine from change, in essence making it non-persistent. This is useful for machines deployed in places where users can invoke changes, download stuff from the Internet, and so forth. Non-persistence offers a means for the enterprise to address these risks, by not letting them happen in the first place. In some respects, this is similar to whitelisting, only allowing approved applications to run.

Snapshots

Snapshots are instantaneous savepoints in time on virtual machines. These allow you to restore the virtual machine to a previous point in time. Snapshots work because a VM is just a file on a machine, and setting the file back to a previous version reverts the VM to the state it was in at that time.

A *snapshot* is a point-in-time saving of the state of a virtual machine. Snapshots have great utility because they are like a savepoint for an entire system. Snapshots can be used to roll a system back to a previous point in time, undo operations, or provide a quick means of recovery from a complex, system-altering change that has gone awry. Snapshots act as a form of backup and are typically much faster than normal system backup and recovery operations.

Snapshots can be very useful in reducing risk, as you can take a snapshot, make a change to the system, and, if the change is bad, revert to the snapshot like the change had never been made. Snapshots can act as a non-persistence mechanism, reverting a system back to a previous known configuration. One danger of snapshot use, is any user data that is stored on the system between the snapshot point and the reversion to it, will be lost. To persist user data, it should be stored on a remote location separate from the VM.

Revert to Known State

Reverting to a known state is an operating system capability that is akin to reverting to a snapshot of a VM. Many OSs now have the capability to produce a restore point, a copy of key files that change upon updates to the OS. If you add a driver or update the OS, and the update results in problems, you can revert the system to the previously saved restore point. This is a very commonly used option in Microsoft Windows, and the system by default creates restore points before it processes updates to the OS, and at set points in time between updates. This enables you to roll back the clock on the OS and restore to an earlier time at which you know the problem did not exist. Unlike snapshots, which record everything, this feature only protects the OS and associated files, but it also does not result in loss of a user's files, something that can happen with snapshots and other non-persistence methods.

Rollback to Known Configuration

Rollback to a known configuration is another way of saying revert to a known state, but it is also the specific language Microsoft uses with respect to rolling back the registry values to a known good configuration on boot. If you make an incorrect configuration change in Windows and now the system won't boot properly, you can select "The Last Known Good Configuration option" during boot from the setup menu and roll back the registry to the last value that properly completed a boot cycle. Microsoft stores most configuration options in the registry, and this is a way to revert to a previous set of configuration options for the machine. Note: Last Known Good Configuration is available only in Windows 7 and earlier. In Windows 8 forward, pressing F8 on bootup is not an option unless you change to Legacy mode. The proper method of backing up and restoring registry settings in Windows 8 through 10, is through the creation of a system restore point.

Live Boot Media

A *live boot media* is an optical disc or USB device that contains a complete bootable system. Live boot media are specially formatted so as to be bootable from the media. This gives you a means of booting the system from an external OS source, should the OS on the internal drive become unusable. This may be used as a recovery mechanism, although if the internal drive is encrypted, you will need backup keys to access it. This is also a convenient method of booting to a task-specific operating system, say with forensic tools or incident response tools, that is separate from the OS on the machine.

Elasticity

Elasticity is the ability of a system to dynamically increase the workload capacity using additional, added-on-demand hardware resources to scale out. If the workload increases, you scale out by adding more resources, and, conversely, when demand wanes, you scale back by removing unneeded resources. This can be set to automatically occur in some environments, where the workload at a given time determines the quantity of hardware resources being consumed. Elasticity is one of the strengths of cloud environments, as you can configure them to scale up and down, only paying for the actual resources you use. In a server farm that you own, you pay for the equipment even when it is not in use.

Scalability

Scalability is a design element that enables a system to accommodate larger workloads by adding resources either making hardware stronger, scale up, or adding additional nodes, scale out. This term is commonly used in server farms and database clusters, as these both can have scale issues with respect to workload. Both elasticity and scalability have an effect on system availability and throughput, which can be significant security- and risk-related issues.

 EXAM TIP   Elasticity and scalability seem to be the same thing, but they are different. Elasticity is related to dynamically scaling a system with workload, scaling out, while scalability is a design element that enables a system both to scale up, to more capable hardware, and to scale out, to more instances.

Distributive Allocation

Distributive allocation is the transparent allocation of requests across a range of resources. When multiple servers are employed to respond to load, distributive allocation handles the assignment of jobs across the servers. When the jobs are stateful, as in database queries, the process ensures that the subsequent requests are distributed to the same server to maintain transactional integrity. When the system is stateless, like web servers, other load-balancing routines are used to spread the work. Distributive allocation directly addresses the availability aspect of security on a system.

Redundancy

Redundancy is the use of multiple, independent elements to perform a critical function, so that if one fails, there is another that can take over the work. When developing a resiliency strategy for ensuring that an organization has what it needs to keep operating, even if hardware or software fails or if security is breached, you should consider other measures involving redundancy and spare parts. Some common applications of redundancy include the use of redundant servers, redundant connections, and redundant ISPs.

The need for redundant servers and connections may be fairly obvious, but redundant ISPs may not be so, at least initially. Many ISPs already have multiple accesses to the Internet on their own, but by having additional ISP connections, an organization can reduce the chance that an interruption of one ISP will negatively impact the organization. Ensuring uninterrupted access to the Internet by employees or access to the organization's e-commerce site for customers is becoming increasingly important.

Many organizations don't see the need for maintaining a supply of spare parts. After all, with the price of storage dropping and the speed of processors increasing, why replace a broken part with older technology? However, a ready supply of spare parts can ease the process of bringing the system back online. Replacing hardware and software with newer versions can sometimes lead to problems with compatibility. An older version of some piece of critical software may not work with newer hardware, which may be more capable in a variety of ways. Having critical hardware (or software) spares for critical functions in the organization can greatly facilitate maintaining business continuity in the event of software or hardware failures.

 EXAM TIP Redundancy is an important factor in both security and reliability. Make sure you understand the many different areas that can benefit from redundant components.

Fault Tolerance

Fault tolerance basically has the same goal as high availability (covered in the next section)—the uninterrupted access to data and services. It can be accomplished by the mirroring of data and hardware systems. Should a "fault" occur, causing disruption in a device such as a disk controller, the mirrored system provides the requested data with no apparent interruption in service to the user. Certain systems, such as servers, are more critical to business operations and should therefore be the object of fault-tolerant measures.

High Availability

One of the objectives of security is the availability of data and processing power when an authorized user desires it. *High availability* refers to the ability to maintain availability of data and operational processing (services) despite a disrupting event. Generally this requires redundant systems, both in terms of power and processing, so that should one system fail, the other can take over operations without any break in service. High availability is more than data redundancy; it requires that both data and services be available.

 EXAM TIP Fault tolerance and high availability are similar in their goals, yet they are separate in application. *High availability* refers to maintaining both data and services in an operational state even when a disrupting event occurs. *Fault tolerance* is a design objective to achieve high availability should a fault occur.

RAID

A common approach to increasing reliability in disk storage is employing a *Redundant Array of Independent Disks (RAID)*. RAID takes data that is normally stored on a single disk and spreads it out among several others. If any single disk is lost, the data can be recovered from the other disks where the data also resides. With the price of disk storage decreasing, this approach has become increasingly popular to the point that many individual users even have RAID arrays for their home systems. RAID can also increase the speed of data recovery as multiple drives can be busy retrieving requested data at the same time instead of relying on just one disk to do the work.

Several different RAID approaches can be considered:

- **RAID 0** (striped disks) simply spreads the data that would be kept on the one disk across several disks. This decreases the time it takes to retrieve data, because the data is read from multiple drives at the same time, but it does not improve reliability, because the loss of any single drive will result in the loss of all the data (since portions of files are spread out among the different disks). With RAID 0, the data is split across all the drives with no redundancy offered.

- **RAID 1** (mirrored disks) is the opposite of RAID 0. RAID 1 copies the data from one disk onto two or more disks. If any one disk is lost, the data is not lost since it is also copied onto the other disk(s). This method can be used to improve reliability and retrieval speed, but it is relatively expensive when compared to other RAID techniques.

- **RAID 2** (bit-level error-correcting code) is not typically used, as it stripes data across the drives at the bit level as opposed to the block level. It is designed to be able to recover the loss of any single disk through the use of error-correcting techniques.

- **RAID 3** (byte-striped with error check) spreads the data across multiple disks at the byte level with one disk dedicated to parity bits. This technique is not commonly implemented because input/output operations can't be overlapped due to the need for all to access the same disk (the disk with the parity bits).

- **RAID 4** (dedicated parity drive) stripes data across several disks but in larger stripes than in RAID 3, and it uses a single drive for parity-based error checking. RAID 4 has the disadvantage of not improving data retrieval speeds, since all retrievals still need to access the single parity drive.

- **RAID 5** (block-striped with error check) is a commonly used method that stripes the data at the block level and spreads the parity data across the drives. This provides both reliability and increased speed performance. This form requires a minimum of three drives.

RAID 0 through 5 are the original techniques, with RAID 5 being the most common method used, as it provides both the reliability and speed improvements. Additional methods have been implemented, such as duplicating the parity data across the disks

(RAID 6) and a stripe of mirrors (RAID 10). Some levels can be combined to produce a two-digit RAID level. RAID 10, then, is a combination of levels 1 (mirroring) and 0 (striping), which is why it is also sometimes identified as RAID 1 + 0. Mirroring is writing data to two or more hard disk drives (HDDs) at the same time—if one disk fails, the mirror image preserves the data from the failed disk. Striping breaks data into "chunks" that are written in succession to different disks.

 EXAM TIP Knowledge of the basic RAID structures by number designation is a testable element and should be memorized for the exam.

Chapter Review

This chapter helped you to formulate strategies to improve resiliency and use automation in an effort to reduce risk. The chapter opened with a discussion of automation and scripting, describing how automated courses of action, continuous monitoring, and configuration validation can help you to reduce risk. The chapter then moved to the subject of templates and master images. Next, the topic of non-persistence covered the role of snapshots, reverting to a known state, rolling back to a known configuration, and live boot media in your strategy.

The chapter then explored elasticity and scalability, and followed with distributive allocation. The chapter closed with topics on resiliency, specifically redundancy, fault tolerance, high availability, and RAID.

Questions

To help you prepare further for the CompTIA Security+ exam, and to test your level of preparedness, answer the following questions and then check your answers against the list of correct answers at the end of the chapter.

1. Which of the following correctly describes a resilient system?

    A. A system with defined configuration and setup strategies

    B. A system using snapshots and reverting to known states

    C. A system with redundancy and fault tolerance

    D. A system that can return to normal operating conditions after an upset

2. Which of the following correctly describes automation as discussed in this chapter?

    A. The configuration of redundant and fault-tolerant systems

    B. The use of short programs to perform tasks otherwise performed manually by keyboard entry.

    C. The proper use of configuration definitions and setup

    D. Processes running autonomously on a given system

3. Which of the following is not an advantage of using scripts?

   A. Reducing the chance of error

   B. Performing change management on the scripts

   C. Avoiding time-consuming activities to correct mistakes

   D. Automating complex tasks by chaining scripts together.

4. What is the Security Content Automation Protocol (SCAP) used for?

   A. To enumerate common vulnerabilities

   B. To secure networks

   C. To provide automation methods for managing vulnerabilities

   D. To define an overarching security architecture

5. Which of the following is a true statement regarding automated courses of action?

   A. They are often unwieldy and error prone.

   B. They induce errors into system management.

   C. They take significant time to design and validate.

   D. They reduce errors.

6. Which of the following correctly defines continuous monitoring?

   A. The operational process by which you can confirm if controls are functioning properly

   B. An ongoing process to evaluate the utility of flat-screen monitors

   C. A dashboard that shows the status of systems

   D. An operations center staffed 24×7, 365 days per year

7. Why is automated testing an important part of configuration validation?

   A. It can scale and be used in continuous monitoring.

   B. It can compare before and after versions of a given system.

   C. It can automatically confirm the validity of a configuration.

   D. It can slow the divergence caused by system updates.

8. What is an advantage of using templates?

   A. They reduce the need for customers to test configurations.

   B. They resolve patching problems.

   C. They allow rapid, error-free creation of systems and services, including configurations, connection of services, testing, and deployment.

   D. They enforce end-user requirements.

9. Which of the following correctly describes master images?

   A. They can regenerate a system, but only after much effort and delays.

   B. They work well for small corporations, but they don't scale.

   C. They require extensive change management efforts.

   D. They are key elements of template-based systems.

10. Which of the following are benefits of using a master image?

    A. They make administrative tasks easier to automate.

    B. They make administrative tasks simpler.

    C. They substantially reduce the number of human errors.

    D. All of the above.

11. Non-persistence systems can reduce risk because?

    A. They can function in constantly evolving environments.

    B. They enable end users to change their computers as much as they want.

    C. They do not allow users to save changes to configuration or applications.

    D. None of the above.

12. What is a major benefit provided by snapshots?

    A. If a change contains errors, it is easy to revert to the previous configuration.

    B. Snapshots can retain a large number of photos.

    C. Because they are instantaneous savepoints on a machine, they do not need to be retained.

    D. They work very well on physical hardware but not so well on virtual machines.

13. What is an important point to understand about reverting to a known state?

    A. Reverting to a known state can result in loss of a user's files.

    B. Reverting to a known state typically only protects the operating system and associated files.

    C. Reverting to a known state does not allow removing an error caused by change.

    D. Creating the known state only occurs after implementing a change.

14. What is the difference between reverting to a known state and rolling back to a known configuration?

    A. Reverting to a known state can effect more than just the OS.

    B. Rolling back to a known configuration is a change to the system configuration, not necessarily what it is working on.

    C. Both A and B.

    D. Neither A nor B.

15. What is a key principle about elasticity?

    A. You can configure systems to scale up and down, so you only pay for the resources used.

    B. Elasticity works very well with on-premises equipment.

    C. Elasticity is not a strength of cloud environments.

    D. Scaling up and down both result in increased charges.

Answers

1. **D.** A resilient system is one that can return to normal operating conditions after a disruption.

2. **B.** Automation in the context of systems administration is the use of tools and methods to perform tasks otherwise performed manually by humans, thereby improving efficiency and accuracy and reducing risk.

3. **B.** Performing change management on the scripts is not an advantage of using them. Reducing the chance of error, avoiding time-consuming activities to correct mistakes, and automating complex tasks by chaining scripts together are all advantages of using scripts.

4. **C.** SCAP provides automation methods for managing vulnerabilities.

5. **D.** The bottom-line statement about the value of automated courses of action is that they reduce errors.

6. **A.** Continuous monitoring is the operational process by which you can confirm if controls are functioning properly.

7. **A.** Automated testing is an important part of configuration validation because it can scale and be used in continuous monitoring.

8. **C.** An important capability of templates is that they allow rapid, error-free creation of systems and services, including configurations, connection of services, testing, and deployment.

9. **D.** Master images are key elements of template-based systems.

10. **D.** Master images make administrative tasks easier to automate, make administrative tasks simpler, and substantially reduce the number of human errors.

11. **C.** Non-persistence does not allow saving changes to configuration or applications.

12. **A.** A major benefit provided by snapshots is that if a change contains errors, it is easy to revert to the previous configuration.

13. B. Reverting to a known state typically only protects the operating system and associated files.

14. C. Reverting to a known state is rolling back to a restore point—this effects the OS and any processes currently running with saved values. Rolling back to a known configuration restores the registry values to a known good configuration, but does not change user values.

15. A. A key principle about elasticity is that you can configure systems to scale up and down, so you only pay for the resources used.

CHAPTER 17

Physical Security Controls

In this chapter, you will

- Explore the importance of physical security controls
- Learn about important environment controls

Physical security is an important topic for businesses dealing with the security of networks and information systems. Businesses are responsible for managing their risk exposure, which requires securing a combination of assets: employees, product inventory, trade secrets, and strategy information. These and other important assets affect the profitability of a company and its future survival. Companies therefore perform many activities to attempt to provide physical security—locking doors, installing alarm systems, using safes, posting security guards, setting access controls, and more.

Environmental controls play an important role in the protection of the systems used to process information. Most companies today have invested a large amount of time, money, and effort in both network security and information systems security. In this chapter, you will learn about how the strategies for securing the network and for securing information systems are linked, and you'll learn several methods by which companies can minimize their exposure to physical security events that can diminish their network security.

Certification Objective   This chapter covers CompTIA Security+ exam objective 3.9, Explain the importance of physical security controls.

Lighting

Proper *lighting* is essential for physical security. Unlit or dimly lit areas allow intruders to lurk and conduct unauthorized activities without a significant risk of observation by guards or other personnel. External building lighting is important to ensure that unauthorized activities cannot occur without being observed and responded to. Internal lighting is equally important, for it enables more people to observe activities and see conditions that are not correct. As described later, in the "Barricades/Bollards" section, windows can play an important role in assisting the observation of the premises. Having sensitive areas well lit and open to observation through windows prevents activities that would otherwise take place in secret. Unauthorized parties in server rooms are more likely to be detected if the servers are centrally located, surrounded in windows, and well lit.

Signs

Signs act as informational devices and can be used in a variety of ways to assist in physical security. Signs can provide information as to areas that are restricted, or indicate where specific precautions, such as keeping doors locked, are required. A common use of signs in high-security facilities is to delineate where visitors are allowed versus secured areas where escorts are required. Visual security clues can assist in alerting users to the need for specific security precautions. Visual clues as to the types of protection required can take the form of different-color name badges that dictate the level of access, visual lanyards that indicate visitors, colored folders, and so forth.

Fencing/Gate/Cage

Fencing serves as a physical barrier around property. It can serve to keep people out and in, preventing the free movement across unauthorized areas. Fencing can be an important part of a physical security plan. Properly employed, it can help secure areas from unauthorized visitors. Outside of the building's walls, many organizations prefer to have a perimeter fence as a physical first layer of defense. Chain-link-type fencing is most commonly used, and it can be enhanced with barbed wire along the top. Anti-scale fencing, which looks like very tall vertical poles placed close together to form a fence, is used for high-security implementations that require additional scale and tamper resistance.

Inside a building fencing can be used to provide a means of restricting entry into areas where separate physical security policies apply. Material storage, servers, networking gear, and other sensitive items can be separated from unauthorized access with simple chain link fences. These areas are typically called a *cage*, and entry/exit to the caged areas is via a *gate*. The gate allows controlled access and makes it easier to monitor who and what enters and leaves the controlled area. Gates are used for external fencing as well. Gates offer a monitoring point for ingress and egress from a controlled area.

Security Guards

Security guards provide an excellent security measure, because guards are a visible presence with direct responsibility for security. Other employees expect security guards to behave a certain way with regard to securing the facility. Guards typically monitor entrances and exits and can maintain access logs of who has entered and departed the building. In many organizations, everyone who passes through security as a visitor must sign the log, which can be useful in tracing who was at what location and why.

Security personnel are helpful in physically securing the machines on which information assets reside, but to get the most benefit from their presence, they must be trained to take a holistic approach to security. The value of data typically can be many times that of the machines on which the data is stored. Security guards typically are not computer security experts, so they need to be educated about the value of the data and be trained in network security as well as physical security involving users. They are the company's eyes and ears for suspicious activity, so the network security department needs to train them to notice suspicious network activity as well. Multiple extensions ringing in sequence during the night, computers rebooting all at once, or strangers parked in the parking lot with laptop computers or other mobile computing devices are all indicators of a network attack that might be missed without proper training.

Alarms

Alarms serve to alert operators to abnormal conditions. Physical security can involve numerous sensors, intrusion alarms, motion detectors, switches that alert to doors being opened, video and audio surveillance, and more. Each of these systems can gather useful information, but it is only truly useful if it is acted upon. When one of these systems has information that can be of use to operational personnel, an alarm is the easiest method of alerting personnel to the condition. Alarms are not simple; if a company has too many alarm conditions, especially false alarms, then the operators will not react to the conditions as desired. Tuning alarms so that they provide useful, accurate, and actionable information is important if you want them to be effective.

 EXAM TIP Lighting, signs, fencing, and alarms are all items readily associated with physical security. The proper answer to an exam question will be based on the specific details of the question—watch for the clues and pick the best answer based on the context of the question.

Safe

Safes are physical storage devices that are intended to impede unauthorized access to their protected contents. Safes come in a wide variety of shapes, sizes, and cost. The higher the level of protection from the physical environment, the better the level of protection against unauthorized access. Safes are not perfect; in fact, they are rated in terms of how long they can be expected to protect the contents from theft or fire. The better the rating, the more expensive the safe.

Secure Cabinets/Enclosures

There are times when a safe is overkill, providing a higher level of security than is really needed. A simpler solution is *secure cabinets* and *enclosures*. Secure cabinets and enclosures provide system owners a place to park an asset until its use. Most secure cabinets/enclosures do not offer all of the levels of protection that one gets with a safe, but they can be useful, especially when the volume of secure storage is large.

Secure enclosures can provide security against some forms of physical access, as in users, yet still provide the proper environmental controls and setting necessary for operation. Safes cannot typically provide these levels of controls.

Protected Distribution/Protected Cabling

Cable runs between systems need to be protected from physical damage to the cables and subsequent communication failures. This is accomplished by *protected distribution/ protected cabling* during the cable installation. This may be something as simple as metal tubes, or as complex a concrete pipes to run buried cables. The objective is to prevent any physical damage to the physical layer portion of the system. Protected distribution/ protected cabling provides physical safeguards to the cabling between systems, from all physical hazards including interception and tapping. The protection of entire systems is covered later in the section "Faraday Cages."

Airgap

An *airgap* is a term used to describe the physical and logical separation of a network from all other networks. This separation is designed to prevent unauthorized data transfers to and from the network. The flaw in this logic is that users will move data by other means, such as a USB drive, to get their work done. Frequently called "sneaker net," this unauthorized bypassing of the airgap, although ostensibly for the purpose of mission accomplishment, increases system risk because it also bypasses checks, logging, and other processes important in development and deployment.

Mantrap

The implementation of a mantrap is one way to combat tailgating. A *mantrap* comprises two doors closely spaced that require the user to card through one and then the other sequentially. Mantraps make it nearly impossible to trail through a doorway undetected—if an intruder happens to catch the first door before it closes, he will be trapped in by the second door as the second door remains locked until the first one closes and locks.

 EXAM TIP A mantrap door arrangement can prevent unauthorized people from following authorized users through an access-controlled door, which is also known as *tailgating*.

Faraday Cages

Electromagnetic interference (EMI) is an electrical disturbance that affects an electrical circuit. EMI is due to either electromagnetic induction or radiation emitted from an external source, either of which can induce currents into the small circuits that make up computer systems and cause logic upsets, and is covered in Chapter 12. EMI can plague any type of electronics, but the density of circuitry in the typical data center can make it a haven for EMI. EMI is defined as the disturbance on an electrical circuit caused by that circuit's reception of electromagnetic radiation. Magnetic radiation enters the circuit by induction, where magnetic waves create a charge on the circuit. The amount of sensitivity to this magnetic field depends on a number of factors, including the length of the circuit, which can act like an antenna. EMI is grouped into two general types:

narrowband and broadband. Narrowband is, by its nature, electromagnetic energy with a small frequency band and, therefore, typically sourced from a device that is purposefully transmitting in the specified band. Broadband covers a wider array of frequencies and is typically caused by some type of general electrical power use such as power lines or electric motors.

In the United States, the Federal Communications Commission (FCC) has responsibility for regulating products that produce EMI and has developed a program for equipment manufacturers to adhere to standards for EMI immunity. Modern circuitry is designed to resist EMI. Cabling is a good example; the twists in unshielded twisted pair (UTP), or Category 5e, 6, 6a, or 7, cable are there to prevent EMI. EMI is also controlled by metal computer cases that are grounded; by providing an easy path to ground, the case acts as an EMI shield. Shielding can be important for network cabling. It is important not to run lengths of network cabling in parallel with power cables. Twisted pair offers some degree of protection, but in electrically noisy environments such as industrial facilities, shielded twisted pair (STP) may be necessary.

A bigger example of shielding would be a *Faraday cage* or Faraday shield, which is an enclosure of conductive material that is grounded. These can be room-sized or built into a building's construction; the critical element is that there is no significant gap in the enclosure material. These measures can help shield EMI, especially in high radio frequency environments.

While we have talked about the shielding necessary to keep EMI radiation out of your circuitry, there is also technology to try and help keep it in. Known by some as TEMPEST, it is a DoD program designed to block Van Eck emissions. A computer's monitor or LCD display produces electromagnetic radiation that can be remotely observed with the correct equipment, called Van Eck emissions. TEMPEST was the code word for a National Security Agency (NSA) program to secure equipment from this type of eavesdropping. While some of the information about TEMPEST is still classified, there are guides on the Internet that describe protective measures, such as shielding and electromagnetic-resistant enclosures. A company has even developed a commercial paint that offers radio frequency shielding. All of these protections are designed to stop electromagnetic energy from carrying a signal beyond a specific physical boundary, either the Faraday cage or paint or other EM barrier. This prevents outside signals from getting in and prevents those outside from monitoring what is happening on the inside.

 EXAM TIP When it comes to shielding, understand the difference between a Faraday cage (large open space) and EMI shielding on cables (very specific shielding) and which is appropriate based on what is being protected from EMI.

Lock Types

Locks are a common security measure that are used with near ubiquity. Everyone is familiar with using a lock to secure something. Many different *lock types* are used in and around the computer security arena. There are types for laptops, for desktops, even servers. Just as locks can keep your car or bike from being stolen, they can secure computers as well.

Figure 17-1
Lock-picking
tools

Laptops are popular targets for thieves and should be locked inside a desk when not in use, or secured with special computer lockdown cables. Laptop thefts from cars can occur in seconds, and thieves have been caught taking laptops from security screening areas at airports while the owner was distracted in screening. If an organization uses desktop towers, it should use computer desks that provide a space in which to lock the computer. In some cases, valuable media are stored in a safe designed for that purpose. All of these measures can improve the physical security of the computers themselves, but most of them can be defeated by attackers if users are not knowledgeable about the security program and do not follow it.

Although locks have been used for hundreds of years, their design has not changed much: a metal "token" is used to align pins in a mechanical device. Because all mechanical devices have tolerances, it is possible to sneak through these tolerances by "picking" the lock. Most locks can be easily picked with simple tools, some of which are shown in Figure 17-1.

Humans are always trying to build a better mousetrap, and that applies to locks as well. High-security locks have been designed to defeat attacks, such as the one shown in Figure 17-2; these locks are more sophisticated than a standard home deadbolt system. Typically found in commercial applications that require high security, these locks are made to resist picking and drilling, as well as other common attacks such as simply pounding the lock through the door. Another common feature of high-security locks is key control, which refers to the restrictions placed on making a copy of the key. For most residential locks, a trip to the hardware store will allow you to make a copy of the key. Key control locks use patented keyways that can only be copied by a locksmith, who will keep records on authorized users of a particular key.

Figure 17-2
A high-security
lock and its key

High-end lock security is more important now that attacks such as "bump keys" are well known and widely available. A bump key is a key cut with all notches to the maximum depth, also known as "all nines." This key uses a technique that has be around a long time, but has recently gained a lot of popularity. The key is inserted into the lock and then sharply struck, bouncing the lock pins up above the shear line and allowing the lock to open. High-security locks attempt to prevent this type of attack through various mechanical means such as nontraditional pin layout, sidebars, and even magnetic keys.

Biometrics

Biometrics is the measurement of biological attributes or processes with the goal of identification of a party possessing the measures. The most well-known biometric factor is the fingerprint. Fingerprint readers have been available for several years in laptops and other mobile devices, such as shown in Figure 17-3, and as stand-alone USB devices.

Other biometric measurements that can be used for physical security purposes include the retina or iris of the eye, the geometry of the hand, and the geometry of the face. When any of these are used for authentication, there is a two-part process: enrollment and then authentication. During enrollment, a computer takes the image of the biological factor and reduces it to a numeric value. When the user attempts to authenticate, his or her feature is scanned by the reader, and the computer compares the numeric value being read to the one stored in the database. If they match, access is allowed. Since these physical factors are unique, theoretically, only the actual authorized person would be allowed access.

Biometrics are frequently used in physical security, and are becoming nearly ubiquitous for controlling access to mobile devices, such as phones and tablets. For many physical security situations, the true question for access is, are you the correct person who should have access? Using biometrics to confirm the identity of the person being presented for access as the same person who went through the identification phase at enrollment is a good way to answer this question. You can't loan your fingerprints, iris, or retina for a scan, or your hand for its geometry. Biometrics bind the identification token to the person.

Figure 17-3
Newer laptop computers often include a fingerprint reader.

Biometrics are not foolproof. Some biometric measures can be duplicated to fool a sensor, and in many cases, the actual biometric is converted to a number that can also be intercepted and used in a software attack. Safeguards exist for most biometric bypass mechanisms, making them a usable security technology.

Barricades/Bollards

The primary defense against a majority of physical attacks are the *barricades* between the assets and a potential attacker—walls, fences, gates, and doors. Barricades provide the foundation upon which all other security initiatives are based, but the security must be designed carefully, as an attacker has to find only a single gap to gain access. Barricades can also be used to control vehicular access to and near a building or structure. The simple post-type barricade that prevents a vehicle from passing but allows people to walk past is called a *bollard*.

EXAM TIP   All entry points to server rooms and wiring closets should be closely controlled, and, if possible, access should be logged through an access control system.

Walls may have been one of the first inventions of humans. Once they learned to use natural obstacles such as mountains to separate them from their enemy, they next learned to build their *own* mountain for the same purpose. Hadrian's Wall in England, the Great Wall of China, and the Berlin Wall are all famous examples of such basic physical defenses. The walls of any building serve the same purpose, but on a smaller scale: they provide barriers to physical access to company assets. In the case of information assets, as a general rule, the most valuable assets are contained on company servers. To protect the physical servers, you must look in all directions. Doors and windows should be safeguarded, and a minimum number of each should be used in a server room when they are all that separate the servers from the personnel allowed to access them. It is very important that any transparent windows or doors do not allow shoulder surfing from outside the server room. It is good to see people in the room, just not what they type on their screens. Less obvious entry points should also be considered: Is a drop ceiling used in the server room? Do the interior walls extend to the actual roof, raised floors, or crawlspaces? Access to the server room should be limited to the people who need access, not to all employees of the organization. If you are going to use a wall to protect an asset, make sure no obvious holes appear in that wall.

NOTE   Windows or no windows? Windows provide visibility, allowing people to observe activities in the server room. This can provide security if those doing the observing have authority to see the activity in the server room. If those outside do not have this authority, then windows should be avoided.

Another method of preventing surreptitious access is through the use of windows. Many high-security areas have a significant number of windows so that people's activities within the area can't be hidden. A closed server room with no windows makes for a quiet place for someone to achieve physical access to a device without worry of being seen. Windows remove this privacy element that many criminals depend upon to achieve their entry and illicit activities.

Tokens/Cards

Controlling physical access to a small facility can be achieved through door locks and physical keys, but that solution is unwieldy for larger facilities with numerous people coming and going. Many organizations rely on a badging system using either *tokens* or *cards* that can be tied to automated ID checks and logging of entry/exit. This can provide much greater detail in tracking who is in a facility and when they have come and gone. Tokens and cards can embed a serialized ID for each user, enabling user-specific logging. Originally designed to augment payroll time cards, these electronic IDs have improved security through the logging of employees' in and out times. Tokens and cards offer the same function as keys, but the system can be remotely updated to manage access in real time, and users can have privilege revoked without having to recover the token or card.

Environmental Controls

While the confidentiality of information is important, so is its availability. Sophisticated *environmental controls* are needed for current data centers. Heating and cooling is important for computer systems as well as users. Server rooms require very specific cooling, usually provided by a series of hot and cold aisles. Fire suppression is an important consideration when dealing with information systems.

 EXAM TIP   Be sure you understand the principles behind environmental control systems such as HVAC and fire suppression, as well as environmental monitoring.

HVAC

Controlling a data center's temperature and humidity is important to keeping servers running. *Heating, ventilating, and air conditioning (HVAC)* systems are critical for keeping data centers cool, because typical servers put out between 1000 and 2000 BTUs of heat (1 BTU equals the amount of energy required to raise the temperature of one pound of liquid water one degree Fahrenheit).

Multiple servers in a confined area can create conditions too hot for the machines to continue to operate. This problem is made worse with the advent of blade-style computing systems and with many other devices shrinking in size. While physically smaller, they tend to still expel the same amount of heat.

Temperature is not the only concern. Humidity needs to be controlled to prevent static issues (too low humidity) or condensation issues (too high humidity). Typically, air pressure in controlled spaces is kept slightly higher than surrounding areas, to ensure air flows out of the controlled space, not in.

Hot and Cold Aisles

The trend toward smaller, denser servers means more servers and devices per rack, putting a greater load on the cooling systems. This encourages the use of a hot aisle/cold aisle layout. A data center that is arranged into *hot and cold aisles* dictates that all the intake fans on all equipment face the cold aisle, and the exhaust fans all face the opposite aisle. The HVAC system is then designed to push cool air underneath the raised floor and up through perforated tiles on the cold aisle. Hot air from the hot aisle is captured by return air ducts for the HVAC system. The use of this layout is designed to control airflow, with the purpose being never to mix the hot and cold air. This requires the use of blocking plates and side plates to close open rack slots. The benefits of this arrangement are that cooling is more efficient and can handle higher density.

Fire Suppression

According to the Fire Suppression Systems Association (www.fssa.net), 43 percent of businesses that close as a result of a significant fire never reopen. An additional 29 percent fail within three years of the event. The ability to respond to a fire quickly and effectively is thus critical to the long-term success of any organization. Addressing potential fire hazards and vulnerabilities has long been a concern of organizations in their risk analysis process. The goal obviously should be never to have a fire, but in the event that one does occur, it is important to have mechanisms in place to limit the damage the fire can cause. *Fire suppression* systems are designed to provide protection against the damage from a fire that spreads in a facility. Because they are suppression systems, they don't prevent the fire from occurring per se, but they do stop it once it begins.

Water-Based Fire Suppression Systems

Water-based fire suppression systems have long been, and still are today, the primary tool to address and control structural fires. Considering the amount of electrical equipment found in today's office environment and the fact that, for obvious reasons, this equipment does not react well to large applications of water, it is important to know what to do with equipment if it does become subjected to a water-based sprinkler system. The 2017 *NFPA 75: Standard for the Protection of Information Technology Equipment* outlines measures that can be taken to minimize the damage to electronic equipment exposed to water. This guidance includes these suggestions:

- Open cabinet doors, remove side panels and covers, and pull out chassis drawers to allow water to run out of equipment.
- Set up fans to move room-temperature air through the equipment for general drying. Move portable equipment to dry, air-conditioned areas.
- Use compressed air at no higher than 50 psi to blow out trapped water.
- Use handheld dryers on the lowest setting to dry connectors, backplane wirewraps, and printed circuit cards.

- Use cotton-tipped swabs for hard-to-reach places. Lightly dab the surfaces to remove residual moisture. Do not use cotton-tipped swabs on wirewrap terminals.

- Use water-displacement aerosol sprays containing Freon-alcohol mixtures as an effective first step in drying critical components. Follow up with professional restoration as soon as possible.

Even if these guidelines are followed, damage to the systems may have already occurred. Since water is so destructive to electronic equipment, not only because of the immediate problems of electronic shorts to the system but also because of longer-term corrosive damage water can cause, alternative fire suppression methods have been sought. One of the more common alternative methods used was halon-based systems. Halon systems have been phased out because of environmental concerns surrounding the release of halon into the atmosphere, as it is a potent greenhouse gas.

Clean-Agent Fire Suppression Systems

Carbon dioxide (CO_2) has been used as a fire suppression agent for a long time. The Bell Telephone Company used portable CO_2 extinguishers in the early part of the 20th century. Carbon dioxide extinguishers attack all three necessary elements for a fire to occur. CO_2 displaces oxygen so that the amount of oxygen remaining is insufficient to sustain the fire. It also provides some cooling in the fire zone and reduces the concentration of "gasified" fuel.

Argon extinguishes fire by lowering the oxygen concentration below the 15 percent level required for combustible items to burn. Argon systems are designed to reduce the oxygen content to about 12.5 percent, which is below the 15 percent needed for the fire but is still above the 10 percent required by the EPA for human safety.

Inergen, a product of Ansul Corporation, is composed of three gases: 52 percent nitrogen, 40 percent argon, and 8 percent carbon dioxide. In a manner similar to pure argon systems, Inergen systems reduce the level of oxygen to about 12.5 percent, which is sufficient for human safety but not sufficient to sustain a fire.

Another chemical used to phase out halon is FE-13, or trifluoromethane. This chemical was originally developed as a chemical refrigerant and works to suppress fires by inhibiting the combustion chain reaction. FE-13 is gaseous, leaves behind no residue that would harm equipment, and is considered safe to use in occupied areas. Other halocarbons are also approved for use in replacing halon systems, including FM-200 (heptafluoropropane), a chemical used as a propellant for asthma medication dispensers.

EXAM TIP The specific chemicals used for fire suppression are not testable; they are included here to provide you with the complete story for the workplace.

Handheld Fire Extinguishers

Although computer security professionals typically do not have much influence over the type of fire suppression system that their office includes, they do need to be aware of what type has been installed, what they should do in case of an emergency, and what they need to do to recover after the release of the system. One area that they can influence, however, is the type of handheld fire extinguisher that is located in their area.

Automatic fire suppression systems designed to discharge when a fire is detected are not the only systems you should be aware of. If a fire can be caught and contained before the automatic systems discharge, it can mean significant savings to the organization in terms of both time and equipment costs (including the recharging of the automatic system). Handheld extinguishers are common in offices, but the correct use of them must be understood or disaster can occur.

There are four different classes of fire, as shown in Table 17-1. Each class of fire has its own fuel source and method for extinguishing it. Class A systems, for example, are designed to extinguish fires with normal combustible material as the fire's source. Water can be used in an extinguisher of this sort, since it is effective against fires of this type. Water, as we've discussed, is not appropriate for fires involving wiring or electrical equipment. Using a Class A extinguisher against an electrical fire not only will be ineffective but can result in additional damage. Some extinguishers are designed to be effective against more than one class of fire, such as the common ABC fire extinguishers. This is probably the best type of system to have in a data processing facility. All fire extinguishers should be easily accessible and should be clearly marked. Before anybody uses an extinguisher, they should know what type of extinguisher it is and what the source of the fire is. When in doubt, evacuate and let the fire department handle the situation.

 EXAM TIP The type of fire distinguishes the type of extinguisher that should be used to suppress it. Remember that the most common type is the ABC fire extinguisher, which is designed to handle all types of fires except flammable-metal fires, which are rare.

Fire Detection Devices

An essential complement to fire suppression systems and devices are fire detection devices (fire detectors). Detectors may be able to detect a fire in its very early stages, before a fire suppression system is activated, and sound a warning that potentially enables employees to address the fire before it becomes serious enough for the fire suppression equipment to kick in.

Class of Fire	Type of Fire	Examples of Combustible Materials	Example Suppression Method
A	Common combustibles	Wood, paper, cloth, plastics	Water or dry chemical
B	Combustible liquids	Petroleum products, organic solvents	CO_2 or dry chemical
C	Electrical	Electrical wiring and equipment, power tools	CO_2 or dry chemical
D	Flammable metals	Magnesium, titanium	Copper metal or sodium chloride

Table 17-1 Types of Fire and Suppression Methods

There are several different types of fire detectors. One type, of which there are two varieties, is activated by smoke. The two varieties of smoke detector are ionization and photoelectric. A photoelectric detector is good for potentially providing advance warning of a smoldering fire. This type of device monitors an internal beam of light. If something degrades the light, for example by obstructing it, the detector assumes it is something like smoke and the alarm sounds. An ionization style of detector uses an ionization chamber and a small radioactive source to detect fast-burning fires. Shown in Figure 17-4, the chamber consists of two plates, one with a positive charge and one with a negative charge. Oxygen and nitrogen particles in the air become "ionized" (an ion is freed from the molecule). The freed ion, which has a negative charge, is attracted to the positive plate, and the remaining part of the molecule, now with a positive charge, is attracted to the negative plate. This movement of particles creates a very small electric current that the device measures. Smoke inhibits this process, and the detector will detect the resulting drop in current and sound an alarm.

Both of these devices are often referred to generically as smoke detectors, and combinations of both varieties are possible. For more information on smoke detectors, see http://home.howstuffworks.com/home-improvement/household-safety/fire/smoke2 .htm. As both of these devices are triggered by the interruption of a signal, without regard to why, they can give false alarms. They are unable to distinguish the difference between the smoke from a kitchen fire and burned toast.

Another type of fire detector is activated by heat. These devices also come in two varieties. Fixed-temperature or fixed-point devices activate if the temperature in the area ever exceeds some predefined level. Rate-of-rise or rate-of-increase temperature devices activate when there is a sudden increase in local temperature that may indicate the beginning stages of a fire. Rate-of-rise sensors can provide an earlier warning but are also responsible for more false warnings.

A third type of detector is flame activated. This type of device relies on the flames from the fire to provide a change in the infrared energy that can be detected. Flame-activated devices are generally more expensive than the other two types but can frequently detect a fire sooner.

Figure 17-4

An ionization chamber for an ionization type of smoke detector

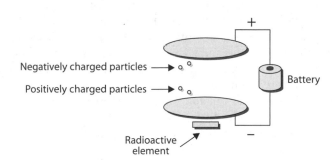

Cable Locks

Portable equipment has a principal feature of being portable. This can also be a problem, as portable equipment—laptops, projectors, and the like—can be easily removed or stolen. *Cable locks* provide a simple means of securing portable equipment to furniture or another fixture in the room where the equipment resides. Cable locks can be used by road warriors to secure laptops from casual theft. They also can be used in open areas such as conference centers or rooms where portable equipment is exposed to a wide range of visitors.

Screen Filters

As discussed in Chapter 2, *shoulder surfing* involves the attacker directly observing an individual entering information on a form, keypad, or keyboard, usually to read passwords or other sensitive information. Given the close physical spacing on today's aircraft and other public conveyances, if you are going to use a laptop, others are going to have access to see the screen. *Screen filters* are optical filters that limit the angle of viewability to a very narrow range, making it difficult for others to visually eavesdrop. Screen filters have a wide range of uses, from road warrior laptops, to kiosks, to receptionists' computers, or places where sensitive data is displayed (medical data in medical environments).

 EXAM TIP Some physical security equipment is used to secure aspects of mobile devices. Screen filters secure screens from observation, while cable locks prevent equipment theft. These are both preventative agents, and you should be ready to match them on the exam to specific threats, such as shoulder surfing or device theft.

Cameras

Video surveillance is typically done through closed-circuit television (CCTV). The use of CCTV *cameras* for surveillance purposes dates back to at least 1961, when cameras were installed in the London Transport train station. The development of smaller camera components and lower costs has caused a boon in the CCTV industry since then.

CCTV cameras are used to monitor a workplace for security purposes. These systems are commonplace in banks and jewelry stores, places with high-value merchandise that is attractive to thieves. As the expense of these systems dropped, they became practical for many more industry segments.

Traditional cameras are analog based and require a video multiplexer to combine all the signals and make multiple views appear on a monitor. IP-based cameras are changing that, as most of them are stand-alone units that are viewable through a web browser, such as the camera shown in Figure 17-5.

These IP-based systems add useful functionality, such as the ability to check on the building from the Internet. This network functionality, however, makes the cameras subject to normal IP-based network attacks. A DoS attack launched at the CCTV system

Figure 17-5
IP-based cameras leverage existing IP networks instead of needing a proprietary CCTV cable.

just as a break-in is occurring is the last thing that anyone would want (other than the criminals). For this reason, IP-based CCTV cameras should be placed on their own separate network that can be accessed only by security personnel. The same physical separation applies to any IP-based camera infrastructure. Older time-lapse tape recorders are slowly being replaced with digital video recorders. While the advance in technology is significant, be careful if and when these devices become IP-enabled, since they will become a security issue, just like everything else that touches the network.

If you depend on the CCTV system to protect your organization's assets, carefully consider camera placement and the type of cameras used. Different iris types, focal lengths, and color or infrared capabilities are all options that make one camera superior to another in a specific location.

Motion Detection

When monitoring an area for unauthorized activity, one potentially useful tool is a *motion detector*. In areas where there is little or no expected traffic, a motion detector can alert an operator to activity in an area. Motion detectors come in a variety of types, but most are based on infrared (heat) radiation and can detect the changes of a warm body moving. They can be tuned for size, ignoring smaller movement such as small animals in outdoor settings. Although not useful in busy office buildings during normal daily use, motion detectors can be useful during off-hours, when traffic is minimal. Motion detectors can be used to trigger video systems, so they do not record large amounts of "empty" activity. Video monitoring of the loading dock area in the back of the building can be triggered in this fashion, using the motion detector to turn on cameras whenever activity is occurring.

Logs

Physical security *logs* provide the same utility as computer logs do for a security investigation. They act as a record of what was observed at specific points in time. Having roving guards check in at various places across a shift via a log entry provides a record of the actual surveillance. Logs of visitors arriving and departing, equipment received and shipped out, and so forth all serve as a record of the physical happenings in a facility.

Remote sensing of badges and equipment utilizing RFID tags can create equipment move logs that include when, where, what, and who—all automatically. Advanced capabilities such as this make inventory of movable equipment easier as its location is tracked and it can be scanned remotely.

 EXAM TIP Cameras, IR detection, motion detection, and logs are all methods associated with detection, and frequently after-the-fact detection at that. These devises and methods provide valuable attribution fact patterns, even when it is after the actual event.

Infrared Detection

Infrared (IR) radiation is not visible to the human eye, but can be used just like a light source to detect a range of things. Motion from living creatures can be seen because of the heat signatures of their bodies. *Infrared detection* is a technical means of looking for things that otherwise may not be noticed. At night, when it is dark, someone can hide in the shadows, but infrared light can point them out to IR-sensing cameras. Infrared detectors can sense differences in temperature, which can be from a person entering a room, even if not visible due to darkness. IR alarms are used extensively to monitor people movement in areas where there should be none.

Key Management

Physical locks have physical keys, and keeping track of who has what keys can be a chore. Add in master keys and maintaining a list of who has physical access to each space, and such tracking can quickly become a task requiring a software solution. *Key management* is the process of keeping track of where the keys are and who has access to what. A physical security environment that does not have a means of key management is not verifiably secure. Key management will be essential when, say, a server in a locked room goes missing and management wants to know "Who has keys that can give them access to that room?"

Chapter Review

In this chapter, you became acquainted with the principles of physical security controls, including environmental controls. The chapter began with lighting, signs, fencing, gates, and cages, all items designed to restrict or guide physical movement. From there the chapter moved into security guards, alarms, safes, secure cabinets, and protected distribution for cables. These elements further refine restrictions on movement and the ability for access to system components. The chapter then examined airgaps, mantraps, and Faraday cages.

Physical lock types, tokens/cards, and biometrics were discussed. Barricades and bollards closed up the core physical protection area. The chapter then moved into environmental controls, HVAC, hot and cold aisles, and fire suppression. The chapter closed with an examination of cable locks, screen filters, cameras, motion detectors, logs, infrared detection, and key management.

Questions

To help you prepare further for the CompTIA Security+ exam, and to test your level of preparedness, answer the following questions and then check your answers against the correct answers at the end of the chapter.

1. Why is physical security important to protecting data?

   A. Physical access to data will negate the security advantages of the cloud.

   B. Information resides on physical assets, linking physical and information security.

   C. Social engineering can negate any information security controls.

   D. None of the above.

2. Proper interior and exterior lighting is important because:

   A. It can detect people who are where they don't belong.

   B. It shows who is in a restricted space.

   C. It allows more people and activities to be observed.

   D. It is needed for the use of closed-circuit television cameras.

3. Your organization has experienced multiple incidents of graffiti tagging and people loitering in the parking lot despite the chain-link fence surrounding it. What is the best solution to the issue?

   A. No Trespassing signage

   B. More guard stations

   C. Additional external lighting

   D. Change the chain-link fencing to anti-scale fencing

4. The supervisor in charge of the security guards wants to increase the guards' awareness of information security and has asked you to provide a training session. List two things that would be included in your curriculum?

   A. _____

   B. _____

5. After a physical security incident, what critical data can security guards commonly provide?

    A. Employee ID information

    B. Access logs of who has entered and exited the building

    C. Alarm codes

    D. Blueprints showing unmonitored areas of the building

6. Alarms are effective only if which of the following is true?

    A. They alert on abnormal conditions.

    B. Every entrance is monitored with a sensor.

    C. They are not tied to the information systems.

    D. They are tuned to provide accurate and useful alerts.

7. You are implementing a test lab at your organization for early alpha software development. To prevent any of the development code from inadvertently getting put on production computers, what should you implement?

    A. Airgap

    B. Strict firewalls

    C. Protected distribution

    D. Patch management

8. What is the security benefit of a Faraday cage?

    A. Prevents attack by EMP

    B. Prevents illicit monitoring of Van Eck emissions

    C. Works better than anti-scale fencing

    D. Prevents stack overflows by EMI

9. The CSO is starting a project to revamp all physical security at the organization. Of particular interest to him are high-security locks on critical infrastructure, and he has asked you to create a PowerPoint presentation to justify the expense to management. What three features would you highlight in your presentation about high-security locks?

    A. _____

    B. _____

    C. _____

10. Biometrics are based upon which of the following?

    A. The original fingerprint studies of the 1880s

    B. Parts of the human body that are unique

    C. The ability to rapidly scan biological markers

    D. Advances in retinal scanning

11. What is a primary problem with biometrics?

    A. Technically biometrics are difficult to implement

    B. The human body changing over time

    C. The ease with which biometrics are faked

    D. Biometrics can't be loaned or delegated

12. The token's primary security advantage over metallic keys is _____.

    A. Tokens are revocable

    B. Tokens can be copied for faster distribution

    C. Tokens are bigger, and thus easier to find than a key

    D. Tokens can be issued to all employees

13. Clean-agent fire suppression systems are designed to replace this traditional fire suppression element: _____.

14. A fire involving which of the following is not covered by the traditional ABC handheld fire extinguisher?

    A. Flammable liquids

    B. Flammable metals

    C. Cloth soaked in accelerant

    D. A computer on fire

15. What should you do to protect your IP-based CCTV system from a DDoS attack?

    A. Reconfigure your firewalls

    B. Connect it to an intrusion detection system

    C. Require multifactor authentication to access the CCTV system

    D. Place all CCTV components on a separate network

Answers

    1. B. Information resides on physical assets, linking physical security with the security of information.

    2. C. Proper lighting allows more people and activities to be observed.

    3. D. A change from chain-link fencing to anti-scale fencing to prevent intruders from climbing the fence is the best solution.

    4. There are several things that you can discuss to assist guards' information security knowledge, such as indicators of a network attack being all computers rebooting at once, several phones ringing at once, and strangers with laptops or other equipment sitting in a vehicle in the parking lot.

5. B. Guards commonly have logs of who has entered and exited a building.

6. D. Alarms are effective only if they are tuned to provide accurate and useful alerting information.

7. A. A lab environment can be airgapped from the rest of the network to prevent software from being accidentally copied to production machines.

8. B. A Faraday cage can prevent illicit monitoring of computer systems through Van Eck emissions.

9. High-security locks have many anti-intrusion features, so your presentation should highlight any three of the following: pick resistance, drill resistance, resistance to pounding it through the door, bump resistance, sidebars, magnetic keys, nontraditional pins, and key control.

10. B. Biometrics are based upon parts of the body that are unique, such as fingerprints, iris, retina, and others.

11. B. Some biometric features can change over time, or with medical conditions making them less reliable and forcing a re-identification phase to resync a user and their biometric.

12. The primary security advantage tokens have over metallic keys is the ability to revoke a key remotely.

13. The most traditional fire suppression agent is water, but that cannot be used on all fires and can cause damage to electrical equipment.

14. B. A fire involving flammable metals is not covered by a typical ABC fire extinguisher.

15. D. The CCTV system should be on a completely separate network, airgapped if possible, with only security personnel having access.

PART IV

Identity and Access Management

CHAPTER 18

Identity, Access, and Accounts

In this chapter, you will

- Examine how to compare and contrast identity and access management concepts
- Explore how to differentiate common account management practices when given a scenario

Access control and authentication are important to control who has access to computer systems and resources. Principles of controlling access and properly authenticating apply to both internal access and remote access. Remote access requirements are more rigorous, but the same principles can be applied to internal access.

Access control mechanisms work together with accounts and account policies to determine the proper level of access for users on systems. The chapter will examine authentication systems, account types, and general concepts associated with access control and authentication.

Certification Objectives   This chapter covers CompTIA Security+ exam objectives 4.1, Compare and contrast identity and access management concepts, and 4.4, Given a scenario, differentiate common account management practices. Objective 4.4 is a good candidate for performance-based questions, which means you should expect questions in which you must apply your knowledge of the topic to a scenario. The best answer to a question will depend upon specific details in the scenario preceding the question, not just the question. The questions may also involve tasks other than just picking the best answer from a list. Instead, they may involve actual simulation of steps to take to solve a problem.

Identification, Authentication, Authorization, and Accounting (AAA)

Identification is the process of ascribing a computer ID to a specific user, computer, network device, or computer process. The identification process is typically performed only once, when a user ID is issued to a particular user. User identification enables authentication and authorization to form the basis for accountability. For accountability purposes, user IDs should not be shared, and for security purposes, user IDs should not be descriptive of job function. This practice enables you to trace activities to individual users or computer processes so that users can be held responsible for their actions. Identification usually takes the form of a logon ID or user ID. A required characteristic of such IDs is that they must be unique.

Authentication is the process of verifying an identity previously established in a computer system. There are a variety of methods of performing this function, each with its advantages and disadvantages. These are the subject of the next section of the chapter.

Authorization is the process of permitting or denying access to a specific resource. Once identity is confirmed via authentication, specific actions can be authorized or denied. Many types of authorization schemes are used, but the purpose is the same: determine whether a given user who has been identified has permissions for a particular object or resource being requested. This functionality is frequently part of the operating system and is transparent to users.

Accounting is the process of ascribing resource usage by account for the purpose of tracking resource utilization. This is a basic accounting function that is still used by some enterprises.

The separation of tasks, from identification to authentication to authorization, has several advantages. Many methods can be used to perform each task, and on many systems several methods are concurrently present for each task. Separation of these tasks into individual elements allows combinations of implementations to work together. Any system or resource, be it hardware (router or workstation) or a software component (database system), that requires authorization can use its own authorization method once authentication has occurred. This makes for efficient and consistent application of these principles.

Multifactor Authentication

Multifactor authentication (or multiple-factor authentication) is simply the combination of two or more types of authentication. Five broad categories of authentication can be used: what you are (for example, biometrics), what you have (for instance, tokens), what you know (passwords and other information), somewhere you are (location), and something you do (physical performance). Two-factor authentication combines any two of these before granting access. An example would be a card reader that then turns on a fingerprint scanner—if your fingerprint matches the one on file for the card, you are granted access. Three-factor authentication would combine all three types, such as a smart card reader that asks for a PIN before enabling a retina scanner. If all three correspond to a valid user in the computer database, access is granted.

 EXAM TIP Two-factor authentication combines any two methods, matching items such as a token with a biometric. Three-factor authentication combines any three, such as a passcode, biometric, and a token.

Multifactor authentication methods greatly enhance security by making it very difficult for an attacker to obtain all the correct materials for authentication. They also protect against the risk of stolen tokens, as the attacker must have the correct biometric, password, or both. More important, multifactor authentication enhances the security of biometric systems by protecting against a spoofed biometric. Changing the token makes the biometric useless unless the attacker can steal the new token. It also reduces false positives by trying to match the supplied biometric with the one that is associated with the supplied token. This prevents the computer from seeking a match using the entire database of biometrics. Using multiple factors is one of the best ways to ensure proper authentication and access control.

Something You Are

Something you are specifically refers to biometrics. One of the challenges with using something you are artifacts as authentication factors is that typically they are hard to change, so once assigned they inevitably become immutable, as you can change fingers, but only a limited number of times and then you run out of changes. Another challenge with biometrics is that cultural or other issues associated with measuring things on a person may exist. For example, people in some cultures object to having their pictures taken. Another example is that physical laborers in some industries tend to lack scannable fingerprints because they are worn down. Some biometrics are not usable in certain environments; for instance, in the case of medical workers, or workers in clean room environments, their personal protective gear inhibits the use of fingerprint readers and potentially other biometrics.

Something You Have

Something you have specifically refers to security tokens and other items that a user can possess physically. One of the challenges with using something you have as an authentication factor is that you have to have it with you whenever you wish to be authenticated, and this can cause issues. It also relies on interfaces that may not be available for some systems, such as mobile devices, although interfaces, such as one-time password (OTP) generators, are device independent. OTP generators generate new passwords on demand, against a known sequence that is known only to the OTP generator and the OTP element on the system accepting the password.

One of the challenges of something you have is the concept of something you lost, such as left in a briefcase, at home, etc. Just as leaving your key ring with your office key can force a return trip back home to get it, so can leaving a dongle or other security element that is something you have in nature. And if something you have becomes something you had stolen, the implications are fairly clear—you don't have access and you have to re-identify yourself to get access again.

Something You Know

Something you know specifically refers to passwords. The most common example of something you know is a password. One of the challenges with using something you know as an authentication factor is that it can be "shared" without the user knowing it because knowledge can be duplicated without the owner's knowledge. Another concern with "something you know" elements is that because of the vast number of different ones a typical user has to remember, they do things to assist with memory. Repeating passwords, slight changes such as incrementing the number from password1 to password2, or writing them down, these are all common methods used to deal with the password sprawl, yet they each introduce new vulnerabilities.

Another form of authentication via what you know is called identity driven authentication. In identity driven authentication, you contact someone to get access, they will respond with a series of challenge questions. Sometimes the questions are based on previously submitted information, sometimes the questions are based on publically known information, such as previous addresses, phone numbers, cars purchase/licensed, etc. Again, the proper respondent will know these answers, while an imposter will not. These tests are timed and if the respondent takes too long, as in performing lookups, they will fail.

Something You Do

Something you do specifically refers to a physical action that you perform uniquely. An example of this is a signature; the movement of the pen and the two-dimensional output are difficult for others to reproduce. This makes it useful for authentication, but challenges exist in capturing the data, as signature pads are not common peripherals on machines. Something you do is one of the harder artifacts to capture without specialized hardware making it less ubiquitous as a method of authentication.

Somewhere You Are

One of the more discriminant authentication factors is your location, *somewhere you are*. When using a mobile device, GPS can identify where the device is currently located. When you are logged on to a local, wired desktop connection, it shows you are in the building. Both of these can be compared to records to see if you are really there, or should be there. If you are badged into your building, and at your desk on a wired PC, then a second connection with a different location would be suspect, as you can only be one place at a time.

 EXAM TIP Be able to differentiate between the five factors for authentication: something you are, have, know, or do, or somewhere you are. These are easily tested on the exam. Be sure you recognize examples for each factor to match to a scenario-type question.

Federation

Federation, or *identity federation*, defines policies, protocols, and practices to manage identities across systems and organizations. Federation's ultimate goal is to allow users to seamlessly access data or systems across domains. Federation is enabled through the use of industry standards such as SAML, discussed in Chapter 19.

Single Sign-on

Single sign-on (SSO) is a form of authentication that involves the transferring of credentials between systems. As more and more systems are combined in daily use, users are forced to have multiple sets of credentials. A user may have to log in to three, four, five, or even more systems every day just to do her job. Single sign-on allows a user to transfer her credentials, so that logging into one system acts to log her into all of them. This has an advantage of reducing login hassles for the user. It also has a disadvantage of combining the authentication systems in such a way that if one login is compromised, they all are for that user.

Transitive Trust

Security across multiple domains is provided through trust relationships. When trust relationships between domains exist, authentication for each domain trusts the authentication for all other trusted domains. Thus, when an application is authenticated by a domain, its authentication is accepted by all other domains that trust the authenticating domain.

It is important to note that trust relationships apply only to authentication. They do not apply to resource usage, which is an access control issue. Trust relationships allow users to have their identity verified (authentication). The ability to use resources is defined by access control rules. Thus, even though a user is authenticated via the trust relationship, it does not provide access to actually use resources.

A *transitive trust* relationship means that the trust relationship extended to one domain will be extended to any other domain trusted by that domain. A two-way trust relationship means that two domains trust each other.

 EXAM TIP Transitive trust involves three parties: If A trusts B, and B trusts C, in a transitive trust relationship, then A will trust C.

Account Types

To manage the privileges of many different people effectively on the same system, a mechanism for separating people into distinct entities (users) is required, so you can control access on an individual level. It's convenient and efficient to be able to lump users together when granting many different people (groups) access to a resource at the same time. At other times, it's useful to be able to grant or restrict access based on a person's job or function within the organization (role). While you can manage privileges on the basis of users alone, managing user, group, and role assignments together is far more convenient and efficient.

User Account

The term *user account* refers to the account credentials that are used when accessing a computer system. In privilege management, a user is a single individual, such as "John

Forthright" or "Sally Jenkins." This is generally the lowest level addressed by privilege management and the most common area for addressing access, rights, and capabilities. When accessing a computer system, each user is generally given a user ID—a unique alphanumeric identifier he or she will use to identify himself or herself when logging in or accessing the system. User IDs are often based on some combination of the user's first, middle, and last names and often include numbers as well. When developing a scheme for selecting user IDs, you should keep in mind that user IDs must be unique to each user, but they must also be fairly easy for the user to remember and use. Because the user ID is used to identify the person who performed specific actions, it is important to not have generic or shared credentials. Either of these situations makes traceability to an authorized user difficult if not impossible.

 EXAM TIP Having unique, nonshared user IDs for all users of a system is important when it comes time to investigate access control issues.

With some notable exceptions, in general a user wanting to access a computer system must first have a user ID created for him on the system he wishes to use. This is usually done by a system administrator, security administrator, or other privileged user, and this is the first step in privilege management—a user should not be allowed to create his own account.

Once the account is created and a user ID is selected, the administrator can assign specific permissions to that user. Permissions control what the user is allowed to do on the system—which files he may access, which programs he may execute, and so on. While PCs typically have only one or two user accounts, larger systems such as servers and mainframes can have hundreds of accounts on the same system.

Account policy enforcement is an important part of user credential systems. Managing credentials begins with policies that state the desired objectives. Key elements of the policy include elements such as prohibition against sharing accounts and against generic accounts not assigned to a user. For users that have multiple roles, multiple accounts may be necessary, but these need to be delineated by policy rather than on an ad hoc basis. Credential management rules, such as password policy, should be enacted, including lockout and recovery procedures. When users no longer are authorized, such as when they leave the firm or change jobs, the accounts should be disabled, not removed.

Shared and Generic Accounts/Credentials

Shared accounts go against the specific premise that accounts exist so that user activity can be tracked. This said, there are times that shared accounts are used for groups like guests. Guest accounts are covered in the next section. Sometimes the shared accounts are called *generic accounts* and exist only to provide a specific set of functionality, such as in a PC running in kiosk mode, with a browser limited to accessing specific sites as an information display. Under these circumstances, being able to trace the activity to a user is not particularly useful.

A common form of a shared account is one created to run nightly batch operations. As every action must be associated to a user account, a shared account in the name of a batch user can be used to run batch jobs. This is a generic set of *credentials*, not actually associated with a single person, but rather is associated with a particular type of process (i.e., batch jobs, backups, etc.). These credentials are maintained by administrators, but are reserved for specific uses, such as executing batch jobs. Because these accounts are in essence local, and are being used to run tasks, they can be restricted in function, not permitted to log in for instance, thus lowering their usefulness for an attacker.

Guest Accounts

Guest accounts are frequently used on corporate networks to provide visitors access to the Internet and to some common corporate resources, such as projectors, printers in conference rooms, and so forth. Again, like generic accounts, these types of accounts are restricted in their network capability to a defined set of machines, with a defined set of access, much like a user visiting the company's public-facing website via the Internet. As such, logging and tracing activity have little to no use, so the overhead of establishing a unique account does not make sense.

Service Accounts

Service accounts are accounts that are used to run processes that do not require human intervention to start, stop, or administer. From running batch jobs in the data center to executing simple tasks that an organization must complete for purposes of regulatory compliance, many reasons exist for running processes with service accounts that don't require an account holder. From a security perspective, administrators can configure service accounts to minimize risks associate with them. For example, in Windows systems, administrators can prevent service accounts from logging in to the system. This limits some of the attack vectors that can be applied to these accounts. Another security provision that can be applied to service accounts that run batch jobs at night is to restrict when they can run. Any service account that has to run in an elevated privilege mode can also be designated to receive extra monitoring and scrutiny.

Privileged Accounts

Privileged accounts are any accounts with greater than normal user access. Privileged accounts are typically root- or administrative-level accounts and represent risk in that they are unlimited in their powers. These accounts require regular real-time monitoring, if at all possible, and should always be monitored when operating remotely. Administrators may need to perform tasks via a remote session in certain scenarios, but when they do, they first need to identify the purpose and get approval.

 EXAM TIP   For the exam, understand the different account types and how they differ, and remember that the principle of least privilege means limiting a user to the least amount of privilege they need to perform their job. Administrator or root accounts can always perform an action, but if a user lacking elevated privileges can perform it as well, then the user is a better choice to perform the action. You should never use elevated privilege unless necessary to do a task.

General Concepts

Account management, frequently called privilege management, is the process of restricting a user's ability to interact with the computer system. A user's interaction with a computer system covers a fairly broad area and includes viewing, modifying, and deleting data; running applications; stopping and starting processes; and controlling computer resources. Essentially, controlling everything a user can do to or with a computer system falls into the realm of account management.

Least Privilege

One of the most fundamental principles in account management is *least privilege*. Least privilege means that an object (which may be a user, application, or process) should have only the rights and privileges necessary to perform its task, with no additional permissions. Limiting an object's privileges limits the amount of harm that it can cause, thus limiting the organization's exposure to damage. Users may have access to the files on their workstations and a select set of files on a file server, but they have no access to critical data that is held within the database. This rule helps an organization protect its most sensitive resources and helps ensure that whoever is interacting with these resources has a valid reason to do so.

Onboarding/Offboarding

Onboarding and *offboarding* refer to the processes of adding personnel to a project or team and removing personnel from a project or team. During onboarding, proper account relationships need to be initiated, including the establishment of accounts. Newly onboarded members should be put into the correct access control groups based on their needed permissions and assigned tasks, and when they are offboarded, they should be removed from the access control groups, and have their account disabled. This is one way in which access control groups can be used to manage permissions and can be very efficient when users move between units and tasks.

Permission Auditing and Review

As with all security controls, an important aspect of security controls that are used to mitigate risk is an auditing component. Just as it is important to periodically verify all users with accounts on the system are still valid users of the system from a business perspective, it is equally important to periodically perform *permission auditing and review*. Permission auditing and review is an action that verifies the user accounts on the system are all needed, justified, and actually represent real authorized users. As users can come and go from groups, it is important to audit periodically to ensure that they have not retained permissions granted to a group they no longer belong to.

Usage Auditing and Review

Logs are the most frequently used auditing component, and with respect to privileged accounts, logging can be especially important. *Usage auditing and review* is just that, an examination of logs to determine user activity. Reviewing access control logs for root-level accounts is an important element of securing access control methods. Because of the power and potential for misuse of administrative- or root-level accounts, they should be closely monitored, particularly the use of an administrative-level account on a production system.

 EXAM TIP Logging and monitoring of failed login attempts provides valuable information during investigations of compromises.

A strong configuration management environment will include the control of access to production systems by users who can change the environment. Root-level changes in a system tend to be significant changes, and in production systems these changes would require approval in advance. A comparison of all root-level activity against approved changes will assist in the detection of activity that is unauthorized.

Time-of-Day Restrictions

Creating *time-of-day restrictions* for access can solve many account management problems. For the majority of workers who work set shifts, having a system whereby their accounts are not active during their nonworking hours reduces the surface of user accounts available for attackers to use. This is even more important for privileged users, as their elevated accounts offer greater risk, and if an authorized user of an account is not working, there is no reason to have it authorized. As with all policies, provisions need to be made for change and emergencies, whereby authorized users can obtain access when needed, even if outside normal working hours.

Recertification

User accounts should be recertified periodically as necessary. The process of *recertification* can be as simple as a check against current payroll records to ensure all users are still employed, or as intrusive as having users come re-identify themselves. The latter method is highly intrusive, interrupting people's work schedules as they have to physically visit the security office, identify themselves, and have their account reactivated. This may be warranted for high-risk accounts, as it ensures there is a legitimate person associated with each account. The process of recertification ensures that only users who need accounts have accounts in the system.

Standard Naming Convention

Establishing a *standard naming convention* for account names, and systems, is a topic that can stir controversy even among professionals who seem to agree on most things. One advantage of having a standard naming convention is that it enables users to extract meaning from a name. For example, having server names with dev, test, and prod as part of the name can help to prevent inadvertent changes by a user because of the misidentification of an asset. The standard name also helps those doing account maintenance functions as it provides easily seen information on the account by way of its name. By the same token, a naming convention that identifies privilege level, say appending SA to the end of usernames with system administrator privileges, results in two potential problems. First, it alerts adversaries to which accounts are the most valuable. Second, it creates a problem when the person is no longer a member of the system administrators group, as the account must be renamed.

One aspect that everyone does agree on is the concept that a naming convention should leave room for future accounts. The simplest example is in numbering of accounts. For instance, for e-mail accounts, an organization's convention may be to use first initial plus last name, plus a single digit if two or more people have the same name, such as jsmith2@*yourorg*.com. Will the organization ever have more than nine John Smiths? Maybe not, but the pool might also include Joan Smiths and Jack Smiths. And the pool is further diluted by the fact that the organization inactivates old accounts and does not reuse them. So, you need to plan ahead to ensure your organization's naming convention supports future growth and change.

Account Maintenance

The job of a traffic cop may seem boring to you, until you discover that roughly half of all arrests of felons occur during routine traffic stops. Account maintenance is somewhat analogous—no, we aren't catching felons, but we do find errors that otherwise only increase risk and, because of their nature, are hard to defend against any other way. *Account maintenance* is the routine screening of all attributes for an account. It involves determining questions such as whether the business purpose for the account is still valid (i.e., is the user still employed?), whether the business process for a system account is still occurring, and whether the actual permissions associated with the account are appropriate for the account holder. Best practice indicates that account maintenance be performed in accordance with the risk associated with the profile. System administrators and other privileged accounts warrant greater scrutiny that normal users. Shared accounts, such as guest accounts, also require scrutiny to ensure that they are not abused.

To ensure that certain high-risk situations do not occur, such as unauthenticated guest accounts being granted administrator privilege, you can configure an automated check that monitors the accounts on a regular basis. In Active Directory, for example, administrators can configure a setting that automatically notifies them anytime a user is granted domain admin privilege. And it is also important to note that account maintenance is a joint responsibility. The job of determining who has what access is actually one that belongs to the business, not the security group. The business side of the house is where the policy decision on who should have access is determined. The security group merely takes the steps to enforce this decision.

Group-Based Access Control

Group-based access control refers to managing access control using groups of users rather than user by user. This can be much more efficient and less prone to error in large enterprises. Under privilege management, a *group* is a collection of users with some common criteria, such as a need for access to a particular data set or group of applications. A group can consist of one user or hundreds of users, and each user can belong to one or more groups. Figure 18-1 shows a common approach to grouping users—building groups

Figure 18-1
Logical
representation
of groups

Sales

Information
Technology

Engineering

based on job function. Role-based access control (RBAC), discussed in Chapter 20, is implemented via groups in a modern OS.

By assigning a user membership in a specific group, you make it much easier to control that user's access and privileges. For example, if every member of the engineering department needs access to product development documents, administrators can place all the users in the engineering department in a single group and allow that group to access the necessary documents. Once a group is assigned permissions to access a particular resource, adding a new user to that group will automatically allow that user to access that resource. In effect, the user "inherits" the permissions of the group as soon as she is placed in that group. As Figure 18-2 shows, a computer system can have many different groups, each with its own rights and privileges.

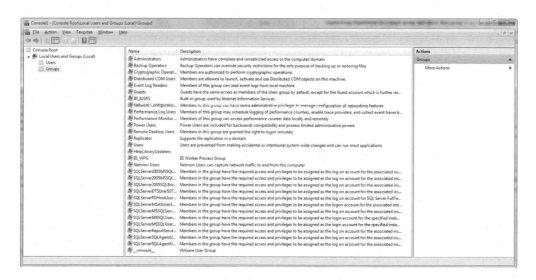

Figure 18-2   Group management screen in Windows

As you can see from the description for the Administrators group in Figure 18-2, this group has complete and unrestricted access to the system. This includes access to all files, applications, and data. Anyone who belongs to the Administrators group or is placed in this group will have a great deal of access and control over the system.

 EXAM TIP   Placing users in groups and managing groups can reduce account management workload and complexity on large systems and domain environments.

Location-Based Policies

In organizations with multiple locations, there may be situations where user access does not translate across different locations. A doctor may have access rights in one clinic's system, but not another he is working in. There is also the issue of whether a user accessing the system via remote access should have the same rights and privileges as a user with local access. *Location-based policies* for access control are risk-based access decisions that are best addressed by examining the business rationale, including risks and rewards for access control at different locations for a user. Once the policies are defined, they can be enforced via the specific access control mechanisms in place.

 EXAM TIP   While policies seem to be less technical and just something extra for management to do, they are the basis for all of the technical actions performed, and as such are foundational to security. Without a policy dictating what is desired, you have no basis to enforce proper actions.

Account Policy Enforcement

The key method used to control access to most systems is still one based on passwords. In conjunction with a strongly enforced account policy that prohibits sharing of passwords and credentials, use of passwords forms the foundation to support the concept that each user ID should be traceable to a single person's activity. Passwords need to be managed to provide appropriate levels of protection. They need to be strong enough to resist attack, and yet not too difficult for users to remember. An account policy can act to ensure that the necessary steps are taken to enact a secure password solution, both by users and by the password infrastructure system.

Credential Management

Credential management refers to the processes, services, and software used to store, manage, and log the use of user credentials. Credential management solutions are typically aimed at assisting end users to manage their growing set of passwords. There are credential management products that provide a secure means of storing user credentials and making them available across a wide range of platforms, from local stores to cloud storage locations.

Group Policy

Microsoft Windows systems in an enterprise environment can be managed via Group Policy objects (GPOs). GPOs act through a set of registry settings that can be managed via the enterprise. A wide range of settings can be managed via GPOs, including numerous settings that are related to security, including user credential settings such as password rules.

Password Complexity

Every organization should have defined *password complexity* requirements that passwords must meet. Typical requirements specify that the password must meet the minimum length requirement and have characters from at least three of the following four groups: English uppercase characters (A through Z), English lowercase characters (a through z), numerals (0 through 9), and nonalphabetic characters (such as !, $, #, %).

 EXAM TIP You may be aware of new research from NIST that indicates that password complexity rules designed to force entropy into passwords do so at the risk of other, less-desirable password behaviors by users, such as writing them down or versioning them with an increasing number element. The latest NIST guidance (Special Publication 800-63B, June 2017) is that long passphrases offer the best protection. However, SP 800-63B, was published after CompTIA released its Security+ exam objectives, so for the exam, you should know the tried and true password complexity requirements listed here.

Expiration

Account *expiration* should occur when a user is no longer authorized to use a system. This requires coordination between those who manage access control lists and accounts and those who manage the need for access. The best solution is to have those who manage users also manage account expiration because they are better situated to know when an employee transfers, quits, or otherwise no longer requires an account. This first line of management should be the first line of notification to the security team as to the disposition of permissions. HR should be the backstop, not the primary. Having first-line management initiate permissions issues also enables the proper transfer of permissions when a person departs to someone who takes over the responsibility for the digital assets. Who assumes ownership over files that the previous person was sole owner of? This is a business decision and best managed by those closest to the business.

To manage temporary and contract worker accounts, Windows systems offer a built-in feature that allows you to create a temporary user account that will expire automatically on the date you specify. Upon reaching the expiration date, the user account expires and the user is unable to log on to Windows after that date.

Recovery

Account *recovery* seems like one of those esoteric topics until you lose the password on your laptop and have no way back in. The same is even more serious if you lose administrator account passwords to key elements of your infrastructure. Having a recovery plan for accounts should something happen to the person who knows the password is important for the enterprise to continue after the loss of that resource. Rather than focus on all the ways one can lose the resource—fired, left on own accord, stepped in front of a bus, coma, and so on—focus on a simple recovery method, such as keeping a list of accounts and passwords in a safe governed by a senior executive. PKI systems have key recovery mechanisms that can be used when emergencies happen. Account recovery is no different; you need to have a plan, and practice executing that plan to prepare for the emergency before the time comes when you need it. Because if you wait until you need the plan, it is too late to create it.

From a technical perspective, recovery is simple. Use a second administrator-level account, reset the lost password, and force it to be changed once the user logs back in. This requires some planning as you need to have the second administrator account before you need to use it. And you need a system by which a user can contact an administrator and after proving their identity to have their account reset. For some cases, this entire process can be automated, using previous security questions for proving identity and scripts to run the rest.

Disablement

Account *disablement* is a step between the account having access and the account being removed from the system. Whenever an employee leaves a firm, all associated accounts should be disabled to prevent further access by the ex-employee. Disabling is preferable to removal as removal may result in permission and ownership problems. Removing an account can orphan items that remain without other forms of ownership, making it more difficult to share the former employee's files. Periodic audits of user accounts to ensure they still need access is also a good security measure. Disabling an account is reversible, but it prohibits the account from being used until the issue that resulted in the disabling is resolved. Account disablement can be an automatic response from a security system if it detects that the account is under attack, say a brute force password-guessing attack.

Lockout

Account *lockout* is akin to disablement, although lockout typically refers to temporarily blocking the user's ability to log in to a system. For example, if a user mistypes her password a certain number of times, she may be forced to wait a set amount of time while her account is locked out before attempting to log in again. These lockouts can be automated on most systems and provide a series of increasing time hurdles for an attacker, while minimizing the inconvenience to legitimate users who have credential problems. We might mistype our password a couple of times, so at worst a minimal lockout hits a legitimate user on rare occasion. An attacker, trying a set of possible passwords, will hit the lockouts multiple times. Lockout after three attempts allows a reasonable error rate and balances risk.

EXAM TIP Accounts have many facets that are governed by both action and policy. Remember policy directs actions, and the specifics of the question give the context by which you can choose the best answer. There is a lot of detail in this section and it is all testable in this manner.

Password History

Password history refers to passwords previously used by an account. It is good security policy to prohibit reuse of passwords, at least for a set number of passwords. In Windows, under Local Group Policy, you can set three elements that work together to manage password history:

- **Enforce password history** Tells the system how many passwords to remember and does not allow a user to reuse an old password in that list
- **Maximum password age** Specifies the maximum number of days a password may be used before it must be changed
- **Minimum password age** Specifies the minimum number of days a password must be used before it can be changed again

The minimum password age is to prevent a user from changing their password 20 times in a row to recycle back to the previous or current password.

Password Reuse

Password reuse is a bad idea in that it reopens an exposure to an adversary who has previously obtained a password. Official guidance is passwords should not be reused for at least a year, and for at least a half dozen changes, whichever comes last. Practically, we should never reuse passwords, for a single account or between accounts. As breaches have released many e-mails and passwords into the open domain, people should never expect old passwords to be secure. Adopting a policy of no reuse makes good sense from a risk perspective. This is to minimize the opportunity for an adversary to take advantage of a reuse case. As described in the previous section, you can restrict password reuse in Windows under Local Group Policy.

Password Length

Password length is critical to password-based security. The true strength of a password lies in its entropy or randomness. The higher the entropy or randomness, the greater the keyspace that must be searched for random matching. Password length and complexity are the easiest way to increase entropy in a password. Recent research has shown that passphrases of 20 characters or more are easier to remember, are not typically written down, and can provide the required entropy to be effective. The only problem is that not all systems take passphrases. That being said, the current standard is at least 10 characters with numbers, mixed case, and special characters, and 12-character length is preferred.

PART IV

EXAM TIP Passwords and password policies are prime targets for questions. Although all aspects of the policies are important, the specifics of the scenario will shift focus to one particular aspect, so focus on the scenario to provide the context for your answer.

Chapter Review

In this chapter, you became acquainted with the breadth and depth of identity and access management systems. The chapter opened with a description of identification, authentication, authorization, and accounting. It then looked at multifactor authentication, including the five factors of something you are, something you have, something you know, something you do, and somewhere you are. The next topics covered were federation, single sign-on, and transitive trust.

The next section covered types of accounts, including user accounts, shared or generic accounts, guest accounts, service accounts, and privileged accounts. The general concepts around authentication and authorization were covered, including least privilege, onboarding/offboarding, permission audits and review, usage auditing and review, time-of-day restrictions, recertification, standard naming conventions, account maintenance, group-based access control, and location-based policies.

The chapter finished with a discussion of account policy enforcement. In this section, the topics of credential management, group policy, password complexity, expiration, recovery, disablement, lockout, password history, reuse, and length were covered.

Questions

To help you prepare further for the CompTIA Security+ exam, and to test your level of preparedness, answer the following questions and then check your answers against the correct answers at the end of the chapter.

1. Which of the following is an account you might use to run processes that do not require human intervention to start or stop?

   A. Guest account

   B. Process account

   C. Service account

   D. Root account

2. A friend of yours who works in the IT department of a bank tells you that tellers are allowed to log in to their terminals only from 9 A.M. to 5 P.M., Monday through Saturday. What is this restriction an example of?

   A. User auditing

   B. Least privilege

C. Time-of-day restrictions

D. Account verification

3. What is the process of ascribing a computer ID to a specific user known as?

   A. Authentication

   B. Validation

   C. Authorization

   D. Identification

4. You are working with a group to develop a new multifactor authentication system for your organization. Which of the following is not a valid category of authentication factors you might use?

   A. Something you know

   B. Something you see

   C. Something you are

   D. Something you do

5. Your organization is revamping its account management policies and you've been asked to clarify the difference between account disablement and account lockout. Which of the following statements best describes that difference?

   A. Account disablement removes the user and all their data files; account lockout does not.

   B. Account lockout typically only affects the ability to log in; account disablement removes all privileges.

   C. Account lockout is permanent; account disablement is easily reversible.

   D. Account disablement requires administrative privileges to execute; account lockout can be performed by any user.

6. Which of the following would most likely be the hardest password to crack?

   A. An eight-character password based on a common dictionary word

   B. A six-character password using only uppercase letters

   C. A seven-character password using a completely random mix of letters, symbols, and numbers

   D. An eight-character password using only lowercase letters

7. What are accounts with greater than "normal" user access called?

   A. Privileged accounts

   B. System accounts

   C. Superuser accounts

   D. Audit accounts

8. You've been tasked to make sure every account on your mail server belongs to a valid, active employee. What is this process often called?

   A. Recertification

   B. Privilege auditing

   C. Password cracking

   D. Payroll auditing

9. In a meeting discussing account management, one of your colleagues suggests you manage access control using collections of users rather than on a user-by-user basis. Your colleague is suggesting you use which type of access control?

   A. Least privilege access control

   B. Location-based access control

   C. Group-based access control

   D. Privilege-based access control

10. When a user no longer needs or is no longer authorized to use a system, which of the following should occur?

    A. Account recovery

    B. Account deletion

    C. Account reset

    D. Account audit

11. Your organization trusts authentication of accounts from a partner organization and your partner organization trusts authentication from your organization. What is this relationship known as specifically?

    A. Two-way trust relationship

    B. Transition trust relationship

    C. Authentication validation relationship

    D. Account auditing relationship

12. Which of the following defines policies, protocols, and practices to manage identities across systems and organizations?

    A. Transitive trust

    B. Single sign-on

    C. Identity federation

    D. Account management

13. Which of the following would not be considered "something you are" when discussing authentication factors?

    A. Fingerprints

    B. Voice

    C. PIN code

    D. Retina pattern

14. In which of the following scenarios might it be acceptable to use a shared account?

    A. On a server maintained by different personnel

    B. On a publicly accessible PC running in kiosk mode

    C. If the account is used only to administer e-mail accounts

    D. If the account is used by the CEO and her assistant

15. The processes of adding a person to a project or team and removing a person from a project or team are known as:

    A. Account creation and account disablement

    B. Intake and outflow

    C. Onboarding and offboarding

    D. Account auditing and account review

Answers

1. **C.** Service accounts are used to run processes that do not require human intervention to start, stop, or administer.

2. **C.** Time-of-day restrictions are often used to limit the hours during which a user is allowed to log into or access a system. This helps prevent unauthorized access outside that user's normal working hours.

3. **D.** Identification is the process of ascribing a computer ID to a specific user, computer, network device, or computer process.

4. **B.** Something you see is not one of the categories of authentication factors.

5. **B.** Account disablement is a step down from removing an account completely. While the account (and associated data files) still exist on the system, the account itself is disabled and has no privileges to access the system. Account lockout typically only affects logon privileges. Performing a temporary account lockout is a common approach to thwarting brute force password-guessing attacks.

6. **C.** Of the examples, C would be the most difficult to crack because it is random and is composed of letters, symbols, and numbers—a much larger character set to brute force.

7. **A.** Privileged accounts are any accounts with greater than normal user access. Privileged accounts are typically root- or admin-level accounts and represent risk in that they are unlimited in their powers.

8. **A.** Recertification is the process of ensuring users are still employed and still require accounts.

9. **C.** Group-based access control manages access control using groups of users rather than user by user.

10. **B.** Account disablement should occur when a user no longer has authorized use privileges on the system. Account deletion can mess with permissions.

11. **A.** When two domains trust each other, this is known as a two-way trust relationship. In this case, your organization trusts the partner organization and they trust your organization in return. An extended trust is a nonsense distractor.

12. **C.** Federation, or identity federation, defines policies, protocols, and practices to manage identities across systems and organizations. Federation's ultimate goal is to allow users to seamlessly access data or systems across domains.

13. **C.** The authentication factor category "something you are" specifically refers to biometrics. These are uniquely identifying characteristics associated with individuals that typically do not change.

14. **B.** In general, shared accounts should be avoided when possible, but in situations where creating individual accounts is neither practical nor feasible and tracking user activity is not critical, shared accounts can be the solution. A publicly accessible PC running in kiosk mode is a good use of a shared account, as you wouldn't be able to issue individual accounts to each person who uses the kiosk and tracking specific user activity is not critical.

15. **C.** Onboarding and offboarding refer to the processes of adding personnel to a project or team and removing them from a project or team.

CHAPTER 19

Identity and Access Services

In this chapter, you will

- Learn how to install and configure identity and access services
- Understand how to compare and contrast the different identity and access services

To use a system, one must identify themselves with the system in some form or fashion. This chapter examines the identity and access services employed by systems to determine whether a user gets access or not. Identity and access services are comprised of hardware, software, and protocol elements that work together to manage the identity and access functions across the enterprise.

Certification Objective   This chapter covers CompTIA Security+ exam objective 4.2, Given a scenario, install and configure identity and access services.

Objective 4.2 is a good candidate for performance-based questions, which means you should expect questions in which you must apply your knowledge of the topic to a scenario. The best answer to a question will depend upon specific details in the scenario preceding the question, not just the question. The questions may also involve tasks other than just picking the best answer from a list. Instead, you may be instructed to order things on a diagram, put options in rank order, match two columns of items, or perform a similar task.

LDAP

A *directory* is a data storage mechanism similar to a database, but it has several distinct differences designed to provide efficient data-retrieval services compared to standard database mechanisms. A directory is designed and optimized for reading data, offering very fast search and retrieval operations. The types of information stored in a directory tend to be descriptive attribute data. A directory offers a static view of data that can be changed without a complex update transaction. The data is hierarchically described in a treelike structure, and a network interface for reading is typical. Common uses of directories include e-mail address lists, domain server data, and resource maps of network resources.

The *Lightweight Directory Access Protocol (LDAP)* is commonly used to handle user authentication and authorization and to control access to Active Directory objects.

To enable interoperability, the X.500 standard was created as a standard for directory services. The primary method for accessing an X.500 directory is through the Directory Access Protocol (DAP), a heavyweight protocol that is difficult to implement completely, especially on PCs and more constrained platforms. This led to LDAP, which contains the most commonly used functionality. LDAP can interface with X.500 services and, most importantly, can be used over TCP with significantly less computing resources than a full X.500 implementation. LDAP offers all of the functionality most directories need and is easier and more economical to implement, hence LDAP has become the Internet standard for directory services. LDAP standards are governed by two separate entities depending upon use: the International Telecommunication Union (ITU) governs the X.500 standard, and LDAP is governed for Internet use by the Internet Engineering Task Force (IETF). Many RFCs apply to LDAP functionality, but some of the most important are RFCs 4510 through 4519.

 EXAM TIP A client starts an LDAP session by connecting to an LDAP server, called a Directory System Agent (DSA), by default on TCP and UDP port 389, or on port 636 for LDAPS (LDAP over SSL).

Kerberos

Developed as part of MIT's project Athena, *Kerberos* is a network authentication protocol designed for a client/server environment. The current release at the time of writing is Kerberos Version 5 release 1.15.2 and is supported by all major operating systems. Kerberos securely passes a symmetric key over an insecure network using the Needham-Schroeder symmetric key protocol. Kerberos is built around the idea of a trusted third party, termed a *key distribution center (KDC)*, which consists of two logically separate parts: an authentication server (AS) and a ticket-granting server (TGS). Kerberos communicates via "tickets" that serve to prove the identity of users.

Taking its name from the three-headed dog of Greek mythology, Kerberos is designed to work across the Internet, an inherently insecure environment. Kerberos uses strong encryption so that a client can prove its identity to a server and the server can in turn authenticate itself to the client. A complete Kerberos environment is referred to as a Kerberos realm. The Kerberos server contains user IDs and hashed passwords for all users that will have authorizations to realm services. The Kerberos server also has shared secret keys with every server to which it will grant access tickets.

The basis for authentication in a Kerberos environment is the ticket. Tickets are used in a two-step process with the client. The first ticket is a ticket-granting ticket (TGT) issued by the AS to a requesting client. The client can then present this ticket to the Kerberos server with a request for a ticket to access a specific server. This client-to-server ticket is used to gain access to a server's service in the realm. Since the entire session can be encrypted, this will eliminate the inherently insecure transmission of items such as a password that can be intercepted on the network. Tickets are time-stamped and have a lifetime, so attempting to reuse a ticket will not be successful.

The steps involved in Kerberos authentication are

1. The user presents credentials and requests a ticket from the Key Distribution Server (KDS).

2. The KDS verifies credentials and issues a TGT.

3. The user presents a TGT and request for service to the KDS.

4. The KDS verifies authorization and issues a client-to-server ticket.

5. The user presents a request and a client-to-server ticket to the desired service.

6. If the client-to-server ticket is valid, service is granted to the client.

To illustrate how the Kerberos authentication service works, think about the common driver's license. You have received a license that you can present to other entities to prove you are who you claim to be. Because other entities trust the state in which the license was issued, they will accept your license as proof of your identity. The state in which the license was issued is analogous to the Kerberos authentication service realm, and the license acts as a client-to-server ticket. It is the trusted entity both sides rely on to provide valid identifications. This analogy is not perfect, because we all probably have heard of individuals who obtained a phony driver's license, but it serves to illustrate the basic idea behind Kerberos.

 EXAM TIP Kerberos is a third-party authentication service that uses a series of tickets as tokens for authenticating users. The steps involved are protected using strong cryptography.

TACACS+

The *Terminal Access Controller Access Control System+ (TACACS+)* protocol is the current generation of the TACACS family. TACACS+ has extended attribute control and accounting processes.

One of the fundamental design aspects is the separation of authentication, authorization, and accounting in this protocol. Although there is a straightforward lineage of these protocols from the original TACACS, TACACS+ is a major revision and is not backward compatible with previous versions of the protocol series.

TACACS+ uses TCP as its transport protocol, typically operating over TCP port 49. This port is used for the login process. Both UDP and TCP port 49 are reserved for the TACACS+ login host protocol.

TACACS+ is a client/server protocol, with the client typically being a network access server (NAS) and the server being a daemon process on a UNIX, Linux, or Windows server. This is important to note, for if the user's machine (usually a PC) is not the client (usually a NAS), then communications between the PC and NAS are typically not encrypted and are passed in the clear. Communications between a TACACS+ client and TACACS+ server are encrypted using a shared secret that is manually configured into each entity and is not shared over a connection. Hence, communications between a TACACS+ client (typically a NAS) and a TACACS+ server are secure, but the communications between a user (typically a PC) and the TACACS+ client are subject to compromise.

TACACS+ Authentication

TACACS+ allows for arbitrary length and content in the authentication exchange sequence, enabling many different authentication mechanisms to be used with TACACS+ clients. Authentication is optional and is determined as a site-configurable option. When authentication is used, common forms include Point-to-Point Protocol (PPP) authentication with either Password Authentication Protocol (PAP), Challenge Handshake Authentication Protocol (CHAP), or Extensible Authentication Protocol (EAP), token cards, and Kerberos. The authentication process is performed using three different packet types: START, CONTINUE, and REPLY. START and CONTINUE packets originate from the client and are directed to the TACACS+ server. The REPLY packet is used to communicate from the TACACS+ server to the client.

The authentication process is illustrated in Figure 19-1, and it begins with a START message from the client to the server. This message may be in response to an initiation from a PC connected to the TACACS+ client. The START message describes the type of authentication being requested (simple plaintext password, PAP, CHAP, and so on). This START message may also contain additional authentication data, such as username and password. A START message is also sent as a response to a restart request from the server in a REPLY message. A START message always has its sequence number set to 1.

When a TACACS+ server receives a START message, it sends a REPLY message. This REPLY message will indicate whether the authentication is complete or needs to be continued. If the process needs to be continued, the REPLY message also specifies what additional information is needed. The response from a client to a REPLY message requesting additional data is a CONTINUE message. This process continues until the server has all the information needed, and the authentication process concludes with a success or failure.

TACACS+ Authorization

TACACS+ authorization is defined as the action associated with determining permission associated with a user action. This generally occurs after authentication, as shown in Figure 19-1, but this is not a firm requirement. A default state of "unknown user" exists before a user is authenticated, and permissions can be determined for an unknown user. As with authentication, authorization is an optional process and may or may not be part of a site-specific operation. When authorization is used in conjunction with authentication, the authorization process follows the authentication process and uses the confirmed user identity as input in the decision process.

The authorization process is performed using two message types: REQUEST and RESPONSE. The authorization process is performed using an authorization session consisting of a single pair of REQUEST and RESPONSE messages. The client issues an authorization REQUEST message containing a fixed set of fields that enumerate the

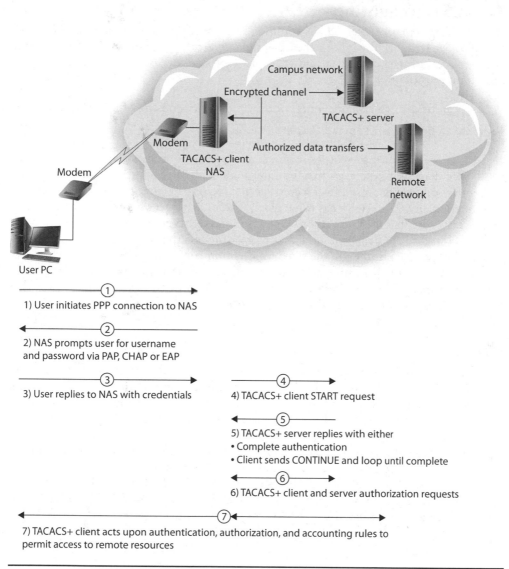

Figure 19-1 TACACS+ communication sequence

authenticity of the user or process requesting permission and a variable set of fields enu-merating the services or options for which authorization is being requested.

The RESPONSE message in TACACS+ is not a simple yes or no; it can also include qualifying information, such as a user time limit or IP restrictions. These limitations have important uses, such as enforcing time limits on shell access or IP access list restrictions for specific user accounts.

TACACS+ Accounting

As with the two previous services, accounting is also an optional function of TACACS+. When utilized, it typically follows the other services. Accounting in TACACS+ is defined as the process of recording what a user or process has done. Accounting can serve two important purposes:

- It can be used to account for services being utilized, possibly for billing purposes.

- It can be used for generating security audit trails.

TACACS+ accounting records contain several pieces of information to support these tasks. The accounting process has the information revealed in the authorization and authentication processes, so it can record specific requests by user or process. To support this functionality, TACACS+ has three types of accounting records: START, STOP, and UPDATE. Note that these are record types, not message types as earlier discussed.

START records indicate the time and user or process that began an authorized process. STOP records enumerate the same information concerning the stop times for specific actions. UPDATE records act as intermediary notices that a particular task is still being performed. Together these three message types allow the creation of records that delineate the activity of a user or process on a system.

CHAP

Challenge Handshake Authentication Protocol (CHAP) is used to provide authentication across a point-to-point link using PPP. In this protocol, authentication after the link has been established is not mandatory. CHAP is designed to provide authentication periodically through the use of a challenge/response system sometimes described as a three-way handshake, as illustrated in Figure 19-2. The initial challenge (a randomly generated number) is sent to the client. The client uses a one-way hashing function to calculate what the response should be and then sends this back. The server compares the response to what it calculated the response should be. If they match, communication continues. If the two values don't match, then the connection is terminated. This mechanism relies on a shared secret between the two entities so that the correct values can be calculated.

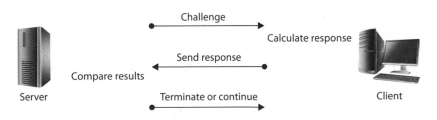

Figure 19-2   The CHAP challenge/response sequence

EXAM TIP CHAP uses PPP, which supports three functions:

—Encapsulate datagrams across serial links

—Establish, configure, and test links using LCP (Link Control Protocol)

—Establish and configure different network protocols using NCP (Network Control Protocol)

PPP supports two authentication protocols:

—Password Authentication Protocol (PAP)

—Challenge Handshake Authentication Protocol (CHAP)

PAP

Password Authentication Protocol (PAP) authentication involves a two-way handshake in which the username and password are sent across the link in clear text. PAP authentication does not provide any protection against playback and line sniffing. PAP is now a deprecated standard.

EXAM TIP PAP is a cleartext authentication protocol and hence is subject to interception. CHAP uses a challenge response handshake protocol to secure the channel.

MSCHAP

Microsoft Challenge Handshake Authentication Protocol (MSCHAP) is the Microsoft variant of CHAP. Microsoft has created two versions of CHAP, modified to increase its usability across their product line. MSCHAPv1, defined in RFC 2433, has been deprecated and dropped in Windows Vista. The current standard is MSCHAPv2, RFC 2759, which was introduced with Windows 2000. MSCHAPv2 offers mutual authentication, verifying both users in an exchange. It also offers improved cryptographic support including separate cryptographic keys for transmitted and received data.

RADIUS

Remote Authentication Dial-In User Service (RADIUS) is a protocol that was developed as an AAA protocol. It was submitted to the IETF as a series of RFCs: RFC 2058 (RADIUS specification), RFC 2059 (RADIUS accounting standard), and updated RFCs 2865–2869 and 3579 are now standard protocols. The IETF AAA Working Group has proposed extensions to RADIUS (RFC 2882) and a replacement protocol called Diameter (RFC 7075).

RADIUS is designed as a connectionless protocol utilizing User Datagram Protocol (UDP) as its transport-level protocol. Connection type issues, such as timeouts, are handled by the RADIUS application instead of the transport layer. RADIUS utilizes UDP ports 1812 for authentication and authorization and 1813 for accounting functions.

RADIUS is a client/server protocol. The RADIUS client is typically a network access server (NAS). The RADIUS server is a process or daemon running on a UNIX or Windows Server machine. Communications between a RADIUS client and RADIUS server are encrypted using a shared secret that is manually configured into each entity and not shared over a connection. Hence, communications between a RADIUS client (typically a NAS) and a RADIUS server are secure, but the communications between a user (typically a PC) and the RADIUS client are subject to compromise. This is important to note, for if the user's machine (the PC) is not the RADIUS client (the NAS), then communications between the PC and the NAS are typically not encrypted and are passed in the clear.

RADIUS Authentication

The RADIUS protocol is designed to allow a RADIUS server to support a wide variety of methods to authenticate a user. When the server is given a username and password, it can support PPP, PAP, CHAP, UNIX login, and other mechanisms, depending on what was established when the server was set up. A user login authentication consists of a query (Access-Request) from the RADIUS client and a corresponding response (Access-Accept or Access-Reject) from the RADIUS server, as you can see in Figure 19-3.

The Access-Request message contains the username, encrypted password, NAS IP address, and port. The message also contains information concerning the type of session the user wants to initiate. Once the RADIUS server receives this information, it searches its database for a match on the username. If a match is not found, either a default profile is loaded or an Access-Reject reply is sent. If the entry is found or the default profile is used, the next phase involves authorization, for in RADIUS, these steps are performed in sequence. Figure 19-3 shows the interaction between a user and the RADIUS client and RADIUS server and the steps taken to make a connection:

1. A user initiates PPP authentication to the NAS.

2. The NAS prompts for
   - username and password (if PAP), or
   - challenge (if CHAP).

3. User replies with credentials.

4. RADIUS client sends username and encrypted password to the RADIUS server.

5. RADIUS server responds with Accept, Reject, or Challenge.

6. The RADIUS client acts upon services requested by user.

RADIUS Authorization

In the RADIUS protocol, the authentication and authorization steps are performed together in response to a single Access-Request message, although they are sequential steps, as shown in Figure 19-3. Once an identity has been established, either known or default, the authorization process determines what parameters are returned to the client. Typical authorization parameters include the service type allowed (shell or framed), the protocols allowed, the IP address to assign to the user (static or dynamic), and the access list to apply or static route to place in the NAS routing table. These parameters are all

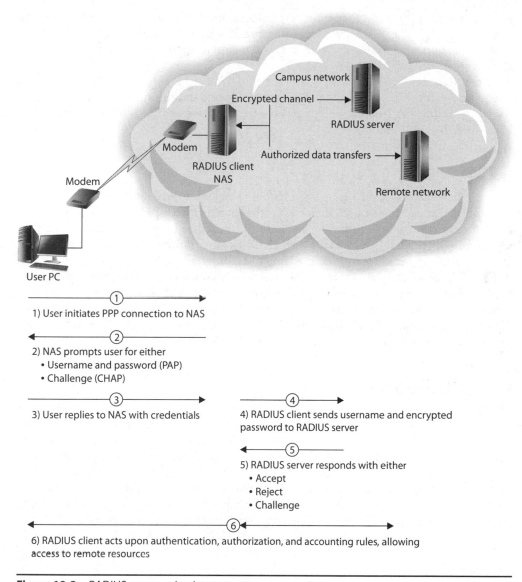

1) User initiates PPP connection to NAS

2) NAS prompts user for either
 • Username and password (PAP)
 • Challenge (CHAP)

3) User replies to NAS with credentials

4) RADIUS client sends username and encrypted password to RADIUS server

5) RADIUS server responds with either
 • Accept
 • Reject
 • Challenge

6) RADIUS client acts upon authentication, authorization, and accounting rules, allowing access to remote resources

Figure 19-3   RADIUS communication sequence

defined in the configuration information on the RADIUS client and server during setup. Using this information, the RADIUS server returns an Access-Accept message with these parameters to the RADIUS client.

RADIUS Accounting

The RADIUS accounting function is performed independently of RADIUS authentication and authorization. The accounting function uses a separate UDP port, 1813. The primary functionality of RADIUS accounting was established to support ISPs in their user accounting, and it supports typical accounting functions for time billing and security logging. The RADIUS accounting functions are designed to allow data to be transmitted at the beginning and end of a session, and it can indicate resource utilization, such as time, bandwidth, and so on.

When RADIUS was first designed in the mid-1990s, the role of ISP NASs was relatively simple. Allowing and denying access to a network and timing usage were the major concerns. Today, the Internet and its access methods have changed dramatically, and so have the AAA requirements.

SAML

Security Assertion Markup Language (SAML) is a single sign-on (SSO) capability used for web applications to ensure user identities can be shared and are protected. It defines standards for exchanging authentication and authorization data between security domains. It is becoming increasingly important with cloud-based solutions and with Software-as-a-Service (SaaS) applications as it ensures interoperability across identity providers.

SAML is an XML-based protocol that uses security tokens and assertions to pass information about a "principal" (typically an end user) with a SAML authority (an "identity provider" or IdP) and the service provider (SP). The principal requests a service from the SP, which then requests and obtains an identity assertion from the IdP. The SP can then grant access or perform the requested service for the principal.

OpenID Connect

OpenID Connect is a simple identity layer on top of the OAuth 2.0 protocol, which is discussed next. OpenID Connect allows clients of all types, including mobile, JavaScript, and web-based clients, to request and receive information about authenticated sessions and end users. OpenID is intended to make the process of proving who you are easier, the first step in the authentication–authorization ladder. To do authorization, a second process is needed, and OpenID is commonly paired with OAuth 2.0. OpenID was created for federated authentication that lets a third party, such as Google or Facebook, authenticate your users for you, by using accounts that the users already have.

OAUTH

OAuth (Open Authorization) is an open protocol that allows secure, token-based authorization on the Internet from web, mobile, and desktop applications via a simple and standard method. OAuth is used by companies such as Google, Facebook, Microsoft, and Twitter to permit users to share information about their accounts with third-party applications or websites. OAuth 1.0 was developed by a Twitter engineer as part of the Twitter OpenID implementation. OAuth 2.0 (not backward compatible) has taken off with support from most major web platforms. OAuth's main strength is that it can be used by an external partner site to allow access to protected data without having to re-authenticate the user.

OAuth was created to remove the need for users to share their passwords with third-party applications, instead substituting a token. OAuth 2.0 expanded this into also providing authentication services, so it can eliminate the need for OpenID.

 EXAM TIP OpenID and OAuth are typically used together, yet have different purposes. OpenID is used for authentication, while OAuth is used for authorization.

Shibboleth

Shibboleth is a service designed to enable single sign-on and federated identity-based authentication and authorization across networks. It began in 2000, has been through several revisions and versions, but has yet to gain any widespread acceptance. Shibboleth is a web-based technology that is built using SAML technologies. Shibboleth uses the HTTP/POST, artifact, and attribute push profiles of SAML, including both identity provider (IdP) and service provider (SP) components to achieve its goals. As such, it is included by many services that use SAML for identity management.

Secure Token

Within a claims-based identity framework, such as OASIS WS-Trust, security tokens are used. A *secure token* service is responsible for issuing, validating, renewing, and cancelling these security tokens. The tokens issued can then be used to identify the holders of the tokens to any services that adhere to the WS-Trust standard. Secure tokens solve the problem of authentication across stateless platforms, for user identity must be established with each request. The basic five-step process to use tokens is as follows:

1. User requests access with username/password.
2. Secure token service validates credentials.
3. Secure token service provides a signed token to the client.
4. Client stores that token and sends it along with every request.
5. Server verifies token and responds with data.

These steps are highly scalable and can be widely distributed and even shared. A user application can use a token for access via another app, allowing someone to validate a login to Twitter via Facebook, as the tokens are transportable.

NTLM

NT LAN Manager (NTLM), also known as Windows Challenge/Response, is a suite of Microsoft security protocols that provides authentication, integrity, and confidentiality to users. NTLM is the successor to the authentication protocol in Microsoft LAN Manager (LANMAN), an older Microsoft product. Both of these suites have been widely replaced by Microsoft's Kerberos implementation, although NTLM is still used for logon authentication on stand-alone Windows machines. NTLM uses an encrypted challenge/response protocol to authenticate a user without sending the user's password over the wire, but the cryptography used for this, MD4, is considered weak and deprecated by today's standards.

Chapter Review

In this chapter, you became acquainted with the principles behind identity and access services. The chapter opened with an exploration of the LDAP protocol and then moved to Kerberos. TACACS+ was explored next, including how it performs authentication, authorization, and accounting. The chapter then examined the CHAP, PAP, and MSCHAP protocols. It then moved back to integrated services, this time looking at RADIUS, including how it does authentication, authorization, and accounting.

The chapter then explored distributed and federated methods such as SAML, OpenID Connect, OAuth, and Shibboleth. The chapter next introduced the use of secure tokens, followed by an examination of NTLM, an old, but still essential service.

Questions

To help you prepare further for the CompTIA Security+ exam, and to test your level of preparedness, answer the following questions and then check your answers against the correct answers at the end of the chapter.

1. You are working with a development group on a new web application that will be hosted in the cloud. They need single sign-on capability to exchange authentication and authorization data between multiple security domains and they prefer working with XML. What would you suggest they use?

   A. PAP

   B. RADIUS

   C. SAML

   D. SecureID

2. A colleague has been tasked to update the authentication protocols for a very old Windows-based application running on a stand-alone system—it's still using LANMAN and running on Windows XP. The colleague would prefer to keep using something from Microsoft, but she can't upgrade the OS past Windows 7 during this effort. Which of the following would you suggest she use?

   A. TACACS+

   B. NTLM

   C. RADIUS

   D. LDAP

3. Which of the following protocols uses a key distribution center and can securely pass a symmetric key over an insecure network?

A. CHAP

B. PAP

C. LDAP

D. Kerberos

4. Your colleague is preparing a talk about TACACS+ authentication and the exchange sequence. He is having trouble remembering the three different packet types used in the authentication process. Which of the following is *not* one of the three packet types used in TACACS+ authentication?

A. REPLY

B. START

C. CONTINUE

D. INITIATE

5. While helping to catalog older servers in your data center, you come across a RADIUS accounting server. Your supervisor asks you what RADIUS accounting was typically used for. You tell him it was used mainly for which of the following?

A. Source and destination IP addresses of network traffic

B. Applications used by users

C. Time billing and security logging

D. Tracking file access

6. Your development team needs an authentication solution that supports authentication across stateless platforms. They want you to explain how other applications use Facebook or Goggle logins for authentication. In your explanation, which of the following concepts would you definitely need to mention?

A. Secure tokens

B. Secure tickets

C. XML requests

D. Request packets

7. You are establishing a point-to-point link and need to provide authentication using PPP. Which of the following protocols would you consider?

A. CHAP

B. RADIUS

C. SAML

D. TCP auth

PART IV

8. What does the "A" in RADIUS stand for?

   A. Application

   B. Authorization

   C. Authentication

   D. Auditing

9. Which of the following statements regarding TACACS+ is true?

   A. Communications between a TACACS+ client (typically a NAS) and a TACACS+ server are not secure.

   B. Communications between a user (typically a PC) and the TACACS+ client are subject to compromise as communications are usually not encrypted.

   C. TACACS+ is an extension of TACACS and is backward compatible.

   D. TACACS+ uses UDP for its transport protocol.

10. Which of the following protocols involves a two-way handshake and sends the username and password in clear text?

    A. SAML

    B. LDAP

    C. PAP

    D. NTLM

11. OpenID Connect allows for which of the following?

    A. A third party can authenticate your users for you using accounts the users already have.

    B. Symmetric keys can be shared across unsecured networks.

    C. Identity can be confirmed with a single UDP packet.

    D. Trusted IP addresses can be used to mitigate brute force attacks.

12. Your IT group is reworking their user authentication and authorization capabilities. They need something that can be used to control access to objects as well as handle user authentication and authorization. Which of the following protocols would you suggest they use?

    A. MSCHAP

    B. TACACS

    C. PPP

    D. LDAP

13. Which of the following is a service designed to enable single sign-on and federated identity-based authentication and authorization across networks?

    A. PAP

    B. Shibboleth

    C. XAML

    D. OASIS

14. Which of the following is a true statement about the NTLM protocol?

    A. It uses an encrypted challenge/response protocol to authenticate a user.

    B. It passes user credentials in clear text only.

    C. It is commonly used to integrate UNIX services into a network.

    D. It is typically used on stand-alone systems.

15. Which of the following is an open protocol that allows secure, token-based authentication and authorization from web, desktop, and mobile applications and is used by companies such as Google and Microsoft to permit users to share information about their accounts with third-party applications?

    A. TKIP

    B. OAuth

    C. SAML

    D. RADIUS

Answers

1. C. Security Assertion Markup Language (SAML) is a single sign-on capability used for web applications to ensure user identities can be shared and are protected. It defines standards for exchanging authentication and authorization data between security domains. It is becoming increasingly important with cloud-based solutions and with Software-as-a-Service (SaaS) applications as it ensures interoperability across identity providers.

2. B. NT LAN Manager (NTLM) is a suite of Microsoft security protocols that provides authentication, integrity, and confidentiality to users and would be the most likely choice from the list of choices. NTLM is the successor to the authentication protocol in Microsoft LAN Manager (LANMAN).

3. D. Kerberos securely passes a symmetric key over an insecure network using the Needham-Schroeder symmetric key protocol. Kerberos is built around the idea of a trusted third party, termed a *key distribution center (KDC)*, which consists of two logically separate parts: an authentication server (AS) and a ticket-granting server (TGS). Kerberos communicates via "tickets" that serve to prove the identity of users.

4. D. The TACACS+ authentication process is performed using three different packet types: START, CONTINUE, and REPLY. START and CONTINUE packets originate from the client and are directed to the TACACS+ server. The REPLY packet is used to communicate from the TACACS+ server to the client.

5. **C.** The primary functionality of RADIUS accounting was established to support ISPs in their user accounting, and it supports typical accounting functions for time billing and security logging.

6. **A.** Secure tokens provide for authentication across stateless platforms and can be used to identify the holder of the token to any services that adhere to the WS-Trust standard. Secure tokens are transportable, which is what allows users to log in to Twitter or other applications via Facebook.

7. **A.** Challenge Handshake Authentication Protocol (CHAP) is used to provide authentication across a point-to-point link using PPP.

8. **C.** The "A" stands for Authentication—Remote Authentication Dial-In User Service (RADIUS).

9. **B.** Communications between a user (typically a PC) and the TACACS+ client are subject to compromise as they are usually not encrypted.

10. **C.** Password Authentication Protocol (PAP) authentication involves a two-way handshake in which the username and password are sent across the link in clear text. PAP authentication does not provide any protection against playback and line sniffing.

11. **A.** OpenID was created for federated authentication that lets a third party authenticate your users for you, by using accounts the users already have.

12. **D.** LDAP is a protocol that is commonly used to handle user authentication/authorization as well as control access to Active Directory objects.

13. **B.** Shibboleth is a service designed to enable single sign-on and federated identity-based authentication and authorization across networks. Shibboleth is a web-based technology that is built using SAML technologies.

14. **A.** NTLM uses an encrypted challenge/response protocol to authenticate a user without sending the user's password over the wire, but the cryptography is considered to be weak and ineffective by today's standards.

15. **B.** OAuth (Open Authorization) is an open protocol that allows secure, token-based authorization on the Internet from web, mobile, and desktop applications via a simple and standard method. OAuth is used by companies such as Google, Facebook, Microsoft, and Twitter to permit the users to share information about their accounts with third-party applications or websites.

Identity and Access Management Controls

In this chapter, you will

- Learn how to implement identity management controls
- Learn how to implement access management controls

One of the core tenets of computer security is the concept that all actions will be controlled via a system of approvals; accessing a resource, operating on a resource, and storing of an item all can only be performed by authorized parties. Identity and access management systems are the mechanisms by which this is accomplished. Identity systems establish a link between users and accounts in the system which represent the user during system operations. Access management controls work to manage what users can do with resources, which actions are allowed, which actions are denied. This chapter examines the specifics of these systems.

Certification Objective   This chapter covers CompTIA Security+ exam objective 4.3, Given a scenario, implement identity and access management controls. This objective is a good candidate for performance-based questions, which means you should expect questions in which you must apply your knowledge of the topic to a scenario. The best answer to a question will depend upon specific details in the scenario preceding the question, not just the question. The questions may also involve tasks other than just picking the best answer from a list. Instead, they may involve actual simulations of steps to take to solve a problem.

Access Control Models

The term *access control* describes a variety of protection schemes. It sometimes refers to all security features used to prevent unauthorized access to a computer system or network. In this sense, it may be confused with *authentication*. More properly, *access* is the ability of a subject (such as an individual or a process running on a computer system) to interact with an object (such as a file or hardware device). Authentication, on the other hand, deals with verifying the identity of a subject.

To understand the difference, consider the example of an individual attempting to log in to a computer system or network. Authentication is the process used to verify to the computer system or network that the individual is who he claims to be. The most common method to do this is through the use of a user ID and password. Once the individual has verified his identity, access controls regulate what the individual can actually do on the system—just because a person is granted entry to the system does not mean that he should have access to all data the system contains.

Consider another example. When you go to your bank to make a withdrawal, the teller at the window will verify that you are indeed who you claim to be by asking you to provide some form of identification with your picture on it, such as your driver's license. You might also have to provide your bank account number. Once the teller verifies your identity, you will have proved that you are a valid (authorized) customer of this bank. This does not, however, mean that you have the ability to view all information that the bank protects—such as your neighbor's account balance. The teller will control what information, and funds, you can access and will grant you access only to the information that you are authorized to see. In this example, your identification and bank account number serve as your method of authentication and the teller serves as the access control mechanism.

In computer systems and networks, access controls can be implemented in several ways. An access control matrix provides the simplest framework for illustrating the process and is shown in Table 20-1. In this matrix, the system is keeping track of two processes, two files, and one hardware device. Process 1 can read both File 1 and File 2 but can write only to File 1. Process 1 cannot access Process 2, but Process 2 can execute Process 1. Both processes have the ability to write to the printer.

While simple to understand, the access control matrix is seldom used in computer systems because it is extremely costly in terms of storage space and processing. Imagine the size of an access control matrix for a large network with hundreds of users and thousands of files. The actual mechanics of how access controls are implemented in a system varies, though access control lists (ACLs) are common. An ACL is nothing more than a list that contains the subjects that have access rights to a particular object. The list identifies not only the subject but the specific access granted to the subject for the object. Typical types of access include read, write, and execute, as indicated in the example access control matrix.

No matter what specific mechanism is used to implement access controls in a computer system or network, the controls should be based on a specific *model* of access. Several different models are discussed in security literature and listed under exam objective 4.3, including mandatory access control (MAC), discretionary access control (DAC), attribute-based access control (ABAC), role-based access control (RBAC), and rule-based access control (also RBAC).

	Process 1	Process 2	File 1	File 2	Printer
Process 1	Read, write, execute		Read, write	Read	Write
Process 2	Execute	Read, write, execute	Read, write	Read, write	Write

Table 20-1 An Access Control Matrix

MAC

A less frequently employed system for restricting access is *mandatory access control (MAC)*. This system, generally used only in environments in which different levels of security classifications exist, is much more restrictive regarding what a user is allowed to do. Referring to the "Orange Book," a mandatory access control is "a means of restricting access to objects based on the sensitivity (as represented by a label) of the information contained in the objects and the formal authorization (i.e., clearance) of subjects to access information of such sensitivity." In this case, the owner or subject can't determine whether access is to be granted to another subject; it is the job of the operating system to decide.

 EXAM TIP Common information classifications include High, Medium, Low, Confidential, Private, and Public.

In MAC, the security mechanism controls access to all objects, and individual subjects cannot change that access. The key here is the label attached to every subject and object. The label will identify the level of classification for that object and the level to which the subject is entitled. Think of military security classifications such as Secret and Top Secret. A file that has been identified as Top Secret (has a label indicating that it is Top Secret) may be viewed only by individuals with a Top Secret clearance. It is up to the access control mechanism to ensure that an individual with only a Secret clearance never gains access to a file labeled as Top Secret. Similarly, a user cleared for Top Secret access will not be allowed by the access control mechanism to change the classification of a file labeled as Top Secret to Secret or to send that Top Secret file to a user cleared only for Secret information. The complexity of such a mechanism can be further understood when you consider today's windowing environment. The access control mechanism will not allow a user to cut a portion of a Top Secret document and paste it into a window containing a document with only a Secret label. It is this separation of differing levels of classified information that results in this sort of mechanism being referred to as *multilevel security*.

Finally, just because a subject has the appropriate level of clearance to view a document does not mean that she will be allowed to do so. The concept of least privilege, or sometimes called "need to know," which is a DAC concept (discussed next), also exists in MAC mechanisms. Least privilege means that a person is given access only to information that she needs in order to accomplish her job or mission.

DAC

Both *discretionary access control (DAC)* and mandatory access control are terms originally used by the military to describe two different approaches to controlling an individual's access to a system. As defined by the "Orange Book," a Department of Defense (DoD) document that at one time was the standard for describing what constituted a trusted computing system, DACs are "a means of restricting access to objects based on the identity of subjects and/or groups to which they belong. The controls are discretionary in the sense that a subject with a certain access permission is capable of passing that permission (perhaps indirectly) on to any other subject." While this might appear to be confusing "government-speak," the principle is rather simple. In systems that employ DACs, the owner of an object can decide which other subjects can have access to the object and what specific access they can have. One common method to accomplish this is the permission bits used in Linux-based systems. The owner of a file can specify what permissions (read/write/execute) members in the same group can have and also what permissions all others can have. ACLs are also a common mechanism used to implement DAC.

 EXAM TIP If you are trying to remember the difference between MAC and DAC, just remember that MAC is associated with multilevel security labels such as Top Secret and Secret, while DAC uses ACLs.

ABAC

Attribute-based access control (ABAC) is a form of access control based on attributes. These attributes can be in a wide variety of forms, such as user attributes, resource or object attributes, and environmental attributes. For instance, a doctor can access medical records, but only for patients to which she is assigned, or only when she is on shift. The major difference between ABAC and role-based access control is the ability to include Boolean logic in the access control decision.

Role-Based Access Control

ACLs can be cumbersome and can take time to administer properly. Another access control mechanism that has been attracting increased attention is *role-based access control (RBAC)*. In this scheme, instead of each user being assigned specific access permissions for the objects associated with the computer system or network, each user is assigned a set of roles that he or she may perform. The roles are in turn assigned the access permissions necessary to perform the tasks associated with the role. Users will thus be granted permissions to objects in terms of the specific duties they must perform—not according to a security classification associated with individual objects.

Rule-Based Access Control

The first thing that you might notice is the ambiguity that is introduced with this access control method also using the acronym RBAC. *Rule-based access control* again uses objects such as ACLs to help determine whether access should be granted or not. In this case, a series of rules are contained in the ACL and the determination of whether to grant access will be made based on these rules. An example of such a rule is one that states that no employee may have access to the payroll file after hours or on weekends. As with MAC, users are not allowed to change the access rules, and administrators are relied on for this. Rule-based access control can actually be used in addition to or as a method of implementing other access control methods. For example, MAC methods can utilize a rule-based approach for implementation.

EXAM TIP Do not become confused between rule-based and role-based access controls, even though they both have the same acronym. The name of each is descriptive of what it entails and will help you distinguish between them.

Physical Access Control

Physical access control is the process of defining and enforcing who can have physical access to a system. Physical access control lists work in the physical world in the same way they work in the electronic world. Access lists define the group of individuals who are authorized to utilize a resource. Entry into a server room, access to equipment rooms, and keys for locks protecting sensitive areas are all examples of elements that require access control.

Many organizations use electronic access control systems to control the opening of doors. The use of proximity readers and contactless access cards provides user information to the control panel. Doorways are electronically controlled via electronic door strikes and magnetic locks. These devices rely on an electronic signal from the control panel to release the mechanism that keeps the door closed. These devices are integrated into an access control system that controls and logs entry into all the doors connected to it, typically through the use of access tokens. Security is improved by having a centralized system that can instantly grant or refuse access based upon access lists and the reading of a token that is given to the user. This kind of system also logs user access, providing nonrepudiation of a specific user's presence in a controlled environment. The system will allow logging of personnel entry, auditing of personnel movements, and real-time monitoring of the access controls.

Proximity Cards

One method of electronic door control is through the use of *proximity cards*, or contactless access cards (such as the example shown in Figure 20-1). A keypad, a combination of the card and a separate PIN code, may also be required to open the door to a secure space.

Many organizations use electronic access control systems to control the opening of doors. The use of proximity readers and contactless access cards provides user information to the control panel. Doorways are electronically controlled via electronic door strikes and magnetic locks. These devices rely on an electronic signal from the control panel to release the mechanism that keeps the door closed. These devices are integrated into an access control system that controls and logs entry into all the doors connected to it, typically through the use of access tokens. Security is improved by having a centralized system that can instantly grant or refuse access based upon access lists and the reading of a token that is given to the user. This kind of system also logs user access, providing nonrepudiation of a specific user's presence in a controlled environment. The system will allow logging of personnel entry, auditing of personnel movements, and real-time monitoring of the access controls.

PART IV

Figure 20-1
Contactless access cards act as modern keys to a building.

Smart Cards

A *smart card* (also known as an *integrated circuit card [ICC]* or *chip card*) is a credit card-sized card with embedded integrated circuits that is used to provide identification security authentication. Smart cards can increase the physical security because they can carry long cryptographic tokens, too long to remember and too large a space to guess. Because of the manner in which they are employed and used, copying the number is not a practical option as well. Smart cards can find use in a variety of situations where you want to combine something you know (a pin or password) together with something you have (and can't be duplicated, a smart card). Many standard corporate-type laptops come with smart card readers installed and their use is integrated into the Windows user access system.

Biometric Factors

Biometric factors are measurements of certain biological factors to identify one specific person from others. These factors are based on parts of the human body that are unique. The most well-known of these unique biological factors is the fingerprint. Fingerprint readers have been available for several years in laptops and other mobile devices, on keyboards, and as stand-alone USB devices.

However, many other biological factors can be used, such as the retina or iris of the eye, the geometry of the hand, and the geometry of the face. When these are used for authentication, there is a two-part process: enrollment and then authentication. During enrollment, a computer takes the image of the biological factor and translates it to a numeric value, called a template. When the user attempts to authenticate, the biometric feature is scanned by the reader, and the computer computes a value in the same fashion as the template, and then compares the numeric value being read to the one stored in the database. If they match, access is allowed. Since these physical factors are unique, theoretically only the actual authorized person would be allowed access.

In the real world, however, the theory behind biometrics breaks down. Tokens that have a digital code work very well because everything remains in the digital realm. A computer checks your code, such as 123, against the database; if the computer finds 123 and that number has access, the computer opens the door. Biometrics, however, take an analog signal, such as a fingerprint or a face, and attempt to digitize it, and it is then matched against the digits in the database. The problem with an analog signal is that it might not encode the exact same way twice. For example, if you came to work with a bandage on your chin, would the face-based biometrics grant you access or deny it? Because of this, the templates are more complex in a manner where there can be a probability of match, or closeness measurement.

Fingerprint Scanner

A *fingerprint scanner* measures the unique pattern of a person's fingerprint and translates that pattern into a numerical value, or template, as discussed in the previous section. Fingerprint readers can be enhanced to assure that the pattern is a live pattern, one with circulating blood or other detectable biological activity, to prevent simple spoofing with a Play-Doh mold of the print. Fingerprint scanners are cheap to produce and have widespread use in mobile devices. One of the challenges of fingerprint scanners is that they don't function if the user is wearing gloves (e.g., medical gloves) or has worn off their fingerprints through manual labor, as many involved in the sheetrock trade do through normal work.

Retinal Scanner

A *retinal scanner* examines blood vessel patterns in the back of the eye. Believed to be unique and unchanging, the retina is a readily detectable biometric. Retinal scanning does suffer from lack of user acceptance, as it involves a laser scanning the inside of the user's eyeball, which raises some psychological issues for some users who are wary of letting a laser scan the inside of their eye. This detection requires the user to be right in front of the device for it to work. It is also more expensive because of the precision of the detector and the involvement of lasers and users' vision.

Iris Scanner

An *iris scanner* works in a means similar to a retinal scanner in that it uses an image of a unique biological measurement, in this case the pigmentation associated with the iris of the eye. This can be photographed and measured from a distance, removing the psychological impediment of placing one's eye up close to a scanner. The downside to being able to capture an iris scan at a distance is that it's easy to do without a person's knowledge, and even construct contact lenses that mimic a pattern. There are also some other issues associated with medical conditions such as pregnancy, and some diseases, which can be detected by changes in a person's iris and if revealed would be a privacy violation.

Voice Recognition

Voice recognition is the use of unique tonal qualities and speech patterns to identify a person. Long the subject of sci-fi movies, this biometric has been one of the hardest to develop into a reliable mechanism, primarily because of problems with false acceptance and rejection rates, which will be discussed a bit later in the chapter.

Facial Recognition

Facial recognition was also mostly the stuff of sci-fi until it was integrated into various mobile phones. A sensor that recognizes when you move the phone in a position to see your face, coupled with a state of not logged in, turns on the forward-facing camera and the system looks for its enrolled owner. This system has proven to have fairly high discrimination, and works fairly well, with only one drawback. Another person can move the phone in front of the registered user and it can unlock; in essence, another user can activate the unlocking mechanism even when the user is unaware. The other minor drawback is that for certain transactions, such as positive identification for financial transactions, the position of the phone on an NFC location, together with the user's face needing to be in a certain orientation with respect to the phone leads to awkward positions. Having to put your face in a proper position on the phone to identify you, while holding it against the counter height NFC credit card reader, can be awkward.

False Positives and False Negatives

Engineers who design biometric systems understand that if a system were set to exact checking, an encoded biometric might never grant access since the system might never scan the biometric exactly the same way twice. Therefore, most systems are designed to allow a certain amount of error in the scan, while not allowing too much. This leads to the concepts of false positives and false negatives. A *false positive* occurs when a biometric is scanned and allows access to someone who is not authorized—for example, two people who have very similar fingerprints might be recognized as the same person by the computer, which grants access to the wrong person. A *false negative* occurs when the system denies access to someone who is actually authorized—for example, a user at the hand geometry scanner forgot to wear a ring he usually wears and the computer doesn't recognize his hand and denies him access.

What is desired is for the system to be able to differentiate the two signals, one being the stored value and the other being the observed value, in such a way that the two curves do not overlap. Figure 20-2 illustrates two probability distributions that do not overlap.

For biometric authentication to work properly, and also be trusted, it must minimize the existence of both false positives and false negatives. But biometric systems are seldom that discriminating, and the curves tend to overlap, as shown in Figure 20-3. For detection to work, a balance between exacting and error must be created so that the machines allow a little physical variance—but not too much.

This leads us to acceptance and rejection rates.

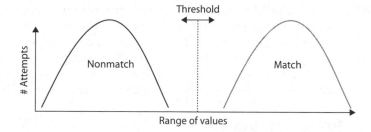

Figure 20-2
Ideal
probabilities

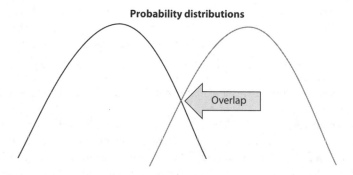

Figure 20-3
Overlapping
probabilities

False Acceptance Rate

The *false acceptance rate (FAR)* is just that, what level of false positives are going to be allowed in the system. A false acceptance/positive is demonstrated by the grayed-out area in Figure 20-4. In this area, the two curves overlap, and the decision has been set that at the threshold or better an accept signal will be given. Thus, if you are not a match, but your measured value falls on the upper end of the nonmatch curve, in the gray area, you will be considered a match, and hence become a false positive. Expressed as probabilities, the false acceptance rate is the probability that the system incorrectly identifies a match between the biometric input and the stored template value.

Figure 20-4
False acceptance
rate

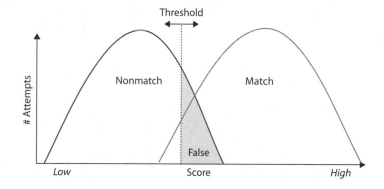

When selecting the threshold value, the designer must be cognizant of two factors: one is the rejection of a legitimate biometric, the area on the match curve below the threshold value. The second consideration is the acceptance of false positives. The more the curves overlap, the larger the problem for once a threshold is chosen, that number defines the FAR. Setting the threshold higher will decrease false positives but increase false negatives or rejections. This would increase the false rejection rate, discussed in the next section.

False Rejection Rate

The *false rejection rate (FRR)* is just that, what level of false negatives, or rejections, are going to be allowed in the system. A false rejection is demonstrated by the grayed-out area in Figure 20-5. In this section, the curves overlap, and the decision has been set that at the threshold or lower a reject signal will be given. Thus, if you are on the lower end of the match curve, in the gray area, you will be rejected, even if you should be a match. Expressed as probabilities, the false rejection rate is the probability that the system incorrectly rejects a legitimate match between the biometric input and the stored template value.

When comparing the FAR and the FRR, one realizes that, in most cases, whenever the curves overlap, they are related. This brings up the issue of the crossover error rate. Both the FAR and the FRR are set by choosing the threshold value. This is done when the system is set up and reflects the choice of which error rate is more important. If you want to make it harder for a false positive, you will cause many failed authorizations of legitimate users as they will be seen by the system as on the other curve. If you want to make sure all legitimate users do not experience troubles during scans, then some unauthorized users will get accepted (false positives) as they will be interpreted by the system as being on the wrong curve based on where the threshold is set.

Crossover Error Rate

The *crossover error rate (CER)* is the rate where both accept and reject error rates are equal. This is the desired state for most efficient operation, and it can be managed by manipulating the threshold value used for matching. In practice, the values may not be

Figure 20-5
False rejection
rate

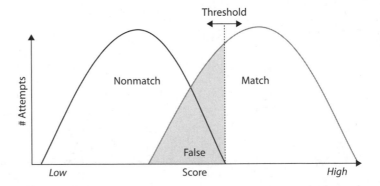

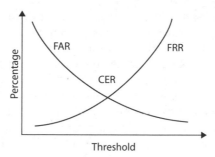

Figure 20-6
FRR, FAR, and
CER compared

exactly the same, but they will typically be close to each other. Figure 20-6 demonstrates the relationship between the FAR, FRR, and CER.

Biometrics Calculation Example

Assume we are using a fingerprint biometric system, and we have 1000 users. During the enrollment stage, 5 users were unable to enroll (the system could not establish a fingerprint signature/template for them). This means the system has a failure to enroll rate (FER) = 0.5 percent. This means only 995 users can use the system, and an alternative means needs to be in place for the users who cannot use the system.

During the testing of the 995 users, 50 users were rejected when the system matched their fingerprint against their enrollment fingerprint template. This makes the FRR = 5.02 percent.

Also, 25 users out of the 995 users were accepted by the system when the system matched their fingerprint against another user's fingerprint template. This means the FAR = 2.51 percent

The lower the FAR and FRR, the better the system, and the ideal situation is setting the thresholds where the FAR and FRR are equal, the crossover error rate.

EXAM TIP   Understand how to calculate FAR and FRR given data. Remember to include those that fail enrollment.

Tokens

An access *token* is a physical object that identifies specific access rights, and in authentication falls into the "something you have" factor. Your house key, for example, is a basic physical access token that allows you access into your home. Although keys have been used to unlock devices for centuries, they do have several limitations. Keys are paired exclusively with a lock or a set of locks, and they are not easily changed. It is easy to add an authorized user by giving the user a copy of the key, but it is far more difficult to give that user selective access unless that specified area is already set up as a separate key. It is also difficult to take access away from a single key or key holder, which usually requires a rekey of the whole system.

In many businesses, physical access authentication has moved to contactless radio frequency cards and proximity readers. When passed near a card reader, the card sends out a code using radio waves. The reader picks up this code and transmits it to the control panel. The control panel checks the code against the reader from which it is being read and the type of access the card has in its database. The advantages of this kind of token-based system include the fact that any card can be deleted from the system without affecting any other card or the rest of the system. In addition, all doors connected to the system can be segmented in any form or fashion to create multiple access areas, with different permissions for each one. The tokens themselves can also be grouped in multiple ways to provide different access levels to different groups of people. All of the access levels or segmentation of doors can be modified quickly and easily if building space is re-tasked. Newer technologies are adding capabilities to the standard token-based systems. Smart cards can also be used to carry identification tokens. The primary drawback of token-based authentication is that only the token is being authenticated. Therefore, the theft of the token could grant anyone who possesses the token access to what the system protects.

The risk of theft of the token can be offset by the use of multifactor authentication (described in Chapter 18). One of the ways that people have tried to achieve multifactor authentication is to add a biometric factor to the system. A less expensive alternative is to use hardware tokens in a challenge/response authentication process. In this way, the token functions as both a something-you-have and something-you-know authentication mechanism. Several variations on this type of device exist, but they all work on the same basic principles. The device has an LCD screen and may or may not have a numeric keypad. Devices without a keypad will display a password (often just a sequence of numbers) that changes at a constant interval, usually about every 60 seconds. When an individual attempts to log in to a system, he enters his own user ID number and then the number that is displayed on the LCD. These two numbers are either entered separately or concatenated. The user's own ID number is secret, and this prevents someone from using a lost device. The system knows which device the user has and is synchronized with it so that it will know the number that should have been displayed. Since this number is constantly changing, a potential attacker who is able to see the sequence will not be able to use it later, since the code will have changed. Devices with a keypad work in a similar fashion (and may also be designed to function as a simple calculator). The individual who wants to log in to the system will first type his personal identification number into the calculator. He will then attempt to log in. The system will then provide a challenge; the user must enter that challenge into the calculator and press a special function key. The calculator will then determine the correct response and display it. The user provides the response to the system he is attempting to log in to, and the system verifies that this is the correct response. Since each user has a different PIN, two individuals receiving the same challenge will have different responses. The device can also use the date or time as a variable for the response calculation so that the same challenge at different times will yield different responses, even for the same individual.

Hardware

There are several forms of *hardware tokens*, from proximity cards and smart cards discussed earlier to Common Access Cards (CACs), USB tokens, and key fobs with RFID chips. These hardware components act as a token, being an authentication factor that typically takes the form of a physical or logical entity that the user must be in possession of to access their account or certain resources.

Most of these tokens are physical tokens that display a series of numbers that changes every 30 to 90 seconds, such as the token pictured in Figure 20-7 from Blizzard Entertainment. These act as one-time password generators, making them impossible to copy as the sequence is tied to each device independently. The displayed sequence of numbers must be entered when the user is attempting to log in or access certain resources. The ever-changing sequence of numbers is synchronized to a remote server such that when the user enters the correct username, password, and matching sequence of numbers, she is allowed to log in. Even if an attacker obtains the username and password, the attacker cannot log in without the matching sequence of numbers.

Software

Access tokens may also be implemented in software. *Software tokens* still provide two-factor authentication but don't require the user to have a separate physical device on hand. Some tokens require software clients that store a symmetric key (sometimes called a seed record) in a secured location on the user's device (laptop, desktop, tablet, and so on). Other software tokens use public key cryptography. Asymmetric cryptography solutions, such as public key cryptography, often associate a PIN with a specific user's token. To log in or access critical resources, the user must supply the correct PIN. The PIN is stored on a remote server and is used during the authentication process so that if a user presents the right token, but not the right PIN, the user's access can be denied. This helps prevent an attacker from gaining access if he gets a copy of or gains access to the software token. The most common form of software tokens is in identifying a specific device in addition to a user, in that the software token is on the device and the user supplies the rest of the details needed to demonstrate authenticity.

Figure 20-7
Token authenticator from Blizzard Entertainment

HOTP/TOTP

HMAC-based One-Time Password (HOTP) is an algorithm that can be used to authenticate a user in a system by using an authentication server. (HMAC stands for Hash-based Message Authentication Code.) It is defined in RFC 4226, dated December 2005. The *Time-based One-Time Password (TOTP)* algorithm is a specific implementation of an HOTP that uses a secret key with a current timestamp to generate a one-time password. It is described in RFC 6238, dated May 2011.

 EXAM TIP Tokens represent 1) something you have with respect to authentication as well as 2) a device that can store more information than a user can memorize, which makes them very valuable for access control. The details in the scenario preceding a question will provide the necessary criteria to pick the best token method for the question.

Certificate-Based Authentication

Certificate-based authentication is a means of proving identity via the presentation of a certificate. Certificates offer a method of establishing authenticity of specific objects such as an individual's public key or downloaded software. A *digital certificate* is a digital file that is sent as an attachment to a message and is used to verify that the message did indeed come from the entity it claims to have come from. Using a digital certificate is a verifiable means of establishing possession of an item, specifically the certificate. When the certificate is held within a store that prevents tampering or extraction, then this becomes a reliable means of identification, especially when combined with an additional factor such as something you know or a biometric.

PIV/CAC/Smart Card

The U.S. federal government has several *smart card* solutions for identification of personnel. The *Personal Identity Verification (PIV) card* is a U.S. government smart card that contains the cardholder's credential data used to determine access to federal facilities and information systems. The *Common Access Card (CAC)* is a smart card used by the U.S. Department of Defense (DoD) for active-duty military, Selected Reserve members, DoD civilians, and eligible contractors. Like the PIV card, it is used for carrying the cardholder's credential data, in the form of a certificate, used to determine access to federal facilities and information systems.

IEEE 802.1x

IEEE 802.1X is an authentication standard that supports port-based authentication services between a user and an authorization device, such as an edge router. IEEE 802.1X is used by all types of networks, including Ethernet, Token Ring, and wireless. This standard describes methods used to authenticate a user prior to granting access to a network and the authentication server, such as a RADIUS server. 802.1X acts through an intermediate device, such as an edge switch, enabling ports to carry normal traffic if the connection is properly authenticated. This prevents unauthorized clients from accessing the publicly available ports on a switch, keeping unauthorized users out of a LAN. Until a client has successfully authenticated itself to the device, only Extensible Authentication Protocol over LAN (EAPoL) traffic is passed by the switch.

CAUTION   One security issue associated with 802.1X is that the authentication occurs only upon initial connection, and that another user can insert themselves into the connection by changing packets or using a hub. The secure solution is to pair 802.1X, which authenticates the initial connection, with a VPN or IPsec, which provides persistent security.

EXAM TIP   Understanding how public key cryptography is used to establish trust for identities is covered partly in this chapter and partly in Chapter 29. But to answer questions regarding objective 4.3, you need to understand both chapters, as Chapter 29 covers the limitations of certificates.

File System Security

File systems need a method of applying security, to prevent unauthorized access and unauthorized alterations. *File system security* is the set of mechanisms and processes employed to ensure this critical function. Using a combination of file storage mechanisms, along with access control lists and access control models, provides a means by which you can secure your file systems. You need a file system capable of supporting user-level access differentiation, something NTFS does, but FAT32 does not. Next, you need to have a functioning access control model, such as MAC, DAC, or ABAC, as previously described in this chapter. Then you need a system to grant users permissions to access and modify the files, which can be handled by the OS, although administering and maintaining this can be a challenge. Modern OSs that are employed in enterprise settings, specifically NTFS for Windows, are designed to enable file system security. This is done through the inner workings of the file system and is invisible to the user as users will not even see files they cannot access.

Database Security

Database security is the application of security functions, who can access what, inside a database system. Data security is a significant concern for many enterprises, as the data in the databases represents valuable information assets. Major database engines have built-in access control provisions and encryption capabilities. Access control is managed by named users and defined permissions, all managed inside the database system. The results are enforced via encryption, which also provides protection should the datafiles be copied or released. This can provide the desired levels of confidentiality and integrity to the contents of the database. The advantage to these encryption schemes is that they can be tailored to the data structure, protecting the essential columns while not impacting columns that are not sensitive. Properly employing database encryption requires that the data schema and its security requirements be designed into the database implementation. The advantage is in better protection against any database compromise, and the performance hit is typically negligible with respect to other alternatives.

Chapter Review

In this chapter, you became acquainted with access control methods for securing information in the enterprise. The chapter opened with an examination of the major access control models, including MAC, DAC, ABAC, role-based, and rule-based access control. It next addressed physical access control through the use of proximity cards and smart cards.

The discussion of biometric factors included both factors and usage. You learned about several different biometric technologies: fingerprint scanning, retinal scanning, iris scanning, voice recognition, and facial recognition. The methods and analytics covered included false positive and false negatives, false acceptance rate, false rejection rate, and the crossover error rate, and you were given an example showing how these factors are interrelated.

The chapter continued with an examination of various tokens used in access control, including hardware and software options, as well as HOTP/TOTP forms of one-time password generators. Certificate-based authentication, including its use in PIV/CAC and smart cards as well as 802.1x, was presented. The chapter concluded with an examination of file system security and database security.

Questions

To help you prepare further for the CompTIA Security+ exam, and to test your level of preparedness, answer the following questions and then check your answers against the correct answers at the end of the chapter.

1. During a visit to a hosting center where your organization keeps some offsite servers, you see a door with an odd-looking panel next to it. You see people approaching the panel and placing their eyes into a hooded viewer. A few seconds after they've done this, the door unlocks. What type of biometric scanner might this be?

   A. Voice recognition scanner

   B. Retinal scanner

   C. Fingerprint scanner

   D. Facial recognition scanner

2. You've spent the last week tweaking a fingerprint scanning solution for your organization. Despite your best efforts, roughly 1 in 50 attempts will fail even if the user is using the correct finger and their fingerprint is in the system. Your supervisor says 1 in 50 is "good enough" and tells you to move onto the next project. Your supervisor just defined which of the following for your fingerprint scanning system?

   A. False rejection rate

   B. False acceptance rate

   C. Critical threshold

   D. Failure acceptance criteria

3. Which of the following algorithms uses a secret key with a current timestamp to generate a one-time password?

   A. Hash-based Message Authentication Code

   B. Date-hashed Message Authorization Password

   C. Time-based One-Time Password

   D. Single sign-on

4. Your organization needs a system for restricting access to files based on the sensitivity of the information in those files. You might suggest which of the following access control systems?

   A. Discretionary access control

   B. Mandatory access control

   C. Confidential access control

   D. File-based access control

5. Which of the following describes a major difference between NTFS and FAT32 file systems?

   A. NTFS supports user-level access differentiation.

   B. FAT32 supports group-level access differentiation.

   C. FAT32 natively encrypts files and directories.

   D. NTFS logs all file access using secure tokens.

6. Your organization has grown too large to support assigning permissions to users individually. Within your organization, you have large groups of users who perform the same duties and need the same type and level of access to the same files. Rather than assigning individual permissions, your organization may wish to consider using which of the following access control methods?

   A. Group-based access control

   B. Shift-based access control

   C. Role-based access control

   D. File-based access control

PART IV

7. With regard to authentication, an access token falls into which factor category?

   A. Something you are

   B. Something you have

   C. Something you know

   D. Something you see

8. Which of the following is NOT a common form of hardware token?

   A. Proximity card

   B. Common Access Card

   C. USB token

   D. Iris scan

9. A client of yours wants a system that will allow them to verify that messages came from specific individuals. In other words, they want to make sure that if a message purports to come from Sally, it really came from Sally. What method of establishing authenticity might you suggest they use?

   A. Digital certificates

   B. One-time passwords

   C. Software tokens

   D. Fingerprint scans

10. The hospital client you are working with needs to do a better job restricting access to patient records. They want doctors to have access only to records for their patients and only when the doctors are in the hospital. What type of access control method might work well in this situation?

    A. Role-based access control

    B. Mandatory access control

    C. Discretionary access control

    D. Attribute-based access control

11. While depositing cash from a charity fundraiser at a local bank, you notice bank employees are holding up cards next to a panel near a door. A light on the panel turns green and the employees are able to open the door. The light on the panel is normally red. What type of electronic door control is this bank using?

    A. Iris scanner

    B. Hardware tokens

    C. Proximity cards

    D. Symmetric key tokens

12. Your colleague is telling you a story she heard about a way to trick fingerprint scanners using gummy bears. She heard that if you press a gummy bear against an authorized user's finger, you can then use that gummy bear as their fingerprint to fool a fingerprint scanner. If this works, the result is an example of which of the following?

    A. False negative

    B. False positive

    C. Crossover positive

    D. Crossover negative

13. The HR department in your organization wants to restrict access to the payroll file such that no one can access the payroll file outside of normal business hours (M–F, 7 A.M. to 6 P.M.). What type of access control method are they asking for?

    A. Rule-based access control

    B. Mandatory access control

    C. Physical access control

    D. Restrictive access control

14. When designing and tweaking biometric systems, the point where both the accept and reject error rates are equal is known as which of the following?

    A. Crossover acceptance rate

    B. Accept-reject overlap rate

    C. Crossover error rate

    D. Overlap acceptance rate

15. Which of the following is a smart card identification typically used by the U.S. Department of Defense?

    A. Personal Identity Verification card

    B. Common Access Card

    C. Symmetric Token Card

    D. Proximity Verification Card

Answers

1. **B.** This is most likely a retinal scanner. Retinal scanners examine blood vessel patterns in the back of the eye. Retinal scanning must be done at short distances; the user has to be right at the device for it to work.

2. **A.** Your supervisor just defined the false rejection rate (FRR) for your system. The FRR is the level of false negatives, or rejections, that are going to be allowed in the system. In this case your supervisor is willing to accept 1 false rejection for every 50 attempts.

3. **C.** The Time-based One-Time Password (TOTP) algorithm is a specific implementation of an HOTP that uses a secret key with a current timestamp to generate a one-time password.

4. **B.** Mandatory access control (MAC) is a system used in environments with different levels of security classifications. Access to objects (like files) is based on the sensitivity of the information contained in those objects and the authorization of the user to access information with that level of sensitivity.

5. **A.** NTFS supports user-level access differentiation and allows you to assign user permissions to files and directories.

6. **C.** Your organization could consider role-based access control. In role-based access control, instead of each user being assigned specific access permissions for the objects associated with the computer system or network, each user is assigned a set of roles that he or she may perform. The roles are in turn assigned the access permissions necessary to perform the tasks associated with the role. Users will thus be granted permissions to objects in terms of the specific duties they must perform—not according to a security classification associated with individual objects.

7. **B.** An access token is a physical object that identifies specific access rights, and in authentication falls into the "something you have" factor category.

8. **D.** An iris scan would be considered a biometric technique and is not a hardware token. A hardware token is a physical item the user must be in possession of to access their account or certain resources.

9. **A.** You might suggest they consider digital certificates. A digital certificate is a digital file that is sent as an attachment to a message and is used to verify that the message did indeed come from the entity it claims to have come from.

10. **D.** The hospital should consider using attribute-based access control (ABAC), a form of access control based on attributes. These attributes can be in a wide variety of forms, such as user attributes, resource or object attributes, and environmental attributes. For instance, a doctor can access medical records, but only for patients to which he is assigned, or only when he is on shift. The major difference between ABAC and role-based access control is the ability to include Boolean logic in the access control decision.

11. **C.** The bank employees are using proximity cards, contactless access cards that provide information to the electronic door control system. Proximity cards just need to be close enough to the scanner to work—they do not need to actually touch the scanner.

12. **B.** This is an example of a false positive. A false positive occurs when a biometric is scanned and allows access to someone who is not authorized.

13. **A.** The HR department is looking for rule-based access control, which uses objects such as ACLs to help determine whether access should be granted or not. In this case, a series of rules are contained in the ACL and the determination of whether to grant access will be made based on these rules.

14. **C.** The crossover error rate (CER) is the rate where both accept and reject error rates are equal. This is the desired state for most efficient operation of a biometric system, and it can be managed by manipulating the threshold value used for matching.

15. **B.** The Common Access Card (CAC) is a smart card identification used by the U.S. Department of Defense (DoD) for active-duty military, Selected Reserve members, DoD civilians, and eligible contractors.

PART V

Risk Management

Policies, Plans, and Procedures

In this chapter, you will

- Understand the importance of policies, plans, and procedures related to organizational security
- Distinguish between the standard types of agreements
- Be introduced to personnel management policies and procedures
- Examine some general security policies

Policies and procedures govern the operation of the organization and represent a set of requirements developed from both internal and external requirements. External requirements may come from laws and regulations, contractual terms such as incorporation of the Payment Card Industry Data Security Standard (PCI DSS), or customer specifications. There are regulatory situations where specific business actions are required by law or regulation. In many cases, the laws or regulations specify that specific policies are in place to govern compliance. Understanding the specific requirements of the business environment may require assistance from supporting business functions, guidance from industry groups, or help from other sources. Determining the relevant security policies and procedures that apply to third-party relationships is a key endeavor in ensuring that all elements of them are met during business operations. The bottom line is simple: in some business situations, policies and procedures may be mandated by outside regulation, and assistance may be required in ensuring compliance.

Certification Objective   This chapter covers CompTIA Security+ exam objective 5.1, Explain the importance of policies, plans and procedures related to organizational security.

Standard Operating Procedure

Procedures are the step-by-step instructions on how to implement policies in the organization. They describe exactly how employees are expected to act in a given situation or to accomplish a specific task. Standards are mandatory elements regarding the implementation of a policy. They are accepted specifications that provide specific details on how a policy is to be enforced. Some standards are externally driven. Regulations for banking and financial institutions, for example, require certain security measures be taken by law. Other standards may be set by the organization to meet its own security goals. *Standard operating procedures* are just that, mandatory step-by-step instructions set by the organization so that in the performance of their duties, employees will meet the stated security objectives of the firm.

Agreement Types

Many business operations involve actions between many different parties—some within an organization, and some in different organizations. These actions require communication between the parties, defining the responsibilities and expectations of the parties, the business objectives, and the environment within which the objectives will be pursued. To ensure an agreement is understood between the parties, written agreements are used. Numerous forms of legal agreements and contracts are used in business, but with respect to security, some of the most common ones are the business partnership agreement, service level agreement, interconnection security agreement, and memorandum of understanding.

BPA

A *business partnership agreement (BPA)* is a legal agreement between partners that establishes the terms, conditions, and expectations of the relationship between the partners. These details can cover a wide range of issues, including typical items such as the sharing of profits and losses, the responsibilities of each partner, the addition or removal of partners, and any other issues. The Uniform Partnership Act (UPA), established by state law and convention, lays out a uniform set of rules associated with partnerships to resolve any partnership terms. The terms in a UPA are designed as "one size fits all" and are not typically in the best interest of any specific partnership. To avoid undesired outcomes that may result from UPA terms, it is best for partnerships to spell out specifics in a BPA.

SLA

A *service level agreement (SLA)* is a negotiated agreement between parties detailing the expectations between a customer and a service provider. SLAs essentially set the requisite level of performance of a given contractual service. SLAs are typically included as part of a service contract and set the level of technical expectations. An SLA can define specific services, the performance level associated with a service, issue management and resolution, and so on. SLAs are negotiated between customer and supplier and represent the agreed-upon terms. Specific security requirements can be specified in an SLA, and enforced once both parties agree. Once entered into, the SLA becomes a legally binding document.

ISA

An *interconnection security agreement (ISA)* is a specialized agreement between organizations that have interconnected IT systems, the purpose of which is to document the security requirements associated with the interconnection. An ISA can be a part of an MOU detailing the specific technical security aspects of a data interconnection.

MOU/MOA

A *memorandum of understanding (MOU)* and *memorandum of agreement (MOA)* are legal documents used to describe a bilateral agreement between parties. It is a written agreement expressing a set of intended actions between the parties with respect to some common pursuit or goal. Typically, an MOU has higher-level descriptions, while an MOA is more specific, but the boundaries between these two legal terms are blurry and they are often used interchangeably. Each is more formal and detailed than a simple handshake, but generally lacks the binding powers of a contract. MOUs/MOAs are also commonly used between different units within an organization to detail expectations associated with the common business interest, including security requirements.

 EXAM TIP   Be sure you understand the differences between the interoperability agreements SLA, BPA, ISA, and MOU/MOA for the CompTIA Security+ exam. All of them can be used to communicate security requirements between parties, but each is specific as to when it should be used. Look at usage for hints as to which would apply.

Personnel Management

A significant portion of human-created security problems results from poor security practices. These poor practices may be those of an individual user who is not following established security policies or processes, or they may be caused by a lack of security policies, procedures, or training within the user's organization. Through the establishment, enforcement, and monitoring of personnel-related policies—*personnel management*—an organization can create a framework that empowers its workers to achieve business objects, yet keeps them constrained within security recommended practices. This section covers a dozen security topics related to the management of personnel.

Mandatory Vacations

Organizations have been providing vacation time for their employees for many years. Until recently, however, few organizations forced employees to take this time if they didn't want to. Some employees are given the choice to either "use or lose" their vacation time, and if they do not take all of their time, they'll lose at least a portion of it. Many arguments can be made as to the benefit of taking time off, but more importantly, from a security standpoint, an employee who never takes time off is a potential indicator of nefarious activity. Employees who never take any vacation time could be involved in activity such as fraud or embezzlement and might be afraid that if they leave on vacation, the organization would discover their illicit activities. As a result, requiring employees to use their vacation time through a policy of *mandatory vacations* can be a security protection mechanism. Using mandatory vacations as a tool to detect fraud will require that somebody else also be trained in the functions of the employee who is on vacation. Having a second person familiar with security procedures is also a good policy in case something happens to the primary.

Job Rotation

Another policy that provides multiple benefits is *job rotation*. Rotating through jobs provides individuals with a better perspective of how the various parts of the organization can enhance (or hinder) the business. Since security is often of secondary concern to people in their jobs, rotating individuals through security positions can result in a much wider understanding of the organization's security problems. A secondary benefit is that it also eliminates the need to rely on one individual for security expertise. If all security tasks are the domain of one employee, security will suffer if that individual is lost from the organization. In addition, if only one individual understands the security domain, should that person become disgruntled and decide to harm the organization, recovering from their attack could be very difficult.

Separation of Duties

Separation of duties is a principle employed in many organizations to ensure that no single individual has the ability to conduct transactions alone. This means that the level of trust in any one individual is lessened, and the ability for any individual to cause catastrophic damage to the organization is also lessened. An example might be an organization in which one person has the ability to order equipment, but another individual makes the payment. An individual who wants to make an unauthorized purchase for his own personal gain would have to convince another person to go along with the transaction.

Separating duties as a security tool is a good practice, but it is possible to go overboard and break up transactions into too many pieces or require too much oversight. This results in inefficiency and can actually be less secure, since individuals may not scrutinize transactions as thoroughly because they know others will also be reviewing them. The temptation is to hurry something along and assume that somebody else will examine it or has examined it.

 EXAM TIP Another aspect of the separation of duties principle is that it spreads responsibilities out over an organization so no single individual becomes the indispensable individual with all of the "keys to the kingdom" or unique knowledge about how to make everything work. If enough tasks have been distributed, assigning a primary and a backup person for each task will ensure that the loss of any one individual will not have a disastrous impact on the organization.

Clean Desk

Preventing access to information is also important in the work area. Firms with sensitive information should have a *clean desk* policy specifying that sensitive information must not be left unsecured in the work area when the worker is not present to act as custodian. Even leaving the desk area and going to the bathroom can leave information exposed and subject to compromise. The clean desk policy should identify and prohibit things that are not obvious upon first glance, such as passwords on sticky notes under keyboards and mouse pads or in unsecured desk drawers.

Background Checks

Personnel are key to security in the enterprise. Hiring good personnel has always been a challenge in the technical field, but it is equally important to hire trustworthy people, especially in key roles that have greater system access. Performing routine *background checks* provides the HR team the necessary information needed to make the correct decisions. Background checks can validate previous employment, criminal backgrounds, and financial background. Depending upon the industry, firm, and position, different elements from these areas may be included.

 NOTE It is commonly heard that hiring a talented security hacker requires accepting someone with a shady past. The veracity of that comment aside, the real question to ask is not "Would I hire this person?" but rather "Would I be afraid of firing them?"

Exit Interviews

Exit interviews can be powerful tools for gathering information when people leave an organization. From a security perspective, the off-boarding process for personnel is very important. Employee termination needs to be modified to include termination of all accounts, including those enabled on mobile devices. It's not uncommon to find terminated employees with accounts or even company devices still connecting to the corporate network months after being terminated. E-mail accounts should be removed promptly as part of the employee termination policy and process. Mobile devices supplied by the company should be collected upon termination. BYOD equipment should have its access to corporate resources terminated as part of the off-boarding process. Regular audits for old or unterminated accounts should be performed to ensure prompt deletion of accounts for terminated employees.

Role-Based Awareness Training

For training to be effective, it needs to be targeted to the user with regard to their role in the subject of the training. While all employees may need general security awareness training, they also need specific *role-based awareness training* in areas where they have individual responsibilities. Role-based training with regard to information security responsibilities is an important part of information security training.

If a person has job responsibilities that may impact information security, then role-specific training is needed to ensure that the individual understands the responsibilities as they relate to information security. Some roles, such as system administrator or developer, have clearly defined information security responsibilities. The roles of others, such as project manager or purchasing manager, have information security impacts that are less obvious, but these roles require training as well. In fact, the less-obvious but wider-impact roles of middle management can have a large effect on the information security culture, and thus if a specific outcome is desired, it requires training.

As in all personnel-related training, two elements need attention. First, retraining over time is necessary to ensure that personnel keep proper levels of knowledge. Second, as people change jobs, a reassessment of the required training basis is needed, and additional training may be required. Maintaining accurate training records of personnel is the only way this can be managed in any significant enterprise.

Data Owner

Data requires a data owner. Data ownership roles for all data elements need to be defined in the business. Data ownership is a business function, where the requirements for security, privacy, retention, and other business functions should be established. Not all data requires the same handling restrictions, but all data requires these characteristics to be defined. This is the responsibility of the data owner. It is important that data owners receive training and understand their responsibilities with respect to this important requirement.

System Administrator

System administrators are administrative users with the responsibility of maintaining a system within its defined requirements. The system owner defines the requirements, such as frequency of backups, whereas the system administrator configures the system to operationally meet these requirements. System administrators have virtually unlimited power over the system, for they can control all functions, but they should not have the power, or the responsibility, to set policies for the system. That falls to the system owner. It is important that system administrators receive training and understand their responsibilities with respect to this important requirement, and the delineation of their responsibilities.

System Owner

Every system requires a system owner. Like data ownership, system ownership is a business function, where the requirements for security, privacy, retention, and other business functions are established for an entire system. Not all systems require the same policies, but the determination of what the policies for a given system are is the responsibility of the system owner. It is important that system owners receive training and understand their responsibilities with respect to this important requirement.

User

Normal users need limited access based on their job role and tasks assigned. This is where the principle of least privilege comes into play. Limiting an object's privileges limits the amount of harm that can be caused, thus limiting an organization's exposure to damage. Users may have access to the files on their workstations and a select set of files on a file server, but they have no access to critical data that is held within the database. This rule helps an organization protect its most sensitive resources and helps ensure that whoever is interacting with these resources has a valid reason to do so. Users should be trained as to the limits of their use and their responsibilities associated with those limits.

Privileged User

A privileged user has more authority than a standard user. Short of full administrative or root access, a privileged user has permissions to do a wider range of tasks, as their job role may require greater responsibilities. For example, a database administrator would need the equivalent of root access to database functions, but not to all servers or other OS options. Aligning privileges to user responsibilities is good standard policy.

Executive User

Executive users are a special type of user. Their business responsibility may be broad and deep, covering many levels and types of business functions. This work level of responsibilities may not translate directly to their needed computer access. Does the CIO, the highest IT level employee, require all of the permissions of all of their subordinates? The true answer is no, for they will not be performing the same level of tasks in their work. And should they on occasion need the access, it can be granted at the time of need.

Limiting the access of executives is not meant to limit their work, but rather limit the range of damage should an account become compromised. Executive users are natural targets for spear phishing attacks, and limiting their system privileges to what is truly needed for them to perform their system-level tasks, limits the damage a hacker could cause by compromising an executive account.

NDA

Non-disclosure agreements (NDAs) are standard corporate documents used to explain the boundaries of company secret material, information which control over should be exercised to prevent disclosure to unauthorized parties. NDAs are frequently used to delineate the level and type of information, and with whom it can be shared. NDAs can be executed between any two parties where one party wishes that the material being shared is not further shared, enforcing confidentiality via contract.

Onboarding

A key element when *on-boarding* personnel is to ensure that the personnel are aware of and understand their responsibilities with respect to securing company information and assets. Agreements with business partners tend to be fairly specific with respect to terms associated with mutual expectations associated with the process of the business. Ensuring the correct security elements are covered during onboarding is essential to setting proper employee expectations. These considerations need to be made prior to the establishment of the relationship, not added at the time that it is coming to an end.

EXAM TIP Onboarding and offboarding business procedures should be well documented to ensure compliance with legal requirements.

Continuing Education

Technology and security practices are far from static environments. They advance every year, and relevant skills can become outdated in as little as a couple of years. Maintaining a skilled workforce in security necessitates ongoing training and education. A *continuing education* program can assist greatly in helping employees keep their skills up to date.

Acceptable Use Policy/Rules of Behavior

An *acceptable use policy (AUP)* outlines what the organization considers to be the appropriate use of its resources, such as computer systems, e-mail, Internet, and networks. Organizations should be concerned about any personal use of organizational assets that does not benefit the company.

The goal of the policy is to ensure employee productivity while limiting potential organizational liability resulting from inappropriate use of the organization's assets. The policy should clearly delineate what activities are not allowed. The AUP should address issues such as the use of resources to conduct personal business, installation of hardware or software, remote access to systems and networks, the copying of company-owned software, and the responsibility of users to protect company assets, including data, software, and hardware. Statements regarding possible penalties for ignoring any of the policies (such as termination) should also be included.

Related to appropriate use of the organization's computer systems and networks by employees is the appropriate use by the organization. The most important of such issues is whether the organization will consider it appropriate to monitor the employees' use of the systems and network. If monitoring is considered appropriate, the organization should include a statement to this effect in the banner that appears at login. This repeatedly warns employees, and possible intruders, that their actions are subject to monitoring and that any misuse of the system will not be tolerated. Should the organization need to use in either a civil or criminal case any information gathered during monitoring, the issue of whether the employee had an expectation of privacy, or whether it was even legal for the organization to be monitoring, is simplified if the organization can point to its repeatedly displayed statement that use of the system constitutes consent to monitoring. Before any monitoring is conducted, or the actual wording on the warning message is created, the organization's legal counsel should be consulted to determine the appropriate way to address this issue.

 EXAM TIP Make sure you understand that an acceptable use policy outlines what is considered acceptable behavior for a computer system's users. This policy often goes hand-in-hand with an organization's Internet usage policy.

Adverse Actions

Punishing employees when they violate policies is always a difficult subject. There are two schools of thought regarding when to take *adverse actions*:

- **Zero-tolerance**   One strike and you are out is the norm. The defense of this view is that by setting the bar high, you get better performers and stricter adherence to policies. The downside is that the lack of flexibility means an otherwise excellent long-term employee who makes an uncharacteristic mistake in judgment must be treated the same as a middling employee who violates the same policy his first week on the job. There is no flexibility to save the employee's career, or their future contributions to the organization. In an environment where highly skilled workers are not readily available, this lack of flexibility can lead to staffing and morale issues.

- **Discretionary action**   Adverse issues are handled using the principle "violations will be punished via a range of HR actions, up to and including termination." The flexibility that this offers makes handling cases more challenging because management must determine the correct level of adverse action, but it also gives the flexibility to salvage good employees who have made an uncharacteristic mistake.

Regardless of which path an organization takes, the key to being legal and ethical is consistency in practice.

 EXAM TIP   Understanding the importance of various policies and procedures is specifically called for in the exam objectives. Learning how to differentiate which policy is relevant to address a specific situation is important from a testing point of view.

General Security Policies

In keeping with the high-level nature of policies, the *security policy* is a high-level statement produced by senior management that outlines what security means to the organization and what the organization's goals are for security. The main security policy can then be broken down into additional policies that cover specific topics. Statements such as "this organization will exercise the principle of least privilege in its handling of client information" would be an example of a security policy. The security policy can also describe how security is to be handled from an organizational point of view (such as describing which office and corporate officer or manager oversees the organization's security program).

In addition to policies related to access control, the organization's security policy should include the specific policies described in this chapter. All policies should be reviewed on a regular basis and updated as needed. Generally, policies should be updated less frequently than the procedures that implement them, since the high-level goals will not change as often as the environment in which they must be implemented. All policies should be reviewed by the organization's legal counsel, and a plan should be outlined describing how the organization will ensure that employees will be made aware of the policies. Policies can also be made stronger by including references to the authority who made the policy (whether this policy comes from the CEO or is a department-level policy) and to any laws or regulations that are applicable to the specific policy and environment.

Social Media Networks/Applications

The rise of *social media networks and applications* has changed many aspects of business. Whether used for marketing, communications, customer relations, or some other purpose, social media networks can be considered a form of third party. One of the challenges in working with social media networks and/or applications is their terms of use. While a relationship with a typical third party involves a negotiated set of agreements with respect to requirements, there is no negotiation with social media networks. The only option is to adopt their terms of service, so it is important to understand the implications of these terms with respect to the business use of the social network.

The use of social media sites by employees at work brings in additional risks, in the form of viruses, worms, and spear phishing data collection. In years past, employers worried about employees using the machines at work to shop on eBay or surf the Web rather than work. Today, the risks are increased beyond just lost time to now include malware introduction to work machines. It is common for firms to use AUPs to restrict employee personal use of things like social media, peer-to-peer (P2P) networking, BitTorrent, and other non-work-related applications.

Personal E-mail

Comingling of personal and work-related materials may not appear to be a real problem when viewed from an employee's perspective … what can be the harm? But the reality of modern e-discovery and other processes raises many concerns from a corporate perspective. While occasional use of work e-mail for personal use probably doesn't add enough data to be a storage concern, what happens when that e-mail becomes involved in a personal legal dispute? Whether the issue is one inherently personal, as in divorce, or financial, as in a case of suspected fraud, when the lawyers get involved and send a litigation hold request to a firm for an employee's personal e-mail on a corporate server, the comingling becomes a problem. The simplest and easiest policy is to disallow use of corporate resources for personal use, including e-mail, storage, devices, and so forth.

Using third-party e-mail services such as Gmail, Hotmail, and so forth also introduces risk to the corporate environment in that this provides yet another channel for malware, including worms, viruses, Trojans, and ransomware. As in other use issues associated with corporate resources, this topic should be covered in the AUP.

 EXAM TIP Employees should be trained to be cognizant of the risks to the organization whenever using computer resources. Because malware, including Trojans and ransomware, is so common on the Web, users are part of the defense in keeping this material off of the organization's network. This duty extends to the use of non-work-related applications, such as social media, P2P networks for file sharing, personal e-mail services, and so forth. Understanding where the risk originates, and that personal accounts and applications are not immune, is important.

Chapter Review

In this chapter, you became acquainted with policies and procedures. The chapter opened with various types of business agreements, including the business partnership agreement (BPA), service level agreement (SLA), interconnection security agreement (ISA), and memorandum of understanding/memorandum of agreement (MOU/MOA), and then ventured into the area of policies associated with personnel management. From work policies such as mandatory vacations, separation of duties, and clean desk, to role-based training, the bulk of the chapter centered on personnel policies. The chapter concluded with some general security policies that affect most users.

Questions

To help you prepare further for the CompTIA Security+ exam, and to test your level of preparedness, answer the following questions and then check your answers against the correct answers at the end of the chapter.

1. What is the name given to the step-by-step instructions on how to implement policies in an organization?

   A. Standards

   B. Guidelines

   C. Regulations

   D. Procedures

2. What is the name given to mandatory elements regarding the implementation of a policy?

   A. Standards

   B. Guidelines

   C. Regulations

   D. Procedures

3. Which of the following is a description of a business partnership agreement (BPA)?

   A. A negotiated agreement between parties detailing the expectations between a customer and a service provider.

   B. A legal agreement between entities establishing the terms, conditions, and expectations of the relationship between the entities.

   C. A specialized agreement between organizations that have interconnected IT systems, the purpose of which is to document the security requirements associated with the interconnection.

   D. A written agreement expressing a set of intended actions between the parties with respect to some common pursuit or goal.

4. Which of the following is used to essentially set the requisite level of performance of a given contractual service?

    A. Memorandum of understanding

    B. Inter-organizational service agreement (ISA)

    C. Memorandum of agreement

    D. Service level agreement (SLA)

5. Which of the following is an issue that must be addressed if an organization enforces a mandatory vacation policy?

    A. Enforcing a mandatory vacation policy in most cases is a costly policy.

    B. Using mandatory vacations as a tool to detect fraud will require that somebody else also be trained in the functions of the employee who is on vacation.

    C. Vacations often occur at the most inopportune time for the organization and can affect its ability to complete projects or deliver services.

    D. Forcing employees to take a vacation if they don't want to often will result in disgruntled employees, which can introduce another security threat.

6. Which of the following are reasons for an organization to have a job rotation policy? (Choose all that apply.)

    A. Since security is often of secondary concern to people in their jobs, rotating individuals through security positions can result in a much wider understanding of the organization's security problems.

    B. It helps to maintain a high level of employee morale.

    C. It ensures all important operations can still be accomplished should budget cuts result in the termination of a number of employees.

    D. It eliminates the need to rely on one individual for security expertise.

7. Which of the following statements are true when discussing separation of duties? (Choose all that apply.)

    A. Separation of duties is a principle employed in many organizations to ensure that no single individual has the ability to conduct transactions alone.

    B. Employing separation of duties means that the level of trust in any one individual is lessened, and the ability for any individual to cause catastrophic damage to the organization is also lessened.

    C. Separating duties as a security tool is a good practice, but it is possible to go overboard and break up transactions into too many pieces or require too much oversight.

    D. Separation of duties spreads responsibilities out over an organization so no single individual becomes the indispensable individual with all of the "keys to the kingdom" or unique knowledge about how to make everything work.

8. Which of the following are true in regard to a clean desk policy for security? (Choose all that apply.)

   A. While a clean desk policy makes for a pleasant work environment, it actually has very little impact on security.

   B. Sensitive information must not be left unsecured in the work area when the worker is not present to act as custodian.

   C. Even leaving the desk area and going to the bathroom can leave information exposed and subject to compromise.

   D. A clean desk policy should identify and prohibit things that are not obvious upon first glance, such as passwords on sticky notes under keyboards and mouse pads.

9. While all employees may need general security awareness training, they also need specific training in areas where they have individual responsibilities. This type of training is referred to as which of the following?

   A. Functional training

   B. User training

   C. Role-based training

   D. Advanced user training

10. Security, privacy, and retention policies for data are important to an organization. Not all data requires the same handling restrictions, but all data requires these characteristics to be defined. Defining these characteristics for specific information is generally the responsibility of which of the following?

    A. The data security office

    B. The privacy office

    C. The data owner

    D. An individual specifically given this responsibility for the organization

11. Which of the following is the name typically given to administrative users with the responsibility of maintaining a system within its defined requirements?

    A. System owner

    B. System administrator

    C. Privileged user

    D. Executive user

12. Which of the following is the term used for a document used to explain the boundaries of company secret material, information which control over should be exercised to prevent disclosure to unauthorized parties, and to obtain agreement to follow these limits?

    A. Non-disclosure agreement (NDA)

    B. Data access agreement (DAA)

    C. Data disclosure agreement (DDA)

    D. Data release agreement (DRA)

13. What is the name given to a policy that outlines what an organization considers to be the appropriate use of its resources, such as computer systems, e-mail, Internet, and networks?

    A. Resource usage policy (RUP)

    B. Acceptable use of resources policy (AURP)

    C. Organizational use policy (OUP)

    D. Acceptable use policy (AUP)

14. What is the greatest risk to an organization when employees comingle corporate and personal e-mail?

    A. Lost work productivity

    B. Introduction of malware to the network

    C. Loss of company data

    D. Use of server resources for personal mail storage

15. What is the term used for a high-level statement produced by senior management that outlines what security means to the organization and what the organization's goals are for security?

    A. Security standard

    B. Statement of security goals (SSG)

    C. Security policy

    D. Security guidance

Answers

1. **D.** Procedures are the step-by-step instructions on how to implement policies in an organization.

2. **A.** Standards is the term given to mandatory elements regarding the implementation of a policy.

3. **B.** A business partnership agreement is a legal agreement between entities establishing the terms, conditions, and expectations of the relationship between the entities.

4. **D.** A service level agreement (SLA) essentially sets the requisite level of performance for a given contractual service.

5. **B.** Using mandatory vacations as a tool to detect fraud will require that somebody else also be trained in the functions of the employee who is on vacation. The organization must therefore ensure that they have a second person who is familiar with the vacationing employee's duties.

6. **A** and **D.** Since security is often of secondary concern to people in their jobs, rotating individuals through security positions can result in a much wider understanding of the organization's security problems. A secondary benefit is that it also eliminates the need to rely on one individual for security expertise. If all security tasks are the domain of one employee, security will suffer if that individual is lost from the organization

7. **A, B, C,** and **D.** All of the statements are true when discussing separation of duties.

8. **B, C,** and **D.** A clean desk policy can actually have a positive impact on security for the reasons listed.

9. **C.** Training targeted to the user with regard to their role in the organization is generally referred to as role-based training or role-based awareness training.

10. **C.** Defining these characteristics is the responsibility of the data owner.

11. **B.** System administrators are administrative users with the responsibility of maintaining a system within its defined requirements.

12. **A.** Non-disclosure agreements (NDA) are standard corporate documents used to explain the boundaries of company secret material, information which control over should be exercised to prevent disclosure to unauthorized parties.

13. **D.** An acceptable use policy (AUP) outlines what the organization considers to be the appropriate use of its resources, such as computer systems, e-mail, Internet, and networks.

14. **B.** Malware can come from personal e-mail as well as corporate e-mail, and serious mail screening on corporate mail servers before users get the mail does not occur with third-party mail apps. While occasional use of work e-mail for personal use probably doesn't add enough data to be a storage concern, nor is the loss of work productivity typically significant, malware should always be a concern.

15. **C.** A security policy is a high-level statement produced by senior management that outlines what security means to the organization and what the organization's goals are for security.

PART V

Risk Management and Business Impact Analysis

In this chapter, you will

- Understand concepts of business impact analysis
- Understand concepts of risk management
- Explore risk management processes
- Compare and contrast various types of controls
- Learn the categories of security controls

Risk management is a core business function of an enterprise, for it is through the risk management process that an enterprise can maximize its return on investments. Understanding the business impact of operations associated with the enterprise is key for business success. This can be accomplished using a business impact analysis. Using the data from the analysis, coupled with a threat analysis and a risk assessment process, the enterprise can come to an understanding of the sources and intensities of the risk elements it faces.

Certification Objective This chapter covers CompTIA Security+ exam objectives 5.2, Summarize business impact analysis concepts, 5.3, Explain risk management processes and concepts, and 5.7, Compare and contrast various types of controls.

Business Impact Analysis Concepts

Business impact analysis (BIA) is the process used to determine the sources and relative impact values of risk elements in a process. It is also the name often used to describe a document created by addressing the questions associated with sources of risk and the steps taken to mitigate them in the enterprise. The BIA also outlines how the loss of any of your critical functions will impact the organization. This section explores the range of terms and concepts related to conducting a BIA.

RTO/RPO

The term *recovery time objective (RTO)* is used to describe the target time that is set for a resumption of operations after an incident. This is a period of time that is defined by the business, based on the needs of the business. A shorter RTO results in higher costs because it requires greater coordination and resources. This term is commonly used in business continuity and disaster recovery operations.

Recovery point objective (RPO), a totally different concept from RTO, is the time period representing the maximum period of acceptable data loss. The RPO defines the frequency of backup operations necessary to prevent unacceptable levels of data loss. A simple example of establishing RPO is to answer the following questions: How much data can you afford to lose? How much rework is tolerable?

RTO and RPO are seemingly related but in actuality measure different things entirely. The RTO serves the purpose of defining the requirements for business continuity, while the RPO deals with backup frequency. It is possible to have an RTO of 1 day and an RPO of 1 hour, or an RTO of 1 hour and an RPO of 1 day. The determining factors are the needs of the business.

 EXAM TIP Although recovery time objective and recovery point objective seem to be the same or similar, they are very different. The RTO serves the purpose of defining the requirements for business continuity, while the RPO deals with backup frequency.

MTBF

Mean time between failures (MTBF) is a common measure of reliability of a system and is an expression of the average time between system failures. The time between failures is measured from the time a system returns to service until the next failure. The MTBF is an arithmetic mean of a set of system failures:

$$\text{MTBF} = \Sigma \text{ (start of downtime − start of uptime) / number of failures}$$

Mean time to failure (MTTF) is a variation of MTBF, one that is commonly used instead of MTBF when the system is replaced in lieu of being repaired. Other than the semantic difference, the calculations are the same, and the meaning is essentially the same.

MTTR

Mean time to repair (MTTR) is a common measure of how long it takes to repair a given failure. This is the average time, and may or may not include the time needed to obtain parts. The CompTIA Security+ Acronyms list indicates mean time to recover is an alternative meaning for MTTR. In either case, MTTR is calculated as follows:

$$\text{MTTR} = \text{(total downtime) / (number of breakdowns)}$$

Availability is a measure of the amount of time a system performs its intended function. Reliability is a measure of the frequency of system failures. Availability is related to, but different than, reliability and is typically expressed as a percentage of time the system is in its operational state. To calculate availability, both the MTBF and the MTTR are needed:

$$\text{Availability} = \text{MTBF} / (\text{MTBF} + \text{MTTR})$$

Assuming a system has an MTBF of 6 months and the repair takes 30 minutes, the availability would be

$$\text{Availability} = 6 \text{ months} / (6 \text{ months} + 30 \text{ minutes}) = 99.9884\%$$

 EXAM TIP Although MTBF and MTTR may seem similar, they measure different things. Exam questions may ask you to perform simple calculations. Incorrect answer choices will reflect simple mistakes in the ratios, so calculate carefully.

Mission-Essential Functions

When examining risk and impacts to a business, it is important to identify mission-essential functions from other business functions. In most businesses, the vast majority of daily functions, although important, are not mission essential. *Mission-essential functions* are those that should they not occur, or be performed improperly, the mission of the organization will be directly affected. In other terms, mission-essential functions are those that must be restored first after a business impact to enable the organization to restore its operations. The reason that identification of these functions is vital for risk management is simple: you should spend the majority of your effort protecting the functions that are essential. Other functions may need protection, but their impairment will not cause the immediate impact that impairment of a mission-essential function would.

Identification of Critical Systems

A part of identifying mission-essential functions is identifying the systems and data that support the functions. *Identification of critical systems* enables the security team to properly prioritize defenses to protect the systems and data in a manner commensurate with the associated risk. It also enables the proper sequencing of restoring operations to ensure proper restoration of services.

Single Point of Failure

As discussed in Chapter 11 and elsewhere, a key principle of security is depense-in-depth. This layered approach to security is designed to eliminate any specific single points of failure. A *single point of failure* any system component whose failure or malfunctioning could result in the failure of the entire system. An example of a single point of failure would be a single connection to the Internet, fine for a small business, but not so for a large enterprise with servers serving content to customers. Redundancies have costs, but if the alternative cost is failure, then implementing levels of redundancy is acceptable. For mission-essential systems, single points of failure are items that need to be called to management's attention, with full explanation of the risk and costs associated with them. In some scenarios, avoiding a single point of failure may not be possible or practical, in which case everyone in the organization with responsibility for risk management should understand the nature of the situation and the resultant risk profile.

Impact

Risk is the chance of something not working as planned and causing an adverse impact. *Impact* is the cost associated with a realized risk. Impact can be in many forms, from human life, as in injury or death, to property loss, to loss of safety, financial loss, or loss of reputation. Losses are seldom absolute, and can come in all sizes and combinations. Different levels of risk can result in different levels of impact. Sometimes external events can have an effect on the impact. If everyone in the industry has been experiencing a specific type of loss, and your firm had time and warning to mitigate it, but didn't, the environment defined by these outside factors may well indeed increase the impact to your firm from this type of event. For instance, failing to patch a system can have serious impacts to an organization as recent data breaches have shown. But failure to patch a system, when you know it will be used against you, is even worse as it almost invites further attacks.

Life

Many IT systems are involved in healthcare, and failures of some of these systems can and have resulted in injury and death to patients. IT systems are also frequently integral to the operation of machines in industrial settings, and their failure can have similar impacts. Injury and loss of *life* are outcomes that backups cannot address and can result in consequences beyond others. As part of a BIA, you would identify these systems and ensure that they are highly redundant, to avoid impact to life.

Property

Property damage can be the result of unmitigated risk. Property damage to company-owned property, property damage to property of others, and even environmental damage from toxic releases in industrial settings are all examples of damage that can be caused by IT security failures. This can be especially true in companies that have manufacturing plants and other cyber physical processes. If you think property damage can't happen to your organization because it only has office computers, consider the Shamoon malware that destroyed the computing resources of Saudi Aramco to the point that the company had to buy replacement equipment, as reimaging to a clean state was not guaranteed, nor was it a timely solution.

Safety

Safety is the condition of being protected from or unlikely to cause danger, risk, or injury. Safety makes sense from both a business risk perspective and when you consider the level of concern one places for the well-being of people. In a manufacturing environment, with moving equipment and machines that can present a danger to workers, government regulations drive specific actions to mitigate risk and make the workplace as safe as possible. Computers are increasingly becoming involved in all aspects of businesses, and they can impact safety. Failures that lead to safety issues will cause work stoppages and increase losses that could otherwise have been avoided. Unsafe conditions that are the result of computer issues will face the same regulatory wrath that unsafe plants have caused in manufacturing—fines and criminal complaints.

Finance

Finance is in many ways the final arbiter of all activities, for it is how we keep score. We can measure the gains through sales and profit, and the losses through unmitigated risks. We can take most events, put a dollar value on them, and settle the books. Where this becomes an issue is when the impacts exceed the expected costs associated with the planned residual risks, for then the costs directly impact profit. Impacts to a business ultimately become a financial impact. What starts as a missed patch allows ransomware to infiltrate a system. This results in a business impact that eventually adds costs, which should have been avoided.

Reputation

Corporate *reputation* is important in marketing. Would you deal with a bank with a shoddy record of accounting or losing personal information? How about online retailing? Would your customer base think twice before entering their credit card information after a data breach? These are not purely hypothetical questions; these events have occurred, and corporate reputations have been damaged as a result. And this has cost the firms in customer base and revenue.

 EXAM TIP Risk is instantiated as impact. Impacts can have effects on life, property, safety, reputation, and finances. Typically, multiple impacts occur from an incident and finance always pays the bill. Be prepared to parse a question to determine whether its focus is risk, impact, or specific consequence.

Privacy Impact Assessment

A *privacy impact assessment (PIA)* is a structured approach to determining the gap between desired privacy performance and actual privacy performance. A PIA is an analysis of how personally identifiable information (PII) is handled through business processes and an assessment of risks to the PII during storage, use, and communication. A PIA provides a means to assess the effectiveness of a process relative to compliance requirements and identify issues that need to be addressed.

Privacy Threshold Assessment

A *privacy threshold assessment* is an analysis of whether PII is collected and maintained by a system. If PII is stored, then the next step in determining privacy risk is a privacy impact assessment, PIA, covered in the preceding section.

Risk Management Concepts

Risk management can best be described as a decision-making process. *Risk management concepts* include elements of threat assessment, risk assessment, and security implementation concepts, all positioned within the concept of business management. In the simplest terms, when you manage risk, you determine what could happen to your business, you assess the impact if it were to happen, and you decide what you could do to control that impact as much as you or your management deems necessary. You then decide to act or not to act, and, finally, you evaluate the results of your decision. The process may be iterative, as industry best practices clearly indicate that an important aspect of effectively managing risk is to consider it an ongoing process.

Threat Assessment

A *threat assessment* is a structured analysis of the threats that confront an enterprise. Threats are important to understand, for you generally cannot change the threat—you can only change how it affects you. A threat assessment begins with an enumeration of the threats that exist, followed by an estimate of the likelihood of success for each threat. Analyzing each threat as to the potential impact to the enterprise provides a prioritized list of threats requiring attention.

Environmental

One of the largest sources of threats is from the environment. *Environmental* changes can come from a wide variety of sources, weather, lightning, storms, and even solar flares, and these can cause changes to the system in a manner that disrupts normal operations. These changes can increase risk. While IT security measures cannot change the environmental factors that can impact operations, they can have an effect on the risk associated with the environmental issue. Making systems resilient can reduce impacts and mitigate these sources of risk to the enterprise. And there are times that these effects can be felt at a distance; for instance, how can you back up to a remote site if the remote site is down due to power outage as a result of a fallen branch from a storm?

Manmade

Manmade threats are those that are attributable to the actions of a person. But these threats aren't limited to hostile actions by an attacker; they include accidents by users. Users can represent one of the greatest risks in an IT system. More files are lost by accidental user deletion than by hackers deleting files, and to the team trying to restore the lost files, the attribution has no bearing on the restoration effort. User actions, such as poor cyber hygiene and reusing passwords, have all been shown to be the starting point for many major cybersecurity events over the past several years. Proper controls to manage the risk to a system must include controls against both accidental and purposeful acts.

Internal vs. External

Threats can come from internal and external sources. *Internal threats* include disgruntled employees, and well-meaning employees who make mistakes or have an accident. Internal threats tend to be more damaging, as the perpetrator has already been granted some form of access. The risk is related to the level of access and the value of the asset being worked on. For instance, if a system administrator working on the domain controller accidently erases a critical value and crashes the system, it can be just as costly as an unauthorized outsider performing a DoS attack against the enterprise.

External threats come from outside the organization, and by definition begin without access to the system. Access is reserved to users who have a business need to know and have authorized accounts on the system. Outsiders must first hijack one of these accounts. These extra steps and the reliance on external connections typically make external attackers easier to detect.

 EXAM TIP When performing a threat assessment, be sure to consider environmental, manmade, and internal threats. On the exam, carefully read the scenario preceding the question to differentiate which of these threat sources is the best answer, as multiple sources are common, but one is usually the higher risk.

Risk Assessment

A *risk assessment* is a method to analyze potential risk based on statistical and mathematical models. You can use any one of a variety of models to calculate potential risk assessment values. A common method is the calculation of the annualized loss expectancy (ALE). Calculating the ALE creates a monetary value of the impact. This calculation begins by calculating a single loss expectancy (SLE).

SLE

The *single loss expectancy (SLE)* is the value of a loss expected from a single event. It is calculated using the following formula:

$$\text{SLE} = \text{asset value} \times \text{exposure factor}$$

Exposure factor is a measure of the magnitude of loss of an asset.

By example, to calculate the exposure factor, assume the asset value of a small office building and its contents is $2 million. Also assume that this building houses the call center for a business, and the complete loss of the center would take away about half of the capability of the company. Therefore, the exposure factor is 50 percent. The SLE is

$$\$2 \text{ million} \times 0.5 = \$1 \text{ million}$$

ALE

After calculating the SLE, the *annual loss expectancy (ALE)* is then calculated simply by multiplying the SLE by the likelihood or number of times the event is expected to occur in a year, which is called the annualized rate of occurrence (ARO):

$$\text{ALE} = \text{SLE} \times \text{ARO}$$

This represents the expected losses over the course of a year based on the ALE. If multiple events are considered, the arithmetic sum of all of the SLEs and AROs can be done to provide a summation amount.

PART V

ARO

The *annualized rate of occurrence (ARO)* is a representation of the frequency of the event, measured in a standard year. If the event is expected to occur once in 20 years, then the ARO is 1/20. Typically, the ARO is defined by historical data, either from a company's own experience or from industry surveys. Continuing our example, assume that a fire at this business's location is expected to occur about once in 20 years. Given this information, the ALE is

$$\$1 \text{ million} \times 1/20 = \$50,000$$

The ALE determines a threshold for evaluating the cost/benefit ratio of a given countermeasure. Therefore, a countermeasure to protect this business adequately should cost no more than the calculated ALE of $50,000 per year.

NOTE Numerous resources are available to help in calculating ALE. There are databases that contain information to help businesses (member institutions) manage exposure to loss from natural disasters such as hurricanes, earthquakes, and so forth. These databases include information on property perils such as fire, lightning, vandalism, windstorm, hail, and so forth, and even include granular information to help evaluate, for example, the effectiveness of your building's sprinkler systems.

Asset Value

The *asset value (AV)* is the amount of money it would take to replace an asset. This term is used with the exposure factor, a measure of how much of an asset is at risk, to determine the single loss expectancy.

EXAM TIP Understand the terms SLE, ALE, and ARO and how they are used to calculate a potential loss. You may be given a scenario, asked to calculate the SLE, ALE, or ARO, and presented answer choices that include values that would result from incorrect calculations.

Risk Register

A *risk register* is a list of the risks associated with a system. It also can contain additional information associated with the risk element, such as categories to group like risks, probability of occurrence, impact to the organization, mitigation factors, and other data. There is no standardized form. The Project Management Institute has one format, other sources have different formats. The reference document *ISO Guide 73:2009 Risk Management—Vocabulary* defines a risk register to be a "record of information about identified risks."

Likelihood of Occurrence

The *likelihood of occurrence* is the chance that a particular risk will occur. This measure can be qualitative or quantitative, as discussed a bit later in the chapter. For qualitative measures, the likelihood of occurrence is typically defined on an annual basis so that it can be compared to other annualized measures. If defined quantitatively, it is used to create rank-order outcomes.

Supply Chain Assessment

The analysis of risk in a supply chain has become an important issue in our connected society. Organizations need to consider not just the risk associated with a system, but the risk embedded in the system as a result of its components that the vendor has obtained through its supply chain, which could span the globe. For instance, if a system has critical components that are not replaceable except from a single source, what happens if that source quits making the component? The term *supply chain assessment* describes the process of exploring and identifying these risks.

Impact

The *impact* of an event is a measure of the actual loss when a threat exploits a vulnerability. Federal Information Processing Standards (FIPS) 199 defines three levels of impact using the terms high, moderate, and low. The impact needs to be defined in terms of the context of each organization, as what is high for some firms may be low for much larger firms. The common method is to define the impact levels in terms of important business criteria. Impacts can be in terms of cost (dollars), performance (service level agreement [SLA] or other requirements), schedule (deliverables), or any other important item. Impact can also be categorized in terms of the information security attribute that is relevant to the problem: confidentiality, integrity, and availability.

Quantitative

Quantitative risk assessment is the process of objectively determining the impact of an event that affects a project, program, or business. Quantitative risk assessment usually involves the use of metrics and models to complete the assessment. Whereas qualitative risk assessment relies on judgment and experience, quantitative risk assessment applies historical information and trends to attempt to predict future performance. This type of risk assessment is highly dependent on historical data, and gathering such data can be difficult. Quantitative risk assessment can also rely heavily on models that provide decision-making information in the form of quantitative metrics, which attempt to measure risk levels across a common scale.

Qualitative

Qualitative risk assessment is the process of subjectively determining the impact of an event that affects a project, program, or business. Qualitative risk assessment usually involves the use of expert judgment, experience, or group consensus to complete the assessment. To assess risk qualitatively, you compare the impact of the threat with the probability of occurrence. For example, if a threat has a high impact and a high probability of occurring, the risk exposure is high and probably requires some action to reduce this threat (see darkest box in Figure 22-1). Conversely, if the impact is low with a low probability, the risk exposure is low and no action may be required to reduce this threat (see white box in Figure 22-1). Figure 22-1 shows an example of a binary assessment, where only two outcomes are possible each for impact and probability. Either it will have

Figure 22-1
Binary
assessment

Impact

High Impact/Low Probability	High Impact/High Probability
Low Impact/Low Probability	Low Impact/High Probability

Probability

an impact or it will not (or it will have a low or high impact), and it can occur or it will not (or it will have a high probability of occurring or a low probability of occurring).

In reality, a few threats can usually be identified as presenting high-risk exposure and a few threats present low-risk exposure. The threats that fall somewhere between (light gray boxes in Figure 22-1) will have to be evaluated by judgment and management experience.

If the analysis is more complex, requiring three levels of analysis, such as low-medium-high or red-green-yellow, nine combinations are possible, as shown in Figure 22-2. Again, the darkest boxes probably require action, the white boxes may or may not require action, and the gray boxes require judgment. (Note that for brevity, in Figure 22-3, the first term in each box refers to the magnitude of the impact, and the second term refers to the probability of the threat occurring.)

Other levels of complexity are possible. With five levels of analysis, 25 values of risk exposure are possible. In this case, the possible values of impact and probability could take on these values: very low, low, medium, high, or very high. Also, note that the matrix does not have to be symmetrical. For example, if the probability is assessed with three values (low, medium, high) and the impact has five values (very low, low, medium, high, very high), the analysis would be as shown in Figure 22-3. (Again, note that the first term in each box refers to the impact, and the second term in each box refers to the probability of occurrence.)

So far, the examples have focused on assessing probability versus impact. Qualitative risk assessment can be adapted to a variety of attributes and situations in combination with each other. For example, Figure 22-4 shows the comparison of some specific risks that have been identified during a security assessment. The assessment identified the risk areas listed in the first column (weak intranet security, high number of modems, Internet attack vulnerabilities, and weak incident detection and response mechanisms). The assessment

Figure 22-2
Three levels of
analysis

Impact

High	Low	High	Medium	High	High
Medium	Low	Medium	Medium	Medium	High
Low	Low	Low	Medium	Low	High

Probability

Figure 22-3
A 3-by-5 level
analysis

Impact

Very High	Low	Very High	Medium	Very High	High
High	Low	High	Medium	High	High
Medium	Low	Medium	Medium	Medium	High
Low	Low	Low	Medium	Low	High
Very Low	Low	Very Low	Medium	Very Low	High

Probability

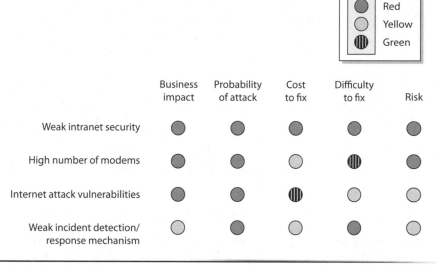

Figure 22-4   Example of a combination assessment

also identified various potential impacts listed across the top (business impact, probability of attack, cost to fix, and difficulty to fix). Each of the impacts has been assessed as low, moderate, or high—depicted using green (G), yellow (Y), and red (R), respectively. Each of the risk areas has been assessed with respect to each of the potential impacts, and an overall risk assessment has been determined in the last column.

Adding Objectivity to a Qualitative Assessment   Making a qualitative assessment more objective can be as simple as assigning numeric values to one of the tables shown in Figures 22-1 through 22-4. For example, the impacts listed in Figure 22-4 can be prioritized from highest to lowest and then weighted, as shown in Table 22-1, with business impact weighted the most and difficulty to fix weighted least.

Next, values can be assigned to reflect how each risk was assessed. Figure 22-4 can thus be made more objective by assigning a value to each color that represents an assessment.

Impact	Explanation	Weight
Business impact	If exploited, would this have a material business impact?	4
Probability of attack	How likely is a potential attacker to try this technique or attack?	3
Cost to fix	How much will it cost in dollars and resources to correct this vulnerability?	2
Difficulty to fix	How hard is this to fix from a technical standpoint?	1

Table 22-1   Adding Weights and Definitions to the Potential Impacts

Table 22-2 Adding Values to Assessments	Assessment	Explanation	Value
	Red	Many critical, unresolved issues	3
	Yellow	Some critical, unresolved issues	2
	Green	Few unresolved issues	1

For example, a red assessment indicates many critical, unresolved issues, and this will be given an assessment value of 3. Green means few issues are unresolved, so it is given a value of 1. Table 22-2 shows values that can be assigned for an assessment using red, yellow, and green.

The last step is to calculate an overall risk value for each risk area (each row in Figure 22-4) by multiplying the weights depicted in Table 22-1 times the assessed values from Table 22-2 and summing the products:

$$Risk = W_1 \times V_1 + W_2 \times V_2 + \ldots W_4 \times V_4$$

The risk calculation and final risk value for each risk area listed in Figure 22-4 have been incorporated into Figure 22-5. The assessed areas can then be ordered from highest to lowest based on the calculated risk value to aid management in focusing on the risk areas with the greatest potential impact.

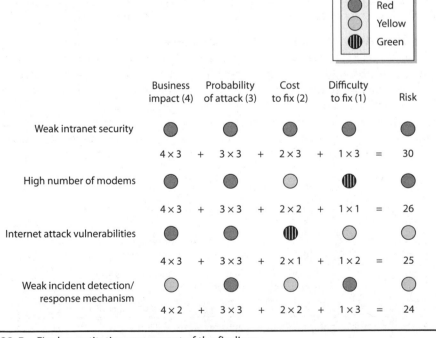

Figure 22-5   Final quantitative assessment of the findings

It is important to understand that key assumptions underlie any model, and different models will produce different results even when given the same input data. Although significant research and development have been invested in improving and refining the various risk analysis models, expert judgment and experience must still be considered an essential part of any risk-assessment process. Models can never replace judgment and experience, but they can significantly enhance the decision-making process.

 EXAM TIP Understand the difference between quantitative and qualitative risk assessments. Quantitative means you can actually count something, whereas qualitative is more subjective, with values such as high, medium, low.

Testing

Understanding what a system's risk exposure is, in actuality, is not a simple task. Using a series of tests, one can determine an estimate of the risk that a system has to the enterprise. Vulnerability tests detail the known vulnerabilities and the degree to which they are exposed. It is important to note that zero day vulnerabilities will not be known and the risk from them still remains unknown. A second form of testing, penetration testing, is used to simulate an adversary to see if the controls in place perform to the desired level.

Penetration Testing Authorization   As covered in detail in Chapter 4, penetration tests are used by organizations that want a real-world test of their security. Unlike actual attacks, penetration tests are conducted with the knowledge of the organization, although some types of penetration tests occur without the knowledge of the employees and departments being tested.

Obtaining *penetration testing authorization* is the first step in penetration testing. The testing team, in advance, obtains permission, in writing with specifics, from the system owner to perform the penetration test. The authorization should explain the full scope of the penetration testing. This penetration testing authorization is used as a communication plan for the test. It should inform the system owner that penetration tests are typically used to verify threats or to test security controls. They do this by bypassing security controls and exploiting vulnerabilities, using a variety of tools and techniques, including the attack methods discussed earlier in this book. Social engineering, malware, and vulnerability exploit tools are all fair game when it comes to penetration testing. Penetration tests actively test security controls by exploiting vulnerabilities and bypassing security controls, and this helps to verify that a risk exists.

Vulnerability Testing Authorization   Vulnerability tests are used to scan for specific vulnerabilities or weaknesses. These weaknesses, if left unguarded, can result in loss. Obtaining *vulnerability testing authorization* from management before commencing the test is the step designed to prevent avoidable misunderstandings, such as triggering an IR response. Just as it is important to obtain authorization for penetration tests, it is important to obtain permission for vulnerability tests of productions machines. This permission is usually a multiperson process and involves explaining the risk of these tests and their purpose to management. The vulnerability tests are then analyzed with respect to how the security controls respond, and management is notified of the adequacy of the defenses in place.

PART V

Risk Response Techniques

Risks are absolutes—they cannot be removed or eliminated. You can take actions to change the effects that a risk poses to a system, but the risk itself doesn't really change, no matter what actions you take to mitigate that risk. A high risk will always be a high risk. However, you can take actions to reduce the impact of that risk if it occurs. A limited number of strategies can be used to manage risk. The risk can be avoided, transferred, mitigated, or accepted.

Avoiding the risk can be accomplished in many ways. Although you can't remove threats from the environment, you can alter the system's exposure to the threats. Not deploying a module that increases risk is one manner of risk avoidance.

A common method of *transferring* risk is to purchase insurance. Insurance allows risk to be transferred to a third party that manages specific types of risk for multiple parties, thus reducing the individual cost. Another common example of risk transfer is the protection against fraud that consumers have on their credit cards. The risk is transferred to another party, so people can use the card in confidence.

Risk can also be *mitigated* through the application of controls that reduce the impact of an attack. Controls can alert operators so that the level of exposure is reduced through process intervention. When an action occurs that is outside the accepted risk profile, a second set of rules can be applied, such as calling the customer for verification before committing a transaction. Controls such as these can act to reduce the risk associated with potential high-risk operations.

When analyzing a specific risk, after weighing the cost to avoid, transfer, or mitigate a risk against the probability of its occurrence and its potential impact, the best response is to *accept* the risk. For example, a manager may choose to allow a programmer to make "emergency" changes to a production system (in violation of good separation of duties) because the system cannot go down during a given period of time. The manager accepts that the risk that the programmer could possibly make unauthorized changes is outweighed by the high-availability requirement of that system. However, there should always be some additional controls, such as a management review or a standardized approval process, to ensure the assumed risk is adequately managed.

Understand that risk cannot be completely eliminated. A risk that remains after implementing controls is termed a *residual risk*. You have to further evaluate residual risks to identify where additional controls are required to reduce risk even more. This reinforces the statement earlier in the chapter that the risk management process is iterative.

 EXAM TIP You can do four things to respond to risk: accept it, transfer it, avoid it, and mitigate it. Understand the differences, as these will all be presented as possible answer choices for a question, and the scenario details will apply to one better than the others.

Change Management

Change management has its roots in system engineering, where it is commonly referred to as configuration management. Most of today's software and hardware change management practices derive from long-standing system engineering configuration management practices. Computer hardware and software development have also evolved to the point that proper management structure and controls must exist to ensure the products operate as planned. It is normal for an enterprise to have a Change Control Board to approve all production changes and ensure the change management procedures are followed before changes are introduced to a system.

Configuration control is the process of controlling changes to items that have been baselined. Configuration control ensures that only approved changes to a baseline are allowed to be implemented. It is easy to understand why a software system, such as a web-based order-entry system, should not be changed without proper testing and control—otherwise, the system might stop functioning at a critical time. Configuration control is a key step that provides valuable insight to managers. If a system is being changed, and configuration control is being observed, managers and others concerned will be better informed. This ensures proper use of assets and avoids unnecessary downtime due to the installation of unapproved changes.

EXAM TIP Change management ensures proper procedures are followed when modifying the IT infrastructure.

Security Controls

Security controls are the mechanisms employed to minimize exposure to risk and mitigate the effects of loss. Using the security attributes of confidentiality, integrity, and availability associated with data, it is incumbent upon the security team to determine the appropriate set of controls to achieve the security objectives.

Controls can be of a variety of types, as described in this section. The different categories of controls do not act as a taxonomy, as there are overlapping descriptions and some controls categories are descendent from third-party policies and procedures.

NOTE NIST provides a catalog of controls in its NIST SP 800-53 series. The current revision, revision 4, lists over 600 controls grouped into 18 functional categories. The 18 functional categories are grouped under three major categories, Management, Technical, and Operational. Although the vast majority of these controls are associated with the electronic security of information, many of them extend into the physical world as well.

Deterrent

A *deterrent control* acts to discourage the attacker by reducing the likelihood of success from the perspective of the attacker. An example would be laws and regulations that increase punishment, increasing risk and costs for the attacker.

Preventive

A *preventative control* is one that prevents specific actions from occurring, such as a man-trap prevents tailgating. Preventative controls act before an event, preventing it from advancing. A firewall is an example of a preventative control, as it can block access to a specific resource.

EXAM TIP The key element in exam objective 5.7 is to compare and contrast various types of controls. How are they alike (compare) and how are they different (contrast)? Understanding the differences can be subtle. For instance, do laws with punishment, if enforced, prevent attacks? Laws may deter attackers, but they do not prevent them from attacking if the deterrent doesn't dissuade them from deciding to attack.

Detective

A *detective control* is one that facilitates the detection of a physical security breach. Detective controls act during an event, alerting operators to specific conditions. Alarms are common examples of detective controls. An IDS is an example of an IT security alarm that detects intrusions.

Corrective

A *corrective control* is used post event, in an effort to minimize the extent of damage. Backups are a prime example of a corrective control, as they can facilitate rapid resumption of operations.

Compensating

A *compensating control* is one that is used to meet a requirement when there is no control available to directly address the threat. Fire suppression systems do not prevent fire damage, but if properly employed, they can mitigate or limit the level of damage from fire.

 EXAM TIP The previous five types of controls tend to be exclusive of each other—they describe the point of interaction of the control with the attacker's tools, techniques, and processes.

Technical

A *technical control* is the use of some form of technology to address a physical security issue. Biometrics are technical controls.

Administrative

An *administrative control* is a policy or procedure used to limit security risk. Instructions to guards act as administrative controls.

Physical

A *physical control* is one that prevents specific physical actions from occurring, such as a mantrap prevents tailgating. Physical controls prevent specific human interaction with a system, and are primarily designed to prevent accidental operation of something. Physical controls act before an event, preventing it from actually occurring. The use of covers over critical buttons is one example, as is a big red "STOP" button, positioned so it is easily reachable. The former stops inadvertent activation, while the latter facilitates easy activation in an emergency. For further information, Chapter 17 has a section devoted to physical security controls.

 EXAM TIP The last three descriptors of controls, technical, administrative, and physical, are separate from the previous descriptors and can be used independently of them. It is possible to have a control that is a technical, physical, and preventative control (for example, a door lock).

 EXAM TIP The types of security controls are commonly tested on the exam—memorization is recommended.

Chapter Review

In this chapter, you first became acquainted with examining risk from a business impact analysis point of view. The chapter examined the analytical methods of RTO/RPO, MTBF, and MTTR including how to calculate these values. It went on to examine the concepts of mission-essential functions, identification of critical systems, single points of failure, and impact. Impact was examined in terms of damage to life, property, safety, finance, and reputation. The chapter continued with topics associated with privacy, specifically privacy impact assessments and privacy threshold assessments and how these items can influence business impacts.

The chapter then moved into risk management concepts, beginning with threat assessments of environmental, manmade, internal, and external threat sources. Moving from threat assessment to risk assessment, the concepts of measuring risk were explored. The methods covered included the analytical calculations associated with SLE, ALE, ARO, and asset value. Additional risk assessment topics included risk registers, likelihood of occurrence, supply chain assessments, impact, and qualitative and quantitative risk assessments. The importance of obtaining authorization before performing testing of systems was addressed, specifically penetration testing and vulnerability testing. The discussion of risk management concepts concluded with risk response techniques and change management.

The chapter wrapped up with an examination of the different classes of security controls, prime targets for exam questions. The categories of security controls were presented, with examples: deterrent, preventive, corrective, compensating, technical, administrative, and physical.

Questions

To help you prepare further for the CompTIA Security+ exam, and to test your level of preparedness, answer the following questions and then check your answers against the correct answers at the end of the chapter.

1. Which of the following is the name often used to describe the process of addressing the questions associated with sources of risk, the impacts and the steps taken to mitigate them in the enterprise?

   A. Risk assessment

   B. Business impact analysis

   C. Threat assessment

   D. Penetration test

2. Which of the following terms is used to describe the target time that is set for a resumption of operations after an incident?

   A. RPO

   B. MTBF

   C. RTO

   D. MTTR

3. Which of the following is a common measure of how long it takes to fix a given failure?

   A. MTTR

   B. RTO

   C. RPO

   D. MTBF

4. Which of the following is a system component whose failure or malfunctioning could result in the failure of the entire system?

   A. Mean time between failures

   B. Single point of failure

   C. Single loss expectancy

   D. Likelihood of occurrence

5. Which type of security control is used post event, in an effort to minimize the extent of damage?

   A. Deterrent

   B. Corrective

   C. Preventative

   D. Detective

6. Which type of security control is used to meet a requirement when the requirement cannot be directly met?

    A. Preventative

    B. Physical

    C. Deterrent

    D. Compensating

7. Which of the following is the process of subjectively determining the impact of an event that affects a project, program, or business?

    A. Likelihood of occurrence

    B. Supply chain assessment

    C. Qualitative risk assessment

    D. Quantitative risk assessment

8. Which of the following describes mission-essential functions? (Choose all that apply.)

    A. Functions that if they do not occur, the mission of the organization would be directly affected.

    B. Functions that if they are not accomplished properly would directly affect the mission of the organization.

    C. Functions that are considered essential to the organization.

    D. The routine business functions.

9. Which security control is a policy or procedure used to limit physical security risk?

    A. Physical

    B. Technical

    C. Administrative

    D. Corrective

10. A mantrap is an example of which security control? (Choose all that apply.)

    A. Physical

    B. Corrective

    C. Administrative

    D. Preventative

11. Which of the following is the best description of *risk*?

    A. The cost associated with a realized risk

    B. The chance of something not working as planned

    C. Damage that is the result of unmitigated risk

    D. The level of concern one places for the well-being of people

12. Which of the following impacts is in many ways the final arbiter of all activities, for it is how we "keep score"?

   A. Reputation

   B. Safety

   C. Finance

   D. Life

13. Which of the following is an analysis of whether PII is collected and maintained by a system?

   A. Privacy threshold assessment

   B. Privacy impact assessment

   C. Risk assessment

   D. Threat assessment

14. Which of the following has its roots in system engineering, where it is commonly referred to as configuration management?

   A. Configuration control

   B. Security control

   C. Administrative control

   D. Change management

15. Which of the following is a representation of the frequency of an event, measured in a standard year?

   A. Annual Loss Expectancy (ALE)

   B. Annualized Rate of Occurrence (ARO)

   C. Single Loss Expectancy (SLE)

   D. Annualized Expectancy of Occurrence (AEO)

Answers

1. **B.** Business impact analysis (BIA) is the name often used to describe a document created by addressing the questions associated with sources of risk and the steps taken to mitigate them in the enterprise. A risk assessment is a method to analyze potential risk based on statistical and mathematical models. A common method is the calculation of the annualized loss expectancy (ALE). A threat assessment is a structured analysis of the threats that confront an enterprise. Penetration tests are used by organizations that want a real-world test of their security.

2. **C.** The term recovery time objective (RTO) is used to describe the target time that is set for a resumption of operations after an incident. Recovery point objective (RPO) is the time period representing the maximum period of

acceptable data loss. Mean time between failures (MTBF) is a common measure of reliability of a system and is an expression of the average time between system failures. Mean time to repair (MTTR) is a common measure of how long it takes to repair a given failure.

3. **A.** Mean time to repair (MTTR) is a common measure of how long it takes to repair a given failure. The term recovery time objective (RTO) is used to describe the target time that is set for a resumption of operations after an incident. Recovery point objective (RPO) is the time period representing the maximum period of acceptable data loss. Mean time between failures (MTBF) is a common measure of reliability of a system and is an expression of the average time between system failures.

4. **B.** A single point of failure is any aspect that, if triggered, could result in the failure of the system. Mean time between failures (MTBF) is a common measure of reliability of a system and is an expression of the average time between system failures. Single loss expectancy (SLE) is the expected loss from the occurrence of a risk on an asset. The likelihood of occurrence is the chance that a particular risk will occur.

5. **B.** Corrective controls are used post event, in an effort to minimize the extent of damage. A deterrent control acts to influence the attacker by reducing the likelihood of success. A preventative control is one that prevents specific actions from occurring. A detective control is one that facilitates the detection of a security breach.

6. **D.** A compensating control is one that is used to meet a requirement when the requirement cannot be directly met. Fire suppression systems do not prevent fire damage, but if properly employed, they can mitigate or limit the level of damage from fire. A preventative control is one that prevents specific actions from occurring. A physical control is one that prevents specific physical actions from occurring, such as a mantrap prevents tailgating. A deterrent control acts to influence the attacker by reducing the likelihood of success.

7. **C.** Qualitative risk assessment is the process of subjectively determining the impact of an event that affects a project, program, or business. The likelihood of occurrence is the chance that a particular risk will occur. A supply-chain assessment considers not just the risk associated with a system, but the risk embedded in a system as a result of its components that the vendor has obtained through its supply chain, which could span the globe. Quantitative risk assessment is the process of objectively determining the impact of an event that affects a project, program, or business.

8. **A, B,** and **C.** Mission-essential functions are those that should they not occur, or be performed improperly, the mission of the organization will be directly affected. This is where you spend the majority of your effort, protecting the functions that are essential. It is important to separate mission-essential functions from other business functions.

PART V

9. **C.** An administrative control is a policy or procedure used to limit security risk. A physical control is one that prevents specific physical actions from occurring. A technical control is the use of some form of technology to address a security issue. Corrective controls are used post event, in an effort to minimize the extent of damage.

10. **A** and **D.** It is possible for a specific security control to fall into more than one category. Because a mantrap is a physical barrier that prevents tailgating, it is both a physical control and a preventative control. Corrective controls are used post event, in an effort to minimize the extent of damage. An administrative control is a policy or procedure used to limit security risk.

11. **B.** Risk is the chance of something not working as planned and causing an adverse impact. Impact is the cost associated with a realized risk.

12. **C.** Finance is in many ways the final arbiter of all activities, for it is how we keep score. The others are important but are not considered the final arbiter.

13. **A.** A privacy threshold assessment is an analysis of whether PII is collected and maintained by a system. A privacy impact assessment (PIA) is a structured approach to determining the gap between desired privacy performance and actual privacy performance. A risk assessment is an analysis of risks based on statistical and mathematical models. A threat assessment is a structured analysis of the threats that confront an enterprise.

14. **D.** Change management has its roots in system engineering, where it is commonly referred to as configuration management. Configuration control is the process of controlling changes to items that have been baselined. Configuration control ensures that only approved changes to a baseline are allowed to be implemented. A security control is a mechanisms employed to minimize exposure to risk and mitigate the effects of loss. An administrative control is a policy or procedure used to limit security risk.

15. **B.** The annualized rate of occurrence (ARO) is a representation of the frequency of the event, measured in a standard year. The annual loss expectancy (ALE) is calculated by multiplying the single loss expectancy (SLE) by the likelihood or number of times the event is expected to occur in a year. The SLE is calculated by multiplying the asset value times the exposure factor. Annualized expectancy of occurrence (AEO) is not a term used in the cybersecurity industry.

Incident Response, Disaster Recovery, and Continuity of Operations

In this chapter, you will

- Understand the incident response process
- Learn the incident response procedures
- Explore disaster recovery preparation
- Examine the process of continuity of operations

Normal operations in an IT enterprise include preparing for when things go wrong. One aspect of things going wrong is when things are not operating correctly, for reasons unknown, and the incident response process is used to determine the what, why, and where of the problem. A bigger problem is a disaster, where disaster recovery is the pressing issue, as well as continuity of operations. Each of these situations is one that requires preparation and readiness for the enterprise to navigate all of the complexities of these types of operations. This chapter looks at the concepts and procedures behind these specialized operations.

Certification Objective   This chapter covers CompTIA Security+ exam objectives 5.4, Given a scenario, follow incident response procedures, and 5.6, Explain disaster recovery and continuity of operation concepts.

Objective 5.6 is a good candidate for performance-based questions, which means you should expect questions in which you must apply your knowledge of the topic to a scenario. The best answer to a question will depend upon specific details in the scenario preceding the question, not just the question. The questions may also involve tasks other than just picking the best answer from a list. Instead, you may be instructed to order things on a diagram, put options in rank order, match two columns of items, or perform a similar task.

Incident Response Plan

An *incident response plan* describes the steps an organization performs in response to any situation determined to be abnormal in the operation of a computer system. The causes of incidents are many, from the environment (storms), to errors on the part of users, to unauthorized actions by unauthorized users, to name a few. Although the causes may be many, the results can be classified into classes. A low-impact incident may not result in any significant risk exposure, so no action other than repairing the broken system is needed. A moderate-risk incident will require greater scrutiny and response efforts, and a high-level risk exposure incident will require the greatest scrutiny and response efforts. To manage incidents when they occur, an IT team needs to create an incident response plan that includes a table of guidelines to assist in determining the level of response.

Two major elements play a role in determining the level of response. Information criticality is the primary determinant, and this comes from the data classification and the quantity of data involved. The loss of one administrator password is less serious than the loss of all of them and thus requires a lower level of response. The second factor is how the incident potentially affects the organization's operations. A series of breaches, whether minor or not, indicates a pattern that can have public relations and regulatory issues.

The incident response plan will cover a wide range of items, which are covered in the next several sections. Although an incident response plan may cover more items in a given enterprise, the Security+ objectives examine incident types and category definitions, roles and responsibilities of personnel, reporting and escalation requirements, cyber-incident response teams, and exercising of the plan.

Documented Incident Types/Category Definitions

To assist in the planning of incident responses and to group the myriad of possible incidents into a manageable set of categories, one step of the incident response planning process is the documentation of incident types/category definitions. *Documented incident types/category definitions* provide planners and responders with a set number of pre-planned scripts that can be applied quickly, minimizing repetitive approvals and process flows. Examples of how categories are defined include items such as interruption of service, malicious communication, data exfiltration, malware delivery, phishing attack, and so on, although this list will be customized to meet the IT needs of each organization.

As this is customized to meet the IT needs of the organization, their onus is on the security group to develop the details for the different types of incident response categories and the materials and procedures to be used in each type. Doing this work before an incident is easy, as there is no time crunch of the actual incident pushing you at every step. The amount of work scales with the size of the IT organization and the services they are providing to the enterprise, but in all cases it is a doable task.

Roles and Responsibilities

A critical step in the incident response planning process is to define the *roles and responsibilities* of the incident response team members. These roles and responsibilities may vary slightly based on the identified categories of incident, but defining them before an incident occurs empowers the team to perform the necessary tasks during the time-sensitive aspects of an incident. Permissions to cut connections, change servers, and start/stop services are common examples of actions that are best defined in advance to prevent time-consuming approvals during an actual incident.

There are several specific roles that are unique to all IR teams, the team leader, the team communicator, and an appropriate bevvy of SMEs. The team leader manages the overall IR process, so they need to be a member of management so they can navigate the corporate chain of command. The team communicator is the spokesperson for the team to all other groups, inside and outside the company. IR team members are typically SMEs, and their time is valuable and should be spent on task. The team communicator shields these members from the time-consuming press interview portion as much as possible.

Reporting Requirements/Escalation

Planning the desired *reporting requirements* including *escalation* steps is an important part of the operational plan for an incident. Who will talk for the incident and to whom, and what will they say? How does the information flow? Who needs to be involved? When does the issue escalate to higher levels of management? These are all questions best handled in the calm of a pre-incident planning meeting where the procedures are crafted rather than on the fly as an incident is occurring.

Reporting requirements can refer to industry, regulatory, and statutory requirements in addition to internal communications. Understanding the reporting requirements to external entities is part of the responsibility of the communications lead on the team. Having the correct information in the hands of the correct people at the correct time is an essential part of reporting, and a prime responsibility of the communications' lead on the team.

Cyber-Incident Response Teams

The *cyber-incident response team* is composed of the personnel who are designated to respond to an incident. The incident response plan should identify the membership and backup members, prior to an incident occurring. Once an incidence response begins, trying to find personnel to do tasks only slows down the function, and in many cases would make it unmanageable. Whether a dedicated team or a group of situational volunteers, the planning aspect of incident response needs to address the topic of who is on the team and what are their duties.

Management needs to appoint the team members and ensure that they have time to be prepared for service. The team leader is typically a member of management who fully understands both the enterprise IT environment and IR process, for their job is to lead the team with respect to the process. Subject matter experts on the various systems that are involved provide the actual working portion of the team, often in concert with operational IT personnel for each system. The team is responsible for all phases of the incident response process, which is covered in the next section of this chapter.

Exercise

One really doesn't know how well a plan is crafted until it is tested. *Exercises* come in many forms and functions, and doing a tabletop exercise where planning and preparation steps are tested is an important final step in the planning process. Having a process and a team is not enough unless the team has practiced the process on the systems of the enterprise.

EXAM TIP If given a scenario, the details of the scenario will point to the appropriate part of the planning process. Pay attention to the details for the best answer.

Incident Response Process

The *incident response process* is the set of actions security personnel perform in response to a wide range of triggering events. These actions are wide and varied, as they have to deal with a wide range of causes and consequences. Incident response activities at times are closely related to other IT activities involving IT operations. Incident response activities can be similar to disaster recovery and business continuity operations. Incident response activities are not performed in a vacuum, but rather are intimately connected to many operational procedures, and this connection is key to overall system efficiency.

EXAM TIP Know the six phases of the incident response process and the order in which they are performed: preparation, identification, containment, eradication, recovery, and lessons learned.

Preparation

Preparation is the phase of incident response that occurs before a specific incident. Preparation includes all the tasks needed to be organized and ready to respond to an incident. Through the use of a structured framework coupled with properly prepared processes, incident response becomes a manageable task. Without proper preparation, this task can quickly become impossible or intractably expensive. Successful handling of an incident is a direct result of proper preparation. Items done in preparation are things like ensuring the correct data events are being logged, that reporting of potential incidents is happening, that people are trained with respect to IR process and their personal responsibilities.

Identification

Identification is the process where a team member suspects that a problem is bigger than an isolated incident and notifies the incident response team for further investigation. An incident is defined as a situation that departs from normal, routine operations. Whether an incident is important or not is the first point of decision as part of an incident response process. A single failed login is technically an incident, but if it is followed by a correct login, then it is not of any consequence. In fact, this could even be considered as normal.

But 10,000 failed attempts on a system, or failures across a large number of accounts, are distinctly different and may be worthy of further investigation. The act of identification is coming to a decision that the information related to the incident is worthy of further investigation by the IR team.

Identification can be done by many on the IT team, from the help desk, to admins, to database personnel, in essence anyone who finds something out of the ordinary that may be a real problem. Some training is required to prevent false alarms, a single failed file access for instance, or a server that resets unexpectedly, these things happen and probably are not a cause for IR alarm. But when the single incidents become multiple incidents, then an investigation may be warranted and the conditions should be identified as a possible IR issue.

A key first step is in the processing of information and the determination of whether or not to invoke incident response processes. Incident information can come from a wide range of sources, including logs, employees, help desk calls, system monitoring, security devices, and more. The challenge is to detect that something other than simple common errors that are routine is occurring. When evidence accumulates, or in some cases specific items such as security device logs indicate a potential incident, the next step is to escalate the situation to the incident response team.

The IR team examines the information, gathering additional information if necessary to determine the cause of the incident. If it meets the defined thresholds of the organization, an incident will be logged and fully investigated. Whatever the root cause, if it is truly more than a random error, the next step is containment.

Containment

Once the IR team has determined that an incident has in fact occurred and requires a response, their first step is to contain the incident and prevent its spread. For example, if the incident involves a virus or worm that is attacking database servers, then protecting uninfected servers is paramount. *Containment* is the set of actions taken to constrain the incident to the minimal number of machines. This preserves as much of production as possible and ultimately makes handling the incident easier. This can be complex, for in many cases, containing the problem requires fully understanding the problem, its root cause, and the vulnerabilities involved.

Eradication

Once the IR team has contained a problem to a set footprint, the next step is to eradicate the problem. *Eradication* involves removing the problem, and in today's complex system environment, this may mean rebuilding a clean machine. A key part of operational eradication is the prevention of reinfection. Presumably, the system that existed before the problem occurred would be prone to a repeat infection, and thus this needs to be specifically guarded against. One of the strongest value propositions for virtual machines is the ability to rebuild quickly, making the eradication step relatively easy.

Recovery

After the issue has been eradicated, the recovery process begins. At this point, the investigation is complete and documented. *Recovery* is the process of returning the asset into the business function and restoration of normal business operations. Eradication, the previous step, removed the problem, but in most cases the eradicated system will be isolated. The recovery process includes the steps necessary to return the systems and applications to operational status. After recovery, the team moves to document the lessons learned from the incident.

Lessons Learned

A post-mortem session should collect *lessons learned* and assign action items to correct weaknesses and to suggest ways to improve. To paraphrase a famous quote, those who fail to learn from history are destined to repeat it. The lessons learned phase serves two distinct purposes. First is to document what went wrong and allowed the incident to occur in the first place. Failure to correct this means a sure repeat. Second is to examine the incident response process itself. Where did it go well, where were the problems, and how can it be improved? Continuous improvement of the actual incident response process is an important task.

 EXAM TIP Two main elements have been covered and they have overlap. Incident response planning and the actual incident response process are multistep items that can easily generate questions. Be sure to pay attention to what aspect, planning or process, the question belongs to, and then what aspect of that topic. Step one, determine if the question is concerning the planning or IR process. Then pick the correct phase.

Disaster Recovery

Many types of disasters, whether natural or caused by people, can stop your organization's operations for some length of time. Such disasters are unlike the threats to your computer systems and networks, because the events that cause the disruption are not specifically aimed at your organization. This is not to say that those other threats won't disrupt operations—they can, and industrial espionage, hacking, disgruntled employees, and insider threats all must be considered. The purpose of this section is to point out additional events that you may not have previously considered.

The amount of time your organization's operations are disrupted depends in part on how prepared it is for a disaster and what plans are in place to mitigate the effects of a disaster. *Disaster recovery* is the process that the organization uses to recover from events that disrupt normal operations. Any of the events in Table 23-1 could cause a disruption in operations.

Fortunately, these types of events do not happen very often. It is more likely that business operations will be interrupted due to employee error (such as accidental corruption of a database, or unplugging a system to plug in a vacuum cleaner—an event that has

Table 23-1 Common Causes of Disasters	Fire	Flood	Tornado	Hurricane
	Electrical storm	Earthquake	Political unrest/riot	Blizzard
	Gas leak/explosion	Chemical spill	Terrorism	War

occurred at more than one organization). A good disaster recovery plan will prepare your organization for any type of organizational disruption.

When disaster occurs, it is typically too late to begin the planning of a response. The following sections, "Recovery Sites," "Hot Sites," "Warm Sites," and "Cold Sites," provides details needed to make appropriate preparations.

Recovery Sites

Related to the location of backup storage is where the restoration services will be located. If the organization has suffered physical damage to its facility, having offsite data storage is only part of the solution. This data will need to be processed somewhere, which means that computing facilities similar to those used in normal operations are required. These sites are referred to as *recovery sites*. The recovery problem can be approached in a number of ways, including hot sites, warm sites, and cold sites.

Hot Sites

A *hot site* is a fully configured environment, similar to the normal operating environment that can be operational immediately or within a few hours depending on its configuration and the needs of the organization.

Warm Sites

A *warm site* is partially configured, usually having the peripherals and software but perhaps not the more expensive main processing computer. It is designed to be operational within a few days.

Cold Sites

A *cold site* will have the basic environmental controls necessary to operate but few of the computing components necessary for processing. Getting a cold site operational may take weeks.

 EXAM TIP Alternate sites are highly tested on the CompTIA Security+ exam. It is also important to know whether the data is available or not at each location. For example, a hot site has duplicate data or a near-ready backup of the original site. A cold site has no current or backup copies of the original site data. A warm site has backups, but they are typically several days or weeks old.

Order of Restoration

Part of the planning for a disaster is to decide the *order of restoration*, which systems should be restored first, second, and ultimately last. There are a couple of distinct factors to consider. First are dependencies. Any system that is dependent upon another for proper operation might as well wait in line to be restored until the prerequisite services are up and running. The second factor is criticality to the enterprise. The most critical service should be brought back up first.

Backup Concepts

A key element in business continuity/disaster recovery (BC/DR) plans is the availability of *backups*. This is true not only because of the possibility of a disaster but also because hardware and storage media will periodically fail, resulting in loss or corruption of critical data. An organization might also find backups critical when security measures have failed and an individual has gained access to important information that may have become corrupted or at the very least can't be trusted. Data backup is thus a critical element in these plans, as well as in normal operation. There are several factors to consider in an organization's data backup strategy:

- How frequently should backups be conducted?
- How extensive do the backups need to be?
- What is the process for conducting backups?
- Who is responsible for ensuring backups are created?
- Where will the backups be stored?
- How long will backups be kept?
- How many copies will be maintained?

Keep in mind that the purpose of a backup is to provide valid, uncorrupted data in the event of corruption or loss of the original file or the media where the data was stored. Depending on the type of organization, legal requirements for maintaining backups can also affect how it is accomplished.

There are four main forms of backups: full, incremental, differential, and snapshots. Each of these has advantages and disadvantages in terms of time to back up and restore as well as complexity. These are described in the coming sections.

Understanding the purpose of the archive bit is important when you read about the backup types. The archive bit is used to indicate whether a file has (1) or has not (0) changed since the last backup. The bit is set (changed to a 1) if the file is modified, or in some cases, if the file is copied, the new copy of the file has its archive bit set. The bit is reset (changed to a 0) when the file is backed up. The archive bit can be used to determine which files need to be backed up when using methods such as the differential backup method.

EXAM TIP When learning the following backup types, be sure to pay attention to details as to how many backups are needed to restore. A typical exam question "With this type of backup (differential or incremental) and a seven-day backup scheme, how many backup tapes are needed for a restore?" is not a simple memorization, for you need the details from the scenario to answer. Also know the "order of restoration" of the backups.

Differential

In a *differential backup*, only the files that have changed since the last full backup was completed are backed up. This also implies that periodically a full backup needs to be accomplished. The frequency of the full backup versus the interim differential backups depends on your organization and needs to be part of your defined strategy. Restoration from a differential backup requires two steps: the last full backup first needs to be loaded, and then the last differential backup performed can be applied to update the files that have been changed since the full backup was conducted. Again, this is not a difficult process, but it does take some time. The amount of time to accomplish the periodic differential backup, however, is much less than that for a full backup, and this is one of the advantages of this method. Obviously, if a lot of time has passed between differential backups, or if most files in your environment change frequently, then the differential backup does not differ much from a full backup. It should also be obvious that to accomplish the differential backup, the system has to have a method to determine which files have been changed since some given point in time. The archive bit is not cleared in a differential backup since the key for a differential is to back up all files that have changed since the last full backup.

Incremental

The *incremental backup* is a variation on a differential backup, with the difference being that instead of copying all files that have changed since the last full backup, the incremental backup backs up only files that have changed since the last full *or* incremental backup occurred, thus requiring fewer files to be backed up. With incremental backups, even less information will be stored in each backup. Just as in the case of the differential backup, the incremental backup relies on the occasional full backup being accomplished. After that, you back up only files that have changed since the last backup of any sort was conducted. To restore a system using this type of backup method requires quite a bit more work. You first need to go back to the last full backup and reload the system with this data. Then you have to update the system with every incremental backup that has occurred since the full backup. The advantage of this type of backup is that it requires less storage and time to accomplish. The disadvantage is that the restoration process is more involved. Assuming that you don't frequently have to conduct a complete restoration of your system, however, the incremental backup is a valid technique. An incremental backup will clear the archive bit.

PART V

Snapshots

A *snapshot is* a copy of a virtual machines at a specific point in time. A snapshot is a created by copying the files that store the virtual machine. One of the advantages of a virtual machine over a physical machine is the ease with which the virtual machine can be backed up and restored—the ability to revert to an earlier snapshot is as easy as clicking a button and waiting for the machine to be restored via a change of the files.

Full

The easiest type of backup to understand is the full backup. In a *full backup*, all files and software are copied onto the storage media. Restoration from a full backup is similarly straightforward—you must copy all the files back onto the system. This process can take a considerable amount of time. Consider the size of even the average home PC today, for which storage is measured in tens and hundreds of gigabytes. Copying this amount of data takes time. In a full backup, the archive bit is cleared.

 EXAM TIP   The amount of data that will be backed up, and the time it takes to accomplish this, has a direct bearing on the type of backup that should be performed. The table outlines the three basic types of backups that can be conducted, the amount of space required for each, and the ease of restoration using each strategy.

	Full	Differential	Incremental
Amount of Space	Large	Medium	Medium
Restoration	Simple	Simple	Involved

Geographic Considerations

An important element to factor into the cost of the backup strategy is the expense of storing the backups. A simple strategy might be to store all your backups together for quick and easy recovery actions. This is not, however, a good idea. Suppose the catastrophic event that necessitated the restoration of backed-up data was a fire that destroyed the computer system the data was processed on. In this case, any backups that were stored in the same facility might also be lost in the same fire.

The solution is to keep copies of backups in separate locations. The most recent copy can be stored locally, as it is the most likely to be needed, while other copies can be kept at other locations. Depending on the level of security your organization desires, the storage facility itself could be reinforced against possible threats in your area (such as tornados or floods). A more recent advance is online backup services. A number of third-party companies offer high-speed connections for storing data in a separate facility. Transmitting the backup data via network connections alleviates some other issues with physical movement of more traditional storage media, such as the care during transportation (tapes do not fare well in direct sunlight, for example) or the time that it takes to transport the tapes.

Off-Site Backups

Off-site backups are just that, backups that are stored in a separate location from the system being backed up. This can be important in the realm of problems that can affect larger areas than a single room. A building fire, a hurricane, a tornado … these are all disasters that occur frequently and typically affect a larger area than a single room or building. Having backups off-site alleviates the risk of losing the backup to the same problem. In today's high-speed network world with cloud services, storing backups in the cloud is an option that can resolve many of the risk issues associated with backup availability.

Distance

The *distance* associated with an off-site backup is a logistics problem. If you need to restore a system and the backup is stored hours away by car, that increases the recovery time. The delay resulting from physical movement of backup tapes has been alleviated in many systems through networks that move the data at the speed of the network. Distance is also critical when examining the reach of a disaster. It is important that the off-site location is far enough away that it is not affected by the same incident. This includes the physical location of a cloud storage provider's servers. If your business is in Puerto Rico and so is your cloud provider's servers, for example, Hurricane Maria likely made your data unavailable for a long time.

Location Selection

Picking a storage location for backups has several key elements. First is physical safety of the backup media. Because of the importance to maintain a proper environmental condition safe from outside harm, this can limit locations. HVAC can be a consideration, as well as issues such as potential flooding and theft. Protecting the backup media is important as damage to it may not be discovered until the media is needed and then the loss becomes potentially catastrophic. Ability to move the backups in and out of storage is also a concern. Again, the cloud and networks come to the rescue. With today's high-speed networks, reasonably priced storage, and the ability to store backups in a redundant array across multiple sites, all while protecting the information via encryption, cloud storage is the ideal solution.

Legal Implications

With regard to location selection, if you are considering cloud storage for your backups, you must take into consideration the *legal implications* of where the data would actually be stored. Different jurisdictions have different laws, rules, and regulations concerning core tools such as encryption. Understanding how these affect data backup storage plans is critical to prevent downstream problems. Some countries require storage of data concerning their citizens to be done within their borders, under their legal jurisdiction. Other countries may have different government regulations concerning privacy that would impact the security of the data. In the end, without proper contracting and review, one may not have any idea where their data is actually stored, for what might be a cloud in Atlanta this week, could be Albania next week.

Data Sovereignty

Data sovereignty is a relatively new type of legislation several countries have enacted recently that mandates data stored within their borders is subject to their laws, and in some cases that data originating within their borders must be stored there. In today's multinational economy, with the Internet's lack of borders, this has become a problem. Several high-tech firms have changed their business strategies and offerings in order to comply with data sovereignty rules and regulations. For example, LinkedIn, a business social network site, recently was told by Russian authorities that it needed to store all of its data on Russian citizens on servers in Russia. LinkedIn took the business decision that the cost was not worth the benefit and has since abandoned the Russian market.

 EXAM TIP Using the information in the given scenario, you should be able to differentiate which geographic consideration is most important. This can change based on how the scenario is worded, so answer per the given criteria.

Continuity of Operation Planning

Ensuring continuity of operations is a business imperative, as it has been shown that businesses that cannot quickly recover from a disruption have a real chance of never recovering and going out of business. The overall goal of *continuity of operation planning* is to determine which subset of normal operations needs to be continued during periods of disruption. Continuity of operations planning involves developing a comprehensive plan to enact during a situation where normal operations are interrupted. This includes identifying critical assets (including key personnel), critical systems, and interdependencies, and ensuring their availability during a disruption.

Developing a continuity of operations plan is a joint effort between the business and the IT team. The business understands which functions are critical for continuity of operations, and which functions can be suspended. The IT team understands how this translates into equipment, data and services and can establish the correct IT functions. Senior management will have to make the major decisions as to the risk balance versus cost versus criticality when examining hot, warm, or cold site strategies.

Exercises/Tabletop

Once a continuity of operations plan is in place, a *tabletop exercise* should be performed to walk through all of the steps and ensure all elements are covered and that the plan does not forget a key dataset or person. This tabletop exercise is a critical final step, for it is this step that validates the planning covered the needed elements. The steps in the exercise should be performed by the principal leaders of the business and IT functions to ensure that all steps are correct. This will take time from senior members, but given the criticality of this business process, as this is being done for operations determined to be critical to the business, this hardly seems like overkill.

This exercise aspect is not a onetime thing, it should be repeated after major changes to systems that impact the continuity of operations plan or other major change such as personnel. As such, major corporations regularly exercise these types of systems on a calendar-based schedule, rotating through day and night shifts, primary and backup people and different systems.

After-Action Reports

Just as identifying and documenting lessons learned is a key element of the incident response process, *after-action reports* should be prepared after invoking the continuity of operations plan. Similar to lessons learned, after-action reports serve two functions. First, they document the level of operations upon transfer to the backup system. Is all of the capability necessary to continue operations up and running? The second question set addresses how the actual change from normal operations to those supported by continuity systems occurred, including documenting what went right and what went wrong?

Failover

Failover is the process for moving from a normal operational capability to the continuity-of-operations version of the business. The required speed and flexibility of the failover depends on the business type, from seamless for most financial sites, to a slightly delayed process where A is turned off and someone goes and turns B on with some period of no service between. Simple transparent failovers can be achieved through architecture and technology choices, but they must be designed into the system. Simpler, slightly delayed failovers cost less but result in less continuity for those connected to the system.

Failover can be a technology driven thing where one system fails and a redundant system takes its place without notice by the rest of the process. Failover can also be an interruption to service, switch to business continuity of operations mode type event that involves technology, people and shifting business processes. In both extremes, and all cases in between, the term failover refers to the shift from primary or original processing to a redundant or secondary form.

Separate from failover, which occurs whenever a problem occurs, is the switch back to the original system. Once a system is fixed, resolving whatever caused the outage, there is a need to move back to the original production system. This "failback" mechanism, by definition, is harder to perform, as primary keys and indices are not easily transferred back. The return to operations is a more complicated process, but the good news is that it can be performed at a time of the organization's choosing, unlike the problem that initiated the initial shift of operations to continuity procedures.

Alternate Processing Sites

One of the key aspects of planning a solid, cost-effective continuity of operations plan is to consider *alternate processing sites*. In the worst case, the action that triggered the shift to the continuity system could also have rendered the physical location of the original business system unusable. Another consideration is the scale and volume of transactions to be processed while in continuity mode of operations. Typically, the volume is smaller, meaning that smaller sites can handle the continuity operations. It is also important to consider the operators, as continuity systems will require people to operate specific aspects of their function and location of the sites where they are physically accessible by the correct personnel is important. If you choose an alternate processing site that is 500 miles away in another major city and you do not have staff or personnel there, you need to have a plan to temporarily move the required personnel, including temporary lodging, etc. In a company with multiple sites, it is not uncommon to use a different geographic office to cover the one that is lost, using local people to run the business continuity processes.

Alternate Business Practices

Because continuity of operations involves maintaining only key systems, the business practices that are appropriate for continuity of operations will most likely be different than those used in normal operations. This leads to *alternate business practices*, an element of continuity of operation that must be planned and tested. These alternate business practices need to meet the objectives of the continuity of operations objectives. There are many operations that are performed in business that may be suspended during alternative operations. For instance, assuming you use an internal clocking system to record employee time, one where they log into an application when they start and stop working. This operation may not be deemed important enough to continue during alternative processing, so an alternative means of logging employee time and paying them is needed.

 EXAM TIP Continuity of operation planning is an important concept with several parts, all of which are easily tested. Do not confuse incident response steps, backups, and continuity of operations. They have items in common, so watch for specific details in a question scenario to select the best answer.

Chapter Review

In this chapter, you became acquainted with incident response procedures as well as concepts related to disaster recovery and continuity of operations. The chapter opened with incident response planning, including documented incident types/categories, defining the roles and responsibilities or responders, the reporting requirements and escalation plans, the composition of the cyber-incident response team, and the necessity of exercising the plans. The chapter then described the six phases of the incident response process: preparation, identification, containment, eradication, recovery, and lessons learned.

The chapter then moved to disaster recovery concepts, beginning with recovery sites, which include hot, warm, and cold sites. The concept of order of restoration was presented next, explaining the importance of identifying the order in which systems should be restored. Backup concepts included the various types of backups: differential backups, incremental backups, snapshots, and full backups. Geographic considerations included off-site backups, distance, location selection, legal implications, and data sovereignty.

The chapter concluded with an examination of continuity of operations planning, including exercises/tabletop, after-action reports, failover, alternate processing sites, and alternate business practices.

Questions

To help you prepare further for the CompTIA Security+ exam, and to test your level of preparedness, answer the following questions and then check your answers against the correct answers at the end of the chapter.

1. What is the term used to describe the steps an organization performs after any situation determined to be abnormal in the operation of a computer system?

   A. Computer/network penetration incident plan

   B. Incident response plan

   C. Backup restoration and reconfiguration

   D. Cyber event response

2. Two major elements play a role in determining the level of response to an incident. Information criticality is the primary determinant. What is the other?

   A. Information sensitivity or the classification of the data

   B. The value of any data lost in the incident

   C. How the incident potentially affects the organization's operations

   D. Whether the organization wishes to pursue a legal settlement against the attacker(s)

3. The designated group of personnel who will respond to an incident is called which of the following?

   A. Incident response red team

   B. Incident action group

   C. Cyber-emergency response group

   D. Cyber-incident response team

4. Which phase of the incident response process occurs before an actual incident?

   A. Preparation

   B. Identification

   C. Containment

   D. Prevention

5. Which phase of the incident response process involves removing the problem?

   A. Identification

   B. Eradication

   C. Recovery

   D. Mitigation

6. In which phase of the incident response process are actions taken to constrain the incident to the minimal number of machines?

   A. Eradication

   B. Identification

   C. Containment

   D. Recovery

7. Which of the following is a fully configured environment similar to the normal operating environment that can be operational immediately or within a few hours depending on its configuration and the needs of the organization?

   A. Cold site

   B. Warm site

   C. Hot site

   D. Recovery site

8. Which of the following is a partially configured location, usually having the peripherals and software but perhaps not a more expensive main processing computer?

   A. Cold site

   B. Warm site

   C. Hot site

   D. Recovery site

9. Which of the following are considerations for an organization's data backup strategy? (Choose all that apply.)

   A. How frequently backups should be conducted

   B. How extensive backups need to be

   C. Where the backups will be stored

   D. How long the backups will be kept

10. Which backup strategy includes only the files and software that have changed since the last full backup?

    A. Incremental

    B. Full

    C. Snapshot

    D. Differential

11. Which backup strategy focuses on copies of virtual machines?

    A. Incremental

    B. Full

    C. Snapshot

    D. Differential

12. When discussing location for storage of backups, which of the following is true? (Choose all that apply.)

   A. The most recent copy should be stored off-site, as it is the one that is most current and is thus the most valuable one.

   B. Off-site storage is generally not necessary except in cases where the possibility of a break-in at the main facility is high.

   C. Off-site storage is a good idea so that you don't lose your backup to the same event that caused you to lose your operational data and thus need the backup.

   D. The most recent copy can be stored locally, as it is the most likely to be needed, while other copies can be kept at other locations.

13. What is the term used to describe the requirement where some countries have enacted laws stating that certain types of data must be stored within their boundaries?

   A. Data sovereignty

   B. International intellectual property

   C. International privacy rights

   D. National data protection rights

14. What is the term for the set of steps needed to develop a comprehensive plan to enact during a situation where normal operations are interrupted?

   A. Disaster recovery

   B. Continuity of operations planning

   C. Incident response planning

   D. Restoration of business functions planning

15. What is the name of the process for moving from a normal operational capability to the continuity-of-operations version of the business?

   A. Disaster recovery

   B. Alternate business practices

   C. Failover

   D. Continuity of business functions

Answers

1. **B.** *Incident response plan* is the term used to describe the steps an organization performs in response to any situation determined to be abnormal in the operation of a computer system.

2. **C.** The second factor involves a business decision on how this incident plays into current business operations. A series of breaches, whether minor or not, indicates a pattern that can have public relations and regulatory issues.

3. **D.** The designated group of personnel who will respond to an incident is known as the cyber-incident response team.

4. **A.** Preparation is the phase of incident response that occurs before a specific incident. Preparation includes all the tasks needed to be organized and ready to respond to an incident. The act of identification is coming to a decision that the information related to the incident is worthy of further investigation by the IR team. Containment is the set of actions taken to constrain the incident to the minimal number of machines. Prevention is not a phase of the incident response process.

5. **B.** Eradication involves removing the problem, and in today's complex system environment, this may mean rebuilding a clean machine. The act of identification is coming to a decision that the information related to the incident is worthy of further investigation by the IR team. The recovery process includes the steps necessary to return the systems and applications to operational status. Mitigation is not a phase in the incident response process.

6. **C.** Containment is the set of actions taken to constrain the incident to the minimal number of machines. Eradication involves removing the problem, and in today's complex system environment, this may mean rebuilding a clean machine. The act of identification is coming to a decision that the information related to the incident is worthy of further investigation by the IR team. The recovery process includes the steps necessary to return the systems and applications to operational status.

7. **C.** A hot site is a fully configured environment similar to the normal operating environment that can be operational immediately or within a few hours depending on its configuration and the needs of the organization. A cold site will have the basic environmental controls necessary to operate but few of the computing components necessary for processing. A warm site is partially configured, usually having the peripherals and software but perhaps not the more expensive main processing computer. A recovery site is any location where restoration of services would take place, whether cold, warm, or hot.

8. **B.** A warm site is partially configured, usually having the peripherals and software but perhaps not the more expensive main processing computer. A cold site will have the basic environmental controls necessary to operate but few of the computing components necessary for processing. A hot site is a fully configured environment similar to the normal operating environment that can be operational immediately or within a few hours depending on its configuration and the needs of the organization. A recovery site is any location where restoration of services would take place, whether cold, warm, or hot.

9. **A, B, C,** and **D.** All of these are considerations for an organization's data backup strategy.

10. **D.** In a differential backup, only the files and software that have changed since the last full backup was completed are backed up. The incremental backup is a variation on a differential backup, with the difference being that instead of copying all files that have changed since the last full backup, the incremental backup backs up only files that have changed since the last full *or* incremental backup occurred, thus requiring fewer files to be backed up. In a full backup, all files and software are copied onto the storage media. Snapshots refer to copies of virtual machines.

11. **C.** Snapshots refer to copies of virtual machines. The incremental backup is a variation on a differential backup, with the difference being that instead of copying all files that have changed since the last full backup, the incremental backup backs up only files that have changed since the last full *or* incremental backup occurred, thus requiring fewer files to be backed up. In a full backup, all files and software are copied onto the storage media. In a differential backup, only the files and software that have changed since the last full backup was completed are backed up.

12. **C** and **D.** Off-site storage is a good idea so that you don't lose your backup to the same event that caused you to lose your operational data and thus need the backup. Additionally, the most recent copy can be stored locally, as it is the most likely to be needed, while other copies can be kept at other locations.

13. **A.** Data sovereignty is a relatively new phenomena, but in the past couple of years several countries have enacted laws stating the certain types of data must be stored within their boundaries. The other terms do not describe any actual situation.

14. **B.** Continuity of operations planning is the set of steps needed to develop a comprehensive plan to enact during a situation where normal operations are interrupted. Disaster recovery is the process that an organization uses to recover from events that disrupt normal operations. An incident response plan describes the steps an organization performs in response to any situation determined to be abnormal in the operation of a computer system. Restoration of business functions planning is not a standard term used in recovery planning.

15. **C.** Failover is the process for moving from a normal operational capability to the continuity-of-operations version of the business. Disaster recovery is the process that an organization uses to recover from events that disrupt normal operations. Alternate business practices are developed in recognition that processes may need to be different in a continuity of operations situation since the focus is only on maintaining key systems. Continuity of business functions is not a term used in industry.

PART V

CHAPTER 24

Digital Forensics

In this chapter, you will
- Study basic concepts of forensics
- Understand the legal basis behind forensic processes
- Understand the steps of digital forensics processes

Computer forensics is certainly a popular buzzword in computer security. The term *forensics* relates to the application of scientific knowledge to legal problems. Specifically, computer forensics involves the preservation, identification, documentation, and interpretation of computer data. In many cases, digital forensics is the technical side of developing proof as to what happened or didn't happen as part of an incident response effort. Digital forensics specifically uses scientific principles to provide assurance in explaining what digital evidence tells you about what either has or hasn't happened with a computer system.

Certification Objective   This chapter covers CompTIA Security+ exam objective 5.5, Summarize basic concepts of forensics.

Order of Volatility

There are many sources of data in a computer system, and if the machine is running, some of these sources are volatile. Things such as the state of the CPU and its registers, RAM, and even storage are always changing, which can make the collection of electronic data a difficult and delicate task. These elements tend to change at different rates, and you should pay attention to the *order of volatility*, or lifetime of the data, so that you can prioritize your collection efforts after a security incident to ensure you don't lose valuable forensic evidence. In some cases, you may have only one chance to collect volatile data, after which it becomes lost forever.

Following is the order of volatility of digital information in a system:

1. CPU, cache, and register contents (collect first)
2. Routing tables, ARP cache, process tables, kernel statistics
3. Live network connections and data flows

4. Memory (RAM)

5. Temporary file system/swap space

6. Data on hard disk

7. Remotely logged data

8. Data stored on archival media/backups (collect last)

 EXAM TIP Understanding the order of volatility of digital information in a system is a testable item—commit it to memory.

When collecting digital evidence, it is important to use proper techniques and tools. Some of the key elements are the use of write blockers when making forensic copies, hashing and verifying hash matches, documenting handling and storage, and protecting media from environmental change factors. Of particular note is that the data present on a system can be a function of both the file system and the hardware being employed. A physical hard disk drive (HDD) will persist data longer than a solid state drive (SSD). And the newer file systems with journaling and shadow copies can have longer persistence of information than older systems such as File Allocation Table (FAT) based systems. Raw disk blocks can be recovered in some file systems long after data has been rewritten or erased, due to the nature of how the file systems manage the data.

 EXAM TIP A common data element needed later in the forensics process is an accurate system time with respect to an accurate external time source. A record time offset is calculated by measuring system time with an external clock such as a Network Time Protocol (NTP) server. The offset between system time and true time can be lost if the system is powered down, so it is best to collect it while the system is still running.

Chain of Custody

After evidence is collected, it must be properly controlled to prevent tampering. The chain of custody accounts for all persons who handled or had access to the evidence. More specifically, the *chain of custody* shows who obtained the evidence, when and where it was obtained, where it was stored, and who had control or possession of the evidence for the entire time since the evidence was obtained.

The following shows the critical steps in a chain of custody:

1. Record each item collected as evidence.

2. Record who collected the evidence along with the date and time it was collected or recorded.

3. Write a description of the evidence in the documentation.

4. Put the evidence in containers and tag the containers with the case number, the name of the person who collected it, and the date and time it was collected or put in the container.

5. Record all message digest (hash) values in the documentation.

6. Securely transport the evidence to a protected storage facility.

7. Obtain a signature from the person who accepts the evidence at this storage facility.

8. Provide controls to prevent access to and compromise of the evidence while it is being stored.

9. Securely transport the evidence to court for proceedings.

 EXAM TIP Never analyze the seized evidence directly. The original evidence must be secured and protected with a chain of custody. It should never be subjected to a forensic examination, because of the fragile nature of digital evidence. A forensic copy, however, can be examined and, if something goes wrong, discarded, and the copy process can be repeated. A good forensics process will prove that the forensic copy is identical to the original at the start and at the end of the examination. From a practical standpoint, investigators usually make multiple forensic copies and perform their analysis in parallel on the multiple copies.

Legal Hold

In the U.S. legal system, legal precedent requires that potentially relevant information must be preserved at the instant a party "reasonably anticipates" litigation or another type of formal dispute. Although this sounds technical, it is fairly easy to grasp: once an organization is aware that it needs to preserve evidence for a court case, it must do it. The mechanism is fairly simple as well: once you realize your organization needs to preserve evidence, you must use a *legal hold*, or litigation hold, the process by which you properly preserve any and all digital evidence related to a potential case. This event is usually triggered by one organization issuing a litigation hold request to another. Once an organization receives this notice, it is required to maintain a complete set of unaltered data including metadata, of any and all information related to the issue causing the litigation hold. This means that ordinary data retention policies no longer are sufficient, and that even alterations to metadata can be considered to be a violation of the hold request. If a judge determines that a violation of a hold request may materially affect the ability of a jury to make a decision, the judge can instruct the jury to consider the act as hiding evidence. Major jury awards have been decided based on failure to retain information as failure to comply can be seen as negligence.

Where does the information subject to a legal hold reside? Everywhere, including e-mail, office documents (electronic and paper), network shares, mobile phones, tablets, databases—everywhere the information is shared, all copies need to be produced unaltered, even if relevant documents were created years ago. Finding and managing all of this information falls under a branch of digital forensics called e-discovery, which deals with the identification, management, and preservation of digital information that is subject to legal hold.

Data Acquisition

Evidence consists of the documents, verbal statements, and material objects admissible in a court of law. Evidence is critical to convincing management, juries, judges, or other authorities that some kind of violation has occurred. It is vitally important to document all the steps taken in the collection of evidence, as these may be challenged in court and the processes followed as evidenced by the documentation will be all that can be used to demonstrate the veracity of the processes.

The submission of evidence is challenging, but it is even more challenging when computers are used, because the people involved may not be technically educated and thus may not fully understand what's happened. Keep these points in mind as you collect evidence:

- Who collected the evidence?
- How was it collected?
- Where was it collected?
- Who has had possession of the evidence?
- How was it protected and stored?
- When was it removed from storage? Why? Who took possession?

Computer evidence presents yet more challenges, because the data itself cannot be sensed with the physical senses—that is, you can see printed characters, but you can't see the bits where that data is stored. Bits of data are merely magnetic pulses on a disk or some other storage technology. Therefore, data must always be evaluated through some kind of "filter" rather than sensed directly by human senses. This is often of concern to auditors, because good auditing techniques recommend accessing the original data or a version as close as possible to the original data.

The next three topics, standards for evidence, types of evidence, and three rules regarding evidence, are covered for topic completeness but are not specifically listed in the exam objectives. Also not specifically covered are the tools used in data acquisition. Because of the need to preserve, unaltered, the metadata of data being acquired, special tools are used to perform this task. Ordinary DOS or system utilities will not work for this task. Three main tool suites used are Encase, Forensic Toolkit (FTK), and the Sleuth Kit (TSK and open source).

Standards for Evidence

For evidence to be credible, especially if it will be used in court proceedings or in corporate disciplinary actions that could be challenged legally, it must meet three standards:

- **Sufficient evidence**   The evidence must be convincing or measure up without question.
- **Competent evidence**   The evidence must be legally qualified and reliable.
- **Relevant evidence**   The evidence must be material to the case or have a bearing on the matter at hand.

Types of Evidence

All evidence is not created equal. Some evidence is stronger and better than other, weaker evidence. Several types of evidence can be germane:

- **Direct evidence**   Oral testimony that proves a specific fact (such as an eyewitness's statement). The knowledge of the facts is obtained through the five senses of the witness, with no inferences or presumptions.
- **Real evidence**   Also known as associative or physical evidence, this includes tangible objects that prove or disprove a fact. Physical evidence links the suspect to the scene of a crime.
- **Documentary evidence**   Evidence in the form of business records, printouts, manuals, and the like. Much of the evidence relating to computer crimes is documentary evidence.
- **Demonstrative evidence**   Used to aid the jury and can be in the form of a model, experiment, chart, and so on, offered to prove that an event occurred.

Three Rules Regarding Evidence

An item officially becomes evidence in a legal proceeding when a judge determines that it is admissible. Three rules guide a judge's determination of whether to admit an item into evidence:

- **Best evidence rule**   Courts prefer original evidence rather than a copy, to ensure that no alteration of the evidence (whether intentional or unintentional) has occurred. In some instances, an evidence duplicate can be accepted, such as when the original is lost or destroyed by a natural disaster or in the normal course of business. A duplicate is also acceptable when a third party beyond the court's subpoena power possesses the original. Copies of digital records, where proof of integrity is provided, can in many cases be used in court.

 NOTE   Evidence rules exist at the federal and state levels and vary. Digital evidence is not always considered a "writing" and is not always subject to the best evidence rule.

- **Exclusionary rule**   The Fourth Amendment to the U.S. Constitution precludes unreasonable search and seizure. Therefore, any evidence collected in violation of the Fourth Amendment is not admissible as evidence. Additionally, if evidence is collected in violation of the Electronic Communications Privacy Act (ECPA) or other related violations of the U.S. Code, or other statutes, it may not be admissible to a court. For example, if no policy exists regarding the company's intent to monitor network traffic or systems electronically, or if such a policy exists but employees have not been asked to acknowledge it by signing an agreement, sniffing employees' network traffic could be a violation of the ECPA.

- **Hearsay rule**   Hearsay is second-hand evidence—evidence offered by the witness that is not based on the personal knowledge of the witness but is being offered to prove the truth of the matter asserted. Hearsay is inadmissible unless it falls under one of the many recognized exceptions (such as those delineated in FRE 803). Typically, computer-generated evidence is considered hearsay evidence, as the maker of the evidence (the computer) cannot be interrogated. Exceptions are being made where items such as logs and headers (computer-generated materials) are being accepted in court. Computer evidence is typically brought into a case by an expert witness who can speak for the data and what it means.

NOTE   The laws mentioned here are U.S. laws. Other countries and jurisdictions may have similar laws that would need to be considered in a similar manner.

Capture System Image

Imaging or dumping the physical memory of a computer system can help identify evidence not available on a hard drive. This is especially appropriate for rootkits, where evidence on the hard drive is hard to find. Once the memory is imaged, you can use a hex editor to analyze the image offline on another system. (Memory-dumping tools and hex editors are available on the Internet.) Note that dumping memory is more applicable for investigative work where court proceedings will not be pursued. If a case is likely to end up in court, do not dump memory without first seeking legal advice to confirm that live analysis of the memory is acceptable; otherwise, the defendant will be able to dispute easily the claim that evidence was not tampered with.

The other system image is that of the internal storage devices. Making forensic duplicates of all partitions is a key step in preserving evidence. A forensic copy is a bit-by-bit copy and has supporting integrity checks in the form of hashes. Hash functions are covered in Chapter 27. The proper practice is to use a write blocker when making a forensic copy of a drive. This device allows a disk to be read, but prevents any writing actions to the drive, guaranteeing that the copy operation does not change the original media. Once a forensic copy is created, working copies from the master forensic copy can be created for analysis and sharing with other investigators. The use of hash values provides a means of demonstrating that all of the copies are true to each other and the original.

EXAM TIP A digital forensic copy can only be made with specific methods designed to perform bit-by-bit copying of the files, free and slack space, making a verifiably true copy of the medium as demonstrated by hash values.

Network Traffic and Logs

An important source of information in an investigation can be the network activity associated with a device. There can be a lot of useful information in the network logs associated with network infrastructure. The level and breadth of this information is determined by the scope of the investigation. While the best data would be from that of a live network forensic collection process, in most cases this type of data will not be available. There are many other sources of network forensic data, including firewall and IDS logs, network flow data, and event logs on key servers and services.

Capture Video

A convenient method of capturing significant information at the time of collection is video capture. Videos allow high-bandwidth data collection that can show what was connected to what, how things were laid out, desktops, and so forth. A picture can be worth a thousand words, so take the time to document everything with pictures. Pictures of serial numbers and network and USB connections can prove invaluable later in the forensics process. Complete documentation is a must in every forensics process, and photographs can assist greatly in capturing details that would otherwise take a long time and be prone to transcription error.

Another source of video data is the CCTVs that are used for security, both in industry and, in growing numbers, homes. Like all other digital information, CCTV video can be copied and manipulated and needs to be preserved in the same manner as other digital information.

 EXAM TIP A digital camera is great for recording a scene and information. Screenshots of active monitor images may be obtained as well. Pictures can detail elements such as serial number plates, machines, drives, cables connections, and more. Photographs are truly worth a thousand words.

Record Time Offset

Record time offset is the difference in time between the system clock and the actual time. To minimize record time offset, most computers sync their time over the Internet with an official time source. Files and events logged on a computer will have timestamp markings that are based on the clock time on the machine itself. It is a mistake to assume that this clock is accurate. To allow the correlation of timestamp data from records inside the computer with any external event, it is necessary to know any time offset between the machine clock and the actual time. When collecting forensic data it is vitally important to collect the record time offset so that local variations in time can be corrected.

Take Hashes

If files, logs, and other information are going to be captured and used for evidence, you need to ensure that the data isn't modified. In most cases, a tool that implements a hashing algorithm to create message digests is used.

A *hashing algorithm* performs a function similar to the familiar parity bits, checksum, or cyclic redundancy check (CRC). It applies mathematical operations to a data stream (or file) to calculate some number that is unique based on the information contained in the data stream (or file). If a subsequent hash created on the same data stream results in a different hash value, it usually means that the data stream was changed.

The mathematics behind hashing algorithms has been researched extensively, and although it is possible that two different data streams could produce the same message digest, it is very improbable. This is an area of cryptography that has been rigorously reviewed, and the mathematics behind Message Digest 5 (MD5) and Secure Hash Algorithm (SHA) is very sound. In 2005, weaknesses were discovered in the MD5 and SHA algorithms leading the National Institute of Standards and Technology (NIST) to announce a competition to find a new cryptographic hashing algorithm named SHA-3. Although MD5 is still used, best practice would be to use SHA-2 series, and SHA-3 once it becomes integrated into tools.

The hash tool is applied to each file or log and the message digest value is noted in the investigation documentation. It is a good practice to write the logs to a write-once media such as a CD-ROM. If the case actually goes to trial, the investigator may need to run the tool on the files or logs again to show that they have not been altered in any way.

 NOTE The number of files stored on today's hard drives can be very large, with literally hundreds of thousands of files. Obviously, this is far too many for the investigator to analyze. However, by matching the message digests for files installed by the most popular software products to the message digests of the files on the drive being analyzed, the investigator can avoid analyzing approximately 90 percent of the files because he can assume they are unmodified. The National Software Reference Library (NSRL) collects software from various sources and incorporates file profiles into a Reference Data Set (RDS) available for download as a service. See www.nsrl.nist.gov.

Screenshots

Pay particular attention to the state of what is on the screen at the time of evidence collection. The information on a video screen is lost once the system changes or power is removed. Take *screenshots*, using a digital camera or video camera, to provide documentation as to what was on the screen at the time of collection. Because you cannot trust the system internals themselves to be free of tampering, do not use internal screenshot capture methods.

Witness Interviews

Remember that witness credibility is extremely important. It is easy to imagine how quickly credibility can be damaged if the witness is asked "Did you lock the file system?" and can't answer affirmatively. Or, when asked "When you imaged this disk drive, did you use a new system?" the witness can't answer that the destination disk was new or had been completely formatted using a low-level format before data was copied to it. Witness preparation can be critical in a case, even for technical experts.

As human memory is not as long lasting as computer files, it is important to get witness testimony and collect that data as early as possible. Having them write down what they remember immediately is very helpful in preserving memory.

Preservation

When information or objects are presented to management or admitted to court to support a claim, that information or those objects can be considered as evidence or documentation supporting your investigative efforts. Senior management will always ask a lot of questions—second- and third-order questions that you need to be able to answer quickly. Likewise, in a court, credibility is critical. Therefore, evidence must be properly acquired, identified, protected against tampering, transported, and stored.

One of the key elements in preservation is to ensure nothing changes as a result of data collection. If a machine is off, do not turn it on—the disk drives can be imaged with the machine off. Turning on the machine causes a lot of processes to run and data elements to be changed. When making a forensic copy of a disk, always use a write blocker, this prevents any changes on the media being imaged. Normal copying leaves traces and changes behind, a write blocker prevents these alterations.

Digital evidence has one huge, glaring issue: it can change, and not leave a record of the change. The fact that the outcome of a case can hinge on information that can be argued as not static leads to the crucial element of preservation. From the initial step in the forensics process, the most important issue must always be *preservation* of the data. There is no recovery from data that has been changed, so from the beginning of the collection process, safeguards must be in place. There are several key steps that assist the forensic investigator in avoiding data spoilage. First, when data is collected, a solid chain of custody is maintained until the case is completed and the materials are released or destroyed. Second, when a forensic copy of the data is obtained, a hash is collected as well, to allow for the verification of integrity. All analysis is done on forensic copies of the original data collection, not the master copy itself. And each copy is verified before and after testing by comparing hash values to the original set to demonstrate integrity.

This process adds a lot of work, and time, to an investigation, but it yields one crucial element—repudiation of any claim that the data was changed, tampered, or damaged in any way. Should a hash value vary, the action is simple. Discard the copy, make a new copy, and begin again. This process shows the courts two key things: process rigor to protect the integrity of the data, and traceability via hash values to demonstrate the integrity of the data and the analysis results derived from the data.

EXAM TIP   Understanding not only the importance of data preservation but the process of assuring it using hash values is a very testable concept.

Recovery

Recovery in a digital forensics sense is associated with determining the relevant information for the issue at hand—simply stated, recover the evidence associated with an act. But what if the act is not precisely known? For example, suppose a sales manager for a company quits and goes to work with a competitor. Because she is a sales manager, she has had access to sensitive information that would benefit the new employer. But how do you know whether she took sensitive information with her? And even if she did, how do you determine for purposes of recovery which information she took, and where to look for it? Since forensics software has yet to invent a "Find Evidence" button, and there is no field in any computer protocol to tell investigators this is the data you are looking for, the act of recovering the necessary information can be a significant challenge. With today's multi-terabyte drives, the volumes of data can be daunting.

Handing a forensic investigator a 1TB drive and saying "Tell me everything that happened on this machine" is tantamount to giving the investigator a never-ending task. The number of events, files, and processes that occur as a normal part of computing leads to literally thousands of events for every logon–work–logoff cycle. This is not a problem of finding a needle in a haystack; it's a problem of finding a needle in the hay fields of Kansas! There are ways to trim the work: establishing timelines within which the suspected activity occurred; identifying keywords to find strings of information that make a record relevant; and, perhaps the most powerful for building a solid dataset, pinpointing specific activities that have associated logs of their occurrence. The latter strategy is associated with the idea of active logging, discussed in the next section.

Strategic Intelligence/ Counterintelligence Gathering

Strategic intelligence gathering is the use of all resources to make determinations. This can make a large difference in whether a firm is prepared for threats or not. The same idea fits into digital forensics. Strategic intelligence can provide information that limits the scope of an investigation to a manageable level. If we have an idea of specific acts for which we would like to have demonstrable evidence of either occurrence or nonoccurrence, we can build a strategic intelligence data set on the information. Where is it, what is it, and what is allowed/not allowed are all pieces of information that, when arranged and analyzed, can lead to a data-logging plan to help support forensic event capture. Consideration of other events, such as: What about things like adding data-wiping programs, then removing these programs, is important to consider. The list of possibilities is long, but just like strategic threat intelligence, it is manageable, and by working not in isolation but in concert with other firms and professionals, a meaningful plan can emerge.

Counterintelligence gathering is the gathering of information specifically targeting the strategic intelligence effort of another entity. Knowing what people are looking at and what information they are obtaining can provide information into their motives and potential future actions. Making and using a tool so that it does not leave specific traces of where, when, or on what it was used is a form of counterintelligence gathering in action.

Active Logging

Ideally, you should minimize the scope of logging so that when you have to search logs, the event you are interested in stands out without being hidden in a sea of irrelevant log items. Before a problem occurs, if as part of the preparation phase the organization limits logging to specific events, such as copying sensitive files, then later, if questions arise as to whether the event happened or not, a log file exists to provide the information. When you have an idea of what information you will want to be able to examine, you can make an active logging plan that assures the information is logged when it occurs, and if at all possible in a location that prevents alteration. *Active logging* is determined during preparation, and when it comes time for recovery, the advance planning pays off in the production of evidence. Strategic intelligence gathering provides the information necessary to build an effective active logging plan.

Track Man-Hours

Demonstrating the efforts and tasks performed in the forensics process may become an issue in court and other proceedings. Having the ability to demonstrate who did what, when they did it, and how long it took can provide information to establish that the steps were taken per the processes employed. Having solid accounting data on man-hours and other expenses can provide corroborating evidence as to the actions performed.

Chapter Review

In this chapter, you became acquainted with the application of digital forensics. The chapter opened with an explanation of the legal basis behind digital forensic work, and then progressed through the steps of data acquisition, preservation, and recovery. The chapter closed with a look at how strategic intelligence and active logging can greatly assist in making the desired digital artifacts available for use.

Questions

To help you prepare further for the CompTIA Security+ exam, and to test your level of preparedness, answer the following questions and then check your answers against the list of correct answers at the end of the chapter.

1. Which of the following purposes for conducting computer forensics is also a description of what is referred to as *incident response*?

   A. Investigating and analyzing computer systems as related to a violation of laws

   B. Investigating computer systems that have been remotely attacked

   C. Investigating and analyzing computer systems for compliance with an organization's policies

   D. None of the above

2. Volatile information locations such as the RAM change constantly and data collection should occur in the order of volatility or lifetime of the data. Order the following list from most volatile (which should be collected first) to least volatile.

   A. Routing tables, ARP cache, process tables, kernel statistics

   B. Memory (RAM)

   C. CPU, cache, and register contents

   D. Temporary file system/swap space

3. A common data element needed later in the forensics process is an accurate system time with respect to an accurate external time source. A record time offset is calculated by measuring system time with an external clock such as a Network Time Protocol (NTP) server. Which of the following must be considered relative to obtaining a record time offset?

   A. The record time offset can be lost if the system is powered down, so it is best collected while the system is still running.

   B. The internal clock may not be recorded to the same level of accuracy, so conversions may be necessary.

   C. External clock times may vary as much as 2 to 3 seconds, so it is best to obtain the time from several NTP servers to gain a more accurate reading.

   D. Recording time to track man-hours is a legal requirement.

4. What is the term used to describe the process that accounts for all persons who handled or had access to a piece of evidence?

   A. Secure e-discovery

   B. Chain of custody

   C. Evidence accountability process

   D. Evidence custodianship

5. In the U.S. legal system, at what point does legal precedent require that potentially relevant information must be preserved?

   A. When the owner is provided with a warrant to seize the storage device

   B. At the instant a party "reasonably anticipates" litigation or another type of formal dispute

   C. The moment any investigation is begun

   D. When a law enforcement official or officer of the court requests that the storage device be secured to ensure no data is modified or destroyed

6. Which standard of evidence states the evidence must be convincing or measure up without question?

   A. Direct evidence

   B. Competent evidence

   C. Relevant evidence

   D. Sufficient evidence

7. Which standard of evidence states the evidence must be material to the case or have a bearing on the matter at hand?

   A. Direct evidence

   B. Competent evidence

   C. Relevant evidence

   D. Sufficient evidence

8. Which type of evidence is oral testimony that proves a specific fact (such as an eyewitness's statement), where the knowledge of the fact is obtained through the recollection of five senses of the witness, with no inferences or presumptions?

   A. Direct evidence

   B. Real evidence

   C. Documentary evidence

   D. Demonstrative evidence

9. Which type of evidence is also known as associative or physical evidence and includes tangible objects that prove or disprove a fact?

   A. Direct evidence

   B. Real evidence

   C. Documentary evidence

   D. Demonstrative evidence

10. Which rule states that evidence is not admissible if it was collected in violation of the Fourth Amendment's prohibition of unreasonable search and seizure?

    A. Best evidence rule

    B. Hearsay rule

    C. Exclusionary rule

    D. Legal hold rule

11. Which rule of evidence addresses the fact that courts prefer original evidence rather than a copy, to ensure that no alteration of the evidence (whether intentional or unintentional) has occurred?

    A. Best evidence rule

    B. Hearsay rule

    C. Exclusionary rule

    D. Direct evidence rule

12. Which of the following would a capture video not be used to collect?

    A. Serial number plates

    B. Cable connections

    C. System image

    D. Physical layout and existence of systems

13. Which of the following performs a function similar to the familiar parity bits, checksum, or cyclic redundancy check?

    A. Record offset

    B. Cryptographic algorithm

    C. Authentication code

    D. Hashing algorithm

14. What type of plan is implemented when you have an idea of what information you will want to be able to examine and want to ensure the information is logged when it occurs, and if at all possible in a location that prevents alteration?

    A. System logging plan

    B. Forensic logging plan

    C. Investigative logging plan

    D. Active logging plan

15. From the initial step in the forensics process, the most important issue must always be which of the following?

    A. Preservation of the data

    B. Chain of custody

    C. Documenting all actions taken

    D. Witness preparation

Answers

1. **B.** Investigating computer systems that have been remotely attacked is often referred to as *incident response* and can be a subset of the other two points.

2. **C, A, B,** and **D.** The most volatile elements should be examined and collected first and in this order.

3. **A.** Record time offset will be lost if the system is powered down, so it is best collected while the system is still running.

4. **B.** The chain of custody accounts for all persons who handled or had access to the evidence.

5. **B.** In the U.S. legal system, legal precedent requires that potentially relevant information must be preserved at the instant a party "reasonably anticipates" litigation or another type of formal dispute.

6. **D.** *Sufficient evidence* states the evidence must be convincing or measure up without question. *Direct evidence* is oral testimony that proves a specific fact (such as an eyewitness's statement). The knowledge of the facts is obtained through the five senses of the witness, with no inferences or presumptions. *Competent evidence* states the evidence must be legally qualified and reliable. *Relevant evidence* states the evidence must be material to the case or have a bearing on the matter at hand.

7. **C.** *Relevant evidence* states the evidence must be material to the case or have a bearing on the matter at hand. *Sufficient evidence* states the evidence must be convincing or measure up without question. *Direct evidence* is oral testimony that proves a specific fact (such as an eyewitness's statement). The knowledge of the facts is obtained through the five senses of the witness, with no inferences or presumptions. *Competent evidence* states the evidence must be legally qualified and reliable.

8. **A.** *Direct evidence* is oral testimony that proves a specific fact (such as an eyewitness's statement). The knowledge of the facts is obtained through the five senses of the witness, with no inferences or presumptions. *Real evidence* is also known as associative or physical evidence and this includes tangible objects that prove or disprove a fact. Physical evidence links the suspect to the scene of a crime. Evidence in the form of business records, printouts, manuals, and similar objects, which make up much of the evidence relating to computer crimes, is *documentary evidence*. *Demonstrative evidence* is used to aid the jury and can be in the form of a model, experiment, chart, and so on, offered to prove that an event occurred.

9. **B.** *Real evidence* is also known as associative or physical evidence and includes tangible objects that prove or disprove a fact. Physical evidence links the suspect to the scene of a crime. *Direct evidence* is oral testimony that proves a specific fact (such as an eyewitness's statement). The knowledge of the facts is obtained through the five senses of the witness, with no inferences or presumptions. Evidence in the form of business records, printouts, manuals, and similar objects, which make up much of the evidence relating to computer crimes, is *documentary evidence*. *Demonstrative evidence* is used to aid the jury and can be in the form of a model, experiment, chart, and so on, offered to prove that an event occurred.

10. **C.** The Fourth Amendment to the U.S. Constitution precludes illegal search and seizure. Therefore, any evidence collected in violation of the Fourth Amendment is not admissible as evidence. This is addressed by the *exclusionary rule*. The *best evidence* rule addresses the fact that courts prefer original evidence rather than a copy, to ensure that no alteration of the evidence (whether intentional or unintentional) has occurred. *Hearsay* rule addesses second-hand evidence— evidence offered by the witness that is not based on the personal knowledge of the witness but is being offered to prove the truth of the matter asserted. There was no discussion of a direct evidence rule.

11. **A.** The *best evidence* rule addresses the fact that courts prefer original evidence rather than a copy, to ensure that no alteration of the evidence (whether intentional or unintentional) has occurred. *Hearsay* rule addresses second-hand evidence—evidence offered by the witness that is not based on the personal knowledge of the witness but is being offered to prove the truth of the matter asserted. The Fourth Amendment to the U.S. Constitution precludes illegal search and seizure. Therefore, any evidence collected in violation of the Fourth Amendment is not admissible as evidence. This is addressed by the *exclusionary rule*. There was no discussion of a direct evidence rule.

12. **C.** A system image is a dump of the physical memory of a computer system and would not be captured in a video. All of the others are static sources of information that a capture video is valuable in recording.

13. **D.** A *hashing algorithm* performs a function similar to the familiar parity bits, checksum, or cyclic redundancy check (CRC). It applies mathematical operations to a data stream (or file) to calculate some number that is unique based on the information contained in the data stream (or file).

14. **D.** When you have an idea of what information you will want to be able to examine, you can make an active logging plan that ensures the information is logged when it occurs, and if at all possible in a location that prevents alteration.

15. **A.** While all of these are important, from the initial step in the forensics process, the most important issue must always be preservation of the data.

CHAPTER 25

Data Security and Privacy Practices

In this chapter, you will

- Study data security practices
- Explore privacy practices

Data security and privacy practices are interrelated because of the basic premise that to have privacy, you must have security. Privacy is defined as the control you exert over your data, and security is a key element of control. Data privacy in an organization is the prevention of unauthorized use of data held by the organization. One method of ensuring privacy is the destruction of data after it is no longer needed. Elements that enable data privacy efforts include properly labeling and handling sensitive data, assigning responsibility for protecting data, and securely storing retained data, all of which are covered in this chapter.

Certification Objective   This chapter covers CompTIA Security+ exam objective 5.8, Given a scenario, carry out data security and privacy practices.

This objective is a good candidate for performance-based questions, which means you should expect questions in which you must apply your knowledge of the topic to a scenario. The best answer to a question will depend upon specific details in the scenario preceding the question, not just the question. The questions may also involve tasks other than just picking the best answer from a list. Instead, you may be instructed to order things on a diagram, put options in rank order, match two columns of items, or perform a similar task.

Data Destruction and Media Sanitization

When data is no longer being used, whether it be on old printouts, old systems being discarded, or broken equipment, it is important to destroy the data before losing physical control over the media it is on. Many criminals have learned the value of dumpster diving to discover information that can be used in identity theft, social engineering, and other malicious activities. An organization must concern itself not only with paper trash, but also the information stored on discarded objects such as computers. Several government organizations have been embarrassed when old computers sold to salvagers proved to contain sensitive documents on their hard drives. It is critical for every organization to have a strong disposal and destruction policy and related procedures. This section covers *data destruction and media sanitization* methods.

Burning

Burning is considered one of the gold-standard methods of data destruction. Once the storage media is rendered into a form that can be destroyed by fire, the chemical processes of fire are irreversible and render the data lost forever. The typical method is to shred the material, even plastic disks and hard drives (including SSDs), and then put the shred in an incinerator and oxidize the material back to base chemical forms. When the material is completely combusted, the information that was on it is gone.

Shredding

Shredding is the physical destruction by tearing an item into many small pieces, which can then be mixed, making reassembly difficult if not impossible. Important papers should be shredded, and *important* in this case means anything that might be useful to a potential intruder or dumpster diver. It is amazing what intruders can do with what appears to be innocent pieces of information. Shredders come in all sizes, from little desktop models that can handle a few pages at a time, or a single CD/DVD, to industrial versions that can handle even phone books and multiple discs at the same time. The ultimate in industrial shredders can even shred hard disk drives, metal case and all. Many document destruction companies have larger shredders on trucks that they bring to their clients location and do on-site shredding on a regular schedule.

Pulping

Pulping is a process by which paper fibers are suspended in a liquid and recombined into new paper. If you have data records on paper, and you shred the paper, the pulping process removes the ink by bleaching, and recombines all the shred into new paper, completely destroying the physical layout of the old paper.

Pulverizing

Pulverizing is a physical process of destruction using excessive physical force to break an item into unusable pieces. Pulverizers are used on items like hard disk drives, destroying the platters in a manner that they cannot be reconstructed. A more modern method of pulverizing the data itself is the use of encryption. The data on the drive is encrypted and the key itself is destroyed. This renders the data non-recoverable based on the encryption strength. This method has unique advantages of scale; a small business can pulverize its own data, whereas they would either need expensive equipment or a third party to pulverize the few disks they need to destroy each year.

Degaussing

A safer method for destroying files on magnetic storage devices (i.e., magnetic tape and hard drives) is to destroy the data magnetically, using a strong magnetic field to degauss the media. *Degaussing* realigns the magnetic particles, removing the organized structure that represented the data. This effectively destroys all data on the media. Several commercial degaussers are available for this purpose.

Purging

Data *purging* is a term that is commonly used to describe methods that permanently erase and remove data from a storage space. The key phrase is "remove data," for unlike deletion, which just destroys the data, purging is designed to open up the storage space for reuse. A circular buffer is a great example of an automatic purge mechanism. It stores a given number of data elements and then the space is reused. A circular buffer that holds 64 MB, once full, as new material is added to the buffer, it overwrites the oldest material.

Wiping

Wiping data is the process of rewriting the storage media with a series of patterns of 1's and 0's. This is not done once, but is done multiple times to ensure that every trace of the original data has been eliminated. There are data-wiping protocols for various security levels of data, with 3, 7, or even 35 passes. Of particular note are solid-state drives, as these devices use a different storage methodology and require special utilities to ensure that all the sectors are wiped.

Data wiping is non-destructive to the media, unlike pulping and shredding, and this makes it ideal for another purpose. Media sanitization is the clearing of previous data off of a media device before the device is reused. Wiping can be used to sanitize a storage device, making it clean before use. This can be important to remove old trace data that will later show up in free and unused space.

 EXAM TIP This section covers several methods of data/media destruction, a couple of which are used together. Learn the details of each method and look for nonsense answer choices that narrow down the possible correct answers, such as options that refer to pulping non-paper items or degaussing non-magnetic media.

Data Sensitivity Labeling and Handling

Effective data classification programs include measures to ensure *data sensitivity labeling and handling* so that personnel know whether data is sensitive and understand the levels of protection required. When the data is inside an information-processing system, the protections should be designed into the system. But when the data leaves this cocoon of protection, whether by printing, downloading, or copying, it becomes necessary to ensure continued protection by other means. This is where data sensitivity labeling assists users in fulfilling their responsibilities. Training to ensure that labeling occurs and that it is used and followed is important for users whose roles can be impacted by this material.

Training plays an important role in ensuring proper data handling and disposal. Personnel are intimately involved in several specific tasks associated with data handling and data destruction/disposal and, if properly trained, can act as a security control. Untrained or inadequately trained personnel will not be a productive security control and, in fact, can be a source of potential compromise.

A key component of IT security is the protection of the information processed and stored on the computer systems and network. Organizations deal with many different types of information, and they need to recognize that not all information is of equal importance or sensitivity. This requires classification of information into various categories, each with its own requirements for its handling. Factors that affect the classification of specific information include its value to the organization (what will be the impact to the organization if it loses this information?), its age, and laws or regulations that govern its protection. The most widely known system of classification of information is that implemented by the U.S. government (including the military), which classifies information into categories such as Confidential, Secret, and Top Secret. Businesses have similar desires to protect information and often use categories such as Confidential, Private, Public, Proprietary, PII, and PHI. Each policy for the classification of information should describe how it should be protected, who may have access to it, who has the authority to release it and how, and how it should be destroyed. All employees of the organization should be trained in the procedures for handling the information that they are authorized to access.

Confidential

Data is labeled *Confidential* if its disclosure to an unauthorized party would potentially cause serious harm to the organization. This data should be defined by policy, and that policy should include details regarding who has the authority to release the data. Common examples of confidential data include trade secrets, proprietary software code, new product designs, etc., as the release of these could result in significant loss to the firm.

Private

Data is labeled *Private* if its disclosure to an unauthorized party would potentially cause harm or disruption to the organization. Passwords could be considered private. The term private data is usually associated with personal data belonging to a person and less often with corporate entities. The level of damage typically associated with private data is lower than confidential, but still significant to the organization.

Public

Public data is data that can be seen by the public and has no needed protections with respect to confidentiality. It is important to protect the integrity of public data, lest one communicate incorrect data as being true. Public facing web pages, press releases, corporate statements—these are examples of public data that still needs protection, but specifically with respect to integrity.

Proprietary

Proprietary data is data that is restricted to a company because of potential competitive use. If a company has data that could be used by a competitor for any particular reason, say internal costs and pricing data, then it needs to be labeled and handled in a manner to protect it from release to competitors. Proprietary data may be shared with a third party that is not a competitor, but in labeling the data Proprietary, you alert the party you have shared with that the data is not to be shared further.

EXAM TIP Learn the differences between the data sensitivity labels so you can compare and contrast the terms confidential, private, public, and proprietary. The differences are subtle, but will be important to determine the correct answer.

PII

When information is about a person, failure to protect it can have specific consequences. Business secrets are protected through trade secret laws, government information is protected through laws concerning national security, and privacy laws protect information associated with people. A set of elements that can lead to the specific identity of a person is referred to as *personally identifiable information (PII)*. By definition, PII can be used to identify a specific individual, even if an entire set is not disclosed.

CAUTION As little information as the ZIP code, gender, and date of birth can resolve to a single person.

PII is an essential element of many online transactions, but it can also be misused if disclosed to unauthorized parties. For this reason, it should be protected at all times, by all parties that possess it. And when PII is no longer needed, it should be destroyed in accordance with the firm's data destruction policy in a complete, nonreversible manner.

PHI

The Health Insurance Portability and Accountability Act (HIPAA) regulations define *Protected Health Information (PHI)* as "any information, whether oral or recorded in any form or medium" that

> *"[i]s created or received by a health care provider, health plan, public health authority, employer, life insurer, school or university, or health care clearinghouse"; and*

> *"[r]elates to the past, present, or future physical or mental health or condition of an individual; the provision of health care to an individual; or the past, present, or future payment for the provision of health care to an individual."*

HIPAA's language is built upon the concepts of PHI and Notice of Privacy Practices (NPP). HIPAA describes "covered entities" including medical facilities, billing facilities, and insurance (third-party payer) facilities. Patients are to have access to their PHI, and an expectation of appropriate privacy and security associated with medical records.

HIPAA mandates a series of administrative, technical, and physical security safeguards for information, including elements such as staff training and awareness, and specific levels of safeguards for PHI when in use, stored, or in transit between facilities.

 EXAM TIP Know the difference between PII and PHI, and don't jump to the wrong one on the exam.

Data Roles

Multiple personnel in an organization are associated with the control and administration of data. These *data roles* include data owners, stewards, custodians, and users. Each of these roles has responsibilities in the protection and control of the data. The leadership of this effort is under the auspices of the privacy officer.

Owner

All data elements in an organization should have defined requirements for security, privacy, retention, and other business functions. It is the responsibility of the designated *data owner* to define these requirements.

Steward/Custodian

A *data custodian* or *data steward* is the role responsible for the day-to-day caretaking of data. The data owner sets the relevant policies, and the steward or custodian ensures they are followed.

Privacy Officer

The *privacy officer* is the C-level executive who is responsible for establishing and enforcing data privacy policy and addressing legal and compliance issues. Data minimization initiatives are also the responsibility of the privacy officer. Storing data that does not have any real business value only increases the odds of disclosure. The privacy officer is responsible for determining the gap between a company's privacy practices and the required actions to close the gap to an approved level. This is called a privacy impact analysis and is covered in Chapter 22.

The privacy officer also plays an important role if information on European customers is involved, for the EU has strict data protection (privacy) rules. The privacy officer who is accountable for the protection of consumer data from the EU must ensure compliance with EU regulations.

Data Retention

Data retention is the storage of data records. One of the first steps in understanding data retention in an organization is the determination of what records require storage and for how long. Among the many reasons for retaining data, some of the most common are for purposes of billing and accounting, contractual obligation, warranty history, and compliance with local, state, and national government regulations, such as IRS rules. Maintaining data stores for longer than is required is a source of risk, as is not storing the information long enough. Some information is subject to regulations requiring lengthy data retention, such as PHI for workers who have been exposed to specific hazards. Some data elements, such as the CVC/CV2 element in a credit card transaction, are never stored. They are used and destroyed to prevent loss after the transaction is concluded.

Failure to maintain the data in a secure state can also be a retention issue, as is not retaining it. In some cases, destruction of data, specifically data subject to legal hold in a legal matter, can result in adverse court findings and sanctions. Even if the data destruction is unintentional or inadvertent, it is still subject to sanction as the firm had a responsibility to protect it. Legal hold, discussed in depth in Chapter 24, can add significant complexity to data retention efforts, as it forces almost separate store of the data until the legal issues are resolved. Once data is on the legal hold track, its retention clock does not expire until the hold is lifted. This makes identifying, labeling, and maintenance of data subject to a legal hold an added dimension to normal storage considerations.

Legal and Compliance

Many data security and privacy practices are guided by *legal* requirements and regulatory *compliance*. Different sectors have differing requirements concerning the use of personal information. The most heavily regulated sectors are medical, finance, and banking. The Health Insurance Portability and Accountability Act (HIPAA), as amended by the HITECH Act, covers PHI and PII associated with medical records. HIPAA has provisions for safeguarding the information in any form, electronic or paper. Administrative, technical, and physical controls are mandated by HIPAA, including workforce training and awareness, encryption of data transfers, and physical barriers to records (locked storage rooms).

In banking, the Fair Credit Reporting Act and its Disposal Rule cover consumer information and its disposal with respect to credit. The Disposal Rule requires businesses and individuals to take appropriate measures to dispose of sensitive information derived from consumer reports. Any business or individual who uses a consumer report for a business purpose is subject to the requirements of the Disposal Rule.

The Federal Trade Commission issues regulations and findings with respect to data privacy. The FTC's Disposal Rule applies to consumer reporting agencies as well as to any individuals and businesses that use consumer reports, such as lenders, insurers, employers, and landlords. The FTC has adopted a set of red flag rules that are invoked to assist entities in determining when extra precautions must be taken concerning PII records. The following are some examples of red flags that should prompt an organization to initiate additional, specific data handling steps to protect data:

- Change of address request. This is a common tool for identity thieves, and as such, firms should provide protection steps to verify change of address requests.

- Sudden use of an account that has been inactive for a long time, or radical changes in use of any account.

- A suspicious address or phone number. Many fraudulent addresses and numbers are known, and repeated applications should be quickly noted and stopped.

- Request for credit on a consumer account that has a credit freeze on a credit reporting record.

Whenever a red flag issue occurs, the business must have special procedures in place to ensure that the event is not fraudulent. Calling the customer and verifying information before taking action is one example of this type of additional action.

In the finance sector, the Gramm-Leach-Bliley Act and its Safeguards Rule and Privacy of Consumer Financial Information Rule require significant protections. The Safeguards Rule requires institutions to have measures in place to keep customer information secure, including taking steps to ensure that their affiliates and service providers also safeguard customer information in their care. The Financial Privacy Rule prohibits the sharing of information with third parties unless a bona fide business relationship and reason for the sharing exists.

Some other interesting information privacy laws include the U.S. Privacy Act of 1974 and the Freedom of Information Act of 1996. The Privacy Act of 1974 was an omnibus act designed to affect the entire federal information landscape. This act has many provisions that apply across the entire federal government, with only minor exceptions for national security (classified information), law enforcement, and investigative provisions. This act has been amended numerous times, and you can find current, detailed information at the Electronic Privacy Information Center (EPIC) website, http://epic.org/privacy/laws/privacy_act.html.

The Freedom of Information Act is one of the most widely used privacy acts in the United States, so much so that its acronym, FOIA (pronounced "foya"), has reached common use. FOIA was designed to enable public access to U.S. government records (federal government records only), and "public" includes the press, which purportedly acts on the public behalf and widely uses FOIA to obtain information. FOIA carries a presumption of disclosure; the burden is on the government, not the requesting party, to substantiate why information cannot be released. Upon receiving a written request, agencies of the U.S. government are required to disclose those records, unless they can be lawfully withheld from disclosure under one of nine specific exemptions in FOIA. The right of access is ultimately enforceable through the federal court system.

When things go wrong and data disclosures occur, a myriad of state regulations take center stage. There is not a single national data disclosure law in the United States, and the current list of U.S. states and territories that require disclosure notices is up to 48, with only Alabama, Mississippi, New Mexico, and South Dakota without bills. Each of these disclosure notice laws is different, making the case for a unifying federal statute compelling, but currently it is low on the priority lists of most politicians. California Senate Bill 1386 (SB 1386) was a landmark law concerning information disclosures. It mandates that Californians be notified whenever PII is lost or disclosed. Since the passage of SB 1386, numerous other states have modeled legislation on this bill, and although national legislation has been blocked by political procedural moves, it will eventually be passed.

Privacy is not a U.S.-centric phenomenon, but it does have strong cultural biases. Legal protections for privacy tend to follow the socio-cultural norms by geography; hence, there are different policies in European nations than in the United States. In the United States, the primary path to privacy is via opt-out, whereas in Europe and other countries, it is via opt-in. What this means is that the fundamental nature of control shifts. In the United States, a consumer must notify a firm that they wish to block the sharing of personal information; otherwise, the firm has permission by default. In the EU, sharing is blocked unless the customer specifically opts in to allow it. The Far East has significantly different cultural norms with respect to individualism versus collectivism and this is reflected in their privacy laws as well. Even in countries with common borders, distinct differences exist, such as the United States and Canada; Canadian laws and customs have strong roots to their UK history, and in many cases follow European ideals as opposed to U.S. ones. One of the primary sources of intellectual and political thought on privacy has been the Organisation for Economic Co-operation and Development (OECD). This multinational entity has for decades conducted multilateral discussions and policy formation on a wide range of topics, including privacy.

Chapter Review

In this chapter, you became acquainted with the issues surrounding data security and privacy practices. The chapter opened with methods of data destruction and media sanitization. These methods include burning, shredding, pulping, pulverizing, degaussing, purging, and wiping. Data sensitivity labeling and handling practices were addressed next. The chapter then examined the corporate personnel who are involved in data privacy, the data owner, data steward/custodian, and the privacy officer. The chapter concluded with an examination of data retention and legal and compliance issues.

Questions

To help you prepare further for the CompTIA Security+ exam, and to test your level of preparedness, answer the following questions and then check your answers against the list of correct answers at the end of the chapter.

1. The Freedom of Information Act applies to which of the following?

    A. All federal government documents, without restrictions

    B. All levels of government documents (federal, state, and local)

    C. Federal government documents, with a few enumerated restrictions

    D. Only federal documents containing information concerning the requester

2. HIPAA requires which of the following controls for medical records?

    A. Encryption of all data

    B. Technical controls only

    C. Physical controls only

    D. Administrative, technical, and physical controls

3. Which of the following is not PII?

    A. Customer name

    B. Customer ID number

    C. Customer Social Security number or taxpayer identification number

    D. Customer birth date

4. A privacy impact assessment:

    A. Determines the gap between a company's privacy practices and required actions

    B. Determines the damage caused by a breach of privacy

    C. Determines what companies hold information on a specific person

    D. Is a corporate procedure to safeguard PII

5. Which of the following is an acceptable PII disposal procedure?

    A. Shredding

    B. Burning

    C. Electronic destruction per military data destruction standards

    D. All of the above

6. In the United States, company responses to data disclosures of PII are regulated by:

    A. Federal law, the Privacy Act

    B. A series of state statutes

    C. Contractual agreements with banks and credit card processors

    D. The Gramm-Leach-Bliley Act (GLBA)

7. The U.S. Privacy Act of 1974 applies to which of the following?

    A. Corporate records for U.S.-based companies

    B. Records from any company doing business in the United States

    C. Federal records containing PII

    D. All levels of government records containing PII

8. Data privacy as applicable to organizations is defined as:

    A. The control the organization exerts over its data

    B. The organization being able to keep its information secret

    C. Making data-sharing illegal without consumer consent

    D. No longer important in the Internet age

9. All but which of the following are items associated with privacy of health records?

    A. Protected Health Information

    B. Personal Health Information

    C. Notice of Privacy Practices

    D. HITECH Act extension of HIPAA

10. The FTC Disposal Rule applies to which of the following?

    A. Small businesses using consumer reporting information

    B. Debt collectors

    C. Individuals using consumer reporting information

    D. All of the above

11. Who is responsible for determining what data is needed by the enterprise?

    A. Data owner

    B. Privacy officer

    C. Data custodian

    D. Data steward

12. Data that is labeled "Private" typically pertains to what category?

    A. Proprietary data

    B. Confidential information

    C. Legal data

    D. Personal information

13. Data that is labeled "Proprietary" typically pertains to what category?

    A. Information under legal hold

    B. Information to be safeguarded by business partners because it contains business secrets

    C. Personal data

    D. PHI and PII together

14. What is the best method to destroy sensitive data on DVDs at a desktop?

    A. Shredding

    B. Burning

    C. Wiping

    D. Pulping

15. Information that could disclose the identity of a customer is referred to as?

    A. Customer identity information (CII)

    B. Personally identifiable information (PII)

    C. Privacy protected information (PPI)

    D. Sensitive customer information (SCI)

PART V

Answers

1. **C.** Nine groups of documents are exempt from FOIA requests.

2. **D.** Administrative, technical, and physical controls are mandated by HIPAA, including workforce training and awareness, encryption of data transfers, and physical barriers to records (locked storage rooms).

3. **B.** A customer ID number generated by a firm to track customer records is meaningful only inside the firm and is generally not considered to be personally identifiable information (PII). It is important not to use the SSN for the customer ID number, for obvious purposes.

4. **A.** A PIA determines the gap between what a company is doing with PII and what its policies, rules, and regulations state it should be doing.

5. **D.** Although using electronic destruction per military data destruction standards might seem excessive (and in many cases it is), all of the options comply with FTC-mandated disposal procedures for PII.

6. **B.** No overarching federal disclosure statute exists, so company responses to data disclosures of PII are regulated by individual statutes in most states and territories.

7. **C.** The Privacy Act is a federal law, affecting federal records only.

8. **A.** The control the organization exerts over its data is the definition of data privacy in an enterprise.

9. **B.** The correct term per HIPAA is Protected Health Information.

10. **D.** All are listed by FTC as responsible for following the Disposal Rule.

11. **A.** The data owner determines the business need. The privacy officer ensures that laws and regulations are followed, and the custodian/steward maintains the data.

12. **D.** Private data frequently refers to personal data.

13. **B.** Proprietary data may be shared with a third party that is not a competitor, but in labeling the data Proprietary, you alert the party you have shared with that the data is not to be shared further.

14. **A.** A desktop shredder can destroy DVDs and CDs. Burning is not wise at a desk. Wiping and pulping don't work on DVDs.

15. **B.** Any information that can be used to determine identity is referred to collectively as personally identifiable information (PII).

PART VI

Cryptography and Public Key Infrastructure

26

Cryptographic Concepts

In this chapter, you will

- Identify the different types of cryptography
- Learn about current cryptographic methods
- Understand how cryptography is applied for security
- Given a scenario, utilize general cryptography concepts
- Compare and contrast basic concepts of cryptography

Cryptography is the science of *encrypting*, or hiding, information—something people have sought to do since they began using language. Although language allowed them to communicate with one another, people in power attempted to hide information by controlling who was taught to read and write. Eventually, more complicated methods of concealing information by shifting letters around to make the text unreadable were developed. These complicated methods are cryptographic algorithms, also known as *ciphers*. The word "cipher" comes from the Arabic word *sifr*, meaning empty or zero.

Certification Objective   This chapter covers CompTIA Security+ exam objective 6.1, Compare and contrast basic concepts of cryptography.

General Cryptographic Concepts

Historical ciphers were simple to use and also simple to break. Because hiding information was still important, more advanced transposition and substitution ciphers were required. As systems and technology became more complex, ciphers were frequently automated by some mechanical or electromechanical device. A famous example of a modern encryption machine is the German Enigma machine from World War II. This machine used a complex series of substitutions to perform encryption, and interestingly enough, it gave rise to extensive research in computers.

When setting up a cryptographic scheme, it is important to use proven technologies. Proven cryptographic libraries and proven cryptographically correct random number generators are the foundational elements associated with a solid program. Homegrown or custom elements in these areas can greatly increase risk associated with a broken system. Most groups don't possess the abilities to develop their own cryptographic algorithms. Algorithms are complex and difficult to create. Any algorithm that has not had public review can have weaknesses. Most good algorithms are approved for use only after a lengthy test and public review phase.

When material, called *plaintext*, needs to be protected from unauthorized interception or alteration, it is encrypted into *ciphertext*. This is done using an algorithm and a key, and the rise of digital computers has provided a wide array of algorithms and increasingly complex keys. The choice of specific algorithm depends on several factors, and they will be examined in this chapter.

Cryptanalysis, the process of analyzing available information in an attempt to return the encrypted message to its original form, required advances in computer technology for complex encryption methods. The birth of the computer made it possible to easily execute the calculations required by more complex encryption algorithms. Today, the computer almost exclusively powers how encryption is performed. Computer technology has also aided cryptanalysis, allowing new methods to be developed, such as linear and differential cryptanalysis. *Differential cryptanalysis* is done by comparing the input plaintext to the output ciphertext to try to determine the key used to encrypt the information. *Linear cryptanalysis* is similar in that it uses both plaintext and ciphertext, but it puts the plaintext through a simplified cipher to try to deduce what the key is likely to be in the full version of the cipher.

Fundamental Methods

Modern cryptographic operations are performed using both an algorithm and a key. The choice of algorithm depends on the type of cryptographic operation that is desired. The subsequent choice of key is then tied to the specific algorithm. Cryptographic operations include encryption for the protection of confidentiality, hashing for the protection of integrity, digital signatures to manage non-repudiation, and a bevy of specialty operations such as key exchanges.

While the mathematical specifics of these operations can be very complex and are beyond the scope of this level of material, the knowledge to properly employ them is not complex and is subject to being tested on the CompTIA Security+ exam. Encryption operations are characterized by the quantity and type of data, as well as the level and type of protection sought. Integrity protection operations are characterized by the level of assurance desired. Data is characterized by its usage: data-in-transit, data-at-rest, or data-in-use. It is also characterized in how it can be used, either in block form or stream form, as described next.

Symmetric Algorithms

Symmetric algorithms are a form of encryption that is older and a simpler method of encrypting information. The basis of symmetric encryption is that both the sender and the receiver of the message have previously obtained the same key. This is, in fact, the basis for even the oldest ciphers—the Spartans needed the exact same size cylinder, making the cylinder the "key" to the message, and in shift ciphers, both parties need to

Figure 26-1
Layout of a
symmetric
algorithm

know the direction and amount of shift being performed. All symmetric algorithms are based upon this shared secret principle, including the unbreakable one-time pad method.

Figure 26-1 is a simple diagram showing the process that a symmetric algorithm goes through to provide encryption from plaintext to ciphertext. This ciphertext message is, presumably, transmitted to the message recipient, who goes through the process to decrypt the message using the same key that was used to encrypt the message. Figure 26-1 shows the keys to the algorithm, which are the same value in the case of symmetric encryption.

Unlike with hash functions, a cryptographic key is involved in symmetric encryption, so there must be a mechanism for key management. Managing the cryptographic keys is critically important in symmetric algorithms because the key unlocks the data that is being protected. However, the key also needs to be known or transmitted in a secret way to the party with whom you wish to communicate. This key management applies to all things that could happen to a key: securing it on the local computer, securing it on the remote one, protecting it from data corruption, protecting it from loss, and, probably the most important step, protecting it while it is transmitted between the two parties. Later in the chapter we will look at public key cryptography, which greatly eases the key management issue, but for symmetric algorithms, the most important lesson is to store and send the key only by known secure means.

 EXAM TIP Common symmetric algorithms are 3DES, AES, Blowfish, Twofish, and RC4.

Symmetric algorithms are important because they are comparatively fast and have few computational requirements. Their main weakness is that two geographically distant parties both need to have a key that matches exactly. In the past, keys could be much simpler and still be secure, but with today's computational power, simple keys can be brute forced very quickly. This means that larger and more complex keys must be used and exchanged. This key exchange is difficult because the key cannot be simple, such as a word, but must be shared in a secure manner. It might be easy to exchange a 4-bit key such as *b* in hex, but exchanging the 128-bit key *4b36402c5727472d5571373d22675b4b* is far more difficult to do securely. This exchange of keys is greatly facilitated by asymmetric, or public key, cryptography, discussed after modes of operation.

Modes of Operation

In symmetric or block algorithms, there is a need to deal with multiple blocks of identical data to prevent multiple blocks of ciphertext that would identify the blocks of identical input data. There are multiple methods of dealing with this, called *modes of operation.*

There are five common algorithmic modes that are detailed in NIST SP 800-38A, *Recommendation for Block Cipher Modes of Operation: Methods and Techniques*. These algorithms are covered in detail in Chapter 27, and are, Electronic Code Book (ECB), Cipher Block Chaining (CBC), Cipher Feedback Mode (CFB), Output Feedback Mode (OFB), and Counter Mode (CTR).

Asymmetric Algorithms

Asymmetric algorithms comprise a type of cryptography more commonly known as *public key cryptography*. Asymmetric cryptography is in many ways completely different from symmetric cryptography. While both are used to keep data from being seen by unauthorized users, asymmetric cryptography uses two keys instead of one. It was invented by Whitfield Diffie and Martin Hellman in 1975. The system uses a pair of keys: a private key that is kept secret and a public key that can be sent to anyone. The system's security relies upon resistance to deducing one key, given the other, and thus retrieving the plaintext from the ciphertext.

Public key systems typically work by using complex math problems. One of the more common methods is through the difficulty of factoring large numbers. These functions are often called *trapdoor functions*, as they are difficult to process without the key, but easy to process when you have the key—the trapdoor through the function. For example, given a prime number, say 293, and another prime, such as 307, it is an easy function to multiply them together to get 89,951. Given 89,951, it is not simple to find the factors 293 and 307 unless you know one of them already. Computers can easily multiply very large primes with hundreds or thousands of digits, but cannot easily factor the product.

The strength of these functions is very important: because an attacker is likely to have access to the public key, he can run tests of known plaintext and produce ciphertext. This allows instant checking of guesses that are made about the keys of the algorithm. RSA, Diffie-Hellman, elliptic curve cryptography (ECC), and ElGamal are all popular asymmetric protocols.

Asymmetric encryption enables digital signatures and also corrects the main weakness of symmetric cryptography. The ability to send messages securely without senders and receivers having had prior contact has become one of the basic concerns with secure communication. Digital signatures enable faster and more efficient exchange of all kinds of documents, including legal documents. With strong algorithms and good key lengths, security can be assured.

Asymmetric cryptography involves two separate but mathematically related keys. The keys are used in an opposing fashion. One key undoes the actions of the other and vice versa. So, as shown in Figure 26-2, if you encrypt a message with one key, the other key is used to decrypt the message. In the top example, Alice wishes to send a private message to Bob. So, she uses Bob's public key to encrypt the message. Then, since only Bob's private key can decrypt the message, only Bob can read it. In the lower example, Bob wishes to send a message, with proof that it is from him. By encrypting it with his private key, anyone who decrypts it with his public key knows the message came from Bob.

Asymmetric keys are distributed using certificates. A digital certificate contains information about the association of the public key to an entity, and additional information that can be used to verify the current validity of the certificate and the key. When keys

Figure 26-2
Using an asymmetric algorithm

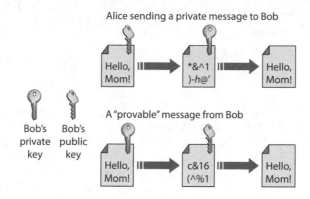

<are exchanged between machines, such as during an SSL/TLS handshake, the exchange
is done by passing certificates.

EXAM TIP Public key cryptography always involves two keys, a public key
and a private key, which together are known as a *key pair*. The public key is
made widely available to anyone who may need it, while the private key is
closely safeguarded and shared with no one.

Symmetric vs. Asymmetric

Both symmetric and asymmetric encryption methods have advantages and disadvantages. Symmetric encryption tends to be faster, is less computationally involved, and is better for bulk transfers. But it suffers from a key management problem in that keys must be protected from unauthorized parties. Asymmetric methods resolve the key secrecy issue with public keys, but add significant computational complexity that makes them less suited for bulk encryption.

Bulk encryption can be done using the best of both systems by using asymmetric encryption to pass a symmetric key. By adding in ephemeral key exchange, you can achieve perfect forward secrecy, discussed later in the chapter. Digital signatures, a highly useful tool, are not practical without asymmetric methods.

Hashing

Hashing functions are commonly used encryption methods. A hashing algorithm is a special mathematical function that performs one-way encryption, which means that once the algorithm is processed, there is no feasible way to use the ciphertext to retrieve the plaintext that was used to generate it. Also, ideally, there is no feasible way to generate two different plaintexts that compute to the same hash value. Figure 26-3 shows a generic hashing process.

Common uses of hashing algorithms are to store computer passwords and to ensure message integrity. The idea is that hashing can produce a unique value that corresponds to the data entered, but the hash value is also reproducible by anyone else running the same algorithm against the data. So you could hash a message to get a message authentication

PART VI

Figure 26-3
How hashes work

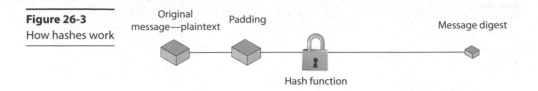

Original
message—plaintext

Padding

Hash function

Message digest

code (MAC), and the computational number of the message would show that no intermediary has modified the message. This process works because hashing methods are typically public, and anyone can hash data using the specified method. It is computationally simple to generate the hash, so it is simple to check the validity or integrity of something by matching the given hash to one that is locally generated. *HMAC*, or *Hashed Message Authentication Code*, is a special subset of hashing technology. It is a hash algorithm applied to a message to make a MAC, but it is done with a previously shared secret. So, the HMAC can provide integrity simultaneously with authentication.

A hash algorithm can be compromised with what is called a *collision attack*, in which an attacker finds two different messages that hash to the same value. This type of attack is very difficult and requires generating a separate algorithm that will attempt to find a text that will hash to the same value of a known hash. This must occur faster than simply editing characters until you hash to the same value, which is a brute-force type attack. The consequence of a hash function that suffers from collisions is that integrity is lost. If an attacker can make two different inputs purposefully hash to the same value, she might trick people into running malicious code and cause other problems. Popular hash algorithms are the *Secure Hash Algorithm (SHA)* series, the *RIPEMD* algorithms, and the *Message Digest (MD)* hash of varying versions (MD2, MD4, MD5).

EXAM TIP The hashing algorithms in common use are MD2, MD4, MD5, SHA-1, SHA-256, SHA-384, and SHA-512.

Hashing functions are very common, and they play an important role in the way information, such as passwords, is stored securely and the way in which messages can be signed. By computing a digest of the message, less data needs to be signed by the more complex asymmetric encryption, and this still maintains assurances about message integrity. This is the primary purpose for which the protocols were designed, and their success will allow greater trust in electronic protocols and digital signatures.

Salt, IV, Nonce

To provide sufficient entropy for low-entropy inputs to hash functions, the addition of a high-entropy piece of data concatenated with the material being hashed can be used. The term *salt* refers to this initial data piece. Salts are particularly useful when the material being hashed is short and low in entropy. For example, the addition of a high-entropy, 30-character salt to a 3-character password greatly increases the entropy of the stored hash.

As introduced in Chapter 2, an *initialization vector*, or *IV*, is used in several ciphers, particularly in the wireless space, to achieve randomness even with normally deterministic inputs. IVs can add randomness and are used in block ciphers to initiate modes of operation.

A *nonce* is similar to a salt or an IV, but it is only used once, and if needed again, a different value is used. Nonces provide random, nondeterministic entropy in cryptographic functions and are commonly used in stream ciphers to break stateful properties when the key is reused.

Elliptic Curve

Elliptic curve cryptography (ECC) works on the basis of elliptic curves. An *elliptic curve* is a simple function that is drawn as a gently looping curve on the X, Y plane. Elliptic curves are defined by this equation:

$$y^2 = x^3 + ax^2 + b$$

Elliptic curves work because they have a special property—you can add two points on the curve together and get a third point on the curve.

For cryptography, the elliptic curve works as a public key algorithm. Users agree on an elliptic curve and a fixed curve point. This information is not a shared secret, and these points can be made public without compromising the security of the system. User 1 then chooses a secret random number, K_1, and computes a public key based upon a point on the curve:

$$P_1 = K_1 \times F$$

User 2 performs the same function and generates P_2. Now user 1 can send user 2 a message by generating a shared secret:

$$S = K_1 \times P_2$$

User 2 can generate the same shared secret independently:

$$S = K_2 \times P_1$$

This is true because

$$K_1 \times P_2 = K_1 \times (K_2 \times F) = (K_1 \times K_2) \times F = K_2 \times (K_1 \times F) = K_2 \times P_1$$

The security of elliptic curve systems has been questioned, mostly because of lack of analysis. However, all public key systems rely on the difficulty of certain math problems. It would take a breakthrough in math for any of the mentioned systems to be weakened dramatically, but research has been done about the problems and has shown that the elliptic curve problem has been more resistant to incremental advances. Again, as with all cryptography algorithms, only time will tell how secure they really are. The big benefit of ECC systems is that they require less computing power for a given bit strength. This makes ECC ideal for use in low-power mobile devices. The surge in mobile connectivity has brought secure voice, e-mail, and text applications that use ECC and AES algorithms to protect a user's data.

PART VI

Weak/Deprecated Algorithms

Over time, cryptographic algorithms fall to different attacks or just the raw power of computation. The challenge is understanding which algorithms have fallen to attacks and avoiding their use, even if they are still available for use in software libraries. Although this list will continue to grow, it is important to consider this topic, for old habits die hard. Hash algorithms, such as MD5, should be considered inappropriate, as manufactured collisions have been achieved. Even newer hash functions have issues, such as SHA-1 (and soon SHA-256). The Data Encryption Standard, DES, and its commonly used stronger form 3DES, have fallen from favor. The good news is that new forms of these functions are widely available, and in many cases, such as AES, are computationally efficient, providing better performance.

Key Exchange

Cryptographic mechanisms use both an algorithm and a key, with the key requiring communication between parties. In symmetric encryption, the secrecy depends upon the secrecy of the key, so insecure transport of the key can lead to failure to protect the information encrypted using the key. *Key exchange* is the central foundational element of a secure symmetric encryption system. Maintaining the secrecy of the symmetric key is the basis of secret communications. In asymmetric systems, the key exchange problem is one of key publication. Because public keys are designed to be shared, the problem is reversed from one of secrecy to one of publicity.

Early key exchanges were performed by trusted couriers. People carried the keys from senders to receivers. One could consider this form of key exchange to be the ultimate in out-of-band communication. With the advent of digital methods and some mathematical algorithms, it is possible to pass keys in a secure fashion. This can occur even when all packets are subject to interception. The Diffie-Hellman key exchange is one example of this type of secure key exchange. The Diffie-Hellman key exchange depends upon two random numbers, each chosen by one of the parties and kept secret. Diffie-Hellman key exchanges can be performed in-band, and even under external observation, as the secret random numbers are never exposed to outside parties.

 EXAM TIP Security+ exam objective 6.1 is to compare and contrast basic concepts of cryptography. Understanding the differences between symmetric, asymmetric, and other concepts from a description of events is important to master.

Cryptographic Objectives

Cryptographic methods exist for a purpose: to protect the integrity and confidentiality of data. There are many associated elements with this protection to enable a system-wide solution. Elements such as perfect forward secrecy, non-repudiation, key escrow, and others enable successful cryptographic implementations.

Digital Signatures

A *digital signature* is a cryptographic implementation designed to demonstrate authenticity and identity associated with a message. Using public key cryptography, a digital signature allows traceability to the person signing the message through the use of their private key. The addition of hash codes allows for the assurance of integrity of the message as well. The operation of a digital signature is a combination of cryptographic elements to achieve a desired outcome. The steps involved in digital signature generation and use are illustrated in Figure 26-4. The message to be signed is hashed, and the hash is encrypted using the sender's private key. Upon receipt, the recipient can decrypt the hash using the sender's public key. If a subsequent hashing of the message reveals an identical value, two things are known: First, the message has not been altered. Second, the sender possessed the private key of the named sender, so is presumably the sender him- or herself.

A digital signature does not by itself protect the contents of the message from interception. The message is still sent in the clear, so if confidentiality of the message is a requirement, additional steps must be taken to secure the message from eavesdropping. This can be done by encrypting the message itself, or by encrypting the channel over which it is transmitted.

Figure 26-4
Digital signature operation

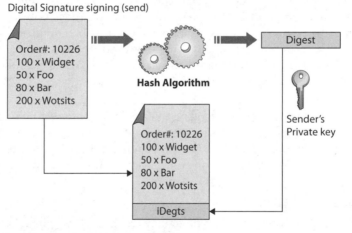

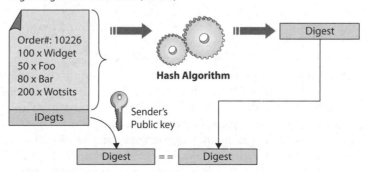

If the digests match, message authenticity and integrity are assured.

Diffusion

Diffusion is a principle that the statistical analysis of plaintext and ciphertext results in a form of dispersion rendering one structurally independent of the other. In plain terms, a change in one character of plaintext should result in multiple changes in the ciphertext in a manner that changes in ciphertext do not reveal information as to the structure of the plaintext.

Confusion

Confusion is a principle to affect the randomness of an output. The concept is operationalized by ensuring that each character of ciphertext depends on several parts of the key. Confusion places a constraint on the relationship between the ciphertext and the key employed, forcing an effect that increases entropy.

Collision

A *collision* is when two different inputs have the same output on a cryptographic function such as a hash. Since inputs to a hash function are technically infinite (unlimited in length) and the number of unique outputs is limited by hash size, collisions have to occur. The issue is whether one can manufacture a collision using cryptanalysis methods. As mentioned earlier in the chapter, this form of attack is known as a collision attack, and practical forms of this attack are possible with the computer power available on a desktop. If two inputs can be generated that produce the same hash value, this enables the movement of a digital signature from an original to a near duplicate, resulting in the failure of the digital signature to protect an original.

 EXAM TIP Understanding the difference between diffusion and confusion is important. Collision seems like it fits with these terms, but it is about something totally different. Do not allow some common words to confuse you in the heat of the exam. Learn the definitions of the vocabulary terms.

Steganography

Steganography, an offshoot of cryptography technology, gets its meaning from the Greek word "steganos," meaning covered. Invisible ink placed on a document and hidden by innocuous text is an example of a steganographic message. Another example is a tattoo placed on the top of a person's head, visible only when the person's hair is shaved off.

Hidden writing in the computer age relies on a program to hide data inside other data. The most common application is the concealing of a text message in a picture file. The Internet contains multiple billions of image files, allowing a hidden message to be located almost anywhere without being discovered. The nature of the image files also makes a hidden message difficult to detect. While it is most common to hide messages inside images, they can also be hidden in video and audio files.

The advantage to steganography over cryptography is that the messages do not attract attention, and this difficulty in detecting the hidden message provides an additional barrier to analysis. The data that is hidden in a steganographic message is frequently also encrypted, so should it be discovered, the message will remain secure. Steganography has many uses, but the most publicized uses are to hide illegal material, often pornography, and allegedly for covert communication by terrorist networks. Terrorists have used steganography to distribute materials via the web, and the techniques have been documented in some of their training materials.

Steganographic encoding can be used in many ways and through many different media. Covering them all is beyond the scope of this book, but we will discuss one of the most common ways to encode into an image file, LSB encoding. LSB, Least Significant Bit, is a method of encoding information into an image while altering the actual visual image as little as possible. A computer image is made up of thousands or millions of pixels, all defined by 1s and 0s. If an image is composed of Red Green Blue (RGB) values, each pixel has an RGB value represented numerically from 0 to 255. For example, 0,0,0 is black, and 255,255,255 is white, which can also be represented as 00000000, 00000000, 00000000 for black and 11111111, 11111111, 11111111 for white. Given a white pixel, editing the least significant bit of the pixel to 11111110, 11111110, 11111110 changes the color. The change in color is undetectable to the human eye, but in an image with a million pixels, this creates a 125KB area in which to store a message.

Obfuscation

Obfuscation is the masking of an item to render it unreadable yet still usable. Consider source code as an example. If the source code is written in a manner that it is easily understood, then its functions can be easily recognized and copied. Code obfuscation is the process of making the code unreadable by adding complexity at the time of creation. This "mangling" of code makes it impossible to easily understand, copy, fix, or maintain. Using cryptographic functions to obfuscate materials is more secure in that it is not reversible without the secret element, but this also renders the code unusable until it is decoded.

Program obfuscation can be achieved in many forms, from tangled C functions with recursion and other indirect references that make reverse engineering difficult, to proper encryption of secret elements. Storing secret elements directly in source code does not really obfuscate them, because numerous methods can be used to find hard-coded secrets in code. Proper obfuscation requires the use of cryptographic functions against a non-reversible element. An example is the storing of password hashes. If the original password is hashed with the addition of a salt, reversing the stored hash is practically not feasible, making the key information, the password, obfuscated.

Stream vs. Block

When encryption operations are performed on data, there are two primary modes of operation, block and stream. Block operations are performed on blocks of data, enabling both transposition and substitution operations. This is possible when large pieces of data are present for the operations. Stream data has become more common with audio and video across the Web. The primary characteristic of stream data is that it is not available in large chunks, but either bit by bit or byte by byte, pieces too small for block operations. Stream ciphers operate using substitution only and therefore offer less robust protection than block ciphers. A table comparing and contrasting block and stream ciphers is presented in Table 26-1.

Block Ciphers	Stream Ciphers
Require more memory to process	Faster than block in operation
Stronger	More difficult to implement correctly
High diffusion	Low diffusion
Resistant to insertions/modifications	Susceptible to insertions and/or modifications
Susceptible to error propagation	Low error propagation
Can provide for authentication and integrity verification	Cannot provide integrity or authentication protections
Common algorithms: 3DES, AES	Common algorithms: A5, RC4

Table 26-1 Comparison of Block and Stream Ciphers

 EXAM TIP Compare and contrast are common objectives in the Security+ exam—comparing and contrasting block and stream ciphers is a prime exam target.

Key Strength

The strength of a cryptographic function typically depends upon the strength of a key: a larger key has more entropy and adds more strength to an encryption. Because different algorithms use different methods with a key, direct comparison of key strength between different algorithms is not easily done. Some cryptographic systems have fixed key lengths, such as 3DES, while others, such as AES have multiple lengths, AES-128, AES-192, and AES-256.

Session Keys

A *session key* is a symmetric key used for encrypting messages during a communication session. It is generated from random seeds and is used for the duration of a communication session. When correctly generated and propagated during session setup, a session key provides significant levels of protection during the communication session and also can afford perfect forward secrecy (described later in the chapter). Session keys offer the advantages of symmetric encryption, speed, strength and simplicity, and, with key exchanges possible via digital methods, significant levels of automated security.

Ephemeral Key

Ephemeral keys are cryptographic keys that are used only once after generation. When an ephemeral key is used as part of the Diffie-Hellman scheme, it forms an Ephemeral Diffie-Hellman (EDH) key exchange. An EDH key exchange generates a temporary key for each connection, never using the same key twice. This provides for perfect forward secrecy.

Secret Algorithm

Algorithms can be broken into two types: those with published details and those whose steps are kept secret. Secrecy has its uses in security. Keeping your password secret, for instance, is an essential element in its proper functionality. Secrecy in how to apply security elements can assist in thwarting reverse engineering. An example of this is the use of multiple rounds of multiple hash functions to provide password security. Although the developers of a secret algorithm must understand how many rounds to use and the proper order of algorithmic application, users don't need to know those details because they are encoded into the application itself. Keeping this secret can enhance security because it makes reverse engineering difficult, if not impossible.

The drawback of keeping a cryptographic algorithm secret is that it reduces the testing of the algorithm by cryptographers. The most secure algorithms are those that have survived over time the onslaught of cryptographic researchers attacking them.

Data-in-Transit

Transport encryption is used to protect *data-in-transit*, or data that is in motion. When data is being transported across a network, it is at risk of interception. An examination of the OSI networking model shows a layer dedicated to transport, and this abstraction can be used to manage end-to-end cryptographic functions for a communication channel. When utilizing the TCP/IP protocol, Transport Layer Security (TLS) is one specific method of managing security at the transport level. Secure Sockets Layer (SSL) is another example. Managing a secure layer of communications is an essential element in many forms of computer operations.

Data-at-Rest

Protecting *data-at-rest* is the most prominent use of encryption, and is typically referred to as data encryption. Whole disk encryption of laptop data to provide security in the event of device loss is an example of data-at-rest protection. The same concept applies to data being stored in the cloud, where encryption can protect against unauthorized reading.

Data-in-Use

Data-in-use is the term used to describe data that is stored in a non-persistent state of either RAM, CPU caches, or CPU registers. Data-in-use is of increasing concern to security professionals as attacks such as RAM scraping malware are occurring. Data-in-use is still data that requires protection, and in modern secure systems, this data can be encrypted. New techniques, such as Intel's Software Guard Extensions (SGX), promise a future where sensitive data can be protected from all other processes on a system, even those with higher levels of authority, such as root.

 EXAM TIP Data-in-transit, data-at-rest, and data-in-use are terms commonly used to describe states of data in a computing system. Understanding how to differentiate these terms based on their similarities and differences when it comes to cryptography is a very testable item.

Random/Pseudo-Random Number Generation

Many cryptographic functions require a random number. A true random number has no correlation to previous random numbers, nor future random numbers, and has a uniform frequency distribution over the range of interest. This means that even given all previous numbers, the next number cannot be predicted with any greater probability than by chance. True random numbers are virtually impossible to generate from physical or algorithmic processes because of the influences associated with the underlying process. This leads to the field of pseudo-random numbers, a set of numbers that while statistically appearing to be random with respect to frequency distribution, because they are algorithmically generated, if one knows the algorithm and the seeds, one can predict future values.

For cryptographic purposes, the importance of the unpredictability cannot be over-stated. This has led to a series of specialized *random/pseudo-random number generation* algorithms that minimize the predictability element, making them nearly perfect from a true randomness point of view. When selecting random number generators to be used in cryptographic algorithms, it is very important to use cryptographically secure random number generation methods to prevent introducing flaws into the encryption protections.

Key Stretching

Key stretching is a mechanism that takes what would otherwise be weak keys and "stretches" them to make the system more secure against brute force attacks. Computers have gained so much computational power that hash functions can be computed very quickly, leading to a need for a manner of increasing the workload when computing hashes so that an attacker can't merely compute them all. In the case of a short key, the chance of randomly matching the hash function by use of computational guessing attacks has increased. To make the problem more difficult, either the keyspace must be increased or the computation must be slowed down. Key stretching involves increasing the computational complexity by adding iterative rounds of computations, rounds that cannot be done in parallel. The increase in computational workload becomes significant when done billions of times, making attempts to use a brute force attack much more expensive.

Implementation vs. Algorithm Selection

When using cryptography for protection of data, several factors need to be included in the implementation plan. One of the first decisions is which algorithm to select. The algorithm must be matched to the intended use, and deprecated algorithms must be avoided.

Crypto Service Provider

A *cryptographic service provider (CSP)* is a software library that implements cryptographic functions. CSPs implement encoding and decoding functions, which computer application programs may use, for example, to implement strong user authentication or for secure e-mail. In Microsoft Windows, the Microsoft CryptoAPI (CAPI) is a CSP for all processes that need specific cryptographic functions. This provides a standard implementation of a complex set of processes.

Crypto Modules

A *cryptographic module* is a hardware or software device or component that performs cryptographic operations securely within a physical or logical boundary. Crypto modules use a hardware, software, or hybrid cryptographic engine contained within the boundary, and cryptographic keys that do not leave the boundary, maintaining a level of security. Maintaining all secrets within a specified protected boundary is a foundational element of a secure cryptographic solution.

Perfect Forward Secrecy

Perfect forward secrecy is a property of a public key system in which a key derived from another key is not compromised even if the originating key is compromised in the future. This is especially important in session key generation, where the security of all communication sessions using the key may become compromised; if perfect forward secrecy were not in place, then past messages that had been recorded could be decrypted.

Security Through Obscurity

Security through obscurity is the concept that security can be achieved by hiding what is being secured. This method alone has never been a valid method of protecting secrets. This has been known for centuries. But this does not mean obscurity has no role in security. For example, naming servers after a progressive set of objects, like Greek gods, planet names, or rainbow colors, provides an attacker an easier path once they start obtaining names. Obscurity has a role, making it hard for an attacker to easily guess critical pieces of information, but should not be relied upon as a singular method of protection.

Common Use Cases

Cryptographic services are being employed in more and more systems, and there are many common use cases associated with them. Examples include implementations to support situations such as low power, low latency, and high resiliency, as well as supporting functions such as confidentiality, integrity, and non-repudiation.

Low Power Devices

Low power devices, such as mobile phones and portable electronics, are ubiquitous and require cryptographic functions. Because cryptographic functions tend to take significant computational power, special cryptographic functions, such as elliptic curve cryptography, are well suited for low-power applications.

Low Latency

Some use cases involve *low latency* operations, requiring specialized cryptographic functions to support operations that have extreme time constraints. Stream ciphers are examples of low latency operations.

High Resiliency

High resiliency systems are characterized by functions that are capable of resuming normal operational conditions after an external disruption. The use of cryptographic modules can support resiliency through a standardized implementation of cryptographic flexibility.

Supporting Confidentiality

Protecting data from unauthorized reading is the definition of confidentiality. Cryptography is the primary means of protecting data confidentiality—at rest, in transit, and in use.

Supporting Integrity

Integrity of data is needed in scenarios such as during transfers. Integrity can demonstrate that data has not been altered. The use of message authentication codes (MACs) supported by hash functions is an example of cryptographic services supporting integrity.

Supporting Obfuscation

There are times where information needs to be obfuscated, protected from casual observation. In the case of a program, *obfuscation* can protect the code from observation by unauthorized parties. It is common for computer programs to have variable and function names changed to random names masking their use. Some people will write down things like PIN codes, but change the order of the digits so it is not immediately obvious.

Supporting Authentication

Authentication is a property that deals with the identity of a party, be it a user, a program, or piece of hardware. Cryptographic functions can be employed to demonstrate authentication, such as the validation that an entity has a specific private key, associated with a presented public key, proving identity.

Supporting Non-repudiation

Non-repudiation is a property that deals with the ability to verify that a message has been sent and received so that the sender (or receiver) cannot refute sending (or receiving) the information. An example of this in action is seen with the private key holder relationship. It is assumed that the private key never leaves the possession of the private key holder. Should this occur, it is the responsibility of the holder to revoke the key. Thus, if the private key is used, as evidenced by the success of the public key, then it is assumed that the message was sent by the private key holder. Thus, actions that are signed cannot be repudiated by the holder.

Resource vs. Security Constraints

Cryptographic functions require system resources. Using the proper cryptographic functions for a particular functionality is important for both performance and resource reasons. Determining the correct set of security and resource constraints is an essential beginning step when planning a cryptographic implementation.

EXAM TIP Understanding the different common use cases for cryptography and being able to identify the applicable use case given a scenario is a testable element associated with this section's objective.

Chapter Review

In this chapter, you became acquainted with the principles of cryptography. The chapter opened with the concepts of cryptography, including the description of vocabulary elements associated with general cryptography. It then examined the fundamental concepts of cryptography, encryption, and hashing in terms of the types of algorithms and the types of data. Next, cryptographic objectives, including digital signatures, steganography, diffusion and confusion, as well as others, were presented, followed by an examination of issues such as session keys, key strength, ephemeral keys, and key stretching. The chapter concluded with topics associated with use cases and implementation details, including an introduction to cryptographic service providers and modules; use of cryptology for confidentiality, integrity, and non-repudiation; and adoptions of cryptology in low-power, high-resiliency, and low-latency situations.

Questions

To help you prepare further for the CompTIA Security+ exam, and to test your level of preparedness, answer the following questions and then check your answers against the correct answers at the end of the chapter.

1. What is the difference between linear and differential cryptanalysis?

   A. Differential cryptanalysis can examine symmetric and asymmetric ciphers, whereas linear cryptanalysis only works on symmetric ciphers.

   B. Linear cryptanalysis puts the input text through a simplified cipher, whereas differential cryptanalysis does not.

   C. Unlike differential cryptanalysis, linear cryptanalysis is deprecated because it does not work on newer ciphers.

   D. Differential cryptanalysis cannot take advantage of computational improvements, whereas linear cryptanalysis makes full use of newer computations.

2. What is the oldest form of cryptography?

   A. Asymmetric

   B. Hashing

   C. Digital signatures

   D. Symmetric

3. What kind of cryptography makes key management less of a concern?

    A. Asymmetric

    B. Hashing

    C. Digital signatures

    D. Symmetric

4. Why are computers helpful in the function of public key systems?

    A. They can store keys that are very large in memory.

    B. They provide more efficient SSL key exchange for servers.

    C. They can easily multiply very large prime numbers.

    D. They can encrypt large amounts of data.

5. What is the best way, if any, to get the plaintext from a hash value?

    A. Use linear cryptanalysis.

    B. Factor prime numbers.

    C. You cannot get the plaintext out of a hash value.

    D. Use an ephemeral key.

6. What does a salt do?

    A. It tells the algorithm how many digits of primes to use.

    B. It primes the algorithm by giving it initial noncritical data.

    C. It adds additional rounds to the cipher.

    D. It provides additional entropy.

7. What makes a digitally signed message different from an encrypted message?

    A. A digitally signed message has encryption protections for integrity and non-repudiation, which an encrypted message lacks.

    B. A digitally signed message uses much stronger encryption and is harder to break.

    C. An encrypted message only uses symmetric encryption, whereas a digitally signed message use both asymmetric and symmetric encryption.

    D. There is no difference.

8. Why is LSB encoding the preferred method for steganography?

    A. It uses much stronger encryption.

    B. It applies a digital signature to the message.

    C. It alters the picture the least amount possible.

    D. It provides additional entropy.

9. Why is the random number used in computing called a pseudo-random number?

   A. They could have an unknown number.

   B. Algorithms cannot create truly random numbers.

   C. The numbers have deliberate weaknesses placed in them by the government.

   D. They follow a defined pattern that can be detected.

10. What is the advantage of a crypto module?

    A. Custom hardware adds key entropy.

    B. It performs operations and maintains the key material in a physical or logical boundary.

    C. It performs encryption much faster than general-purpose computing devices.

    D. None of the above.

11. If you need to ensure authentication, confidentiality, and non-repudiation when sending sales quotes, which method best achieves the objective?

    A. Key stretching

    B. Asymmetric encryption

    C. Digital signature

    D. Ephemeral keys

12. Given a large quantity of data in the form of a streaming video file, what is the best type of encryption method to protect the content from unauthorized live viewing?

    A. Symmetric block

    B. Hashing algorithm

    C. Stream cipher

    D. Asymmetric block

13. Why does ECC work well on low-power devices?

    A. Less entropy is needed for a given key strength.

    B. Less computational power is needed for a given key strength.

    C. Less memory is needed for a given key strength.

    D. None of the above.

14. What does Diffie-Hellman allow you to do?

    A. Exchange keys in-band

    B. Exchange keys out-of-band

    C. Both A and B

    D. Neither A nor B

15. In developing a system with a logon requirement, you need to design the system to store passwords. To ensure that the passwords being stored do not divulge secrets, which of the following is the best solution?

   A. Key stretching

   B. Salt

   C. Obfuscation

   D. Secret algorithms

Answers

1. **B.** Differential cryptanalysis works by comparing the input plaintext to the output ciphertext, while linear cryptanalysis runs plaintext through a simplified version of the cipher to attempt to deduce the key.

2. **D.** Symmetric is the oldest form of cryptography.

3. **A.** Asymmetric cryptography makes key management less of a concern because the private key material is never shared.

4. **C.** Computers can easily multiply prime numbers that are many digits in length, improving the security of the cipher.

5. **C.** Hash ciphers are designed to reduce the plaintext to a small value and are built to not allow extraction of the plaintext. This is why they are commonly called "one-way" functions.

6. **D.** The salt adds additional entropy, or randomness, to the encryption key.

7. **A.** The digital signature includes a hash of the message to supply message integrity and uses asymmetric encryption to demonstrate non-repudiation, the fact that the sender's private key was used to sign the message.

8. **C.** LSB, or Least Significant Bit, is designed to place the encoding into the image in the least significant way to avoid altering the image.

9. **B.** Random numbers in a computer are generated by an algorithm, and it is not possible to create truly random numbers, so only numbers that are very close to being random, called pseudo-random numbers, are possible.

10. **B.** Crypto modules, such as smartcards, maintain the key material inside a physical or logical boundary and perform cryptographic operations inside the boundary. This ensures that private key material is kept secure.

11. **C.** Digital signatures can support confidentiality, integrity, and authentication of "signed" materials.

12. C. Stream ciphers work best when the data is in very small chunks to be processed rapidly, such as live streaming video. Block ciphers are better for large chunks of data.

13. B. ECC uses less computational power for a given key strength than traditional asymmetric algorithms.

14. A. Diffie-Hellman allows an in-band key exchange even if the entire data stream is being monitored, because the shared secret is never exposed.

15. B. Salts are used to provide increased entropy and eliminate the problem of identical passwords between accounts.

Cryptographic Algorithms

27

In this chapter, you will
- Identify the different types of cryptography
- Learn about current cryptographic methods
- Understand how cryptography is applied for security
- Given a scenario, utilize general cryptography concepts

Cryptographic systems are composed of two main elements, an algorithm and a key. The key exists to provide a means to alter the encryption from message to message, while the algorithm provides the method of converting plaintext to ciphertext and back. This chapter examines the types and characteristics of cryptographic algorithms.

Certification Objective   This chapter covers CompTIA Security+ exam objective 6.2, Explain cryptography algorithms and their basic characteristics.

Symmetric Algorithms

Symmetric algorithms are characterized by using the same key for both encryption and decryption. Symmetric encryption algorithms are used for bulk encryption because they are comparatively fast and have few computational requirements. Common symmetric algorithms are DES, 3DES, AES, Blowfish, Twofish, RC2, RC4, RC5, and RC6.

EXAM TIP   Ensure you understand DES, 3DES, AES, Blowfish, Twofish, and RC4 symmetric algorithms for the exam.

DES

The *Data Encryption Standard (DES)* was developed in response to the National Bureau of Standards (NBS), now known as the National Institute of Standards and Technology (NIST), issuing a request for proposals for a standard cryptographic algorithm in 1973.

NBS specified that DES had to be recertified every five years. While DES passed without a hitch in 1983, the National Security Agency (NSA) said it would not recertify it in 1987. However, since no alternative was available for many businesses, many complaints ensued, and the NSA and NBS were forced to recertify DES. The algorithm was then recertified in 1993. NIST has now certified the Advanced Encryption Standard (AES) to replace DES.

3DES

Triple DES (3DES) is a follow-on implementation of DES. Depending on the specific variant, it uses either two or three keys instead of the single key that DES uses. It also spins through the DES algorithm three times via what's called *multiple encryption.*

Multiple encryption can be performed in several different ways. The simplest method of multiple encryption is just to stack algorithms on top of each other—taking plaintext, encrypting it with DES, then encrypting the first ciphertext with a different key, and then encrypting the second ciphertext with a third key. In reality, this technique is less effective than the technique that 3DES uses, which is to encrypt with one key, then decrypt with a second, and then encrypt with a third.

This greatly increases the number of attempts needed to retrieve the key and is a significant enhancement of security. The additional security comes with a price, however. It can take up to three times longer to compute 3DES than to compute DES. However, the advances in memory and processing power in today's electronics make this problem irrelevant in all devices except for very small, low power devices.

The only weaknesses of 3DES are those that already exist in DES. However, because different keys are used with the same algorithm in 3DES, the effective key length is longer than the DES keyspace, which results in greater resistance to brute force attack, making 3DES stronger than DES to a wide range of attacks. While 3DES has continued to be popular and is still widely supported, AES has taken over as the symmetric encryption standard.

AES

Because of the advancement of technology and the progress being made in quickly retrieving DES keys, NIST put out a request for proposals (RFP) for a new *Advanced Encryption Standard (AES)*. NIST called for a block cipher using symmetric key cryptography and supporting key sizes of 128, 192, and 256 bits. After evaluation, NIST had five finalists:

- **MARS** IBM
- **RC6** RSA
- **Rijndael** Joan Daemen and Vincent Rijmen
- **Serpent** Ross Anderson, Eli Biham, and Lars Knudsen
- **Twofish** Bruce Schneier, John Kelsey, Doug Whiting, David Wagner, Chris Hall, and Niels Ferguson

In the fall of 2000, NIST picked Rijndael to be the new AES. It was chosen for its overall security as well as its good performance on limited-capacity devices. AES has three different standard key sizes, 128, 192, and 256, designated AES-128, AES-192, and AES-256, respectively.

While no efficient attacks currently exist against AES, more time and analysis will tell if this standard can last as long as DES did.

EXAM TIP In the world of symmetric cryptography, AES is the current gold standard of algorithms. It is considered secure and is computationally efficient.

RC4

RC is a general term for several ciphers all designed by Ron Rivest—RC officially stands for *Rivest Cipher*. RC1, RC2, RC3, RC4, RC5, and RC6 are all ciphers in the series. RC1 and RC3 never made it to release, but RC2, RC4, RC5, and RC6 are all working algorithms.

RC4 was created before RC5 and RC6, but it differs in operation. *RC4* is a stream cipher, whereas all the symmetric ciphers we have looked at so far have been block-mode ciphers. A stream cipher works by enciphering the plaintext in a stream, usually bit by bit. This makes stream ciphers faster than block-mode ciphers. Stream ciphers accomplish this by performing a bitwise XOR with the plaintext stream and a generated key stream. RC4 can use a key length of 8 to 2048 bits, though the most common versions use 128-bit keys. The algorithm is fast, sometimes ten times faster than DES. The most vulnerable point of the encryption is the possibility of weak keys. One key in 256 can generate bytes closely correlated with key bytes. Proper implementations of RC4 need to include weak key detection.

EXAM TIP RC4 is the most widely used stream cipher and is used in popular protocols such as Transport Layer Security (TLS) and Wi-Fi Protected Access (WPA).

Blowfish/Twofish

Blowfish was designed in 1994 by Bruce Schneier. It is a block-mode cipher using 64-bit blocks and a variable key length from 32 to 448 bits. It was designed to run quickly on 32-bit microprocessors and is optimized for situations with few key changes. The only successful cryptanalysis to date against Blowfish has been against variants that used reduced rounds. There does not seem to be a weakness in the full 16-round version.

Twofish was one of the five finalists in the AES competition. Like other AES entrants, it is a block cipher utilizing 128-bit blocks with a variable-length key of up to 256 bits. This algorithm is available for public use, and has proven to be secure. Twofish is an improvement over Blowfish in that it is less vulnerable to certain classes of weak keys.

Cipher Modes

In symmetric or block algorithms, there is a need to deal with multiple blocks of identical data to prevent multiple blocks of ciphertext that would identify the blocks of identical input data. There are multiple methods of dealing with this, called *modes of operation*. This section describes the common modes listed in exam objective 6.2, ECB, CBC, CTM, and GCM.

CBC

Cipher Block Chaining (CBC) is a block mode where each block is XORed with the previous ciphertext block before being encrypted. To obfuscate the first block, an initialization vector (IV) is XORed with the first block before encryption. CBC is one of the most common modes used, but it has two major weaknesses. First, because there is a dependence on previous blocks, the algorithm cannot be parallelized for speed and efficiency. Second, because of the nature of the chaining, a plaintext block can be recovered from two adjacent blocks of ciphertext. An example of this is in the POODLE (Padding Oracle On Downgraded Legacy Encryption) attack. This type of padding attack works because a one-bit change to the ciphertext causes complete corruption of the corresponding block of plaintext, and inverts the corresponding bit in the following block of plaintext, but the rest of the blocks remain intact.

GCM

Galois Counter Mode (GCM) is an extension of CTM with the addition of a Galois mode of authentication. Galois fields are a mathematical representation that has significant utility in practical encoding. The addition of a Galois mode adds an authentication function to the cipher mode. Because the Galois field used in the process can be parallelized, GCM provides an efficient method of adding this capability. GCM is employed in many international standards, including IEEE 802.1ad and 802.1AE. NIST recognized AES-GCM, as well as GCM and GMAC.

ECB

Electronic Code Book (ECB) is the simplest mode operation of all. The message to be encrypted is divided into blocks, and each block is encrypted separately. This has several major issues, most notable of which is that identical blocks yield identical encrypted blocks, telling the attacker that the blocks are identical. ECB is not recommended for use in cryptographic protocols.

 EXAM TIP   ECB is not recommended for use in any cryptographic protocol because it does not provide protection against input patterns or known blocks.

CTM/CTR

Counter Mode (CTM) uses a "counter" function to generate a nonce that is used for each block encryption. The sequence of operations is to take the counter function value

Block Ciphers	Stream Ciphers
Require more memory to process	Faster than block in operation
Stronger	More difficult to implement correctly
High diffusion	Low diffusion
Resistant to insertions/modifications	Susceptible to insertions and/or modifications
Susceptible to error propagation	Low error propagation
Can provide for authentication and integrity verification	Cannot provide integrity or authentication protections
Common algorithms: 3DES, AES	Common algorithms: A5, RC4

Table 27-1   Comparison of Block and Stream Ciphers

(nonce), encrypt using the key, then XOR with plaintext. Each block can be done independently, resulting in the ability to multithread the processing. CTM is also abbreviated CTR in some circles.

 EXAM TIP   CBC and CTM/CTR are considered to be secure and are the most widely used modes.

Stream vs. Block

When encryption operations are performed on data, there are two primary modes of operation, block and stream. *Block* operations are performed on blocks of data, enabling both transposition and substitution operations. This is possible when large pieces of data are present for the operations. Stream operations have become more common with the streaming of audio and video across the Web. The primary characteristic of stream data is that it is not available in large chunks, but rather either bit by bit or byte by byte, pieces too small for block operations. Stream ciphers operate using substitution only and therefore offer less robust protection than block ciphers. Table 27-1 compares and contrasts block and stream ciphers.

Asymmetric Algorithms

Asymmetric cryptography is in many ways completely different from symmetric cryptography. Also known as public key cryptography, *asymmetric algorithms* are built around hard-to-reverse math problems. The strength of these functions is very important: because an attacker is likely to have access to the public key, he can run tests of known plaintext and produce ciphertext. This allows instant checking of guesses that are made about the keys of the algorithm. RSA, DSA, Diffie-Hellman, elliptic curve cryptography (ECC), and PGP/GPG are all popular asymmetric protocols. We will look at all of them and their suitability for different functions.

PART VI

EXAM TIP   Asymmetric methods are significantly slower than symmetric methods and thus are typically not suitable for bulk encryption.

RSA

RSA, one of the first public key cryptosystems ever invented, can be used for both encryption and digital signatures. RSA is named after its inventors, Ron Rivest, Adi Shamir, and Leonard Adleman, and was first published in 1977. This algorithm uses the product of two very large prime numbers and works on the principle of difficulty in factoring such large numbers. It's best to choose large prime numbers from 100 to 200 digits in length that are equal in length.

This is a simple method, but its security has withstood the test of more than 30 years of analysis. Considering the effectiveness of RSA's security and the ability to have two keys, why are symmetric encryption algorithms needed at all? The answer is speed. RSA in software can be 100 times slower than DES, and in hardware, it can be even slower.

As mentioned, RSA can be used for both regular encryption and digital signatures. Digital signatures try to duplicate the functionality of a physical signature on a document using encryption. Typically, RSA and the other public key systems are used in conjunction with symmetric key cryptography. Public key, the slower protocol, is used to exchange the symmetric key (or shared secret), and then the communication uses the faster symmetric key protocol. This process is known as *electronic key exchange*.

DSA

A digital signature is a cryptographic implementation designed to demonstrate authenticity and identity associated with a message. Using public key cryptography, the *digital signature algorithm (DSA)* allows traceability to the person signing the message through the use of their private key. The addition of hash codes allows for the assurance of integrity of the message as well. The operation of a digital signature is a combination of cryptographic elements to achieve a desired outcome. The steps involved in digital signature generation and use are illustrated in Chapter 26.

The common implementation of DSA is a derivative of the ElGamal signature method and is detailed in Federal Information Processing Standard 186 series. It is covered by a patent that the U.S. government has released royalty free worldwide. The most important element in the signature is the per message random signature value k, which needs to change with every signed message and must be kept secret. Reusing this value can lead to the discovery of the private key as demonstrated by an attack on Sony's improper implementation of DSA when signing software for PS3.

Diffie-Hellman

Diffie-Hellman, introduced in Chapter 26, is one of the most common encryption protocols in use today. It plays a role in the electronic key exchange method of the Secure Sockets Layer (SSL) and TLS protocols. It is also used by the Secure Shell (SSH) and

IP Security (IPsec) protocols. Diffie-Hellman is important because it enables the sharing of a secret key between two people who have not contacted each other before.

EXAM TIP Diffie-Hellman is the gold standard for key exchange, and for the exam, you should understand the subtle differences between the forms DHE and ECDHE.

DH Groups

Diffie-Hellman (DH) groups determine the strength of the key used in the key exchange process. Higher group numbers are more secure, but require additional time to compute the key. DH group 1 consists of a 768-bit key, group 2 consists of a 1024-bit key, and group 5 comes with a 1536-bit key. Higher number groups are also supported, with correspondingly longer keys.

DHE

There are several variants of the Diffie-Hellman key exchange. *Diffie-Hellman Ephemeral (DHE)* is a variant where a temporary key is used in the key exchange rather than reusing the same key over and over.

ECDHE

Elliptic Curve Diffie-Hellman (ECDH) is a variant of the Diffie-Hellman protocol that uses elliptic curve cryptography. ECDH can also be used with ephemeral keys, becoming *Elliptic Curve Diffie-Hellman Ephemeral (ECDHE)*, to enable perfect forward secrecy (described in Chapter 26).

Elliptic Curve

Elliptic curve cryptography (ECC) was covered in detail in Chapter 26. What is important to note from a use perspective is that ECC is well suited for platforms with limited computing power, such as mobile devices.

The security of elliptic curve systems has been questioned, mostly because of lack of analysis. However, all public key systems rely on the difficulty of certain math problems. It would take a breakthrough in math for any of the mentioned systems to be weakened dramatically, but research has been done about the problems and has shown that the elliptic curve problem has been more resistant to incremental advances. Again, as with all cryptography algorithms, only time will tell how secure they really are. The big benefit of ECC systems is that they require less computing power for a given bit strength. This makes ECC ideal for use in low power mobile devices. The surge in mobile connectivity has brought secure voice, e-mail, and text applications that use ECC and AES algorithms to protect a user's data.

EXAM TIP Ensure you understand RSA, DSA, ECC, and Diffie-Hellman variants of asymmetric algorithms for the exam.

PGP/GPG

Pretty Good Privacy (PGP), created by Philip Zimmermann in 1991, passed through several versions that were available for free under a noncommercial license. PGP is now a commercial enterprise encryption product offered by Symantec. It can be applied to popular e-mail programs to handle the majority of day-to-day encryption tasks using a combination of symmetric and asymmetric encryption protocols. One of the unique features of PGP is its use of both symmetric and asymmetric encryption methods, accessing the strengths of each method and avoiding the weaknesses of each as well. Symmetric keys are used for bulk encryption, taking advantage of the speed and efficiency of symmetric encryption. The symmetric keys are passed using asymmetric methods, capitalizing on the flexibility of this method.

Gnu Privacy Guard (GPG), also called *GnuPG*, is an open source implementation of the OpenPGP standard. This command-line–based tool is a public key encryption program designed to protect electronic communications such as e-mail. It operates similarly to PGP and includes a method for managing public/private keys.

Hashing Algorithms

Hashing algorithms are cryptographic methods that are commonly used to store computer passwords and to ensure message integrity.

MD5

Message Digest (MD) is the generic version of one of several algorithms that are designed to create a message digest or hash from data input into the algorithm. MD algorithms work in the same manner as SHA (discussed next) in that they use a secure method to compress the file and generate a computed output of a specified number of bits. The MD algorithms were all developed by Ronald L. Rivest of MIT. The current version is MD5, while previous versions were MD2 and MD4. MD5 was developed in 1991 and is structured after MD4 but with additional security to overcome the problems in MD4. In November 2007, researchers published their findings on the ability to have two entirely different Win32 executables with different functionality but the same MD5 hash. This discovery has obvious implications for the development of malware. The combination of these problems with MD5 has pushed people to adopt a strong SHA version for security reasons.

SHA

Secure Hash Algorithm (SHA) refers to a set of hash algorithms designed and published by the National Institute of Standards and Technology (NIST) and the National Security Agency (NSA). These algorithms are included in the SHA standard Federal Information Processing Standards (FIPS) 180-2 and 180-3. Individually, each standard is named SHA-1, SHA-224, SHA-256, SHA-384, and SHA-512. The latter four variants are occasionally referred to as SHA-2. Because of collision-based weaknesses in the SHA-1 and SHA-2 series, NIST conducted a search for a new version, the result of which is known as SHA-3.

SHA-1

SHA-1, developed in 1993, was designed as the algorithm to be used for secure hashing in the U.S. Digital Signature Standard (DSS). It is modeled on the MD4 algorithm and implements fixes in that algorithm discovered by the NSA. It creates a message digest 160 bits long that can be used by the Digital Signature Algorithm (DSA), which can then compute the signature of the message. This is computationally simpler, as the message digest is typically much smaller than the actual message—smaller message, less work. SHA-1 works, as do all hashing functions, by applying a compression function to the data input.

At one time, SHA-1 was one of the more secure hash functions, but it has been found vulnerable to a collision attack. Thus, most implementations of SHA-1 have been replaced with one of the other, more secure SHA versions. The added security and resistance to attack in SHA-1 does require more processing power to compute the hash. In spite of these improvements, SHA-1 is still vulnerable to collisions and is no longer approved for use by government agencies.

SHA-2

SHA-2 is a collective name for SHA-224, SHA-256, SHA-384, and SHA-512. SHA-2 is similar to SHA-1, in that it will also accept input of less than 2^{64} bits and reduces that input to a hash. The SHA-2 series algorithm produces a hash length equal to the number after SHA, so SHA-256 produces a digest of 256 bits. The SHA-2 series became more common after SHA-1 was shown to be potentially vulnerable to a collision attack.

SHA-3

SHA-3 is the name for the SHA-2 replacement. In 2012, the Keccak hash function won the NIST competition and was chosen as the basis for the SHA-3 method. Because the algorithm is completely different from the previous SHA series, it has proved to be more resistant to attacks that are successful against them. Because the SHA-3 series is relatively new, it has not been widely adopted in many cipher suites yet.

 EXAM TIP The SHA-2 and SHA-3 series are currently approved for use. SHA-1 has been discontinued.

HMAC

HMAC, or Hashed Message Authentication Code, is a special subset of hashing technology. Message authentication codes are used to determine if a message has changed during transmission. Using a hash function for message integrity is common practice for many communications. When you add a secret key and crypto function, the MAC becomes a HMAC and you also have the ability to determine authenticity in addition to integrity. Popular hash algorithms are Message Digest (MD5), the Secure Hash Algorithm (SHA) series, and the RIPEMD algorithms.

EXAM TIP The commonly used hash functions in HMAC are MD5, SHA-1, and SHA-256. Although MD5 has been deprecated because of collision attacks, when used in the HMAC function, the attack methodology is not present and the hash function still stands as useful.

RIPEMD

RACE Integrity Primitives Evaluation Message Digest (RIPEMD) is a hashing function developed by the RACE Integrity Primitives Evaluation (RIPE) consortium. It originally provided a 128-bit hash and was later shown to have problems with collisions. RIPEMD was strengthened to a 160-bit hash known as RIPEMD-160 by Hans Dobbertin, Antoon Bosselaers, and Bart Preneel.

RIPEMD-160

RIPEMD-160 is an algorithm based on MD4, but it uses two parallel channels with five rounds. The output consists of five 32-bit words to make a 160-bit hash. There are also larger output extensions of the RIPEMD-160 algorithm. These extensions, RIPEMD-256 and RIPEMD-320, offer outputs of 256 bits and 320 bits, respectively. While these offer larger output sizes, this does not make the hash function inherently stronger.

Key Stretching Algorithms

As described in Chapter 26, *key stretching* is a mechanism that takes what would otherwise be weak keys and "stretches" them to make the system more secure against brute force attacks. A typical methodology used for key stretching involves increasing the computational complexity by adding iterative rounds of computations. To extend a password to a longer length of key, you can run it through multiple rounds of variable-length hashing, each increasing the output by bits over time. This may take hundreds or thousands of rounds, but for single-use computations, the time is not significant. Two common forms of key stretching employed in use today include BCRYPT and Password-Based Key Derivation Function 2.

BCRYPT

BCRYPT is a key-stretching mechanism that uses the Blowfish cipher and salting, and adds an adaptive function to increase the number of iterations. The result is the same as other key-stretching mechanisms (single use is computationally feasible), but when attempting to brute force the function, the billions of attempts make it computationally unfeasible.

PBKDF2

Password-Based Key Derivation Function 2 (PBKDF2) is a key derivation function designed to produce a key derived from a password. This function uses a password or passphrase and a salt and applies an HMAC to the input thousands of times. The repetition makes brute force attacks computationally unfeasible.

Obfuscation

Obfuscation is the purposeful hiding of the meaning of a communication. By itself, obfuscation is weak, because once the method/algorithm used for hiding is discovered, the protection is gone. But it still has use in increasing the complexity of solving the hidden message problem.

XOR

XOR (exclusive OR) is a simple cipher operation and is performed by the addition of the text and the key, using modulus 2 arithmetic. A string of text can be encrypted by applying the bitwise XOR operator to every character using a given key. To decrypt the output, merely reapplying the XOR function with the key will remove the cipher. Both of these operations are exceedingly fast on chips, making this a true line-speed method. XOR is a common component inside many of the more complex cipher algorithms.

The weakness of using the XOR method is when the text length is significantly longer than the key, forcing reuse of the key across the length of the cipher. If the key is as long as the text being encrypted and is never reused, then this forms a perfect cipher from a mathematical perspective.

ROT13

ROT13 is a special case of a Caesar substitution cipher where each character is replaced by a character 13 places later in the alphabet. Because the basic Latin alphabet has 26 letters, ROT13 has the property of undoing itself when applied twice. The following illustration demonstrates ROT13 encoding of "HelloWorld." The top two rows show encoding, while the bottom two show decoding replacement.

	A	B	C	D	E	F	G	H	I	J	K	L	M	N	O	P	Q	R	S	T	U	V	W	X	Y	Z
Encode ↓																										
	N	O	P	Q	R	S	T	U	V	W	X	Y	Z	A	B	C	D	E	F	G	H	I	J	K	L	M
Decode ↓																										
	A	B	C	D	E	F	G	H	I	J	K	L	M	N	O	P	Q	R	S	T	U	V	W	X	Y	Z
Plaintext ↓	H	E	L	L	O	W	O	R	L	D																
Encode ↓																										
Ciphertext ↓	U	R	Y	Y	B	J	B	E	Y	Q																

Substitution Ciphers

Substitution ciphers substitute characters on a character-by-character basis via a specific scheme. The order of the characters in each block is maintained. A transposition cipher is one where the order of the characters is changed per a given algorithm. A simple substitution cipher replaces each character with a corresponding substitute character, the length of the message. Although this has an entropy of 88 bits, because of structures in language, this is relatively easily broken using frequency analysis of the substituted characters.

PART VI

A more complex method is a polyalphabetic substitution, of which the Vigenère cipher is an example, where the substitution alphabet changes with each use of a character. This increases the complexity and thwarts basic frequency analysis as it obscures repeated letters and frequency analysis in general across a message.

Chapter Review

In this chapter, you became acquainted with cryptographic algorithms and their application. The chapter opened with an examination of the symmetric algorithms, AES, DES, 3DES, RC4, and Blowfish/Twofish. Next, the concept of block cipher modes was covered, including ECB, CBC, CTM, and GCM.

The chapter further explored encryption through asymmetric methods, RSA, DSA, Diffie-Hellman, ECC, and PGP/GPG. Hashing algorithms were then covered, including MD5, SHA, and RIPEMD. The chapter then presented key stretching algorithms and closed with an examination of obfuscation using XOR and ROT13.

Questions

To help you prepare further for the CompTIA Security+ exam, and to test your level of preparedness, answer the following questions and then check your answers against the correct answers at the end of the chapter.

1. Your organization wants to deploy a new encryption system that will protect the majority of data with a symmetric cipher of at least 256 bits in strength. What is the best choice of cipher for large amounts of data at rest?

   A. RC4

   B. 3DES

   C. AES

   D. Twofish

2. A colleague who is performing a rewrite of a custom application that was using 3DES encryption asks you how 3DES can be more secure than the DES it is based on. What is your response?

   A. 3DES uses a key that's three times longer.

   B. 3DES loops through the DES algorithm three times, with different keys each time.

   C. 3DES uses transposition versus the substitution used in DES.

   D. 3DES is no more secure than DES.

3. What cipher mode is potentially vulnerable to a POODLE attack?

   A. ECB

   B. CBC

   C. CTR

   D. GCM

4. What cipher mode is used in the IEEE 802.1AE standard and recognized by NIST?

    A. CTR

    B. GCM

    C. CBC

    D. ECB

5. Your manager wants you to spearhead the effort to implement digital signatures in the organization and to report to him what is needed for proper security of those signatures. You likely have to study which algorithm?

    A. RC4

    B. AES

    C. SHA-1

    D. RSA

6. Hashing is most commonly used for which of the following?

    A. Digital signatures

    B. Secure storage of passwords for authentication

    C. Key management

    D. Block cipher algorithm padding

7. A friend at work asks you to e-mail him some information about a project you have been working on, but then requests you "to hide the e-mail from the monitoring systems by encrypting it using ROT13." What is the weakness in this strategy?

    A. ROT13 is a very simple substitution scheme and is well understood by anyone monitoring the system, providing no security.

    B. ROT13 is not an algorithm.

    C. The monitoring system will not allow anything but plaintext to go through.

    D. ROT13 is more secure than is needed for an internal e-mail.

8. Why would you use PBKDF2 as part of your encryption architecture?

    A. To use the speed of the crypto subsystems built into modern CPUs

    B. To increase the number of rounds a symmetric cipher has to perform

    C. To stretch passwords into secure-length keys appropriate for encryption

    D. To add hash-based message integrity to a message authentication code

9. Why are hash collisions bad for malware prevention?

    A. Malware could corrupt the hash algorithm.

    B. Two different programs with the same hash could allow malware to be undetected.

    C. The hashed passwords would be exposed.

    D. The hashes are encrypted and cannot change.

10. What has made the PGP standard popular for so long?

    A. Its flexible use of both symmetric and asymmetric algorithms

    B. Simple trust model

    C. The ability to run on any platform

    D. The peer-reviewed algorithms

11. What is a key consideration when implementing an RC4 cipher system?

    A. Key entropy

    B. External integrity checks

    C. Checks for weak keys

    D. Secure key exchange

12. Why are ephemeral keys important to key exchange protocols?

    A. They are longer than normal keys.

    B. They add entropy to the algorithm.

    C. They allow the key exchange to be completed faster.

    D. They increase security by using a different key for each connection.

Answers

1. **C.** The most likely utilized cipher is AES. It can be run at 128-, 192-, and 256-bit strengths and is considered the gold standard of current symmetric ciphers, with no known attacks, and is computationally efficient.

2. **B.** 3DES can be more secure because it loops through the DES algorithm three times, with a different key each time: encrypt with key 1, decrypt with key 2, and then encrypt with key 3.

3. **B.** Cipher Block Chaining (CBC) mode is vulnerable to a POODLE (Padding Oracle On Downgraded Legacy Encryption) attack, where the system freely responds to a request about a message's padding being correct. Manipulation of the padding is used in the attack.

4. **B.** Galois Counter Mode (GCM) is recognized by NIST and is used in the 802.1AE standard.

5. **D.** Digital signatures require a public key algorithm, so most likely you need to study RSA to provide the asymmetric cryptography.

6. **B.** Hashing is most commonly used to securely store passwords on systems so that users can authenticate to the system.

7. **A.** ROT13 is a simple substitution cipher that is very well known and will be simple for any person or system to decode.

8. **C.** PBKDF2 is a key stretching algorithm that stretches a password into a key of suitable length by adding a salt and then performing an HMAC to the input thousands of times.

9. **B.** The ability to create a program that has the same hash as a known-good program would allow malware to be undetected by detection software that uses a hash list of approved programs.

10. **A.** Pretty Good Privacy (PGP) is a popular standard because of its use of both symmetric and asymmetric algorithms when best suited to the type of encryption being done.

11. **C.** As RC4 is susceptible to weak keys, one key in 256 is considered weak and should not be utilized. Any implementation should have a check for weak keys as part of the protocol.

12. **D.** Ephemeral keys are important to key exchange protocols because they ensure that each connection has its own key for the symmetric encryption, and if an attacker compromises one key, he does not have all the traffic for this connection.

CHAPTER 28

Wireless Security

In this chapter, you will

- Learn about the security implications of wireless networks
- Learn about the security built into different versions of wireless protocols
- Identify the different 802.11 versions and their security controls
- Install and configure wireless security settings

Wireless is increasingly the way people access the Internet. Because wireless access is considered a consumer benefit, many businesses add wireless access points to lure customers into their shops. With the rollout of third-generation (3G) and fourth-generation (4G) cellular networks, people are also increasingly accessing the Internet from their mobile phones. The massive growth in popularity of nontraditional computers such as netbooks, e-readers, and tablets has also driven the popularity of wireless access.

As wireless use increases, the security of the wireless protocols has become a more important factor in the security of the entire network. As a security professional, you need to understand wireless network applications because of the risks inherent in broadcasting a network signal where anyone can intercept it. Sending unsecured information across public airwaves is tantamount to posting your company's passwords by the front door of the building. This chapter looks at several current wireless protocols and their security features.

Certification Objective   This chapter covers CompTIA Security+ exam objective 6.3, Given a scenario, install and configure wireless security settings. This is a good candidate for performance-based questions, which means you should expect questions in which you must apply your knowledge of the topic to a scenario. The best answer to a question will depend upon specific details in the scenario preceding the question, not just the question. The question may also involve tasks other than just picking the best answer from a list. Instead, it may involve actual simulation of steps to take to solve a problem.

Cryptographic Protocols

Wireless networks, by their very nature, make physical security protections against rogue connections difficult. This lack of a physical barrier makes protection against others eavesdropping on a connection also a challenge. *Cryptographic protocols* are the standards used to describe cryptographic methods and implementations to ensure interoperability between different vendors equipment.

WEP

The designers of the 802.11 protocol also attempted to maintain confidentiality in wireless systems by introducing *Wired Equivalent Privacy (WEP)*, which uses a cipher to encrypt the data as it is transmitted through the air. WEP was initially a success, but over time several weaknesses were discovered in this protocol. WEP has been shown to have an implementation problem that can be exploited to break security. WEP encrypts the data traveling across the network with an RC4 stream cipher, attempting to ensure confidentiality. (The details of the RC4 cipher are covered in Chapter 27.) This synchronous method of encryption ensures some method of authentication. The system depends on the client and the access point (AP) having a shared secret key, ensuring that only authorized people with the proper key have access to the wireless network. WEP supports two key lengths, 40 and 104 bits, though these are more typically referred to as 64 and 128 bits. In 802.11a and 802.11g, manufacturers extended this to 152-bit WEP keys. This is because in all cases, 24 bits of the overall key length are used for the initialization vector (IV).

The IV is the primary reason for the weaknesses in WEP. The IV is sent in the plaintext part of the message, and because the total keyspace is approximately 16 million keys, the same key will be reused. Once the key has been repeated, an attacker has two ciphertexts encrypted with the same key stream. This allows the attacker to examine the ciphertext and retrieve the key. This attack can be improved by examining only packets that have weak IVs, reducing the number of packets needed to crack the key. Using only weak IV packets, the number of required captured packets is reduced to around four or five million, which can take only a few hours on a fairly busy AP. For a point of reference, this means that equipment with an advertised WEP key of 128 bits can be cracked in less than a day, whereas to crack a normal 128-bit key would take roughly 2,000,000,000,000,000,000 years on a computer able to attempt one trillion keys a second. AirSnort is a modified sniffing program that can take advantage of this weakness to retrieve the WEP keys.

The biggest weakness of WEP is that the IV problem exists, regardless of key length, because the IV always remains at 24 bits. Most APs also have the ability to lock in access only to known MAC addresses, providing a limited authentication capability. Given sniffers' capacity to grab all active MAC addresses on the network, this capability is not very effective. An attacker simply configures his wireless cards to a known good MAC address.

 EXAM TIP WEP is no longer listed under any Security+ exam objectives, but the facts and background are relevant to WPA and WPA2 and illustrate how we got to where we are.

WPA

The first standard to be used in the market to replace WEP was *Wi-Fi Protected Access (WPA)*. This standard uses the flawed WEP algorithm with the Temporal Key Integrity Protocol (TKIP). TKIP works by using a shared secret combined with the card's MAC address to generate a new key, which is mixed with the IV to make per-packet keys that encrypt a single packet using the same RC4 cipher used by traditional WEP. This overcomes the WEP key weakness, as a key is used on only one packet. The other advantage to this method is that it can be retrofitted to current hardware with only a software change, unlike Advanced Encryption Standard (AES) and 802.1X (an authentication protocol discussed later in the chapter).

While WEP uses a 40-bit or 104-bit encryption key that must be manually entered on wireless access points and devices and does not change, TKIP employs a per-packet key, generating a new 128-bit key for each packet. This can generally be accomplished with only a firmware update, enabling a simple solution to the types of attacks that compromise WEP.

WPA also suffers from a lack of forward secrecy protection. If the WPA key is known, as in a public Wi-Fi password, then an attacker can collect all the packets from all of the connections and decrypt packets later. This is why, when using public Wi-Fi, you should always use a secondary means of protection, either a VPN or a TLS-based solution, to protect your content. These flaws have resulted in WPA being considered a stopgap measure until WPA2 is widely adopted.

WPA2

IEEE 802.11i is the standard for security in wireless networks and is also known as *Wi-Fi Protected Access 2 (WPA2)*. It uses 802.1X to provide authentication and uses AES as the encryption protocol. WPA2 uses the AES block cipher, a significant improvement over WEP's and WPA's use of the RC4 stream cipher. The 802.11i standard specifies the use of CCMP, discussed next.

CCMP

CCMP stands for *Counter Mode with Cipher Block Chaining–Message Authentication Code Protocol* (or Counter Mode with CBC-MAC Protocol). CCMP is a data encapsulation encryption mechanism designed for wireless use. CCMP is actually the mode in which the AES cipher is used to provide message integrity. Unlike WPA, CCMP requires new hardware to perform the AES encryption.

TKIP

Temporal Key Integrity Protocol (TKIP) was created as a stopgap security measure to replace the WEP protocol without requiring the replacement of legacy hardware. The breaking of WEP had left Wi-Fi networks without viable link-layer security, and a solution was required for already deployed hardware. TKIP works by mixing a secret root key with the IV before the RC4 encryption. WPA/TKIP uses the same underlying mechanism as WEP, and consequently is vulnerable to a number of similar attacks. TKIP is no longer considered secure and has been deprecated with the release of WPA2.

 EXAM TIP Understanding which protocol to use based on a scenario requires you to know the differences and reasons for each of the protocols on the exam. The question will focus on the scenario, not the protocols, so you need to be able to apply that logic.

Authentication Protocols

Authentication protocols are the standardized methods used to provide authentication services, and in the case of wireless networks, remotely. Wireless networks have a need for secure *authentication protocols*. You need to understand the following authentication protocols for the Security+ exam: EAP, PEAP, EAP-FAST, EAP-TLS, EAP-TTLS, IEEE 802.1X, and RADIUS via RADIUS Federation sources.

EAP

The *Extensible Authentication Protocol (EAP)* is a protocol for wireless networks that expands on authentication methods used by the Point-to-Point Protocol (PPP). PPP is a protocol that was commonly used to directly connect devices to each other. EAP is designed to support multiple authentication mechanisms, including tokens, smart cards, certificates, one-time passwords, and public key encryption authentication. EAP has been expanded into multiple versions, some of which are covered in the following sections. EAP is defined in RFC 2284 (obsoleted by 3748).

PEAP

PEAP, or *Protected EAP*, was developed to protect the EAP communication by encapsulating it with TLS. This is an open standard developed jointly by Cisco, Microsoft, and RSA. EAP was designed assuming a secure communication channel. PEAP provides that protection as part of the protocol via a TLS tunnel. PEAP is widely supported by vendors for use over wireless networks.

EAP-FAST

The Wi-Fi Alliance added EAP-FAST to its list of supported protocols for WPA/WPA2 in 2010. *EAP-FAST (EAP Flexible Authentication via Secure Tunneling)* is described in RFC 4851 and proposed by Cisco to be a replacement for LEAP, a previous Cisco version of EAP. It offers a lightweight tunneling protocol to enable authentication. The distinguishing characteristic is the passing of a Protected Access Credential (PAC) that is used to establish a TLS tunnel through which client credentials are verified.

EAP-TLS

The Wi-Fi Alliance also added EAP-TLS to its list of supported protocols for WPA/WPA2 in 2010. *EAP-TLS* is an IETF open standard (RFC 5216) that uses the Transport Layer Security (TLS) protocol to secure the authentication process. EAP-TLS relies on Transport Layer Security (TLS), an attempt to standardize the SSL structure to pass credentials. This is still considered one of the most secure implementations, primarily because common implementations employ client-side certificates. This means that an attacker must also possess the key for the client-side certificate to break the TLS channel.

EAP-TTLS

The Wi-Fi Alliance also added EAP-TTLS to its list of supported protocols for WPA/WPA2 in 2010. EAP-TTLS (the acronym stands for EAP–Tunneled TLS Protocol) is a variant of the EAP-TLS protocol. EAP-TTLS works much the same way as EAP-TLS, with the server authenticating to the client with a certificate, but the protocol tunnels the client side of the authentication, allowing the use of legacy authentication protocols such as Password Authentication Protocol (PAP), Challenge-Handshake Authentication Protocol (CHAP), MS-CHAP, or MS-CHAP-V2. In EAP-TTLS, the authentication process is protected by the tunnel from man-in-the-middle attacks, and although client-side certificates can be used, they are not required, making this easier to set up than EAP-TLS to clients without certificates.

 EXAM TIP There are two key elements concerning EAP. First, it is only a framework to secure the authentication process, not an actual encryption method. Second, many variants exist, and understanding the differences, and how to recognize them in practice, between EAP, EAP-FAST, EAP-TLS, and EAP-TTLS is important for the exam.

IEEE 802.1X

IEEE 802.1X is an authentication standard that supports port-based authentication services between a user and an authorization device, such as an edge router. IEEE 802.1X is commonly used on wireless access points as a port-based authentication service prior to admission to the wireless network. IEEE 802.1X over wireless uses either IEEE 802.11i or EAP-based protocols, such as EAP-TLS or PEAP-TLS.

RADIUS Federation

Using a series of RADIUS servers in a federated connection has been employed in several worldwide *RADIUS federation* networks. One example is the EDUROAM project that connects users of education institutions worldwide. The process is relatively simple in concept, although the technical details to maintain the hierarchy of RADIUS servers and routing tables is daunting at worldwide scale. A user packages their credentials at a local access point using a certificate-based tunneling protocol method. The first RADIUS server determines which RADIUS server to send the request to, and from there the user is authenticated via their home RADIUS server and the results are passed back, permitting a joining to the network.

Because the credentials must pass multiple different networks, the EAP methods are limited to those with certificates and credentials to prevent loss of credentials during transit. This type of federated identity at global scale demonstrates the power of RADIUS and EAP methods.

Methods

As previously described, historically, multiple protocols have been developed to support the securing of wireless networks, including WEP, WPA, and WPA2. WEP is by all practical means no longer a viable method of maintaining any significant security. WPA is not much better, which leaves us primarily with WPA2. WPA2 has several modes, PSK and Enterprise, which will be discussed below. In an attempt to simplify setup for home users, WPS was created and it will be covered in the next section. The final method is the captive portal, a means of capturing a guest user and forcing a sign-in process across a web-based connection to establish a connection to an open Wi-Fi network.

 EXAM TIP CompTIA expects you to understand several methods of installing and configuring wireless security settings, including the WPA2 options, Wi-Fi Protected Setup, and the captive portal, a means of capturing a guest user and forcing a sign-in process across a web-based connection to establish a connection to an open Wi-Fi network.

PSK vs. Enterprise vs. Open

When building out a wireless network, you must decide how you are going to employ security on the network. Specifically, you need to address who will be allowed to connect, and what level of protection will be provided in the transmission of data between mobile devices and the access point.

Both WPA and WPA2, discussed in detail earlier in the chapter, have two methods to establish a connection, PSK and Enterprise. *PSK* stands for pre-shared key, which is exactly what it sounds like, a secret that has to be shared between users. A PSK is typically entered as a passphrase of up to 63 characters. This key must be securely shared between users, as it is the basis of the security provided by the protocol. The PSK is converted to a 256-bit key that is then used to secure all communications between the device and access point. PSK has one particular vulnerability: simple and short PSKs are at risk of brute force attempts. Keeping the PSK at least 20 random characters long or longer should mitigate this attack vector.

In *Enterprise* mode, the devices use IEEE 802.1X and a RADIUS authentication server to enable a connection. This method allows the use of usernames and passwords and provides enterprise-class options such as network access control (NAC) integration, multiple random keys, instead of everyone sharing the same PSK. If everyone has the same PSK, then secrecy between clients is limited to other means, and in the event of one client failure, others could be compromised.

In WEP-based systems, there are two options, *Open System* authentication and shared key authentication. Open System authentication is not truly authentication, for it is merely a sharing of a secret key based on the SSID. The process is simple: the mobile client matches SSID with the access point and requests a key (called authentication) to the access point. Then the access point generates an authentication code (the key, as there is no specific authentication of the client), a random number intended for use only during that session. The mobile client uses the authentication code and joins the network. The session continues until disassociation either by request or loss of signal.

 EXAM TIP Understand the differences between PSK, Enterprise, and Open authentication.

WPS

Wi-Fi Protected Setup (WPS) is a network security standard that was created to provide users with an easy method of configuring wireless networks. Designed for home networks and small business networks, this standard involves the use of an eight-digit PIN to configure wireless devices. WPS consists of a series of EAP messages and has been shown to be susceptible to a brute force attack. A successful attack can reveal the PIN and subsequently the WPA/WPA2 passphrase and allow unauthorized parties to gain access to the network. Currently, the only effective mitigation is to disable WPS.

Setting Up WPA2

If WPS is not safe for use, how does one set up WPA2? To set up WPA2, you need to have several parameters. Figure 28-1 shows the screens for a WPA2 setup in Windows.

The first element is to choose a security framework. When configuring an adapter to connect to an existing network, you need to match the choice of the network. When setting up your own network, you can choose whichever option you prefer. There are many selections, but for security purposes, you should choose WPA2-Personal (PSK) or WPA2-Enterprise. Both of these require the choice of an encryption type, either TKIP or AES. TKIP has been deprecated, so choose AES. The last element is the choice of the network security key—the secret that is shared by all users. WPA2-Enterprise, which is designed to be used with an 802.1X authentication server that distributes different keys to each user, is typically used in business environments. These elements set up Windows for connection to the router, whose settings are shown in Figure 28-2. In reality, the settings are established by the router, so the clients need to match what the access point is offering if they are to connect, so the "master" is the access point or router.

Captive Portals

Captive portal refers to a specific technique of using an HTTP client to handle authentication on a wireless network. Frequently employed in public hotspots, a captive portal opens a web browser to an authentication page. This occurs before the user is granted admission to the network. The access point uses this simple mechanism by intercepting

PART VI

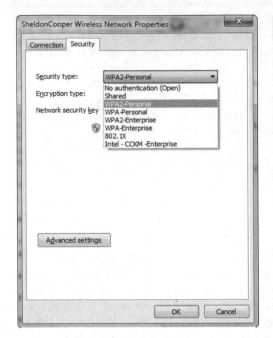

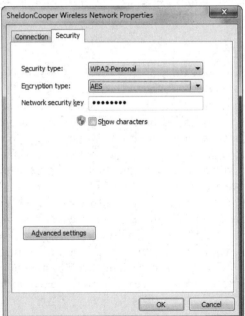

Figure 28-1   WPA2 setup options in Windows

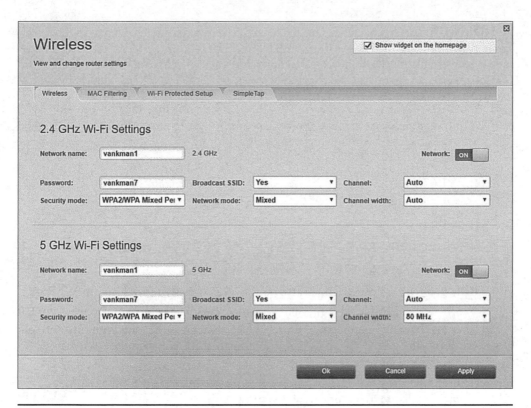

Figure 28-2 WPA2 setup options on an access point/wireless router.

all packets and returning the web page for login. The actual web server that serves up the authentication page can be in a walled-off section of the network, blocking access to the Internet until the user successfully authenticates.

Chapter Review

In this chapter, you became acquainted with the cryptographic protocols, authentication protocols, and methods utilized to secure wireless traffic. Wireless networking uses a specific set of cryptographic protocols, beginning with the now deprecated WEP, and progressing through WPA and WPA2. The protocols of CCMP and TKIP are utilized in securing wireless connections.

Authentication is achieved via EAP and a whole host of variants of EAP, including PEAP, EAP-FAST, EAP-TLS, and EAP-TTLS. Additionally, IEEE 802.1X and RADIUS federation can be employed for authentication.

Setting up the correct set of protocols to secure wireless is done by using one of several methods. Both WPA and WPA2 offer PSK and Enterprise options, whereas WEP-based systems offer Open System authentication and shared key authentication. WEP should be avoided today because of its inherent weaknesses. Other methods include WPS or manually setting up WPA2, or in the case of third-party providers, the use of captive portals.

Questions

To help you prepare further for the CompTIA Security+ exam, and to test your level of preparedness, answer the following questions and then check your answers against the correct answers at the end of the chapter.

1. You are building out a corporate Wi-Fi network that is intended for use only by corporate employees using corporate laptops (no guest access) and must be highly secure. Which of the following is the best solution?

   A. WPA

   B. WPA2-PSK

   C. WPA2-Enterprise

   D. WPS

2. Why would WPA be considered a stopgap fix for the issues with WEP?

   A. It modernizes Wi-Fi with a new encryption cipher.

   B. It provides for using temporary WEP keys to avoid the weakness in WEP, but does not replace the underlying encryption cipher.

   C. It overlays TLS connections on top of the existing WEP encryption to tunnel all traffic back to the access point, but it does not enhance the underlying encryption cipher.

   D. It enforces the use of long-key WEP while having an autogenerated MAC filtering list to avoid potential eavesdropping.

3. List four Wi-Fi authentication protocols:

   _____

   _____

   _____

   _____

4. You are tasked with the implementation of Wi-Fi in Enterprise mode. The initial network diagram shows only the updated access points and network switches. What component is missing from the diagram?

   A. Guest wireless

   B. NAC server

   C. Authentication server

   D. Certificate authority

5. Why is WPA2-Personal not ideal for a large organization?

   A. It has weak encryption.

   B. The pre-shared key must be securely shared with all users.

    C. It has only an eight-digit pin.

    D. It uses Open System authentication.

6. How does Open System authentication differ from a pre-shared key?

    A. Open System authentication only matches the SSID of the system, which is part of all the Wi-Fi packets, so there is no real authentication as with a pre-shared key.

    B. Open System authentication uses a more complex hashing algorithm to pad the encryption key.

    C. Open System authentication requires a RADIUS server.

    D. Open System authentication is best suited for Enterprise applications.

7. Why is enabling WPS not recommended?

    A. It uses WEP-based encryption.

    B. The lack of support for AES.

    C. The use of an eight-digit PIN makes it susceptible to brute force attacks.

    D. All of the above.

8. You are implementing a new wireless system to allow access in all buildings of your corporate campus. You have selected WPA2-Enterprise with 802.1X and a RADIUS server. What is the most efficient way to allow visitors access to the wireless network?

    A. Set up an air-gapped wireless network with Open System authentication enabled so that visitors can easily get access.

    B. Have a series of one-time-use authentication tokens available at the front guard desk so that visitors can use 802.1X and the RADIUS server.

    C. Add all visitors to your Active Directory so they can log onto the wireless natively.

    D. Implement a captive portal.

9. What is the primary vulnerability of pre-shared keys?

    A. They have a weak initialization vector.

    B. They could have too low a key strength.

    C. They can be brute forced.

    D. All of the above.

10. What allows RADIUS to scale to a worldwide authentication network?

    A. Strong encryption

    B. Certificate-based tunneling and EAP

    C. CCMP-delegated authentication

    D. Two-factor authentication

11. Why should you use a VPN when attached to a public WPA hotspot?

    A. Anyone with the key can store all the packets for later decryption.

    B. Public Wi-Fi networks are set up for man-in-the-middle attacks.

    C. To ensure browser secrecy.

    D. An attacker could sniff your RADIUS packets.

12. How does TKIP improve security?

    A. It uses stronger authentication.

    B. It changes the WEP padding algorithm.

    C. It uses a different key for each packet.

    D. It uses SSL VPN tunneling.

13. What makes EAP-TLS so hard for an attacker to break?

    A. The user's key is held by the RADIUS server.

    B. The encryption keys are escrowed.

    C. The access point enforces client isolation as part of the protocol.

    D. The client-side key is needed to break the TLS tunnel.

14. Which authentication protocol uses a Protected Access Credential (PAC)?

    A. PEAP

    B. EAP-FAST

    C. EAP-TLS

    D. EAP-TTLS

15. Which authentication protocol uses mandatory client-side certificates, making it more challenging to maintain if guest access is provided to visitors?

    A. PEAP

    B. EAP-FAST

    C. EAP-TLS

    D. EAP-TTLS

Answers

1. **C.** WPA2-Enterprise is the correct version of WPA2 for this setup, as it uses enterprise-grade options to establish a shared secret.

2. **B.** WPA is a stopgap due to its software-only implementation in that it still uses the flawed WEP RC4 cipher, albeit with temporary keys.

3. The Wi-Fi authentication protocols listed in the exam objectives include EAP, PEAP, EAP-FAST, EAP-TLS, EAP-TTLS, IEEE 802.1X, and RADIUS.

4. C. Enterprise mode mandates authentication, so an authentication server, typically RADIUS, is required.

5. B. WPA2 in Personal mode uses a pre-shared key, and this key must be shared with all users, which is challenging in a large organization.

6. A. Open System authentication only matches to the SSID and generates a random number from that. Because the SSID is part of the Wi-Fi packets, there is no real authentication.

7. C. WPS uses an eight-digit pin and is subject to brute force attacks.

8. D. Implementing a captive portal will ensure that users can easily authenticate and gain access.

9. C. Any pre-shared keys can be configured to be short, and therefore susceptible to a brute force attack. The defense against this is to always use long and complex PSKs.

10. B. The use of SSL-based tunneling and EAP packets makes the distributed authentication of RADIUS possible.

11. A. The reason to use a VPN on any public Wi-Fi network is that, as a shared network, attackers may be attempting to capture all the traffic. In a public Wi-Fi configured with WEP or WPA, using a shared key also allows attackers to easily decrypt the traffic.

12. C. TKIP uses temporal keys, so there is a new key for every packet.

13. D. The TLS connection uses a client key, so the attacker would need this key before being able to break the TLS tunnel.

14. B. EAP-FAST uses the Protected Access Credential (PAC) to create the TLS tunnel.

15. C. EAP-TLS uses client-side certificates.

CHAPTER 29

Public Key Infrastructure

In this chapter, you will

- Learn about the different components of a PKI system
- Learn about the concepts to employ a PKI system
- Understand how certificates are used as part of a security solution
- Given a scenario, implement public key infrastructure components

A *public key infrastructure (PKI)* provides all the components necessary for different types of users and entities to be able to communicate securely and in a predictable manner. A PKI is made up of hardware, applications, policies, services, programming interfaces, cryptographic algorithms, protocols, users, and utilities. These components work together to allow communication to manage asymmetric keys facilitating the use of public key cryptography for digital signatures, data encryption, and integrity. Although many different applications and protocols can provide the same type of functionality, constructing and implementing a PKI boils down to establishing a level of trust.

Certification Objective   This chapter covers CompTIA Security+ exam objective 6.4, Given a scenario, implement public key infrastructure. This is a performance-based question testable objective, which means expect a question in which one must employ the knowledge based on a scenario. The best answer to a question will depend upon details in the scenario, not just the question. The question may also involve tasks other than just picking the best answer from a list. Instead, it may involve actual simulation of steps to take to solve a problem.

PKI Components

A PKI is composed of several components, all working together to handle the distribution and management of keys in a public key cryptosystem. Keys are carried via a digital structure known as a *certificate*. Other components, such as certificate authorities and registration authorities, exist to manage certificates. Working together, these components enable seamless use of public key cryptography between systems.

If, for example, John and Diane want to communicate securely, John can generate his own public/private key pair and send his public key to Diane, or he can place his public key in a directory that is available to everyone. If Diane receives John's public key, either from him or from a public directory, how does she know it really came from John? Maybe another individual is masquerading as John and has replaced John's public key with her own, as shown in Figure 29-1. If this took place, Diane would believe that her messages could be read only by John and that the replies were actually from him. However, she would actually be communicating with Katie. What is needed is a way to verify an individual's identity, to ensure that a person's public key is bound to their identity and thus ensure that the previous scenario (and others) cannot take place.

In PKI environments, entities called *registration authorities (RAs)* and *certificate authorities (CAs)* provide services similar to those of the Department of Motor Vehicles (DMV). When John goes to register for a driver's license, he has to prove his identity to the DMV by providing his passport, birth certificate, or other identification documentation. If the DMV is satisfied with the proof John provides (and John passes a driving test), the DMV will create a driver's license that can then be used by John to prove his identity. Whenever John needs to identify himself, he can show his driver's license. Although many people may not trust John to identify himself truthfully, they do trust the third party, the DMV.

Figure 29-1
Without PKIs, individuals could spoof others' identities, a man-in-the-middle attack.

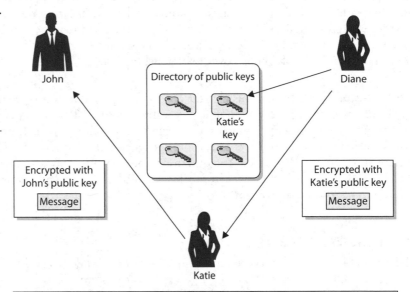

John

Directory of public keys

Katie's key

Diane

Encrypted with John's public key

Message

Encrypted with Katie's public key

Message

Katie

Man-in-the Middle Attack

1. Katie replaces John's public key with her key in the publicly accessible directory.
2. Diane extracts what she thinks is John's key, but it is in fact Katie's key.
3. Katie can now read messages Diane encrypts and sends to John.
4. After Katie decrypts and reads Diane's message, she encrypts it with John's public key and sends it on to him so he will not be the wiser.

In the PKI context, while some variations exist in specific products, the RA will require proof of identity from the individual requesting a certificate and will validate this information. The RA will then advise the CA to generate a certificate, which is analogous to a driver's license. The CA will digitally sign the certificate using its private key. The use of the private key assures the recipient that the certificate came from the CA. When Diane receives John's certificate and verifies that it was actually digitally signed by a CA that she trusts, she will believe that the certificate is actually John's—not because she trusts John, but because she trusts the entity that is vouching for his identity (the CA).

This is commonly referred to as a *third-party trust model*. Public keys are components of digital certificates, so when Diane verifies the CA's digital signature, this verifies that the certificate is truly John's and that the public key the certificate contains is also John's. This is how John's identity is bound to his public key.

This process allows John to authenticate himself to Diane and others. Using the third-party certificate, John can communicate with her, using public key encryption, without prior communication or a preexisting relationship. Once Diane is convinced of the legitimacy of John's public key, she can use it to encrypt and decrypt messages between herself and John, as illustrated in Figure 29-2.

Numerous applications and protocols can generate public/private key pairs and provide functionality similar to what a PKI provides, but no trusted third party is available for both of the communicating parties. For each party to choose to communicate this way without a third party vouching for the other's identity, the two must choose to trust each other and the communication channel they are using. In many situations, it is impractical and dangerous to arbitrarily trust an individual you do not know, and this is when the components of a PKI must fall into place—to provide the necessary level of trust you cannot, or choose not to, provide on your own.

Figure 29-2
Public keys are components of digital certificates.

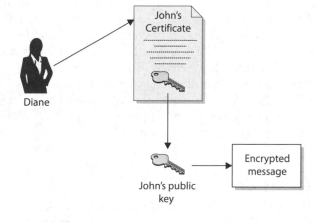

1. Diane validates the certificate.
2. Diane extracts John's public key.
3. Diane uses John's public key for encryption purposes.

What does the "infrastructure" in "public key infrastructure" really mean? An infrastructure provides a sustaining groundwork upon which other things can be built. So an infrastructure works at a low level to provide a predictable and uniform environment that allows other, higher-level technologies to work together through uniform access points. The environment that the infrastructure provides allows these higher-level applications to communicate with each other and gives them the underlying tools to carry out their tasks.

 EXAM TIP Make sure you understand the role of PKI in managing certificates and trust associated with public keys.

Certificate Authority

As just described, the CA is the trusted authority that certifies individuals' identities and creates electronic documents indicating that individuals are who they say they are. The electronic document is referred to as a *digital certificate*, and it establishes an association between the subject's identity and a public key. The private key that is paired with the public key in the certificate is stored separately.

The CA is more than just a piece of software, however; it is actually made up of the software, hardware, procedures, policies, and people who are involved in validating individuals' identities and generating the certificates. This means that if one of these components is compromised, it can negatively affect the CA overall and can threaten the integrity of the certificates it produces.

Every CA should have a certification practices statement (CPS) that outlines how identities are verified; the steps the CA follows to generate, maintain, and transmit certificates; and why the CA can be trusted to fulfill its responsibilities. It describes how keys are secured, what data is placed within a digital certificate, and how revocations will be handled. If a company is going to use and depend on a public CA, the company's security officers, administrators, and legal department should review the CA's entire CPS to ensure that it will properly meet the company's needs, and to make sure that the level of security claimed by the CA is high enough for their use and environment. A critical aspect of a PKI is the trust between the users and the CA, so the CPS should be reviewed and understood to ensure that this level of trust is warranted.

The certificate server is the actual service that issues certificates based on the data provided during the initial registration process. The server constructs and populates the digital certificate with the necessary information and combines the user's public key with the resulting certificate. The certificate is then digitally signed with the CA's private key.

Intermediate CA

Intermediate CAs function to transfer trust between different CAs. These CAs are also referred to as subordinate CAs because they are subordinate to the CA that they reference. The path of trust is walked up from the subordinate CA to the higher-level CA; in essence, the subordinate CA is using the higher-level CA as a reference.

Revocation

A certificate can be revoked when its validity needs to be ended before its actual expiration date is met, and this can occur for many reasons: for example, a user may have lost a laptop or a smart card that stores a private key; an improper software implementation may have been uncovered that directly affects the security of a private key; a user may have fallen victim to a social engineering attack and inadvertently given up a private key; data held within the certificate may no longer apply to the specified individual; or perhaps an employee has left a company and should not be identified as a member of an in-house PKI any longer. In the last instance, the certificate, which was bound to the user's key pair, identified the user as an employee of the company, and the administrator would want to ensure that the key pair could not be used in the future to validate this person's affiliation with the company. *Revocation* of the certificate prevents use in the future.

If any of the previously listed things happens, a user's private key has been compromised or should no longer be mapped to the owner's identity. A different individual may have access to that user's private key and could use it to impersonate and authenticate as the original user. If the impersonator used the key to digitally sign a message, the receiver would verify the authenticity of the sender by verifying the signature by using the original user's public key, and the verification would go through perfectly—the receiver would believe it came from the proper sender and not the impersonator. If receivers could look at a list of certificates that had been revoked before verifying the digital signature, however, they would know not to trust the digital signatures on the list. Because of issues associated with the private key being compromised, revocation is permanent and final—once revoked, a certificate cannot be reinstated. If this were allowed and a user revoked his certificate, the unauthorized holder of the private key could use it to restore the certificate validity.

For example, if Joe stole Mike's laptop, which held, among other things, Mike's private key, Joe might be able to use it to impersonate Mike. Suppose Joe writes a message, digitally signs it with Mike's private key, and sends it to Stacy. Stacy communicates with Mike periodically and has his public key, so she uses it to verify the digital signature. It computes properly, so Stacy is assured that this message came from Mike, but in truth it did not. If, before validating any certificate or digital signature, Stacy could check a list of revoked certificates, she might not fall victim to Joe's false message.

CRL

The CA provides this type of protection by maintaining a *Certificate Revocation List (CRL)*, a list of serial numbers of certificates that have been revoked. The CRL also contains a statement indicating why the individual certificates were revoked and a date when the revocation took place. The list usually contains all certificates that have been revoked within the lifetime of the CA. Certificates that have expired are not the same as those that have been revoked. If a certificate has expired, it means that its end validity date was reached.

The CA is the entity that is responsible for the status of the certificates it generates; it needs to be told of a revocation, and it must provide this information to others. The CA is responsible for maintaining the CRL and posting it in a publicly available directory.

EXAM TIP The Certificate Revocation List is an essential item to ensure a certificate is still valid. CAs post CRLs in publicly available directories to permit automated checking of certificates against the list before certificate use by a client. A user should never trust a certificate that has not been checked against the appropriate CRL.

What if Stacy wants to get back at Joe for trying to trick her earlier, and she attempts to revoke Joe's certificate herself? If she is successful, Joe's participation in the PKI can be negatively affected because others will not trust his public key. Although we might think Joe may deserve this, we need to have some system in place to make sure people cannot arbitrarily have others' certificates revoked, whether for revenge or for malicious purposes.

When a revocation request is submitted, the individual submitting the request must be authenticated. Otherwise, this could permit a type of denial-of-service attack, in which someone has another person's certificate revoked. The authentication can involve an agreed-upon password that was created during the registration process, but authentication should not be based on the individual proving that he has the corresponding private key, because it may have been stolen, and the CA would be authenticating an imposter.

The CRL's integrity needs to be protected to ensure that attackers cannot modify data pertaining to a revoked certification from the list. If this were allowed to take place, anyone who stole a private key could just delete that key from the CRL and continue to use the private key fraudulently. The integrity of the list also needs to be protected to ensure that bogus data is not added to it. Otherwise, anyone could add another person's certificate to the list and effectively revoke that person's certificate. The only entity that should be able to modify any information on the CRL is the CA.

The mechanism used to protect the integrity of a CRL is a *digital signature*. The CA's revocation service creates a digital signature for the CRL. To validate a certificate, the user accesses the directory where the CRL is posted, downloads the list, and verifies the CA's digital signature to ensure that the proper authority signed the list and to ensure that the list was not modified in an unauthorized manner. The user then looks through the list to determine whether the serial number of the certificate that he is trying to validate is listed. If the serial number is on the list, the private key should no longer be trusted, and the public key should no longer be used. This can be a cumbersome process, so it has been automated in several ways that are described in the next section.

One concern is how up to date the CRL is—how often is it updated and does it actually reflect *all* the certificates currently revoked? The actual frequency with which the list is updated depends upon the CA and its CPS. It is important that the list is updated in a timely manner so that anyone using the list has the most current information. CRL files can be requested by individuals who need to verify and validate a newly received certificate, or the files can be periodically pushed down (sent) to all users participating within a specific PKI. This means the CRL can be pulled (downloaded) by individual users when needed or pushed down to all users within the PKI on a timed interval.

The actual CRL file can grow substantially, and transmitting this file and requiring PKI client software on each workstation to save and maintain it can use a lot of resources, so the smaller the CRL is, the better. It is also possible to first push down the full CRL, and after that initial load, the following CRLs pushed down to the users are delta CRLs, meaning that they contain only the changes to the original or base CRL. This can greatly reduce the amount of bandwidth consumed when updating CRLs.

In implementations where the CRLs are not pushed down to individual systems, the users' PKI software needs to know where to look for the posted CRL that relates to the certificate it is trying to validate. The certificate might have an extension that points the validating user to the necessary CRL distribution point. The network administrator sets up the distribution points, and one or more points can exist for a particular PKI. The distribution point holds one or more lists containing the serial numbers of revoked certificates, and the user's PKI software scans the list(s) for the serial number of the certificate the user is attempting to validate. If the serial number is not present, the user is assured that it has not been revoked. This approach helps point users to the right resource and also reduces the amount of information that needs to be scanned when checking that a certificate has not been revoked.

One last option for checking distributed CRLs is an online service. When a client user needs to validate a certificate and ensure that it has not been revoked, he can communicate with an online service that will query the necessary CRLs available within the environment. This service can query the lists for the client instead of pushing down the full CRL to each and every system. So if Joe receives a certificate from Stacy, he can contact an online service and send it the serial number listed in the certificate Stacy sent. The online service would query the necessary CRLs and respond to Joe by indicating whether or not that serial number was listed as being revoked.

OCSP

One of the protocols used for online revocation services is the *Online Certificate Status Protocol (OCSP)*, a request and response protocol that obtains the serial number of the certificate that is being validated and reviews CRLs for the client. The protocol has a responder service that reports the status of the certificate back to the client, indicating whether it has been revoked, it is valid, or its status is unknown. This protocol and service saves the client from having to find, download, and process the right lists.

 EXAM TIP Certificate revocation checks are done either by examining the CRL or using OCSP to see if a certificate has been revoked.

Suspension

Instead of being revoked, a certificate can be suspended, meaning it is temporarily put on hold. *Suspension* of a certificate has the same immediate effect as revocation, but it can be reversed. If, for example, Bob is taking an extended vacation and wants to ensure that his certificate will not be used during that time, he can make a suspension request to the CA. The CRL would list this certificate and its serial number, and in the field that describes why the certificate is revoked, it would instead indicate a hold state. Once Bob returns to work, he can make a request to the CA to remove his certificate from the list.

Another reason to suspend a certificate is if an administrator is suspicious that a private key might have been compromised. While the issue is under investigation, the certificate can be suspended to ensure that it cannot be used.

CSR

A *certificate signing request (CSR)* is the actual request to a CA containing a public key and the requisite information needed to generate a certificate. The CSR contains all of the identifying information that is to be bound to the key by the certificate generation process.

Certificate

A digital *certificate* binds an individual's identity to a public key, and it contains all the information a receiver needs to be assured of the identity of the public key owner. After an RA verifies an individual's identity, the CA generates the digital certificate, but how does the CA know what type of data to insert into the certificate?

The certificates are created and formatted based on the X.509 standard, which outlines the necessary fields of a certificate and the possible values that can be inserted into the fields. As of this writing, X.509 version 3 is the most current version of the standard. X.509 is a standard of the International Telecommunication Union (www.itu.int). The IETF's Public-Key Infrastructure (X.509), or PKIX, working group has adapted the X.509 standard to the more flexible organization of the Internet, as specified in RFC 3280, and is commonly referred to as PKIX for Public Key Infrastructure (X.509).

The following fields are included within an X.509 digital certificate:

- **Version number** Identifies the version of the X.509 standard that was followed to create the certificate; indicates the format and fields that can be used.
- **Subject** Specifies the owner of the certificate.
- **Public key** Identifies the public key being bound to the certified subject; also identifies the algorithm used to create the private/public key pair.
- **Issuer** Identifies the CA that generated and digitally signed the certificate.
- **Serial number** Provides a unique number identifying this one specific certificate issued by a particular CA.
- **Validity** Specifies the dates through which the certificate is valid for use.
- **Certificate usage** Specifies the approved use of the certificate, which dictates intended use of this public key.
- **Signature algorithm** Specifies the hashing and digital signature algorithms used to digitally sign the certificate.
- **Extensions** Allows additional data to be encoded into the certificate to expand the functionality of the certificate. Companies can customize the use of certificates within their environments by using these extensions. X.509 version 3 has extended the extension possibilities.

Figure 29-3 shows the actual values of these different certificate fields for a particular certificate in Internet Explorer. The version of this certificate is V3 (X.509 v3), and the serial number is also listed—this number is unique for each certificate that is created by a specific CA. The CA used the MD5 hashing algorithm to create the message digest value, and it then signed with its private key using the RSA algorithm. The actual CA that issued the certificate is Root SGC Authority, and the valid dates indicate how long this certificate is valid. The subject is MS SGC Authority, which is the entity that registered this certificate and is the entity that is bound to the embedded public key. The actual public key is shown in the lower window and is represented in hexadecimal.

The subject of a certificate is commonly a person, but it does not have to be. The subject can be a network device (router, web server, firewall, and so on), an application, a department, a company, or a person. Each has its own identity that needs to be verified and proven to another entity before secure, trusted communication can be initiated. If a network device is using a certificate for authentication, the certificate may contain the network address of that device. This means that if the certificate has a network address of 10.0.0.1, the receiver will compare this to the address from which it received the certificate to make sure a man-in-the-middle attack is not being attempted.

Figure 29-3
Fields within a
digital certificate

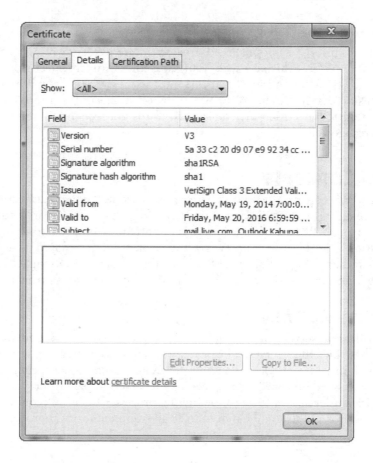

Public Key

Public keys are the key from the key pair that are intended to be freely shared with the message—to everyone, hence the term public. As the purpose of a PKI system is to manage keys and identities using certificates, the distribution or publishing of public keys is done through public communication channels, for nothing is lost if other parties get a public key. By definition, public keys can be shared freely. The use of the public key depends on what action is being performed, but what the public key does, the private key can undo, and vice versa. This provides the great utility of asymmetric encryption.

Private Key

The *private key* is the key from the key pair that is to be protected from all outside actors. It seldom leaves the machine upon which it was generated, for it is the entire strength of the key pair. The most sensitive and critical public/private key pairs are those used by CAs to digitally sign certificates. These need to be highly protected because if they were compromised, the trust relationship between the CA and all of the end-entities would be threatened. In high-security environments, these keys are often kept in a tamper-proof hardware encryption store, only accessible to individuals with a need to access.

Object Identifiers

Each extension, or optional field, to a certificate has its own ID, expressed as an *object identifier (OID)*, which is a set of values, together with either a critical or noncritical indication. The system using a certificate must reject the certificate if it encounters a critical extension that it does not recognize, or that contains information that it cannot process. A noncritical extension may be ignored if it is not recognized, but must be processed if it is recognized.

PKI Concepts

PKI systems are composed of the items discussed in the previous section as well as methods of using and employing those items to achieve the desired functionality. When employing a PKI-based solution, it is important to understand that the security of the solution is as dependent upon how the elements are employed as it is on how they are constructed. This section describes several important operational elements, such as pinning, stapling, and certificate chaining, and examines various trust models.

Online vs. Offline CA

Certification servers must be online to provide certification services, so why would anyone have an offline server? The primary reason is security. If a given certificate authority is used only for periodic functions—for example, signing of specific certificates that are rarely reissued or signed—then keeping the server offline except when needed provides a significant level of security to the signing process. Other CA requests, such as CRL and validation requests, can be moved to a validation authority approved by the CA.

Stapling

Stapling is the process of combining related items to reduce communication steps. An example is that when someone requests a certificate, stapling sends both the certificate and OCSP responder information in the same request to avoid the additional fetches the client would have to perform during path validations.

Pinning

When a certificate is presented for a host, either identifying the host or providing a public key, this information can be saved in an act called pinning. *Pinning* is the process of associating a host with a previously provided X.509 certificate or public key. This can be important for mobile applications that move between networks frequently and are much more likely to be associated with hostile networks where levels of trust are low and risks of malicious data are high. Pinning assists in security through the avoidance of the use of DNS and its inherent risks when on less than secure networks.

The process of reusing a certificate or public key is called key continuity. This provides protection from an attacker, assuming that the attacker was not in position to attack on the initial pinning. If an attacker is able to intercept and taint the initial contact, then the pinning will preserve the attack. You should pin anytime you want to be relatively certain of the remote host's identity, relying upon your home network security, and you are likely to be operating at a later time in a hostile environment. If you choose to pin, you have two options: pin the certificate or pin the public key.

Trust Model

A *trust model* is a construct of systems, personnel, applications, protocols, technologies, and policies that work together to provide a certain level of protection. All of these components can work together seamlessly within the same trust domain because they are known to the other components within the domain and are trusted to some degree. Different trust domains are usually managed by different groups of administrators, have different security policies, and restrict outsiders from privileged access.

Most trust domains (whether individual companies or departments) are not usually islands cut off from the world—they need to communicate with other, less-trusted domains. The trick is to figure out how much two different domains should trust each other, and how to implement and configure an infrastructure that would allow these two domains to communicate in a way that will not allow security compromises or breaches. This can be more difficult than it sounds.

One example of trust considered earlier in the chapter is the driver's license issued by the DMV. Suppose, for example, that Bob is buying a lamp from Carol and he wants to pay by check. Since Carol does not know Bob, she does not know if she can trust him or have much faith in his check. But if Bob shows Carol his driver's license, she can compare the name to what appears on the check, and she can choose to accept it. The trust anchor (the agreed-upon trusted third party) in this scenario is the DMV, since both Carol and Bob trust it more than they trust each other. Since Bob had to provide documentation to prove his identity to the DMV, that organization trusted him enough to generate a license, and Carol trusts the DMV, so she decides to trust Bob's check.

Consider another example of a trust anchor. If Joe and Stacy need to communicate through e-mail and would like to use encryption and digital signatures, they will not trust each other's certificate alone. But when each receives the other's certificate and sees that they both have been digitally signed by an entity they both do trust—the CA—then they have a deeper level of trust in each other. The trust anchor here is the CA. This is easy enough, but when we need to establish trust anchors between different CAs and PKI environments, it gets a little more complicated.

When two companies need to communicate using their individual PKIs, or if two departments within the same company use different CAs, two separate trust domains are involved. The users and devices from these different trust domains will need to communicate with each other, and they will need to exchange certificates and public keys. This means that trust anchors need to be identified, and a communication channel must be constructed and maintained.

A trust relationship must be established between two issuing authorities (CAs). This happens when one or both of the CAs issue a certificate for the other CA's public key, as shown in Figure 29-4. This means that each CA registers for a certificate and public key from the other CA. Each CA validates the other CA's identification information and generates a certificate containing a public key for that CA to use. This establishes a trust path between the two entities that can then be used when users need to verify other users' certificates that fall within the different trust domains. The trust path can be unidirectional or bidirectional, so either the two CAs trust each other (bidirectional) or only one trusts the other (unidirectional).

As illustrated in Figure 29-4, all the users and devices in trust domain 1 trust their own CA 1, which is their trust anchor. All users and devices in trust domain 2 have their own trust anchor, CA 2. The two CAs have exchanged certificates and trust each other, but they do not have a common trust anchor between them.

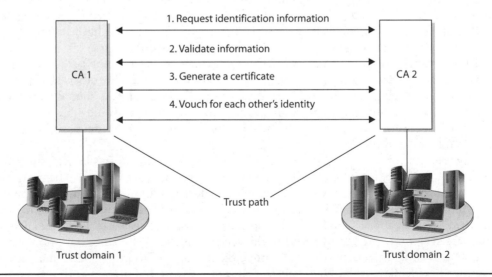

Figure 29-4 A trust relationship can be built between two trust domains to set up a communication channel.

The trust models describe and outline the trust relationships between the different CAs and different environments, which will indicate where the trust paths reside. The trust models and paths need to be thought out before implementation to restrict and control access properly and to ensure that as few trust paths as possible are used. Several different trust models can be used: the hierarchical, peer-to-peer, and hybrid models are discussed in the following sections.

Hierarchical Trust Model

The first type of trust model we'll examine is a basic hierarchical structure that contains a root CA, an intermediate CA, leaf CAs, and end-entities. The configuration is that of an inverted tree, as shown in Figure 29-5. The root CA is the ultimate trust anchor for all other entities in this infrastructure, and it generates certificates for the intermediate CAs, which in turn generate certificates for the leaf CAs, and the leaf CAs generate certificates for the end-entities.

As introduced earlier in the chapter, intermediate CAs function to transfer trust between different CAs. These CAs are referred to as subordinate CAs, as they are subordinate to the CA that they reference. The path of trust is walked up from the subordinate CA to the higher-level CA; in essence, the subordinate CA is using the higher-level CA as a reference.

As shown in Figure 29-5, no bidirectional trusts exist—they are all unidirectional trusts, as indicated by the one-way arrows. Since no other entity can certify and generate certificates for the root CA, it creates a self-signed certificate. This means that the certificate's issuer and subject fields hold the same information, both representing the root CA, and the root CA's public key will be used to verify this certificate when that time comes. This root CA certificate and public key are distributed to all entities within this trust model.

Figure 29-5
The hierarchical trust model outlines trust paths.

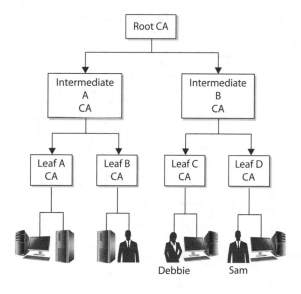

Walking the Certificate Path   When a user in one trust domain needs to communicate with another user in another trust domain, one user will need to validate the other's certificate. This sounds simple enough, but what it really means is that each certificate for each CA, all the way up to a shared trusted anchor, also must be validated. If Debbie needs to validate Sam's certificate, as shown in Figure 29-5, she actually also needs to validate the Leaf D CA and Intermediate B CA certificates, as well as Sam's.

So in Figure 29-5, we have a user, Sam, who digitally signs a message and sends it and his certificate to Debbie. Debbie needs to validate this certificate before she can trust Sam's digital signature. Included in Sam's certificate is an issuer field, which indicates that the certificate was issued by Leaf D CA. Debbie has to obtain Leaf D CA's digital certificate and public key to validate Sam's certificate. Remember that Debbie validates the certificate by verifying its digital signature. The digital signature was created by the certificate issuer using its private key, so Debbie needs to verify the signature using the issuer's public key.

Debbie tracks down Leaf D CA's certificate and public key, but she now needs to verify this CA's certificate, so she looks at the issuer field, which indicates that Leaf D CA's certificate was issued by Intermediate B CA. Debbie now needs to get Intermediate B CA's certificate and public key.

Debbie's client software tracks this down and sees that the issuer for the Intermediate B CA is the root CA, for which she already has a certificate and public key. So Debbie's client software had to follow the *certificate path*, meaning it had to continue to track down and collect certificates until it came upon a self-signed certificate. A self-signed certificate indicates that it was signed by a root CA, and Debbie's software has been configured to trust this entity as her trust anchor, so she can stop there. Figure 29-6 illustrates the steps Debbie's software had to carry out just to be able to verify Sam's certificate.

This type of simplistic trust model works well within an enterprise that easily follows a hierarchical organizational chart, but many companies cannot use this type of trust model because different departments or offices require their own trust anchors. These demands can be derived from direct business needs or from inter-organizational politics. This hierarchical model might not be possible when two or more companies need to communicate with each other. Neither company will let the other's CA be the root CA, because each

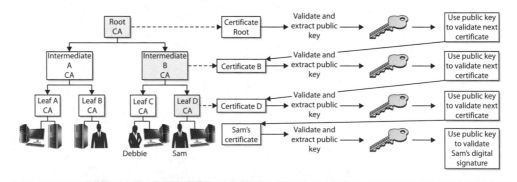

Figure 29-6   Verifying each certificate in a certificate path

does not necessarily trust the other entity to that degree. In these situations, the CAs will need to work in a peer-to-peer relationship instead of in a hierarchical relationship.

Peer-to-Peer Trust Model

In a *peer-to-peer trust model*, one CA is not subordinate to another CA, and no established trusted anchor between the CAs is involved. The end-entities will look to their issuing CA as their trusted anchor, but the different CAs will not have a common anchor.

Figure 29-7 illustrates this type of trust model. The two different CAs will certify the public key for each other, which creates a bidirectional trust. This is referred to as *cross-certification*, since the CAs are not receiving their certificates and public keys from a superior CA, but instead are creating them for each other.

One of the main drawbacks to this model is scalability. Each CA must certify every other CA that is participating, and a bidirectional trust path must be implemented, as shown in Figure 29-8. If one root CA were certifying all the intermediate CAs, scalability would not be as much of an issue. Figure 29-8 represents a fully connected mesh architecture, meaning that each CA is directly connected to and has a bidirectional trust relationship with every other CA. As you can see in this illustration, the complexity of this setup can become overwhelming.

Hybrid Trust Model

A company can be complex within itself, and when the need arises to communicate properly with outside partners, suppliers, and customers in an authorized and secured manner, this complexity can make sticking to either the hierarchical or peer-to-peer trust model difficult, if not impossible. In many implementations, the different model types have to be combined to provide the necessary communication lines and levels of trust. In a *hybrid trust model*, the two companies have their own internal hierarchical models and are connected through a peer-to-peer model using cross-certification.

Figure 29-7
Cross-certification creates a peer-to-peer PKI model.

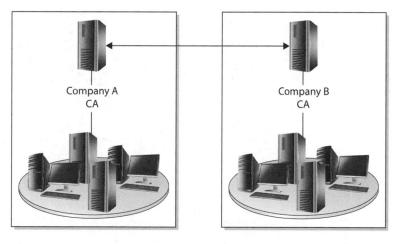

Company A
CA

Company B
CA

PART VI

Figure 29-8
Scalability is
a drawback
in cross-
certification
models.

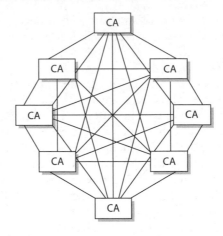

Another option in this hybrid configuration is to implement a *bridge CA*. Figure 29-9 illustrates the role that a bridge CA could play—it is responsible for issuing cross-certificates for all connected CAs and trust domains. The bridge CA is not considered a root or trust anchor, but merely the entity that generates and maintains the cross-certification for the connected environments.

 EXAM TIP Three trust models exist: hierarchical, peer-to-peer, and hybrid. Hierarchical trust is like an upside-down tree. Peer-to-peer is a lateral series of references, and hybrid is a combination of hierarchical and peer-to-peer trust.

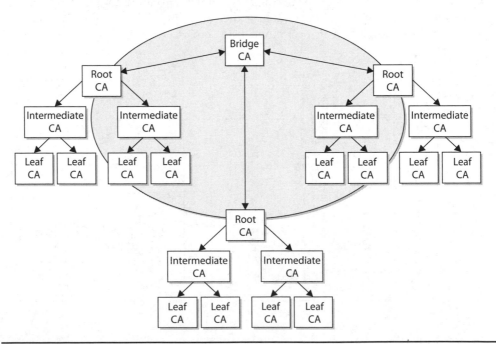

Figure 29-9   A bridge CA can control the cross-certification procedures.

Key Escrow

The impressive growth of the use of encryption technology has led to new methods for handling keys. *Key escrow* is a system by which your private key is kept both by you and by a third party. Encryption is adept at hiding secrets, and with computer technology being affordable to everyone, criminals and other ill-willed people began using encryption to conceal communications and business dealings from law enforcement agencies. Because they could not break the encryption, government agencies began asking for key escrow. Key escrow in this circumstance is a system by which your private key is kept both by you and by the government. This allows people with a court order to retrieve your private key to gain access to anything encrypted with your public key. The data is essentially encrypted by your key and the government key, giving the government access to your plaintext data.

Key escrow is also used by corporate enterprises, as it provides a method of obtaining a key in the event that the key holder is not available. There are also key recovery mechanisms to do this, and the corporate policies will determine the appropriate manner in which to safeguard keys across the enterprise.

Key escrow that involves an outside agency can negatively impact the security provided by encryption, because the government requires a huge, complex infrastructure of systems to hold every escrowed key, and the security of those systems is less efficient than the security of your memorizing the key. However, there are two sides to the key escrow coin. Without a practical way to recover a key if or when it is lost or the key holder dies, for example, some important information will be lost forever. Such issues will affect the design and security of encryption technologies for the foreseeable future.

 EXAM TIP   Key escrow can solve many problems resulting from an inaccessible key, and the nature of cryptography makes the access of the data impossible without the key.

Certificate Chaining

Certificates are used to convey identity and public key pairs to users, but this raises the question: why trust the certificate? The answer lies in the *certificate chain*, a chain of trust from one certificate to another, based on signing by an issuer, until the chain ends with a certificate that the user trusts. This conveys the trust from the trusted certificate to the certificate that is being used. Examining Figure 29-10, we can look at the ordered list of certificates from the one presented to one that is trusted.

Certificates that sit between the presented certificate and the root certificate are called chain or intermediate certificates. The intermediate certificate is the signer/issuer of the presented certificate, indicating that it trusts the certificate. The root CA certificate is the signer/issuer of the intermediate certificate, indicating that it trusts the intermediate certificate. The chaining of certificates is a manner of passing trust down from a trusted root certificate. The chain terminates with a root CA certificate, which is always signed by the CA itself. The signatures of all certificates in the chain must be verified up to the root CA certificate.

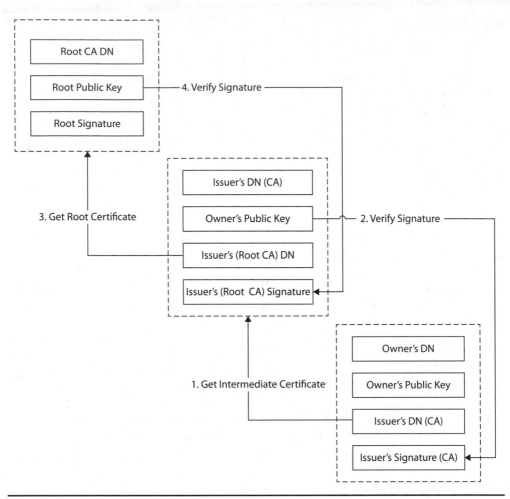

Figure 29-10   Certificate chaining

Types of Certificates

Four main types of certificates are used:

- End-entity certificates
- CA certificates
- Cross-certification certificates
- Policy certificates

End-entity certificates are issued by a CA to a specific subject, such as Joyce, the Accounting department, or a firewall, as illustrated in Figure 29-11. An end-entity certificate is the identity document provided by PKI implementations.

Figure 29-11
End-entity and
CA certificates

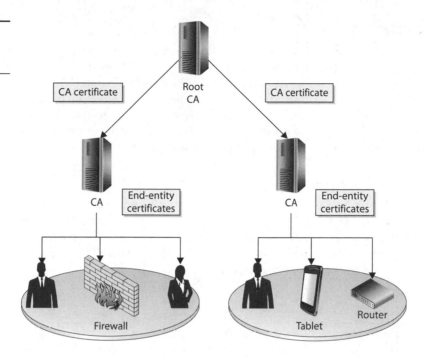

A *CA certificate* can be self-signed, in the case of a stand-alone or root CA, or it can be issued by a superior CA within a hierarchical model. In the model in Figure 29-11, the superior CA gives the authority and allows the subordinate CA to accept certificate requests and generate the individual certificates itself. This may be necessary when a company needs to have multiple internal CAs, and different departments within an organization need to have their own CAs servicing their specific end-entities (users, network devices, and applications) in their sections. In these situations, a representative from each department requiring a CA registers with the more highly trusted CA and requests a CA certificate.

Cross-certification certificates, or *cross-certificates*, are used when independent CAs establish peer-to-peer trust relationships. Simply put, they are a mechanism through which one CA can issue a certificate allowing its users to trust another CA.

Within sophisticated CAs used for high-security applications, a mechanism is required to provide centrally controlled policy information to PKI clients. This is often done by placing the policy information in a *policy certificate*.

Wildcard

Certificates can be issued to an entity such as example.com. But what if there are multiple entities under example.com that need certificates? There are two choices: issue distinct certificates for each specific address, or use *wildcard* certificates. Wildcard certificates work exactly as one would expect. A certificate issued for *.example.com would be valid for one.example.com as well as two.example.com.

SAN

Subject Alternative Name (SAN) is a field (extension) in a certificate that has several uses. In certificates for machines, it can represent the fully qualified domain name (FQDN) of the machine; for users, it can be the user principal name (UPN); or in the case of an SSL certificate, it can indicate multiple domains across which the certificate is valid. Figure 29-12 shows the two domains covered by the certificate in the box below the field details. SAN is an extension that is used to a significant degree because it has become a standard method used in a variety of circumstances.

Code Signing

Certificates can be designated for specific purposes, such as code signing. This is to enable the flexibility of managing certificates for specific functions and reducing the risk in the event of compromise. *Code signing certificates* are designated as such in the certificate itself, and the application that uses the certificate adheres to this policy restriction to ensure proper certificate usage.

Figure 29-12
Subject
Alternative Name

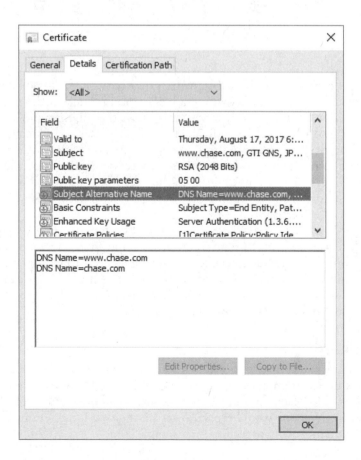

Self-Signed

Certificates are signed by a higher-level CA, providing a root of trust. As with all chains, there is a final node of trust, the root node. Not all certificates have to have the same root node. A company can create its own certificate chain for use inside the company, and thus it creates its own root node. This certificate is an example of a CA certificate mentioned above, and must be *self-signed*, as there is no other "higher" node of trust. What prevents one from signing their own certificates? The trust chain would begin and end with the certificate, and the user would be presented with the dilemma of whether or not to trust the certificate, for in the end, all a certificate does is detail a chain of trust to some entity that an end user trusts. Self-signing is shown for the root certificate in Figure 29-10 (the upper-left certificate).

Machine/Computer

Certificates bind identities to keys and provide a means of authentication, which at times is needed for computers. Active Directory Domain Services can keep track of machines in a system via machines identifying themselves using *machine certificates*, also known as *computer certificates*. When a user logs in, the system can use either the machine certificate, identifying the machine, or the user certificate, identifying the user—whichever is appropriate for the desired operation. This is an example of an end-entity certificate.

E-mail

Digital certificates can be used with e-mail systems for items such as digital signatures associated with e-mails. Just as other specialized functions such as code signing have their own certificates, it is common for a separate *e-mail certificate* to be used for identity associated with e-mail. This is an example of an end-entity certificate.

User

User certificates are just that—certificates that identify a user. They are an example of an end-entity certificate.

 NOTE User certificates are used by users for EFS, e-mail, and client authentications, whereas computer certificates help computers to authenticate to the network.

Root

A *root certificate* is a certificate that forms the initial basis of trust in a trust chain. All certificates are signed by the CA that issues them, and CAs can be chained together in a trust structure. Following the chain, one climbs the tree of trust until they find a self-signed certificate, indicating it is a root certificate. What determines whether or not a system trusts a root certificate is whether or not the root certificate is in the system's store of trusted certificates. Different vendors, such as Microsoft and Apple, have trusted root certificate programs that determine by corporate policy which CAs they will label as trusted. Root certificates, because they form anchors of trust for other certificates, are examples of CA certificates as explained earlier.

Domain Validation

Domain validation is a low trust means of validation based on an applicant demonstrating control over a DNS domain. Domain validation is typically used for TLS and has the advantage that it can be automated via checks against a DNS record. A domain validation–based certificate, typically free, offers very little in assurance that the identity has not been spoofed, for the applicant need not directly interact with the issuer. Domain validation scales well and can be automated with little if no real interaction between an applicant and the CA, but in return it offers little assurance. Domain validation is indicated differently in different browsers, primarily to differentiate it from extended validation certificates.

Extended Validation

Extended validation (EV) certificates are used for HTTPS websites and software to provide a high level of assurance as to the originator's identity. EV certificates use the same methods of encryption to protect certificate integrity as do domain- and organization-validated certificates. The difference in assurance comes from the processes used by a CA to validate an entity's legal identity before issuance. Because of the additional information used during the validation, EV certificates display the legal identity and other legal information as part of the certificate. EV certificates support multiple domains, but do not support wildcards.

To assist users in identifying EV certificates and the enhanced trust, several additional visual clues are provided to users when EVs are employed. When implemented in a browser, the legal entity name is displayed, in addition to the URL and a lock symbol, and in most instances, the entire URL bar is green. All major browser vendors provide this support, and because the information is included in the certificate itself, this function is web server agnostic.

Certificate Formats

Digital certificates are defined in RFC 5280, *Internet X.509 Public Key Infrastructure Certificate and Certificate Revocation List (CRL) Profile.* This RFC describes the X.509 v3 digital certificate format in detail. There are numerous ways to encode the information in a certificate before instantiation as a file, and the different methods result in different file extensions. Common extensions include .der, .pem, .crt, .cer, .pfx, .p12, and .p7b. Although they all can contain certificate information, they are not all directly interchangeable. While in certain cases some data can be interchanged, the best practice is to identify how your certificate is encoded and then label it correctly.

DER

Distinguished Encoding Rules (DER) is one of the Abstract Syntax Notation One (ASN.1) encoding rules that can be used to encode any data object into a binary file. With respect to certificates, the data associated with the certificate, a series of name-value pairs, needs to be converted to a consistent format for digital signing. DER offers a consistent mechanism for this task. A DER file (.der extension) contains binary data and can be used for a single certificate.

PEM

Privacy-enhanced Electronic Mail (PEM) is the most common format used by certificate authorities when issuing certificates. PEM comes from RFC 1422 and is a Base64-encoded ASCII file that begins with -----BEGIN CERTIFICATE-----, followed by the Base64 data, and closing with -----END CERTIFICATE-----. A PEM file supports multiple digital certificates, including a certificate chain. A PEM file can contain multiple entries, one after another, and can include both public and private keys. Most platforms, however, such as web servers, expect the certificates and private keys to be in separate files.

The PEM format for certificate data is used in multiple file types, including .pem, .cer, .crt, and .key files.

 EXAM TIP If you need to transmit multiple certificates, or a certificate chain, use PEM for encoding. PEM encoding can carry multiple certificates, whereas DER can only carry a single certificate.

CER

The .cer file extension is used to denote an alternative form, from Microsoft, of CRT files. The .cer/.crt extension is used for certificates and may be encoded as binary DER or as ASCII PEM. The .cer and .crt extensions are nearly synonymous. The .cer extension is most commonly associated with Microsoft Windows systems, while .crt is associated with Unix systems.

 NOTE The only time .crt and .cer can safely be interchanged is when the encoding type can be identical (e.g., PEM-encoded CRT = PEM-encoded CER).

 EXAM TIP .cer is a file extension for an SSL certificate file format used by web servers to help verify the identity and security of the site in question.

KEY

A KEY file, denoted by the file extension .key, can be used both for public and private PKCS#8 keys. The keys may be encoded as binary DER or as ASCII PEM.

PFX

A PKCS#12 file is a portable file format with a .pfx extension. It is a binary format for storing the server certificate, intermediate certificates, and the private key in one file. PFX files are typically used on Windows machines to import and export certificates and private keys.

P12

P12 is an alternative file extension for a PKCS#12 file format.

P7B

The PKCS#7 or P7B format is stored in Base64 ASCII format and has a file extension of .p7b or .p7c. A P7B file begins with -----BEGIN PKCS7----- and only contains certificates and chain certificates (intermediate CAs), not the private key. The most common platforms that support P7B files are Microsoft Windows and Java Tomcat.

Chapter Review

In this chapter, you became acquainted with the principles of public key infrastructure. The chapter opened with a description of the components of a PKI system, including certificate authorities, certificate lifecycle including revocation and suspension, and the components of a certificate itself. Concepts of PKI usage, including stapling and pinning, were presented. An examination of trust models followed, including hierarchical, peer-to-peer, and hybrid trust models. Key escrow and certificate chaining were also presented.

The chapter concluded with topics associated with different types of certificates, including wildcard, root, SAN, code signing, self-signed, machine, e-mail, user, domain validation, and extended validation. The final topic was an examination of the formats used to store certificates on systems.

Questions

To help you prepare further for the CompTIA Security+ exam, and to test your level of preparedness, answer the following questions and then check your answers against the correct answers at the end of the chapter.

1. You are asked by the senior system administrator to refresh the SSL certificates on the web servers. The process is to generate a certificate signing request (CSR), send it to a third party to be signed, and then apply the return information to the CSR. What is this an example of?

   A. Pinning

   B. Borrowed authority

   C. Third-party trust model

   D. MITM hardening

2. A certificate authority consists of which of the following?

    A. Hardware and software

    B. Policies and procedures

    C. People who manage certificates

    D. All of the above

3. Your manager wants you to review the company's internal PKI system's CPS for applicability and verification and to ensure that it meets current needs. What are you most likely to focus on?

    A. Revocations

    B. Trust level provided to users

    C. Key entropy

    D. How the keys are stored

4. You are preparing an e-mail to send to a colleague at work, and because the message information is sensitive, you decide you should encrypt it. When you attempt to apply the certificate that you have for the colleague, the encryption fails. The certificate was listed as still valid for another year, and the certificate authority is still trusted and working. What happened to this user's key?

    A. It was using the wrong algorithm.

    B. You are querying the incorrect certificate authority.

    C. Revocation.

    D. The third-party trust model failed.

5. Which of the following is a requirement for a CRL?

    A. It must have the e-mail addresses of all the certificate owners.

    B. It must contain a list of all expired certificates.

    C. It must contain information about all the subdomains that are covered by the CA.

    D. It must be posted to a public directory.

6. What does OCSP do?

    A. It reviews the CRL for the client and provides a status about the certificate being validated.

    B. It outlines the details of a certificate authority, including how identities are verified, the steps the CA follows to generate certificates, and why the CA can be trusted.

    C. It provides for a set of values to be attached to the certificate.

    D. It provides encryption for digital signatures.

PART VI

7. The X.509 standard applies to which of the following?

   A. SSL providers

   B. Digital certificates

   C. Certificate Revocation Lists

   D. Public key infrastructure

8. You are browsing a website when your browser provides you with a warning message that "There is a problem with this website's security certificate." When you examine the certificate, it indicates that the root CA is not trusted. What most likely happened to cause this error?

   A. The certificate was revoked.

   B. The certificate does not have enough bit length for the TLS protocol.

   C. The server's CSR was not signed by a trusted CA.

   D. The certificate has expired.

9. Taking a root CA offline is important for security purposes, but with the root CA offline, how does the PKI operate?

   A. It has to be started periodically to provide CSR signing and CRL updates.

   B. All services are delegated to an intermediate CA.

   C. The endpoints cache the trust model until the root CA comes back online.

   D. Pinning.

10. Why is pinning more important on mobile devices?

    A. It uses elliptic curve cryptography.

    B. It uses less power for pinned certificate requests.

    C. It reduces network bandwidth usage by combining multiple CA requests into one.

    D. It allows caching of a known good certificate when roaming to low-trust networks.

11. Your organization has recently acquired another company and needs to enable secure communications with them. You register your CA for a certificate from the other CA and the other organization registers for a certificate from your CA and they each trust the other CA. What is this an example of?

    A. Third-party trust model

    B. Bidirectional trust model

    C. Unidirectional trust model

    D. Secure key exchange model

12. Which of the following models best describes Internet SSL public key infrastructure?

    A. Third-party trust model

    B. Bidirectional trust model

    C. Unidirectional trust model

    D. Secure key exchange model

13. You are the lead architect of the new encryption project. In a meeting one of your management staff members asks why she will be implementing key escrow as part of the encryption solution. Which reason or reasons would be important with the implementation of key escrow?

    A. Prevent data loss when a user forgets their private key passphrase

    B. Legal action in the form of court ordered discovery

    C. Satisfy security audit findings

    D. Both A and B

14. What issue does a wildcard certificate solve?

    A. The need for separate certificates for multiple, potentially dynamic subdomains

    B. The failure of proper reverse DNS configurations

    C. The need for certificates to be reissued after expiration

    D. The need for the root CA to have intermediate CAs

15. You are issued a certificate from a CA, delivered by e-mail, but the file does not have an extension. The e-mail notes that the root CA, the intermediate CAs, and your certificate are all attached in the file. What format is your certificate likely in?

    A. DER

    B. CER

    C. PEM

    D. None of the above

Answers

1. **C.** This is an example of the third-party trust model. Although you are generating the encryption keys on the local server, you are getting these keys signed by a third-party authority so that you can present the third party as the trusted agent for users to trust your keys.

2. **D.** A certificate authority is the hardware and software that manage the actual certificate bits, the policies and procedures that determine when certificates are properly issued, and the people who make and monitor the policies for compliance.

3. **B.** You are most likely to focus on the level of trust provided by the CA to users of the system, as providing trust is the primary purpose of the CA.

4. **C.** The certificate has likely been revoked, or removed from that user's identity and no longer marked valid by the certificate authority.

5. **D.** Certificate Revocation Lists must be posted to a public directory so that all users of the system can query it.

6. **A.** Online Certificate Status Protocol (OCSP) is an online protocol that will look for a certificate's serial number on CRLs and provide a status message about the certificate to the client.

7. **B.** The X.509 standard is used to define the properties of digital certificates.

8. **C.** In this case, the server's CSR was not signed by a CA that is trusted by the endpoint computer, so no third-party trust can be established. This could be an indication of an attack, so the certificate should be manually verified before providing data to the web server.

9. **B.** You can take a root CA offline if all its normal services, such as signing CSRs and generating CRLs, are delegated to an intermediate CA. Because root CA certificates tend to have very long timelines, 20 years, and those of intermediate CAs are much shorter, 3 to 5 years, this solution works much better to avoid the problem of a compromised CA certificate.

10. **D.** Pinning is important on mobile devices because they are much more likely to be used on various networks, many of which have much lower trust than their home network.

11. **B.** This is an example of the bidirectional trust model, allowing each CA to trust certificates issued by the other CA, and allowing users to trust the certificates issued by the other CA.

12. **C.** SSL PKI is based largely on the unidirectional trust model, where the lower servers in the certificate chain all trust the higher ones in the certificate chain.

13. **D.** Both a forgotten key passphrase and a court-ordered government action could be remediated when the system design uses key escrow.

14. **A.** The wildcard certificate will be valid for all possible subdomains of the primary domain. This is good for organizations that have multiple potentially dynamic subdomains.

15. **C.** Because the certificate includes the entire certificate chain, it is most likely delivered to you in PEM format.

PART VII

Appendixes and Glossary

OSI Model and Internet Protocols

In this appendix, you will

- Learn about the OSI model
- Review the network protocols associated with the Internet

Networks are interconnected groups of computers and specialty hardware designed to facilitate the transmission of data from one device to another. The basic function of the network is to allow machines and devices to communicate with each other in an orderly fashion.

Networking Frameworks and Protocols

Today's networks consist of a wide variety of types and sizes of equipment from multiple vendors. To ensure an effective and efficient transfer of information between devices, agreements as to how the transfer should proceed between vendors are required.

The term protocol refers to a standard set of rules developed to facilitate a specific level of functionality. In networking, a wide range of protocols have been developed, some proprietary and some public, to facilitate communication between machines. Just as speakers need a common language to communicate, or they must at least understand each other's language, computers and networks must agree on a common protocol.

Communication requires that all parties have a common understanding of the object under discussion. If the object is intangible or not present, each party needs some method of referencing items in such a way that the other party understands. A model is a tool used as a framework to give people common points of reference when discussing items. Mathematical models are common in science, because they give people the ability to compare answers and results. In much the same way, models are used in many disciplines to facilitate communication. Network models have been developed by many companies as ways to communicate among engineers what specific functionality is occurring when and where in a network.

As the Internet took shape, a series of protocols was needed to ensure interoperability across this universal network structure. The Transmission Control Protocol (TCP), User

Datagram Protocol (UDP), and Internet Protocol (IP) are three of the commonly used protocols that enable data movement across the Internet. As these protocols work in concert with one another, you typically see TCP/IP or UDP/IP as pairs in use. A basic understanding of the terms and of the usage of protocols and models is essential to discuss networking functionality, for it provides the necessary points of reference to understand what is happening where and when in the complex stream of operations that are involved in networking.

OSI Model

To facilitate cross-vendor and multicompany communication, in 1984, the International Organization for Standardization (ISO) created the Open Systems Interconnection (OSI) model for networking. The OSI model is probably the most referenced and widely discussed model in networking. Although it never fully caught on in North America, portions of it have been adopted as reference points, even to the extent of being incorporated into company names. Layer 2, layer 3, network layer, level 3—these are all references to portions of the OSI model. These references allow people to communicate in a clear and unambiguous fashion when speaking of abstract and out-of-context issues. These references provide context to detail in the complex arena of networking. The terms *level* and *layer* have been used interchangeably to describe the sections of the OSI model, although layer is the more common term.

The OSI model is composed of seven layers stacked in a linear fashion. These layers are, from top to bottom, application, presentation, session, transport, network, data-link, and physical. You can use a mnemonic to remember them: All People Seem To Need Data Processing. Each layer has defined functionality and separation designed to allow multiple protocols to work together in a coordinated fashion.

Although the OSI model is probably the most referenced, standardized network model, a more common model, the Internet model, has risen to dominate the Internet. The OSI model enjoys the status of being a formal, defined international standard, while the Internet model has never been formally defined. The Internet model is basically the same as the OSI model, with the top three OSI layers combined into a single application layer, leaving a total of five layers in the Internet model. Both models are shown in Figure A-1.

One aspect of these models is that they allow specific levels of functionality to be broken apart and performed in sequence. This delineation also determines which layers can communicate with others. At each layer, specific data forms and protocols can exist, which makes them compatible with similar protocols and data forms on other machines at the same layer. This makes it seem as if each layer is communicating with its counterpart on the same layer in another computer, although this is just a virtual connection. The only real connection between boxes is at the physical layer of these models. All other connections are virtual—although they appear real to a user, they do not actually exist in reality.

The true communication between layers occurs vertically, up and down—each layer can communicate only with its immediate neighbor above and below. In Figure A-2, the direct communication path is shown as a bold line between the two physical layers.

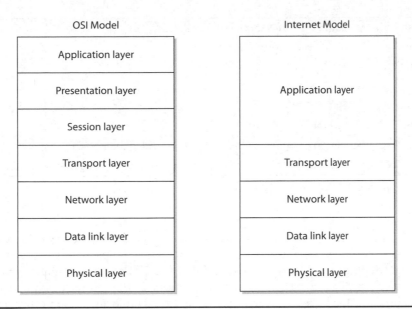

Figure A-1   OSI and Internet network models

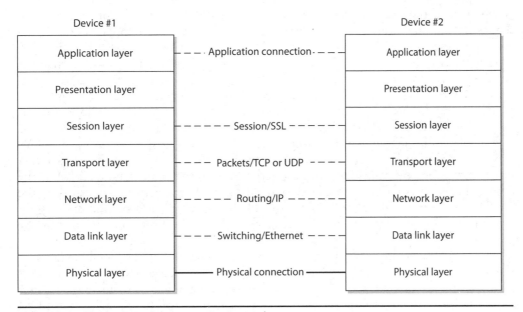

Figure A-2   Network model communication paths

Layer	Commonly Used Protocols
Application	HTTP, SNMP, SMTP, FTP, Telnet
Presentation	XDR
Session	SSL, TLS
Transport	TCP, UDP
Network	IP, ICMP
Data link	IEEE 802.3 (Ethernet), IEEE 802.5 (Token Ring), ARP, RARP
Physical	IEEE 802.3 (Ethernet) hardware, IEEE 802.5 (Token Ring) hardware

Table A-1   Common Protocols by OSI Layer

All data between the boxes traverses this line. The dotted lines between higher layers represent virtual connections, and the associated activities and protocols are also listed for most layers (the protocols are also listed in Table A-1). These dotted lines are virtual—data does not actually cross them, although it appears as though it does. The true path of data is down to the physical layer and back up to the same layer on another machine.

Application Layer

The application layer is the typical interface to the actual application being used. This is the layer of the communication stack that is typically responsible for initiating the request for communication. For example, Internet Explorer is an application program that operates in the application layer using HTTP to move data between systems. This layer represents the user's access to the system and the network. While it appears that the application is communicating directly with an application on another machine, this is actually a virtual connection. The application layer is also sometimes referred to as layer 7 in the OSI model. Several protocols are commonly found in the application layer, including Hypertext Transfer Protocol (HTTP), Simple Mail Transfer Protocol (SMTP), and Simple Network Management Protocol (SNMP).

In the OSI model, the application layer actually communicates with the presentation layer only on its own machine. In the Internet model, the immediate level below the application layer is the transport layer, and this is the only layer directly called by the application layer in this model. As a result of the "missing" presentation and session layers in the Internet model, the functionality of these OSI layers is performed by the application layer.

The session layer functionality present in the Internet model's application layer includes the initiation, maintenance, and termination of logical sessions between endpoints in the network communication. The session layer functionality also includes session-level accounting and encryption services. The presentation layer functionality of the OSI model is also included in the Internet model's application layer, specifically functionality to format the display parameters of the data being received. Any other functions not specifically included in the lower layers of the Internet model are specifically included in the application layer.

Presentation Layer

The presentation layer gets its name from its primary function: preparing for the presentation of data. It is responsible for preparing the data for different interfaces on different types of terminals or displays so the application does not have to deal with this task. Data compression, character set translation, and encryption are found in this layer.

The presentation layer communicates with only two layers—the application layer above it and the session layer below it. The presentation layer is also known as layer 6 of the OSI model.

Session Layer

The primary responsibility of the session layer is the managing of communication sessions between machines. The management functions include initiating, maintaining, and terminating sessions. Managing a session can be compared to making an ordinary phone call. When you dial, you initiate a session. The session must be maintained in an open state during the call. At the completion of the call, you hang up and the circuit must be terminated. As each session can have its own parameters, the session layer is responsible for setting them up, including security, encryption, and billing or accounting functions.

The session layer communicates exclusively with the presentation layer above it and the transport layer below it. The session layer is also known as layer 5 of the OSI model.

Transport Layer

The transport layer is responsible for dealing with the end-to-end transport of data across the network connection. To perform this task, the transport layer handles data entering and leaving the network through logical connections. It can add and use address-specific information, such as ports, to accomplish this task. A port is an address-specific extension that enables multiple simultaneous communications between machines. Should the data transmission be too large for a single-packet transport, the transport layer manages breaking up the data stream into chunks and reassembling it. It ensures that all packets are transmitted and received, and it can request lost packets and eliminate duplicate packets. Error checking can also be performed at this level, although this function is usually performed at the data link layer.

Protocols can be either connection oriented or connectionless. If the protocol is connection oriented, the transport layer manages the connection information. In the case of TCP, the transport layer manages missing packet retransmission requests via the sliding window algorithm.

The transport layer communicates exclusively with the session layer above it and the network layer below it. The transport layer is also known as layer 4 of the OSI model.

Network Layer

The network layer is responsible for routing packets across the network. Routing functions determine the next best destination for a packet and will determine the full address of the target computer if necessary. Common protocols at this level include IP and Internet Control Message Protocol (ICMP).

PART VII

The network layer communicates exclusively with the transport layer above it and the data link layer below it. The network layer is also known as layer 3 of the OSI model.

Data Link Layer

The data link layer is responsible for the delivery and receipt of data from the hardware in layer 1, the physical layer. Layer 1 only manipulates a stream of bits, so the data link layer must convert the packets from the network layer into bit streams in a form that can be understood by the physical layer. To ensure accurate transmission, the data link layer adds end-of-message markers onto each packet and also manages error detection, correction, and retransmission functions. This layer also performs the media-access function, determining when to send and receive data based on network traffic. At this layer, the data packets are technically known as *frames*, although many practitioners use *packet* in a generic sense.

The data link layer communicates exclusively with the network layer above it and the physical layer below it. The data link layer is also known as layer 2 of the OSI model, and it is where LAN switching based on machine-address functionality occurs.

Physical Layer

The physical layer is the realm of communication hardware and software, where 1s and 0s become waves of light, voltage levels, phase shifts, and other physical entities as defined by the particular transmission standard. This layer defines the physical method of signal transmission between machines in terms of electrical and optical characteristics. The physical layer is the point of connection to the outside world via standard connectors, again determined by signal type and protocol.

The physical layer communicates with the physical layer on other machines via wire, fiber-optics, or radio waves. The physical layer also communicates with the data link layer above it. The physical layer is also referred to as OSI layer 1.

Internet Protocols

To facilitate cross-vendor product communication, protocols have been adopted to standardize methods. The Internet brought several new protocols into existence, a few of which are commonly used in the routing of information. Two protocols used at the transport layer are TCP and UDP, whereas IP is used at the network layer. In each session, one transport layer protocol and one network layer protocol is used, making the pairs TCP/IP and UDP/IP.

TCP

TCP is the primary transport protocol used on the Internet today, accounting for more than 80 percent of packets on the Internet.

TCP begins by establishing a virtual connection through a mechanism known as the TCP handshake. This handshake involves three signals: a SYN signal sent to the target, a SYN/ACK returned in response, and then an ACK sent back to the target to complete the circuit. This establishes a virtual connection between machines over which the data will be transported, and that is why TCP is referred to as being *connection oriented*.

TCP is classified as a reliable protocol and will ensure that packets are sent, received, and ordered using sequence numbers. Some overhead is associated with the sequencing of packets and maintaining this order, but for many communications, this is essential, such as in e-mail transmissions, HTTP, and the like.

TCP has facilities to perform all the required functions of the transport layer. TCP has congestion- and flow-control mechanisms to report congestion and other traffic-related information back to the sender to assist in traffic-level management. Multiple TCP connections can be established between machines through a mechanism known as ports. TCP ports are numbered from 0 to 65,535, although ports below 1024 are typically reserved for specific functions. TCP ports are separate entities from UDP ports and can be used at the same time.

UDP

UDP is a simpler form of transport protocol than TCP. UDP performs all of the required functionality of the transport layer, but it does not perform the maintenance and checking functions of TCP. UDP does not establish a connection and does not use sequence numbers. UDP packets are sent via the "best effort" method, often referred to as "fire and forget," because the packets either reach their destination or they are lost forever. It offers no retransmission mechanism, which is why UDP is called an unreliable protocol.

UDP does not have traffic-management or flow-control functions as TCP does. This results in much lower overhead and makes UDP ideal for streaming data sources, such as audio and video traffic, where latency between packets can be an issue. Essential services such as Dynamic Host Configuration Protocol (DHCP) and Domain Name Service (DNS) use UDP, primarily because of the low overhead. When packets do get lost, which is rare in modern networks, they can be resent.

Multiple UDP connections can be established between machines via ports. UDP ports are numbered from 0 to 65,535, although ports below 1024 are typically reserved for specific functionality. UDP ports are separate entities from TCP ports and can be used at the same time.

IP

IP is a connectionless protocol used for routing messages across the Internet. Its primary purpose is to address packets with IP addresses, both destination and source, and to use these addresses to determine the next hop to which the packet will be transmitted. As IP is connectionless, IP packets can take different routes at different times between the same hosts, depending on traffic conditions. IP also maintains some traffic-management information, such as time-to-live (a function to give packets a limited lifetime) and fragmentation control (a mechanism to split packets en route if necessary).

The current version of IP is version 4, referred to as IPv4, and it uses a 32-bit address space. The newer IPv6 protocol adds significant levels of functionality, such as security, improved address space, 128 bits, and a whole host of sophisticated traffic-management options. IPv4 addresses are written as four sets of numbers in the form v.x.y.z, with

PART VII

each of these values ranging from 0 to 255. Since this would be difficult to remember, a naming system for hosts was developed around domains, and DNS servers convert the host names, such as www.ietf.org, to IP addresses, such as 4.17.168.6.

Message Encapsulation

As a message traverses a network from one application on one host, down through the OSI model, out through the physical layer, and up another machine's OSI model, the data is encapsulated at each layer. This can be viewed as an envelope inside an envelope scheme. Since only specific envelopes are handled at each layer, only the necessary information for that layer is presented on the envelope. At each layer, the information inside the envelope is not relevant, and previous envelopes have been discarded—only the information on the current envelope is used. This offers efficient separation of functionality between layers. This concept is illustrated in Figure A-3.

As a message traverses the OSI model from the application layer to the physical layer, envelopes are placed inside bigger envelopes. This increases the packet size, but this increase is known and taken into account by the higher-level protocols. At each level, a header is added to the front end, and it acts to encapsulate the previous layer as data.

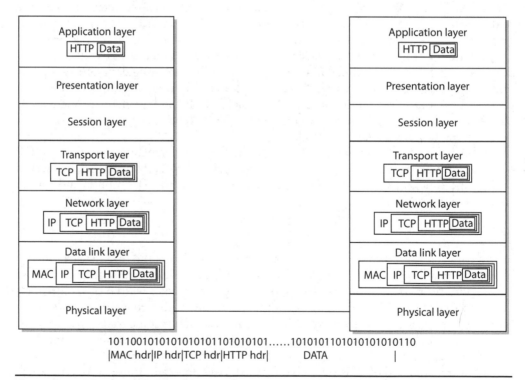

Figure A-3   OSI message encapsulation

At the physical level, the bits are turned into the physical signal and are transmitted to the next station.

At the receiving station, the bits are turned into one large packet, which represents the original envelope-within-envelope concept. Then each envelope is handled at the appropriate level. This encapsulation exists at the transport layer and lower, as this is the domain of a packet within a session.

Common Port Assignments

There are a set of common TCP and UDP port assignments (see Table A-2) that should be committed to memory for the exam. Several of these ports serve multiple services, for instance all SSH secured protocols go over TCP port 22. SSL/TLS secured protocols use

TCP Port Number	UDP Port Number	Keyword	Protocol
20		FTP-Data	File Transfer (Default Data)
21		FTP	File Transfer Control
22		SSH	Secure Shell Login
22		SCP	SCP uses SSH
22		SFTP	SFTP uses SSH
23		TELNET	Telnet
25		SMTP	Simple Mail Transfer
53	53	DNS	Domain Name Server
80		HTTP	Web
110		POP3	e-mail
139		NetBIOS	NetBIOS
143		IMAP	e-mail
161		SNMP	SNMP
162		SNMP	SNMP
443		HTTPS	HTTPS
465		Encrypted SMTP	SMTP over SSL/TLS
636		LDAPS	LDAPS
989		FTPS	FTPS
990		FTPS	FTPS
993		Secure IMAP	Secure IMAP over SSL/TLS
995		Secure POP3	Secure POP3 over SSL/TLS
3269		LDAPS	LDAPS
3389	3389	RDP	Remote Desktop Protocol

Table A-2 Common TCP/UDP Port Assignments

PART VII

a wide variety of TCP ports, different for each associated protocol. Note that all secured protocols use TCP, as the handshake and packet sequencing are essential for encrypted protocols.

Review

To help variable systems understand the functions performed in network communication, a common framework is necessary. This framework is provided by the OSI and Internet network models, which specify which functions occur, and in what order, in the transmission of data from one application to another across a network.

An understanding of the OSI model and thus the state in which the data exists as it transits a network enables a deeper understanding of issues related to security. Understanding that SSL occurs before TCP and IP allows you to understand how SSL protects TCP and IP from outside sniffing. Understanding the different protocols and what happens with data loss gives you a better understanding of how certain types of attacks are performed.

The essence of a framework is to allow enhanced understanding of relationships, and these network models perform this function for network professionals.

About the CD-ROM

The CD-ROM included with this book comes complete with Total Tester customizable practice exam software with 200 practice exam questions and a secured PDF copy of the book.

System Requirements

The software requires Windows Vista or later and 30MB of hard disk space for full installation, in addition to a current or prior major release of Chrome, Firefox, Internet Explorer, or Safari. To run, the screen resolution must be set to 1024×768 or higher. The secured book PDF requires Adobe Acrobat, Adobe Reader, or Adobe Digital Editions to view.

Installing and Running Total Tester Premium Practice Exam Software

From the main screen you may install the Total Tester by clicking the Total Tester Practice Exams button. This will begin the installation process and place an icon on your desktop and in your Start menu. To run Total Tester, navigate to Start | (All) Programs | Total Seminars, or double-click the icon on your desktop.

To uninstall the Total Tester software, go to Start | Control Panel | Programs And Features, and then select the Total Tester program. Select Remove, and Windows will completely uninstall the software.

Total Tester Premium Practice Exam Software

Total Tester provides you with a simulation of the CompTIA Security+ SY0-501 exam. Exams can be taken in Practice Mode, Exam Mode, or Custom Mode. Practice Mode provides an assistance window with hints, references to the book, explanations of the correct and incorrect answers, and the option to check your answer as you take the test. Exam Mode provides a simulation of the actual exam. The number of questions, the types of questions, and the time allowed are intended to be an accurate representation of the exam environment. Custom Mode allows you to create custom exams from selected domains or chapters, and you can further customize the number of questions and time allowed.

To take a test, launch the program and select Security+ AIO5 from the Installed Question Packs list. You can then select Practice Mode, Exam Mode, or Custom Mode. All exams provide an overall grade and a grade broken down by domain.

Secured Book PDF

The entire contents of the book are provided in secured PDF format on the CD-ROM. This file is viewable on your computer and many portable devices.

- **To view the PDF on a computer**, Adobe Acrobat, Adobe Reader, or Adobe Digital Editions is required. A link to Adobe's website, where you can download and install Adobe Reader, has been included on the CD-ROM.

 NOTE For more information on Adobe Reader and to check for the most recent version of the software, visit Adobe's website at www.adobe.com and search for the free Adobe Reader or look for Adobe Reader on the product page. Adobe Digital Editions can also be downloaded from the Adobe website.

- **To view the book PDF on a portable device**, copy the PDF file to your computer from the CD-ROM and then copy the file to your portable device using a USB or other connection. Adobe offers a mobile version of Adobe Reader, the Adobe Reader mobile app, which currently supports iOS and Android. For customers using Adobe Digital Editions and an iPad, you may have to download and install a separate reader program on your device. The Adobe website has a list of recommended applications, and McGraw-Hill Education recommends the Bluefire Reader.

Technical Support

For questions regarding the Total Tester software or operation of the CD-ROM, visit **www.totalsem.com** or e-mail **support@totalsem.com**.

For questions regarding the secured book PDF, visit **http://mhp.softwareassist.com** or e-mail **techsolutions@mhedu.com**.

For questions regarding book content, e-mail **hep_customer-service@mheducation .com**. For customers outside the United States, e-mail **international_cs@mheducation .com**.

3DES   Triple DES encryption—three rounds of DES encryption used to improve security.

802.11   A family of standards that describe network protocols for wireless devices.

802.1X   An IEEE standard for performing authentication over networks.

AAA   *See* authentication, authorization, and accounting.

ABAC   *See* attribute-based access control.

acceptable use policy (AUP)   A policy that communicates to users what specific uses of computer resources are permitted.

access   A subject's ability to perform specific operations on an object, such as a file. Typical access levels include read, write, execute, and delete.

access control   Mechanisms or methods used to determine what access permissions subjects (such as users) have for specific objects (such as files).

access control list (ACL)   A list associated with an object (such as a file) that identifies what level of access each subject (such as a user) has—what they can do to the object (such as read, write, or execute).

access point (AP)   Shorthand for wireless access point, the device that allows devices to connect to a wireless network.

Active Directory   The directory service portion of the Windows operating system that stores information about network-based entities (such as applications, files, printers, and people) and provides a structured, consistent way to name, describe, locate, access, and manage these resources.

ActiveX   A Microsoft technology that facilitates rich Internet applications, and therefore extends and enhances the functionality of Microsoft Internet Explorer. Like Java, ActiveX enables the development of interactive content. When an ActiveX-aware browser encounters a web page that includes an unsupported feature, it can automatically install the appropriate application so the feature can be used.

Address Resolution Protocol (ARP)   A protocol in the TCP/IP suite specification used to map an IP address to a Media Access Control (MAC) address.

Address Space Layout Randomization (ASLR)   A memory-protection process employed by operating systems where the memory space is block randomized to guard against targeted injections from buffer-overflow attacks.

Advanced Encryption Standard (AES)   The current U.S. government standard for symmetric encryption, widely used in all sectors.

Advanced Encryption Standard 256-bit   An implementation of AES using a 256-bit key.

advanced persistent threat (APT)   A threat vector whose main objective is to remain on the system stealthily, with data exfiltration as a secondary task.

adware   Advertising-supported software that automatically plays, displays, or downloads advertisements after the software is installed or while the application is being used.

AES   *See* Advanced Encryption Standard.

AES256   *See* Advanced Encryption Standard 256-bit.

air gap   The forced separation of networks, resulting in an air gap between systems. Communications across an air gap require a manual effort to move data from one network to another, as no network connection exists between the two networks.

algorithm   A step-by-step procedure—typically an established computation for solving a problem within a set number of steps.

amplification   An act of leveraging technology to increase the volume of an attack, such as pinging a network address to get all attached devices to respond.

annualized loss expectancy (ALE)   How much an event is expected to cost the business per year, given the dollar cost of the loss and how often it is likely to occur. ALE = single loss expectancy × annualized rate of occurrence.

annualized rate of occurrence (ARO)   The frequency with which an event is expected to occur on an annualized basis.

anomaly   Something that does not fit into an expected pattern.

antivirus (AV)   A software program designed to detect, mitigate, or remove malware and viruses from a system or network.

application   A program or group of programs designed to provide specific user functions, such as a word processor or web server.

application programming interface (API)   A set of instructions as to how to interface with a computer program so that developers can access defined interfaces in a program.

application service provider (ASP)   A company that offers entities access over the Internet to applications and services.

APT   *See* advanced persistent threat.

ARP   *See* Address Resolution Protocol.

ARP poisoning An attack on the ARP table where values are changed to result in misdirected traffic.

asset A resource or information that an organization needs to conduct its business.

asset value (AV) The value of an asset that is at risk.

asymmetric encryption Also called public key cryptography, a data encryption system that uses two mathematically derived keys to encrypt and decrypt a message—a public key, available to everyone, and a private key, available only to the owner of the key.

attribute-based access control (ABAC) An access control mechanism that grants access based on attributes of a user.

audit trail A set of records or events, generally organized chronologically, that records what activity has occurred on a system. These records (often computer files) are often used in an attempt to re-create what took place when a security incident occurred, and they can also be used to detect possible intruders.

auditing Actions or processes used to verify the assigned privileges and rights of a user, or any capabilities used to create and maintain a record showing who accessed a particular system and what actions they performed.

authentication The process by which a subject's (such as a user's) identity is verified.

authentication, authorization, and accounting (AAA) Three common functions performed upon system login. Authentication and authorization almost always occur, with accounting being somewhat less common. Authentication and authorization are parts of the access control system.

Authentication Header (AH) A portion of the IPsec security protocol that provides authentication services and replay-detection ability. AH can be used either by itself or with Encapsulating Security Payload (ESP). Refer to RFC 2402.

availability Part of the "CIA" of security, applies to hardware, software, and data, specifically meaning that each of these should be present and accessible when the subject (the user) wants to access or use them.

backdoor A hidden method used to gain access to a computer system, network, or application. Often used by software developers to ensure unrestricted access to the systems they create. Synonymous with *trapdoor*.

backup Refers to copying and storing data in a secondary location, separate from the original, to preserve the data in the event that the original is lost, corrupted, or destroyed.

baseline A system or software as it is built and functioning at a specific point in time. Serves as a foundation for comparison or measurement, providing the necessary visibility to control change.

Basic Input/Output System (BIOS)   A firmware element of a computer system that provides the interface between hardware and system software with respect to devices and peripherals. BIOS is being replaced by Unified Extensible Firmware Interface (UEFI), a more complex and capable system.

BGP   *See* Border Gateway Protocol.

biometrics   Used to verify an individual's identity to the system or network using something unique about the individual, such as a fingerprint, for the verification process. Examples include fingerprints, retinal scans, hand and facial geometry, and voice analysis.

BIOS   *See* Basic Input/Output System.

birthday attack   An attack methodology based on combinations rather than linear probability. In a room of thirty people, one doesn't have to match a specific birthday, rather match any two birthdays in the room match, making the problem a combinatorial match, which is much more likely.

Blowfish   A free implementation of a symmetric block cipher developed by Bruce Schneier as a drop-in replacement for DES and IDEA. It has a variable-bit-length scheme from 32 to 448 bits, resulting in varying levels of security.

bluebugging   The use of a Bluetooth-enabled device to eavesdrop on another person's conversation using that person's Bluetooth phone as a transmitter. The bluebug application silently causes a Bluetooth device to make a phone call to another device, causing the phone to act as a transmitter and allowing the listener to eavesdrop on the victim's conversation in real life.

bluejacking   The sending of unsolicited messages over Bluetooth to Bluetooth-enabled devices such as mobile phones, tablets, or laptop computers.

bluesnarfing   The unauthorized access of information from a Bluetooth-enabled device through a Bluetooth connection, often between mobile phones, desktops, laptops, and tablets.

Border Gateway Protocol (BGP)   The interdomain routing protocol implemented in Internet Protocol (IP) networks to enable routing between autonomous systems.

botnet   A collection of software robots, or *bots*, that run autonomously and automatically and, commonly, invisibly in the background. The term is most often associated with malicious software, but it can also refer to the network of computers using distributed computing software.

bridge protocol data unit (BPDU)   BPDUs are a type of data messages that are exchanged across the switches within an extended LAN that uses a Spanning Tree Protocol (STP) topology.

bring your own device (BYOD)   A term used to describe an environment where users bring their personally owned devices into the enterprise and integrate them into business systems.

buffer overflow   A specific type of software coding error that enables user input to overflow the allocated storage area and corrupt a running program.

business availability center (BAC)   A software platform that allows the enterprise to optimize the availability, performance, and effectiveness of business services and applications.

business continuity plan (BCP)   The plan a business develops to continue critical operations in the event of a major disruption.

business impact analysis (BIA)   An analysis of the impact to the business of a specific event.

business partnership agreement (BPA)   A written agreement defining the terms and conditions of a business partnership.

BYOD   *See* bring your own device.

cache   The temporary storage of information before use, typically used to speed up systems. In an Internet context, refers to the storage of commonly accessed web pages, graphic files, and other content locally on a user's PC or a web server. The cache helps to minimize download time and preserve bandwidth for frequently accessed websites, and it helps reduce the load on a web server.

Capability Maturity Model (CMM)   A structured methodology helping organizations improve the maturity of their software processes by providing an evolutionary path from ad hoc processes to disciplined software management processes. Developed at Carnegie Mellon University's Software Engineering Institute.

CAPTCHA   Completely Automated Public Turing Test to Tell Computers and Humans Apart (CAPTCHA), software that is designed to pose tests that require human ability to resolve, preventing robots from filling in and submitting web pages.

centralized management   A type of privilege management that brings the authority and responsibility for managing and maintaining rights and privileges into a single group, location, or area.

CERT   *See* Computer Emergency Response Team.

certificate   A cryptographically signed object that contains an identity and a public key associated with this identity. The certificate can be used to establish identity, analogous to a notarized written document.

certificate authority (CA)   An entity responsible for issuing and revoking certificates. CAs are typically not associated with the company requiring the certificate, although they exist for internal company use as well (such as Microsoft). This term is also applied to server software that provides these services. The term *certificate authority* is used interchangeably with *certification authority*.

PART VII

Certificate Enrollment Protocol (CEP)   Originally developed by VeriSign for Cisco Systems to support certificate issuance, distribution, and revocation using existing technologies.

certificate revocation list (CRL)   A digitally signed object that lists all of the current but revoked certificates issued by a given certification authority. This allows users to verify whether a certificate is currently valid even if it has not expired. A CRL is analogous to a list of stolen charge card numbers that allows stores to reject bad credit cards.

certificate signing request (CSR)   A message sent from an applicant to a certificate authority in order to apply for a digital identity certificate.

chain of custody   Rules for documenting, handling, and safeguarding evidence to ensure no unanticipated changes are made to the evidence.

Challenge Handshake Authentication Protocol (CHAP)   Used to provide authentication across point-to-point links using the Point-to-Point Protocol (PPP).

change (configuration) management   A standard methodology for performing and recording changes during software development and operation.

change control board (CCB)   A body that oversees the change management process and enables management to oversee and coordinate projects.

Channel Service Unit (CSU)   A device used to link local area networks (LANs) into a wide area network (WAN) using telecommunications carrier services.

CHAP   *See* Challenge Handshake Authentication Protocol.

choose your own device (CYOD)   A mobile device deployment methodology where each person chooses their own device type.

CIA of security   Refers to confidentiality, integrity, and availability, the basic functions of any security system.

cipher   A cryptographic system that accepts plaintext input and then outputs ciphertext according to its internal algorithm and key.

Cipher Block Chaining (CBC)   A method of adding randomization to blocks, each block of plaintext is XORed with the previous ciphertext block before being encrypted.

cipher feedback   A method to make a block cipher into a self-synchronizing stream cipher.

ciphertext   The output of an encryption algorithm—the encrypted data.

CIRT   *See* Computer Emergency Response Team.

clickjacking   An attack against a user interface where the user clicks on something without knowing it, triggering a browser action unbeknownst to the user at the time.

closed circuit television (CCTV)   A private television system, usually hardwired in security applications to record visual information.

cloud computing   The automatic provisioning of computational resources on demand across a network.

cloud service provider (CSP)   A company that offers cloud-based network services, infrastructure, or business applications.

cold site   An inexpensive form of backup site that does not include a current set of data at all times. A cold site takes longer to get your operational system back up, but it is considerably less expensive than a warm or hot site.

collisions   Used in the analysis of hashing cryptography, it is the outcome situation that occurs when a hash algorithm will produce the same hash value from two different sets of data.

Common Access Card (CAC)   A smart card used to access U.S. federal computer systems, and to also act as an ID card.

Computer Emergency Response Team (CERT)   Also known as a Computer Incident Response Team (CIRT), the group responsible for investigating and responding to security breaches, viruses, and other potentially catastrophic incidents.

computer security   In general terms, the methods, techniques, and tools used to ensure that a computer system is secure.

computer software configuration item   *See* configuration item.

confidentiality   Part of the CIA of security, refers to the security principle that states that information should not be disclosed to unauthorized individuals.

configuration auditing   The process of verifying that configuration items are built and maintained according to requirements, standards, or contractual agreements.

configuration control   The process of controlling changes to items that have been baselined.

configuration identification   The process of identifying which assets need to be managed and controlled.

configuration item   Data and software (or other assets) that are identified and managed as part of the software change management process. Also known as *computer software configuration items*.

configuration status accounting   Procedures for tracking and maintaining data relative to each configuration item in the baseline.

content management system (CMS)   A management system to manage the content for a specific system, such as a website.

contingency planning (CP)   The act of creating processes and procedures that are used under special conditions (contingencies).

continuity of operations planning (COOP)   The creation of plans related to continuing essential business operations after any major disruption.

Controller Area Network (CAN)   A bus standard for use in vehicles to connect microcontrollers.

cookie   Information stored on a user's computer by a web server to maintain the state of the connection to the web server. Used primarily so preferences or previously used information can be recalled on future requests to the server.

COOP   *See* continuity of operations planning.

corporate owned, personally enabled (COPE)   A form of mobile device ownership/management.

corrective action report (CAR)   A report used to document the corrective actions taken on a system.

Counter Mode (CTM)   Turns a block cipher into a stream cipher.

Counter Mode with Cipher Block Chaining–Message Authentication Code Protocol (CCMP)   An enhanced data cryptographic encapsulation mechanism based upon the Counter Mode with CBC-MAC from AES, designed for use over wireless LANs.

countermeasure   *See* security control.

cracking   A term used by some to refer to malicious hacking, in which an individual attempts to gain unauthorized access to computer systems or networks. *See also* hacking.

CRC   *See* cyclic redundancy check.

CRL   *See* Certificate Revocation List.

cross-site request forgery (CSRF or XSRF)   A method of attacking a system by sending malicious input to the system and relying upon the parsers and execution elements to perform the requested actions, thus instantiating the attack. XSRF exploits the trust a site has in the user's browser.

cross-site scripting (XSS)   A method of attacking a system by sending script commands to the system input and relying upon the parsers and execution elements to perform the requested scripted actions, thus instantiating the attack. XSS exploits the trust a user has for the site.

cryptanalysis   The process of attempting to break a cryptographic system.

cryptography   The art of secret writing that enables an individual to hide the contents of a message or file from all but the intended recipient.

crypto-malware   Malware that uses cryptography to encrypt files for ransom.

CTR   *See* Counter Mode (CTM)—an alternative abbreviation.

cyclic redundancy check (CRC)   An error detection technique that uses a series of two 8-bit block check characters to represent an entire block of data. These block check characters are incorporated into the transmission frame and then checked at the receiving end.

DAC   *See* discretionary access control.

data encryption key (DEK)   An encryption key whose function it is to encrypt and decrypt data.

Data Encryption Standard (DES)   A private key encryption algorithm adopted by the U.S. government as a standard for the protection of sensitive but unclassified information. Commonly used in 3DES, where three rounds are applied to provide greater security.

data execution prevention (DEP)   A security feature of an OS that can be driven by software, hardware, or both, designed to prevent the execution of code from blocks of data in memory.

data loss prevention (DLP)   Technology, processes, and procedures designed to detect when unauthorized removal of data from a system occurs. DLP is typically active, preventing the loss either by blocking the transfer or dropping the connection.

data service unit   *See* channel service unit.

datagram   A packet of data that can be transmitted over a packet-switched system in a connectionless mode.

decision tree   A data structure in which each element is attached to one or more structures directly beneath it.

demilitarized zone (DMZ)   A network segment that exists in a semi-protected zone between the Internet and the inner, secure trusted network.

denial-of-service (DoS) attack   An attack in which actions are taken to deprive authorized individuals from accessing a system, its resources, the data it stores or processes, or the network to which it is connected.

Destination Network Address Translation (DNAT)   A one-to-one static translation from a public destination address to a private address.

DES   *See* Data Encryption Standard.

DHCP   *See* Dynamic Host Configuration Protocol.

Diffie-Hellman   A cryptographic method of establishing a shared key over an insecure medium in a secure fashion.

PART VII

Diffie-Hellman Ephemeral (DHE)   A cryptographic method of establishing a shared key over an insecure medium in a secure fashion using a temporary key to enable perfect forward secrecy.

digital forensics and investigation response (DFIR)   Another name for the incident response process.

digital signature   A cryptography-based artifact that is a key component of a public key infrastructure (PKI) implementation. A digital signature can be used to prove identity because it is created with the private key portion of a public/private key pair. A recipient can decrypt the signature and, by doing so, receive the assurance that the data must have come from the sender and that the data has not changed.

digital signature algorithm (DSA)   A U.S. government standard for implementing digital signatures.

direct-sequence spread spectrum (DSSS)   A method of distributing a communication over multiple frequencies to avoid interference and detection.

disassociation   An attack on a wireless network whereby the attacker sends a deauthentication frame in a wireless connection, to break an existing connection.

disaster recovery plan (DRP)   A written plan developed to address how an organization will react to a natural or manmade disaster in order to ensure business continuity. Related to the concept of a business continuity plan (BCP).

discretionary access control (DAC)   An access control mechanism in which the owner of an object (such as a file) can decide which other subjects (such as other users) may have access to the object, and what access (read, write, execute) these objects can have.

Distinguished Encoding Rules (DER)   A method of providing exactly one way to represent any ASN.1 value as an octet string.

distributed denial-of-service (DDoS) attack   A special type of DoS attack in which the attacker elicits the generally unwilling support of other systems to launch a many-against-one attack.

diversity of defense   The approach of creating dissimilar security layers so that an intruder who is able to breach one layer will be faced with an entirely different set of defenses at the next layer.

dll injection   An attack that uses the injection of a dll onto a system, altering the processing of a program by in essence recoding it.

DNS poisoning   The changing of data in a DNS table to cause misaddressing of packets.

Domain Hijacking   The act of changing the registration of a domain name without the permission of its original registrant.

Domain Name Service/Server (DNS)   The service that translates an Internet domain name (such as www.mhprofessional.com) into IP addresses.

DRP *See* disaster recovery plan.

DSSS *See* direct-sequence spread spectrum.

dumpster diving The practice of searching through trash to discover material that has been thrown away that is sensitive, yet not destroyed or shredded.

Dynamic Host Configuration Protocol (DHCP) An Internet Engineering Task Force (IETF) Internet Protocol (IP) specification for automatically allocating IP addresses and other configuration information based on network adapter addresses. It enables address pooling and allocation and simplifies TCP/IP installation and administration.

dynamic link library (DLL) A shared library function used in the Microsoft Windows environment.

EAP *See* Extensible Authentication Protocol.

electromagnetic interference (EMI) The disruption or interference of electronics due to an electromagnetic field.

electromagnetic pulse (EMP) The disruption or interference of electronics due to a sudden, intense electromagnetic field in the form of a spike or pulse.

Electronic Code Book (ECB) A block cipher mode where the message is divided into blocks, and each block is encrypted separately.

electronic serial number (ESN) A unique identification number embedded by manufacturers on a microchip in wireless phones.

elliptic curve cryptography (ECC) A method of public key cryptography based on the algebraic structure of elliptic curves over finite fields.

Elliptic Curve Diffie-Hellman Ephemeral (ECDHE) A cryptographic method using ECC to establish a shared key over an insecure medium in a secure fashion using a temporary key to enable perfect forward secrecy.

Elliptic Curve Digital Signature Algorithm (ECDSA) A cryptographic method using ECC to create a digital signature.

Encapsulating Security Payload (ESP) A portion of the IPsec implementation that provides for data confidentiality with optional authentication and replay-detection services. ESP completely encapsulates user data in the datagram and can be used either by itself or in conjunction with Authentication Headers for varying degrees of IPsec services.

Encrypted File System (EFS) A security feature of Windows, from Windows 2000 onward, that enables the transparent encryption/decryption of files on the system.

escalation auditing The process of looking for an increase in privileges, such as when an ordinary user obtains administrator-level privileges.

evidence The documents, verbal statements, and material objects admissible in a court of law.

evil twin   An attack involving an attacker-owned router in a wireless system, configured to match a legitimate router.

exposure factor (EF)   A measure of the magnitude of loss of an asset. Used in the calculation of single loss expectancy (SLE).

Extensible Authentication Protocol (EAP)   A universal authentication framework used in wireless networks and point-to-point connections. It is defined in RFC 3748 and has been updated by RFC 5247.

Extensible Markup Language (XML)   A text-based, human-readable data markup language.

false acceptance rate (FAR)   The rate of false positives acceptable to the system.

false positive   Term used when a security system makes an error and incorrectly reports the existence of a searched-for object. Examples include an intrusion detection system that misidentifies benign traffic as hostile, an antivirus program that reports the existence of a virus in software that actually is not infected, or a biometric system that allows system access to an unauthorized individual.

false rejection rate (FRR)   The acceptable level of legitimate users rejected by the system.

FHSS   *See* frequency-hopping spread spectrum.

file system access control list (FACL)   The implementation of access controls as part of a file system.

File Transfer Protocol (FTP)   An application layer protocol used to transfer files over a network connection.

File Transfer Protocol Secure (FTPS)   An application layer protocol used to transfer files over a network connection, which uses FTP over an SSL or TLS connection.

firewall   A network device used to segregate traffic based on rules.

flood guard   A network device that blocks flooding-type DoS/DDoS attacks, frequently part of an IDS/IPS.

forensics (or computer forensics)   The preservation, identification, documentation, and interpretation of computer data for use in legal proceedings.

free space   Sectors on a storage medium that are available for the operating system to use.

frequency-hopping spread spectrum (FHSS)   A method of distributing a communication over multiple frequencies over time to avoid interference and detection.

full disk encryption (FDE)   The application of encryption to an entire disk, protecting all of the contents in one container.

Galois Counter Mode (GCM)   A mode of operation for symmetric key cryptographic block ciphers that has been widely adopted because it can be parallelized to increase efficiency and performance.

Generic Routing Encapsulation (GRE)   A tunneling protocol designed to encapsulate a wide variety of network layer packets inside IP tunneling packets.

Global Positioning System (GPS)   A satellite-based form of location services and time standardization.

Gnu Privacy Guard (GPG)   An application program that follows the OpenPGP standard for encryption.

GPG   *See* Gnu Privacy Guard.

GPO   *See* Group Policy object.

graphic processing unit (GPU)   A chip designed to manage graphics functions in a system.

Group Policy object (GPO)   A method used by Windows for the application of OS settings enterprise-wide.

hacking   The term used by the media to refer to the process of gaining unauthorized access to computer systems and networks. The term has also been used to refer to the process of delving deep into the code and protocols used in computer systems and networks. *See also* cracking.

hard disk drive (HDD)   A mechanical device used for the storing of digital data in magnetic form.

hardware security module (HSM)   A physical device used to protect but still allow use of cryptographic keys. It is separate from the host machine.

hash   A form of encryption that creates a digest of the data put into the algorithm. These algorithms are referred to as one-way algorithms because there is no feasible way to decrypt what has been encrypted.

hash value   *See* message digest.

hashed message authentication code (HMAC)   The use of a cryptographic hash function and a message authentication code to ensure the integrity and authenticity of a message.

HDD   *See* hard disk drive.

heating, ventilation, air conditioning (HVAC)   The systems used to heat and cool air in a building or structure.

HIDS   *See* host-based intrusion detection system.

high availability   A system design to provide assured availability.

PART VII

HIPS   *See* host-based intrusion prevention system.

HMAC-based one time password (HOTP)   A method of producing one-time passwords using HMAC functions.

honeypot   A computer system or portion of a network that has been set up to attract potential intruders, in the hope that they will leave the other systems alone. Since there are no legitimate users of this system, any attempt to access it is an indication of unauthorized activity and provides an easy mechanism to spot attacks.

host-based intrusion detection system (HIDS)   A system that looks for computer intrusions by monitoring activity on one or more individual PCs or servers.

host-based intrusion prevention system (HIPS)   A system that automatically responds to computer intrusions by monitoring activity on one or more individual PCs or servers and responding based on a rule set.

hot site   A backup site that is fully configured with equipment and data and is ready to immediately accept transfer of operational processing in the event of failure on the operational system.

HSM   *See* hardware security module.

Hypertext Markup Language (HTML)   A protocol used to mark up text for use across HTTP.

Hypertext Transfer Protocol (HTTP)   A protocol for transfer of material across the Internet that contains links to additional material.

Hypertext Transfer Protocol over SSL/TLS (HTTPS)   A protocol for transfer of material across the Internet that contains links to additional material that is carried over a secure tunnel via SSL or TLS.

ICMP   *See* Internet Control Message Protocol.

identification (ID)   The first step in the authentication process where the user establishes a secret with the authentication system and is bound to a userid.

identity provider (IdP)   A system that creates, maintains, and manages identity information, including authentication services.

IEEE   *See* Institute for Electrical and Electronics Engineers.

IETF   *See* Internet Engineering Task Force.

impact   The result of a vulnerability being exploited by a threat, resulting in a loss.

impersonation   A social engineering technique that can occur in person, over a phone, or online, where the attacker assumes a role that is recognized by the person being attacked, and in assuming that role, the attacker uses the potential victim's biases against their better judgment to follow procedures.

incident response The process of responding to, containing, analyzing, and recovering from a computer-related incident.

incident response plan (IRP) The plan used in responding to, containing, analyzing, and recovering from a computer-related incident.

industrial control system (ICS) Term used to describe the hardware and software that controls cyber-physical systems.

information security Often used synonymously with computer security, but places the emphasis on the protection of the information that the system processes and stores, instead of on the hardware and software that constitute the system.

infrared (IR) A set of wavelengths past the red end of the visible spectrum used as a communication medium.

Infrastructure as a Service (IaaS) The automatic, on-demand provisioning of infrastructure elements, operating as a service; a common element of cloud computing.

initialization vector (IV) A data value used to seed a cryptographic algorithm, providing for a measure of randomness.

instant messaging (IM) A text-based method of communicating over the Internet.

Institute for Electrical and Electronics Engineers (IEEE) A nonprofit, technical, professional institute associated with computer research, standards, and conferences.

intangible asset An asset for which a monetary equivalent is difficult or impossible to determine. Examples are brand recognition and goodwill.

integrity Part of the CIA of security, the security principle that requires that information is not modified except by individuals authorized to do so.

interconnection security agreement (ISA) An agreement between parties to establish procedures for mutual cooperation and coordination between them with respect to security requirements associated with their joint project.

intermediate distribution frame (IDF) A system for managing and interconnecting the telecommunications cable between end-user devices, typically workstations.

International Data Encryption Algorithm (IDEA) A symmetric encryption algorithm used in a variety of systems for bulk encryption services.

Internet Assigned Numbers Authority (IANA) The central coordinator for the assignment of unique parameter values for Internet protocols. The IANA is chartered by the Internet Society (ISOC) to act as the clearinghouse to assign and coordinate the use of numerous Internet protocol parameters.

Internet Control Message Protocol (ICMP) One of the core protocols of the TCP/IP protocol suite, used for error reporting and status messages.

PART VII

Internet Engineering Task Force (IETF)   A large international community of network designers, operators, vendors, and researchers, open to any interested individual concerned with the evolution of Internet architecture and the smooth operation of the Internet. The actual technical work of the IETF is done in its working groups, which are organized by topic into several areas (such as routing, transport, and security). Much of the work is handled via mailing lists, with meetings held three times per year.

Internet Key Exchange (IKE)   A standard key exchange protocol used on the Internet, an implementation of Diffie-Hellmann algorithm.

Internet Message Access Protocol version 4 (IMAP4)   One of two common Internet standard protocols for e-mail retrieval, the other being POP.

Internet of Things (IoT)   The networking of large numbers of devices via the Internet to achieve a business purpose.

Internet Protocol (IP)   The network layer protocol used by the Internet for routing packets across a network.

Internet Protocol Security (IPsec)   A protocol used to secure IP packets during transmission across a network. IPsec offers authentication, integrity, and confidentiality services and uses Authentication Headers (AH) and Encapsulating Security Payload (ESP) to accomplish this functionality.

Internet Relay Chat (IRC)   An application layer protocol that facilitates communication in the form of text across the Internet.

Internet Security Association and Key Management Protocol (ISAKMP)   A protocol framework that defines the mechanics of implementing a key exchange protocol and negotiation of a security policy.

Internet service provider (ISP)   A telecommunications firm that provides access to the Internet.

intrusion detection system (IDS)   A system to identify suspicious, malicious, or undesirable activity that indicates a breach in computer security.

IPsec   *See* Internet Protocol Security.

ISA   *See* interconnection security agreement.

IT contingency plan (ITCP)   The plan used to manage contingency operations in an IT environment.

Kerberos   A network authentication protocol designed by MIT for use in client/server environments.

key   In cryptography, a sequence of characters or bits used by an algorithm to encrypt or decrypt a message.

key distribution center (KDC) A component of the Kerberos system for authentication that manages the secure distribution of keys.

key encrypting key (KEK) An encryption key whose function it is to encrypt and decrypt the DEK.

keyspace The entire set of all possible keys for a specific encryption algorithm.

Layer 2 Tunneling Protocol (L2TP) A Cisco switching protocol that operates at the data link layer.

LDAP *See* Lightweight Directory Access Protocol.

least privilege A security principle in which a user is provided with the minimum set of rights and privileges that he or she needs to perform required functions. The goal is to limit the potential damage that any user can cause.

Lightweight Directory Access Protocol (LDAP) An application protocol used to access directory services across a TCP/IP network.

Lightweight Extensible Authentication Protocol (LEAP) A version of EAP developed by Cisco prior to 802.11i to push 802.1X and WEP adoption.

load balancer A network device that distributes computing across multiple computers.

local area network (LAN) A grouping of computers in a network structure confined to a limited area and using specific protocols, such as Ethernet for OSI Layer 2 traffic addressing.

logic bomb A form of malicious code or software that is triggered by a specific event or condition. *See also* time bomb.

loop protection The requirement to prevent bridge loops at the Layer 2 level, which is typically resolved using the Spanning Tree algorithm on switch devices.

MAC *See* mandatory access control, Media Access Control, or Message Authentication Code.

Main Distribution Frame (MDF) Telephony equipment that connects customer equipment to subscriber carrier equipment.

man-in-the-browser attack A man-in-the-middle attack involving browser helper objects and browsers to conduct the attack.

man-in-the-middle attack (MITM) Any attack that attempts to use a network node as the intermediary between two other nodes. Each of the endpoint nodes thinks it is talking directly to the other, but each is actually talking to the intermediary.

managed service provider (MSP) A third party that manages aspects of a system under some form of service agreement.

mandatory access control (MAC)   An access control mechanism in which the security mechanism controls access to all objects (files), and individual subjects (processes or users) cannot change that access.

master boot record (MBR)   A strip of data on a hard drive in Windows systems meant to result in specific initial functions or identification.

maximum transmission unit (MTU)   A measure of the largest payload that a particular protocol can carry in a single packet in a specific instance.

MD5   Message Digest 5, a hashing algorithm and a specific method of producing a message digest.

mean time between failures (MTBF)   The statistically determined period of time between failures of the system.

mean time to failure (MTTF)   The statistically determined time to the next failure.

mean time to repair/recover (MTTR)   A common measure of how long it takes to repair a given failure. This is the average time, and may or may not include the time needed to obtain parts.

Media Access Control (MAC)   A protocol used in the data link layer for local network addressing.

memorandum of agreement (MOA)   A document executed between two parties that defines some form of agreement.

memorandum of understanding (MOU)   A document executed between two parties that defines some form of agreement.

message authentication code (MAC)   A short piece of data used to authenticate a message. *See* hashed message authentication code.

message digest   The result of applying a hash function to data. Sometimes also called a hash value. *See* hash.

metropolitan area network (MAN)   A collection of networks interconnected in a metropolitan area and usually connected to the Internet.

Microsoft Challenge Handshake Authentication Protocol (MSCHAP)   A Microsoft-developed variant of the Challenge Handshake Authentication Protocol (CHAP).

mitigation   Action taken to reduce the likelihood of a threat occurring.

mobile device management (MDM)   An application designed to bring enterprise-level functionality onto a mobile device, including security functionality and data segregation.

Monitoring as a Service (MaaS)   The use of a third party to provide security monitoring services.

MSCHAP   *See* Microsoft Challenge Handshake Authentication Protocol.

MTBF   *See* mean time between failures.

MTTF   *See* mean time to failure.

MTTR   *See* mean time to repair.

multifactor authentication (MFA)   The use of more than one different factor for authenticating a user to a system.

multifunction device (MFD)   A device, such as a printer, with multiple functions, such as printing and scanning.

Multimedia Message Service (MMS)   A standard way to send multimedia messages to and from mobile phones over a cellular network.

NAC   *See* network access control.

NAP   *See* Network Access Protection.

NAT   *See* Network Address Translation.

National Institute of Standards and Technology (NIST)   A U.S. government agency responsible for standards and technology.

NDA   *See* non-disclosure agreement.

Near Field Communication (NFC)   A set of standards and protocols for establishing a communication link over very short distances. Used in mobile devices.

network access control (NAC)   An approach to endpoint security that involves monitoring and remediating endpoint security issues before allowing an object to connect to a network.

Network Access Protection (NAP)   A Microsoft approach to network access control.

Network Address Translation (NAT)   A method of readdressing packets in a network at a gateway point to enable the use of local, nonroutable IP addresses over a public network such as the Internet.

network-based intrusion detection system (NIDS)   A system for examining network traffic to identify suspicious, malicious, or undesirable behavior.

network-based intrusion prevention system (NIPS)   A system that examines network traffic and automatically responds to computer intrusions.

Network Basic Input/Output System (NetBIOS)   A system that provides communication services across a local area network.

network operating system (NOS)   An operating system that includes additional functions and capabilities to assist in connecting computers and devices, such as printers, to a local area network.

Network Time Protocol (NTP)   A protocol for the transmission of time synchronization packets over a network.

New Technology File System (NTFS)   A proprietary file system developed by Microsoft, introduced in 1993, that supports a wide variety of file operations on servers, PCs, and media.

New Technology LANMAN (NTLM)   A deprecated security suite from Microsoft that provides authentication, integrity, and confidentiality for users. Because it does not support current cryptographic methods, it is no longer recommended for use.

Next Generation Access Control (NGAC)   One of the primary methods of implementing attribute-based access control (ABAC). The other method is XACML.

NFC   *See* Near Field Communication.

NIST   *See* National Institute of Standards and Technology.

non-disclosure agreement (NDA)   A legal contract between parties detailing the restrictions and requirements borne by each party with respect to confidentiality issues pertaining to information to be shared.

non-repudiation   The ability to verify that an operation has been performed by a particular person or account. This is a system property that prevents the parties to a transaction from subsequently denying involvement in the transaction.

Oakley protocol   A key exchange protocol that defines how to acquire authenticated keying material based on the Diffie-Hellman key exchange algorithm.

object identifier (OID)   A standardized identifier mechanism for naming any object.

object reuse   Assignment of a previously used medium to a subject. The security implication is that before it is provided to the subject, any data present from a previous user must be cleared.

one-time pad (OTP)   An unbreakable encryption scheme in which a series of nonrepeating, random bits is used once as a key to encrypt a message. Since each pad is used only once, no pattern can be established and traditional cryptanalysis techniques are not effective.

Online Certificate Status Protocol (OCSP)   A protocol used to request the revocation status of a digital certificate. This is an alternative to certificate revocation lists.

Open Authorization (OAUTH)   An open standard for token-based authentication and authorization on the Internet.

Open Vulnerability and Assessment Language (OVAL)   An XML-based standard for the communication of security information between tools and services.

operating system (OS)   The basic software that handles input, output, display, memory management, and all the other highly detailed tasks required to support the user environment and associated applications.

OVAL   *See* Open Vulnerability and Assessment Language.

Over the Air (OTA)   Refers to performing an action wirelessly.

P12   *See* PKCS #12

PAC   *See* Proxy Auto Configuration.

Packet Capture (PCAP)   The methods and files associated with the capture of network traffic in the form of text files.

Padding Oracle on Downgraded Legacy Encryption (POODLE)   A vulnerability in SSL 3.0 that can be exploited.

PAM   *See* Pluggable Authentication Modules.

pan-tilt-zoom (PTZ)   A term used to describe a video camera that supports remote directional and zoom control.

pass the hash attack   An attack where the credentials are passed in hashed form to convince an object that permission has been granted.

password   A string of characters used to prove an individual's identity to a system or object. Used in conjunction with a user ID, it is the most common method of authentication. The password should be kept secret by the individual who owns it.

Password Authentication Protocol (PAP)   A simple protocol used to authenticate a user to a network access server.

Password-Based Key Derivation Function 2 (PBKDF2)   A key derivation function that is part of the RSA Laboratories Public Key Cryptography Standards, published as IETF RFC 2898.

patch   A replacement set of code designed to correct problems or vulnerabilities in existing software.

PBX   *See* private branch exchange.

peer-to-peer (P2P)   A network connection methodology involving direct connection from peer to peer.

penetration testing   A security test in which an attempt is made to circumvent security controls in order to discover vulnerabilities and weaknesses. Also called a pen test.

perfect forward security (PFS)   A property of a cryptographic system whereby the loss of one key does not compromise material encrypted before or after its use.

permissions Authorized actions a subject can perform on an object. *See also* access controls.

personal electronic device (PED) A term used to describe an electronic device, owned by the user and brought into the enterprise, that uses enterprise data. This includes laptops, tablets, and mobile phones, to name a few.

personal exchange format (PFX) A file format used when exporting certificates.

personal health information (PHI) Information related to a person's medical records, including financial, identification, and medical data.

Personal Identity Verification (PIV) Policies, procedures, hardware, and software used to securely identify federal workers.

personally identifiable information (PII) Information that can be used to identify a single person.

phreaking Used in the media to refer to the hacking of computer systems and networks associated with the phone company. *See also* cracking.

PKCS #12 A commonly used member of the family of standards called Public-Key Cryptography Standards (PKCS) published by RSA Laboratories.

Plain Old Telephone Service (POTS) The term used to describe the old analog phone service and later the "land-line" digital phone service.

plaintext In cryptography, a piece of data that is not encrypted. It can also mean the data input into an encryption algorithm that would output ciphertext.

Platform as a Service (PaaS) A third-party offering that allows customers to build, operate, and manage applications without having to manage the underlying infrastructure.

Pluggable Authentication Modules (PAM) A mechanism used in Linux systems to integrate low-level authentication methods into an API.

Point-to-Point Protocol (PPP) The Internet standard for transmission of IP packets over a serial line, as in a dial-up connection to an ISP.

Point-to-Point Protocol Extensible Authentication Protocol (PPP EAP) A PPP extension that provides support for additional authentication methods within PPP.

Point-to-Point Protocol Password Authentication Protocol (PPP PAP) A PPP extension that provides support for password authentication methods over PPP.

Point-to-Point Tunneling Protocol (PPTP) The use of generic routing encapsulation over PPP to create a methodology used for virtual private networking.

Port Address Translation (PAT) The manipulation of port information in an IP datagram at a point in the network to map ports in a fashion similar to Network Address Translation's change of network address.

Post Office Protocol (POP)   A standardized format for the exchange of e-mail.

pre-shared key (PSK)   A shared secret that has been previously shared between parties and is used to establish a secure channel.

Pretty Good Privacy (PGP)   A popular encryption program that has the ability to encrypt and digitally sign e-mail and files.

preventative intrusion detection   A system that detects hostile actions or network activity and prevents them from impacting information systems.

privacy   Protecting an individual's personal information from those not authorized to see it.

Privacy-enhanced Electronic Mail (PEM)   Internet standard that provides for secure exchange of e-mail using cryptographic functions.

private branch exchange (PBX)   A telephone exchange that serves a specific business or entity.

privilege auditing   The process of checking the rights and privileges assigned to a specific account or group of accounts.

privilege escalation   The step in an attack where an attacker increases their privilege, preferably to administrator or root level.

privilege management   The process of restricting a user's ability to interact with the computer system.

Protected Extensible Authentication Protocol (PEAP)   A protected version of EAP developed by Cisco, Microsoft, and RSA Security that functions by encapsulating the EAP frames in a TLS tunnel.

Proxy Auto Configuration (PAC)   A method of automating the connection of web browsers to appropriate proxy services to retrieve a specific URL.

PSK   *See* pre-shared key.

PTZ   *See* pan-tilt-zoom.

public key cryptography   *See* asymmetric encryption.

public key infrastructure (PKI)   Infrastructure for binding a public key to a known user through a trusted intermediary, typically a certificate authority.

qualitative risk assessment   The process of subjectively determining the impact of an event that affects a project, program, or business. It involves the use of expert judgment, experience, or group consensus to complete the assessment.

quantitative risk assessment   The process of objectively determining the impact of an event that affects a project, program, or business. It usually involves the use of metrics and models to complete the assessment.

PART VII

RADIUS   Remote Authentication Dial-In User Service, a standard protocol for providing authentication services. It is commonly used in dial-up, wireless, and PPP environments.

RAID   *See* Redundant Array of Inexpensive Disks.

rainbow tables   A precomputed set of hash tables for matching passwords by searching rather than computing each on the fly.

rapid application development (RAD)   A software development methodology that favors the use of rapid prototypes and changes as opposed to extensive advanced planning.

RAS   *See* Remote Access Service/Server.

RBAC   *See* rule-based access control or role-based access control.

RC4   A stream cipher used in TLS and WEP.

real-time operating system (RTOS)   An operating system designed to work in a real-time environment.

Real-time Transport Protocol (RTP)   A protocol for a standardized packet format used to carry audio and video traffic over IP networks.

Recovery Agent (RA)   In Microsoft Windows environments, the entity authorized by the system to use a public key recovery certificate to decrypt other users' files using a special private key function associated with the Encrypted File System (EFS).

recovery point objective (RPO)   The amount of data that a business is willing to place at risk. It is determined by the amount of time a business has to restore a process before an unacceptable amount of data loss results from a disruption.

recovery time objective (RTO)   The amount of time a business has to restore a process before unacceptable outcomes result from a disruption.

Redundant Array of Inexpensive Disks (RAID)   The use of an array of disks arranged in a single unit of storage for increasing storage capacity, redundancy, and performance characteristics.

refactoring   The process of restructuring existing computer code without changing its external behavior to improve nonfunctional attributes of the software, such as improving code readability and/or reducing complexity.

registration authority (RA)   Part of the PKI system responsible for establishing registration parameters during the creation of a certificate.

Remote Access Service/Server (RAS)   A combination of hardware and software used to enable remote access to a network.

remote-access Trojan (RAT)   A set of malware designed to exploit a system providing remote access.

remotely triggered black hole (RTBH)   A popular and effective filtering technique for the mitigation of denial-of-service attacks.

replay attack   The reusing of data during an attack to cause a system to respond based on previous acts.

repudiation   The act of denying that a message was either sent or received.

residual risk   Risks remaining after an iteration of risk management.

return on investment (ROI)   A measure of the effectiveness of the use of capital.

RFID   Radio frequency identification, a technology used for remote identification via radio waves.

RIPEMD   A hash function developed in Belgium. The acronym expands to RACE Integrity Primitives Evaluation Message Digest, but this name is rarely used. The current version is RIPEMD-160.

risk   The possibility of suffering a loss.

risk assessment or risk analysis   The process of analyzing an environment to identify the threats, vulnerabilities, and mitigating actions to determine (either quantitatively or qualitatively) the impact of an event affecting a project, program, or business.

risk management   Overall decision-making process of identifying threats and vulnerabilities and their potential impacts, determining the costs to mitigate such events, and deciding what cost-effective actions can be taken to control these risks.

Rivest, Shamir, Adleman (RSA)   The names of the three men who developed a public key cryptographic system and the company they founded to commercialize the system.

role-based access control (RBAC)   An access control mechanism in which, instead of the users being assigned specific access permissions for the objects associated with the computer system or network, a set of roles that the user may perform is assigned to each user.

RTP   *See* Real-time Transport Protocol.

rule-based access control (RBAC)   An access control mechanism based on rules.

safeguard   *See* security controls.

SAN   *See* storage area network.

SCADA   *See* supervisory control and data acquisition.

SCEP   *See* Simple Certificate Enrollment Protocol.

Secure Copy Protocol (SCP)   A network protocol that supports secure file transfers.

PART VII

Secure FTP   A method of secure file transfer that involves the tunneling of FTP through an SSH connection. This is different than SFTP, which is the Secure Shell File Transfer Protocol.

Secure Hash Algorithm (SHA)   A hash algorithm used to hash block data. The first version is SHA-1, with subsequent versions detailing hash digest length: SHA-256, SHA-384, and SHA-512.

Secure Hypertext Transfer Protocol (SHTTP)   An alternative to HTTPS, in which only the transmitted pages and POST fields are encrypted. Rendered moot, by and large, by widespread adoption of HTTPS.

Secure/Multipurpose Internet Mail Extensions (S/MIME)   An encrypted implementation of the MIME protocol specification.

Secure Real-time Transport Protocol (SRTP)   A secure version of the standard protocol for a standardized packet format used to carry audio and video traffic over IP networks.

Secure Shell (SSH)   A set of protocols for establishing a secure remote connection to a computer. This protocol requires a client on each end of the connection and can use a variety of encryption protocols.

Secure Shell File Transfer Protocol (SFTP)   A secure file transfer subsystem associated with Secure Shell (SSH).

Secure Sockets Layer (SSL)   An encrypting layer between the session and transport layers of the OSI model designed to encrypt above the transport layer, enabling secure sessions between hosts. SSL has been replaced by TLS.

Security Assertion Markup Language (SAML)   An XML-based standard for exchanging authentication and authorization data.

security association (SA)   An instance of security policy and keying material applied to a specific data flow. Both IKE and IPsec use SAs, although these SAs are independent of one another. IPsec SAs are unidirectional and are unique in each security protocol, whereas IKE SAs are bidirectional. A set of SAs is needed for a protected data pipe, one per direction per protocol. SAs are uniquely identified by destination (IPsec endpoint) address, security protocol (AH or ESP), and security parameter index (SPI).

security baseline   The end result of the process of establishing an information system's security state. It is a known good configuration resistant to attacks and information theft.

security content automation protocol (SCAP)   A method of using specific protocols and data exchanges to automate the determination of vulnerability management, measurement, and policy compliance across a system or set of systems.

security controls   A group of technical, management, or operational policies and procedures designed to implement specific security functionality. Access controls are an example of a security control.

security information and event management (SIEM)   The name used for a broad range of technological solutions to the collection and analysis of security-related information across the enterprise.

segregation or separation of duties   A basic control that prevents or detects errors and irregularities by assigning job responsibilities for increased risk tasks to different individuals so that no single individual can commit fraudulent or malicious actions.

self-encrypting drive (SED)   A data drive that has built-in encryption capability on the drive control itself.

Sender Policy Framework (SPF)   An e-mail validation system designed to detect e-mail spoofing by verifying that incoming mail comes from a host authorized by that domain's administrators.

service level agreement (SLA)   An agreement between parties concerning the expected or contracted uptime associated with a system.

service set identifier (SSID)   Identifies a specific 802.11 wireless network. It transmits information about the access point to which the wireless client is connecting.

session hijacking   An attack against a communication session by injecting packets into the middle of the communication session.

shielded twisted pair (STP)   A physical network connection consisting of two wires twisted and covered with a shield to prevent interference.

shimming   The process of putting a layer of code between the driver and the OS to allow flexibility and portability.

Short Message Service (SMS)   A form of text messaging over phone and mobile phone circuits that allows up to 160-character messages to be carried over signaling channels.

shoulder surfing   Stealing of credentials by looking over someone's shoulder while they type them into a system.

signature database   A collection of activity patterns that have already been identified and categorized and that typically indicate suspicious or malicious activity.

Simple Certificate Enrollment Protocol (SCEP)   A protocol used in PKI for enrollment and other services.

Simple Mail Transfer Protocol (SMTP)   The standard Internet protocol used to transfer e-mail between hosts.

Simple Mail Transfer Protocol Secure (SMTPS)   The secure version of the standard Internet protocol used to transfer e-mail between hosts.

Simple Network Management Protocol (SNMP)   A standard protocol used to remotely manage network devices across a network.

PART VII

Simple Object Access Protocol (SOAP)   An XML-based specification for exchanging information associated with web services.

single loss expectancy (SLE)   Monetary loss or impact of each occurrence of a threat. SLE = asset value × exposure factor.

single point of failure (SPoF)   A single system component whose failure can result in system failure.

single sign-on (SSO)   An authentication process by which the user can enter a single user ID and password and then move from application to application or resource to resource without having to supply further authentication information.

slack space   Unused space on a disk drive created when a file is smaller than the allocated unit of storage (such as a sector).

small computer system interface (SCSI)   A protocol for data transfer to and from a machine.

SMS   *See* Short Message Service.

sniffer   A software or hardware device used to observe network traffic as it passes through a network on a shared broadcast media.

social engineering   The art of deceiving another person so that he or she reveals confidential information. This is often accomplished by posing as an individual who should be entitled to have access to the information.

Software as a Service (SaaS)   The provisioning of software as a service, commonly known as on-demand software.

software-defined networking (SDN)   The use of software to act as a control layer separate from the data layer in a network to manage traffic.

software development kit (SDK)   A set of tools and processes used to interface with a larger system element when programming changes to an environment.

software development lifecycle (SDLC)   The processes and procedures employed to develop software.

software development lifecycle methodology (SDLM)   The processes and procedures employed to develop software. Sometimes also called *secure development lifecycle model* when security is part of the development process.

solid-state drive (SSD)   A mass storage device, such as a hard drive, that is composed of electronic memory as opposed to a physical device of spinning platters.

SONET   *See* Synchronous Optical Network Technologies.

spam   E-mail that is not requested by the recipient and is typically of a commercial nature. Also known as unsolicited commercial e-mail (UCE).

spam filter   A security appliance designed to remove spam at the network layer before it enters e-mail servers.

spear phishing   A phishing attack aimed at a specific individual.

spim   Spam sent over an instant messaging channel.

spoofing   Making data appear to have originated from another source so as to hide the true origin from the recipient.

SSD   *See* solid-state drive.

storage area network (SAN)   A dedicated network that provides access to data storage.

STP   *See* shielded twisted pair.

Structured Exception Handler (SEH)   The process used to handle exceptions in the Windows OS core functions.

Structured Query Language (SQL)   A language used in relational database queries.

Subject Alternative Name (SAN)   A field on a certificate that identifies alternative names for the entity to which the certificate applies.

Subscriber Identity Module (SIM)   An integrated circuit or hardware element that securely stores the International Mobile Subscriber Identity (IMSI) and the related key used to identify and authenticate subscribers on mobile telephones.

supervisory control and data acquisition (SCADA)   A generic term used to describe the industrial control system networks used to interconnect infrastructure elements (such as manufacturing plants, oil and gas pipelines, power generation and distribution systems, and so on) and computer systems.

symmetric encryption   Encryption that needs all parties to have a copy of the key, sometimes called a shared secret. The single key is used for both encryption and decryption.

Synchronous Optical Network Technologies (SONET)   A set of standards used for data transfers over optical networks.

system on a chip (SoC)   The integration of complete system functions on a single chip, simplifying construction of devices.

tailgating   The act of following an authorized person through a doorway without using your own credentials.

tangible asset   An asset for which a monetary equivalent can be determined. Examples are inventory, buildings, cash, hardware, software, and so on.

Telnet   A network protocol used to provide cleartext bidirectional communication over TCP.

Temporal Key Integrity Protocol (TKIP)   A security protocol used in 802.11 wireless networks.

Terminal Access Controller Access Control System Plus (TACACS+)   A remote authentication system that uses the TACACS+ protocol, defined in RFC 1492, and TCP port 49.

threat   Any circumstance or event with the potential to cause harm to an asset.

ticket-granting ticket (TGT)   A part of the Kerberos authentication system that is used to prove identity when requesting service tickets.

Time-based One-Time Password (TOTP)   A password that is used once and is only valid during a specific time period.

time bomb   A form of logic bomb in which the triggering event is a date or specific time. *See also* logic bomb.

TKIP   *See* Temporal Key Integrity Protocol.

token   A hardware device that can be used in a challenge-response authentication process.

Transaction Signature (TSIG)   A protocol used as a means of authenticating dynamic DNS records during DNS updates.

Transmission Control Protocol/Internet Protocol (TCP/IP)   A connection-oriented protocol for communication over IP networks.

Transport Layer Security (TLS)   A replacement for SSL that is currently being used to secure communications between servers and browsers.

trapdoor   *See* backdoor.

Trivial File Transfer Protocol (TFTP)   A simplified version of FTP used for low-overhead file transfers using UDP port 69.

Trojan horse   A form of malicious code that appears to provide one service (and may indeed provide that service) but that also hides another purpose. This hidden purpose often has a malicious intent. This code may also be simply referred to as a *Trojan*.

Trusted Platform Module (TPM)   A hardware chip to enable trusted computing platform operations.

typo squatting   An attack form that involves capitalizing upon common typo errors at the URL level, hoping the browser user will not notice they end up on a different site.

Unified Extensible Firmware Interface (UEFI)   A specification that defines the interface between an OS and the hardware firmware. This is a replacement to BIOS.

unified threat management (UTM)   The aggregation of multiple network security products into a single appliance for efficiency purposes.

Uniform Resource Identifier (URI)   A set of characters used to identify the name of a resource in a computer system. A URL is a form of URI.

uninterruptible power supply (UPS)   A source of power (generally a battery) designed to provide uninterrupted power to a computer system in the event of a temporary loss of power.

Universal Resource Locator (URL)   A specific character string used to point to a specific item across the Internet.

Universal Serial Bus (USB)   An industry-standard protocol for communication over a cable to peripherals via a standard set of connectors.

Universal Serial Bus On the Go (USB OTG)   A USB standard that enables mobile devices to talk to one another without an intervening PC

unmanned aerial vehicle (UAV)   A remotely piloted flying vehicle.

unshielded twisted pair (UTP)   A physical connection consisting of a pair of twisted wires forming a circuit.

usage auditing   The process of recording who did what and when on an information system.

user acceptance testing (UAT)   The application of acceptance-testing criteria to determine fitness for use according to end-user requirements.

User Datagram Protocol (UDP)   A protocol in the TCP/IP protocol suite for the transport layer that does not sequence packets—it is "fire and forget" in nature.

user ID   A unique alphanumeric identifier that identifies individuals who are logging in or accessing a system.

vampire tap   A tap that connects to a network line without cutting the connection.

Variable Length Subnet Masking (VLSM)   The process of using variable length subnets, creating subnets in subnets.

video teleconferencing (VTC)   A business process of using video signals to carry audio and visual signals between separate locations, thus allowing participants to meet via a virtual meeting instead of traveling to a physical location. Modern videoconferencing equipment can provide very realistic connectivity when lighting and backgrounds are controlled.

Virtual Desktop Environment (VDE)   The use of virtualization technology to host desktop systems on a centralized server.

virtual desktop infrastructure (VDI)   The use of servers to host virtual desktops by moving the processing to the server and using the desktop machine as merely a display terminal. VDI offers operating efficiencies as well as cost and security benefits.

virtual local area network (VLAN) A broadcast domain inside a switched system.

virtual machine (VM) A form of a containerized operating system that allows a system to be run on top of another OS.

virtual private network (VPN) An encrypted network connection across another network, offering a private communication channel across a public medium.

virus A form of malicious code or software that attaches itself to other pieces of code in order to replicate. Viruses may contain a payload, which is a portion of the code that is designed to execute when a certain condition is met (such as on a certain date). This payload is often malicious in nature.

vishing A form of social engineering attack over voice lines (VoIP).

Voice over IP (VoIP) The packetized transmission of voice signals (telephony) over Internet Protocol.

vulnerability A weakness in an asset that can be exploited by a threat to cause harm.

watering hole attack The infecting of a specific target website, one that users trust and go to on a regular basis, with malware.

whaling A phishing attack targeted against a high value target like a corporate officer or system administrator.

wireless access point (WAP) A network access device that facilitates the connection of wireless devices to a network.

war dialing An attacker's attempt to gain unauthorized access to a computer system or network by discovering unprotected connections to the system through the telephone system and modems.

war driving The attempt by an attacker to discover unprotected wireless networks by wandering (or driving) around with a wireless device, looking for available wireless access points.

web application firewall (WAF) A firewall that operates at the application level, specifically designed to protect web applications by examining requests at the application stack level.

WEP *See* Wired Equivalent Privacy.

wide area network (WAN) A network that spans a large geographic region.

Wi-Fi Protected Access/Wi-Fi Protected Access 2 (WPA/WPA2) A protocol to secure wireless communications using a subset of the 802.11i standard.

Wi-Fi Protected Setup (WPS) A network security standard that allows easy setup of a wireless home network.

Wired Equivalent Privacy (WEP)   The encryption scheme used to attempt to provide confidentiality and data integrity on 802.11 networks.

Wireless Application Protocol (WAP)   A protocol for transmitting data to small hand-held devices such as cellular phones.

wireless intrusion detection system (WIDS)   An intrusion detection system established to cover a wireless network.

wireless intrusion prevention system (WIPS)   An intrusion prevention system established to cover a wireless network.

Wireless Transport Layer Security (WTLS)   The encryption protocol used on WAP networks.

worm   An independent piece of malicious code or software that self-replicates. Unlike a virus, it does not need to be attached to another piece of code. A worm replicates by breaking into another system and making a copy of itself on this new system. A worm can contain a destructive payload but does not have to.

write once read many (WORM)   A data storage technology where things are written once (permanent) and then can be read many times, as in optical disks.

X.509   The standard format for digital certificates.

XML   *See* Extensible Markup Language.

XOR   Bitwise exclusive OR, an operation commonly used in cryptography.

XSRF   *See* cross-site request forgery.

XSS   *See* cross-site scripting.

zero day   A vulnerability for which there is no previous knowledge.

INDEX